Allan Kaprow

Allan Kaprow—Art as Life

Edited by
Eva Meyer-Hermann
Andrew Perchuk
and
Stephanie Rosenthal

Published by the Getty Research Institute

The Getty Research Institute Publications Program
Thomas W. Gaehtgens, *Director, Getty Research Institute*
Gail Feigenbaum, *Associate Director, Programs*
Julia Bloomfield, *Head, Publications Program*

Thomas Crow, Jeffrey M. Hurwit, Jacqueline Lichtenstein, Alex Potts, and Mimi Hall Yiengpruksawan, *Publications Committee*

Allan Kaprow—Art as Life
Rebecca Frazier and Michele Ciaccio, *Manuscript Editors*
Michele Ciaccio, *Production Editor*
Designed by Meryl Pollen
Production coordinated by Suzanne Watson
Type composed by Meryl Pollen in Helvetica Neue
Printed in China through Asia Pacific Offset, Inc., on 140 gsm Gold East Matte

Eva Meyer-Hermann's and Stephanie Rosenthal's essays were translated by Fiona Elliott

Published by the Getty Research Institute, Los Angeles
Getty Publications
1200 Getty Center Drive, Suite 500
Los Angeles, California 90049-1682
www.getty.edu

12 11 10 09 08 5 4 3 2 1

Back cover: Allan Kaprow sitting in *Apple Shrine* (detail), 1960. Allan Kaprow Papers (box 72, folder 5). Photograph by Charles Reynolds

Library of Congress Cataloging-in-Publication Data
Allan Kaprow—art as life / edited by Eva Meyer-Hermann, Andrew Perchuk, and Stephanie Rosenthal.
p. cm.
Includes bibliographical references and index.
ISBN 978-0-89236-890-7 (hardcover)
1. Kaprow, Allan—Criticism and interpretation. 2. Kaprow, Allan—Archives. I. Meyer-Hermann, Eva. II. Perchuk, Andrew. III. Rosenthal, Stephanie. IV. Kaprow, Allan. V. Getty Research Institute. VI. Title: Allan Kaprow.
NX512.K37A45 2008
700.92—dc22
2007028709

Acknowledgments

A volume like this one is only possible through the encouragement and contributions of the many institutions and individuals who have supported us in diverse ways.

We are most grateful to Coryl Crane Kaprow and Barry Rosen. We owe a special thanks to Tamara Bloomberg of the Allan Kaprow Estate for her painstaking research. We would also like to thank Chris Dercon, Elena Heitsch, Tina Köhler, Julienne Lorz, and Marco von Matuschka of Haus der Kunst, Munich; Charles Esche, Inge Borsje, Martha Fritzsche, and Theo Wajon of the Van Abbemuseum, Eindhoven; and Iwan Wirth, Marc Payot, Florian Berktold, Sylvia Bandi, Laura Bechter, and Anna Krayer of Hauser & Wirth, Zurich and London. We are indebted to Magdalena Jetelová, Hermann Pitz, Stefan Römer, Jörg von Brincken, and Regina Wohlfarth for leading the reinventions of the Environments and Happenings in Munich in 2006 and allowing us to reproduce images from them in this publication.

We are sincerely indebted to Paul and Karen McCarthy, Jeff Kelley, and Peter Kirby for sharing with us their knowledge about Kaprow, gained from years of profound engagement with the artist. Our deepest appreciation goes to the authors whose scholarship has expanded our understanding of the life and work of Allan Kaprow: Annette Leddy, Glenn Phillips, Alex Potts, and Paul Schimmel. While we had always intended to include a chronology, Annette Leddy developed its substance and form far beyond what we had originally envisioned. In addition, Glenn Phillips contributed to the editorial and selection process, and Kelly Nipper worked on the initial design concept.

We thank Thomas Crow, Gail Feigenbaum, and Julia Bloomfield at the Getty Research Institute for their support for this publication. We are particularly thankful for the meticulous thoroughness and persistence of production editor Michele Ciaccio, who has organized and coordinated the publication and whose intelligent research has led to significant corrections to the historical record. Her attention to detail, along with that of her colleague Jonlin Wung, has made an extraordinary difference throughout the process of producing this book. The photography of the Allan Kaprow Papers at the Getty Research Institute was superbly executed by Jobe Benjamin, John Kiffe, Christine Nguyen, and Stacey Rain Strickler and was facilitated by Lena Watanabe of Visual Media Services. Their commitment to perfection and visual acuity is in evidence throughout this book. The manuscript has been very much improved due to the patient and attentive editing of Rebecca Frazier. Our thanks also go to Fiona Elliott for her sensitive translations, Suzanne Watson for the high standards of press production visible in this volume, and Meryl Pollen for creating such an innovative, thoughtful, and lively design.

—Eva Meyer-Hermann, Andrew Perchuk, and Stephanie Rosenthal

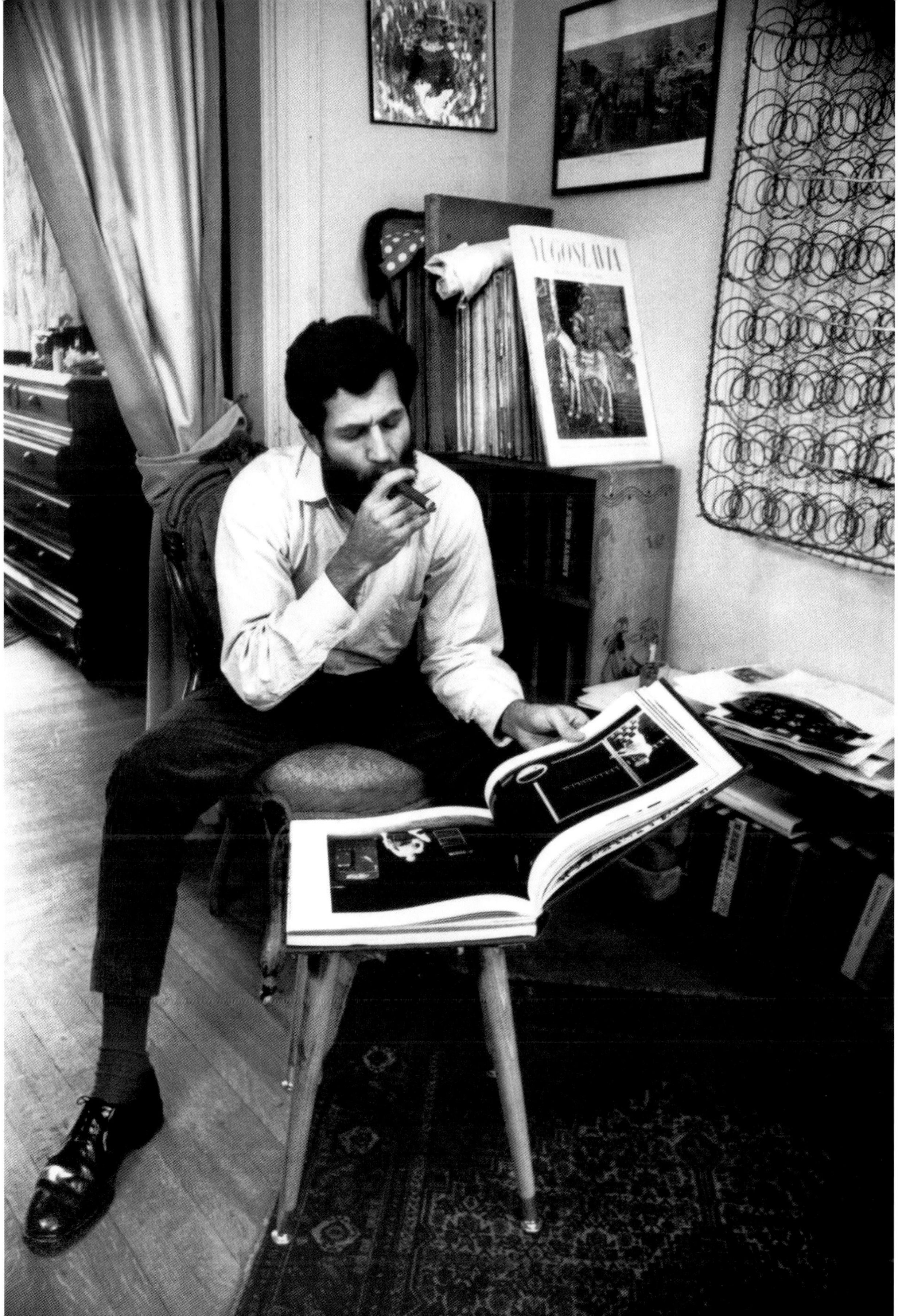
YUGOSLAVIA

Introduction

Eva Meyer-Hermann,
Andrew Perchuk,
and
Stephanie Rosenthal

The immediate occasion for this publication was the realization of the international traveling retrospective *Allan Kaprow—Art as Life*, which draws heavily on the archive of the artist's papers held by the Getty Research Institute. But this is a particularly apt time to reexamine Allan Kaprow's work for other reasons as well. His death, in 2006, brought conclusion to a remarkably broad and diverse oeuvre, created over a span of nearly sixty years. He has, as a number of contributors to this volume assert, been described as the best-known unknown artist among the major postwar practitioners in the United States. There has been a slow acknowledgment on both the scholarly and the institutional level that ephemeral, performative, and notational practices such as Kaprow's are increasingly central to any adequate account of art from the late twentieth and early twenty-first centuries. And, in the midst of one of the longest of the periodic booms in the postwar art market, a state in which commerce makes the values of scholarship, context, and criticality often seem irrelevant, Kaprow's work offers a strong counterpractice, coming from an artist who more resolutely resisted the strictures of the art world than perhaps any other artist of his era.

While there are very few visual artists who have invented an art form whose name has entered common parlance—as did the Happening—Kaprow has been identified far too reductively with that singular invention. A primary goal of this book is to extend the parameters of scholarly investigation of Kaprow's work beyond the roughly ten years of the classic Happenings. Kaprow's career can usefully be conceptualized—at the risk of being overly simplistic—in several phases. From the late 1940s through the late 1950s, Kaprow produced what he retrospectively called "gallery art," beginning with paintings and drawings, then assemblages and action-collages, and finally Environments, in which the incorporation of elements from everyday life increasingly strained traditional exhibition contexts. In 1958, while studying with John Cage, Kaprow invented the Happening, a form in which a number of events take place together in space and time, never to be repeated in exactly the same manner. Within this loose framework, the Happenings evinced a great deal of variety, ranging from the highly scripted and theatrical to the spare and conceptual, and moving from the gallery to commercial and industrial spaces to the outdoors. In the late 1960s, Kaprow began using the term *Activity,* rather than *Happening,* to denote his practice, signaling

Contents

a change from large, public events to ones whose participants were mainly family, friends, fellow artists, and his students. In the 1970s, these works were often accompanied by Activity booklets—a published set of photos and texts that outlined the actions of the Activity and made Kaprow's presence unnecessary to the realization of the piece. From the 1980s until the end of his life, Kaprow's work became private and introspective, to be enacted by a couple or an individual. These developments in Kaprow's art are visually documented by the lengthy chronology, compiled by Annette Leddy, that comprises the bulk of this book. Composed of an illustrated list of his works (as complete as possible from 1958 on), and a list of related events, the chronology provides some of the flavor of Kaprow's practice while offering both a useful introduction for the casual reader and invaluable research material for the dedicated scholar.

The essays in this publication have been grouped into three sections: "Early Works and Writings," "From the Archive," and "The Making of a Retrospective." Paul Schimmel locates Kaprow in the 1950s as negotiating between the legacy of Jackson Pollock and the influence of John Cage, both as a scholar—Kaprow studied art history with Meyer Schapiro—and as an artist. For Schimmel, the crucial work that initiates many of the key issues of Kaprow's mature practice is *Rearrangeable Panels* (1957–59), for which he offers a sustained description and interpretation. Alex Potts discusses Kaprow's invention of the Happening as outgrowth of his assemblage practice, focusing on Kaprow's writing itself as a form of assemblage. He examines Kaprow's written scores and published essays through the mid-1960s, ultimately arguing that the Happenings exist as a missing physical immediacy between two verbal articulations—Kaprow's written scores and the participants' recollections.

Both Glenn Phillips's and Annette Leddy's essays are drawn "From the Archive." Phillips's essay examines the problem, engendered by Kaprow's work, of maintaining the traditional distinction between artwork and archive. It specifically focuses on the material related to one Activity—*Time Pieces*—beginning with the Activity booklet for the piece, and proceeding through the photographic and video documentation of its enactment in Berlin, its reconfiguration for exhibition, and the second video of the work made several years later. Leddy's contribution is a broader survey of the Allan Kaprow Papers that locates a theme of intimacy in an archive that on its surface is intentionally impersonal.

As the curators of the retrospective exhibition *Allan Kaprow—Art as Life,* Stephanie Rosenthal and Eva Meyer-Hermann are concerned with the enormous challenges posed by any presentation of Kaprow's work in the institutional context of the museum. Rosenthal describes the process of working with Kaprow and the ultimate decision to reinvent a number of Happenings in Munich. Meyer-Hermann provides an account of the fraught history between the museum and the work of artists who blur the boundaries between art and life, details the strategies for the in-gallery presentation of Kaprow's work, and offers a plea to reform museological practice to make it more hospitable to nontraditional work.

While the essays and chronology offer a range of approaches to Kaprow's work, this publication is by no means meant to be definitive. Very few artistic practices call out for a true catalogue raisonné more than Kaprow's. It is our hope that this book will be the beginning of a more intensive museological and scholarly engagement with Kaprow's oeuvre, a project in which a great deal of work is still to be done.

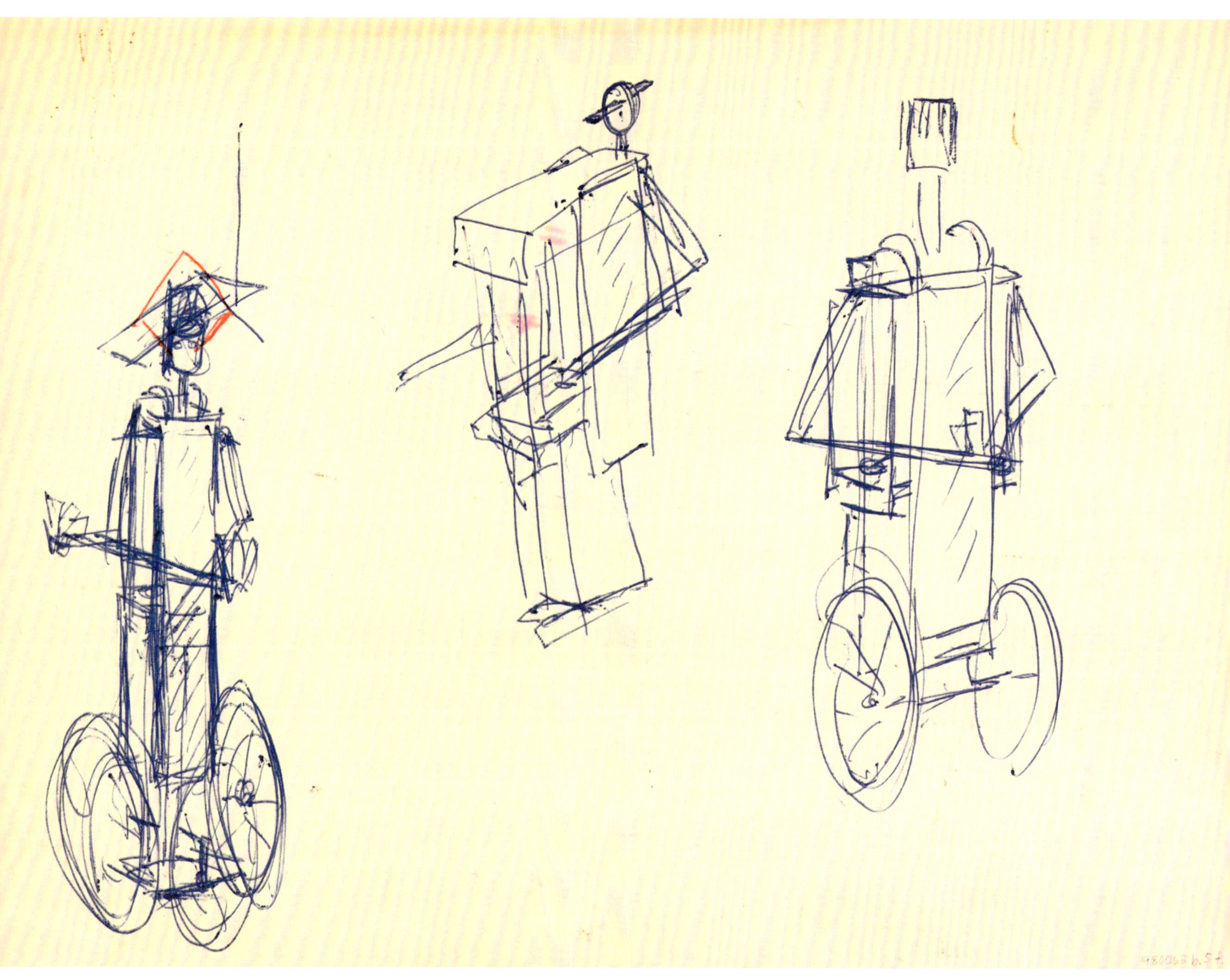

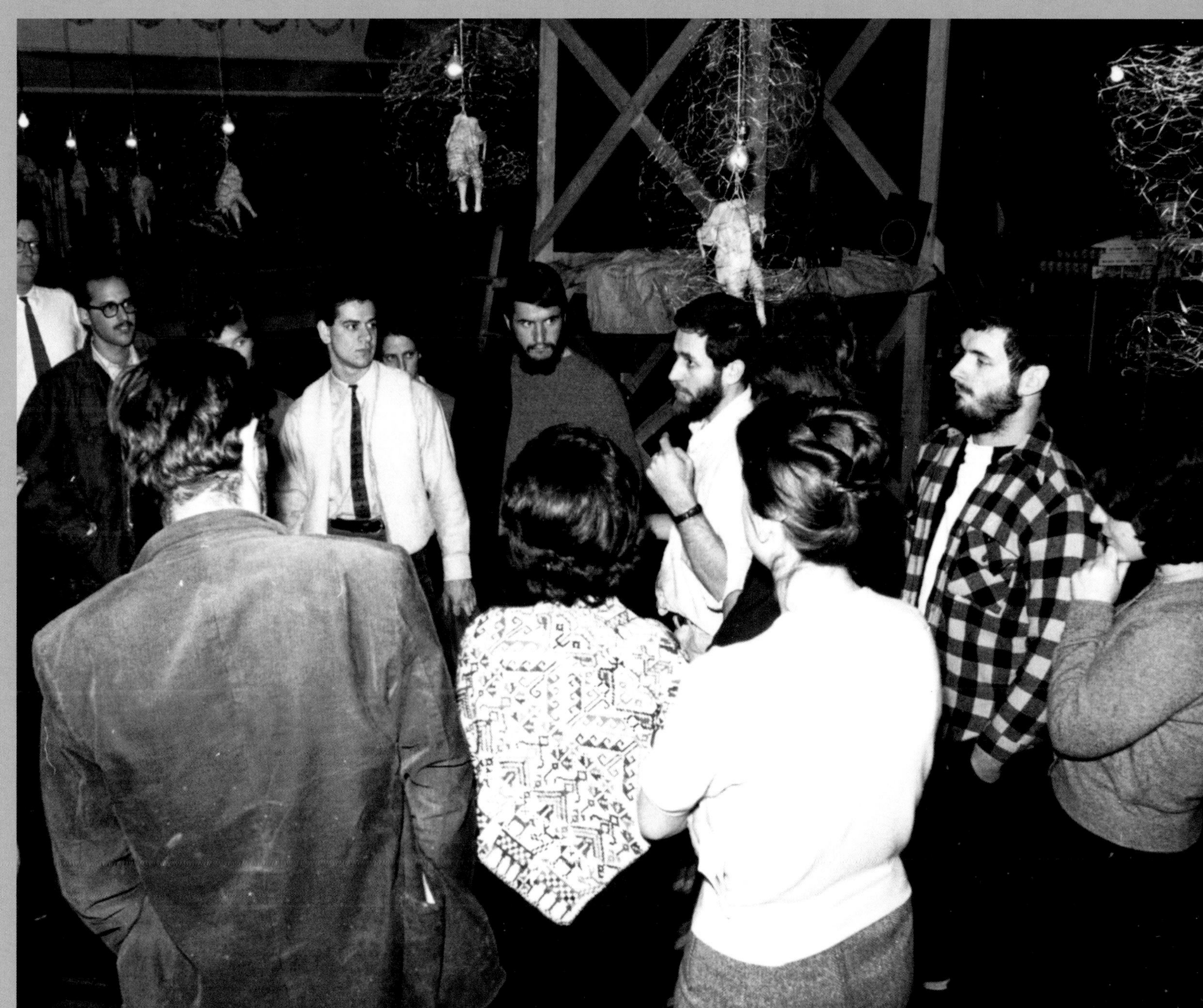

Part One **Early Works and Writings**

"Only memory can carry it into the future": Kaprow's Development from the Action-Collages to the Happenings

Paul Schimmel

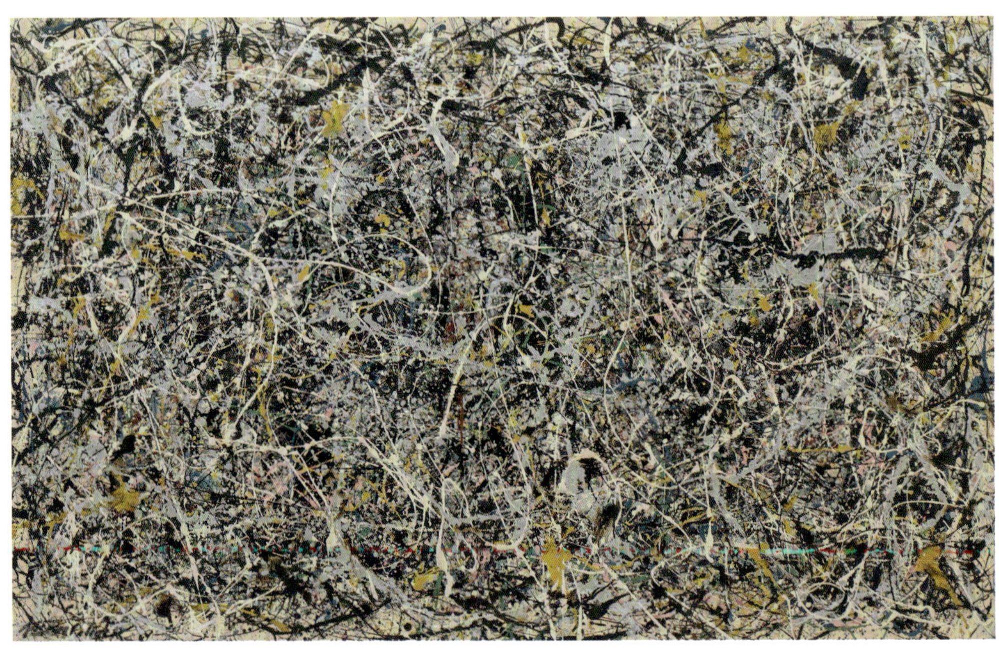

Allan Kaprow willed Happenings into being. Emerging as a painter at the same time as the second-generation New York School was coming to the fore, he rigorously conceptualized his own practice in order to move art in a new direction. His revolutionary creation of Happenings, which erased the boundaries between object, installation, and performance, derived from two contradictory tendencies. Intuitive, open-ended, and time-based on the one hand, they reflected his rigorous practice as an art historian, critic, and teacher on the other. He received his master's degree in art history from Columbia University in 1952, wrote prolifically, and was an influential teacher throughout his career, beginning with his appointment at Rutgers University in 1953. Arguably, no work traces his evolution from painting to sculpture to installation to Happening more powerfully than *Rearrangeable Panels* (1957–59), which he incorporated into the Happening, *18 Happenings in 6 Parts,* in 1959.

Kaprow's artistic development was strongly influenced by his efforts to reconcile the achievements of Jackson Pollock and John Cage. His essay "The Legacy of Jackson Pollock" (1958) reveals his vivid understanding of Pollock's significance as a "liberator" who demonstrated to subsequent generations the primacy of action in the process of artistic creation. Kaprow began to engage with Pollock's work in the late 1940s, in part through his study of painting with Hans Hofmann. In 1952, he and some of Hofmann's other former students, including Jan Müller, Jane Wilson, George Segal, and Robert Whitman, cofounded Hansa Gallery, an artists' cooperative on East Twelfth Street in New York, to provide a forum to explore the legacies of gestural abstraction, assemblage, and other forms. They hoped to find an escape from abstract expressionism, which had degenerated into a mode of art-making that, Kaprow claimed, "invariably seeks the past and drowns itself in its sobs, bitterness and fastidiousness."[1]

Although the Hansa Gallery artists were wedded to the rich, painterly, gestural qualities of Pollock, many were perhaps closer in spirit to the more conceptual practice of Cage. From 1957 to 1958, Kaprow was a student in the weekly experimental music composition class that Cage taught at the New School for Social Research in New York. Other students included George Brecht, Al Hansen, Dick Higgins, Jackson Mac Low, and La Monte Young. Cage showed Kaprow that one of the ways in which he could work through Pollock's legacy was to explore the significance of the act in painting and sculpture in ways that Pollock had only anticipated, such as by incorporating time-based practices, employing new modes of nonnarrative composition, and requiring the participation of the audience for the realization of a work < FIGS. 1, 2 >. Of Cage, Kaprow later wrote:

> A less passionate personality than Pollock, perhaps more ironic, Cage nevertheless has the same vast sense of naturism. His welcome of accident and his taste for blurring the edges between his art and the world beyond are as great as Pollock's or even greater. Just as Pollock's painting has no definite frame, so the sounds and silences in Cage's music could be continued indefinitely. Musical sound and noise (customarily divided) are really one; so are art and life.[2]

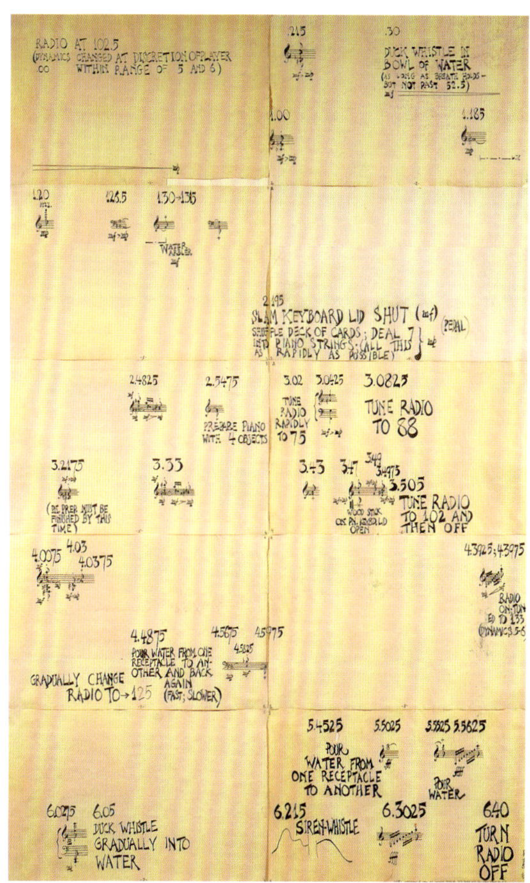

Fig. 2. **John Cage (American, 1912–92)**
Water Music, 1952
India ink on paper, 10 sheets, each sheet: 43.2 × 27.9 cm (17 × 11 in.)
Whitney Museum of American Art, New York

Fig. 1. **Jackson Pollock (American, 1912–56)**
Number 1, 1949
Enamel and metallic paint on canvas, 160 × 259.1 cm (63 × 102 in.)
The Museum of Contemporary Art, Los Angeles

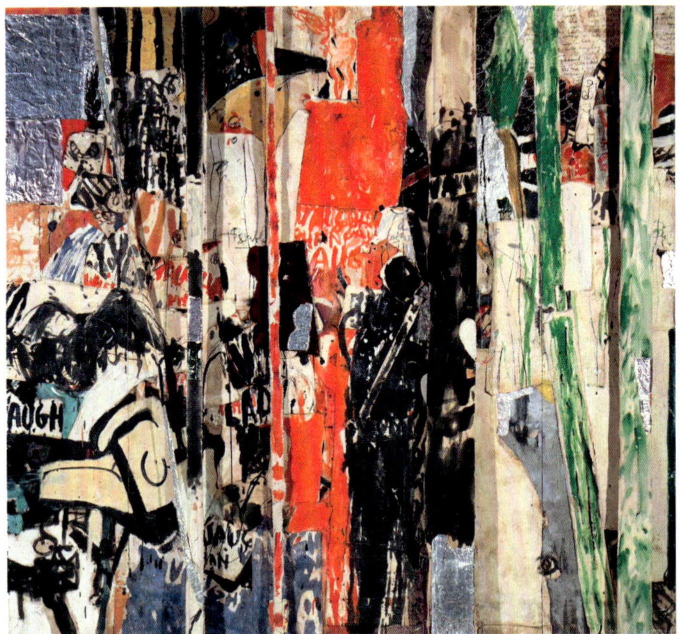

Fig. 3. **Allan Kaprow**
Baby, 1957
Collage: paper, aluminum foil, carpet pieces, oil and synthetic paint, chalk, and rope on masonite plates, 282 × 306 × 17 cm (111 × 120½ × 6¾ in.)
Museum Moderner Kunst Stiftung Ludwig, Vienna

In the mid-1950s, Kaprow perceived himself as equipped to move beyond the narrow-mindedness and banality of the second-generation New York School, which he characterized—wrongly, I believe—as consisting of the followers of Pollock. (In fact, Willem de Kooning was far more influential for painters such as Michael Goldberg, Grace Hartigan, Al Held, Alfred Leslie, and Joan Mitchell, among others.) One of his first steps was to incorporate elements from everyday life into a series of works that he called "action-collages."[3] In these works, gestural painting counterpoints collage and assemblage. Influenced by Pollock's emphasis on the primacy of the act, Kaprow produced the collages "as rapidly as possible by grasping . . . great hunks of varied matter: tin foil, straw, canvas, photos, newspaper, etc. [and placing them] . . . in the ritual of my own rapid action [with] an acting out of the drama of tin soldiers, stories, and musical structures that I had once tried to embody in paint alone."[4] But while a painting by Pollock can be read as a unified field, in Kaprow's collages each element remains distinct within the overall composition, so that the centrality and coherence so important to the monumentality of Pollock's painting are in abeyance—a tendency that reflects Cage's influence. In this respect, the action-collages diverge from the carefully composed narrative and autobiographical Combines of Robert Rauschenberg, another artist who struggled to absorb the dual influences of Pollock and Cage. The elements that make up Kaprow's *Baby* <FIG. 3>—cardboard, foil, torn paper, cut-up sections of his own paintings, and bits of text and image—are fragmented and incoherent; Kaprow achieves formal clarity in the work only by rigorously organizing these elements as a series of vertical bands. His inclusion of found objects was in some ways a direct assault on the homogeneity of the abstract expressionist picture plane—a mythic coherence that lends the ethereal quality that separates it from the visceral world. As Segal, one of Kaprow's closest friends, observed years later, "We found it amazing that so much avant-garde twentieth-century art was rooted in physical experiences of the real world and suddenly the abstract expressionists were legislating any reference to the physical world totally out of art. This was outrageous to us."[5] Nevertheless, during this period Kaprow, like Rauschenberg, remained both indebted to and enamored of the bravura and seemingly unencumbered freedom that the New York School represented, even as he attempted literally to cut this tradition apart in his action-collages.

Kaprow observed in 1965 that his collages "became bigger and I introduced the flashing lights and thicker hunks of matter. These parts projected farther and farther from the wall into the room and included more and more audible elements: sounds of ringing buzzers, bells, toys, etc., until I had accumulated nearly all the sensory elements I was to work for during the following years."[6] Although the use of objects that invited the sensory participation of the audience was not unique to Kaprow (in 1959, Rauschenberg incorporated a working radio into his Combine painting *Broadcast*), his predilection for the lowbrow was distinguishing. Works such as *Penny Arcade* <FIG. 4> suggest the American vernacular exemplified by the arcade, the carnival, and the circus in contrast to that of the refined commercial culture of Madison Avenue that appealed to many of his contemporaries. The development of his aesthetic from *Baby* to *Arcade* is apparent not only in the displacement of the functionality of the incorporated objects rather than the sublimation of their use value but also in the expansion of scale, with the consequent potential to immerse the audience more fully in the experience of the work—a tendency that he would develop further. "I just simply filled the whole gallery up," he stated,

> starting from one wall and ending with the other. When you opened the door you found yourself in the midst of an entire Environment. . . . I immediately saw that every visitor to the Environment was part of it. I had not really thought of it before. And so I gave him occupations like moving something, turning switches on—just a few things. Increasingly during 1957 and 1958, this suggested a more "scored" responsibility for that visitor. I offered him more and more to do, until there developed the Happening.[7]

Kaprow later made the connection between assemblage, Environment, and Happening explicit: "An Environment is a large assemblage, usually to be physically entered, like a forest or a junk-yard. Those entering an Environment may be encouraged to move its material about, thus changing its composition. As more moves are encouraged, the Environment becomes a Happening. Normally, such an Environment is thrown away after a time and its materials may be perishable, like flowers or food."[8]

Kaprow's crucial shift from action-collages to Environments occurred as he was developing *Rearrangeable Panels* between 1957 and 1959. This work lies at the intersection of his efforts to reconcile Pollock and Cage, the painterly and the conceptual, the physical and the theoretical. The work is a large-scale assemblage comprising nine rectangular panels, each approximately eight feet high. The panels, covered with paint, tar, plastic apples, leaves, paper, and mirror fragments, and strung with colored lightbulbs at the top, can be displayed in any configuration, including leaning them against the wall, aligning them side by side to make a wall, or arranging them in the form of a kiosk-like structure. *Rearrangeable Panels* asserts itself as an art object even as it simultaneously denies its own permanence by virtue of the fact that its components may be rearranged. And, as Jeff Kelley observed, this aspect of the work "was an early nod in the direction of what would later become a central principle of Kaprow's work: the participation of others. Kaprow was comfortable with collaboration and ensemble performance—activities typically associated with art forms other than the visual, especially music."[9]

Although there are historical antecedents for *Rearrangeable Panels,* it is clear through Kaprow's writings that he understood better than most the major implications of the move from object to action and the significance of the hybrid, in-between form with which he was wrestling. Some of the most significant precursors were the walk-in environments and objects of Kurt Schwitters—particularly his *Merzbau,* a series of rooms in which a variety of objects and materials were installed, which he originally constructed in his home in Hannover in the 1920s. Marcel Duchamp was also influential, but not as an objectmaker; rather, he was meaningful for his relationship to the found object and for the relationship of his life (including his renowned

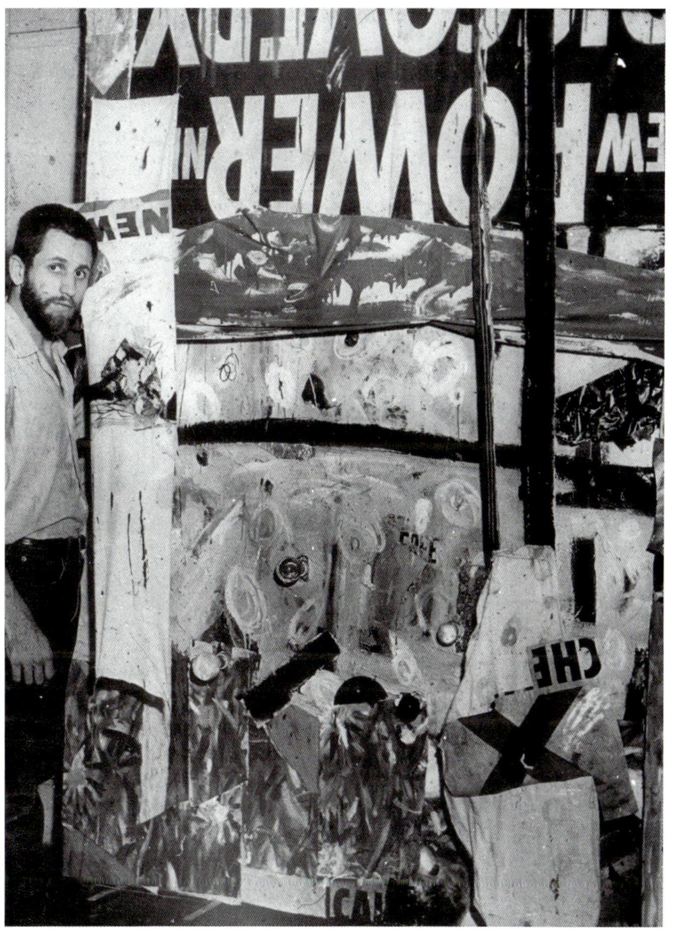

Fig. 4. **Allan Kaprow**
Penny Arcade, 1956
Assemblage with lights and sounds, 243.8 × 182.9 × 60.9 cm (96 × 72 × 24 in.)
Destroyed

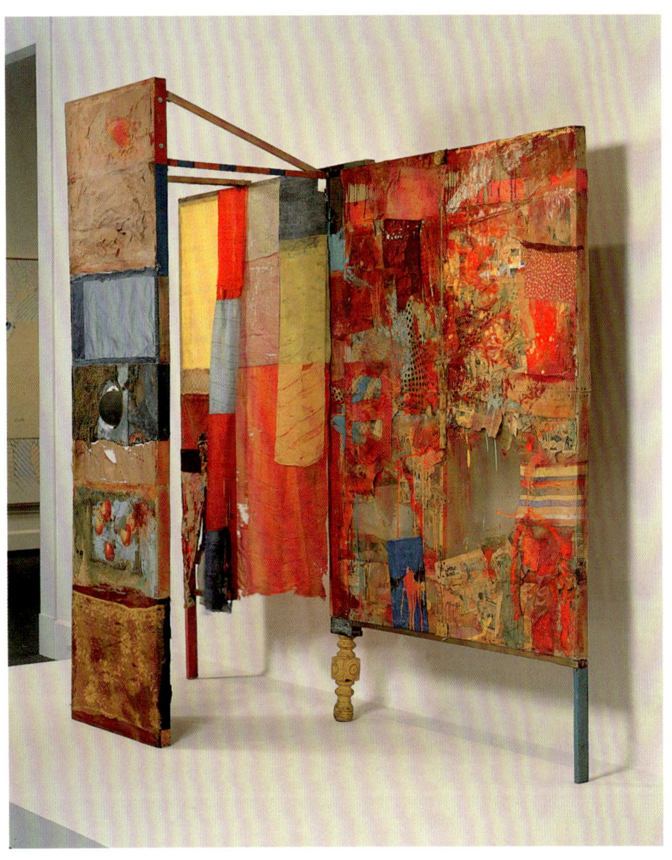

Fig. 5. **Robert Rauschenberg** **(American, born 1925)**

Minutiae, 1954

Combine: oil, paper, fabric, newspaper, wood, metal, and plastic, with mirror on braided wire, on wood structure, 214.6 × 205.7 × 77.4 cm (84½ × 81 × 30½ in.)

Private collection, Switzerland

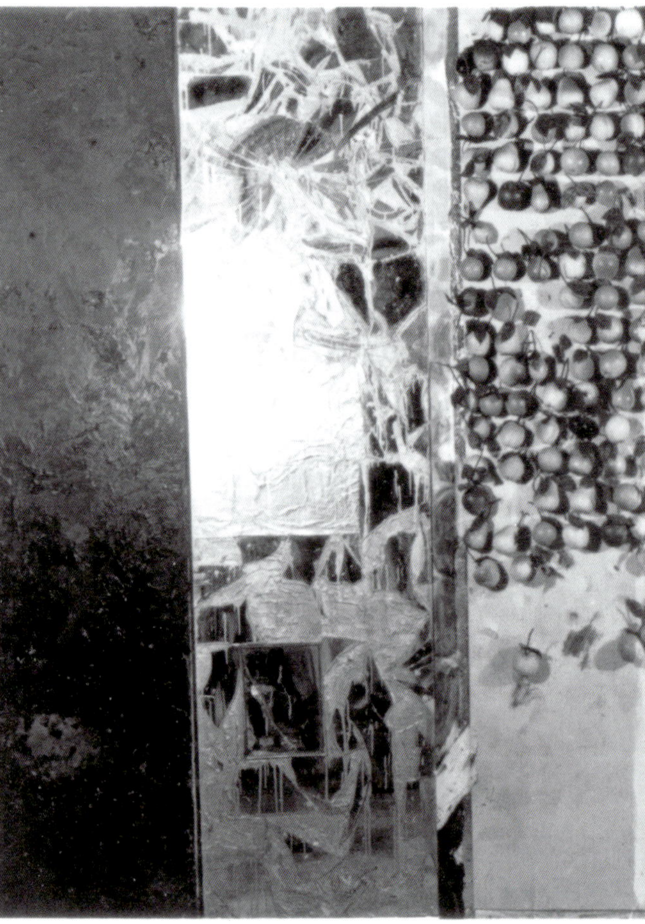

Fig. 6. **Allan Kaprow**

Rearrangeable Panels, 1957–59

Assemblage: oil, leaves, lightbulbs, plastic apples, and mirror on canvas and wood, nine panels, dimensions variable

Musée national d'art moderne, Centre Georges Pompidou, Paris

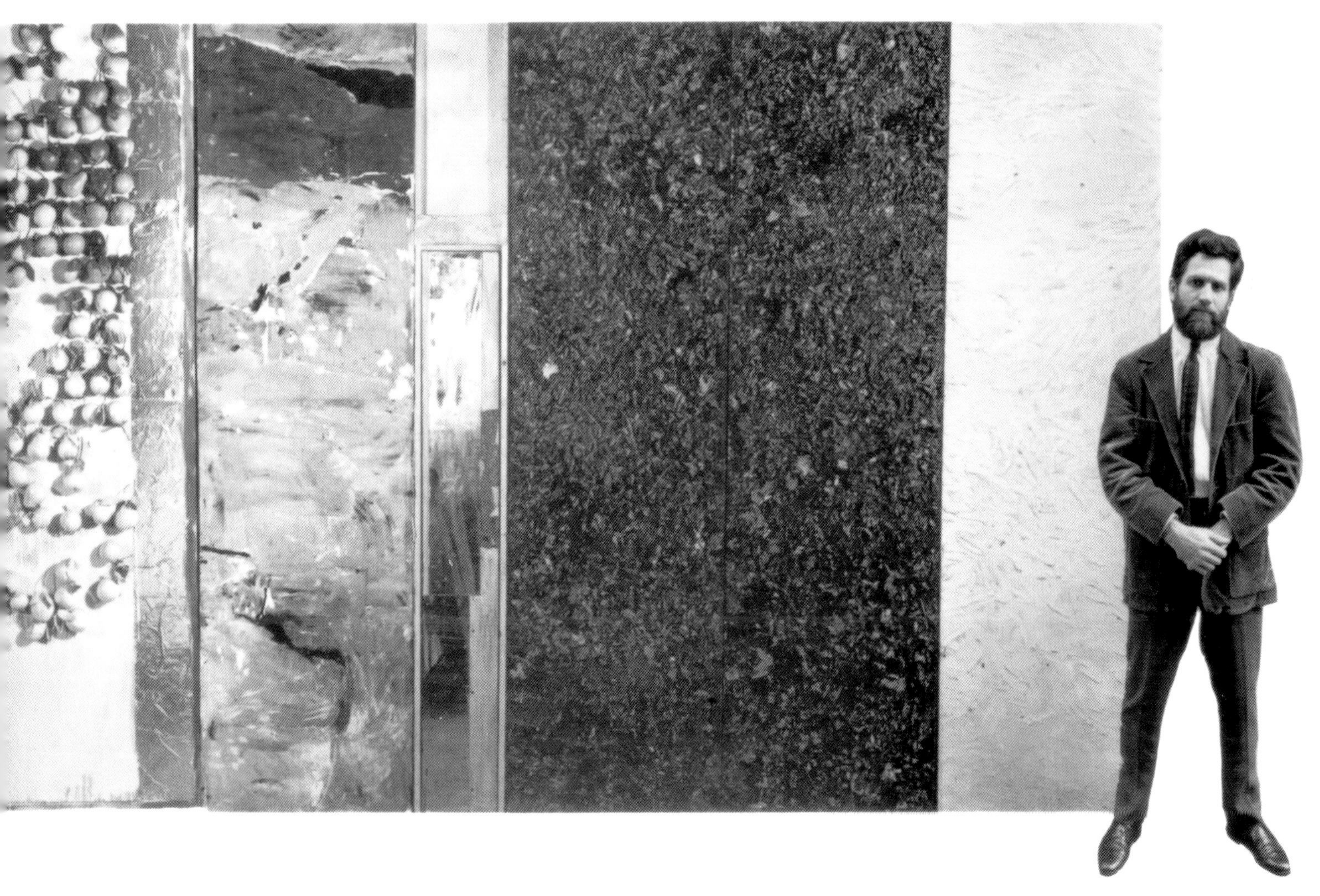

and committed chess playing) to his art. More immediate were Rauschenberg's Combines, such as *Minutiae* < FIG. 5 >, an extraordinary work that articulates the gray area between object and performance in spite of the fact that it was created as a prop for Merce Cunningham, whose dancers moved through, around, and under it for a 1954 performance of the same name.

As envisioned by Kaprow, *Rearrangeable Panels* can be read as a field painting, an installation that wraps around the viewer, or an assemblage that the viewer walks around < FIG. 6; SEE CHRONOLOGY, FIGS. 16–19 >. The panels do not have a fixed order. They are easily moved and rearranged (by the artist, initially), and moving the panels was encouraged by the artist as a way to vary its presentation. In this respect, *Rearrangeable Panels* has as its conceptual foundation Chinese and Japanese screen paintings, which are similarly composed as multiple panels of essentially human scale, both in height and width. Such paintings have architectural implications and a sense of being apart from, yet also defining, the environment in which they exist. It is likely that Kaprow was familiar with Japanese screen painting and its impact on Gutai, a group of avant-garde artists active in Osaka during the 1950s < FIG. 7 >, since he did much to bring these artists to international attention in the early 1960s. Surely Kaprow was subliminally or directly influenced by the screens that had provided a flexible and rearrangeable format for Shimamoto Shōzō, Murakami Saburō, and other Japanese artists.

Although *Rearrangeable Panels* is made up of nine distinct panels, they can be grouped. Most dramatic are the two panels that are overlaid with plant material. The dry, brittle fall leaves that adhere to these panels produce a relatively consistent and uniformly textured surface. The unfinished, process-oriented quality of *Rearrangeable Panels* arises from the dimensional qualities of the imitation apples that are spread across two other panels. Unlike the leaves, which cover their panels, the apples occupy the upper two-thirds of this two-panel composition, with the lower third left blank. A large passage of white paint begins at the bottom of the composition and moves upward, providing visual support for the apples and then obscuring approximately one quarter of them. The stripe of white gives these two panels the feel of an ongoing process and, in a way, of spontaneity.

Although it is obvious that the leaves and the apples are meant to go together, or to be seen in relationship to each other, the other two groupings are less obvious but in some ways more interesting. The black panel, which has clear references to Rauschenberg and Ad Reinhardt's black paintings, is a counterpart to the painted white panel with its exquisitely textured marks and strokes—references to the abstract impressionists of the New York School. More interesting is how the white panel anticipates the early works of Robert Ryman, who, responding to abstract expressionism and Rauschenberg's white paintings, created textured fields of white with contrasting bits of color.

The remaining three panels seem at first glance to have little to do with each another. One is a composition of fractured mirrored glass. One is a collage of scraps of paper with seemingly random applications of black, white, and red paint. One is a very narrow panel, divided horizontally into sections of bare canvas and mirror. The qualities of reflectivity and opacity tie these panels together, most obviously by the mirror, which refers to the broken mirrored surface. Less apparent is the similar use of bits of found material, whether glass or paper.

The lights on top of each panel are an obvious reference to funhouses, circuses, and fairs, but they have a more important function as a visual lintel that ties together the disparate materials that Kaprow used < SEE CHRONOLOGY, FIG. 19 >. The lights create an architectural element that strings together, both visually and metaphorically, the "randomness" of the work. Kaprow leaves it up to the curator or installer to make the final decision about how the panels will be viewed. It is in the installation of *Rearrangeable Panels* that Kaprow's vision was truly revolutionary. Nonetheless, certain elements

Fig. 7. **Kazuo Shiraga (Japanese, born 1924)**
Work 1, 1954
Oil on paper, 109 × 77.5 cm (43 × 30½ in.)
Hyogo Prefectural Museum of Modern Art, Hyogo

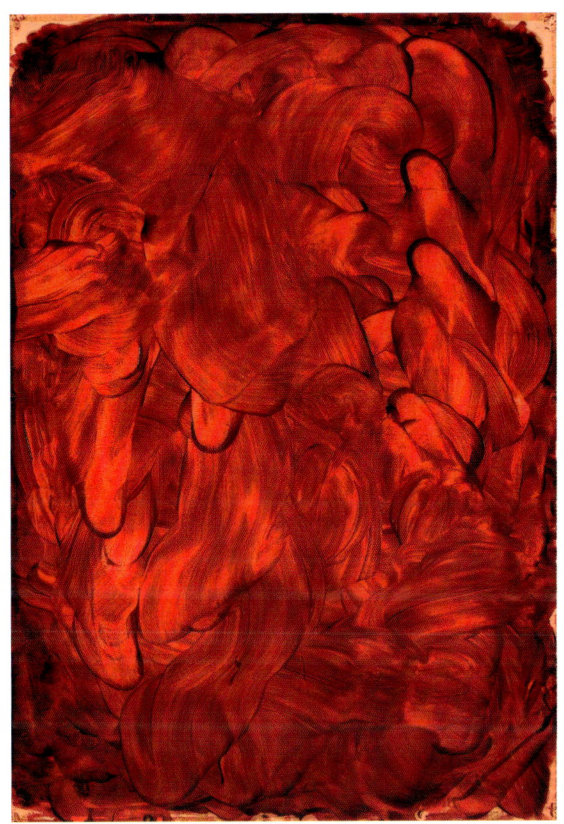

demand the recognition of particular pairings and sequencings, and to arrange them differently would be a deliberate strike against them.

Shortly after he completed *Rearrangeable Panels,* Kaprow wrote that artists were increasingly thinking of the work of art as "a situation, an action, an environment or an event."[10] His description of such a work is easily applied to *Rearrangeable Panels:* "Its shape is sprawling and irregular, sometimes made up of units that are infinitely rearrangeable, expandable and reduceable [*sic*] to adjust to different areas, which gives the whole an ambiguous, fluid existence."[11] Whether the work is presented as a freestanding sculptural object, an environment that fills the field of vision, or a fieldlike painting, the revolutionary decision that Kaprow makes is to define any arrangement of the panels as only one of a large group of possibilities.

With *Rearrangeable Panels,* Kaprow no doubt took cues from his studies with Cage, whose time-based experiments with chance and randomness had greatly influenced him. Through his choice of materials, construction of the visual elements, and pairing of the panels, Kaprow created a work that incorporated an element of randomness and chance, but within predetermined parameters. With *18 Happenings in 6 Parts,* presented at the Reuben Gallery in New York in 1959, Kaprow expanded on the legacy of Pollock by creating a work in which gesture occurred in real time <FIGS. 8–11>. Pioneered simultaneously by New York artists such as Jim Dine, Red Grooms, Claes Oldenburg, and Robert Whitman, Happenings were soon internationally embraced. Initially presented in a limited space for a limited audience, they differed from traditional theatrical productions in that they did not follow conventional narratives and typically invited the viewers' participation. Indeed, the frequent presentation of Happenings in art galleries underscored their origins in modern painting and sculpture (specifically, action painting and assemblage), filtered through the works of Cage. In his Happenings, Kaprow instituted the idea of organizing a series of events in a changeable order.

> For example, we will write down this set: 7 smiles, 3 crumpled papers, 19 lunch-box latch sounds. Element one will have seven kinds of smile in this order: happy, trance-like, benign, silly, disarming, insidious, fearful. Element two will have three kinds of crumpled paper: a panel 6 feet by 8 feet with irregular folds pasted on it in cadmium yellow medium, a box-kite affair of 3 feet by 7 feet with torn patches and bits of high, crumpled newspaper with the sides painted each in three shades of cadmium yellow on bands of unequal size (these can be numerically assigned) and lastly, a hanging group of nine balls of crumpled tissue paper colored zinc yellow, and cream yellow, all different in size. Each of these three variations is conceived as a unit, even though one has nine parts. These parts may be organized with a separate row. These can be fixed or can be presented and removed at certain times on the score.[12]

Identifying a relationship between performance and object making, Kaprow stated that, "just as space in painting and sculpture has become equivalent to the solids formerly considered inviolate, so silence and literal space between events are held to be equally important as the events."[13]

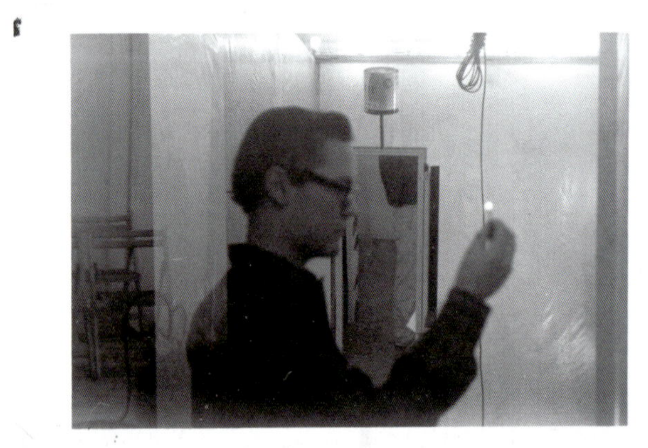

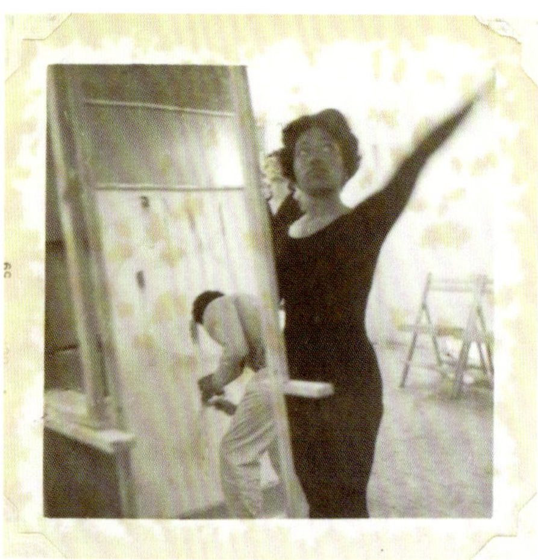

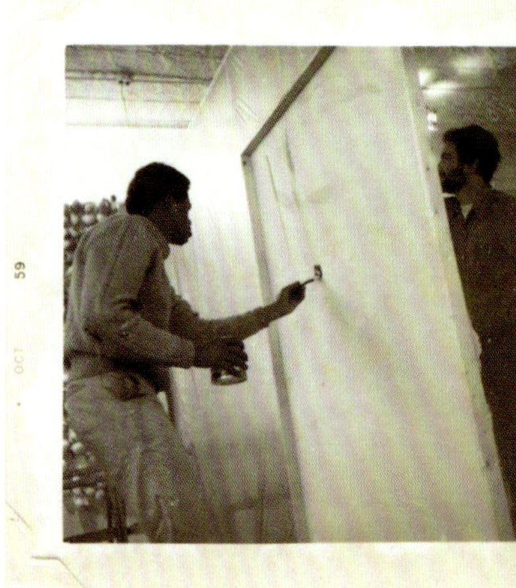

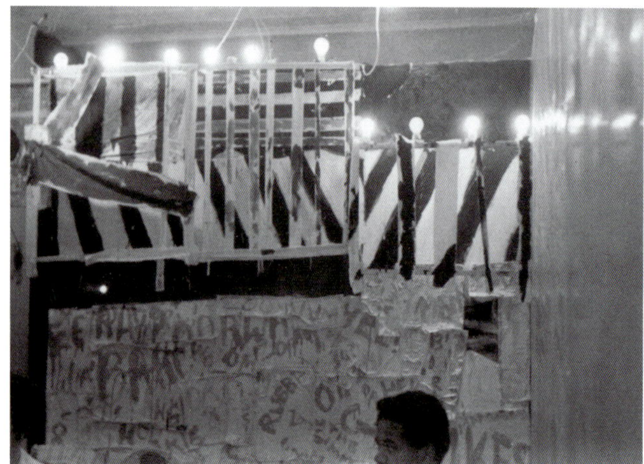

Figs. 8–11. **Views of *18 Happenings in 6 Parts* (1959)**

For *18 Happenings in 6 Parts,* Kaprow created an interactive environment that manipulated the audience to a degree unprecedented in modern art. Indeed, this manipulation constituted one of his most important contributions to contemporary art forms. The work comprised a series of closely timed actions performed by Kaprow and participating actors and artists—including Sam Francis, Leslie, and Segal—who worked from a carefully conceived and tightly scripted score. Kaprow choreographed the movement of bodies, flashing of lights, playing or making of sounds, and projection of slides and films < SEE CHRONOLOGY, FIGS. 29–50 >. Although these "happenings" were plotted out one after another on a grid, they did not relate to one another in a traditional narrative sense. The performance was staged in six parts in three rooms that were defined by semi-transparent plastic sheets, painted and collaged with references to his previous works. *Rearrangeable Panels* formed the north wall of one of the rooms.

While Cage's encouragement of audience participation was motivated by his desire to relinquish authorial control, the audience members of Kaprow's Happenings were the participants and props through which his vision was executed. Prior to the staging of *18 Happenings in 6 Parts,* each audience member received an invitation consisting of a plastic envelope containing an assortment of images and objects, including bits of paper, photographs, painted fragments, and wood.[14] On the evening of the performance, each received programs and three stapled cards printed with an explanation and instructions: "The performance is divided into six parts. Each part contains three happenings which occur at once. The beginning and end of each will be signalled by a bell. At the end of the performance two strokes of the bell will be heard. . . . There will be *no applause after each set,* but you may applaud after the sixth set if you wish."[15] The program also stipulated when audience members would be required to change seats or move between the rooms.

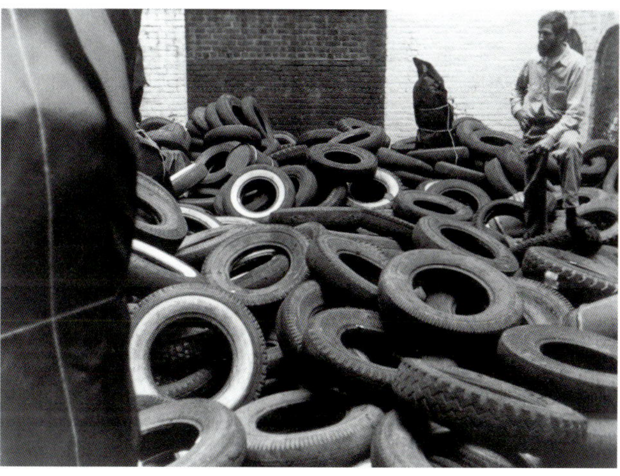

Fig. 12. **Kaprow in *Yard*** (1961)
Photo: Robert R. McElroy

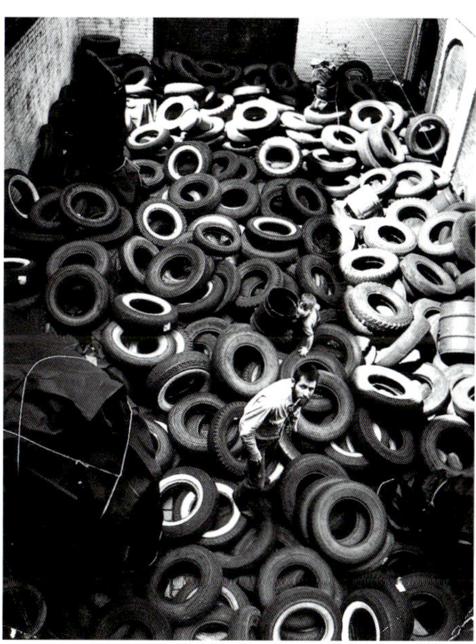

Fig. 13. **Kaprow in *Yard*** (1961) **with his son Anton**

If the manipulation of the audience in *18 Happenings in 6 Parts* was a move away from Cage, Kaprow's work in the following years drew closer to the broad, gestural, physical qualities of the action painters, a trajectory evident in the progression from works such as *Hysteria* (1956) and *Rearrangeable Panels* to the immersive Environments such as *Yard* (1961). In *Yard,* first presented at the Martha Jackson Gallery in New York as part of the group exhibition *Environments, Situations, Spaces,* Kaprow created a field of used tires in the tight confines of the backyard of the townhouse in which the gallery was situated < FIGS. 12, 13; SEE CHRONOLOGY, FIGS. 66–70 >. The work existed as art only when audience members entered the space and interacted with the tires by, for example, climbing on them or rearranging them. Viewers were encouraged to believe that they were playing, but Kaprow established very controlled parameters within which they were required to act. Kaprow was being heralded by critics as a radical on the art horizon, but his audiences found that the abandonment of the traditional object and the open-endedness of the Happenings made his works extraordinarily difficult to comprehend.

In fall 1960, Howard Moody, pastor of the Judson Memorial Church in New York, invited Kaprow to serve as the director of the church's art gallery. The artist's first project for the Judson Gallery, *Apple Shrine* < FIGS. 14, 15; SEE CHRONOLOGY, FIGS. 55–58 >, was, even more than *Yard,* an Environment that expanded on some of the more expressive and situational aspects of *18 Happenings in 6 Parts.* Like the action-collages, this Environment was densely packed with materials, some of which reflected the influence of *Rearrangeable Panels.* Kaprow created a labyrinth of narrow passageways from chicken wire, cardboard, tar paper, straw, and crumpled newspaper, which formed a structure that stretched from ceiling to floor, playing off the site's identity as a church. Viewers navigated through the work to reach an inner sanctum, a private chapel of sorts, with a three-tiered wooden altar, suspended above the floor, that featured a

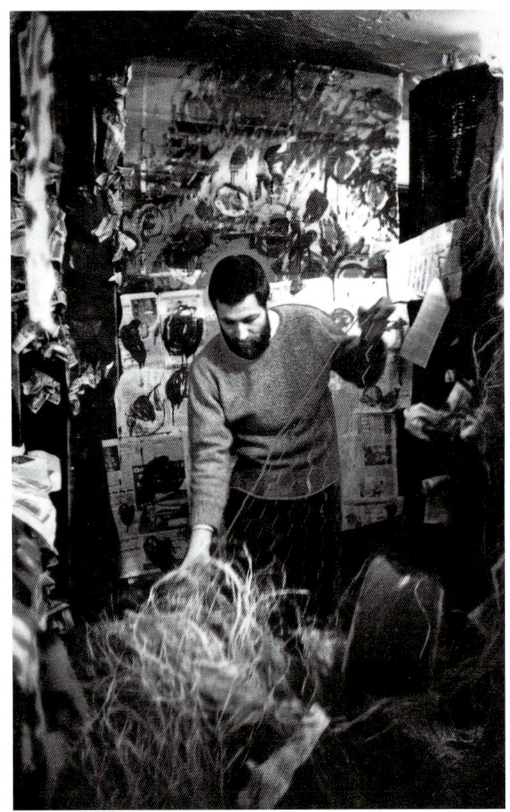

mixture of fresh and plastic apples—very much like those attached to *Rearrangeable Panels*—that they were invited to pick. As Kelley noted, "Originally, Kaprow had not intended to use real apples, planning instead to reuse the plastic ones that had fallen off *Rearrangeable Panels* over the years. As the Environment took shape, however, the symbolic potential of the 'temptation' to pick an apple, either real or fake, became central to his thinking."[16]

The exhibition received no significant critical attention. Indeed, a critic for the *Village Voice* reported that it "was hardly noticed by the public or much of the professional art world." He wrote that Kaprow had been well known for some years for his Environments and Happenings and that he was "an exceptionally original artist and a leader who has seen a movement develop around him." The critic described the Environment in great detail, noting specific features such as the mirror embedded in a cluster of paper and wire that, upon first viewing, was mistaken for an opening in the rough wall, only to reveal itself in the viewer's encounter with his own face, as if he were meeting a stranger. Finally, he explained that "Mr. Kaprow's art poses problems. The exhibition is now dismantled, its materials have been carted away by the junk man, and it will be not seen again. If its vocabulary is unfamiliar, it will not remain to be judged at a later, more knowledgeable year. Its life is a present one, and only memory can carry it into the future."[17]

Of course, we now know that this account, which accurately depicted not only the work but also Kaprow's place within the New York art world, was written by Kaprow under the pseudonym "Theodore Tucker, South Lincoln, Massachusetts" <SEE CHRONOLOGY, FIGS. 59–60>. For Kaprow, the insertion into the public domain of a response written with first-person knowledge but seemingly delivered in another's voice was consistent with his bifurcated role as both thinker and objectmaker. "Far beyond the 'Apple Shrine's' actual content in humanity," he concluded, "stands Kaprow's inadvertent quarrel with all the rapid glories, qualities and eternities which we think are History." As Kaprow and other truly innovative artists of the era discovered, the only sure way to place their work in the historical record was by their own hands. At the end of his pseudonymous review, Kaprow included this prescient note: "Dear Sir, I have written the enclosed critique of Allan Kaprow's work in the hope that the *Village Voice* might publish it free of charge. I think your readers are owed an account of this truly important art being created in the Village. Sincerely."[18]

Pollock, the gestural action-oriented painter, and Cage, the conceptually oriented teacher, had a remarkably generative impact on Kaprow. While their influence is instantiated in *Apple Shrine,* equally significant is Kaprow's articulation of the work's meaning and position within art history in the *Village Voice* review. *Apple Shrine* exists because of Kaprow's desire to embrace two distinct art historical legacies, and he played an active (though anonymous) role in shaping the critical discourse around it.

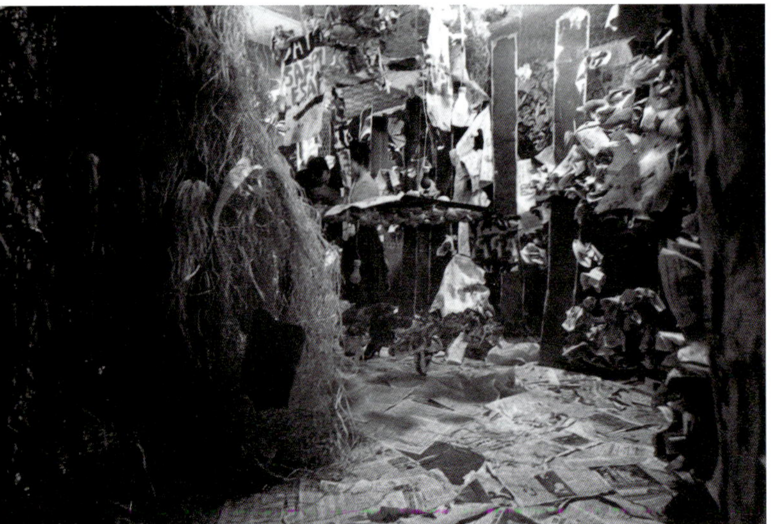

Figs. 14, 15. **Views of *Apple Shrine* (1960)**
Photos: Robert R. McElroy

Notes

1. Allan Kaprow, "The Principles of Modern Art," typescript, 1959, Allan Kaprow Papers, ca. 1940–1997, accession no. 980063 (box 46, folder 11); hereafter Allan Kaprow Papers.
2. Allan Kaprow, "Formalism: Flogging a Dead Horse (1974)," in idem, *Essays on the Blurring of Art and Life,* ed. Jeff Kelley (Berkeley: Univ. of California Press, 1993), 159–60.
3. Although many painters, ranging from Robert Rauschenberg to Jasper Johns to Willem de Kooning, are recognized for introducing the "real" into art during the mid-1950s, often overlooked are sculptors of the early part of the decade, such as David Smith, Richard Peter Stankiewicz, and the rarely remembered Jean Follett. In Follett's work, for example, objects began to take center stage on a two-dimensional surface as abstracted compositional elements with no specific meaning or narrative.
4. Allan Kaprow, "A Statement," in Michael Kirby, *Happenings: An Illustrated Anthology* (New York: E.P. Dutton, 1965), 44–45.
5. George Segal, as cited in Barbara Haskell, "The Aesthetics of Junk," in idem, *Blam! The Explosion of Pop, Minimalism, and Performance, 1958–1964,* exh. cat. (New York: Whitney Museum of American Art, 1984), 15.
6. Kaprow, "A Statement" (note 4), 45.
7. Kaprow, "A Statement" (note 4), 45–46.
8. "Definition of an Environment," statement provided by the Allan Kaprow Studio, 2004.
9. Jeff Kelley, *Childsplay: The Art of Allan Kaprow* (Berkeley: Univ. of California Press, 2004), 14–15.
10. Allan Kaprow, "Some Observations on Contemporary Art" in *New Forms—New Media 1* (New York: Martha Jackson Gallery, 1960), n.p.
11. Kaprow, "Some Observations on Contemporary Art" (note 10), n.p.
12. Kaprow, "Principles of Modern Art" (note 1).
13. Kaprow, "Principles of Modern Art" (note 1). Kaprow stated that, at least for himself, the free and spontaneous organization of form is a method of composition with the greatest risk of becoming dependent on "inspiration" and thus of falling into the trap of devolving into cliché or habit.
14. RoseLee Goldberg, *Performance Art from Futurism to the Present* (New York: Harry N. Abrams, 1988), 128.
15. Allan Kaprow, program notes for *18 Happenings in 6 Parts,* as quoted in RoseLee Goldberg, *Performance Art from Futurism to the Present* (New York: Harry N. Abrams, 1988), 129.
16. Kelley, *Childsplay* (note 9), 53.
17. Theodore Tucker [pseud., Allan Kaprow], "Kaprow's 'Apple Shrine,'" *Village Voice,* 12 January 1961, 7.
18. I am grateful to Kelly Nipper for bringing this quote to my attention. In addition, I would like to thank Kelly Nipper and Tamara Bloomberg for guidance and review of an early draft of this text.

Writing the Happening: The Aesthetics of Nonart

Alex Potts

Allan Kaprow has been a significant presence in the American art world since he first came to public notice in the late 1950s. The reason for this, however, does not lie primarily in the reputation acquired by the art that he produced. Happenings, after all, had a relatively brief life span and were soon marginalized by other performance-based and conceptual forms that became established in the late 1960s and early 1970s as the leading alternatives to traditional, object-based art. Kaprow's attempt to resist the co-optive power of the art world and to position his works so that they operated not within the arena of art, but on the boundary between art and nonart, had its most pervasive impact as an ethical and artistic ideal propounded through his writing and teaching. Starting with his famous essay, "The Legacy of Jackson Pollock," which came out in 1958, he published regularly during the 1960s and 1970s in *ARTnews* and, later, *Artforum,* and his ideas enjoyed a second lease on life with the publication of *Essays on the Blurring of Art and Life* in 1993.[1]

Kaprow's writings were not just commentaries on his practice. They were integral to his art, and in an important sense they constituted what it represented for a larger public. His Happenings were generated by way of written scores and talks delivered to participants,[2] and they lived on after they "happened" not only by way of these scores, carefully preserved by Kaprow in his archive and in some cases published by him, but also in the written recollections of participants and Kaprow himself.[3] Writing, then, played an integral role in the genesis and realization of his Happenings, just as it is essential to how we imagine them today. The verbal testimony and the photographic documentation constitute not only the form in which they exist for us as works of art but also their representation as works of art with some kind of public profile from the moment they were enacted. That Kaprow has a substantial presence as an artist has much to do with his evident talents as a writer—with, that is, his ability to conjure up scenarios and convey in words what the physical, sensory impact of these scenarios might be. What is more, it is within his writings that he played out a paradox central to his conception of nonart. His resonant verbal evocations constitute his Happenings as events disencumbered of the formal and aesthetic pretensions of conventional artwork and, yet, also as phenomena that have a powerful aesthetic effect.[4]

This essay focuses on the writings Kaprow produced up until the late 1960s, when writing, for him, existed in creative tension with an artistic practice that still had a fairly high profile—before he retreated to informal stagings of his works among friends or on the home territory of educational establishments, such as the colleges where he taught. A complex and ultimately precarious negotiation between engaging with the art world and keeping it at bay fed his most substantive and intriguing endeavors. His nonart initiatives, as he observed on several occasions, were not to be seen as entirely disassociated from art.[5] The point was to devise works that escaped the self-referentiality within which modern art was trapped, and this could not be done merely by creating works that either alluded to or directly incorporated realities lying outside the sphere of art. What was needed was a procedure for effecting a compelling transition from materials and situations that were genuinely nonartistic—that were, as he put it, "lifelike"—to an art that momentarily existed outside the context of the art world.

Such a close interplay between art and nonart was consistent with the way he conceived of his own artistic trajectory: as tracing a move toward ever more lifelike and less artlike materials and situations, but without utterly negating his earlier conception of art. As he saw it, the assemblage aesthetic with which he had experimented in his first object-based works in the 1950s was taken up and elaborated in his slightly later environmental art and then redeployed in the structuring of his subsequent Happenings, which were in effect informal assemblages of events and situations played out over space as well as over time. This aesthetic also informed the compositional procedures used in his score writing. Kaprow was quite explicit about such continuities, spelling

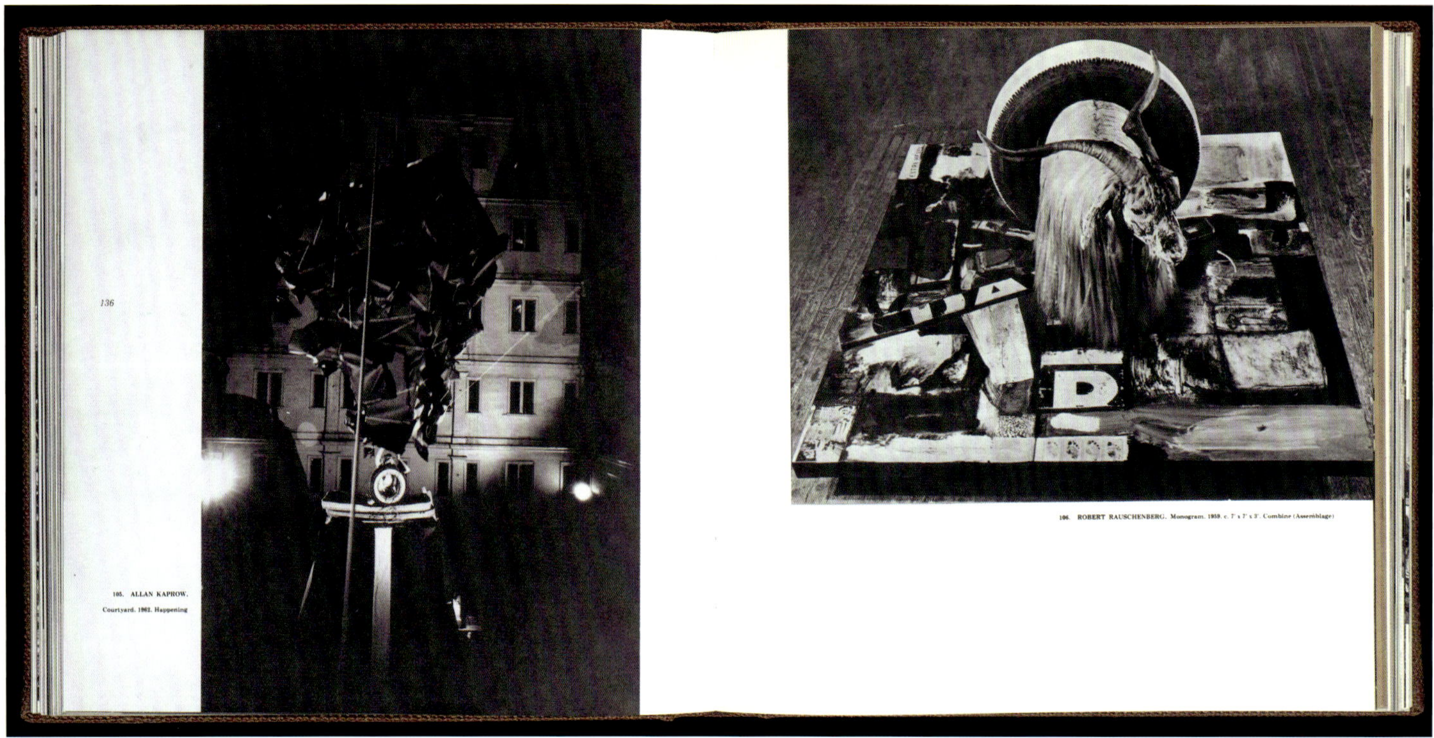

Fig. 1. **Allan Kaprow's *Courtyard* (1962) and Robert Rauschenberg's *Monogram* (1959)**
From Allan Kaprow, *Assemblage, Environments & Happenings* (Harry N. Abrams, 1966), 136–37

them out most fully in *Assemblage, Environments & Happenings* (1966), a publication that included a survey of junk art assemblages by himself and other artists such as Robert Rauschenberg < FIG. 1 >. In the press release for *Courtyard,* staged in New York in 1962, he made the point that his Happenings had "evolved in logical stages, by advancing as far as possible the implications inherent in *Assemblage,* the visual and tactile art that combines diverse materials into unexpected wholes."[6]

In Kaprow's view, genuine experimenters like himself were committed not to eradicating art, but to realizing a "conversion of nonart to art" that would be "electrifying."[7] They could succeed in this endeavor only if they were to "ruthlessly rip out the last shred of artistry in their every thought and enthusiasm."[8] In other words, he saw the extreme measures he took to break away from the closed circuits of object-based art as the only viable basis on which he could sustain a genuinely credible and significant art in present-day circumstances. He was not denying the significance of earlier art made in a very different context. Indeed, he stressed that it was with the aim of preserving the larger existential purposes driving the last wave of avant-garde painting, represented by artists such as Pollock, that he was impelled to abandon painting and anything that smacked of the procedures and conventions of object-based art.

Happenings, as he explained in an essay published in 1961, were to be thought of, "like American art of the late 1940s," as "a moral act, a human stand of great urgency, whose professional status as art is less a criterion than their certainty as an ultimate existential commitment."[9] As he put it more grandiosely in *Assemblage, Environments & Happenings,* the nonart initiatives he was championing "proceeded on the assumption that at present any avant-garde art is primarily a philosophical quest and a finding of truths, rather than purely an aesthetic activity."[10] In a situation of "extraordinary and rapid change" such as the present, the idea of a "perfect work of art" had become "irrelevant," and "great works" might "only be looked forward to . . . in the sense that they may be moments of profound vision into the workings of things, an imitation of life, so to speak, rather than artistic tours de force, i.e., cosmetics."[11] To be anything more than superfluous "artistic tours de force" or "cosmetics," artworks had to take something categorically nonartistic as their point of departure.

Far from being "anti-aesthetic," Kaprow was fascinated and compelled by moments when art and life momentarily became indistinguishable, when something with the reality and density of the nonartistic happened to take on an aesthetic charge. This interest, which stimulated some of his most perceptive writings, emerges clearly in his analysis of the aesthetics of the junk materials that played such an important role in the assemblage art of the time. An artwork made out of impermanent, disregarded, and expendable everyday materials that "will pass into dust or garbage very quickly," he explained, could exist as something much more suggestive than "a fixed, enduring object to be placed in a locked case."[12] Its essential mutability, its truthfulness as a phenomenon caught up in a larger cycle of "creation—decay—creation," was partly determined by the realities of the modern world of consumer capitalism—a world of junk and throwaway products. But it also had to do with a deeper sense of temporality, an ephemerality that subtended the very fabric of everyday living and thinking.

> The use of debris, waste products . . . has, of course, a clear range of allusions with obvious sociological implications, the simplest being the artist's positive involvement, on the one hand with an everyday world, and on the other with a group of objects which, being expendable, might suggest that corresponding lack of status which is supposed to be the fate of anything creative today. These choices must not be ignored, for they reveal what in our surroundings charges the imagination as well as what is most human in our art. But beyond this is the larger issue of reality understood as *constant metamorphosis.* This viewpoint, this metaphysics, is more fundamental than our "throwaway" culture. The latter is the topical vehicle for the former and, while important, should become something else in time.[13]

Kaprow envisaged here, albeit vaguely, the possibility of moving beyond a throwaway culture, as well as beyond a culture that assigns particular value to things and works of art specially preserved and possessed as pieces of property.[14] A radical anarchist and egalitarian politics emerges from time to time in Kaprow's meditations on what a new conception of art might be: one not fixated on objects. This stance also appears in the more laid-back writings of John Cage, who, if anyone could be named as such, was the guru of experimental art in the late 1950s and early 1960s. Cage strove to create a new music that would, in its negation of conventional compositional structures, help fashion a world liberated from individual possession and private property. As he put it in his somewhat gnomic but elegant formulation: "Our poetry now is the reali-zation that we possess nothing. Anything therefore is a delight (since we do not pos-sess it)."[15]

The materials that Kaprow incorporated into his assemblages, Environments, and Happenings—such as cardboard boxes and pieces of paper or foil—were often relatively neutral, certainly more so than the lacerated posters and worn-out artifacts that other assemblage artists used in their work. Kaprow noted how he alternated between things that have "a high degree of associational meaning" because of their function, social use, and psychological associations, such as "machine parts, baby carriages, clothing," and more "generalized" materials, such as "cloth," "cardboard," and "wood," that "are somewhat less specific in meaning."[16] These materials were not necessarily used or rejected, even if they often became rubbish in the course of a Happening. They might be seen to accord with the open neutrality of a world undivided and undisrupted by private property or psychological obsession. In one somewhat uncharacteristic moment, Kaprow imagined a quasi-utopian, purely formal art, in which materials and situations could be "freely manipulated without jarring the overtones of the imagery within them." He explained, however, that this was impossible to realize in present circumstances, where any everyday material—any material that makes up the fabric of our lives, even one as common as Kleenex—would, when attention was focused on it, "push into relief all that we have only half consciously thought about [it] and its intimate uses."[17]

Kaprow has a reputation as one of the more significant opponents of high modernist formalism. He was so effective in this role, however, because he understood formalist principles from the inside and had a real feeling for the dialectic between purity and impurity that sustained his commitment to formal rigor. In "Impurity" (1963), the essay in which he presents his possibly most striking argument against formalism, he made the telling point that "the impure aspect of pure painting like Mondrian's is not some hidden compositional flaw but rather the psychological setting which must be impure for the notion of purity to make any sense at all."[18] He also overturned the common distinction between Pollock's courting of chaos and Barnett Newman's apparent purism and clarity. His detailed formal analysis of the two artists' works led him to the conclusion that, once we engage closely with Newman's larger paintings, we become aware of a "flood of utter chaos, of sheer color inundating us, of lines crashing into splinters and vanishing into the vibrating deluge."[19] The "terror" and "passion" this induces, he claimed, "are as close to our marrow, as unsettling to us emotionally, as anything of Pollock's."[20]

His conception of nonart, then, is not to be confused with a conventional celebration of antiform at the expense of form. The most recent proponents of radical antiform, he noted in an analysis of Robert Morris's felt pieces of the late 1960s, in reality produced only "antigeometry"; their works were "a rephrasing of the formlessness that preoccupied the ancients from the Egyptians onward."[21] Kaprow made it clear that a formal organizing and framing of things enters into our most ordinary engagement with objects and environments. In his view, it was the larger physical and social context within which a work was enacted, not its greater or lesser formlessness of shape, that was at issue in any true "deemphasis of formal esthetics" that might lead to a "palpable experience of the measureless, the indeterminate."[22] For the experimental artist, giving "the heave" to conventional compositional practices was not a matter of abandoning form.[23] Rather, it entailed ridding oneself of the formal patternings peculiar to art and adopting instead those forms inherent in the substance of the nonart materials with which one was working. (Remember here that a number of Kaprow's Happenings from this period incorporated live chickens.)

> The only form a thing has is what it looks like or does. That is, if a chicken runs, eats chicken feed, and roosts, that is all the composition required and all the composition the experimenter needs to think about. This is not nonform, for the brain can only function in patterned ways. It is simply an avoidance of the familiar artistic distinction between matter (the medium) and its malleability (the form).[24]

In this passage, Kaprow argued for the deployment of the real forms (as distinct from conventionalized forms) that we see once we do away with our habitual reliance on the framings and compositional structurings of art. The broader philosophical question—whether these real forms are ones that exist in the things themselves or whether they are structurings inherent in the operations of our mental and perceptual apparatuses that we unself-consciously bring to bear when engaging in nonart activities—is left open. Kaprow was above all concerned with a kind of work whose forms do not present themselves as deliberately imposed by an aesthetic attitude. Rather, they are integral to our ordinary nonart interactions with the world we inhabit and, as a result, seem embedded in our everyday lives. This is in conformity with his conception of a nonart that momentarily blurs the boundaries between art and what is not art, making art come alive as something truly imbricated in the substance of our lives.

Kaprow made extensive use of highly formalized procedures in his practice as an artist. Like the structures deployed by Cage when composing his music, these procedures embraced the possibility of chance occurrences while also blocking the artist from imposing his own aesthetic choices on all aspects of a work. A clear recognition of the formal basis of his practice does come to the fore from time to time in his published writings. Perhaps most notable is a revealing passage at the end of "Assemblage, Environments, and Happenings," a long essay in which he talked about the compositional procedures he might use in generating a score for a Happening. Here he explained how, in "composing" an imagined scenario that he was presenting to the reader, he "played around with images on paper, shifting them this way and that, letting one thing suggest another."[25] He then pointed out that "shifting things around can be an excellent mode of *performance* as much as of composition."[26] He also quite explicitly noted that the assemblage aesthetic of his Happenings was played out in the compositional format of his written scores. In the latter, he combined a set of self-contained segments of text, each denoting a single event or action, in a sequence that is divested of conventional narrative flow.

The extent of his commitment to formal procedure emerges most clearly in the unpublished notes he made for the talks he gave to participants prior to the enactment of his Happenings, in which he described the tasks and the logic that informed them. In one such note related to *Household,* a Happening from 1964 that was showcased in *Assemblage, Environments & Happenings,* he explained how

> happenings function in three customary ways (which are, however, mutually dependant). They are
>
> 1. A fantasy performed
> 2. A formal structure and sub-structure (which seems to make the fantasy performable in direct images, and which also permits the third function to be realized, namely:)
> 3. pattern of meanings.[27]

The "formal structure," he went on to explain, should be composed from "relationships determined by [the] nature of [the] images" being deployed, a view that echoes the published comments quoted above about the nonart forms he was seeking to realize in his work.[28] The unpublished notes, however, make much more explicit the extent to which Kaprow was preoccupied with formal procedures. Moreover, his claim that the nonart forms incorporated into his works were inherent in the materials that he used represented a leap of faith just as great as the one demanded by the early modernists' assumption that the abstract forms in their work were not arbitrarily imposed artistic patternings but were grounded in the larger structuring of things over which the artist had no control. In both cases, the impulse to realize a formal structure that would be experienced as pure immediacy was fundamental.

Kaprow's writing did not function just as a formulation of generative ideas for his art, nor did it serve simply to explain his works to a larger public. It was an essential, constitutive element of his art. This was true for many artists of his generation, as it was for those of a slightly later generation who first came to prominence in the mid-to-late 1960s. The very existence of his art as a public phenomenon that could reach beyond the restricted circle of people who were participants in or direct witnesses of his Happenings depended on his verbal skills and on the written representations of his work and its informing principles. It is through the documents relating to his Happenings that one gains a sense of how expressive and symbolically loaded these early works were, and how they were enacted in very different registers of experience, with the tensions between these registers being central to the compelling nature of his artistic project. Reading through the earlier scores, created before he turned to a Zen-like conceptual simplicity in the later 1960s, one finds a focus on commonplace, junky materials and banal, ordinary actions coexisting with epic pretensions and blatant melodrama.

This disparity is also evident in his general characterizations of the nature of Happenings. On the one hand, he presented Happenings as laid-back and lifelike alternatives to the expressive intensity of conventional high art: "Happenings are events that, put simply, happen . . . . Their form is open-ended and fluid; nothing obvious is sought and therefore nothing is won, except the certainty of a number of occurrences to which we are more than normally attentive. They exist for a single performance, or only a few, and are gone forever as new ones take their place."[29] On the other hand, he saw melodrama as the defining condition of an authentic contemporary American art practice in general and of Happenings in particular.[30] There is certainly more than a touch of melodrama in the scenarios that Kaprow created, in which he invited the reader to imagine the new possibilities that would reveal themselves as the materials of art came off the wall and entered into the environment inhabited by the spectator: "Suddenly there were jungles, crowded streets, littered alleys, dream spaces of science fiction, rooms of madness, and junk-filled attics of the mind."[31] Consider too this list he presented of the nonart materials from which an artist might gain inspiration: "A United States Marine Corps manual on jungle-fighting tactics [by this point, America was already heavily involved in the Vietnam war], a tour of a laboratory where polyethylene kidneys are made, the daily traffic jams on the Long Island Expressway."[32] Such lists, like the Happenings themselves and the earlier assemblage works and Environments, form an almost arbitrary-seeming yet oddly suggestive conjuncture of disparate items that alternate between being utterly flat and mundane in tenor and having an intensity that is often disturbing as well as blatantly melodramatic.

The peculiar concatenation of the everyday with excess and "epic" pretension is vividly staged in a hypothetical score that Kaprow devised to give readers of his 1966 book on Happenings a "kaleidoscope sampling of occurrences typical of Happenings."

> Long maze of wall-size mirrors (as at oldtime carneys). Rows of blinking yellow, blue, and white lights. Quiet neons. Everybody wanders aimlessly. Rubbish on floors of passageways. Five janitors come in with vacuum sweepers, sucking up debris. Crackling sounds. Janitors leave. From above, whistling of some sad pop tune like "Don't Play It No More." More debris is dropped into passages. Crackling sounds again. Janitors rush around handing out brooms and everybody sweeps. Lots of dust, coughs. Mirrors begin to sway and shake. Whistling continues as high whine enters louder and louder. Wheelbarrows and shovels rolled in. Frenzied loading of trash, much noise. Brooms are grabbed from people, are held up close to mirrors and examined. Fellow comes in with wide brush and pail of soapy water and wipes over reflections. Janitors sweep and shout at each other from different passageways, *but their words are backwards.* They yell louder and faster. Then work and noise wears out and finally stops, dust settles, cans of beer are brought in for everybody. Workmen take a swig, burp, and pour beer on the floor. They go. Dead silence. Three pneumatic trip-hammers are dragged in. Compressors start. Floor is drilled into, noise is deafening, mirrors shatter.[33]

The scenario consists of a destabilizing array of events and eruptions of sound, incipiently violent and oppressively close, that disperse any sustained or clearly identifiable affective response. In contrast with melodrama, the playing out of these destructive impulses is interrupted before they can fully define or realize themselves—such interruption is fundamental to the strategies deployed by Kaprow. The sequences of low-key actions and the crescendos of frenzied activity suddenly stall, or drift off into inconsequentiality, framed within blocks of time that halt abruptly, usually at strictly cued points. These cuts prevent any developmental thrust or play of impulse from continuing into the next segment of extended durational occurrence, except as recollections existing entirely in the mind. Kaprow imagined here a very realist art, one echoing the jumble of contradictory possibilities and constraints and impulses that operated in contemporary society.

The realism of the scenario also invokes a distinctive and oddly familiar form of ritualized, everyday activity in the modern world, although it is one that is hard to categorize. The scene is one of laboring, but the working environment lacks definition. It is not the factory or any other characteristically modern workplace nor is it a domestic setting. Participants do ordinary maintenance, or sweeping, or basic construction work—tasks that are never-ending and do not give rise to even a provisionally fixed product. Here perhaps is a curious instantiation of Hannah Arendt's conception of the endless, organic-seeming labor processes of a modern consumer society, which she contrasted with traditional work processes directed to the fashioning of clearly defined, and reified, products.[34]

Exposed here through Kaprow's evident literary talent is something fundamental to the whole enterprise of the Happening as he conceived it. The ability of those beyond the circle of immediate participants or initiates to imagine the physical immediacy of a Happening was necessarily constituted to a large degree through language, particularly given the fact that one of the key principles of Happenings was that they were one-time, ephemeral events that could not be reenacted. Unrecorded, they would soon sink into oblivion. Kaprow was too canny and self-aware as an artist to allow this to happen and all too well able to use his writings to endow his oxymoronic ideal of nonart with a public presence, even if this meant throwing into question his commitment to the living immediacy of the passing moment.

The actual Happening lives on in Kaprow's writings as a phenomenon located in the gap between two verbal articulations: the scenario or projection of what the Happening might be, and the recollection of, or commentary on, what it was. In the case of a conventional artwork, some kind of object fills this gap—something that can be preserved and staged in a museum and that gives the illusion that it fully embodies its artistic essence. In actual fact, the object comes alive and gains real significance for us because we are prompted to imagine the mental and psychological processes and the artistic gestures that once brought it into being and, afterward, to keep recollecting and pondering it as something that sticks in our minds and gathers around it a host of associated thoughts and feelings. With Kaprow's Happenings, this process is laid bare. Happenings do not offer a definable, publicly available physical object that we can identify as embodying the sensuous immediacy of the work. We are obliged to attend to the flux of narrative that makes the artwork into something other than a fixed, inert thing.

The objectlessness of a Kaprow artwork presents us with something that cannot be fully assimilated within the public arena of the museum or gallery. It is always, in part, "something purely imaginary" that we, like the artist, are "free to explore" in "a beautiful privacy."[35] At the same time, the work has a curiously paradoxical status as a phenomenon that is both unmediated and utterly mediated. There is nothing palpably present to which we can return to test our projection of the work as a physical phenomenon. In fact, there never really was, even for participants, who after the work's momentary enactment were left only with their recollections. As readers of Kaprow's writings, we must imagine something that is supposedly very immediate and physical entirely within our minds, taking our cue from the staging of the phenomenon in language or in documentary photographs—materials conventionally seen as mediated records of a work's physical reality. The mostly casual, commonplace rhetoric of the photographs of Kaprow's Happenings tends to block us from seeing them as works of visual art in their own right. Moreover, the published record often consists of only one or a very few photographs. Although they are on occasion oddly captivating and even curiously resonant images < FIGS. 2–4 >, they hardly encapsulate the profusion of events and actions that composed an actual Happening < FIGS. 5, 6 >. For the most part, these photographs function more like conceptual clues than vivid images, and they are generally considerably less evocative than the texts through which Kaprow conjured up the sensory experiences and physical situations of his Happenings.

What is a Happening, then? It is not simply a lost phenomenon that was real for one moment for a small group of participants. Neither is it embodied in the written score or the descriptions that narrate it, as if, in the final analysis, a Happening is like a poem or a story. Its status as an artwork is stubbornly unresolved. The designation of the work as a piece of conceptual art may seem apposite, but in the end it does not fit. If Happenings have a continued existence largely as conceptual phenomena, the nonconceptual immediacy central to Kaprow's imagining of them undercuts any categorization of the scores and the photographs as relatively self-sufficient conceptual works of art.

Figs. 2–4. **Views of *Courtyard* (1962)**

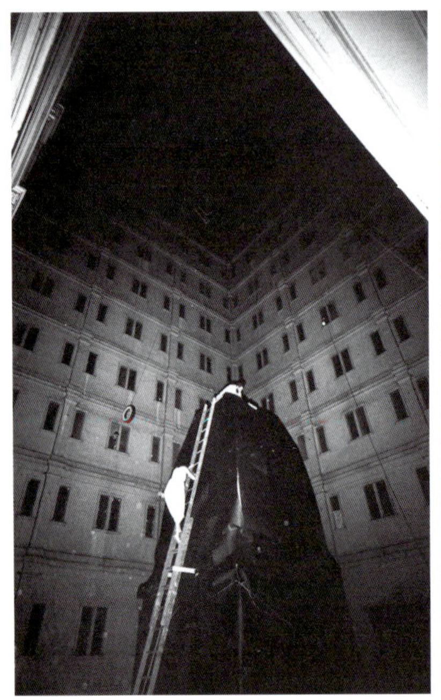

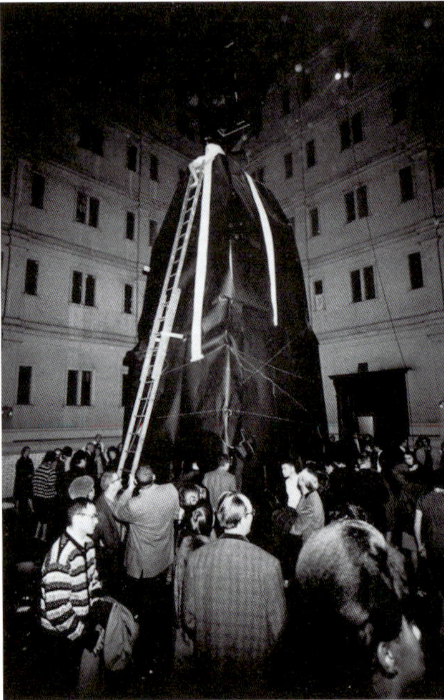

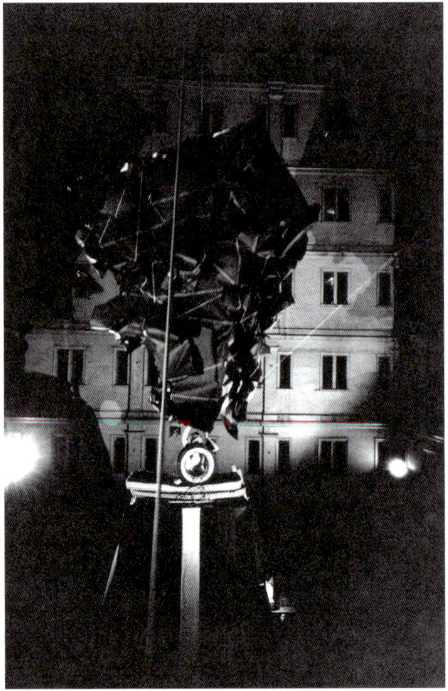

There is a further paradox. The aesthetic status of the Happening is consistently undercut by Kaprow, even as he seduces his readers with the fantasy of an "advanced art" that "approaches a fragile but marvelous life, one that maintains itself by a mere thread, melting the surroundings, the artist, the work, and everyone who comes to it into an elusive, changeable configuration."[36] Kaprow presents us with not only extravagant, lushly romantic fantasies but also hardheaded negations of the aesthetic mythologies surrounding "the enduring and the stable" work of art, mythologies fostered by the reifying and co-opting imperatives of the art world.[37] What is more, while claiming that we must now face up to the fact that "only the changing is really enduring and all else is whistling in the dark," he teases us by ensuring, through the evocativeness of his writing, a continuing presence for artworks that supposedly were, of their very nature, "fragile and impermanent."[38]

In a move that mimics the highly productive perversities of much of the more experimental work of the time, Kaprow sets up a self-canceling and at the same time self-activating dialectic between two diametrically opposing conceptions of what art should be. On the one hand are his romantic projections of aesthetically resonant experiences that can be shamelessly melodramatic, even kitschy. On the other hand is his insistently anti-aesthetic flat-footedness, which he paraded quite blatantly—consider, for example, the clumsy lettering he fashioned for works that incorporated words <FIG. 7>—and his unerring predilection for the blandly commonplace. In his scores, these contradictions are reenacted in the very texture of the writing, both in the verbal rhetoric that veers between the blandly spare and the emotively overblown and in the combinatorial procedures in which a prosaic, uninflected succession of tasks alternates with highly charged and often ludicrously excessive interruptions. The scores, however, lose interest and potency when simply seen as verbal poetry. Kaprow's scores compel us because they present themselves not as self-contained works of art, but as recollections or projections of artistic phenomena that once were, and could possibly be thought of as being, vividly concrete.

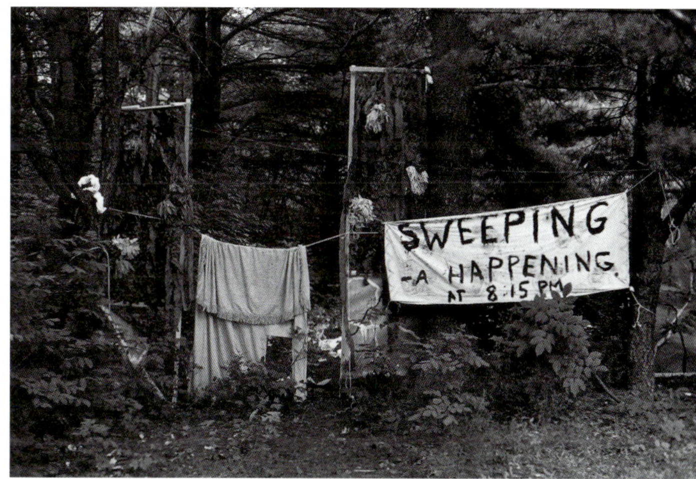

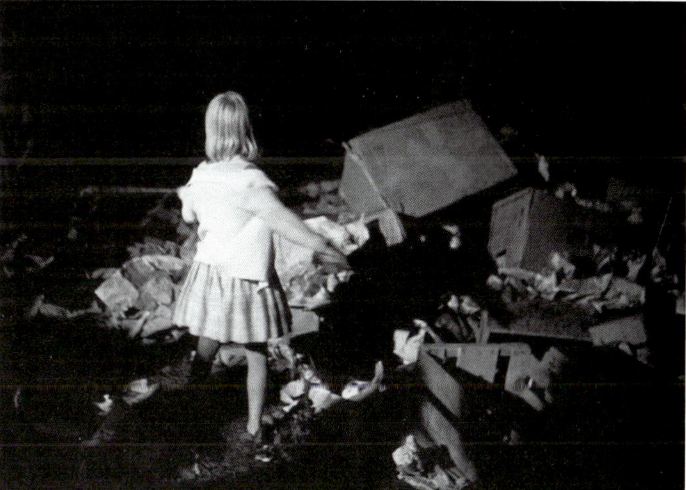

Fig. 5. **View of *Sweeping* (1962)**
Photo: Robert R. McElroy

Fig. 6. **View of *Sweeping* (1962)**
Photo: Peter Moore

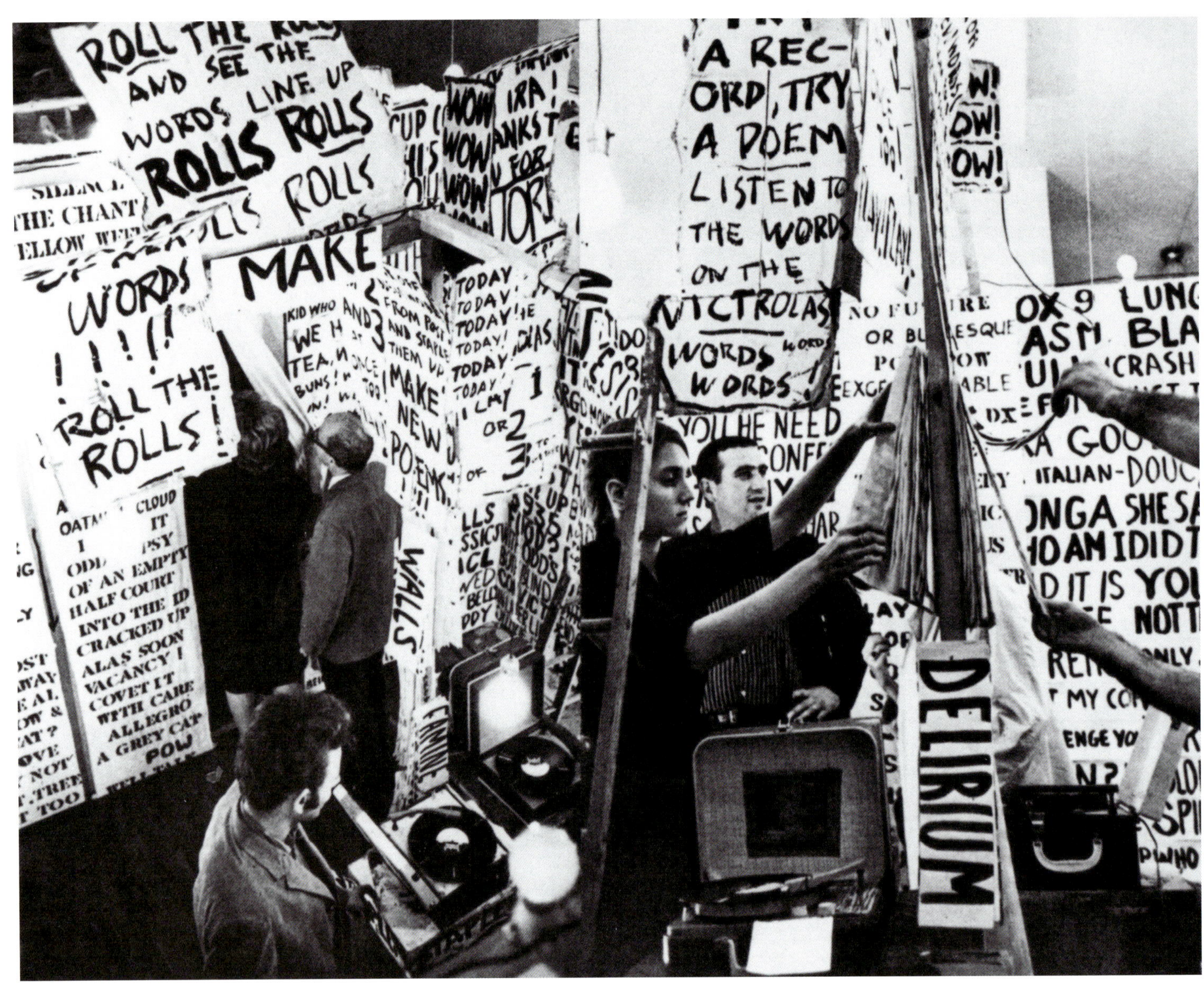

Fig. 7. **View of *Words* (1962) at the Smolin Gallery, New York**
Photo: Robert R. McElroy

Notes

1. Allan Kaprow, *Essays on the Blurring of Art and Life*, ed. Jeff Kelley (Berkeley: Univ. of California Press, 1993), of which a new edition with two further essays came out in 2003. This book did not claim to be a complete collection of Kaprow's writings. It did not include a number of his more significant publications, most notably the major essay he wrote for his book *Assemblage, Environments & Happenings* (New York: Harry N. Abrams, 1966), 151–208, of which there is only the very short and incomplete summary found in his essay "The Happenings Are Dead: Long Live the Happenings! (1966)" (see pp. 59–65).
2. See, for example, the very full notes Kaprow made for the preparatory talks he gave prior to the Happenings *Household* in May 1964 and *Paper* in March 1964, Allan Kaprow Papers, ca. 1940–1997, accession no. 980063 (box 9, folders 1, 3), Research Library, Getty Research Institute, Los Angeles; hereafter Allan Kaprow Papers.

   Several scores were published by Kaprow in his book, *Assemblage, Environments & Happenings* (note 1). Others appeared in more informal publications, such as Kaprow's *Untitled Essay and Other Works,* a Great Bear pamphlet (New York: Something Else, 1967). Some scores took the form of the very barest outline of a sequence of events, while others offered fairly elaborate descriptions of the proposed settings and the intended outcomes.
3. Kaprow typed up a detailed commentary for the New York–based critic Brian O'Doherty on the Happening *Bon Marché* after it took place in Paris; see Allan Kaprow to Brian O'Doherty, 30 July 2003, Allan Kaprow Papers (box 8, folder 4). He sometimes "reviewed" his own work, most notably in the very fulsome account of his Environment *Apple Shrine* that he published under the pseudonym Theodore Tucker in *Village Voice* (12 January 1961); for the handwritten draft of this review, see Allan Kaprow Papers (box 6, folder 4). One of the more intriguing features of the surviving written recollections of his Happenings is their very disparate nature. See, for example, the quite different recollections of Michael Kirby in his *Happenings: An Illustrated Anthology* (New York: E.P. Dutton, 1965), 67–83, and those of Samuel R. Delaney in Gavin Butt, "Happenings in History, or The Epistemology of the Memoir," *Oxford Art Journal* 24, no. 2 (2001): 113–26. It is important to remember that, even if one were a participant in a Happening, there would have been no privileged position from which one would have been able to gain a full, overall sense of the work. Viewed in retrospect, the Happening very evidently becomes something without clearly delimited form, existing as it does in no one fixed location but instead spread across its various manifestations in existing written and photographic records, with Kaprow's scores possibly providing a basis for imagining what it might be.
4. I am grateful to Andrew Perchuk for his perceptive comments on an early draft of this essay.
5. Allan Kaprow, "The Artist as a Man of the World (1964)," in idem, *Essays on the Blurring of Art and Life,* ed. Jeff Kelley (Berkeley: Univ. of California Press, 1993), 52–53.
6. Allan Kaprow, press release for *Courtyard,* 1962, Allan Kaprow Papers (box 7, folder 6).
7. Allan Kaprow, "Experimental Art (1966)," in idem, *Essays on the Blurring of Art and Life,* ed. Jeff Kelley (Berkeley: Univ. of California Press, 1993), 77.
8. Kaprow, "Experimental Art" (note 7), 77.
9. Allan Kaprow, "Happenings in the New York Scene (1961)," in idem, *Essays on the Blurring of Art and Life,* ed. Jeff Kelley (Berkeley: Univ. of California Press, 1993), 21.
10. Kaprow, *Assemblage* (note 1), 207–8.
11. Kaprow, *Assemblage* (note 1), 208.
12. Kaprow, *Assemblage* (note 1), 168.
13. Kaprow, *Assemblage* (note 1), 169.
14. Kaprow, *Assemblage* (note 1), 168–69.
15. John Cage, *Silence: Lectures and Writings* (Middletown, Conn.: Wesleyan Univ. Press, 1961), 110; the text is from a lecture given in 1949 and was first published in 1959.
16. Kaprow, *Assemblage* (note 1), 161.
17. Kaprow, *Assemblage* (note 1), 201.
18. Allan Kaprow, "Impurity (1963)," in idem, *Essays on the Blurring of Art and Life,* ed. Jeff Kelley (Berkeley: Univ. of California Press, 1993), 34.
19. Kaprow, "Impurity" (note 18), 45.
20. Kaprow, "Impurity" (note 18), 45.
21. Allan Kaprow, "The Shape of the Art Environment (1968)," in idem, *Essays on the Blurring of Art and Life,* ed. Jeff Kelley (Berkeley: Univ. of California Press, 1993), 93.
22. Kaprow, "Shape of the Art Environment" (note 21), 93.
23. Kaprow, "Experimental Art" (note 7), 77.
24. Kaprow, "Experimental Art" (note 7), 77.
25. Kaprow, *Assemblage* (note 1), 203–4.
26. Kaprow, *Assemblage* (note 1), 204.
27. Allan Kaprow, note for *Household,* 1964, Allan Kaprow Papers (box 9, folder 1a). Kaprow's elaborate formal structuring of this Happening is evident in the diagram included in this volume, where he mapped out not only the "large structure" of the work but also the patterning of its "substructures" and the "thematic relations" these structures articulated < SEE CHRONOLOGY, FIG. 115 >.
28. Kaprow, note for *Household* (note 27).
29. Kaprow, "Happenings in the New York Scene" (note 9), 16–17.
30. Kaprow, "Happenings in the New York Scene" (note 9), 24–25.
31. Kaprow, *Assemblage* (note 1), 165.
32. Kaprow, *Assemblage* (note 1), 190.
33. Kaprow, *Assemblage* (note 1), 185, 186–87.
34. Hannah Arendt, *The Human Condition* (Chicago: Univ. of Chicago Press, 1958). See part 3, "Labor," 79–135 (particularly chapter 17, "A Consumers' Society," 126–35), and part 4, "Work," 136–74.
35. Kaprow, "Happenings in the New York Scene" (note 9), 26.
36. Kaprow, "Happenings in the New York Scene" (note 9), 18.
37. Allan Kaprow, "Notes on the Creation of a Total Art (1958)," in idem, *Essays on the Blurring of Art and Life,* ed. Jeff Kelley (Berkeley: Univ. of California Press, 1993), 12.
38. Kaprow, "Notes on the Creation of a Total Art" (note 37), 12.

Part Two **From the Archive**

Time Pieces

Glenn Phillips

An artist's archive typically contains any number of documents and ancillary materials surrounding the development and history of the artist's works without actually containing the original works of art themselves, which, if still extant, likely remain in the care of museums or other collections. However, with the archives of conceptual and performance artists—Allan Kaprow among them—this distinction becomes fraught. Unlike a painting or sculpture, most conceptual and performance art lacks an original, fully present and self-contained object. These works, if contained in art collections at all, tend to be assembled into a form that is nearly, if not entirely, indistinguishable from the types of documents and items that have typically been the domain of the archive.

Whereas many artists associated with movements such as Fluxus began at an early point to assemble documentation and remnants from their projects into thoughtfully designed and commercially viable artworks, exhibition-ready documentation of ephemeral pieces—particularly performance-based projects—has more often than not been created after the fact, and sometimes after the artist's death. The types of institutional support that were eventually given to these bodies of work carried with them a corollary need to have something permanent and visual to stand in for the ephemeral work. An unforeseen consequence has been the rise of a parallel and primarily aesthetic criterion by which conceptual and performance art documents have been both assembled and judged. In the museum and the market, these works are often regarded not as documentation but—as with traditional artworks—as self-sustaining *representations* that can be unhinged from, and thus are unhindered by, the larger network of materials that relate to the works purely as archival documentation. Documentary photographs of ephemeral works (often taken by an unaffiliated bystander and only later brought to the artist's attention) are judged not solely by their ability to convey the facts of an event but also by their beauty and compelling nature as photography. Handwritten notes and scores are assessed not as thought processes but as drawings, and more elaborate assemblages of image and text are evaluated by standards of design and presentation that might be completely unrelated to the original nature or intellectual force of the event to which they refer.

This parallel aesthetic emerged strongly in Allan Kaprow's work in the 1970s, not as part of an attempt to create more commercially viable work but as part of Kaprow's struggles to deal with changes in his work that made documentation problematic. Most of Kaprow's Happenings and Environments in the 1960s had operated as highly visual spectacles, with plenty of room to accommodate large numbers of participants and observers. This created a less-immediate need to be concerned about careful documentation of the event. Photographic documentation of these early events was sometimes a bit haphazard, but it nearly always occurred, and often times participants and observers later gave or sold their photographs to Kaprow. By 1973, however, Kaprow was moving more and more toward excluding an audience altogether. His pieces became much smaller in scale and were primarily designed for individuals, couples, or other small groups to complete more or less in private, and usually without Kaprow's supervision. These works required the creation not only of easy-to-follow instructions for participants but also of some sort of visual record that was related to the event.

With *Time Pieces* in 1973 < SEE CHRONOLOGY, FIGS. 220–43 >, Kaprow arrived at a solution that involved producing documentation of the performance event, *before* the performance had officially taken place, in the form of Activity booklets, which functioned as photographically illustrated scores for a piece. The photographs in these booklets were not to be considered as documentation of the event, however, but rather as a representation of the Activity that was yet to happen. In Kaprow's words, an Activity booklet "contains text and photos arranged to outline what is to occur. They function together as an instruction manual or diagrammed play for a football game. Thus, the photos are *illustrations* rather than documents of the actual event."[1] Kaprow was initially pleased with this solution, and in a letter to Willoughby Sharp dated 19 July 1973, Kaprow inquired about the possibility of a spread in an upcoming issue of *Avalanche,* noting that "I'm finally getting to an adequate format for publishing what has for so long been purely ephemeral, and it seems as though it would fit into the general format of your magazine."[2] One week prior to this, on 12 July, Kaprow had completed the final draft of the score for *Time Pieces,* which was developed in response to an invitation from the Neuer Berliner Kunstverein to contribute a piece to the exhibition *ADA: Aktionen der Avantgarde,* which was to open in September of that year.[3] Each artist included in this exhibition was offered a stipend to produce three components: a performance, a gallery display, and a sixteen-page spread in the exhibition catalog. Thus, the very nature of the invitation asked artists to develop multiple formats to convey a single work, and previous drafts of Kaprow's score for *Time Pieces* clearly show that he conceived this piece as a printed visual layout almost from the beginning.

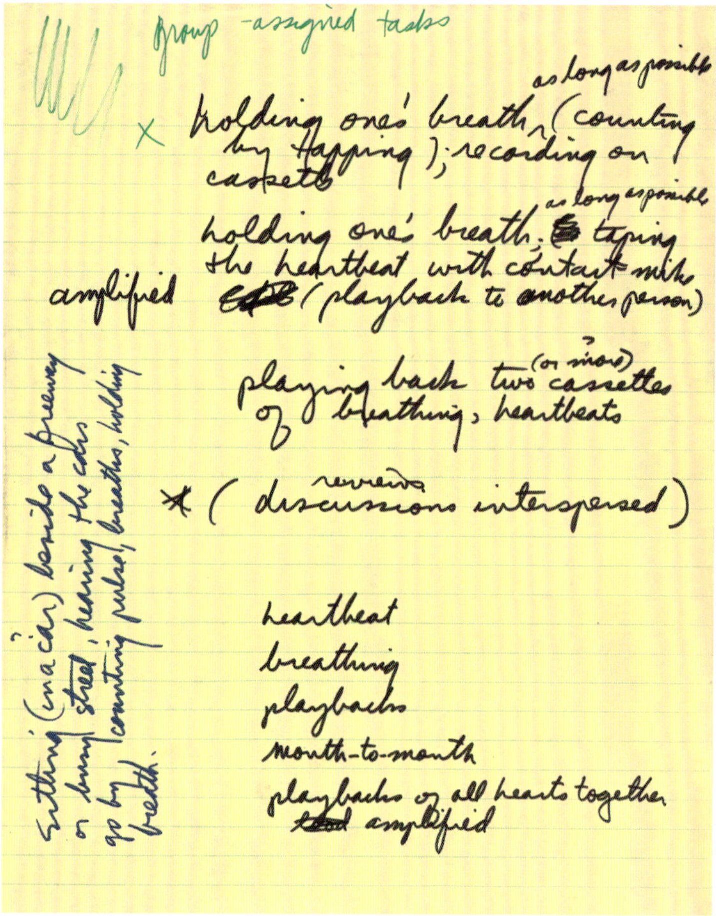

The score for *Time Pieces* asks couples to engage in an elaborate series of more than forty private and shared activities that revolve around monitoring and modifying one's own and one's partner's pulse and breathing rate. Participants are asked to note their pulse and breathing rates during states of rest and after exertion (climbing stairs), as well as to hold both inhaled and exhaled breaths for one minute, to breathe rapidly for one minute, and to exchange breaths by breathing directly into each other's mouths for one minute, or by breathing into plastic bags and exchanging the bags. The production and use of documentation pervade the work, as participants are constantly asked to use a tape recorder to record the sound of their breath or their pulse (registered as counting or tapping) and then immediately listen to the tape or else later play the tape for their partner, either in person or over the telephone.

While the tone of the score for *Time Pieces* is quite measured, the work was constructed to create mild states of anxiety in its participants. Earlier drafts of the piece asked participants to hold their breath not for one minute, but to their physical limit, and to breathe rapidly until they actually hyperventilated. An abandoned portion of the script asked participants to park their cars along a busy freeway and count their pulse and hold their breath while listening to the cars going by < FIG. 1 >.[4] Despite limiting the physical demands of the piece, Kaprow nonetheless was certain of the effect it would produce in his participants. In an introductory lecture that aimed to prepare the group of volunteers who would be performing *Time Pieces* in Berlin, Kaprow noted that the work

> concerns human feelings, that is, each participant's personal feelings. . . . It is a framework of *objective* moves designed to tap *subjective* states, states which are, however, unknown at the beginning. . . . These moves are intentionally clinical . . . but the content of the moves are basic to our existence: our heart beat and our breath. Without them we die, and each of us has learned to subtly

Fig. 1. **Draft score for *Time Pieces* (1973)**

Figs. 2, 3. **Photos illustrating how to perform *Time Pieces***
From the Activity booklet (pub. 1973)

monitor these internal rhythms as signs of how we feel. . . . Thus, *Time Pieces* can be viewed as a "container" which we fill with the discovery of ourselves. . . . And what we will be doing, of course, throughout the Activity is watching ourselves and each other. What we don't know, however, is the effect upon our feelings of *conscious involvement* in such time segments. This remains to be discovered and reported when we reconvene on Sunday.[5]

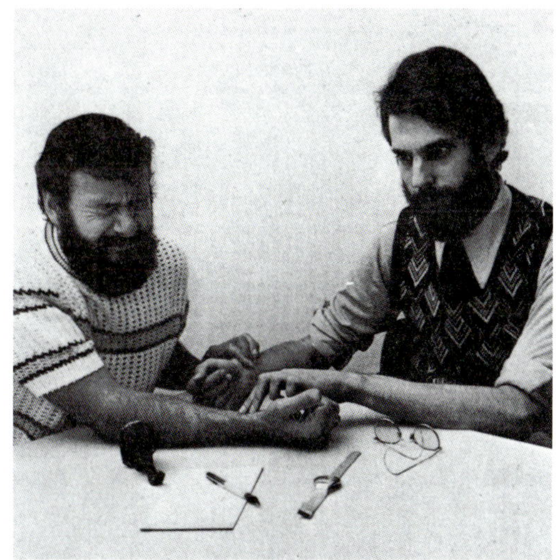

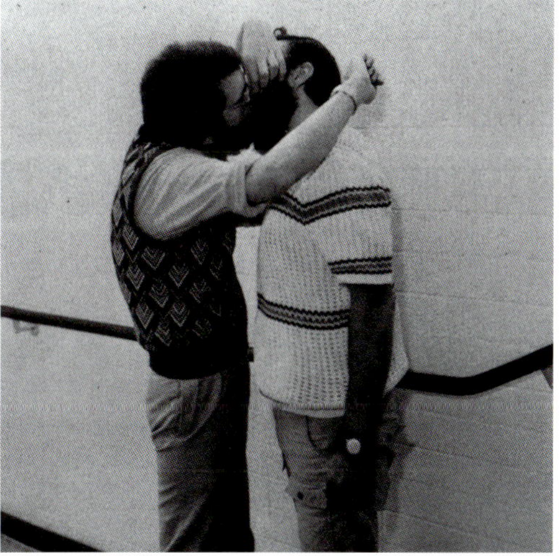

Kaprow clearly hoped that *Time Pieces* would evoke deeply subjective responses in its participants, yet the photographic illustrations in the Activity booklet tell an altogether different story. Aiming to be as objective, spare, and deadpan as possible, the photographs (one for each of the thirteen main sections of the Activity) nonetheless take on a highly visual quality that creates a separate subtext and narrative for the piece. It is, after all, extremely difficult to convey in a single photograph such time-based activities as breathing or increasing one's pulse, let alone the activity of holding your breath and blinking your eyes in rhythm to your pulse while someone else notes the count < FIG. 2 >. Thus an image depicting the activity of breathing into another person's mouth (while timing the event) just as easily suggests an illicit affair between two nervous, time-conscious lovers < FIG. 3 >, and other images take on an air of a taped confession or excruciating pain that, while making the photograph humorous or interesting, is unrelated to the actual experiences the participants were expected to have.

This was not a dilemma that could easily be solved, as *Time Pieces* deals at least in part with the impossibility of representation. Like so many of Kaprow's works from this period, it was meant to be an activity of directed, phenomenological perception, in which participants, engaged with their physical sensations, become aware of the emotional and social import of their actions—"objective moves designed to tap subjective states." There are no spectators, and nowhere in the Activity is one asked to look—only to listen, to count, to breathe, or to hold breath. Vision plays only a supporting role, and even then it is geared toward empathy rather than image, as one observes a partner only to imagine the sensation of his or her heartbeat or breath.

Time Pieces was realized in Berlin by thirty people, divided into fifteen couples, from 14 to 16 September 1973. Kaprow held an initial meeting with the volunteers, at which he distributed to each of them the bilingual instruction booklet and an audio tape recorder and talked to them about the nature and intentions of the piece. One couple was asked to volunteer to have their actions documented by a photographer, and another was asked to volunteer to be videotaped. A second photographer documented Kaprow's own performance of the piece, although these photographs were never used in a project. Couples were given two days to complete the Activity, after which they reconvened to discuss their experiences. No record was kept of the discussions following the performance, but a number of participants did return to Kaprow various charts they had made that documented their pulse and breathing rates throughout the Activity < FIG. 4 >. While we can imagine that the participants aimed to be accurate, and while, visually, the charts bear comparison to other sorts of conceptual art documents from the period,

Fig. 4. **Participants' charts from *Time Pieces* (1973)**

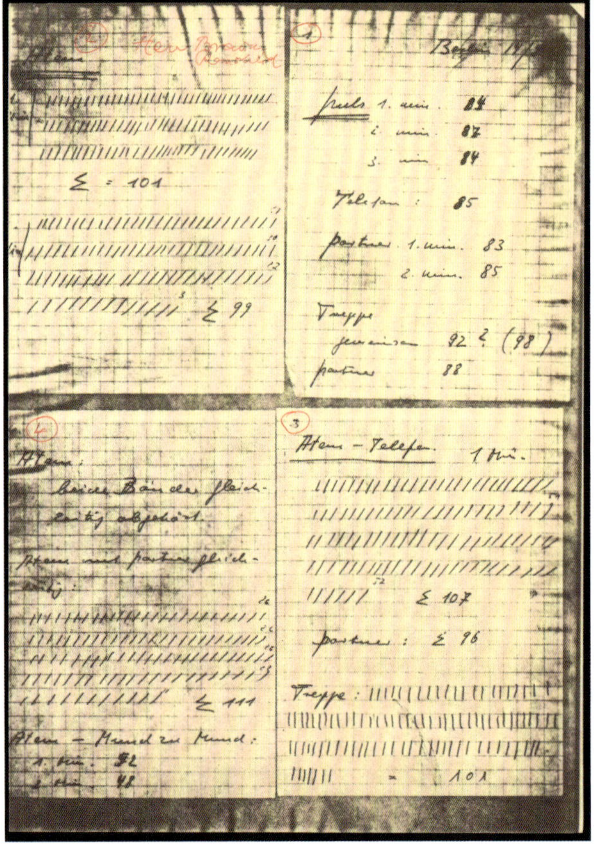

the most compelling documentation of the event is an annotated Activity booklet, in which a participant (probably German artist Wolf Vostell) noted a series of failures that interrupted the Activity throughout its enactment. At various points the tape recorder gave out, or someone's breath gave out, or, in one case, the participant's phone call was interrupted by angry, impatient callers waiting outside the telephone booth < FIG. 5 >.

In addition to executing *Time Pieces,* Kaprow also had to create a gallery display for *ADA: Aktionen der Avantgarde* < FIG. 6 >. The objects he chose suggest that he was torn between displaying the sort of preemptive representation of the yet-to-occur event, as in the Activity booklet, and the straightforward documentation of the performance. One wall of the gallery featured the individual pages of the booklet. Photographs from the recent performance were displayed not on the privileged space of the walls but inside low vitrines in the middle of the room. Above these vitrines were hung plastic bags that had been inflated, sealed, and marked with each participant's name, as if waiting to be inhaled by another participant. Neither the video documentation of the piece nor the audiotapes or the written documentation that had been produced by the participants were included. Instead, and most strangely of all, around the perimeter of the room was a case displaying the tape recorders that the participants had used in the creation of the piece.

The video documentation of the performance was edited at the Kunstverein's Videothek into a work resembling a hybrid of the dense schematics contained in the Activity booklet and the vagaries of the local execution of the piece. A poster produced for the video has this same dual character. The front of the poster < FIG. 7 > features a large image of a telephone, a watch, and a tape recorder that is typical of the didactic clarity of the Activity booklet, but the back of the poster contains a rather jumbled design featuring the full layout of the Activity booklet, mixed with documentary images from the Berlin performance and a short interview with Kaprow about the piece < FIG. 8 >. The video strictly follows the score for the Activity, although the individual sequences that demonstrate its performance do not always have the clarity of composition typical of the Activity booklet—as would be expected, given that the actors were two unsupervised people who were quite earnestly trying to perform the piece and had simply volunteered to be videotaped while doing so.

Kaprow must have been dissatisfied with the video, as he decided to remake the *Time Pieces* video in 1975, this time featuring his wife, Vaughan Rachel, as one of the models. This marked the fifth time that Kaprow had produced new photomechanical imagery relating to the *Time Pieces* project. Kaprow had often used film and video to document his Activities, and he had experimented with different techniques of representing his work as a moving image. These ranged from straightforward, unedited compilations of raw footage to more composed and narrative endeavors that aimed to document all the aspects of a piece that would have been visible to its participants, including his introductory lecture and discussion, prep work by participants, the event itself, and participants discussing the performance once it was over. It was not until 1974, however, with his production of the video *Then* < SEE CHRONOLOGY, FIGS. 247–50 >, that Kaprow produced what could be called single-channel video art—a self-contained work meant to stand alone. The experience of producing *Then* may have influenced Kaprow's thinking, for the remake of the *Time Pieces* video places it firmly in the realm of single-channel video art. This final version of *Time Pieces* is extremely clean, finished, and highly visual, having all the condensed and illustrative appeal of the original Activity booklet. In fact, the video is the booklet come to life: individual scenes in the *Times Pieces* video are strongly related to the photographic compositions of the booklet. The tone of the video feels entirely earnest and serious, as if one is being instructed about the need for rigor

Fig. 5. **Annotated score for *Time Pieces***
From the Activity booklet (pub. 1973)

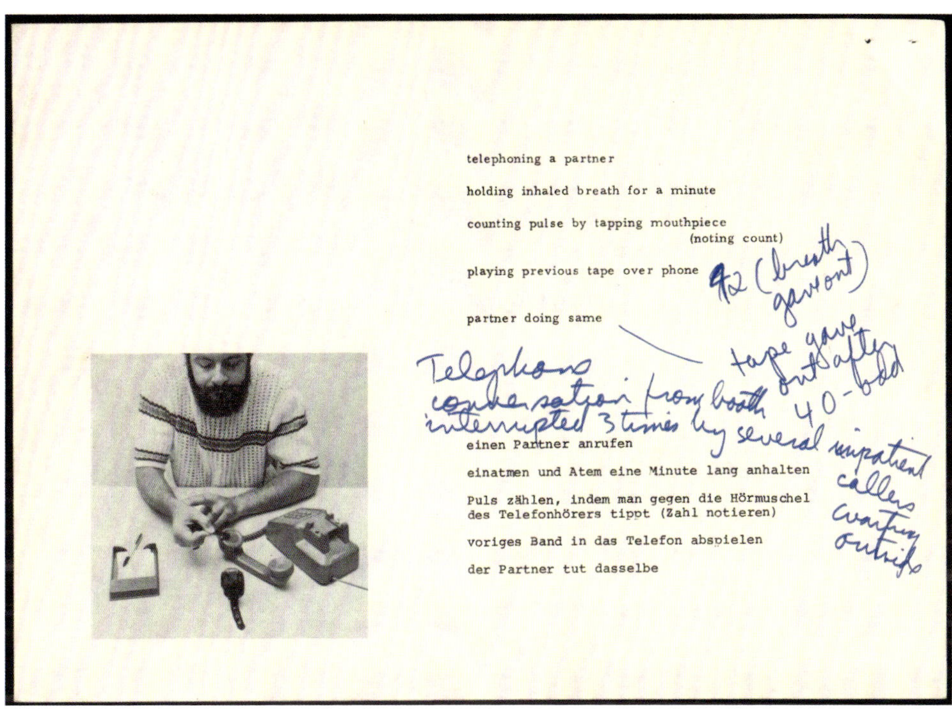

telephoning a partner

holding inhaled breath for a minute

counting pulse by tapping mouthpiece
(noting count)

playing previous tape over phone

partner doing same

einen Partner anrufen

einatmen und Atem eine Minute lang anhalten

Puls zählen, indem man gegen die Hörmuschel
des Telefonhörers tippt (Zahl notieren)

voriges Band in das Telefon abspielen

der Partner tut dasselbe

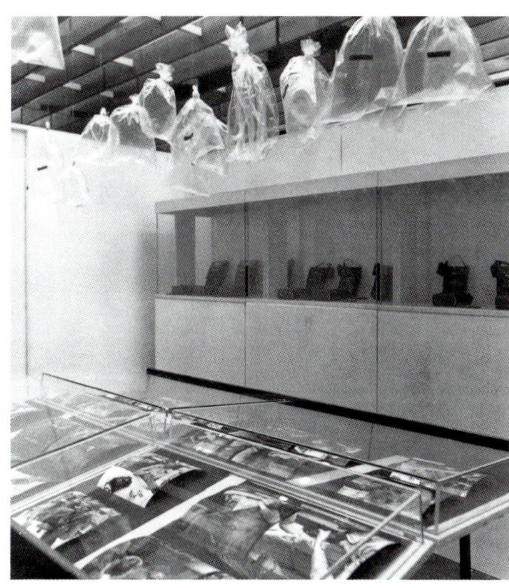

Fig. 6. **Gallery display of *Time Pieces***
Presented for *ADA: Aktionen der Avantgarde*
Neuer Berliner Kunstverein, Berlin

when employing the scientific method. And yet, like the booklet, the video also has a comedic and slightly campy quality that carries it far from the existential intentions of the original score, as the videotaped participants carry on panting, counting, tapping, blinking, and breathing into bags in the most deadpan and absurd manner.

Throughout these several iterations of *Time Pieces,* Kaprow modified only the means of documentation or presentation of the work. The textual score itself remained completely unchanged, and it seems clear that Kaprow's struggles stemmed not from a dissatisfaction with the score, but from his desire to create a more material and visual means of presenting a score, so that it could function as fully communicable performance instructions while also functioning independently as an artwork. For a time, it seemed that the Activity booklets provided the solution, and Kaprow continued to produce them throughout the 1970s.[6] However, finding that participants often took the illustrations in these works quite literally and tended to mimic the photographs or videos when performing the works themselves, Kaprow abandoned the Activity booklets and ultimately forbid them to be used for any "official" performances of his Activities. After all, like so much other phenomenologically oriented work from this era, the Activities were in part designed to trigger awareness of one's own subjectivity as it emerged from one's individual experiences and physical reactions to the work—a process that could be crippled by straightforward mimicry of an illustration.

As a visual experience, both the Activity booklet and the 1975 video of *Time Pieces* stand as some of Kaprow's more pleasurable works. Watching the video or reading the booklet today feels satisfying and complete. Nonetheless, *Time Pieces,*

Fig. 7. **Poster for *Time Pieces***
Double-sided, 79.4 × 57.8 cm (31¼ × 22¾ in.)
Getty Research Institute, Los Angeles

as a score, is not about *watching* an activity, but about *experiencing* an activity that one performs oneself. In this sense, one could view the booklet and video of *Time Pieces* as having fallen prey to the second, purely aesthetic criterion by which ephemeral artworks have come to be judged. These works employ a visual system that is so finished and self-contained that the viewer also feels "finished" after reading the illustrated instructions or watching the video and, thus, does not necessarily feel any urge or need to undertake the Activity to truly experience the artwork. This could in part explain why Kaprow's Activity booklets and videos from the 1970s, when examined at all, have tended to be considered as simply aestheticized and commemorative documentation rather than as tools that could be used by anyone to enact the work. Yet, as the general development of his work throughout the 1970s and 1980s toward ever more private and personal Activities makes clear, Kaprow certainly felt that the importance of these works depended entirely on the physical and emotional experience of a participant who actually performed the Activity. This is not to say that only those who have performed Kaprow's Activities can understand them, but any reconsideration of Kaprow's work from this period might best be driven not by examining a relationship between text and image (as the Activity booklets might suggest) but by examining a relationship between text and *sensation,* as one might be prone to realize through the performance of a score. With a work like *Time Pieces,* such an examination would require one to consider every historical iteration of the piece as secondary to one's direct engagement with the original score itself. It is likely that only a methodology that considers Kaprow's work in this way will be able to fully appreciate the extent of his education as an "Un-artist."

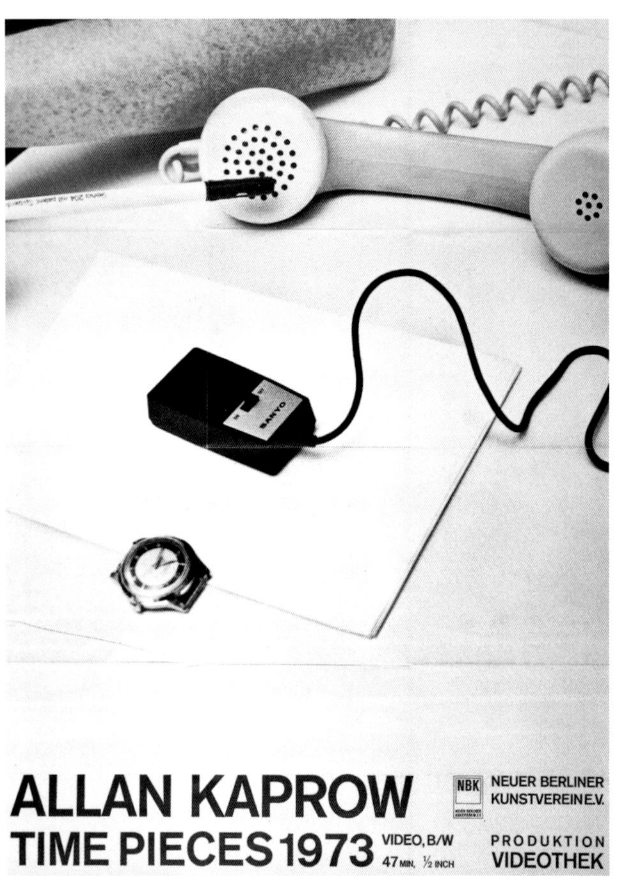

Fig. 8. **Poster for *Time Pieces*** (verso of fig. 7, rotated 90°)

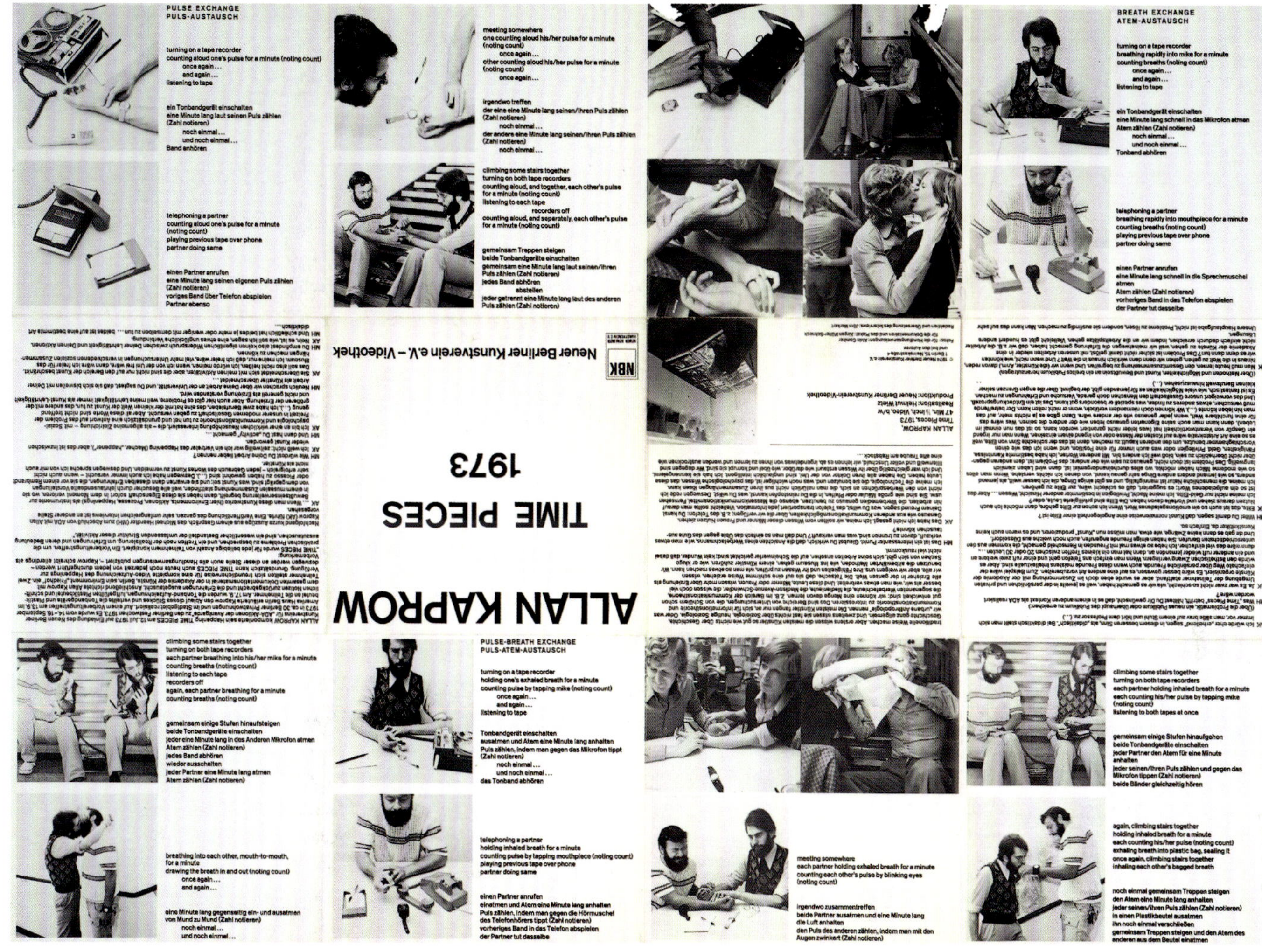

Notes

1. Allan Kaprow, addendum to the *Time Pieces* Activity booklet, 1973, Allan Kaprow Papers, ca. 1940–1997, accession no. 980063 (box 24, folder 3), Research Library, Getty Research Institute, Los Angeles; hereafter Allan Kaprow Papers. Although many Activity booklets were produced after or in commemoration of the first "official" performance of an Activity (and thus did not involve producing documentation before the event had first taken place), they nonetheless involved the same process of carefully staging poses to illustrate the instructions rather than photographing a performance that was actually taking place.
2. Allan Kaprow to Willoughby Sharp, 19 July 1973, Allan Kaprow Papers (box 24, folder 3).
3. Kaprow seems to have begun sketching his ideas for *Time Pieces* prior to the Berlin invitation, but the most substantial work for the piece was completed in preparation for the exhibition.
4. Allan Kaprow, note for *Time Pieces,* 1973, Allan Kaprow Papers (box 24, folder 3).
5. Allan Kaprow, manuscript of lecture for *Time Pieces,* 1973, Allan Kaprow Papers (box 24, folder 3).
6. He also, on occasion, continued to produce films or videos similar in format to the 1975 version of *Time Pieces.*

Intimate: The Allan Kaprow Papers

Annette Leddy

I . . . became aware that artworks of any kind could be autobiographical and prophetic. You could read paintings like handwriting, and over a period of time chart the painter's abiding fantasies, just as you might chart writers' thoughts from collections of personal letters or diaries. Happenings, and later Activities, being less specialized than paintings, poems, and other traditional arts, readily lent themselves to such psychological insights. — Allan Kaprow[1]

In the Allan Kaprow Papers, there are no love letters, no journals containing secret thoughts, no honeymoon snapshots. There are none of the casual, accidentally revealing tokens of a life found in other collections—no airplane slippers in a clear plastic envelope, no foreign currency from a defunct regime, no marijuana cigarettes, no itemized bills from the pharmacist.[2] There are no anecdotes about how unrestrained social life in the 1960s intersected with Happenings. The enticingly labeled "Series IX: Personal" consists solely of awards, photographs of a monument dedicated to Tom Mix, birthday cards a young Kaprow made for his father, and three files of photographs of Kaprow at work locations. Among these are views of him with his first wife taken by a *Life* magazine photographer in 1967 <FIG. 1>. These not quite candid shots are both more dramatic and less revealing than faded images from a bedside table drawer.

Few archives hold astonishing revelations—the true paternity of a sister or a previously undiscovered marriage—but many attest to the inseparability of the personal and the creative. In the Clement Greenberg Papers, for example, Greenberg's diary entries about Helen Frankenthaler reflect at once on their love affair and her painting.[3] The David Tudor Papers contain letters between Tudor and M.C. Richards that portray the anguished life choices embedded in creative work.[4] An archive focused on a "professional" life is, however, possibly more consonant with the philosophy of Kaprow's generation of artists, who rejected the abstract expressionists' dramatic construction of artistic practice and pursued a conscious diminution of the artist's biography. Indeed, the archive testifies that Kaprow pushed this antiromanticism into new forms. "Series VIII: Artists' Files" contains letters between Kaprow and Claes Oldenburg, who accuses Kaprow of having a "person-eliminative" approach to discussing art: "Art can't be talked about the way you talk about [it]. . . . It doesn't exist outside the artist like an object."[5] And Oldenburg vehemently objects to Kaprow's notion that the new artist does not so much create as frame certain objects from the world around him: "An art of non-artistic reality or philosophical reality is impossible."[6]

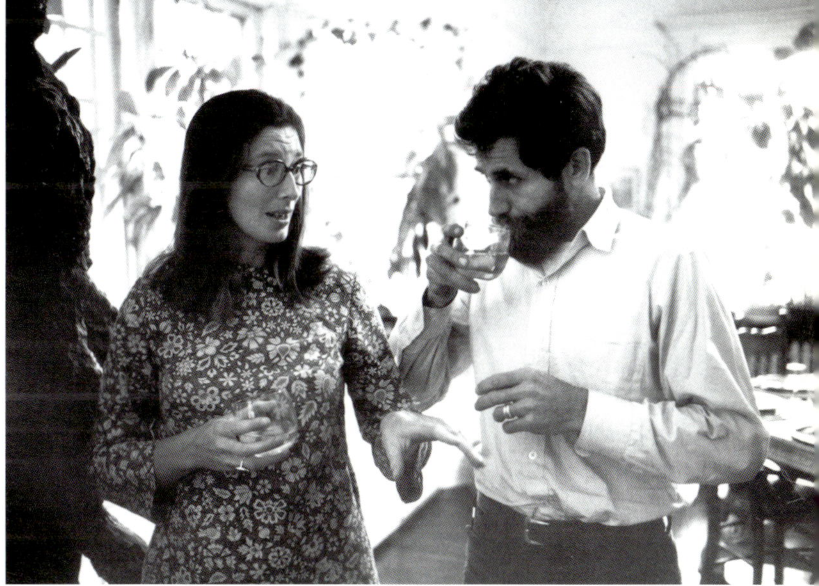

Kaprow eventually honed this person-eliminative approach into a tool of inquiry about human interaction that over the course of his life evolved, paradoxically, into a methodology that explored increasingly intimate relationships. His archive allows us to consider in sequence this evolution to a focus on intimacy as a theme of his work and as an autobiographical issue because it so amply documents an entire oeuvre of ephemeral works, most of which were enacted only once.

Fig. 1. **Vaughan Rachel and Allan Kaprow,** 1967

The prehistory of Kaprow's Environments, Happenings, and Activities may be found in "Series III: Project Files, 1946–1999." Photographs and slides of his figurative paintings from the first half of the 1950s evince his early interest in group interaction. In his rapid progression through collage and assemblage, Kaprow located materials that would soon constitute the tools of his inquiry into human interaction: tires, crumpled paper, aluminum foil, cardboard cartons, cheap mirrors, and plastic strips, apples, and oranges. In his studies with John Cage, he found the essential sounds for this exploration: an electric razor's buzz, a cat's meow, dripping water, a whisper—ordinary, background sounds commensurate with preconscious or half-conscious contact among people.

The project files also contain Kaprow's scores, which David Antin has called "a novel kind of 'concrete poetry.'"[7] Whether they are typed or mimeographed pages, creased and stained with inky cross-outs, or sheets of yellow legal paper filled with Kaprow's handwriting and graced with an occasional hasty sketch, these plans for his works may initially seem a sorry substitute for the heartfelt ruminations found in other artists' archives. Persistence is rewarded, however, as thematic clusters emerge. Underlying the impersonal surface of the scores—which move from the highly scripted, ritualistic Happenings to spare pieces about manual labor to skeletal ones about "pink collar" jobs—is a consistent focus on interpersonal communication. With the early pieces emphasizing the group and the later ones the couple, Kaprow's work eventually arrived at a full disclosure of the desire, fear, and convention that infuse our every word and glance.

Kaprow created the Happening in 1958, and by 1962 it was firmly established as an art form. When Kaprow's fellow artists gave up Happenings and became, for the most part, Pop artists, Kaprow stayed with the form, exploring and refining it, traveling to the institutions in the United States and Europe that would sponsor his pieces. As we move through the project files, the subtleties of Kaprow's thematic trajectory become apparent. We see how the codified behavior and gesture in *18 Happenings in 6 Parts* (1959) had to be located in, or worked through, history and culture < SEE CHRONOLOGY, FIGS. 29–50 >. The Happenings of the early 1960s concerned archetypal group dynamics: scapegoating, sacrifice, objectification, compartmentalization—the hierarchical behaviors through which the unreflecting self is formed. *Calling* (1965), a Happening from this period, addresses a range of human brutalities: rape, desecration, kidnapping, and execution.

> In the city, people stand at street corners and wait.
>
> For each of them:
>
> A car pulls up, someone calls out a name, the person gets in, they drive off.
>
> During the trip, the person is wrapped in aluminum foil. The car is parked at a meter somewhere, is left there, locked; the silver person sitting motionless in the front seat.
>
> Someone unlocks the car, drives off. The foil is removed from the person; he or she is wrapped in cloth or tied into a laundry bag. The car stops, the person is dumped in a public wastebasket, and the car goes away.
>
> A waiting auto pulls over to the curb, the person is removed from the wastebasket, is hauled into the car, is taken to the information booth at Grand Central Station. The person is propped up against it and left.

> The person calls out names, and hears the others brought there also call. They call out for some time. Then they work loose from their wrappings and leave the train station.
>
> They telephone certain numbers. The phone rings and rings. Finally it is answered, a name is asked for, and immediately the other end clicks off.
>
> • • •
>
> In the woods, the persons call out names and hear hidden answers. Here and there, they come upon people dangling upside down from ropes. They rip the people's clothes off and go away.
>
> The naked figures call to each other in the woods for a long time until they are tired. Silence.[8]

Like all Kaprow's works, *Calling* occurred primarily within the minds of the participants. The notes in the file, neatly typed on thin paper, show that the participants who drove the cars were to be those hanging from trees the next day. They may have discovered that being a perpetrator—dumping a body into a trash can or walking among people hanging upside down in a forest filled with cries—produced more complicity in group psychosis than they had anticipated. Conversely, as victims, they may have experienced the extreme isolation that can be mitigated only by empathy, which is always denied. Although this Happening involved a group interaction, it focused on the moment of the (de-individuated) individual's supplication: the attempt—through calling—to communicate anguish. Even the amusing photographs of participants wrapped in aluminum foil fail to dispel the score's chilling effect <SEE CHRONOLOGY, FIGS. 118–23>.

Around 1967, the paradigm of Kaprow's work shifted to how an array of social and natural systems forms the self. The ostensible content of these pieces is manual labor—the work of bricklayers, stonecutters, streetpavers, housepainters, woodworkers. Kaprow abandoned elaborate scripting in these Happenings in favor of a simple set of instructions, such as the one for *Fluids* (1967).

> During three days, about twenty rectangular enclosures of ice blocks (measuring about 30 feet long, 10 wide and 8 high) are built throughout the city. Their walls are unbroken. They are left to melt.[9]

Criticism of *Fluids* has focused on the allegories for work that are implicit in it. Robert Haywood has argued that it "transformed collective participatory labor into a dystopian allegory of capitalist production, consumption and obsolescence," and Kaprow himself alluded to the theme of planned obsolescence.[10] *Fluids*, however, marks the first appearance of frozen water, which was to become a recurrent material and image in Kaprow's works. In *Warm-Ups* (1975), for example, two participants press an ice cube between their foreheads until their body heat melts it <SEE CHRONOLOGY, FIGS. 264–68>; in *Basic Thermal Units* (1973), participants in a warm bath put ice cubes in the water until it grows cold, then add warm water <SEE CHRONOLOGY, FIGS. 211–19>. In these and similar pieces, the melting ice is a metaphor for overcoming emotional distance. Perhaps *Fluids*—a work which involved large blocks of ice that were heavy, unwieldy, and painfully cold to hold and carry—uses the fantasy of communal work as a means to dissolve the walls between individuals.

Homemovies (1969) was a wedding gift to Kaprow's friends Catherine and Daniel Schmidt <SEE CHRONOLOGY, FIGS. 167, 168>. A temporary departure from the labor pieces, it anticipated later works about communication in the intimate context of love, passion, and marriage. Like other Kaprow "firsts," the work expressed an overweening excitement about a new variant of his art, although he would not return to this sort of piece for several years. The first phase of *Homemovies* consisted of videotaping the Schmidts as they greeted each other, took leave of each other, and left together. Then the videotapes were shown to a group of their friends, who were asked to imitate the couple. The imitations were videotaped and shown to the couple, who then imitated the imitations in the presence of their friends. In addition to the score, the project file contains the list of participants (which included Kaprow, his wife Vaughan Rachel, and their children), suggesting that the event was orchestrated to comic extreme < FIGS. 2, 3 >. It also may have been the most tender of wedding gifts. There are no photos of this Happening, and the videotape is irreparably damaged, but the score directs the participants to mirror the glances, caresses, intonations, and other myriad ineffable elements of lovers' communication. The interplay of behavior would be reflected in these imitations, and the couple's imitation of the imitation would manifest the receipt of Kaprow's gift: a new awareness of their love through an understanding of the ways they express it.

In 1970, Kaprow created *Level,* an Activity in which the concerns of *Homemovies* and the labor pieces begin to converge. The project file contains two drafts, one that is inscribed "for Vaughan," Kaprow's wife, and another that is not dedicated. It is not clear which came first < FIG. 4 >. The undedicated version is written in passive voice, the dedicated version in active voice.

placing a block of ice and bale of straw

near each other somewhere

ice melting slowly

reducing bale, straw by straw

(keeping pace with the ice)

until nothing remains[11]

The piece—two blocks of ice next to two bales of straw set in a Colorado field in late summer—had a formal austerity < SEE CHRONOLOGY, FIGS. 175–77 >. Because of the dedication and the pairing of the objects, it is tempting to see *Level* as a portrait of Kaprow's marriage, then in its fourteenth year. If so, it is a grim one, worthy of Robert Frost, in which marriage is a leveling process that reduces both people "until nothing remains."

In the early 1970s, Kaprow began to focus specifically on communication systems while shifting his model from manual labor to service-sector jobs, such as the work of nurses, orderlies, housekeepers, janitors, and mothers, perhaps reflecting the shift to a postindustrial economy in the United States. In these pieces Kaprow examined group behavior through gesture on an even more microcosmic level than that in *18 Happenings in 6 Parts*—through body language as basic as breathing. The booklets that accompany these pieces, which are designed to look like corporate or industrial training manuals, pursue to the point of absurdity the idea of "training" participants to smile, shake hands, or gaze into another person's eyes. Repeated use of tape recorders, mirrors, video cameras, and other reflexive devices emphasized the questions implied in the score: How does the task make you feel? How does it make you think about your everyday activities, gestures, and how and why you do them? If you let go of your conventional gestures, what's behind them? Who are you?

HOMEMOVIES

(A marriage Happening for Catherine and Daniel Schmidt some time after their marriage)

Hello

TV recording of couple greeting each other somewhere

Friends of couple watch recording, imitate them

TV recording of imitation

Trip

TV recording of couple getting on bus to go somewhere

Friends of couple watch recording, imitate them

TV recording of imitation

Goodbye

TV recording of couple saying goodbye somewhere

Friends of couple watch recording, imitate them

TV recording of imitation

Hello

TV recording of couple again greeting each other somewhere

Friends of couple watch recording, imitate them

TV recording of imitation

Copycat

Everybody watches whole TV coverage

Couple imitates imitations

— Allan Kaprow July/69

Fig. 2. **Score for *Homemovies* (1969)**

HOMEMOVIES - A MARRIAGE HAPPENING JULY 11,12,13, 1969
ALLAN KAPROW

I. First Hello - the Schmidt's home on Maple Avenue in Metuchen, N.J.
1. Original - Cathy and Daniel Schmidt
2. Imitations
a. Vaughan and Allan Kaprow
b. Dorothy and Carrel Morgan
c. Nancy Morgan and Eric Martz
d. Barbara and John Vandertuin
3. Copycat - Cathy and Daniel Schmidt imitate the imitations of:
a. Vaughan and Allan Kaprow
b. Dorothy and Carrel Morgan

II. Bus Trip - from Main and Middlesex Aves in Metuchen to New York City.
1. Original - Cathy and Daniel Schmidt
2. Imitations (en masse)
a. Nancy Morgan and Eric Martz
b. Amy and Anton Kaprow
c. Vaughan and Allan Kaprow (with Marisa)
d. Larry Morgan and Dr. Seiler
e. Carrel and Dorothy Morgan
f. Barbara and John Vandertuin
3. Copycat - Cathy and Daniel Schmidt imitate the imitations of:
a. Vaughan and Allan Kaprow
b. Barbara and John Vandertuin

III. Goodby - Bleeker St Cinema, New York City.
1. ~~Original - Cathy and Daniel Schmidt~~
2. Imitations
a. Dorothy and Carrel Morgan
b. Barbara and John Vandertuin
c. Dr. Seiler and Allan Kaprow
d. Nancy Morgan and Eric Martz
3. Copycat - Cathy and Daniel Schmidt imitate the imitations of:
a. Dr. Seiler and Allan Kaprow
(extras include: Eric, New Girl, and Anton Kaprow)
b. Nancy Morgan and Eric Martz

IV. Second Hello - Unitarian Colonial House in Wayne, New Jersey.
1. Original - Cathy and Daniel Schmidt
2. Imitations
a. Barbara and John Vandertuin
b. New Girl and Eric Martz
c. Vaughan and Allan Kaprow
d. Dorothy and Carrel Morgan
e. Nancy and Larry Morgan
3. Copycat - Cathy and Daniel Schmidt imitate the imitations of:
a. Barbara and John Vandertuin
b. Dorothy and Carrel Morgan
c. Nancy and Larry Morgan

Fig. 3. **Participant score for *Homemovies* (1969)**

Activities such as *Basic Thermal Units* (1973) and *Time Pieces* (1973) directed participants to measure and record one another's bodily responses in different environments and then to record their emotional responses to these "experiments." The focus on the personal information that emerged in these works was emphasized by Kaprow's use of family members and friends in the pieces and in the booklets that accompanied them. Although the structure of these Activities differed somewhat from that of *Homemovies,* these works still aimed to invoke intimate experience through the negation of conventional gesture. As Kaprow stated in his notes for *Time Pieces,* these works were built on "a framework of *objective* moves designed to tap *subjective* states, states which are, however, unknown at the beginning"[12] < SEE CHRONOLOGY, FIGS. 220–43 >. *Affect* (1974) was another in this series.

A (at home), putting both hands in water
(one in hot, one in cold),
until a hand feels hot and a hand feels cold

removing hands, waiting for them to dry
tape recording feelings throughout

• • •

B (also at home), doing same

A and B (meeting), playing to each other
their tapes
B, putting face in hot water,
until face feels hot

sitting in front of electric fan,
until face is dry

A, tape recording feelings about B, throughout

B, putting face in cold water,
until face feels cold

blowing hot air on face with hair dryer,
until face is dry

A, tape recording feelings about B, throughout

A and B, listening to tapes

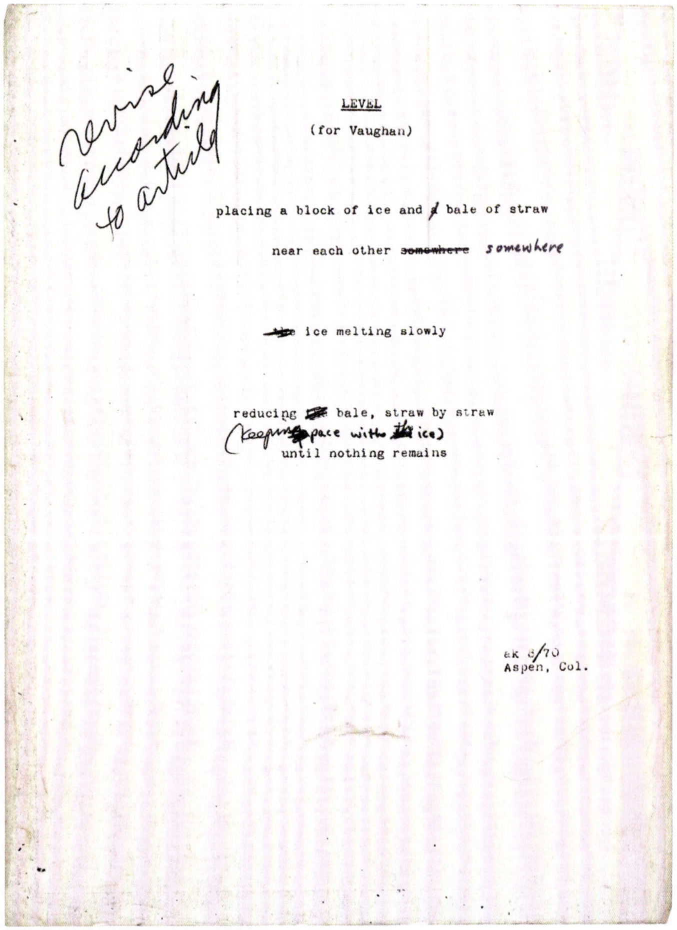

revise according to article

LEVEL
(for Vaughan)

placing a block of ice and a bale of straw
near each other ~~somewhere~~ somewhere

~~the~~ ice melting slowly

reducing ~~the~~ bale, straw by straw
(keeping pace with ~~the~~ ice)
until nothing remains

ak 6/70
Aspen, Col.

Fig. 4. **Score for *Level* (1970)**

A, putting a hand in cold water,
until hand feels cold

clasping B's dry hand

separating hands,
waiting for them to dry

B, tape recording feelings about A and B
throughout

A, getting into hot water,
until the body feels hot

pressing body to B's dry body

separating, waiting for bodies to dry

B, tape recording feelings about A and B,
throughout

A and B, listening to tapes[13]

Affect is documented in an Activity booklet illustrated with photos of Rachel and Kaprow performing the work <FIGS. 5, 6; SEE CHRONOLOGY, FIGS. 253–55>. Kaprow's statement about the piece alters the way we look at the images of the couple speaking into the recorder while gazing at each other or standing naked and embracing. Published at the end of the Activity booklet, the statement suggests that Kaprow created it as a piece about a disharmonious relationship.

> AFFECT, like another recent piece, is composed of our familiar notions of warmth and coldness in personalities; or ardor and distance in connection with body temperature; and of dry moments of life and moist ones. It plays with American verbal expressions that refer to these traits, such as "freezing a person out" (excluding them from a particular group), telling someone to "dry up" (meaning she or he is "all wet" or wrong), saying someone is "dry as dust" (dull) or is "in hot water" (trouble).
>
> In AFFECT, these references are nearly literalized; they are compartmented by separating them from ordinary motivation, and then are brought together either in one person or in a partnership of two persons.[14]

"Doing life, consciously," which Kaprow defined as the method of his art, here seems to have been applied to a tense domestic situation.[15] The archive does not reveal whether Kaprow and Rachel's performance of the Activity was a way of addressing marital difficulties or simply a performance for the purposes of illustrating the Activity booklet. What we do know is that the psychologically laden work of this period was influenced by their involvement in feminist consciousness-raising seminars.[16]

By the end of the decade, Kaprow had let go of the work metaphor but continued to focus on interpersonal communication, always suggesting that even the tiniest gestures carry the imprint of the group, the social system, the culture. The "situations"—the bracketed experiences—that Kaprow presented from the middle to

Figs. 5, 6. **Photos illustrating how to perform *Affect***
From the Activity booklet *2 Measures* (pub. 1974)

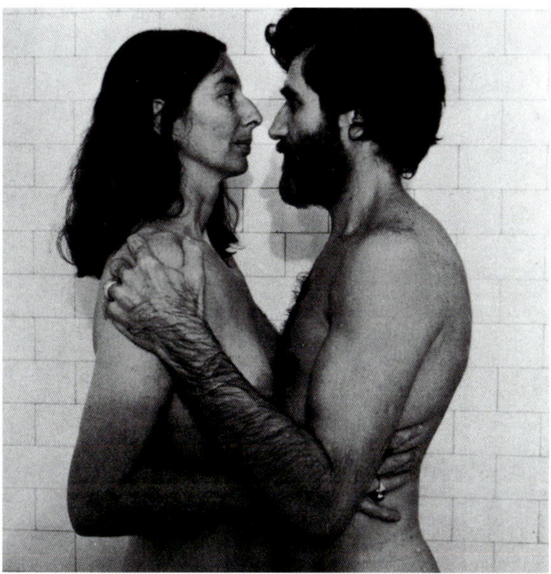

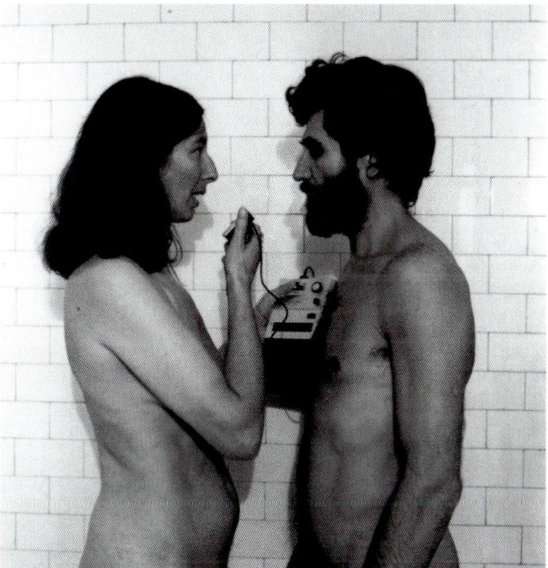

late 1970s were those of a man having encounters with women in an altered personal and social context. In works like *3rd Routine* (1974), *Take-Off* (1974), *Comfort Zones* (1975), *Warm-Ups* (1975), and *Maneuvers* (1976), each partner in turn dressed and undressed while the other tape recorded their feelings; falsified evidence to conceal adultery; and obsessively prepared for reunions and departures. All are actions that reflect a consideration of what makes a relationship good or enduring.

Satisfaction (1976) employed telephone dialogue in its introductory and concluding sequences. Here the desire for connection was repeatedly expressed by the participant couple < FIG. 7 >:

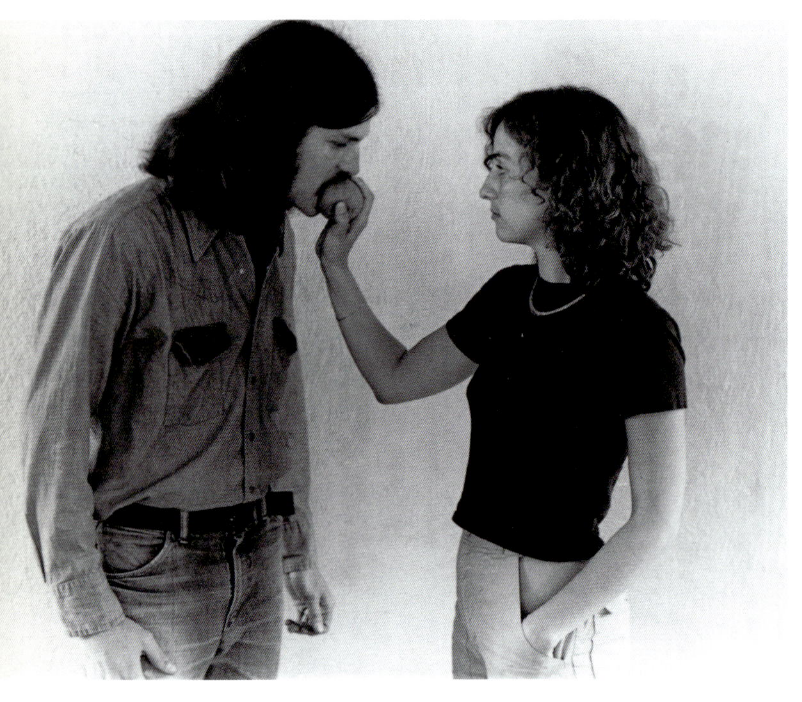

praise me

(or)

look at me

(or)

comfort me

(or)

feed me

(or)

kiss me

(or)

bathe me

showing how[17]

These sequences, repeated again and again in slightly different variations "until options are exhausted," demonstrated the "childish" needs that must be satisfied in a viable relationship.[18] The project file contains a first draft that, perhaps significantly, has a childlike look: the questions are scrawled in orange felt-tip pen on yellow legal paper, with the replies in red ballpoint pen; marginalia identify statements as "public" or "private." The piece's concluding phone dialogue suggests the difficulty of sustaining a state of satisfaction, or perhaps simply the ambivalence of the adult self toward these insatiable desires < SEE CHRONOLOGY, FIGS. 278–84 >. Participants in *Satisfaction* attested to its effective duality, as seen in reviews from "Series IV: Clippings." Pierre Restany observed that the piece's "psychosomatic message" was "infinitely stronger than the verbal message."[19] John Perrault wrote that "what is impor-

Fig. 7. **Photo illustrating how to perform *Satisfaction***
From the Activity booklet (pub. 1976)

tant is what you feel before and what you feel afterwards. The middle is performed by robots." He then concluded: "I only hope that [Kaprow] learned as much from his piece as I did. I suppose not. But who am I to suppose? Who am I?"[20]

Beginning in the 1980s, Kaprow's works were increasingly performed privately, for the enlightenment of himself or his friends. *Team* (1980) was enacted by Kaprow and Coryl Crane, whom he married in 1987 < SEE CHRONOLOGY, FIGS. 299, 300 >. Separated by a mile or so of desert terrain and communicating by walkie-talkies, each unrolled a five-mile line and then directed the other to the end of his or her line. The score specified that they were to rewind each other's lines, but it did not work out that way. Crane's recollection of the Activity is the first personal statement in the project files by a participant who was intimate with Kaprow.

> I was able to see the structure of the piece as a map of my relationship with Allan. In the desert we had tried to "be" with each other while physically being a mile apart. In the everyday world, we lead independent lives which we try to share while living, half of the time, 120 miles from each other. The act of communicating was central to the piece as it is in our lives—without it we both got lost and met up again only by chance and not by design, at least not by our design. The walkie-talkies, our communication tool, were unreliable, and distorted and blocked what we had to say to each other. The telephone is that symbol in our private lives and rather than bringing us together, usually exaggerates the fact that we are apart. . . . Allan often gets lost in "my" life, as I do in "his."[21]

In 1985, Kaprow handwrote *Piece for Coryl's Birthday* in blue pen on yellow unlined paper in two drafts; the first has many cross-outs and inserts, the second only a few small ones. The score, a gift from a Happening artist to his girlfriend, employs many of Kaprow's usual devices: mirrors, tracing, isolation of body parts, tape recording. At once a love letter and a work of art, it was not announced, reviewed, photo-documented, or published. It is the most personal and intimate item in the archive.

> Dear Coryl,
>
> As you and I planned, we'll spend this afternoon and evening together. We'll do some shopping, have dinner at a restaurant, maybe later stop off at the Harrisons' party. During this time, which will be considered in all respects normal time, we'll do the following piece. It will weave in and out of the everyday aspects of our day together.
>
> Each of us will carry with us in a plastic bag a mirror (about 15" square). During this day, whenever either of us wishes to do so, we will ask the other to be still for a moment and will look into our mirror and focus on the reflection of a part of the other's body: an eye, a mouth, the whole face, a hand, a foot or knee, etc.
>
> How much of the part of the body is reflected of course depends on how close or far away we are from the other, and how close our eyes are from the mirror itself. The angle of reflection also will make a difference: whether high, or very low, or from a side, or tipped. This will be a kind of editing. And it will obviously require us to turn away from each other to see each other.
>
> When we've got the part of the body we want, we'll trace [on the mirror] with our finger tip, as slowly or rapidly as we wish, the outline of that body part; or

we can fill in the outline as if painting it. When we're finished we'll put the mirror back in the bag and go on doing our shopping or whatever.

Alternatively, we may want to carry out a variation of this activity. One of us will decide at some particular time to ask the other to be still for a moment, will look at a part of the other's body directly: an ear, a hip or back, a crotch, a finger. Then instead of tracing the outline of that part on the mirror, or filling it in, we'll trace it on the other's body.

This, too, will be a kind of editing or choosing; and how we do it will depend on how we feel and what we're thinking. Our touch can [be] detached, or tender, or absorbed in curiosity; it can be very brief or extended. And during all these times we'll be free to talk as usual, and to talk about what's happening. These two alternative activities can be carried out in any order or repetition.

Throughout the day, and depending on where we are in public or alone, we can also ask one another to modify how a particular part of our body is to be seen: by changing a position, adding or removing an object like a glass of water, adding or removing some clothes. If we're asked to take off our clothes, sexual feelings are not necessarily the point of the piece, but neither are they excluded.

We'll add one more kind of attention to the day: that of an audio-recorder. We'll record the sounds of these reflections and tracings, and our talking about them, turning on the tape machine at whatever point in advance we want, and shutting it off afterwards as the activity moves into other more "normal" things like shopping or preparing a cup of tea. Where the "piece" is and where it isn't is up to each of us to decide. Later, listening to the sequences of recordings may be a kind of retracing, and maybe another reflection of some value.

Finally, the piece is meant to honor your birthday this December 21st. But if we wish we can extend it beyond this day.

with love,
your Allan[22]

Notes

1. Allan Kaprow, "Performing Life (1980)," in idem, *Essays on the Blurring of Art and Life,* ed. Jeff Kelley (Berkeley: Univ. of California Press, 1993), 195–96.
2. All these items are in archives held at the Getty Research Institute, Los Angeles slippers, Harold Rosenberg Papers, 1923–1984, accession no. 980048 (box 58, folder 9); currency, Luciano Folgore Papers, 1890–1966, accession no. 910141 (box 32, folder 14); cigarettes, Dick Higgins Papers, 1960–1994 (bulk 1972–1993), accession no. 870613; bills, Marcia Tucker Papers, 1957–2004, accession no. 2004.M.3.
3. Clement Greenberg Papers, 1928–1995, accession no. 950085 (box 20, folders 1, 2), Research Library, Getty Research Institute, Los Angeles.
4. David Tudor Papers, 1884–1998 (bulk 1940–1996), accession no. 980039 (box 58, folders 5–10), Research Library, Getty Research Institute, Los Angeles.
5. Claes Oldenburg to Allan Kaprow, 31 August 1961, Allan Kaprow Papers, ca. 1940–1997, accession no. 980063 (box 69, folder 7), Research Library, Getty Research Institute, Los Angeles; hereafter Allan Kaprow Papers.
6. Claes Oldenburg to Allan Kaprow, 15 July 1961, Allan Kaprow Papers (box 69, folder 7).
7. David Antin, foreword to Jeff Kelley, *Childsplay: The Art of Allan Kaprow* (Berkeley: Univ. of California Press, 2004), xix.
8. Allan Kaprow, typewritten score for *Calling,* 1965, Allan Kaprow Papers (box 9, folder 7).
9. Allan Kaprow, poster for *Fluids,* 1967, Allan Kaprow Papers (box 12, folder 10).
10. See Robert Haywood, "Critique of Instrumental Labor: Meyer Schapiro's and Allan Kaprow's Theory of Avant-Garde Art," in Benjamin H. D. Buchloh and Judith F. Rodenbeck, eds., *Experiments in the Everyday: Allan Kaprow and Robert Watts—Events, Objects, Documents,* exh. cat. (New York: Columbia University, 1999), 43.
11. Allan Kaprow, typewritten score for *Level,* 1970, Allan Kaprow Papers (box 18, folder 3).
12. Allan Kaprow, note for *Time Pieces,* 1973, Allan Kaprow Papers (box 24, folder 3).
13. Allan Kaprow, typewritten score for *Affect,* 1974, Allan Kaprow Papers (box 25, folder 7).
14. Allan Kaprow, *2 Measures,* Activity booklet, 1974, Allan Kaprow Papers (box 25, folder 7).
15. Kaprow, "Performing Life" (note 1).
16. See Jeff Kelley, *Childsplay: The Art of Allan Kaprow* (Berkeley: Univ. of California Press, 2004), 190–97.
17. Allan Kaprow, typewritten score for *Satisfaction,* 1976, Allan Kaprow Papers (box 27, folder 5).
18. Allan Kaprow, typewritten score for *Satisfaction* (note 17).
19. Pierre Restany, "Allan Kaprow," *Domus,* no. 566 (1977): 52.
20. John Perrault, "Experience with an Experience," *Soho Weekly News,* 6 May 1976.
21. Coryl Crane, transcript of participant account of *Team,* 1980, Allan Kaprow Papers (box 29, folder 11).
22. Allan Kaprow, handwritten score for *Piece for Coryl's Birthday,* 1985, Allan Kaprow Papers (box 31, folder 14).

Part Three **The Making of a Retrospective**

Agency for Action

Stephanie Rosenthal

> Being an artist today is to know oneself, to know oneself is to forget oneself (which is the image one has of one's "self"). — Allan Kaprow[1]

All his life, Allan Kaprow, the inventor of Happenings, had an ambivalent attitude toward exhibitions, and the institutions that presented them. He saw himself as an "Un-Artist/Non-Artist" and wanted to realize his own work somewhere removed from the conventional art discourse.[2] He regarded art as a social instrument. His aim was to encourage active participation, not passive observation. He demanded that art and life should become one, and he remained true to this principle—but the consequence was the disappearance of his art, at least as far as the art market and the wider public were concerned. A recent upsurge of interest in Happenings and other ephemeral art forms has prompted curators, art historians, and art critics to reappraise and recognize the significance of Kaprow's work.[3] The exhibition *Allan Kaprow—Art as Life* aimed to present the artist's work in a way that would preserve his synthesis of art and everyday life.[4] As Eva Meyer-Hermann and I developed the exhibition, we were guided by Kaprow's longstanding desire that the museum be turned into "an educational institute, a computerized bank of cultural history, and an agency for action."[5]

Throughout his life Kaprow challenged the validity of attempts to exhibit his works. As a last resort he could show his early paintings and collages—since they did not require participation on the part of the viewer, the dividing line between art and life was not an issue. He categorically dismissed the museum as a site for his new works of art, however. In the catalog for his exhibition at the Pasadena Art Museum in 1967, he stated that museums effectively killed art by isolating it from life.[6] This position would have been unthinkable without conventional art and its institutional setting as a point of reference—a paradox that permeated his work: "Leaving art *is* the art. But you must have it to leave it. I define it as that act or thought whose identity as art must forever remain unknown. That is, to answer the initial question What is Art?, art could (but might not) be simply doing art, whatever that is, as long as it can't be identified."[7]

In 1988, Kaprow and curator Jeff Kelley had to find a way of presenting Kaprow's oeuvre as a whole for *Allan Kaprow: Precedings,* a retrospective of his work at the Center for Research in Contemporary Art at the University of Texas at Arlington. The problem is outlined and a solution suggested in the proposal for the exhibition.

> How can Allan Kaprow, known for non-conservable events which drift in and out of esthetic and everyday frames, have a retrospective? Obviously, he cannot assemble and display the so-called original "happenings." Nor can he conjure up the times and places which framed them. He can, however, engage in playful retrospection, investigating the role of an artist's memory in the fabrication of art history, especially in the relative absence of historical artifacts; he can explore the changed social, personal, and artistic conditions through which retrospection is necessarily filtered, and in which the events of "then" and "now" take place; and he can open to question the conventional notion of retrospective, insofar as the re-creation of one's past *is* the transformation of a present self.[8]

This was how things stood on 14 December 2004, when Meyer-Hermann and I met Kaprow in Encinitas, California, to talk about an exhibition of his work. Meyer-Hermann was representing the Van Abbemuseum in Eindhoven, and I was there on behalf of Haus der Kunst in Munich. His eyes gleaming like diamonds, Kaprow set the tone of our discussion with these words: "Here's the problem: I don't want to have a show!"[9] This statement was wholly at odds with the fact that he had invited us to visit him and had already expressed his interest, in principle, in an exhibition of his work. From that point onward our discussions revolved around this paradox and our realization that Kaprow's resistance was deeply rooted in his artistic outlook. To our question "Do you want to have a wider public?" he answered, "No. . . . The public want to be entertained." To our question "Should we give the public what it wants?" he replied, "The public doesn't have to get what it wants. That's the added value of art. . . . Everything is art and art is everything and I don't care about everything. I don't care about art. . . . To do what I want to do, I had to leave the art world." At one point he said, "I don't know what I want." And when we asked, "Do you want the public to understand?" he responded, flatly, "No."[10]

The following day he greeted us with these words: "What did we discuss yesterday? . . . What kind of decisions did we make?" We wondered whether he was testing us or trying to confuse us, or whether he might have been confused himself. Whatever the case, it felt as though we were sitting an exam and had just come to the question "What makes a good curator?" Later, when he asked, "How can I make confusion meaningful?" we had our explanation. Kaprow wanted to sustain a state of confusion—a situation in which everything is still completely open—for as long as possible.[11]

By the end of this first visit, Kaprow had agreed to the exhibition. We had passed his test, no doubt because we had not arrived with a preconceived idea of what we wanted, and also because we did not act as if we would abandon the plans for the exhibition if our terms were not met. In the end, we dismissed several plans—making a film called "How To Fail To Do an Exhibition with Allan Kaprow," turning the exhibition into a workshop—and we also rejected the idea of presenting a traditional exhibition of his paintings. Apparently, there was a certain significance in the fact that we were Europeans, representing a continent that had shown considerably more interest in Kaprow's work in recent years than his native land had done. The crucial outcome of our discussion was our decision to realize new versions of some of Kaprow's Environments, Happenings, and Activities—to "reinvent" them. He would have to separate his art from his life, although the two had always been inextricably connected. This was a radical step on Kaprow's part, one that would give his whole output a new dimension. His art would not to come to an end, for he was now prepared to let go. The exhibition would mark this change. Kaprow bid us farewell by saying, "I have to take a risk. I have to trust the public."

Kaprow was a brilliant speaker and a groundbreaking theorist. No one could articulate his ideas or reveal the paradoxical nature of his work better than he. So Kaprow's own words feature prominently in what follows.

WHAT IS A HAPPENING?

Happenings are events that, put simply, happen. Though the best of them have a decided impact—that is, we feel "here is something important"—they appear to go nowhere and do not make any particular literary point.

— Allan Kaprow[12]

In 1959, Allan Kaprow presented *18 Happenings in 6 Parts* at the Reuben Gallery in New York, one of his first "Happenings."[13] For this rather theatrical work, Kaprow divided the gallery space into three distinct rooms separated by wooden frames and plastic sheeting. Cards were passed out as the audience entered the gallery, instructing people to take seats in specific rooms for specific parts. Each of the six parts comprised three Happenings. These Happenings presented both absolutely quotidian activities, such as a girl squeezing oranges, and more contrived actions, such as performers entering the room and executing a series of stiff, choreographed movements. At the end of each part, a bell would sound, signaling that the audience should move to a different room to experience the next set of Happenings < SEE CHRONOLOGY, FIGS. 29–50 >. The Happenings evolved from the Environments, which, as he said in 1962,

> developed quite naturally from the collages and assemblages I made in the years 1953 to 1956. . . . Following the implications inherent in the very impurity and inclusiveness of the process, . . . materials multiplied in number and density, extending away from the flat canvas surface, until that pictorial point of departure was eliminated entirely and the whole gallery was filled. I termed this an environment. . . . That is, I had in mind the totality of most everyday environments and used many of these as models: a subway station, penny-arcade, a forest, kitchen, etc. . . . Connected with this kind of thinking, of course, were the gallery-goers; for since they were encompassed by the environment in which they found themselves, their bodies, colors of clothing, movements, and voices became a part of the whole (whether or not they realized it in those days). It seemed clear to me that a passive and separated onlooker was not only undesirable for my needs, but was literally impossible.[14]

Soon after this, Kaprow decided that the world and everyday life should provide the backdrop to his Happenings—that an artificially created setting was not necessary. Accordingly, in the early 1960s Kaprow relocated his activities to the outside world: "The move to the outside of the gallery was part of a series of steps I had been taking since 1956. I wanted to develop an art which would depart radically from the art history and contexts we traditionally associate with art. . . . What was needed, I believed, was to leave the galleries, museums, stages . . . for the everyday world. (Later, I would include the inner 'spaces' of our heads and bodies.)"[15] Part of the impetus for this move came from Jackson Pollock's paintings: "I said that Happenings would be the heritage of Pollock's work."[16] Kaprow now treated everyday life as his canvas, and ordinary events were the paints that were spattered onto it. Kaprow's Happenings required participants—not spectators—who determined the composition through their actions, which were the colors and the forms of the artwork.

> Now if the models for these early Happenings were not the arts, then there were abundant alternatives in everyday life routines: brushing teeth. . . . The new art genre therefore came about, or more accurately, gradually became an art/life genre, reflecting equally the artificial aspects of everyday life and the lifelike qualities of created art. For example, it was clear to me how formal and culturally learned the act of shaking hands is; just try to pump a hand five or six times instead of two times and you'll cause instant anxiety.[17]

Kaprow's decision to base his works on participation set them apart from stage shows and later performances by Fluxus, but it also made his art unmarketable and impossible to exhibit.[18]

There is a widespread misapprehension that Kaprow's Happenings were restricted to the 1960s and 1970s. In fact, they spanned the years from 1959 until shortly before his death in 2006, although by the early 1970s Kaprow preferred to talk of "Activities." The programs for the Happenings and Activities were always outlined in what Kaprow called a "score"—instructions committed to paper by Kaprow and distributed to the participants.

Kaprow's early scores bore a striking resemblance to those of John Cage, with whom he had studied from 1957 to 1958 < SEE CHRONOLOGY, FIGS. 21, 22, 24, 25 >. Soon, however, the elements of notation disappeared, leaving only the text. At first, Kaprow's directions were detailed and structured rather like stage dramas or screenplays. Over the years, the directions were distilled into shorter forms, much like concrete poetry, that allowed the participants more room to maneuver. In the mid-1970s Kaprow began designing and producing illustrated Activity booklets < SEE CHRONOLOGY, FIGS. 253–55, 259–62, 270–74, 282 >. The combination of score and photographs was intended to suggest how the Activity might be presented.[19] Later Kaprow became dissatisfied with the results: people were too easily drawn into copying the photographs in the booklets, and their approach to the Activity lost any independence.

Starting in the mid-1960s, on the evening before a Happening, Kaprow would give a public lecture (advertised by fliers that had been posted on college campuses and around town) about the work. From the 1970s on, each event was also followed by a workshop that offered participants a chance to discuss the experience—an idea Kaprow borrowed from feminist art, which he first encountered as a faculty member at the California Institute of the Arts.[20] Up until the late 1960s, Kaprow's Happenings predominantly took place in public spaces in the city or in the open countryside. The participants were fellow artists, festival audiences, and, later, his students. The Happenings of the mid-1960s were more overtly political and socially critical than the later works, and between 1968 and 1973 the natural world was a major consideration: "I was interested to draw the obvious parallels between natural cycles such as the seasons, and human ones such as the digestive process. But I was also interested in the fact that consciousness of this tends to separate humans (at least Western humans) from nature, rather than the other way around....Needless to say, on the natural side of things the group was imitating in condensed time typical geological changes of the earth's surface: the land rises and water erodes it, carrying up what was down and down what was up. In the unstable, earthquake country of southern California this was self-evident to everybody."[21]

By mid-1969, Happenings had become too spectacular and were too obviously in vogue for Kaprow's liking; in response the private sphere became increasingly central to his works.[22] He started to use the term *Activity* for these works, which were intended to be enacted by smaller groups in less public places. Nevertheless, the element of participation was just as crucial.

> I've written any number of times that a primary feature of Activities is their participatory function. . . . Without such participation, it could not exist. "Doing" an Activity is to bring it into factual being. I don't (to use a pietistic word) "create" an Activity; rather I arrange its "program". . . . In its doing, in real time and in real environments, the program is fleshed out, and a thousand unforeseeable experiences occur, specifics which neither could have been, nor need to be, pre-planned.[23]

The number of participants was gradually reduced to just two; in the end, he often realized his works in private and all but alone. As the years passed, he steadily contracted the circle around himself until he "occupied" the entire space of the Activity. His immediate surroundings became his only stage, and the event became meditation.

> I was always interested in Zen, but in a philosophical sense. . . . Some of these Happenings had as their main principle the blurring of the line between art and life. That meant leaving the art galleries and museums in favor of everyday spaces such as streets, cellars, kitchens, city dumps and the countryside. . . .

One of the teachings of Zen, as I see it, is that the practice extends activity into everyday life. We may sit in the Zendo but we can carry that practice and all it brings to us into washing the dishes.[24]

In presenting his Happenings and Activities, Kaprow was in effect posing a number of questions: How do I communicate with myself and with others? How can I express myself? Is it possible to explain and to comprehend the functions of the human body by drawing parallels with the natural world? How can I explore nonverbal communication between people? Kaprow's works were almost like scientific experiments in their attempt to devise ways of communicating better with the outside world, ways of connecting his internal and external worlds. One of his earliest Happenings, *Communication,* realized in 1958 after several similar but smaller events for John Cage's class at the New School for Social Research, revolved around just such issues. In *Communication,* which Kaprow identified as his first public Happening, he chose to "enlarge and complicate the idea of communicating by turning a speaking occasion into a multimedia activity," rejecting what he called "then-fashionable appeals to sentimental 'togetherness.'" His "speech" was recorded on audiotape and played back to the audience from three tape recorders positioned in the balconies of the auditorium.[25] In the recording, he identified communication as

one of the most hateful words. I have dedicated my best energies to retaining this disgust. I am offended by the smug and complacent techniques designed to facilitate the passage of one man's thought to another, served up as they are in a syrup-sauce of democracy and smiling optimism. I am convinced that at least in the realm of ideas and values this results only in the preservation of miles of cliché, carrying us further and further from what is true experience. . . . I am only interested in that experience for which I alone am responsible and to which I alone respond. . . . The only "communication" that interests me is the communication of non-communication. This alone is potent, variable, fresh and communicable. Beyond that there is only the simple art.[26]

REINVENTION—NOT REENACTMENT

As time passed, Kaprow became increasingly aware that his Happenings and Activities would come to a halt when his life ended if he did not find a new approach for their realization. Since the Happenings and Activities were about participation, it seemed logical to allow new versions to be made. In 1984, he described a project for the exhibition *Blam! The Explosion of Pop, Minimalism, and Performance, 1958–1964,* to Barbara Haskell, curator at the Whitney Museum of American Art in New York, that suggested how a Happening might be reinvented.

So my proposal is this: to *create* 1960 wholesale, *not* to re-create it in any sense. The idea stems from the plan I'm currently working out with Al Nodal at Otis/Parsons in LA. Al wanted to present a retrospective of my work back to 1947. I suggested instead the invention of my past and he was enthusiastic. The central point of the retrospective would be not retrospecting; and it would

> be made clear right from the beginning in all public communication, for example: "Inventing 1958, 1960, 1963, 1969, 1970, 1974, 1980, and so on . . ." might appear as the catalog title. Almost nothing will appear in the gallery, since the key focus will be the site-specific work after 1957. And for each "older" piece that is created, I plan several versions in different places and at different times.[27]

In 1988, in the context of the retrospective in Arlington, Kaprow started to put on new versions of his Happenings and Activities himself.[28] In 1996, when he was planning his contribution to the exhibition *Out of Actions: Between Performance and the Object, 1949–1979,* held at the Museum of Contemporary Art in Los Angeles in 1998, he defined the parameters for a new version of *18 Happenings,* for which he would be the leader.

> 1) The new version would be markedly different from its earliest form, but would emerge from at least 3 previous versions. 2) It would not occur in the museum, but in the daily environs. 3) It would be for participants (voluntary) not for audiences. 4) I would conduct a workshop, in advance, for about 20 persons in the nature of Happening-type actions, to culminate with the new version of "18 Happenings." 5) The museum, however, could certainly exhibit various documents and reportage about the new piece (and the workshop). 6) I would give a public lecture on Happenings and Performances, and would include descriptions of the workshop and the new "18 Happenings."[29]

By contrast, Kaprow's Environments were specifically designed so that they could also be realized by other people. *Stockroom* (1961), for instance, was planned so that even the first version did not require Kaprow's presence < SEE CHRONOLOGY, FIGS. 61–65 >. Visitors, following posted instructions, were invited to use charcoal or paint to mark the used boxes, which were hanging from the ceiling and lying on the floor, or to rearrange the boxes.

> Basically, the work is to be conceived organically rather than geometrically, though one should not interpret these words in any absolute way. The "feel" of it should be one of artlessness or stylelessness, therefore. This of course requires of the composer the utmost in responsibility and devotion to his job. While flexibility is intended within certain limits, license is to be discouraged. The composer's sense of responsibility to what he does, furthermore, may be conceived in a spirit of either fun or gravity, as long as his feelings are natural and spontaneous.[30]

Kaprow was preoccupied with one question, to which there was no simple answer: Would it be more consistent to let the Happenings and Activities cease? Were the answer "yes," Kaprow would forever remain the best-known unknown artist. Were the answer "no," there was a danger that the core of his artistic practice would be compromised, since his active participation in his art would no longer be possible. Sooner or later, exhibition makers would unearth photographs from the archives that would lead to reenactments, and Kaprow would have no say in these future presentations of his works. By deciding in favor of reinventions rather than reenactments, he was guiding his work in a direction that could be sustained even in his absence. Kaprow deliberately chose the term *reinvention* for new versions of his works, which, unlike *reenactment,* does not typically have a historical flavor.[31] The term underlined the fact that Kaprow did not intend the new versions to be replicas of the versions he had realized in the past, and that change was the order of the day.

Although Kaprow gained something when he made this decision, he also lost something. In reinventions, the form that a work takes is less important than hitherto because it is no longer directed by the artist himself. In the original works, the action was always paramount, but photographs of Kaprow's works show that he also valued how they were executed. Nevertheless, he was always acutely aware of one thing in particular: "I do not think that either art or any value or a life-situation of any intensity could result if I were to start off and end up with a purely aesthetic problem in mind."[32] At the core of Kaprow's work were the exchange of ideas, communication, and collective decision making among the participants. Ultimately, it was the process, not the result, that mattered.

Before *Allan Kaprow—Art as Life,* Kaprow had provided a score to someone else for a realization of a work on only a few occasions; in these instances, he had sent or faxed a score to someone else to present. When Kaprow granted permission for some of his Happenings and Environments to be reinvented in Munich, he was allowing his art to be experienced by a new generation as well as making provisions for his works to live on after his death. Nevertheless, the new versions remained true to the principle he had established in the early 1960s:

> Moreover, so far, Happenings, once presented, are not repeated. Even an account such as the foregoing is nothing like a magazine reproduction of a painting or an LP, stamped out by the thousands. The framework of the event is written out but there is still a wide margin of mystery about what it actually felt like to be there. No more than "red" can be described to a blind man can that experience be conveyed, nor even filmed, accurately. For the time being, the Happening seems incapable of easy standardization.[33]

ALLAN KAPROW—ART AS LIFE

Meyer-Hermann and I resolved to mount an exhibition that would reflect the paradox of Kaprow's desire for an exhibition coupled with his rejection of the idea. Our aim was to find an appropriate vehicle for an artist who defined himself as an un-artist/non-artist. Might the result be an unexhibition/nonexhibition? At the same time, we were aware that Kaprow now had a place in art history and that his life's work deserved to be mediated and presented in an art historical context and at an institutional level. While this was very much in keeping with Kaprow's thinking, it was important that the presentation not be overly documentary, with each of the works being accompanied by detailed instructions, photographs, reviews, and videos that might make them appear misleadingly simplistic or straightforward. We felt it would be more productive to present the various media separately, so that an overview would ultimately exist only in the viewer's mind.

We divided the exhibition into two distinct parts. "Agency for Action" was devoted to the reinvented Environments, Happenings, and Activities, and "Museum as Mediation" took the form of an archive of Kaprow's work, containing scores, videos, and documentary materials such as photographs and films.[34] Our aim was not to present the definitive Kaprow exhibition; on the contrary, we wanted to take Kaprow's own principles for the reinvention of his works—"site-specificity," "impermanence," and "doubt in art"—and apply these to the making of the exhibition <FIGS. 1–4>.[35]

Fig. 1. **Opening night of *Allan Kaprow—Kunst als Leben,***
17 October 2006
Environments, Middle Hall, Haus der Kunst, Munich

Fig. 2. **Opening night of *Allan Kaprow—Kunst als Leben,***
17 October 2006
Environments, Middle Hall, Haus der Kunst, Munich

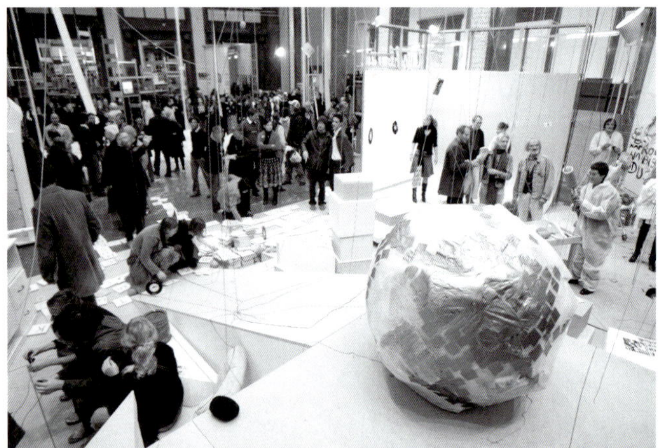

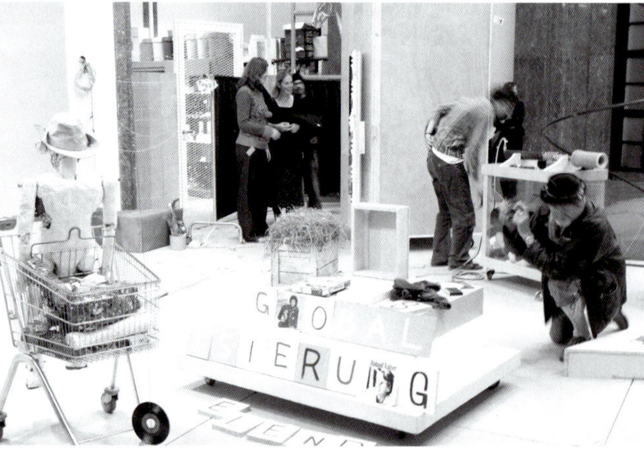

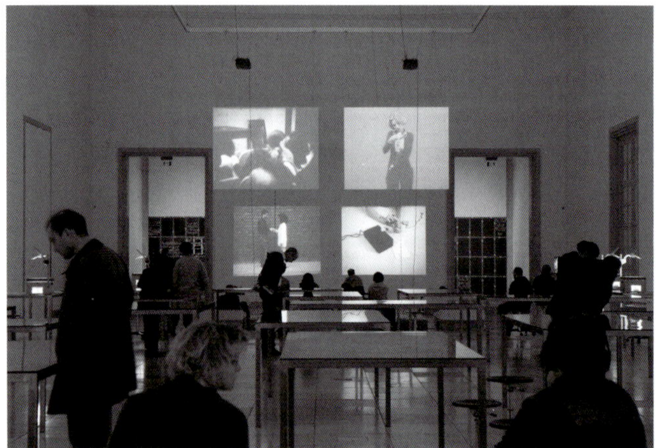

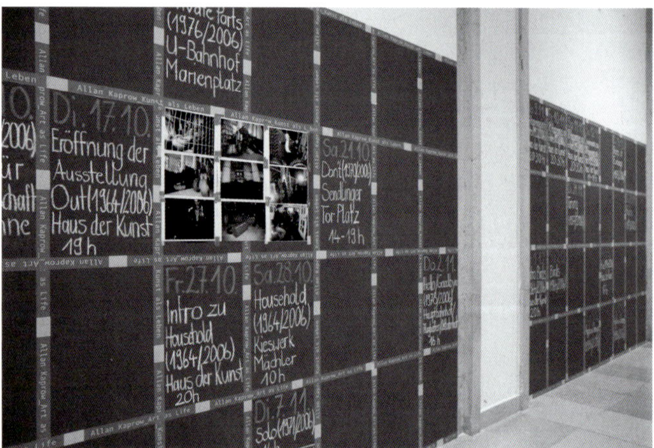

Fig. 3. **Opening night of *Allan Kaprow—Kunst als Leben,***
17 October 2006
View of the East Wing, Haus der Kunst, Munich

Fig. 4. **Calendar of reinvented Happenings**
Haus der Kunst, Munich

In the "Agency for Action" reinventions, Kaprow was no longer solely responsible for the reinventions of his work, for another individual would take on the role of leader, fundamentally affecting the form of the work and its subsequent reception. An artist might choose a focus quite different from that of an art critic, a musician, a dancer, and so on. Kaprow's artistic work was now concerned with issuing invitations to others to realize new versions of his works, as long as his three principles remained sacrosanct.

Kaprow stipulated that wherever possible, responsibility should be given to a single leader. The form of the new version would be dependent on the leader, the time, the place, and the participants. This delegation of control was the logical outcome of his own experience: control creates freedom.[36] Kaprow's guidelines gave the new leader a point of reference to work with and against, so that he or she could avoid being overwhelmed by possibilities. Kaprow's only request was that he not be personally involved or asked for advice, although he wanted to be kept informed of events.[37]

What fascinated me about Kaprow's decision was not only its radicalism but also the fact that he did not hide the pain and effort it cost him. It was impossible for him to think about the reinventions without facing his own mortality. In that sense, I became part of a process of separation: Kaprow was gradually disconnecting his life from his work, preparing to allow his works to lead a life of their own, and it was only his acceptance of his own mortality that made this step possible.

REINVENTIONS—MUNICH

During the run-up to the exhibition, I constantly found myself wondering if our plans could really work without the artist. Now, having led some reinventions myself and having participated in others, I find myself wondering, "But what could have gone wrong?" In a sense, we had already fulfilled Kaprow's wishes before the exhibition opened. The exchange of ideas, the discussions, and the collective decision making that preceded the official opening were crucial to the project as a whole. And, as Kaprow had said very early on, "There is no wrong or right."[38]

For over two years, I talked with colleagues, artists, art historians, critics, friends, theater experts, and others about Kaprow's works, and I found numerous kindred spirits who wanted to realize new versions of Environments, Happenings, and Activities.[39] Working initially with Kaprow and then, following his death, in close consultation with the Kaprow Estate, we decided which works could best be reinvented. In Munich, three professors from Akademie der Bildenden Künste München, Magdalena Jetelová, Hermann Pitz, and Stefan Römer, with the participation of a number of students, reinvented three Environments: *Stockroom* (1961), *Words* (1962), and *Push and Pull* (1963) < SEE CHRONOLOGY, FIGS. 74–77, 93–97 >. For the Happenings and Activities, the leader was to determine for each work the place and the date and whether it should be realized only by the selected participants or by a group that anyone might join. The dates were publicized on a website, where would-be participants could apply to take part. In addition, several scores were distributed as handouts, giving visitors to the exhibition the means to reinvent the work at home. Kaprow and the Kaprow Estate had reserved the right to receive and publish any materials that documented the reinventions.

The leaders found it relatively simple to fulfill at least two of Kaprow's three premises: it was impossible not to take a site-specific approach to the work, and impermanence was also intrinsic to the concept. But what is "doubt in art"? Did Kaprow mean that his works were not about art in the narrower sense? Whatever the case, the artist's words prompted participants to think seriously about art itself.

Our version of *18 Happenings in 6 Parts* provided a unique opportunity to uncover—in practice rather than in theory—the roots of Kaprow's thinking. It was the only work that we reenacted rather than reinvented for the purposes of the exhibition <FIGS. 5, 6>.[40] A transitional work, *18 Happenings* had a structure that differed significantly from the later Happenings. Designed so that it could be reenacted, *18 Happenings* follows a highly detailed score that consists of a complicated sequence of actions and pauses, combined with music and light. It took over two years for Kaprow to develop. Our reenactment cast a particularly interesting light on Kaprow's decision to allow new versions of his works to be made.

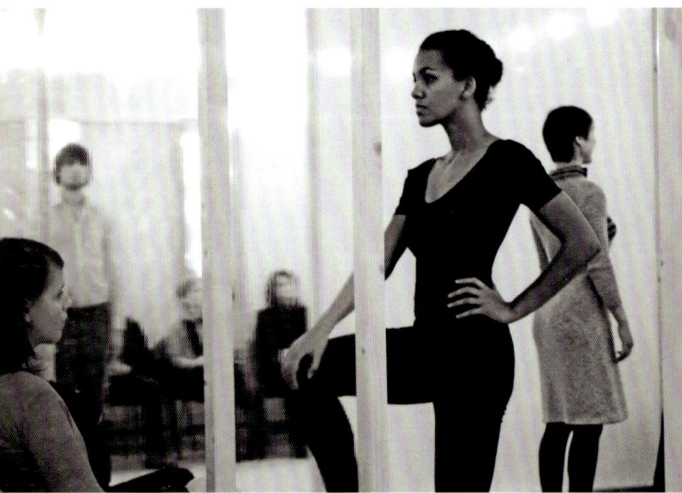

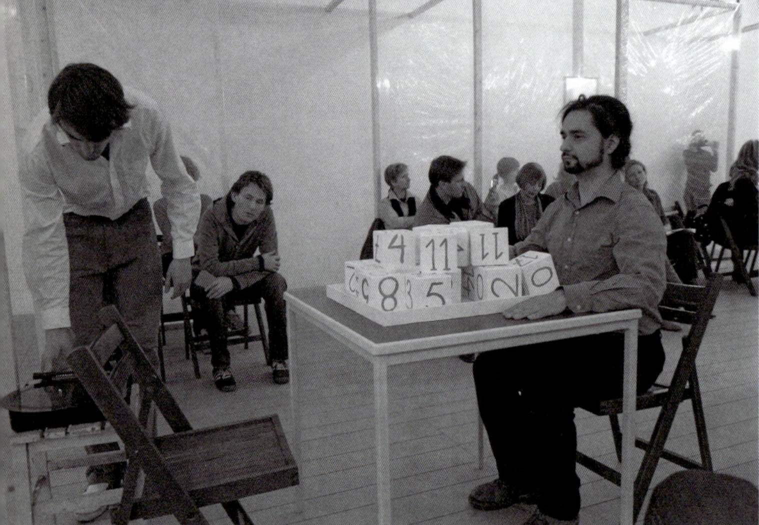

Much has been written about *18 Happenings,* but it has to be experienced to be comprehended.[41] The "intermissions" take more time than the blocks of action, with the result that they take on a tangible presence, becoming as important as the action. The pauses assume an even greater significance when one takes Kaprow's later works into account. The things that occur spontaneously during the pauses—people conversing, moving around, reflecting—are an essential part of the event as a whole. The actions in later Happenings and Activities, when people stacked blocks of ice, shifted concrete slabs, or washed cars, were of course important, but in principle these tasks were interchangeable. Kaprow's invitation to others to interpret his scores as they wished was entirely in keeping with this. His scores are a practical aid to the performance of an action by a group, a couple of people, or a single person, as well as a source of inspiration. It is precisely the unforeseeable factors that emerge during a Happening or Activity, the things that are *not* in the score, that often turn out to be crucial.

In *Round Trip* (1968/2006), for which I led a group of students from the Ludwig-Maximilians-Universität, it was the sudden, spontaneous climax that took on particular importance. An excerpt from Kaprow's score hints at how repetitious the activity could become.

> Tiny ball of paper, cardboard,
> string, rolled several blocks.
> Ball enlarged with more materials.
> Rolled several blocks again. Enlarged . . .
> Rolled several blocks again.
> Process repeated until ball is too
> Large to roll.

Figs. 5, 6. **Views of *18 Happenings in 6 Parts* (1959/2006)**
Reenactment for *Allan Kaprow—Kunst als Leben*
Haus der Kunst, Munich

Some paper, cardboard and string,
Removed. Ball rolled several
Blocks. More material removed.
Rolled several blocks. More removed.
Rolled several blocks. More removed.
Rolled . . . Process repeated until
there is no ball.[42]

Having spent over two hours collecting and rolling garbage into a large ball, we were now rolling the ball back to the university, where we would dismantle the ball and dispose of the rubbish <FIG. 7>. Perspiring and tired, we wished we could just dump it in a trash bin, but we were uneasy at the thought of taking such an easy way out. Were we not taking the task—and, by definition, art—seriously? No one wanted to take responsibility for this radical decision, so, as we made our way back, we just threw bits of the ball into trash bins we found standing on the sidewalk. At the fourth or fifth bin, outside a public building, the caretaker caught us and vociferously scolded us for trying to get rid of our trash in his bin. We explained to him that it was not our trash but that we had collected it in the street and in the park—at which point the caretaker lifted up the ball and stuffed the entire thing into "his" bin. He had taken the decision out of our hands. The whole group breathed a sigh of relief. This turn of events led to a discussion on responsibility and taking things seriously. It became clear that everyone tried to avoid difficult decisions or to put them off as long as possible; we preferred to hope for a lucky chance, such as the one we had experienced.

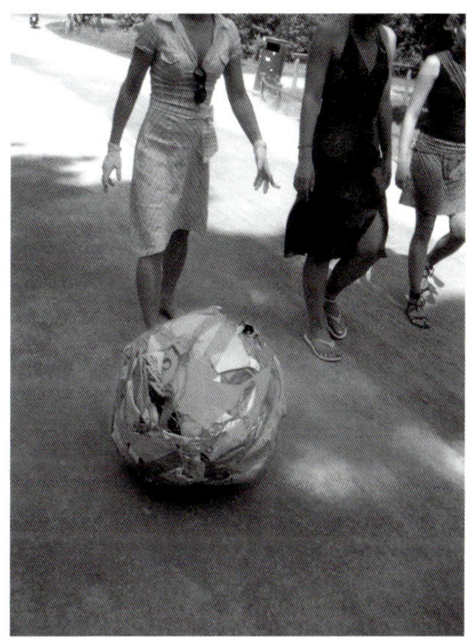

Fig. 7. **View of *Round Trip* (1968/2006)**
Version by Stephanie Rosenthal
Reinvention for *Allan Kaprow—Kunst als Leben*
Munich

Participants drew their own conclusions from this experience. For my part, I learned more about the individual qualities of my students during the Happening than during the two semesters that I had been teaching them. To me, the moment of self-examination and self-observation was a crucial part of the Happening. I discovered that collecting the trash only started to be fun when I stopped trying to make sense of it or worrying about the absurdity of the situation. During a Happening, one is aware of participating in an art action, and thus views oneself and the surroundings from exactly this standpoint—which is not to say that it is impossible to take the Happening seriously. Rather, the experience can sharpen one's eye for aspects of ordinary life—I became more, or perhaps differently, aware of myself, of those around me, and of the way people treat each other.

During the reinvention of *Scales* (1971/2006), I was astonished to find myself captivated by its formal aspects. The score for *Scales* instructs participants to place cement blocks on the steps of a stairway, forming new steps, and then to climb them to the next level <SEE CHRONOLOGY, FIG. 193>. They repeat the task several more times, ascending up two more stairways before reversing course and descending the stairways that they have climbed. The act of placing the concrete slabs and walking up and down on them was wonderful <FIG. 8>. We, as participants, were so conscious of the action that it took on the air of a perfect choreography. The sound made by the slabs as they were set down, depending on the type of step (concrete or marble) that they were laid down on, was a kind of music. And then one's mind turned to the circular nature of the action, its absurdity, and the physical effort it required; these were thoughts that could arise from a reading of the score, but the aesthetic response ensued only during the live performance.

The Swedish artist Bo Christian Larsson realized a new version of *Household* (1964/2006) in which I participated. The original score distinguished three groups, two of which were structured by sex. Set in a dump, *Household* begins with the men building a tower, the women a nest. Then the "people" arrive several hours later, in

Fig. 8. **View of *Scales* (1971/2006)**
Version by Stephanie Rosenthal
Reinvention for *Allan Kaprow—Kunst als Leben*
Haus der Kunst, Munich

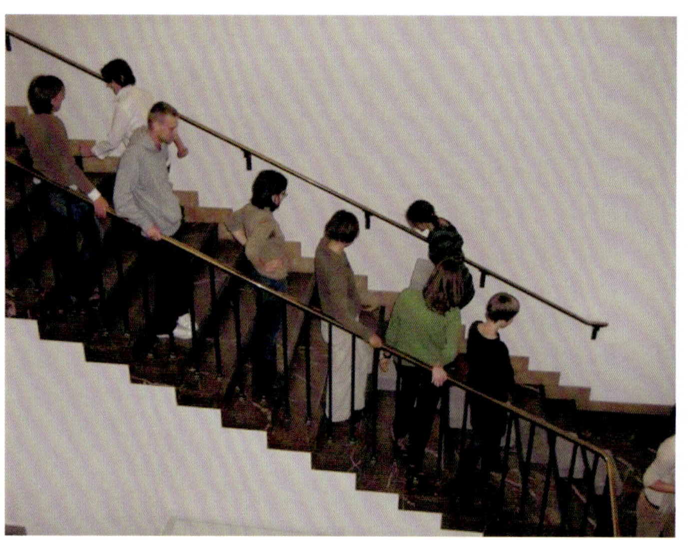

a smoky car. A series of actions ensues, including licking strawberry jam from a car, eating bread, blowing police whistles, screeching, rolling about, disrobing, and destroying the nest, the tower, and the car <SEE CHRONOLOGY, FIGS. 109–17>. Larsson had made some slight changes to the score and had added a group of "newcomers." Even my decision as to which group I should attach myself was revealing. During the introduction on the evening prior to the Happening, I had decided to join the newcomers because it was the smallest group, but I soon noticed that I did not feel at ease there. I had no desire to be in this neutral zone. I wanted to adopt a gendered role, to be a "woman." So the next morning I switched groups. Once again I realized that it was only when I took the game seriously that it worked for me. As long as I remained in the role of observer, be it out of shyness or for practical reasons, I felt emotionally excluded. Our job in the women's group was to build a nest, in accordance with the classic understanding of the female role. Meanwhile, the men were busy building their tower <FIGS. 9, 10; SEE CHRONOLOGY, FIGS. 364, 365>. By and large, we women happily set about constructing our nest from fence posts, foil, and leaves, making it "nice" for ourselves. Those of us in our twenties and thirties had no problem fulfilling this domestic role. We did not feel it impinged on our emancipation as feminists. Not so the women born around 1950: they could not understand why we younger women so willingly accepted the "clichéd" female role. While the men concentrated on building their tower, we settled down and enjoyed ourselves, eating bread and jam in our new "home." We younger women were aware of demonstrating a new type of female self-confidence.

All the Happenings that I led or participated in took a similar course. Excited anticipation was followed by uncertainty as to how one should actually behave. Then "normality"—a routine, even boredom—set in. One found oneself longing for it to be over; then the end approached and one felt oneself relaxing. Afterward I felt strangely uplifted, and it turned out that others felt the same—almost as though we had been playing a game. For what is a Happening, if not that? It is "a game, an adventure, a number of activities, engaged in by participants for the sake of playing," as Kaprow wrote in 1967.[43]

There is no question that Happenings today make as much or as little sense as they did when they were first enacted. Now, as then, concrete slabs are normally dragged to building sites; they are not moved around otherwise, or not without good reason. And Kaprow's own conclusion still holds true today: "Of course, when you do live consciously, life becomes pretty strange—paying attention changes the thing attended—so the Happenings were not nearly as lifelike as I supposed they might be. But I learned something about life and 'life.'"[44]

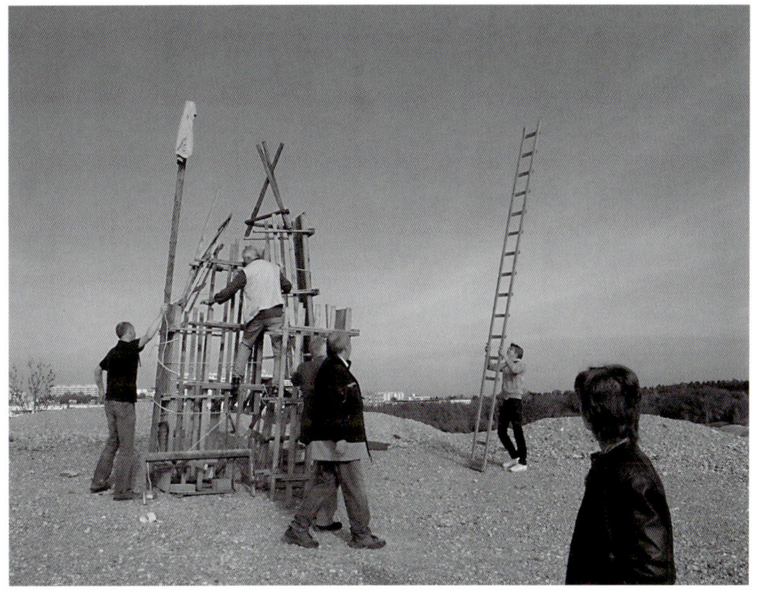

Figs. 9, 10. **Views of *Household*** **(1964/2006)**
Version by Bo Christian Larsson
Reinvention for *Allan Kaprow—Kunst als Leben*
Suburbs of Munich

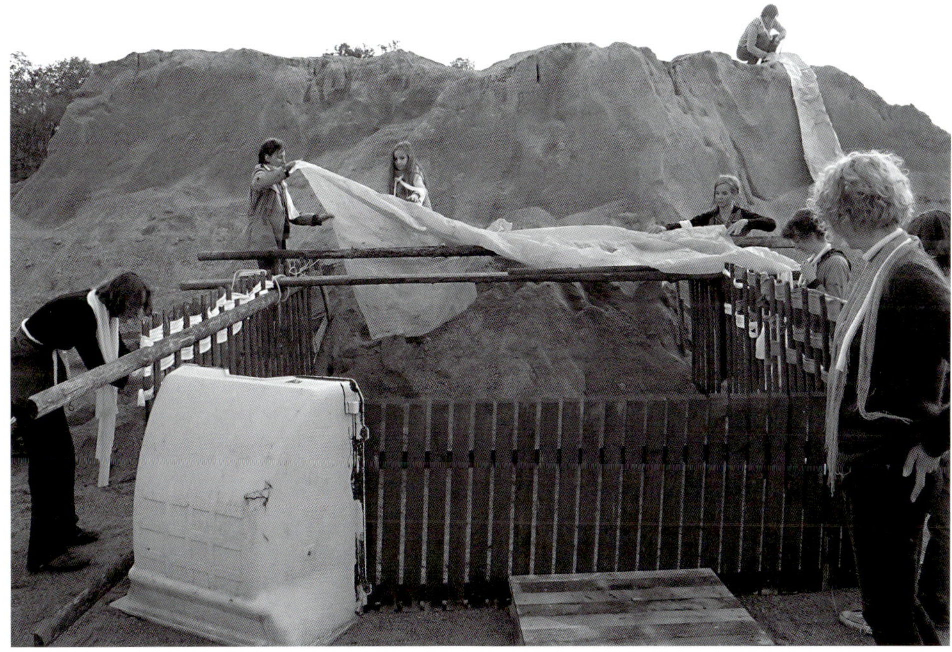

Notes

1. Allan Kaprow, *Bull Shit,* a journal published on the occasion of the exhibition at the Fondazione Mudima, Milan, 1991, Allan Kaprow Papers, ca. 1940–1997, accession no. 980063 (box 32, folder 14), Research Library, Getty Research Institute, Los Angeles; hereafter Allan Kaprow Papers.
2. See Allan Kaprow, "The Education of the Un-Artist, Part I (1971)," in idem, *Essays on the Blurring of Art and Life,* ed. Jeff Kelley (Berkeley: Univ. of California Press, 2003), 97–109.
3. Recent performances and exhibitions that have explored ephemeral forms include: *A Little Bit of History Repeated,* Kunst-Werke Institute for Contemporary Art, Berlin, 16–18 November 2001; *A Short History of Performance I–III,* Whitechapel Art Gallery, London, 15–21 April 2002, 18–23 November 2003, 4–9 October 2005; *Re-Enact,* performance event organized by Casco and Mediamatic, Amsterdam, 12 December 2004; *Life, Once More—Forms of Reenactment in Contemporary Art,* Witte de With, Center for Contemporary Art, Rotterdam, 27 January–25 March 2005; *Seven Easy Pieces,* Marina Abramović, Solomon R. Guggenheim Museum, New York, 9–15 November 2005; *After the Act: Die Re(präsentation) der Performancekunst,* Museum Moderner Kunst Stiftung Ludwig, Vienna, November 2005 and symposium of the same name, 4–11 November 2005; "How to Perform? Wiederaufführung und Dokumentation in der Performance-Kunst" (symposium), Kunsthalle Fridericianum, Kassel, 6 May 2006.
4. The exhibition opened on 17 October 2006 at the Haus der Kunst in Munich and on 10 February 2007 at the Van Abbemuseum in Eindhoven. The exhibition then traveled to the Kunsthalle Bern, the Museo di Arte Contemporanea di Villa Croce in Genoa, and the Museum of Contemporary Art in Los Angeles.
5. Statement by Allan Kaprow, in *Allan Kaprow,* exh. cat. (Pasadena: Pasadena Art Museum, 1967), 3.
6. Statement by Kaprow (note 5), 3: "I'm put off by museums in general; they reek of a holy death which offends my sense of reality. Moreover, apart from my personal view, most advanced art of the last half-dozen years is, in my view, inappropriate for museum display. . . . Museums do more than isolate such work from life, they subtly *sanctify* it and thus kill it."
7. Allan Kaprow, "Preface to the Expanded Edition: On the Way to Un-Art," in idem, *Essays on the Blurring of Art and Life,* ed. Jeff Kelley (Berkeley: Univ. of California Press, 2003), xxix.
8. Jeff Kelley in consultation with Allan Kaprow, typescript, 1988, Allan Kaprow Papers (box 32, folder 3).
9. Allan Kaprow in conversation with Stephanie Rosenthal and Eva Meyer-Hermann, 14 December 2004.
10. Kaprow in conversation (note 9).
11. Kaprow in conversation (note 9).
12. Allan Kaprow, "Happenings in the New York Scene (1961)," in idem, *Essays on the Blurring of Art and Life,* ed. Jeff Kelley (Berkeley: Univ. of California Press, 1993), 16.
13. Kaprow wrote on the historical context of the Happening in "Happenings in the New York Scene" (note 12), 15–26. For more on Happenings, see also RoseLee Goldberg, *Performance Art: From the Future to the Present* (New York: Thames & Hudson, 2001), 128–34.
14. Allan Kaprow, typewritten score for *A Service for the Dead I,* 1962, Allan Kaprow Papers (box 7, folder 1). A modified version was published in *Art International* 7, no. 1 (1963): 46–47.
15. Allan Kaprow, typescript, 1982, Allan Kaprow Papers (box 31, folder 7).

16. Allan Kaprow, as cited in Douglas M. Davis, "'To What Purpose? I Am Still Thinking': Following the Script for a Happening," *National Observer,* 12 June 1967, Allan Kaprow Papers (box 12, folder 3).
17. Allan Kaprow, typescript for the essay "Performing Life," 1979, Allan Kaprow Papers (box 29, folder 5).
18. Kaprow, "Happenings in the New York Scene" (note 12), 25.
19. The videos were also made with the same intention: "The paste-ups, booklets, video tapes and films shown here are neither documentations nor conceptual art. Instead, they are made as an artificial language to be read and applied—like a music score or industry flow chart—which schematizes real events, places and people. . . . The visitor should view the linked texts and images as a kind of short-hand program of transactions that have taken place in the ordinary environment. . . . In addition, each piece is a plan of action that can be realized by anyone who wishes to carry it out." Allan Kaprow, introduction to *Natural Distances,* 1976, Allan Kaprow Papers (box 27, folder 2).
20. Kaprow in conversation (note 9).
21. Allan Kaprow, introduction to *Easy,* 1972, Allan Kaprow Papers (box 20, folder 2).
22. For more on this, see Sven Lütticken, "An Arena in Which To Reenact," in idem, ed., *Life, Once More: Forms of Reenactment in Contemporary Art* (Rotterdam: Witte de With, Center for Contemporary Art, 2005), 23.
23. Allan Kaprow, note for *Population,* 1968, Allan Kaprow Papers (box 13, folder 8).
24. Allan Kaprow, typewritten score for *Meditation Piece,* ca. 1981, Allan Kaprow Papers (box 30, folder 1).
25. Allan Kaprow, handwritten score for *Communication,* 1958, Allan Kaprow Papers (box 5, folder 2).
26. Kaprow, handwritten score for *Communication* (note 25).
27. Allan Kaprow to Barbara Haskell, 10 April 1984, Allan Kaprow Papers (box 32, folder 3).
28. From 1988 to 1989, new versions were realized of *18 Happenings in 6 Parts* (1959); *Sweeping* (1962); *Record II* (1968); *Self-Service* (1966); *Pose* (1969); *Routine* (1973); *Blindsight* (1979); *Company* (1984); and *Trading Dirt* (1983–85).
29. Allan Kaprow to Paul Schimmel, 27 June 1996, Allan Kaprow Papers (box 34, folder 1). *18 Happenings* was ultimately not reinvented for *Out of Actions.*
30. Kaprow was unable to travel to the Moderna Museet, Stockholm, to install the work. As a result the work was installed by the museum's director Pontus Hulten and his staff. See Allan Kaprow, typewritten score for *Stockroom*, 1961, Allan Kaprow Papers (box 6, folder 5).
31. The term *reenactment* is used specifically with reference to historical events; it is also used in criminology. For more on this term see Lütticken, "An Arena in Which To Reenact" (note 22), 25–42. Kaprow's approach was fundamentally different from those of other artists, such as that taken by Marina Abramović in 2005 when she presented *Seven Easy Pieces* at the Solomon R. Guggenheim Museum in New York. From 9 to 15 November, each day from 5 P.M. to 12 A.M. Abramović reenacted a performance from the 1960s and 1970s that had been performed by Vito Acconci, Joseph Beuys, Valie Export, Bruce Nauman, Gina Pane, and herself. It was impossible to replicate events since the date of the performance necessarily affects the performance.
32. Allan Kaprow, handwritten score for *Yard,* 1961, Allan Kaprow Papers (box 6, folder 7).
33. Allan Kaprow to Brian O'Doherty, July 1963, Allan Kaprow Papers (box 8, folder 4).
34. See Eva Meyer-Hermann's essay "Museum as Mediation" in this volume.
35. Kaprow in conversation (note 9).
36. Allan Kaprow in conversation with Stephanie Rosenthal, 27 April 2005.
37. Kaprow in conversation (note 36). Kaprow was aware that any statement he made would have a strong influence on us.
38. Kaprow in conversation (note 36).
39. It was important to identify who was leading the piece. Accordingly, we decided on the following formula for clarifying the circumstances of the reinvented works: Allan Kaprow, *Household* (1964/date of new version), version by (leader's name).
40. Our version was directed by André Lepecki, with the help of Christin Vahl, Noémie Solomon, Shawn Greenlee, and Swantje Grundler.
41. See Philip Ursprung, *Grenzen der Kunst: Allan Kaprow und das Happening, Robert Smithson und die Land Art* (Munich: Verlag Silke Schreiber, 2003), 76–86; and Jeff Kelley, *Childsplay: The Art of Allan Kaprow* (Berkeley: Univ. of California Press, 2004), 29–42.
42. Allan Kaprow, handwritten score for *Round Trip,* 1968, Allan Kaprow Papers (box 14, folder 3).
43. Allan Kaprow, handwritten note for *Watching,* 1967, Allan Kaprow Papers (box 12, folder 8).
44. Kaprow, typescript for the essay "Performing Life" (note 17).

Museum as Mediation

Eva Meyer-Hermann

Having decided to prepare an exhibition on the work of Allan Kaprow, Stephanie Rosenthal and I found ourselves confronted with an almost insurmountable mountain of bound and unbound texts; handwritten and typed documents on white, yellow, blue, and pink paper; old and new descriptions of the same projects with crystal-clear or hopelessly blurred marginalia; diverse correspondence with and without dates; disintegrating reviews taken from newspapers; black-and-white photographs on cards; torn duplicate photographs; yellowed small-format slides and Polaroids; hissing and flickering audio- and videotapes; crumpled exhibition posters; faded invitation cards; and dusty books.

As we sorted through the stacks of materials, we found ourselves constantly asking the same questions: Is it possible to exhibit this body of work at all? What does "exhibition" mean in this context? Can we really exhibit something that has staunchly resisted being exhibited since the 1960s? Has Kaprow's art—in keeping with its declared intention—migrated into daily life? Is it possible to capture the spirit of this art in an art institution, thereby confirming that the museum can also play a part in daily life? Our search for answers in the archive, and in conversation with the artist, shaped *Allan Kaprow—Art as Life,* held at the Haus der Kunst in Munich in 2006 and the Van Abbemuseum in Eindhoven in 2007.

KNOWN YET UNKNOWN?

Kaprow is one of the best-known unknown artists. Despite his writings and his many years of teaching, his is a household name only to fellow artists and art historians. Very few people actually witnessed his legendary Happenings in the late 1950s and 1960s, and it is only through hearsay that they have become part of the collective artistic consciousness. Exhibitions in public institutions or commercial galleries were a rarity. Did the artist resist the idea of exhibiting his work? Was his art simply not suited to the museum context? Or did the fault lie with the institutions, because they were unwilling to accommodate Kaprow's unusual attitude toward what a work of art should be?

Museums have a problem with the art that they are supposed to research, preserve, and mediate. On a visit to the Whitney Museum of American Art in New York in 1982, Kaprow reacted with some bemusement to one of the exhibits, *TV Chair* by Nam June Paik. To Kaprow's surprise even he—who had lent the work to the museum—was not allowed to sit on the chair, no doubt in keeping with the insurers' conditions. This, however, made it impossible to use the chair as the artist had intended: viewers were to sit on the chair and look through their legs at the flickering images on the television monitor under the seat <FIG. 1>. Kaprow was appalled: "The dumb museums."[1]

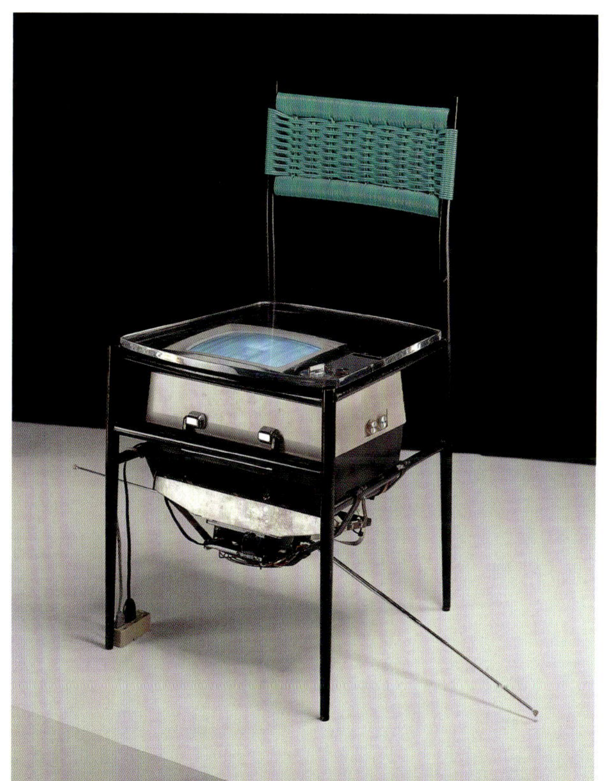

Fig. 1. **Nam June Paik (American, 1932–2006)**
TV Chair, 1968
Standard metal-frame chair, lucite seat, plastic backing, suspended TV set, 76.2 × 50.8 × 50.8 cm (30 × 20 × 20 in.)
Private collection

Similar things happen to exhibition-goers all the time. Carl Andre laid a covering of metal plates on a museum floor in 1968 and invited people to walk across the newly defined area <FIGS. 2, 3>. People have been plagued with doubts ever since: walk on the plates, or walk around? Those who dare to set foot on this strangely delineated terrain often do so only after glancing hesitantly at the security staff. Of course, the works of Paik and Andre consist of much more than a chair and a television monitor in one case and industrial metal plates in the other. Both artists, typically for their generation, take account of human perceptions in their work. Paik creates closed circuits connecting real objects and human beings, while Andre uses his materials to ground the exhibition-goer in the space, both literally and symbolically. It seems, however, that while art has long sought to connect more closely with reality—and hence with life itself—museums have increasingly distanced themselves from art.

This paradox is not a recent development. In 1917, Marcel Duchamp created an uproar even among his fellow artists when he submitted *Fountain*—a common urinal that he signed "R. Mutt"—for an exhibition in New York, thus turning the everyday object into art. Other artists at this time were including quotidian materials—scraps of newspaper, for instance—in their collages. They were creating a framework for reality, so to speak, challenging art critics and historians, museum-goers, and other artists to consider reality in the context of art.

Kaprow, for his part, hoped for a "new concrete art," and in "The Legacy of Jackson Pollock" (1958), he listed some of the materials that new generations of artists would utilize—"paint, chairs, food, electric and neon lights, smoke, water, old socks, a dog, movies"—and touched on the content of their art: "unheard-of happenings and events, found in garbage cans, police files, hotel lobbies; seen in store windows and on the streets; and sensed in dreams and horrible accidents. An odor of crushed strawberries, a letter from a friend, or a billboard selling Drano."[2]

Kaprow thought that as art changed, how it was perceived would also change. In 1950, he wrote an essay for Meyer Schapiro's class at Columbia University in which he discussed the viewer's perception of a painting by Pollock, which he likened to contemplating a Chinese landscape painting:

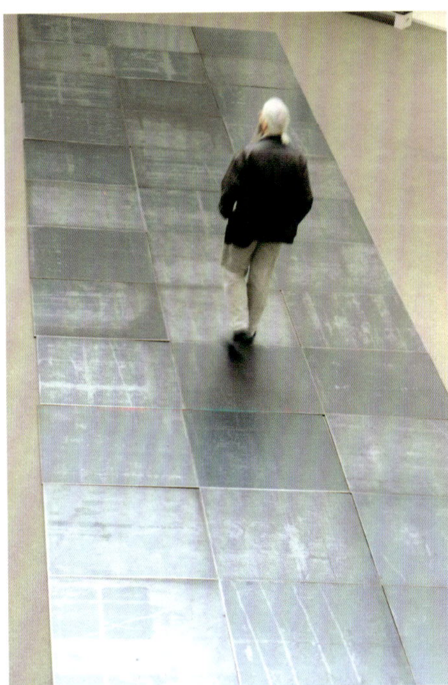

Figs. 2, 3. **Carl Andre (American, born 1935)**
Köln Steel Lock, Den Haag 1968, 1968
Hot-rolled steel, 36-unit rectangle (3 × 12), on the floor
Each plate: 1 × 100 × 100 cm (½ × 39⅜ × 39⅜ in.)
Overall: 1 × 300 × 1200 cm (½ × 118⅛ × 472½ in.)
Museum Ludwig, Cologne
Installed in 1990 at Kunsthalle Düsseldorf, Dusseldorf

"There are landscapes in which one can travel, landscapes which can be gazed upon, landscapes in which one may ramble, and landscapes in which one may dwell." In this new mode of perception, he explained, the viewer would connect individual components by "rambling" through them, without necessarily having to achieve an overview of the work as a physical whole.[3]

In Kaprow's eyes, the role of the viewer was concerned with creatively filling the "gaps" that arose from the changed interrelationships of the various components. He noted in his master's thesis, which was subtitled "A Study in Seeing," that the works of Piet Mondrian came alive only when a "process of seeing" took place in the space between the painting and the viewer.[4] Years later, in a lecture for a panel titled "The Futility of New Museums," Kaprow ascribed the loss of the uninterrupted whole to the new production methods of the computer age, which yielded "a myriad of alternative assemblies almost at once and before our eyes."[5] Marshall McLuhan also noted the influence of the electronic age on art, holding it responsible for the fact that the continuous story line had been replaced by symbolic and musical structures. In his view, the alternative to this lost narrative was "the art of the interval," which he saw in the art of flower arranging, Zen poetry, James Joyce's *Finnegans Wake*—and the Happening.

> The Happening is an artistic event of all-at-onceness in which there is no story line. It nearly resembles the newspaper and also the ordinary human environment. To put a tomato can in the Guggenheim Museum or to bring the unintended noises of the ordinary environment into the concert hall is an important way of announcing that in the electric age we must begin to consider the environment itself as an art form. We approach a time when the total human situation must be considered as a work of art . . . . The world of the Happening announces that our involvement in the conditions of life on this planet is such that we must begin to do . . . not some things, but everything as well as possible . . . . When I say that "the medium is the message" I am merely stating the fact that "meaning" is a Happening, the multitudinous interplay of events.[6]

KILLING ART?

By the mid-twentieth century, the frames around pictures and the plinth beneath sculptures had disappeared from many contemporary works, and the museum had increasing difficulty justifying its existence as a context for art. Lawrence Weiner pointed out that art now had more to do with the interrelationships between objects and the relationships of objects and people than with a material display.[7] The museum was no longer necessary—according to Daniel Buren, the museum itself could even be "exhibited."[8] Kaprow had no desire to do away with museums altogether; he thought that they had their place for art from the past, including his own early work, which had been made as "gallery art." Moreover, museums occasionally offered opportunities—and funding—for his works. One of his Happenings, *Moving,* was presented in conjunction with the inaugural exhibition at the Museum of Contemporary Art in Chicago in 1967 < SEE CHRONOLOGY, FIGS. 143, 144 >. It took place at "some unused houses in different parts of the city":

Fig. 4. **Views of the Whitney Museum of American Art in New York and Lenin's mausoleum in Moscow**

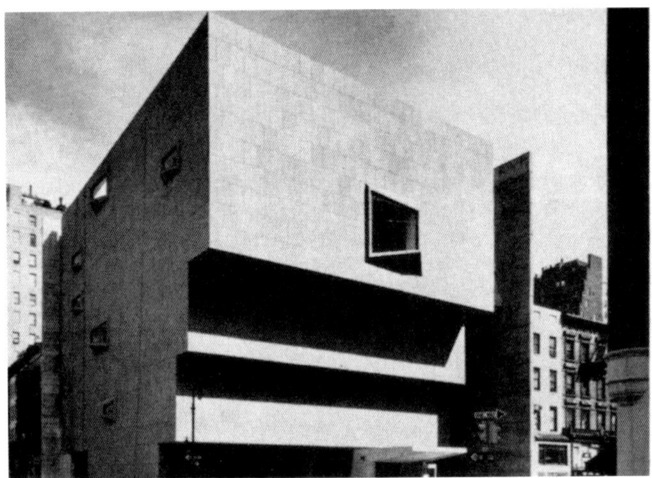

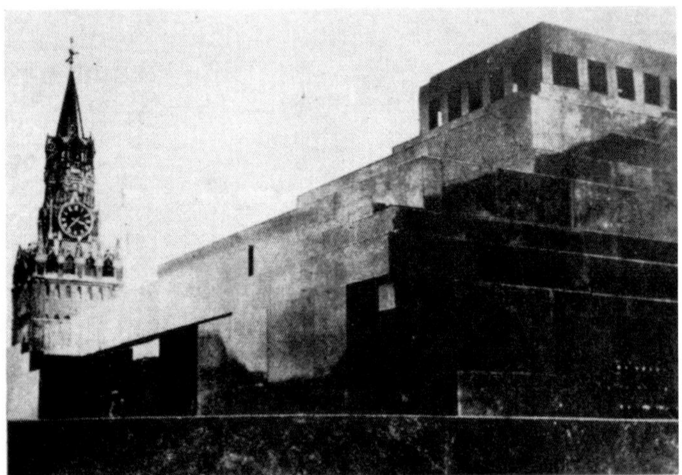

> On each of four days, old furniture is obtained, and is pushed through the streets to the houses. The furniture is installed.
> On the first day, bedrooms are furnished, and slept in that night.
> On the second day, dining rooms are furnished, and a meal is eaten.
> On the third day, living rooms are furnished, and guests are invited to cocktails.
> On the fourth day, attics are filled and their doors are locked.[9]

In 1967, the Pasadena Art Museum presented Kaprow's first retrospective. The museum was one of the most important venues for avant-garde art worldwide, renowned for its exhibitions of the work of artists from Duchamp to Andy Warhol.[10] The artist expressed his distrust of the institution in a statement that appeared in the catalog that accompanied the exhibition.

> I am put off by museums in general, they reek of a holy death which offends my sense of reality. Moreover, apart from my personal view, most advanced art of the last half-dozen years is, in my view, inappropriate for museum display. It is an art of the world: enormous scale, environmental scope, mixed media, spectator participation, technology, themes drawn from the daily milieu, and so forth. Museums do more than isolate such work from life, they subtly *sanctify* it and thus kill it.[11]

Nevertheless, Kaprow lived in the pragmatic hope that the museum would adjust its function by becoming "an educational institute, a computerized bank of cultural history, and an agency for action."[12]

Kaprow went more deeply into his critique of museums in "What Is a Museum?" (1967), a published conversation with Robert Smithson. Embedded in some evocative imagery is a clear expression of his discomfiture: "Museums tend to make increasing concessions to the idea of art and life as being related. What's wrong with their version of this is that they provide canned life, an aestheticized illustration of life. 'Life' in the museum is like making love in a cemetery."[13] The text is accompanied by pairs of photographs that were chosen by the speakers, including a juxtaposition of the Whitney Museum with Lenin's mausoleum in Moscow < FIG. 4 >. Kaprow even suggested that the splendid architecture of the Solomon R. Guggenheim Museum in New York should be left standing entirely empty and exhibited as a sculpture in its own right.

This theoretical critique, repeatedly expressed in a variety of contexts, stands in contrast to Kaprow's apparently muted approach to his own exhibition in Pasadena, where he presented not only a conventional hanging of a number of his canvases, collages, assemblages, and three-dimensional works from the late 1940s through the late 1950s but also new versions of three of the Environments that he had made between 1958 and 1964—*Yard* (1961), *Words* (1962), and *Push and Pull* (1963). At the same time, however, a truly spectacular event, *Fluids,* was taking place outside the museum. At fifteen sites in greater Los Angeles, fifteen groups working under the artist's supervision erected thirty-foot-long, nonfunctional structures made of solid blocks of ice; the minimalist forms were strikingly reminiscent of ancient Egyptian tombs < SEE CHRONOLOGY, FIGS. 133–42 >.

This endeavor to construct transient forms in the warm California sun can be read as an attempt to symbolically deconstruct the museum. The edifices literally melted away. Here art was neither architectural nor sculptural, but procedural, located in the interaction of people and materials. In addition to attacking the existing order of the institution, *Fluids* was a literal dissolution of the concept of what art is.

Kaprow continued to accept invitations from museums to develop new works, but this support was rare—and his radical approach had little effect on the way art was presented inside the established institutions. In the 1970s, Pierre Restany noted that Kaprow's works were "performed throughout the world, . . . carefully avoiding the sanctioned cultural environments."[14] His Happenings and Activities (as he called these works from mid-1969 on) were mainly promoted by universities, theater festivals, and other avant-garde enterprises. Nevertheless, museums and galleries in Italy, France, and Germany were relatively interested in his work.

In 1976, Kunsthalle Bremen presented the exhibition *Allan Kaprow: Activity-Dokumente 1968–1976,* which concentrated on the formal instructions and illustrative photographs in the booklets that Kaprow produced for his Activities. In 1976—almost ten years after *Fluids*—Bremen was also the venue for the Activity *Durations.* Once again, a huge modular ice structure was erected and left to melt and dissipate naturally < SEE CHRONOLOGY, FIGS. 285–89 >. Significantly, this event was not supported by any museum, but by Radio Bremen's experimental series Pro Musica Nova.

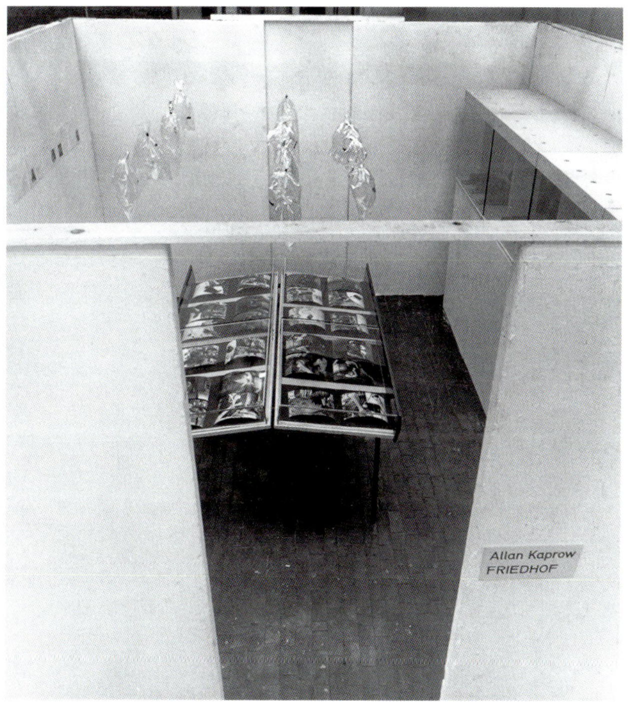

Fig. 5. **Gallery display of *Time Pieces***
Presented for *ADA: Aktionen der Avantgarde*
Neuer Berliner Kunstverein, Berlin

In 1973, *Time Pieces,* one of Kaprow's complex Activities, was at the center of *ADA: Aktionen der Avantgarde,* a group show at the Neuer Berliner Kunstverein. Over the course of three days and at times of their own choosing, thirty participants, working in pairs, examined the processes of their bodies: they counted and made audio recordings of their own and their partner's heart and breathing rates <SEE CHRONOLOGY, FIGS. 220–43, AND PHILLIPS, FIGS. 1–8>.[15] Those who did not participate in the event could only view the various items that were left over: documentary photographs in display cases; the cassette recorders that were used during the Activity, also housed in the cases; and clear plastic bags filled with air, hanging from the ceiling. These items were displayed in a secluded, separate area. At the entrance were the words "Allan Kaprow. FRIEDHOF"—"Allan Kaprow. CEMETERY" <FIG. 5>.

In 1977, during preparations for *Museum Portraits,* an Activity that was to take place at the Hamburger Kunsthalle, Kaprow insisted that he needed certain information on the museum's personnel and finances. The Activity, intended to reveal the group dynamic of the museum's staff, was structured around the arrangement and use of museum employees' desk chairs. The whole exhibition foundered. The director of the museum, Werner Hofmann, felt there was too great a danger that his institution might somehow be compromised <SEE CHRONOLOGY, FIGS. 290–92>. Years of experience had taught Kaprow how sensitive the museum world can be, yet it was not unusual that a Kaprow project, born of an institution's enthusiasm for his artistic approach, came to nothing because of the artist's stubbornness and impossible demands. In 1981, circumstances of this kind became too much for Karl Ruhrberg, the director of the Museum Ludwig in Cologne, with the result that he canceled a retrospective that was already in the planning stages. In 1986, a Kaprow retrospective at the Museum am Ostwall in Dortmund, West Germany, was organized along more conventional lines: visitors could see not only work from the early days of the artist's career but also new interpretations of old Environments and Happenings. Events took place on the streets around the museum and in towns around Dortmund <SEE CHRONOLOGY, FIGS. 327–33>. The Dortmund exhibition certainly did not offer a groundbreaking, structural rethink of Kaprow's work. These museums had neither the infrastructure nor the finances to function as Kaprow's hoped-for "agency for action."

RETROSPECTIVE ACTIVITIES?

Allan Kaprow: Precedings, conceived two years later, brought with it a marked, hitherto-unheard-of change in Kaprow's chosen form of mediation. *Precedings* was described as a "retrospective consideration of the works of Allan Kaprow, 1957–1987." The term *retrospective* was interpreted not as a type of exhibition but as a set of tasks: the project would be a process, not a static event.[16] *Precedings* was presented by the Center for Research in Contemporary Art at the University of Texas at Arlington under the leadership of its director, Jeff Kelley.[17]

Precedings comprised a yearlong series of events, consisting of three main segments. First, nine historic Happenings and Activities from 1959 through 1985 were reinvented in five locations. Second, five days were declared a "retrospective period," during which Kaprow presented four lecture-performances and artists and critics participated in a symposium titled "Precedings: Art as Participation, 1958–1988"[18]

<SEE CHRONOLOGY, FIG. 339>. The third program segment was a comprehensive book, never published, that was intended to contain transcripts from *Precedings,* scholarly essays, and Kaprow's collected critical texts.[19]

Prompted by *Precedings,* in 1988 Kaprow turned his attention to "retrospective questions." Besides looking at the "how" and the "what," he reflected on his work, devising a "body of ideas about the self" to match his "body of work as objects."[20] For this, he divided the self into a public and private artistic persona. In his view, his natural, private self was timeless, whereas his created, artistic self had a past, a present, and a future. And yet his ideas about exhibiting his art remained a tangle of impossibilities and uncertainties: "It's obvious, once you say the economy is built on goods industries and service industries, that we're talking about services—like janitorial work or cooking. The art industry traditionally produces goods. I try to provide service. What services? Play. Being invited, and agreeing, to have a 'retrospective.' But what's to retrospect? Nothing. So, stories about that. True stories and made-up ones when memory or interest fades (mine and others). Playing with the past."[21]

Two exhibitions in the early 1990s seemed to undermine Kaprow's earlier statements that his works were ephemeral. In these exhibitions—*7 Environments* in Milan in 1991 and Naples in 1992, and *4 Environments* in Paris in 1992—he created elaborate new versions of earlier Environments. Moreover, the lavish catalog for the exhibitions in Italy reinforced the physical, in-the-world aspect of the exhibition.[22] At first sight, the reinterpretations of the Environments bore little relation to their forerunners in the 1960s. The new versions took into account the exhibition venues and contemporary tastes <SEE CHRONOLOGY, FIGS. 345–50>. The reinvention of *Yard* (1961), for example, included a Fiat, with the tires properly stored in racks, framed by a dominating red wall; the provisional "poor" look of the 1960s was exchanged for a more design-oriented look that resonated with current Italian style. None of Kaprow's earlier Environments had such a powerful material presence. Was Kaprow further extending the divide between himself and his art?

At this point, in 1993, Kaprow had just come to the end of a long period of intense teaching in Los Angeles and San Diego. His works had followed a clear course since the 1960s, and by now they had little physicality. Kaprow was no longer dependent on institutional support or the cooperation of large groups of people, and from the 1980s onward, Activities had taken place within the artist's private sphere. Kaprow had completely withdrawn from the business of official exhibitions. The exhibitions in Naples and Paris constituted a magnificent yet oddly static monument to this farewell.

ROLE OF THE NEW MUSEUM

Kaprow's initial reservations regarding the museum world and his critical attitude to its procedures led to his later, enduring skepticism. But were his polemical attacks ever followed by constructive suggestions as to how the situation might be improved? What exactly did he mean when he referred to the museum as an "agency for action" with a commitment to education? In the past, this function had been fulfilled by offering programs of accompanying events that had no real effect on the internal structure of the exhibition.

Kaprow was interested in a qualitative commitment to art and its effectiveness in society and felt that this commitment should come from museums and schools. In his lectures in the 1960s, Kaprow outlined concepts and plans—including the makeup of academic boards—for high school and college arts curricula.[23] And he saw elementary schools as the place where artistic role models would find the greatest acceptance: "What school children need is a Pied Piper, lots of Pied Pipers, not social workers and lab technicians. The Pied Piper had magic and this is what is important about his story. Like magicians, artists deal in a sort of magic and it is proposed here that some of them can double as Pied Pipers and lead school children along roads they are pressured to avoid and soon forget."[24] In 1969, in connection with Project Other Ways in Berkeley, Kaprow presented *Six Ordinary Happenings,* which were very much in line with his educational principles < SEE CHRONOLOGY, FIGS. 163, 164 >.[25] For *Charity,* for example, a group of children purchased secondhand clothing at a thrift store, washed and pressed the clothes, then attempted to donate them to the same store. It is easy to imagine the disbelieving, dismissive gestures of the thrift shop owner when the children returned. What better way to teach the structures and values of society?

Kaprow's role as a Pied Piper, and the large public events that he led, came to an end after the Happenings in Berkeley. The invitation to become a founding member of the faculty of the now legendary California Institute of the Arts in 1969 and his subsequent appointment at the University of California in San Diego in 1974 had a marked effect on the character of his work. From this point, his Activities were planned in close consultation with his students and were realized by specifically chosen, psychologically charged groups of like-minded individuals.

Kaprow became a member of the board of trustees at the Pasadena Museum of Modern Art in 1973, only to resign within a few months because of his disappointment with the museum's education committee.[26] As he saw it, the committee's remit was not clear, it had no authority, and, in any case, it had no funds. The museum's reluctance to accept change and provide funding would not have surprised a museum professional, but Kaprow—an artist—quickly became impatient. He wanted the museum to immediately reclassify all its departments as "educational," to provide financial support for local artists, and to engage them as educators in the museum and in local schools. Kaprow was convinced that "making and experiencing art is a profound way of learning." The museum, already recognized as a "cultural symbol," could now be reconfigured as an "educational agency" by interconnecting the forces of education and artistic creativity.[27] In addition to putting on exhibitions, concerts, and other events, the museum would also engage in outreach work—for example, running art classes in local schools and the community.

In a lecture delivered in 1978, Kaprow criticized the notion of "alternative art spaces," whose history went back to the nineteenth century when artists first reacted against established galleries and museums. As Kaprow pointed out, these supposedly new spaces were still dominated by the same traditional tastes: "The one ironic difference between the past and now is that such spaces today are neither 'underground' nor rare." He even described them as "junior establishment." For Kaprow, the typical studio or gallery—what he described as a "box"—was only one of seven possible experimental art spaces. He listed urban spaces and explicitly public and private locations (from the city center to someone's bedroom) as spaces for art and even included the human body as a possible display area. Immaterial spaces, like telecommunications networks, and other spiritual, religious, or metaphorical spaces created by the human intellect also had a place on his list.[28] For Kaprow, art had long ceased to be what went on in art galleries and museums. All the artist needed, he said, was "a typewriter, a public relations budget and some airplane tickets. Compared to the cash required to support a 'house' for several years, the outlay would be minimal."[29]

Kaprow returned to the same idea in 1982 in a lecture delivered for "The Futility of New Museums," in which he surveyed the historical dimension of the museum as an institution that had arisen from private and ecclesiastical collections amassed during the eighteenth and nineteenth centuries. Kaprow noted that the circumstances governing the museum had changed: "Context is the real subject and meaning-carrier of modern culture. . . . The major issues of today: the new and rich range of consciousness of our internal experience and our bodies, new awareness of the range of ways we communicate with each other and with the world around us." In our urgent need to communicate with one another and with the world—upon which, he stated, our survival depends—the "gallery and museum as cultural framing devices are as obsolete as the kings and queens of yesteryear." In Kaprow's view, museums were no longer fit for the purpose of communication because they operated according to an entirely self-referential logic. Even if elements of the "outside" world were introduced into the museum, they were interpreted in the context of art history: "You can have a live cow about to give birth in a museum but she will be seen as part of the history of rural paintings from Hobbema to Warhol."[30]

This paradox shaped Kaprow's work throughout his life. Kaprow appealed to the individual and encouraged group discussions and debate. His works posed philosophical questions ranging from "Where do we stand?" to "How do we see our social responsibility?" As we strive to answer, we learn about life through art, and we come to understand that art is life. This positive, didactic approach is deeply rooted in the American history of ideas. How does the socialization of the individual as part of a group come about? Can creative individuality—developed through work—serve as a survival strategy, and can discussion benefiting from group dynamics be a way to learn reason and responsibility?[31]

FROM EXHIBITION TO PRESENTATION

Although Allan Kaprow often spoke of the functions of the museum and of education in general, it seems that this particular topic barely impinged on his artistic output. He was not interested in developing exhibition concepts; indeed, he was so suspicious of any possible outcome that he was reluctant to engage in the process at all. Kaprow withdrew from the institutional context more determinedly than almost any other artist of his generation, yet even Kaprow needed the mechanisms of the art institution to be noticed. It was simply not enough that something happened once and that the existence of the event was confirmed by word of mouth (the reliability of which, according to Kaprow, is always open to doubt).

During the planning of *Allan Kaprow—Art as Life,* the artist constantly questioned all possibilities. We, as cocurators, agreed with the artist to refer to our project as a "presentation" rather than an "exhibition." From the outset of our discussions, it was clear that we had to find an approach that would do justice both to the artist's philosophy and to the public's need for information and enlightenment. We wanted to counter Kaprow's assertion that museums are "dumb" with something that derived directly from his work.[32] We always took Kaprow's critical position as our main point of reference. Why, for instance, did he regard his Activity booklets from the 1970s as an idea that never really worked? In part, it was because he saw that the Activity booklets were often treated as a manual of sorts. Kaprow's works were not intended to have a fixed, immutable form, but he discovered that frequently the people carrying out his Activities merely copied the text and photographs in the booklets, mimicking the outward appearance of the works. Consequently, it was important that our exhibition not present fixed forms as some kind of fait accompli. And we made every attempt to avoid what had happened in so many other, related exhibitions of conceptual art such as Fluxus—namely, that artists' works were reconstructed solely according to surviving records and embellished with fetish objects that had been left behind here and there.

Kaprow's conception of a work of art was much more open and generous than any documentation could ever convey. The participants in his events were always afforded the greatest possible freedom even as the artist exercised a high degree of control over them. Right from the outset, in the early Happenings, with their distinctly theatrical or filmic scripts and narrative structures, Kaprow was always at the center of proceedings, even when tasks were carried out at multiple sites and he was unable to be present. He claimed the artistic high ground in the sense that there was a difference between Kaprow placing an apple on a table and someone else doing the same thing. There will always be a gap between the artist's concept, what he asks of the participants (from whom he expects at least an adequate artistic act), and the realization of the piece. But since the realization should not be confused with any final result, this mismatch is not really a problem. Kaprow's pieces were never intended to be works of art that would be preserved (or embalmed) in a museum for all eternity—Kaprow was interested in the human activities that ensue from them. His playful mediation and absorption of an artistic philosophy will continue to have a place in people's thinking.

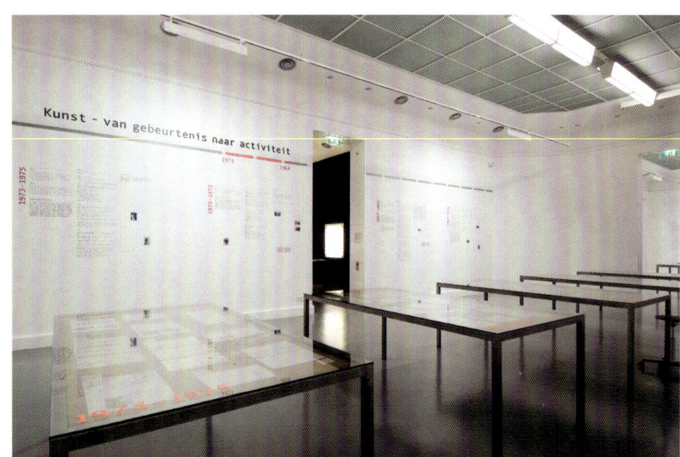

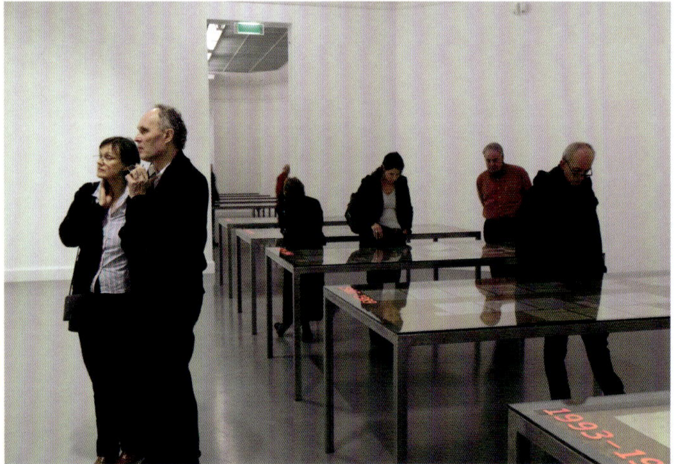

The exhibition we conceived for Munich and Eindhoven was structured around two principles: Kaprow's phrase "Agency for Action," and, as our paraphrase, "Museum as Mediation." Our premise was that visitors would perceive the exhibition as a whole in much the same way that they would an individual work. No longer a mere consumer, the viewer would be an active participant instead. The material items that would be shown would not be "works of art"; they would be merely the artist's materials. "Museum as Mediation" pertained to the way in which the exhibition was ordered; "Agency for Action" pertained to the events that the exhibition entailed. The phrase *museum as mediation* is taken from the museum world and from art history. Similar to a musical score that is displayed rather than played, the objects related to museum as mediation were intended to invite viewers to reflect on comparisons, presence, and what remains from the past. By contrast, the phrase *agency for action* connotes the music rather than the score. This aspect of the exhibition connected with life and temporal, human actions. It is not hard to see the paradox inherent in this pair of opposites: the material objects that represented museum as mediation

Figs. 6, 7. **Tables with Allan Kaprow's scores and manuscripts**
Presented for *Allan Kaprow—Kunst als leven*
Van Abbemuseum, Eindhoven

lay claim to the present; they existed in the here and now even though they had come from the past. At the same time, the Environments, Happenings, and Activities that represented agency for action were of the present, yet they instantly dissipated and became part of the past. The dichotomy in this pairing cannot be resolved; it was our paradoxical response to the challenge of satisfactorily conveying Kaprow's concept of a work of art in an exhibition—or, rather, presentation. "Museum as Mediation" presented the active presence of the past; "Agency for Action" turned the present into the past before our eyes.[33]

The order implied by the phrase *museum as mediation* was realized in the presentation of individual media. Since we never aimed to create a historical reconstruction, the exhibition did not adhere to the usual chronological sequence associated with a retrospective. The idea was not to create the impression that "this" is how it was back then, or that "these things" are what is left of that time. Consequently, there were no relics from past Activities on display. We agreed that trying to reconstruct an image from the past in order to explain the nature of a work would be no more than sentimentalism. An important step toward sustaining the presence of Kaprow's works was his decision to relinquish his hitherto exclusive control of his works and to allow others to take responsibility for the reinvention of Happenings, Activities, and Environments.

Ordering the presentation according to media rather than individual works introduced redundancies that were intended to unsettle viewers and encourage them to question the status of the various documents. At the conceptual heart of the presentation were Kaprow's own handwritten notes and sketches for Environments, Happenings, and Activities <FIGS. 6, 7>. These included his scores—the instructions for the actions that the event comprised—as well as notes reflecting on or interpreting the event. The focus here was not so much on the detail of these accounts as on the formal nature of the language used to define, prepare, and document the events. A comparative display of more than 300 pages spanning over thirty years—an overwhelming amount of information—shed at least some light on Kaprow's artistic spirit. Although these documents were closely tied to individual events, they also pointed beyond them. They are like musical scores—anyone who learns to read their "notation" will hear music.

In addition, out of hundreds of Kaprow's scores thirty-one were reproduced and offered to visitors as handouts. These texts formed an interface with "Agency for Action": visitors were able to take the newly typed instructions away with them and realize them either in the museum or elsewhere, as they pleased. New versions of Happenings and Activities that needed considerable preparation and organization—and the cooperation of museum staff as well—were generated in the "Agency for Action" area, and visitors were also invited to submit feedback by means of a "photo wall" and email.

One aspect of the exhibition was devoted to film and video, and another to photography. Past Happenings and Activities were documented in both. Typological differences emerged between the "staged" scenarios (as seen in the 1970s in the Activity booklets) and the "documentary" images.[34] Once again, a deliberately overwhelming number of photographs was presented for the visitor to peruse. Thus, optical stimulation preceded cognitive recognition. At the same time, it was possible, but not necessary, for visitors to make connections with information gleaned from the scores. The moving images of film and video, beholden to time, demanded a different kind of attention. Visitors were able to choose from a number of viewing options, depending on their particular interests <FIGS. 8, 9>.

Audio documents occupied an important position in the exhibition. For Kaprow, the incorporation of a whole spectrum of sounds into his Environments ultimately led to the development of the Happenings. The acoustic material ranged from original audio materials used in early works and Happenings to recorded documentary accounts and commentaries <FIG. 10>. Here, completeness or the precise ordering

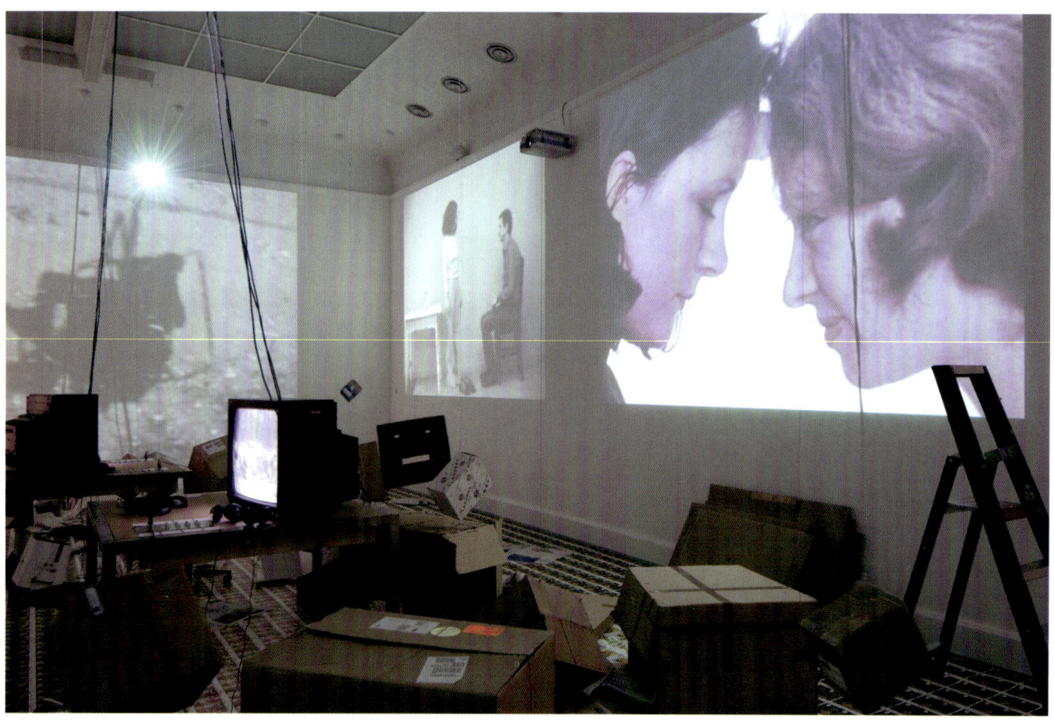

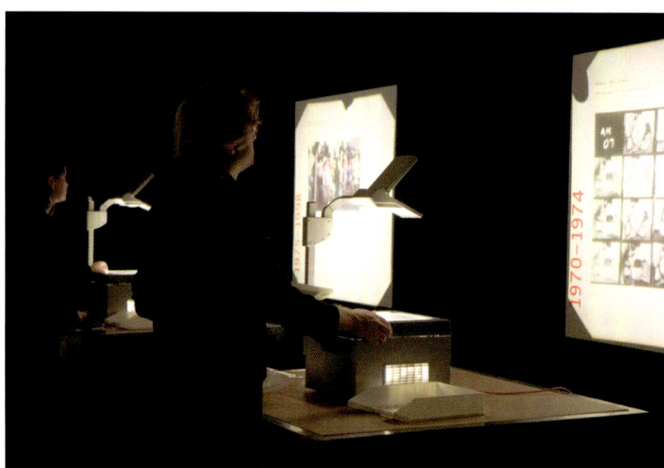

Fig. 8. **Reinvented Environment *Stockroom*** **(1961/2007) with screenings of Allan Kaprow's videos**
Presented for *Allan Kaprow—Kunst als leven*
Van Abbemuseum, Eindhoven

Fig. 9. **Overhead projectors for photo reproductions on acetates**
Presented for *Allan Kaprow—Kunst als leven*
Van Abbemuseum, Eindhoven

of the audio documents was much less important than stimulating the visitor's sense of hearing < FIG. 11 >.

The reinvented Environments enjoyed a special status. By definition semi-static, the Environments marked the transition from Kaprow's early works to the first of his Happenings. In a sense, they are large-scale assemblages with an additional—albeit strictly controlled—element of action. In Munich, responsibility for the Environments was delegated to a group of professors and students from the Akademie der Bildenden Künste München; in Eindhoven, the Environments formed part of the curatorial dramaturgy that was intended to "lure" spectators into participating.[35] The Environments were deliberately organized to playfully break down the divisions between different aspects of the exhibition and to reduce the visitor's natural inhibitions < FIGS. 12–15 >.

The area devoted to Kaprow's early works contained a comparatively conventional presentation of canvases that revealed his interest in human beings and how they behave at home, in a studio, or in the city. This aspect of the exhibition was related to art history—one could imagine that this group of early works might lead into a room with a selection of other objects representing turning points in the development of art: perhaps a spiky bottle rack by Duchamp; a silent, black-and-white Mondrian; and a window-sized, all-over universe by Pollock, perhaps with a grating Dada nonsense poem issuing quietly from a loudspeaker. The presentation did not make—indeed, could not have made—things easy for the viewer. *Allan Kaprow—Art as Life* did not follow a typical format, but it provided a wealth of information by grouping materials and relating contexts. It had no story line, in keeping with Kaprow's desire: "Oddly enough, the disappearance of the story line creates a much higher degree of involvement for the viewer or reader."[36] We chose, to paraphrase McLuhan, to present an exhibition of the interval—an exhibition whose meaning emerged in the space between the physical aspect of the exhibition and the viewer, the point where the viewer became a participant.[37]

Museums in the present day will be compromised if they are not able and willing to be engaged with all forms of contemporary art and to develop exhibition concepts that suit each of them. Art now occupies all sorts of locations that once were considered experimental. The museum has become an alternative venue, although one that is essential to the art that has attacked and questioned it. Art that appears only by arrangement for small groups in secret locations or is restricted to the ivory towers of academia reaches a very limited public. It is up to the museum, with its history and accumulated knowledge, to continue undaunted, making the most of its role and its status, so that it may remain at the center of the discourse on art and life. For everyone.

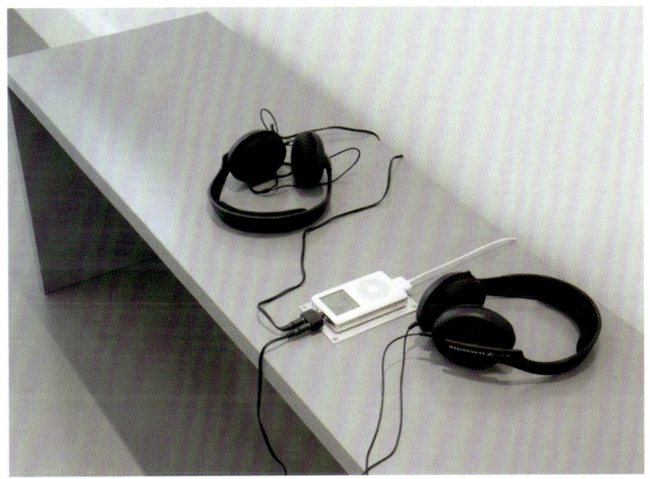

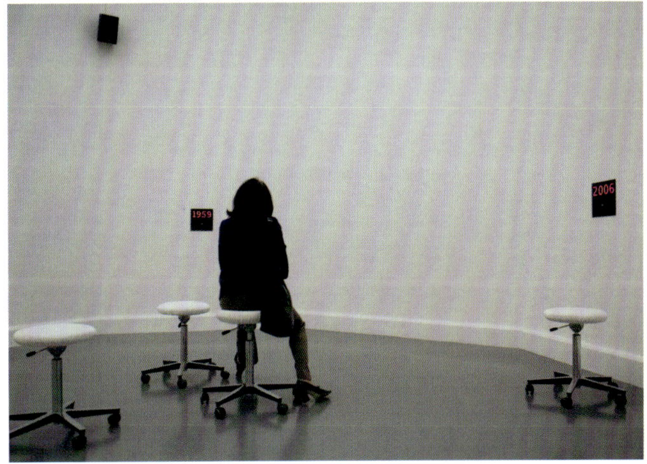

Fig. 10. **Listening devices for various audio documents from early Happenings**
Presented for *Allan Kaprow—Kunst als leven*
Van Abbemuseum, Eindhoven

Fig. 11. **Room with ambient audio sound documents from the 1959 and the 2006 reenacted version of *18 Happenings in 6 Parts***
Presented for *Allan Kaprow—Kunst als leven*
Van Abbemuseum, Eindhoven

Fig. 12. **Partial view of reinvented Environment *Push and Pull* (1963/2007), used as activity zone**
Presented for *Allan Kaprow—Kunst als leven*
Van Abbemuseum, Eindhoven

Fig. 13. **Participants in activity zone**
Presented for *Allan Kaprow—Kunst als leven*
Van Abbemuseum, Eindhoven

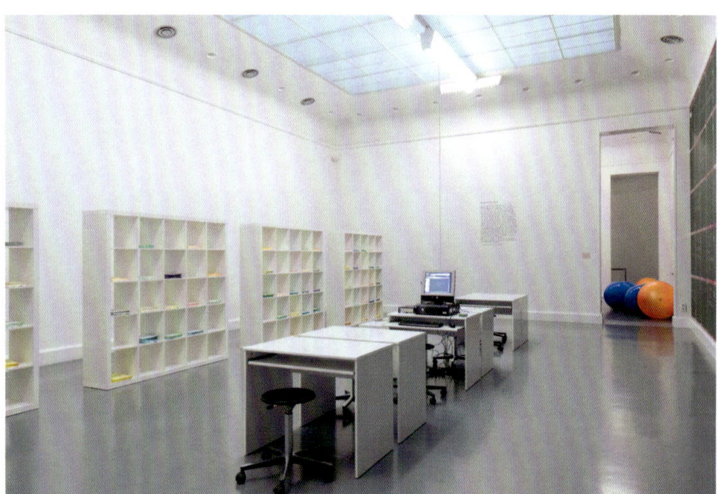

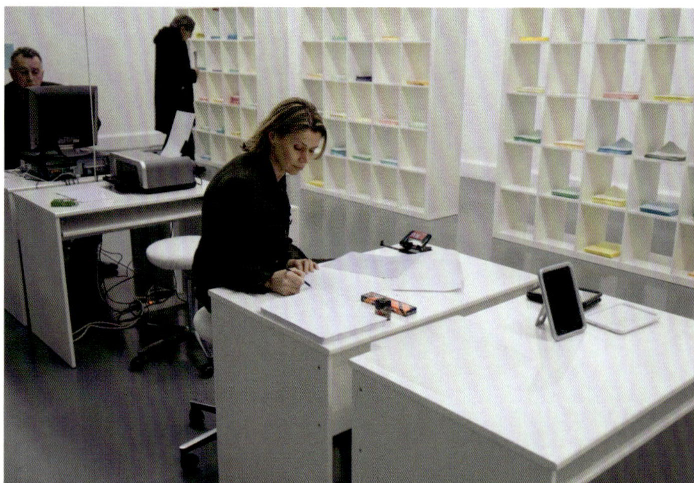

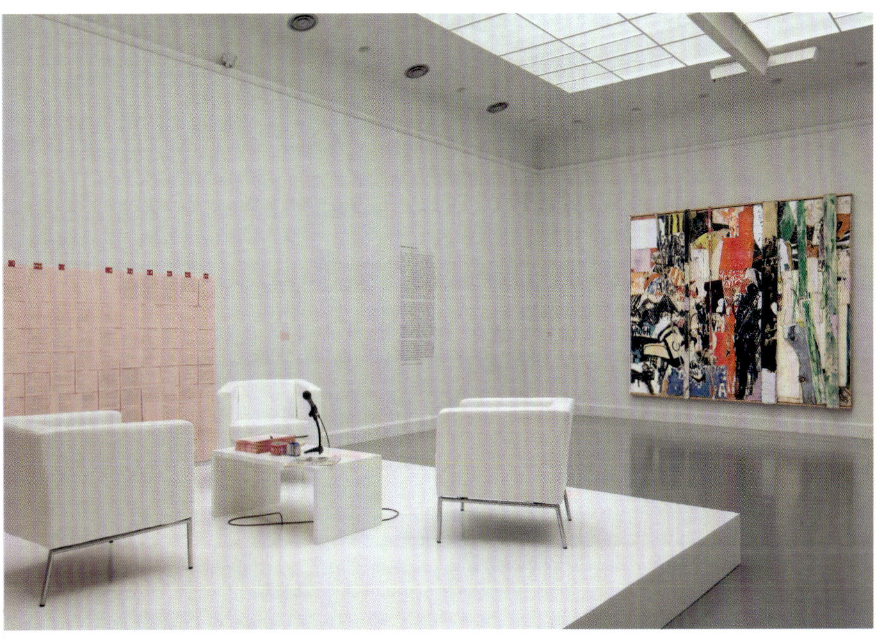

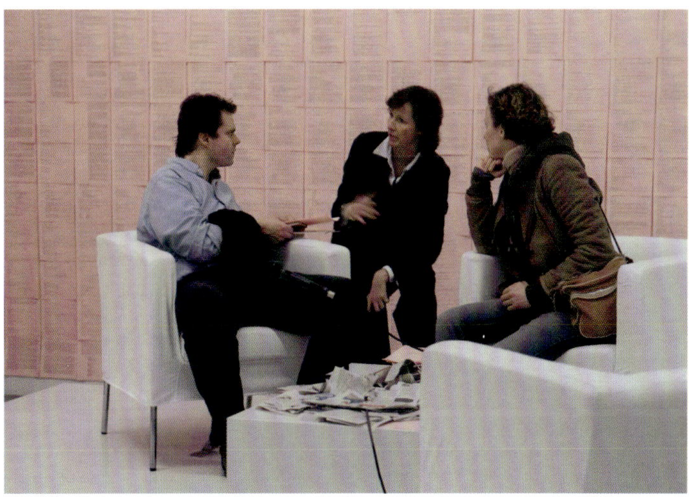

Fig. 14. **Partial view of reinvented Environment *Words* (1962/2007), with the collage *Baby* (1957) in the background**
Presented for *Allan Kaprow—Kunst als leven*
Van Abbemuseum, Eindhoven

Fig. 15. **Participants in reinvented Environment *Words* (1962/2007)**
Presented for *Allan Kaprow—Kunst als leven*
Van Abbemuseum, Eindhoven

19 (side view)

C RON

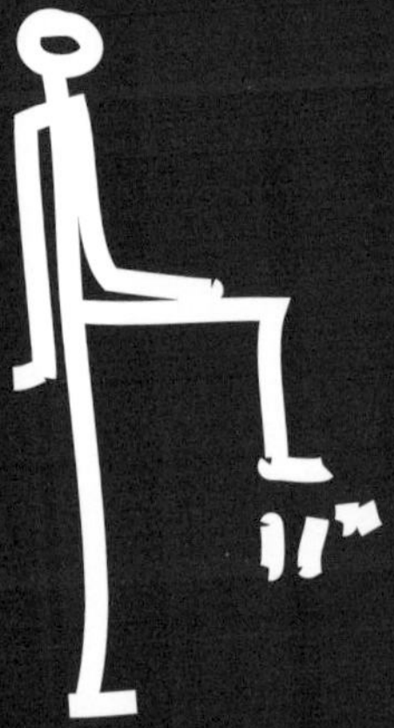

leg raised
forearm
resting
on thighs

OLOGY

by Annette Leddy

Selected Drawings, Paintings, Collages, Sculptures, Assemblages, Scores, Environments, Happenings, Activities, Activity Booklets, Videos, and Films

1927 Born 23 August, Atlantic City, New Jersey. **1933–42** Attended school, Tucson, Arizona. **1942–45** High School of Music and Art, New York, New York. **1945–49** BA in Philosophy and Art History, New York University, New York. **1947–48** Studied painting at Hans Hofmann School of Fine Arts, New York. **July 1947** Group exhibition, Woodstock Arts Association, Woodstock, New York. **1949–50** Graduate coursework in Philosophy, New York University, New York. **1950–52** MA in Art History, Columbia University, New York. **April 1951** Group exhibition, Columbia University Graduate School of Art, New York.

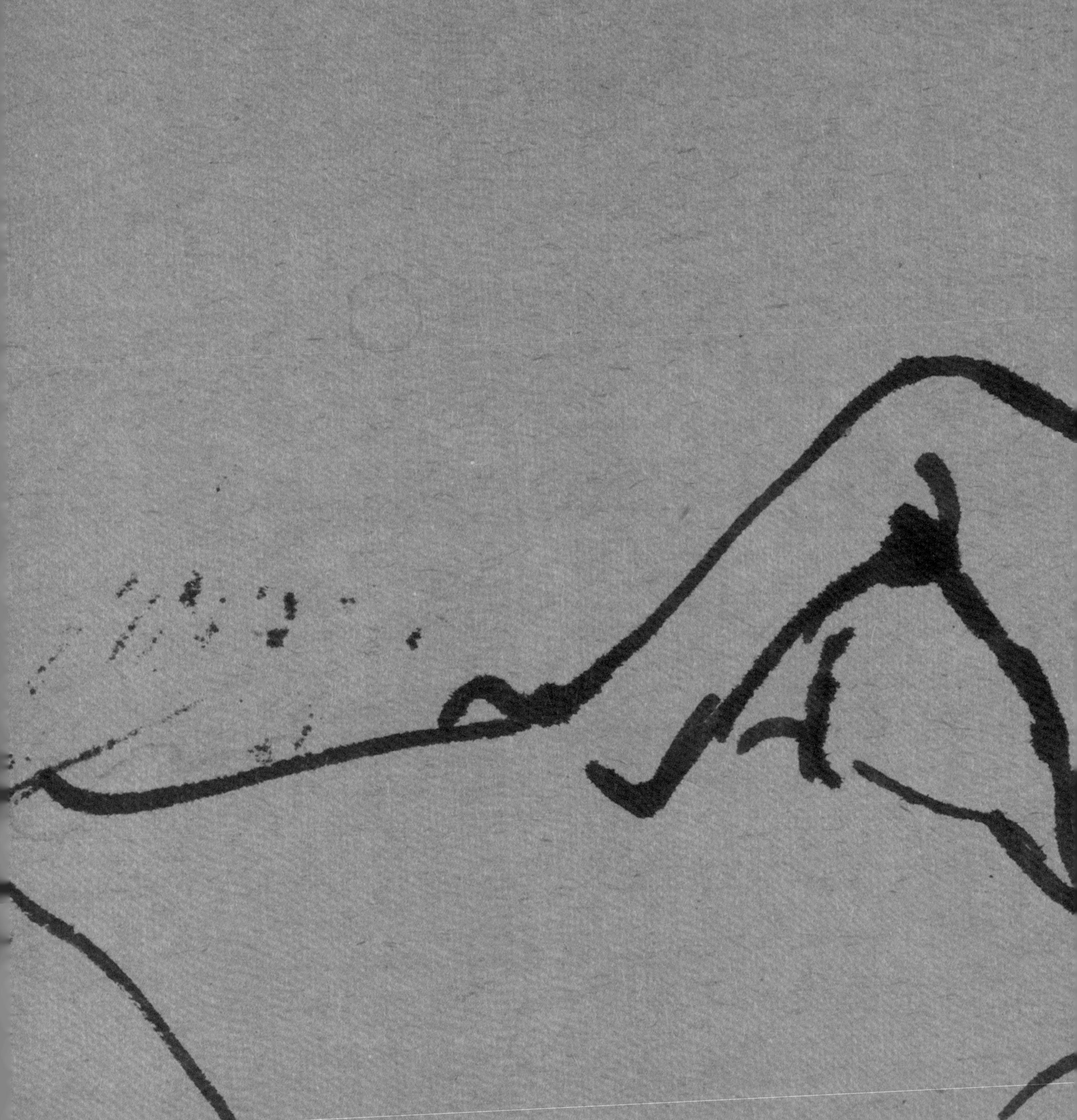

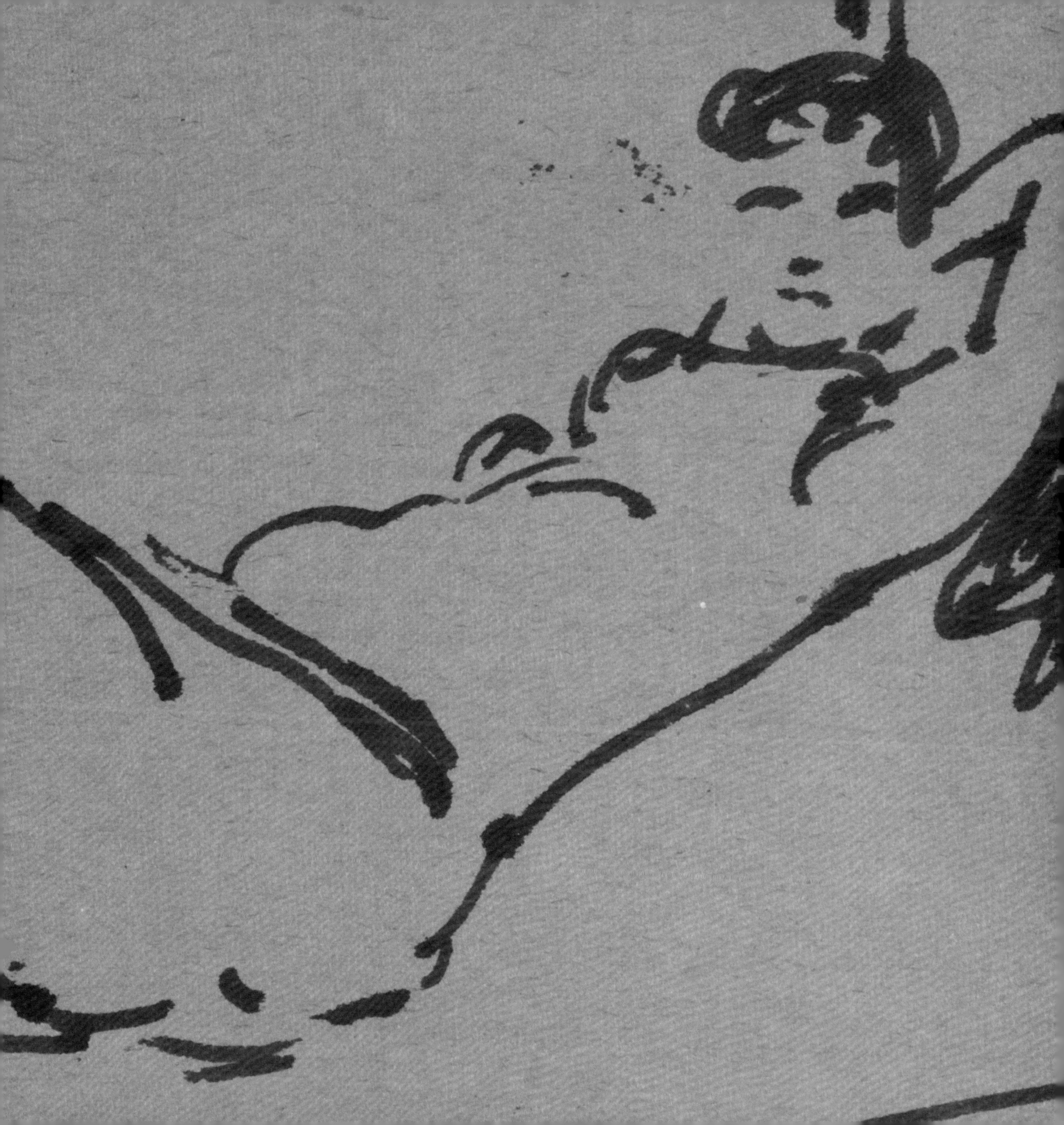

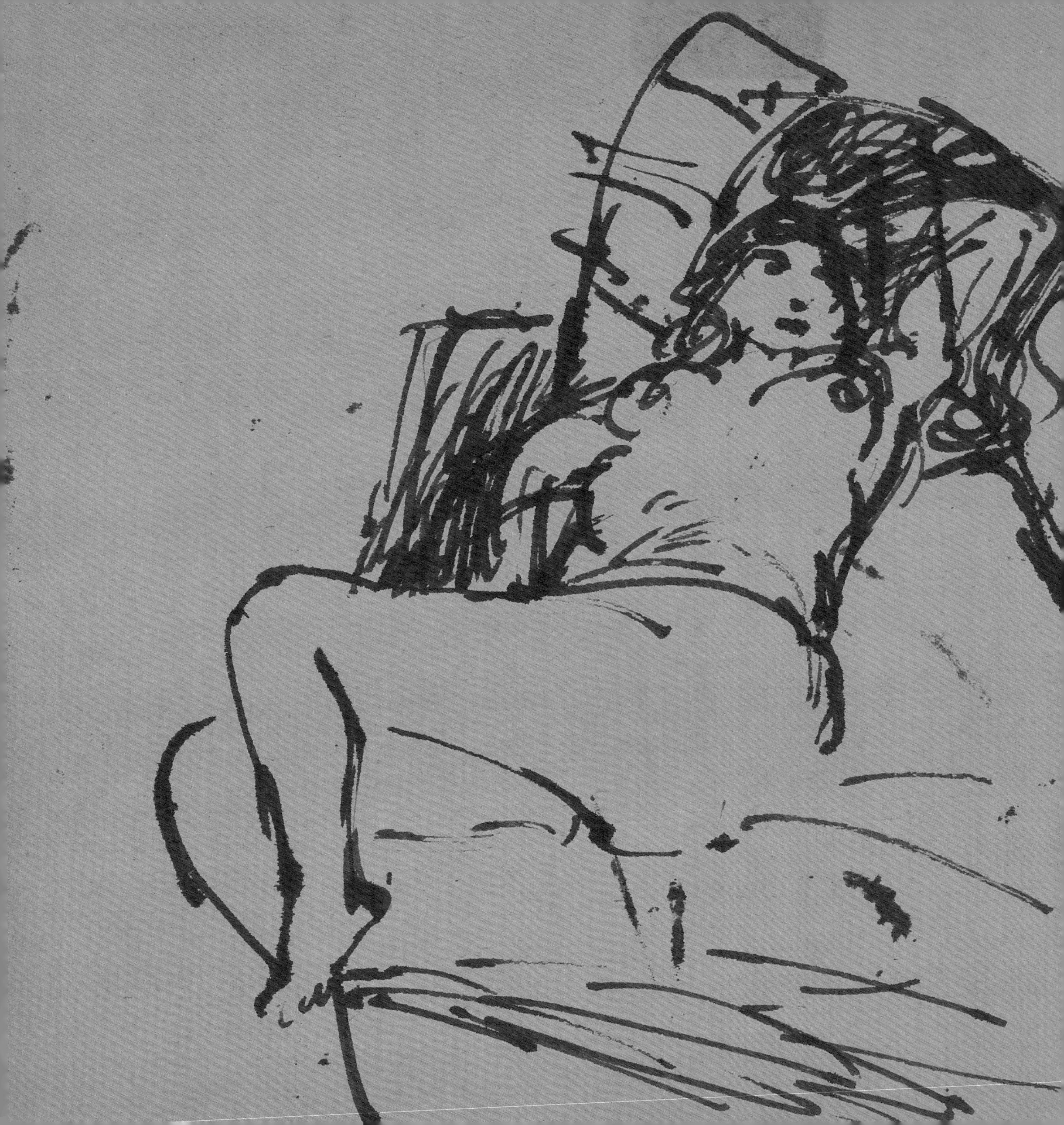

AWARDS Katherine White Award. ¶ GALLERY ADMINISTRATION Cofounder, Hansa Gallery, New York. ¶ GROUP EXHIBITIONS Jabberwocky Gallery, New York, February. Hansa Gallery, New York, Fall. Ramapo Gallery, Suffern, New York, November. Rienzi Gallery, New York, November. Gallery 201, Brooklyn, December. ¶ WRITINGS "Piet Mondrian: A Study in Seeing," MA thesis, Columbia University.

1952

1

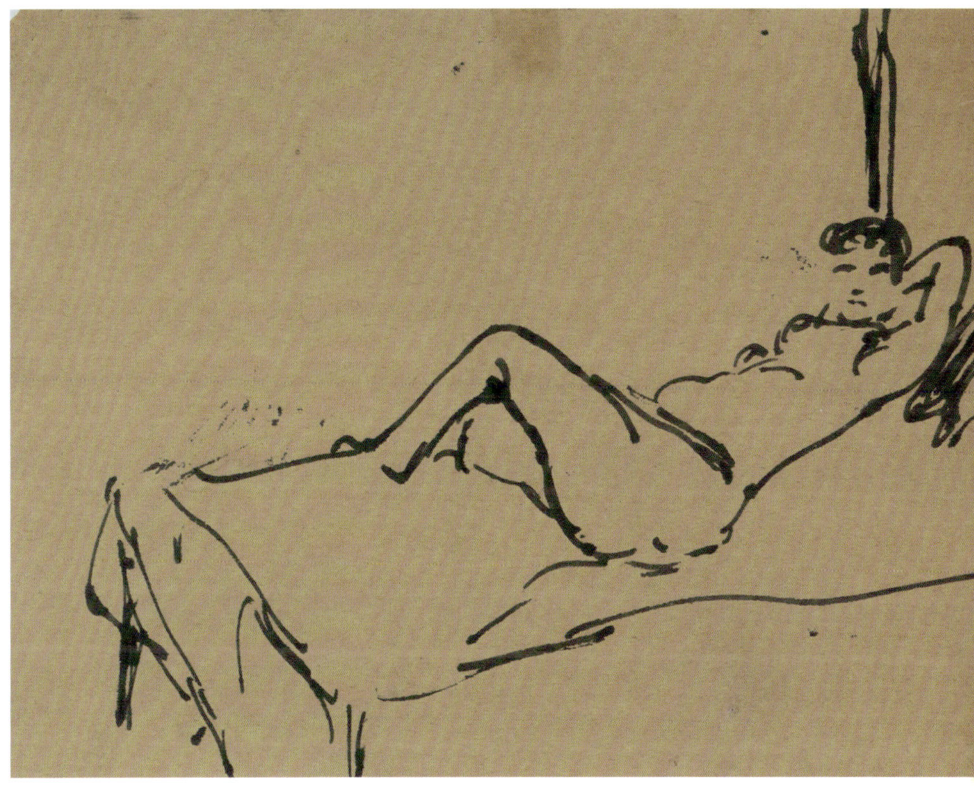

2

Abstracted Still Life
Oil on board, 1952
32.4 × 40 cm (12 3/4 × 15 3/4 in.)
Allan Kaprow Estate

Two Fighting Bulls
Oil on wood panel, 1952
29.2 × 37.8 cm (11 1/2 × 14 7/8 in.)
Allan Kaprow Estate

1 **Reclining Nude, Head on Cushion**
Pen and ink on paper, 1952–53
22.2 × 29.7 cm (8 3/4 × 11 3/4 in.)
Allan Kaprow Estate

2 **Reclining Nude Gazing Out**
(detail previous spread)
Pen and ink on paper, 1952–53
22.2 × 29.5 cm (8 3/4 × 11 5/8 in.)
Allan Kaprow Estate

TEACHING POSITIONS Instructor, Department of Fine Arts, Rutgers University. ¶ **SOLO EXHIBITIONS** Art House, Rutgers University, Spring. *Allan Kaprow: Paintings and Drawings,* Hansa Gallery, New York, May. ¶ **GROUP EXHIBITIONS** *Southern State Touring Group Exhibition of New York Artists* (arranged through Kootz Gallery, New York), April. *Allan Kaprow and Lester Johnson,* Earl Pilgrim Gallery, Provincetown, Massachusetts, August. Contemporary Americans series, Hansa Gallery, New York, September–October. New York City Center Gallery, New York, November. *Hansa Gallery Members,* Art House, Rutgers University, December. *Xmas Show,* Hansa Gallery, New York, December.

1953

3 **Figures in Landscape**
Oil on canvas, 1953
169.2 × 213 cm (66⅝ × 83⅞ in.)
Allan Kaprow Estate

4 **Red Forest**
Oil on canvas, 1953
154.9 × 195.6 cm (61 × 77 in.)
Collection Sergio and Andrea Siani, Concord, Massachusetts

Still Life on Table
Oil on board, 1953
40.3 × 31.7 cm (15⅞ × 12½ in.)
Allan Kaprow Estate

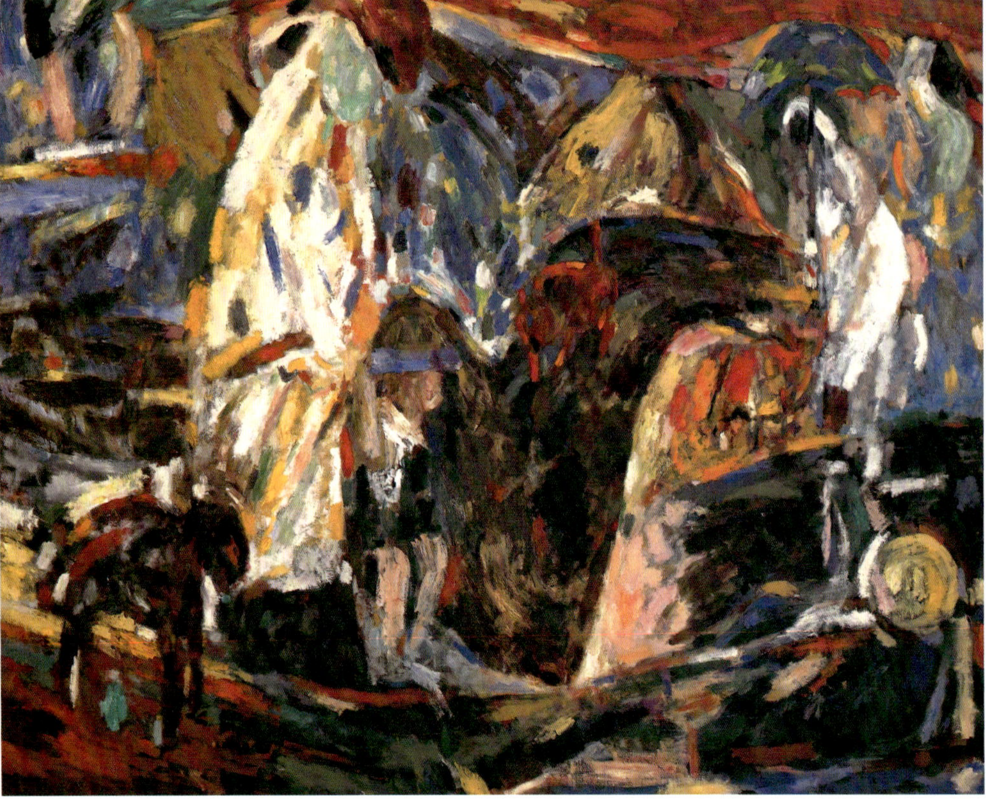
3

4

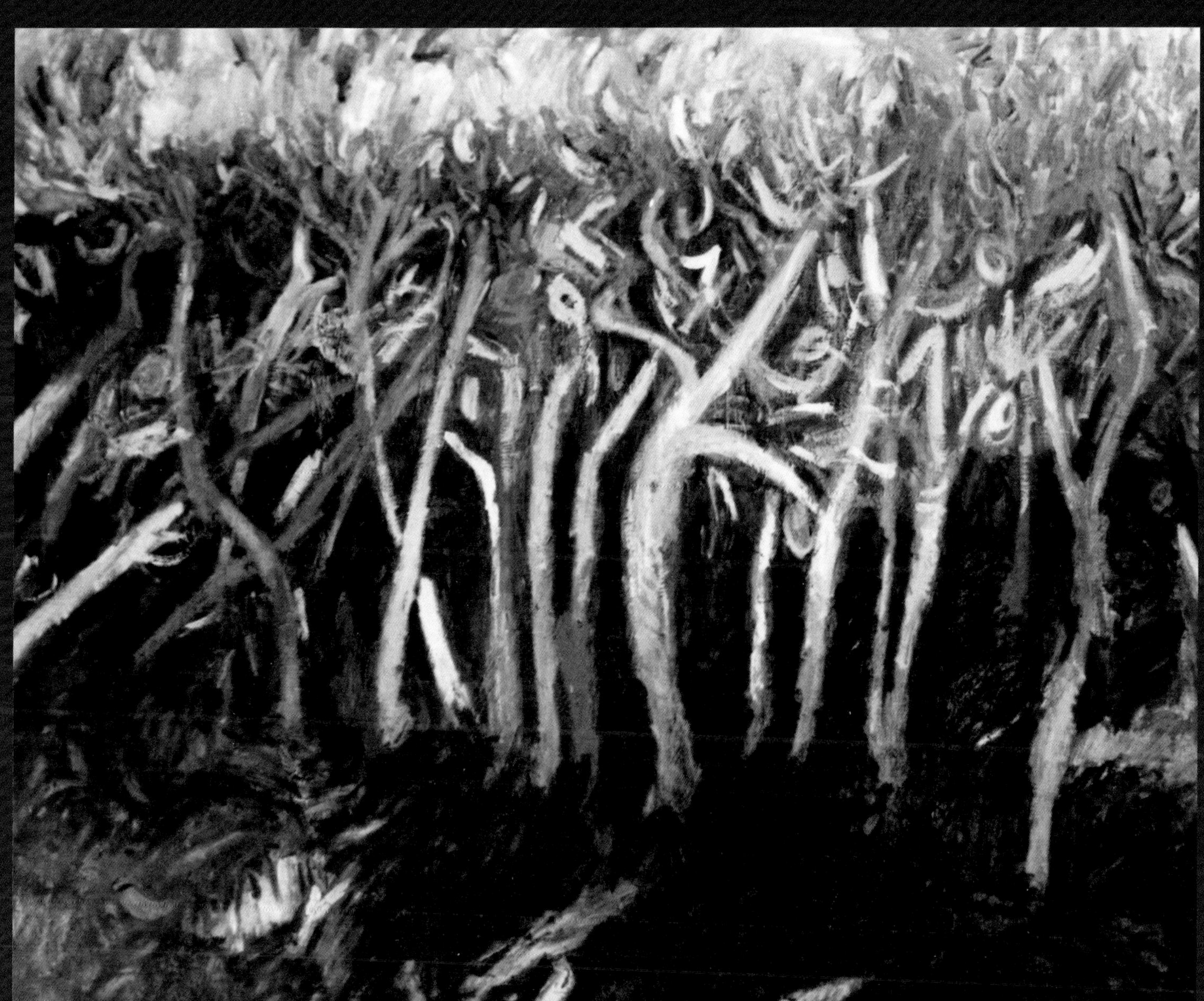

TEACHING POSITIONS Instructor, Department of Fine Arts, Rutgers University. ¶ SOLO EXHIBITIONS *Allan Kaprow: Paintings and Drawings,* Hansa Gallery, New York, April. Jewish Community Center, New Brunswick, New Jersey, Winter. ¶ GROUP EXHIBITIONS *Invitation Group Exhibition,* Hansa Gallery, New York, January. Urban Gallery, New York, April. *Contemporary Art by Younger New York Artists,* George Washington University, May. New Brunswick Art Association, New Brunswick, New Jersey, May. Earl Pilgrim Gallery, Provincetown, Massachusetts, July. Beryl-Lush Gallery, Provincetown, Massachusetts, August. Gallery 256, Provincetown, Massachusetts, August. Urban Gallery, New York, September. *Benefit Group Exhibition,* New York City Center Gallery, New York, December.

1954

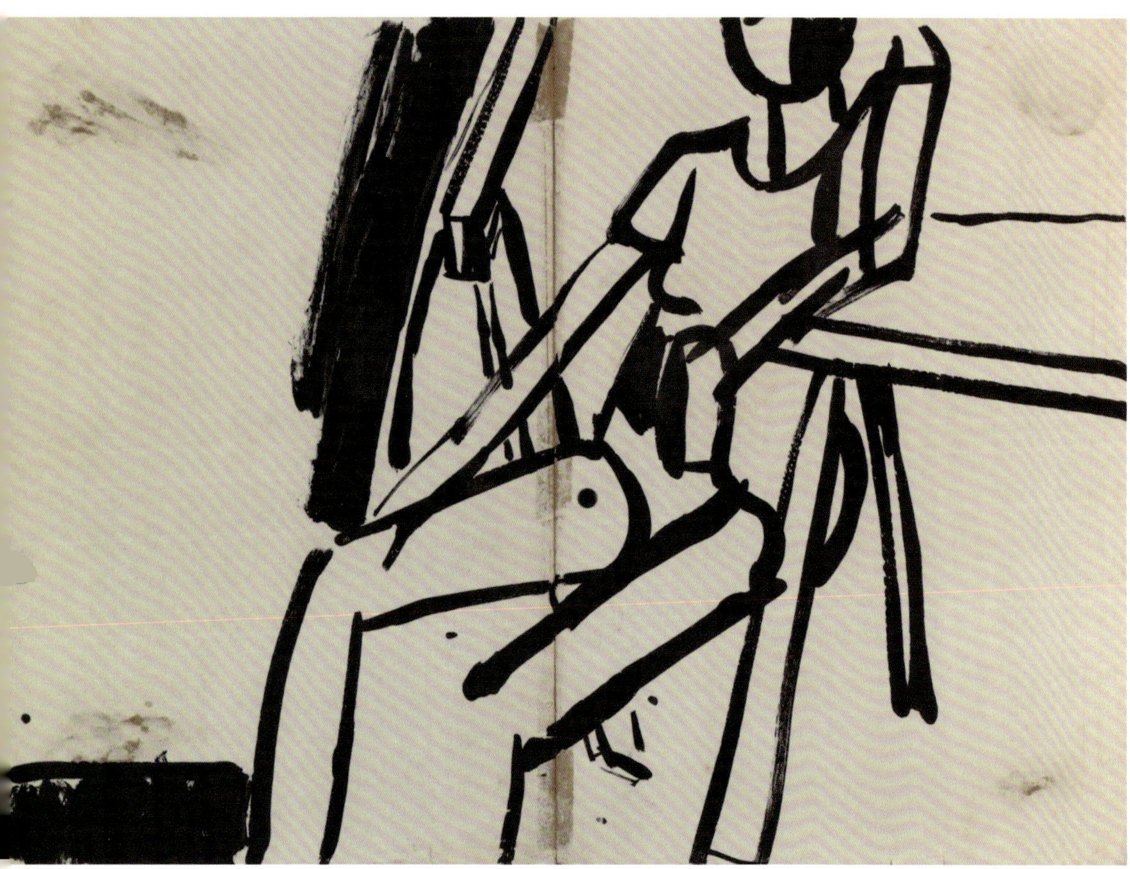

5

5 **Seated Model in Leotard in Studio**
Ink on paper, 1954
43.5 × 60 cm (17 1/8 × 23 5/8 in.)
Allan Kaprow Estate

6 **Model in Leotard Leaning on Sawhorse**
Ink on paper, 1954
43.2 × 30 cm (17 × 11 7/8 in.)
Allan Kaprow Estate

7 **Model in Leotard Leaning on Sawhorse**
Ink on paper, 1954
43.5 × 30 cm (17 1/8 × 11 7/8 in.)
Allan Kaprow Estate

White and Brown Figures
Oil on canvas, 1954
117.5 × 101.3 cm (46 1/4 × 39 7/8 in.)
Allan Kaprow Estate

Seated White Figure
Oil on canvas, 1954
101.6 × 76.2 cm (40 × 30 in.)
Allan Kaprow Estate

Artist in Studio
Oil on canvas, 1954
152.7 × 119.4 cm (60 1/8 × 47 in.)
Allan Kaprow Estate

Figures in Yellow Interior
Oil on canvas, 1954
123.8 × 153 cm (48 3/4 × 60 1/4 in.)
Allan Kaprow Estate

Magenta Nude
Oil on canvas, 1954
38 × 71 cm (15 × 28 in.)
Collection Leah Patricia Schneider, Pacific Beach, California

6

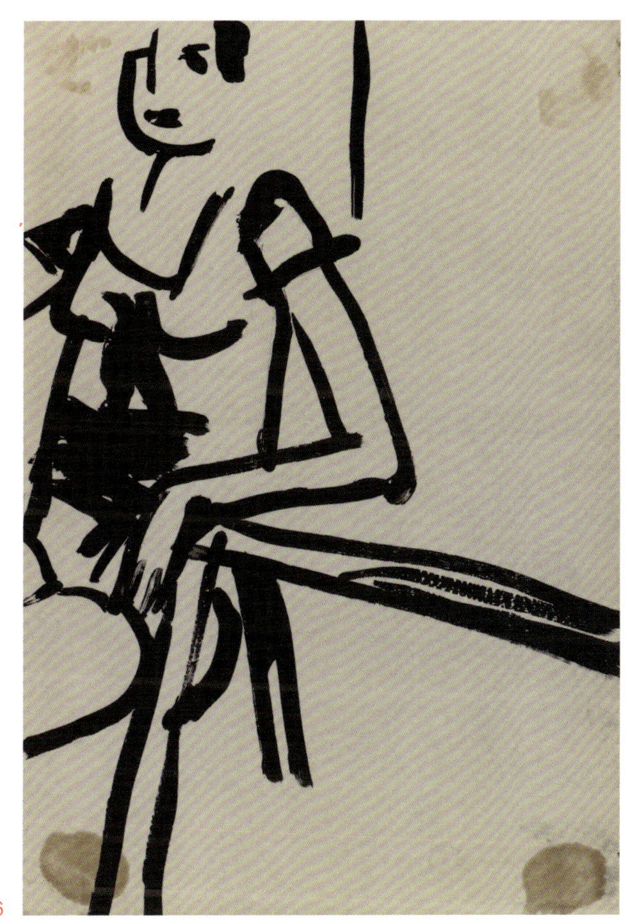

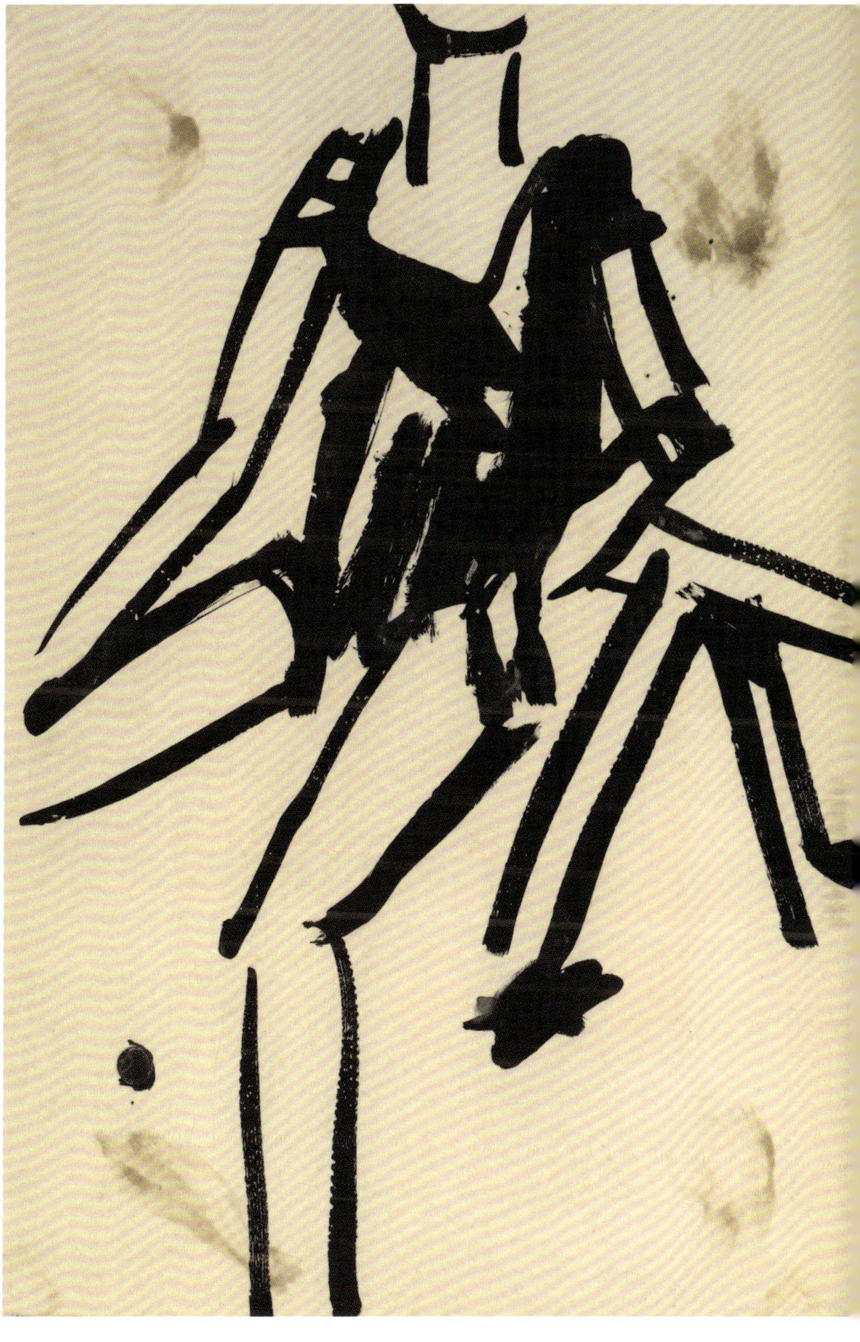

7

Alan Kaprow

A forthright and vigorous expressionist, Alan Kaprow sustains the intensity of his initial impetuous attack throughout each canvas. Throbbing, vibrant color, cadmiums and violets vying with each other, and vehemence of application, abrupt, slashing strokes and thick crests of pigment, lend these canvases an impassioned violence almost worthy of Soutine, although the violence seems to concern the act of painting itself rather than the outpouring of emotion. The figure appears in all of these paintings, in repose or in the wild motions and gyrations of a raucous dance, always delineated with the same bold strokes which ignore refinements of contour or variation of shape, emphasizing posture and gesture, indicating direction and motion more than form and substance. Often the figures operate in relief fashion within a very shallow space against solid grounds, while in some compositions indications of setting are arranged to establish an ambiguous, explosive space which leads the eye in many simultaneous directions. There is an immediacy here which conveys the impression of a headlong and almost hasty approach, but underlying the rapid execution of each painting is a backlog of experiment and experience which gives richness and conviction to the work. (Urban, to June 4.)—M.S. Art Digest '55

8 Review of Urban Gallery solo exhibition

Blue and White Nudes in Interior
Oil on canvas, 1955
29.8 × 30.2 cm (11¾ × 11⅞ in.)
Allan Kaprow Estate

9 **Red Dancers**
Oil on canvas, 1955
149.9 × 125.4 cm (59 × 49⅜ in.)
Allan Kaprow Estate

Small Red Dancers
Oil on canvas, 1955
25.7 × 30.7 cm (10⅛ × 12⅛ in.)
Hirshhorn Museum and Sculpture Garden, Washington, D.C.

Untitled (The Cherry Orchard)
Oil on canvas, 1955
107 × 140 cm (42⅛ × 55⅛ in.)
Collection Amy Kaprow Mezey, Berkeley

Untitled (Still Life)
Oil on canvas, 1955
51 × 110 cm (20⅛ × 43⅜ in.)
Collection Amy Kaprow Mezey, Berkeley

Three White Dancers
Oil on canvas, 1955
25.7 × 30.5 cm (10⅛ × 12 in.)
Allan Kaprow Estate

Homage to Monet
Oil on canvas, 1955
76.2 × 74 cm (30 × 29⅛ in.)
Allan Kaprow Estate

George Washington Bridge (Front View)
Oil on burlap, 1955
52.7 × 72.4 cm (20¾ × 28½ in.)
Allan Kaprow Estate

George Washington Bridge (Side View)
Oil on canvas, 1955
95.7 × 117.5 cm (37¾ × 46¼ in.)
Allan Kaprow Estate

LIFE EVENTS Married Vaughan Rachel, March. ¶ TEACHING POSITIONS Instructor, Department of Fine Arts, Rutgers University. ¶ SOLO EXHIBITIONS *Kaprow*, Urban Gallery, New York, May–June. ¶ GROUP EXHIBITIONS *Drawings, Water Colors, Pastels*, Hansa Gallery, New York, January. Urban Gallery, New York, January. Art House, Rutgers University, March. Art House, Rutgers University, April. *Community Art Day*, Douglass College, Rutgers University, May. Bernard-Ganymede Gallery, New York, September. *Xmas Group Show*, Hansa Gallery, New York, December. ¶ WRITINGS "Three Drawings by George Bogdanovitch," *Anthologist* 26, no. 3: 17–19.

1955

9

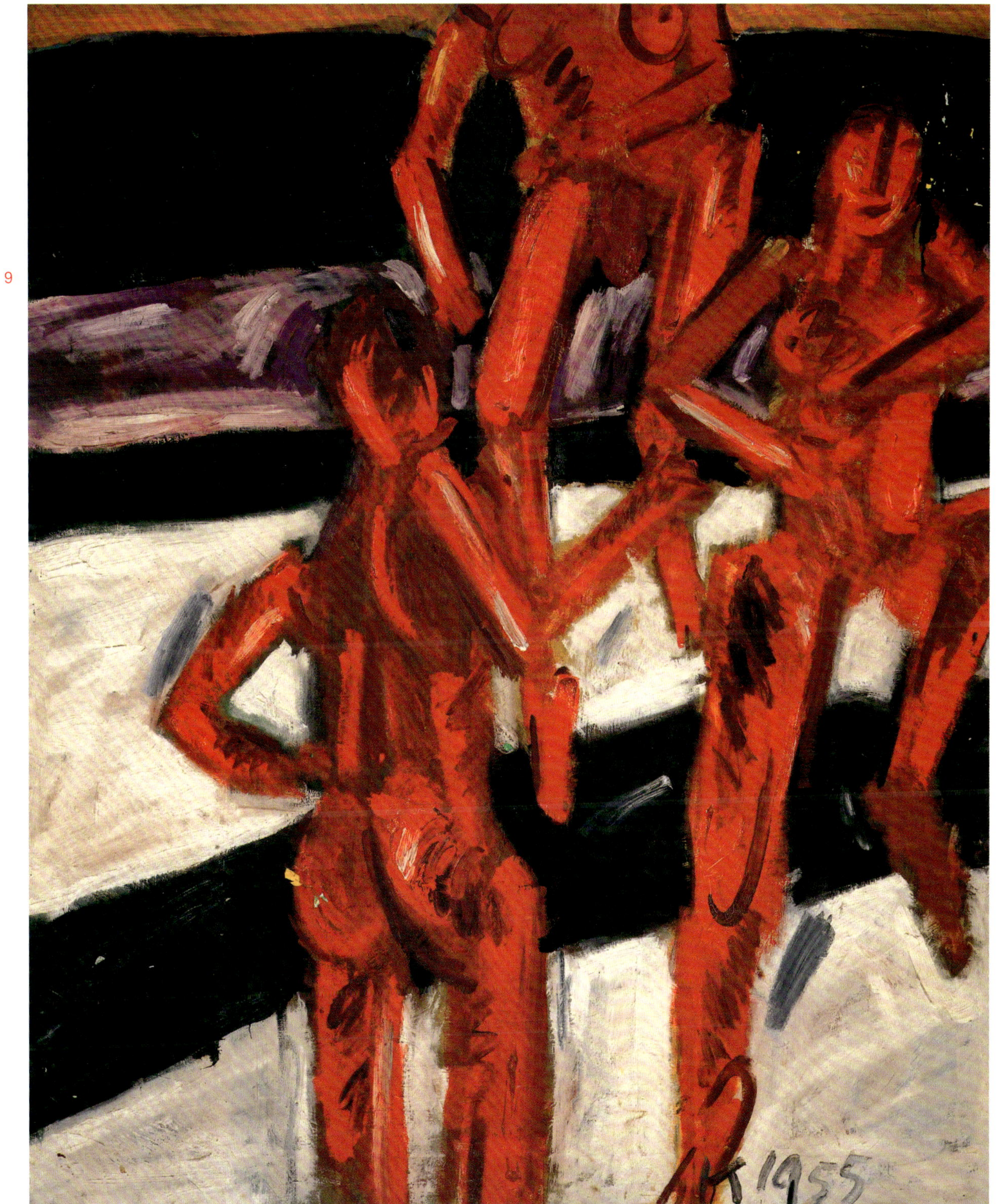

10 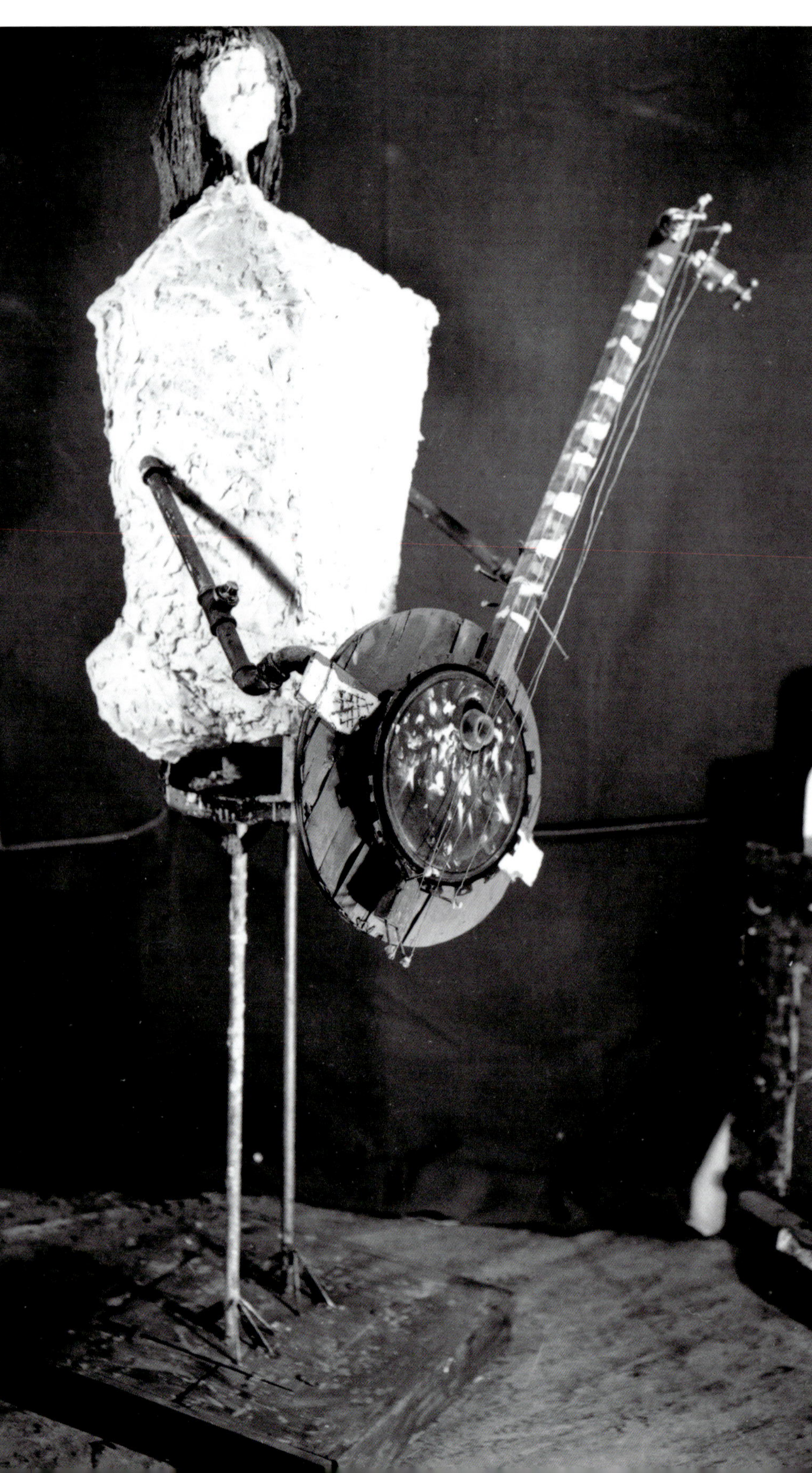

Yellow Flowers
Collage on canvas, 1955
126 × 140 cm (49⅝ × 55⅛ in.)
Museum Bochum, Bochum

Hero
Assemblage: metal, paper, and plaster covered with roofing cement, ca. 1955–56
198.8 × 48.3 × 58.1 cm
(78¼ × 19 × 22⅞ in.)
Allan Kaprow Estate

10 **Banjo Player**
Assemblage: iron, plaster, and mixed media, 1955–56
200 × 80 cm (78¾ × 31½ in.)
base: 50 × 60 × 14 cm
(19¾ × 23⅝ × 5½ in.)
Archivio F. Conz, Verona

11 **Woman out of Fire**
Assemblage: metal, paper, and plaster covered with roofing cement, 1955–56
172.7 × 62.9 × 62.2 cm
(68 × 24¾ × 24½ in.)
Allan Kaprow Estate

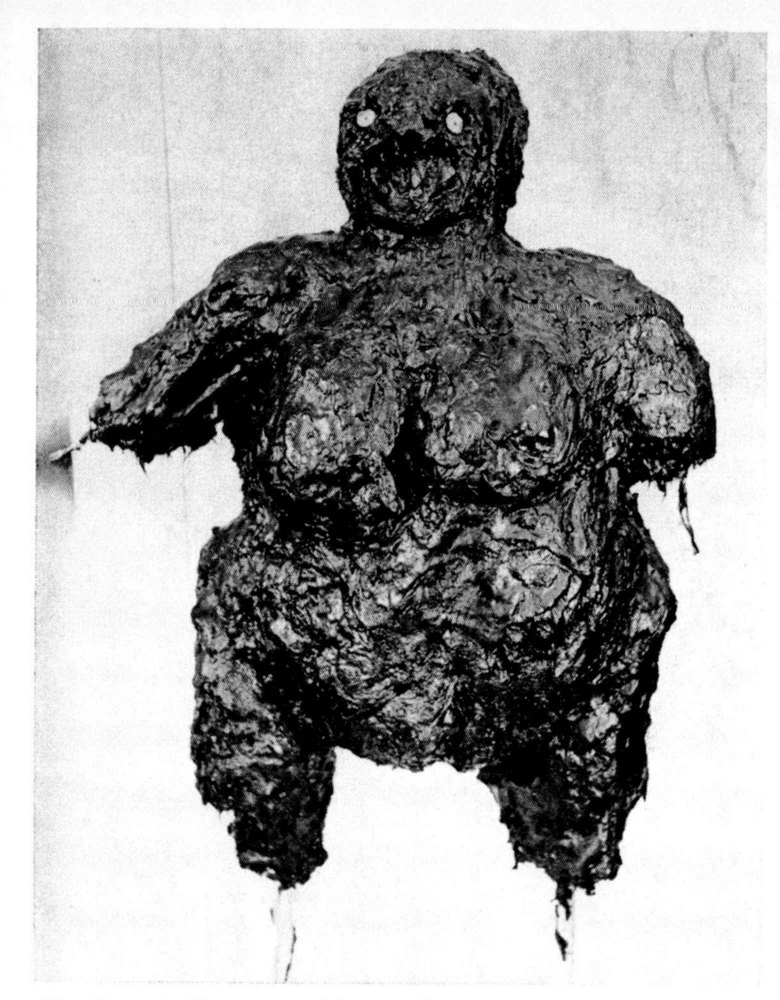

Allan Kaprow's *Woman Out of Fire*, roofing cement: "frenetic paroxysm"

Allan Kaprow [Hansa; Feb. 11-March 2], a disciple of Hans Hofmann, composes painted collages

TEACHING POSITIONS Assistant Professor, Department of Fine Arts, Rutgers University. ¶ **SOLO EXHIBITIONS** *Allan Kaprow,* Bernard-Ganymede Gallery, New York, February–March. Jewish Community Center, Highland Park, New Jersey, November. Art House, Rutgers University, December. ¶ **GROUP EXHIBITIONS** Mills College, New York, April. *June Salon Group Show,* Camino Gallery, New York, June. H.C.E. Gallery, Provincetown, Massachusetts, August. *Allan Kaprow and George Segal,* Z & Z Delicatessen, New Brunswick, New Jersey, September. Contemporary Americans series, Hansa Gallery, New York, October. Studio Gallery, New Brunswick, New Jersey, November. *Mid-Season Salon Group Exhibition,* Camino Gallery, New York, December. ¶ **FESTIVALS** Boston Arts Festival, Boston, June. ¶ **WRITINGS** *Chagall, Modigliani, Pissaro and Soutine: Four Introductory Essays* (Santa Susana, Calif.: Brandeis Youth Foundation Art Program), pamphlet. "Hans Hofmann," introduction to the Hans Hofmann exhibition, Art House, Rutgers University.

1956

12 Poster for Hansa Gallery group exhibition

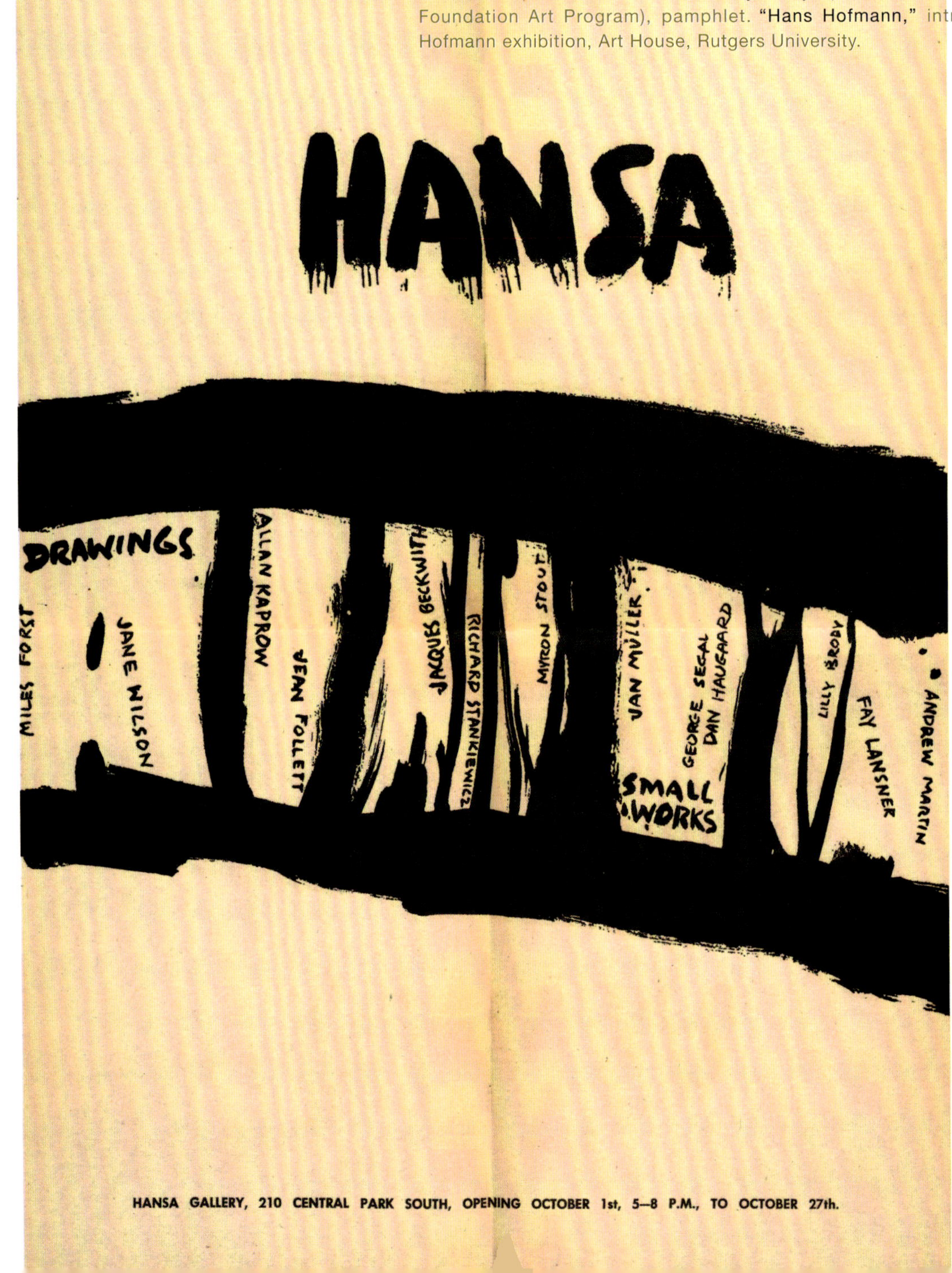

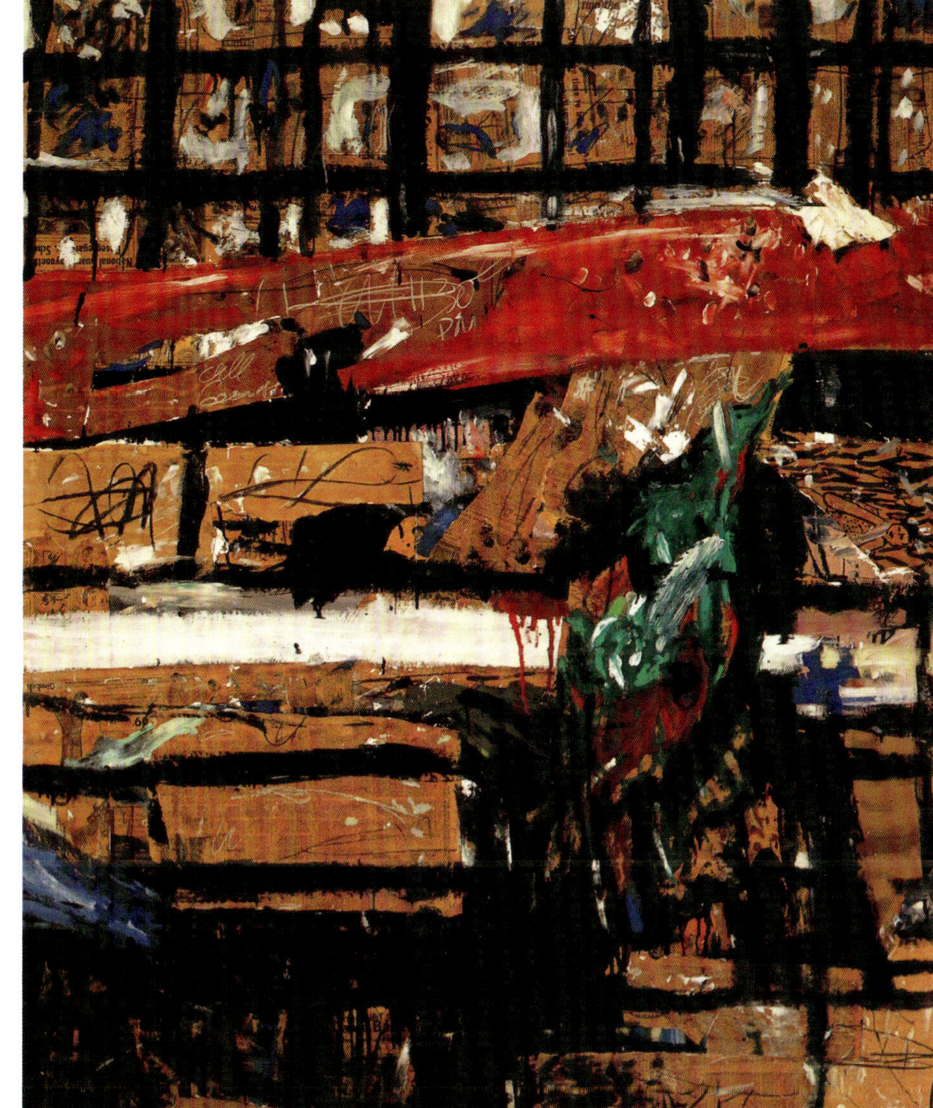

13

Leaning into the Light
Oil on wood panel, 1956
14.4 × 17.5 cm (5¾ × 6⅞ in.)
Collection Feelisch, Remscheid, Germany

Subway with Self-Portrait
Oil on canvas, 1956
127 × 91.4 cm (50 × 36 in.)
Allan Kaprow Estate

From James Joyce's *Ulysses*
Oil on canvas, 1956
212.3 × 194.3 cm (83⅝ × 76½ in.)
Allan Kaprow Estate

13 **Caged Pheasant #1**
Collage and paint on canvas, 1956
152.4 × 127 cm (60 × 50 in.)
Allan Kaprow Estate

Caged Pheasant #2
Collage and paint on canvas, 1956
177.5 × 121.9 cm (69⅞ × 48 in.)
Allan Kaprow Estate

14

14 **Stained Glass Window**
Collage and paint on canvas, 1956
266 × 175.3 cm (104¾ × 69 in.)
Museum Ludwig, Cologne

15 **Blue Blue Blue**
Collage and paint on canvas, 1956
152.4 × 120.6 cm (60 × 47½ in.)
Allan Kaprow Estate

Veronica
Collage and paint on canvas, 1956
145 × 120 cm (57⅛ × 47¼ in.)
Carré d'art, Musée d'art contemporain de Nîmes, Nîmes

In the Art
Collage and paint on board, 1956
34 × 32 cm (13⅜ × 12⅝ in.)
Collection Amy Kaprow Mezey, Berkeley

People
Collage and paint on board, 1956
42 × 30 cm (16⅝ × 11⅞ in.)
Collection Amy Kaprow Mezey, Berkeley

Hysteria
Collage: oil paint, aluminum foil, and canvas on canvas, 1956
200.7 × 182.9 cm (79 × 72 in.)
Private collection

Tobacco King
Collage: cloth, paint, and photograph, 1956
58.5 × 28 cm (23 × 11 in.)
Private collection

Untitled
Collage and paint on paper, 1956
187.7 × 188 cm (74 × 74 in.)
Städtisches Museum Abteiberg, Mönchengladbach, Germany

Penny Arcade
Assemblage with lights and sounds, 1956
243.8 × 182.9 × 60.9 cm
(96 × 72 × 24 in.)
Destroyed

Bouquet
Collage and paint on board, 1956
45.7 × 55.9 cm (18 × 22 in.)
Location unknown

15

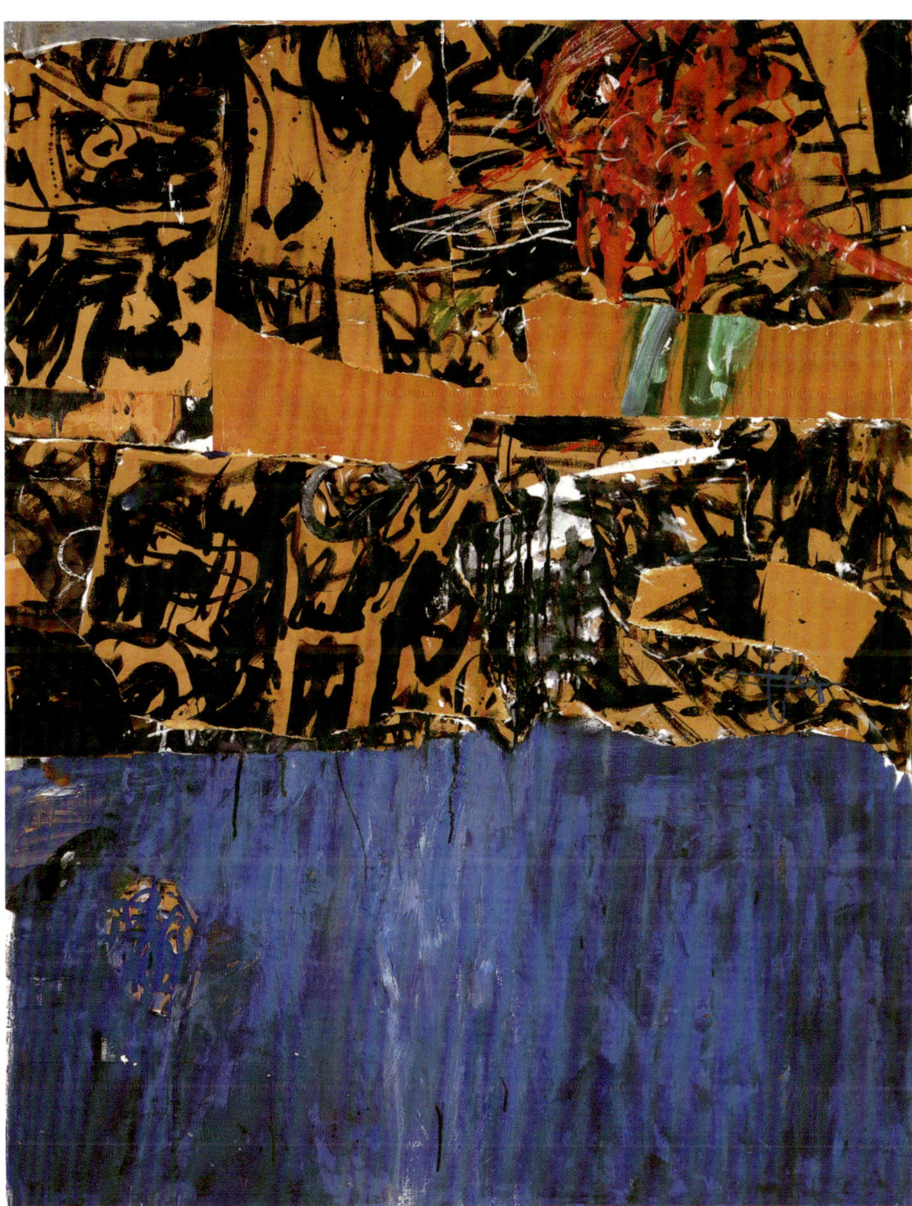

Baby
Collage: paper, aluminum foil, carpet pieces, oil and synthetic paint, chalk, and rope on masonite plates, 1957
282 × 306 × 17 cm
(111 × $120\frac{1}{2}$ × $6\frac{3}{4}$ in.)
Museum Moderner Kunst Stiftung Ludwig, Vienna

Grandma's Boy
Assemblage: mattress ticking, broken furniture, mirror, and found snapshot, 1957
47 × 71.8 × 4.8 cm
($18\frac{1}{2}$ × $28\frac{1}{4}$ × $1\frac{7}{8}$ in.), open
47 × 40 × 7.6 cm
($18\frac{1}{2}$ × $15\frac{3}{4}$ × 3 in.), closed
Newark Museum, Newark

Collage No. 2
Collage: wood, wire, cloth, and paint, 1957
96.5 × 45.7 cm (38 × 18 in.)
Location unknown

The Oldtimer
Collage: fabric, wood, and paper, 1957
30.3 × 25.4 cm (12 × 10 in.)
Location unknown

Music
Tape score, 1957
Getty Research Institute, Los Angeles

Roulette
Tape score, 1957
Getty Research Institute, Los Angeles

Saw
Tape score, 1957
Getty Research Institute, Los Angeles

Throat and Cough Piece
Sound score, 1957–58
Getty Research Institute, Los Angeles

16–19 **Rearrangeable Panels**
Assemblage: oil, leaves, lightbulbs, plastic apples, and mirror on canvas and wood, 1957–59, nine panels:
(1) Tar, 244.5 × 66 × 5.5 cm ($96\frac{1}{4}$ × 26 × $2\frac{1}{4}$ in.)
(2) Pieces of broken mirror, 244 × 56.4 × 6 cm ($96\frac{1}{8}$ × $22\frac{1}{4}$ × $2\frac{3}{8}$ in.)
(3) Apples on a silver panel, 246.2 × 76.5 × 13 cm (97 × $30\frac{1}{8}$ × $5\frac{1}{8}$ in.)
(4) Apples on a green panel, 247 × 75.6 × 5 cm ($97\frac{1}{4}$ × $29\frac{3}{4}$ × 2 in.)
(5) Collage, 244.5 × 66.6 × 5.4 cm ($96\frac{1}{4}$ × $26\frac{1}{4}$ × $2\frac{1}{8}$ in.)
(6) Mirror and collage, 246.4 × 27.5 × 4.4 cm (97 × $10\frac{7}{8}$ × $1\frac{3}{4}$ in.)
(7) Elm leaves, 244 × 66.4 × 5 cm ($96\frac{1}{8}$ × $26\frac{1}{8}$ × 2 in.)
(8) Elm leaves with gaps, 244 × 66.4 × 4.4 cm ($96\frac{1}{8}$ × $26\frac{1}{8}$ × $1\frac{3}{4}$ in.)
(9) White paint, 244.5 × 66.3 × 5.7 cm ($96\frac{1}{4}$ × $26\frac{1}{8}$ × $2\frac{1}{4}$ in.)
Musée national d'art moderne, Centre Georges Pompidou, Paris

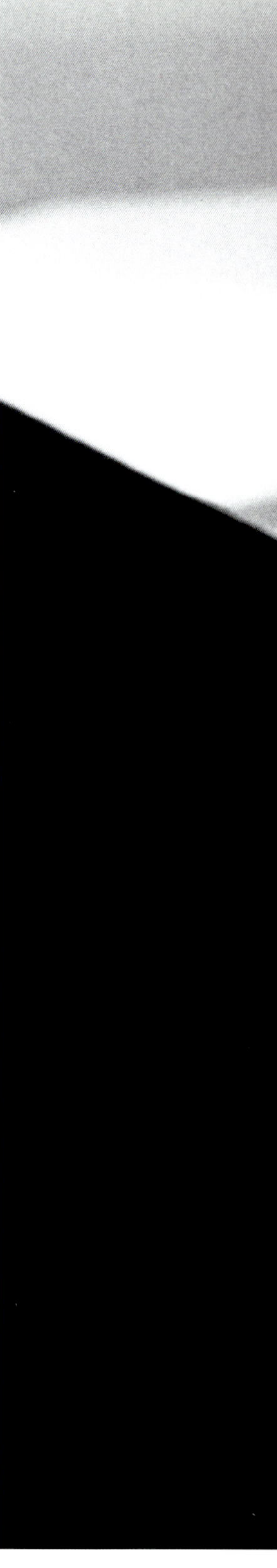

1957

LIFE EVENTS Anton Michael Kaprow, son, born March. ¶ TEACHING POSITIONS Assistant Professor, Department of Fine Arts, Rutgers University. ¶ EDUCATION Studied music composition with John Cage, New School for Social Research, New York. ¶ SOLO EXHIBITIONS *Allan Kaprow: Collages and Sculpture,* Hansa Gallery, New York, February–March. Sun Gallery, Provincetown, Massachusetts, August. ¶ GROUP EXHIBITIONS *Artists of the New York School: Second Generation,* Jewish Museum, New York, March–April. *13 Members, 13 Guests,* March Gallery, New York, April. *James Gallery Invitation Annual,* James Gallery, New York, May. *Sculpture: May Salon,* Camino Gallery, New York, May. *Second Generation of the New York School,* Landau Gallery, Los Angeles, July. *New York Artists,* Tuxedo Park, New York, August. *6 Exemplary Paintings and 1 Sculpture,* Hansa Gallery, New York, October. *Old and New Works,* Hansa Gallery, New York, November. *Traveling Group Show of Younger New York Artists* (arranged by the Hansa Gallery), Nashville Museum, Nashville, November. *Collage in America* (sponsored by the American Federation of Arts), Zabriskie Gallery, New York, December. *Tenth Street Christmas Show,* March Gallery, New York, December. ¶ WRITINGS "Rub-A-Dub, Rub-A-Dub!" *Anthologist* 29, no. 2: 16–18.

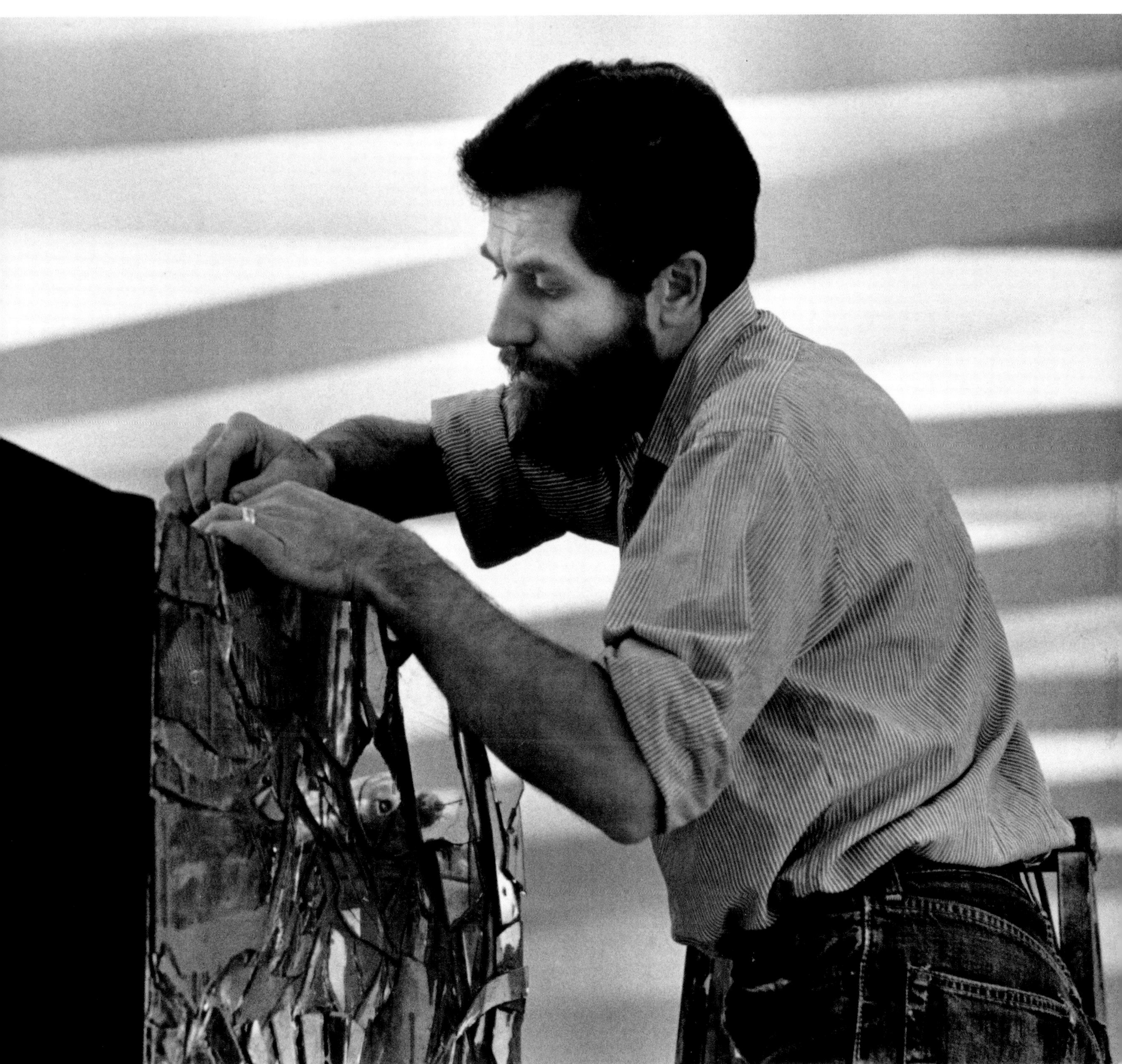

16 Kaprow constructing broken mirror panel
Photo: Robert R. McElroy

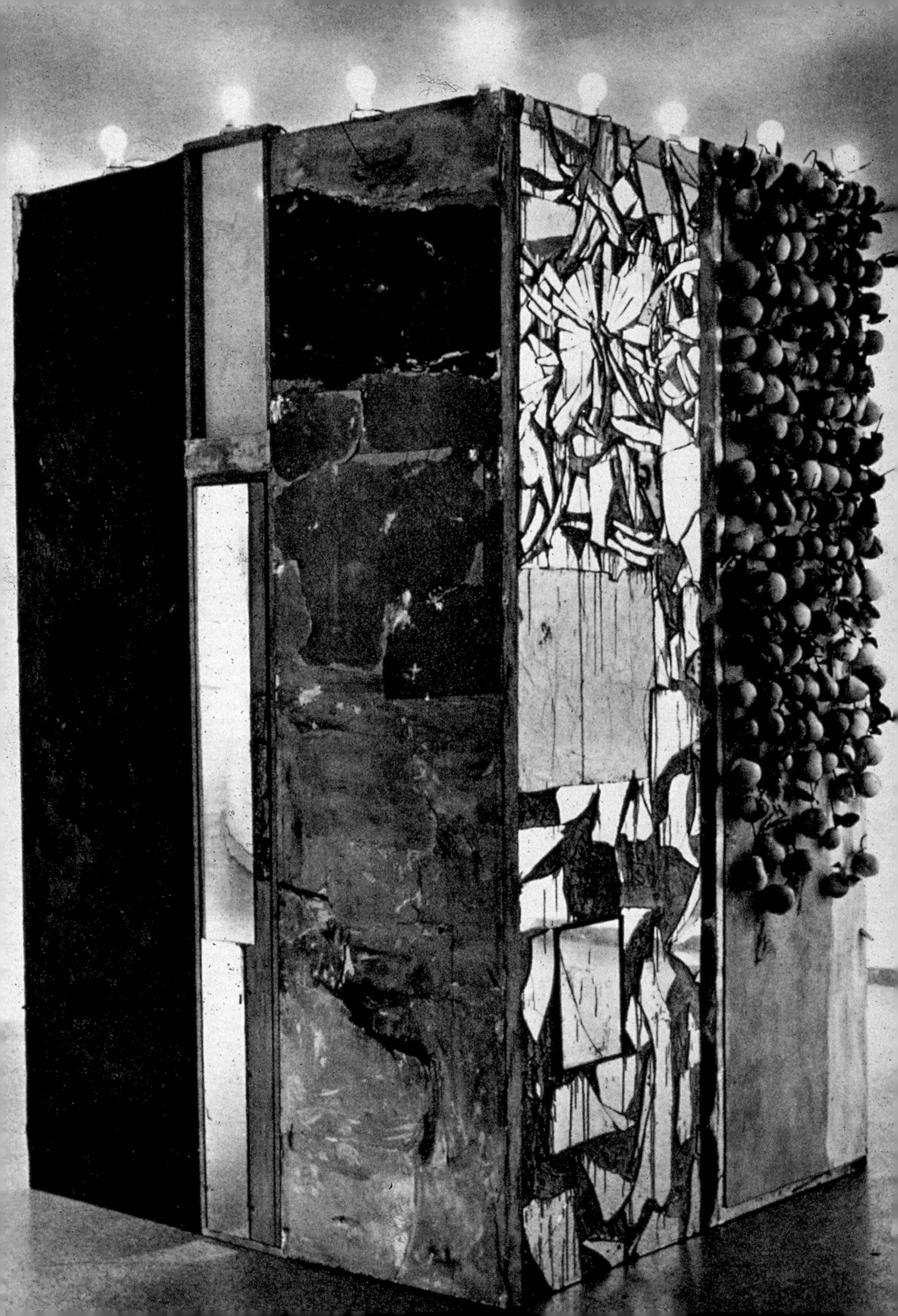

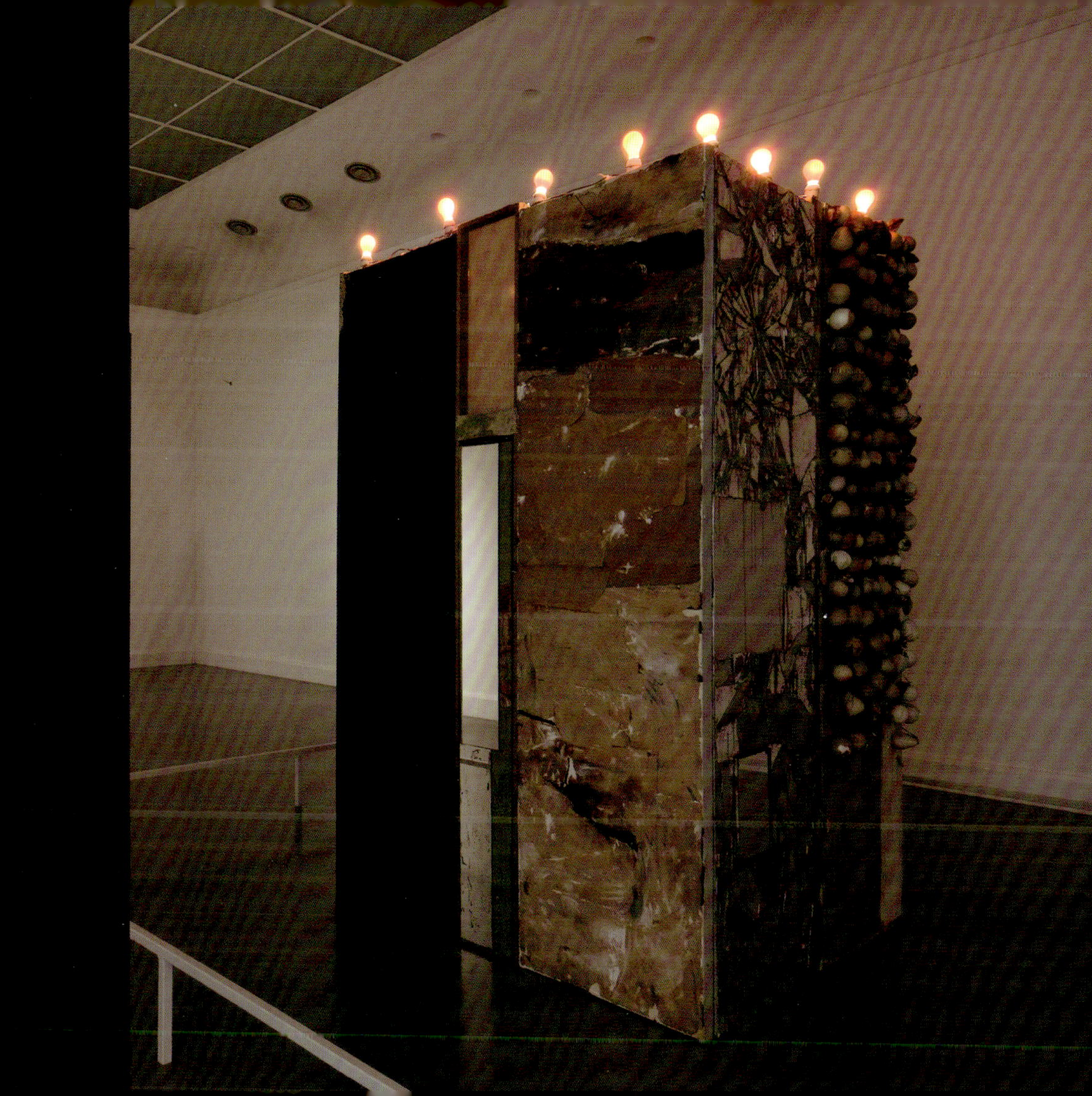

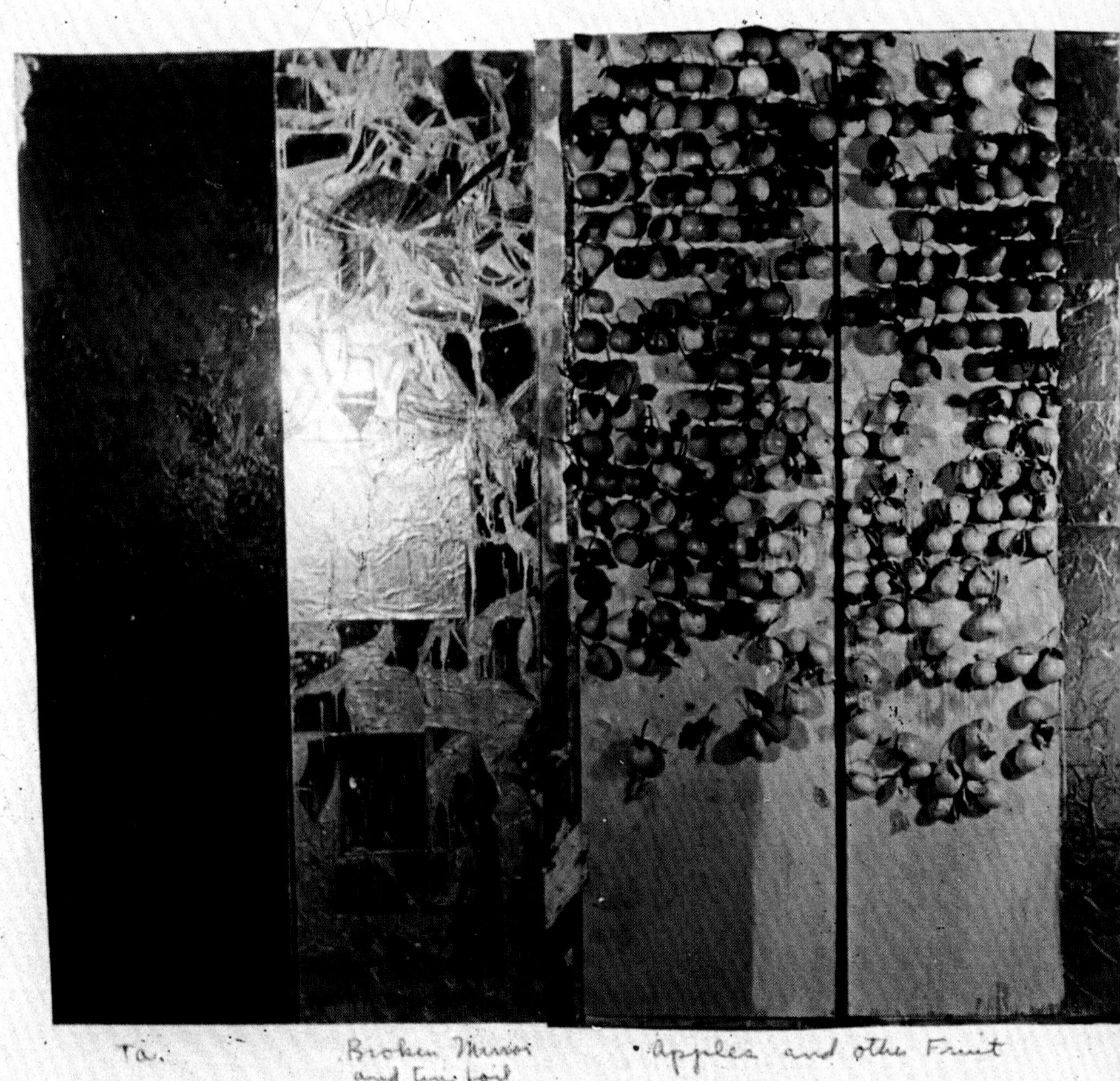
Broken Mirror and tin foil
Apples and other Fruit
ALLAN KAPROW, PANELS 1957-9, 8' x 21'

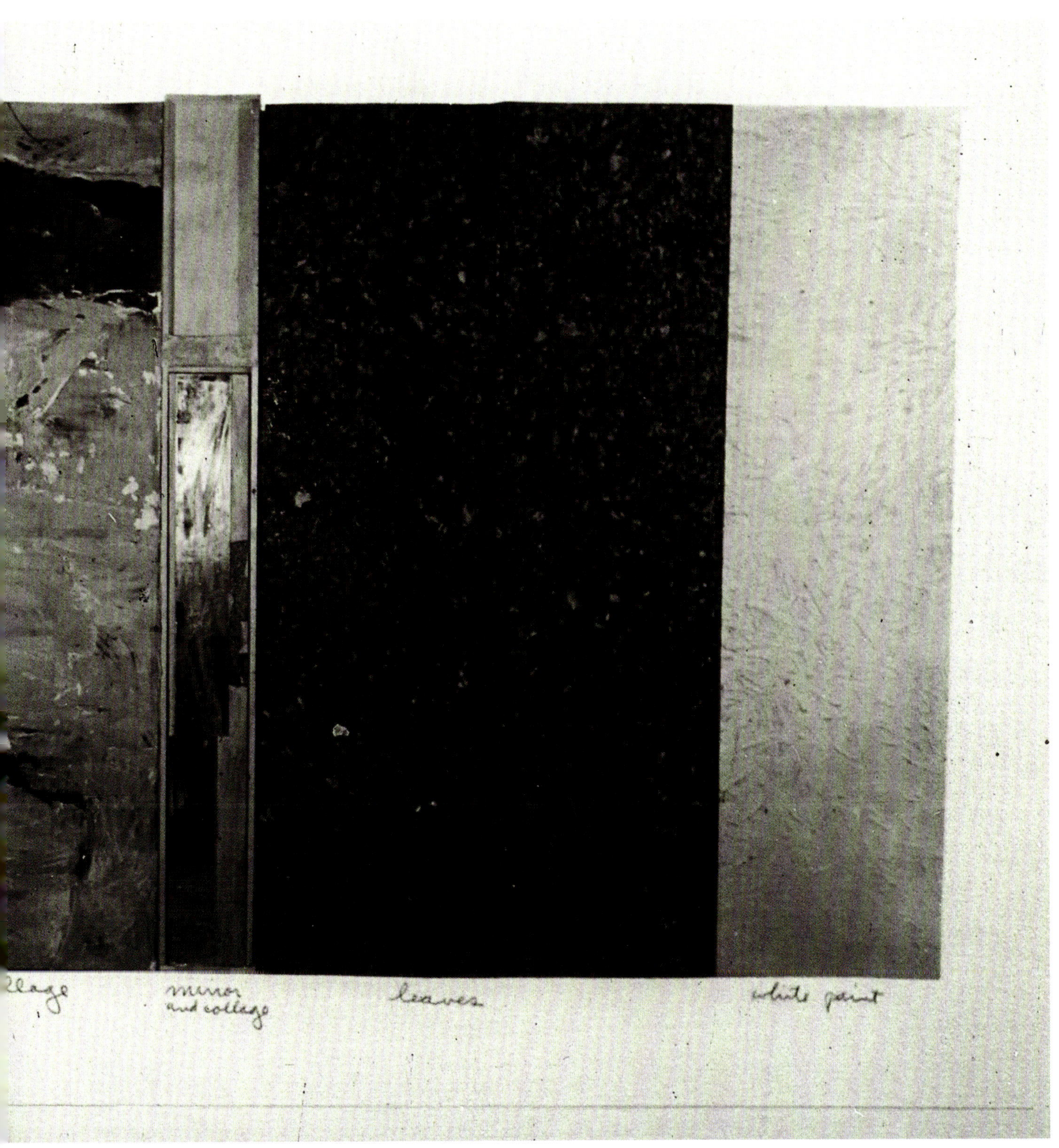

19 *Rearrangeable Panels* (wall configuration with Kaprow's captions)
Photo: Robert R. McElroy

TEACHING POSITIONS Assistant Professor, Department of Fine Arts, Rutgers University. ¶ **EDUCATION** Studied music composition with John Cage, New School for Social Research, New York. ¶ **AWARDS** Research grant from Rutgers University. ¶ **SOLO EXHIBITIONS** *Allan Kaprow,* Hansa Gallery, New York, March. Centaur Restaurant, New York, August. *Allan Kaprow: An Exhibition,* Hansa Gallery, New York, November–December. ¶ **GROUP EXHIBITIONS** *Collages and Constructions,* Festival XII Exhibition, White Art Museum, Cornell University, April–May. Independent Gallery, New York, May. *Intro-Bulletin Benefit,* Hansa Gallery, New York, May. *New York School Artists,* Art House, Rutgers University, May. *Exhibition of Paintings,* Eleventh Annual Creative Arts Program, University of Colorado, Boulder, June–August. Hansa Gallery, New York, September–October. *24,* Contemporary Americans series, Hansa Gallery, New York, November. *1958 Pittsburgh International Exhibition of Contemporary Painting and Sculpture,* Carnegie Institute, Pittsburgh, December–February. ¶ **WRITINGS** "The Legacy of Jackson Pollock," *ARTnews* 57, no. 6: 24–26, 55–57. "Notes on the Creation of a Total Art," published in the mimeographed pamphlet for *Untitled Environment,* Hansa Gallery, New York, November–December.

1958

20–28 **Untitled Environment**
Environment, March 1958
Hansa Gallery, New York
Reinvented in 1958, 1966, and 1980
Reinvented as *Fresh Air* in 1986; as *Beauty Parlor* in 1991; as *Dead End* in 1992; as *Short Circuit* in 1992; as *Beauty Parlor 2* in 1993; and as *Vital Fluids* in 1997

Untitled Environment
Environment, November–December 1958
Hansa Gallery, New York

Communication
Happening, April 1958
Voorhees Chapel, Douglass College, Rutgers University

Pastorale
Happening, Spring 1958
George Segal's farm, South Brunswick, New Jersey

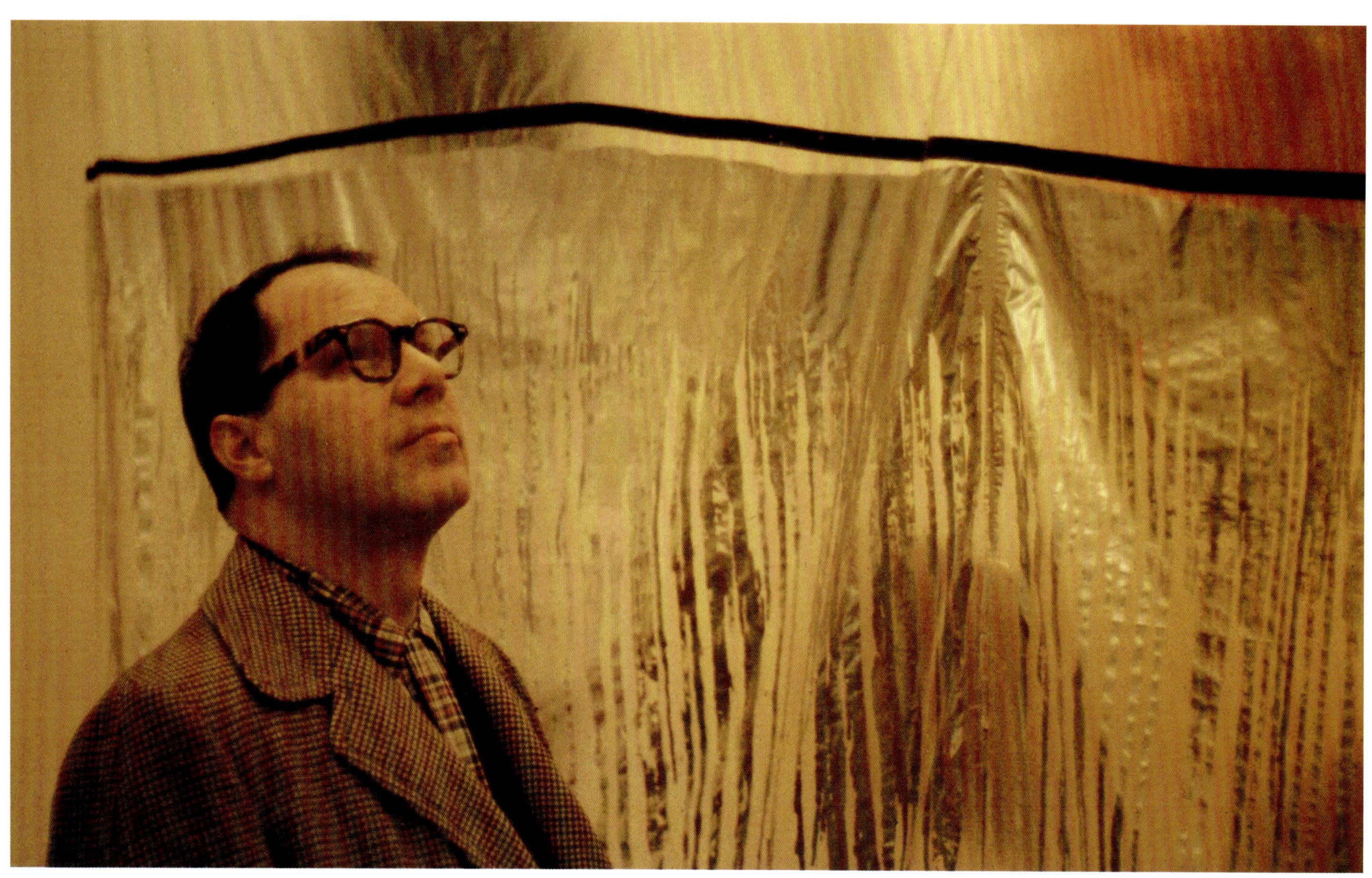

20 John Hermansader wanders through the Environment

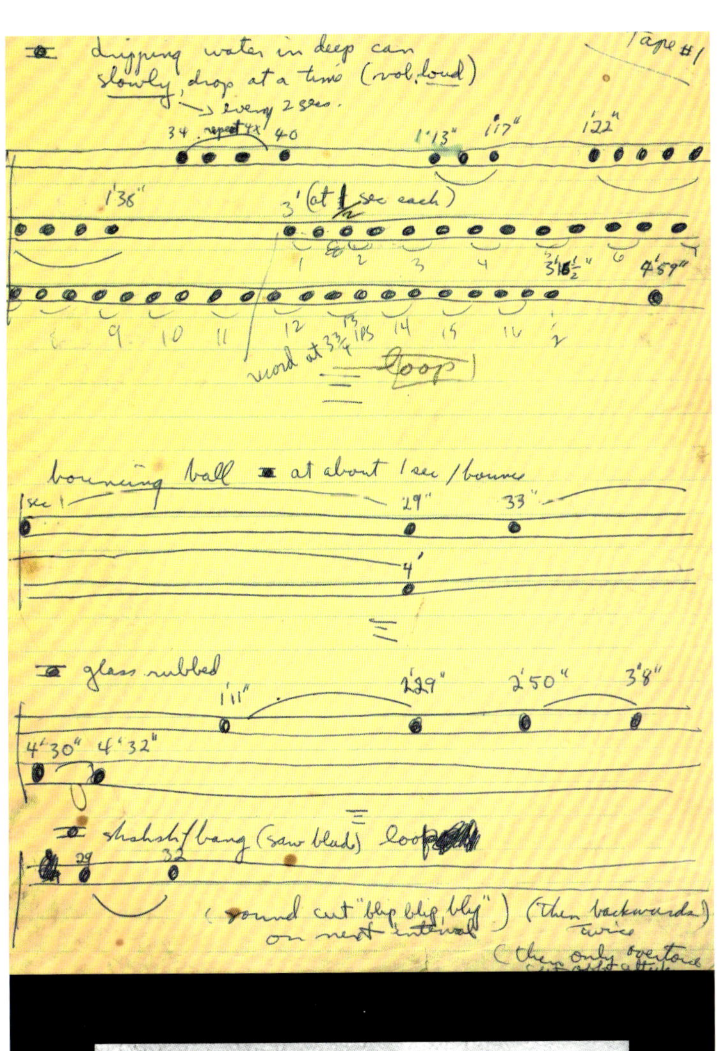

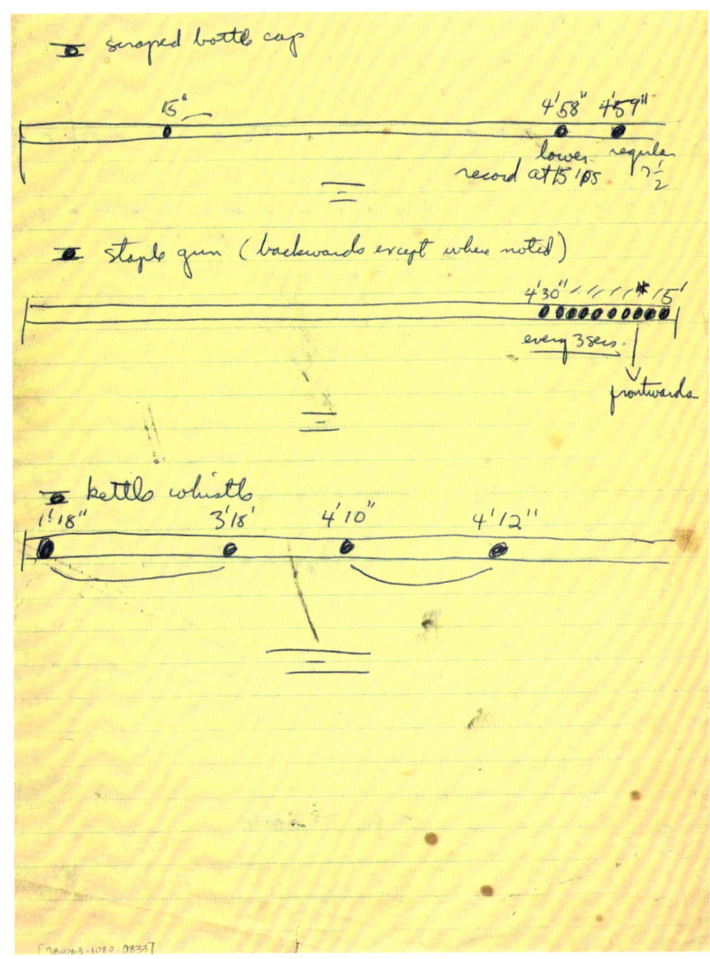

21 Score for Tape #1, recto

22 Score for Tape #2, verso

You are invited to a performance of a work by Allan Kaprow at the Hansa Gallery, 210 Central Park South, New York City. The performance is at 3 P.M. daily, Monday through Saturday, from Tuesday, March 11th to March 29th. The work may be viewed, however, during the regular Gallery hours, 11 A.M. to 6 P.M.

23 Invitation to *Untitled Environment*

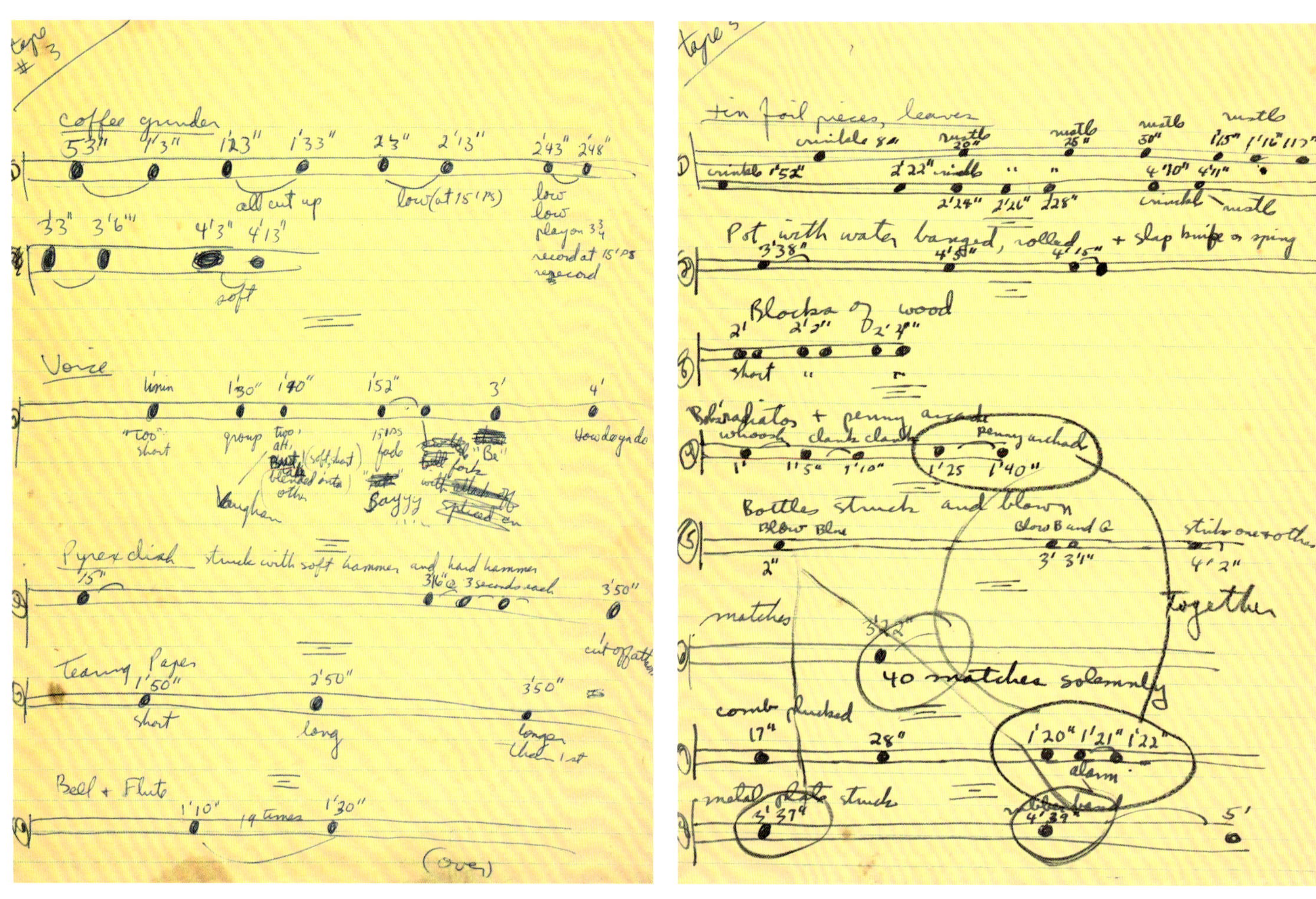

24 Score for Tape #3, recto
25 Score for Tape #5, recto

26

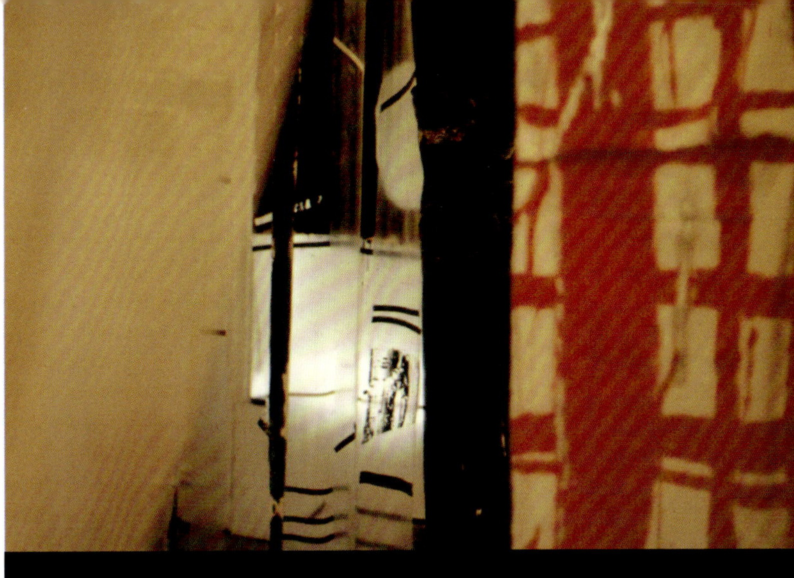

27 Review of *Untitled Environment*

Allan Kaprow: Strips and hangings of translucent plastic and cloth decorated with paint or varied with cutouts, the whole assemblage was arranged in aisles through which one was invited to walk. Here and there, one's excursion was rewarded by a diaphanous little inner sanctum blocked off by scrim or strung with Christmas lights. For those who preferred the artist packaged, so to speak, in the midst of his work, a performance was arranged each afternoon. (Hansa, Mar. 10-29.)—J.R.M.

ARTS / *May 1958*

28

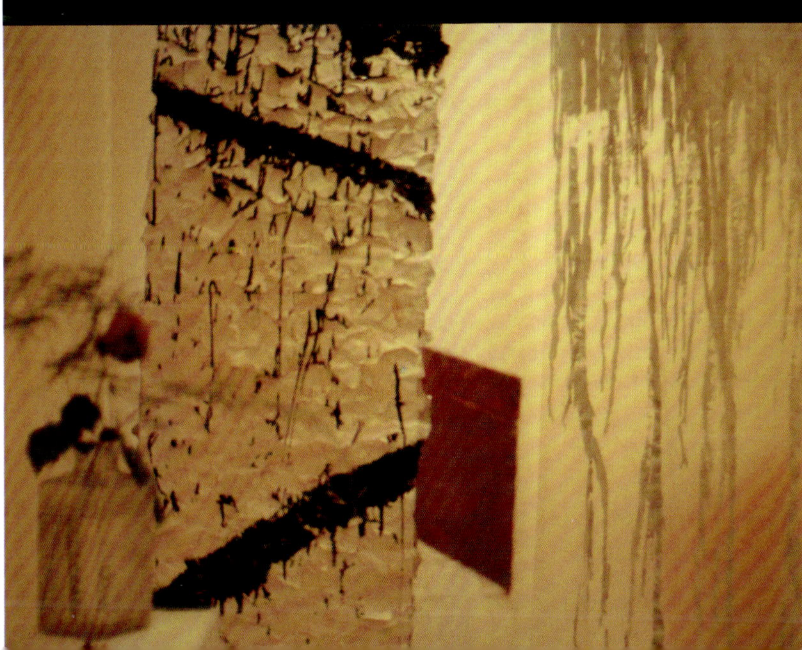

18 HAPPENINGS
IN SIX PARTS
BY ALLAN KAPROW

THE REUBEN GALLERY
61 4th AVE., N.Y.C.
OCT. 4,6,7,8,9,10--8:30 p.m.

CAST OF PARTICIPANTS

Allan Kaprow - who speaks and plays a musical instrument

Rosalyn Montague - who speaks and moves

Shirley Prendergast - who moves and plays a musical instrument

Lucas Samaras - who speaks, plays a game and a musical instrument

Janet Weinberger - who moves and plays a musical instrument

Robert Whitman - who moves, speaks and plays a game

Sam Francis, Red Grooms, Dick Higgins, Lester Johnson, Alfred Leslie, Jay Milder, George Segal, Robert Thompson - each of whom paints

The visitors - who sit in various chairs

INSTRUCTIONS

The performance is divided into six parts. Each part contains three happenings which occur at once. The beginning and end of each will be signalled by a bell. At the end of the performance two strokes of the bell will be heard.

You have been given three cards. Be seated as they instruct you. That is, be sure to change your place for set three and for set five.

Between part one and part two there is a two minute interval. Remain seated.

Between part two and part three there is a fifteen minute interval. You may move about freely.

Between part three and part four there is a two minute interval when you will remain in your seats.

Between part four and part five there is a fifteen minute interval. You may move about.

Between part five and part six there is a two minute interval. Remain seated.

There will be no applause after each set. You may applaud after the sixth set if you wish, although there will be no "curtain call".

The visitors are please asked not to smoke at all in the loft. They are also asked not to leave the building during the longer intermissions.

31 Cast and instructions for *18 Happenings in 6 Parts*

29–50 **18 Happenings in 6 Parts**

Happening, October 1959
Reuben Gallery, New York
Reinvented in 1988; reenacted in 2006

Laughs and Balloons

Happening, November 1959
Reuben Gallery, New York

Untitled (Mountain)

Assemblage: stepladder, chicken wire, newspaper, and tape, 1959
Dimensions variable
Destroyed

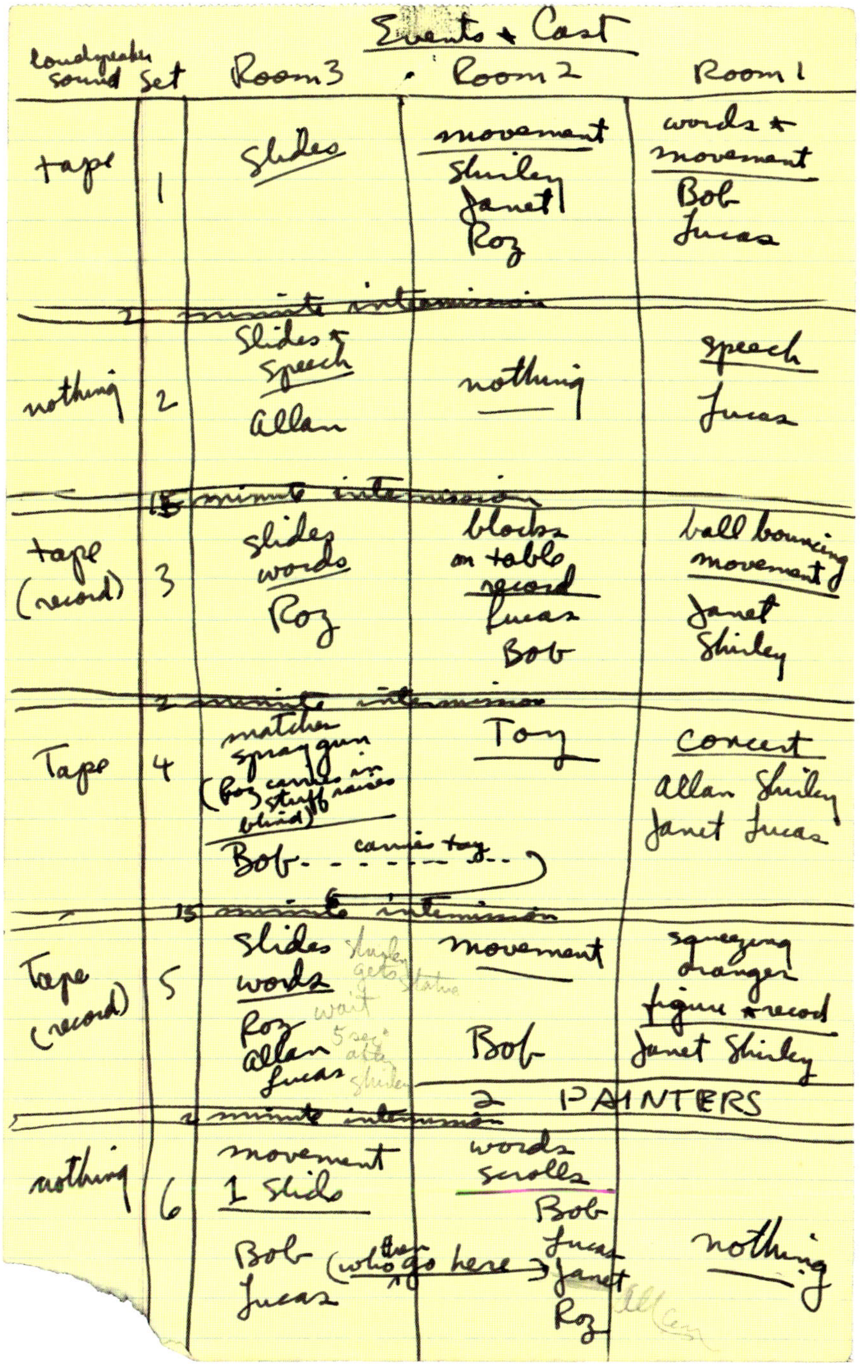

Events + Cast

Loudspeaker sound	Set	Room 3	Room 2	Room 1
tape	1	slides	movement Shirley Janet Roz	words + movement Bob Lucas
2 minute intermission				
nothing	2	Slides + speech Allan	nothing	speech Lucas
15 minute intermission				
tape (record)	3	slides words Roz	blocks on table record Lucas Bob	ball bouncing movement Janet Shirley
2 minute intermission				
Tape	4	matches spray gun (Roz carries in stuff raises blind) Bob - carries toy - - -	Toy	concert Allan Shirley Janet Lucas
15 minute intermission				
Tape (record)	5	slides words Roz Allan Lucas	movement Bob	squeezing oranges figure + record Janet Shirley
			2 PAINTERS	
2 minute intermission				
nothing	6	movement 1 slide Bob Lucas (who go here →)	words scrolls Bob Lucas Janet Roz	nothing

32 Score for *18 Happenings in 6 Parts*

Room 1 Set 1

Person 1

All movements will be made according to the cardinal axes ✥

walks slowly along corridor (ahead of those going to Room 2), stops at entrance 5", walks slowly, in a straight line, eyes ahead, to within 3 feet of the person seated ~~in front~~ opposite, stops there for 7" turns around for 2"; takes one step to the left and proceeds as follows:

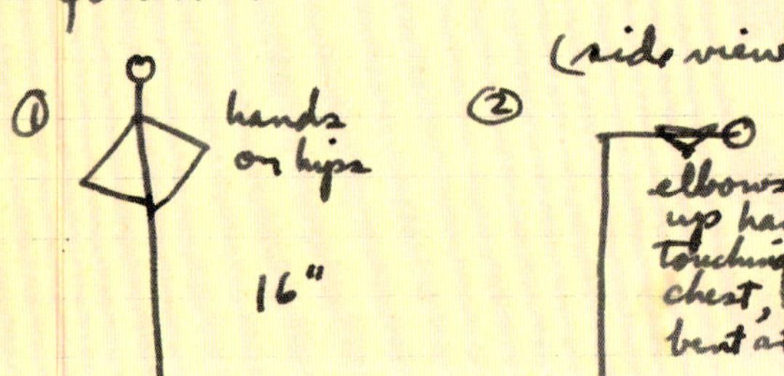

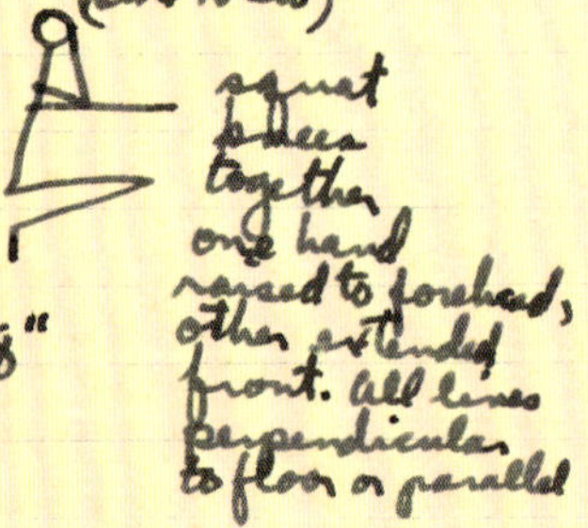

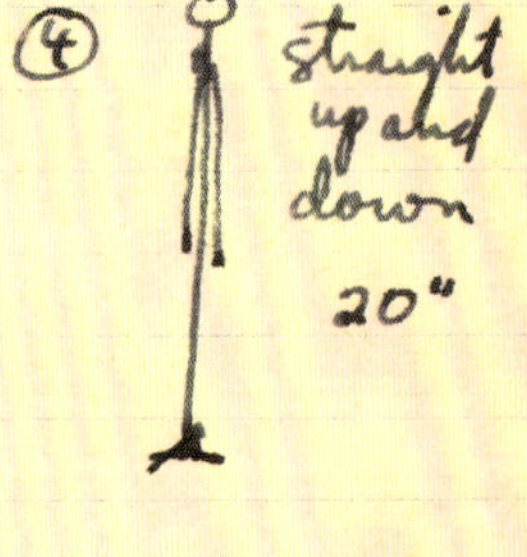

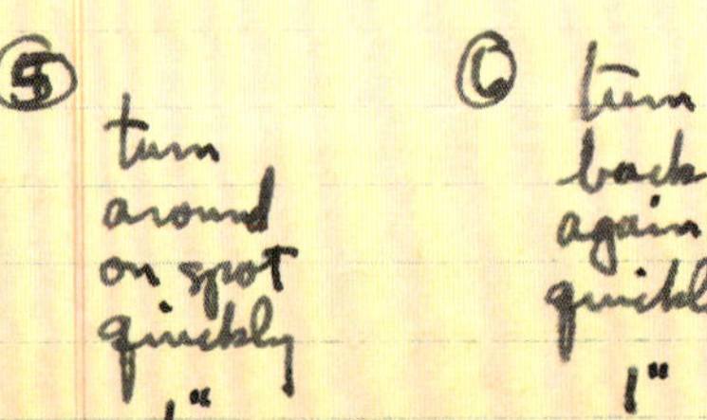

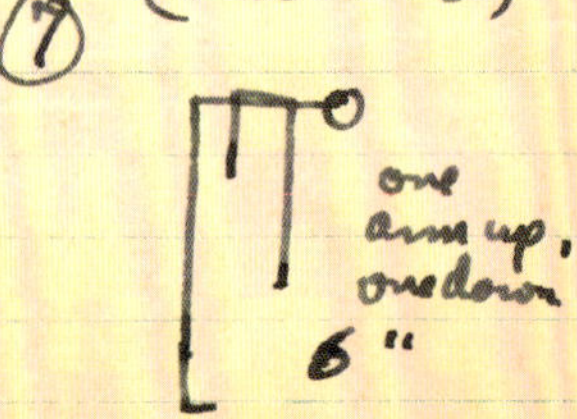

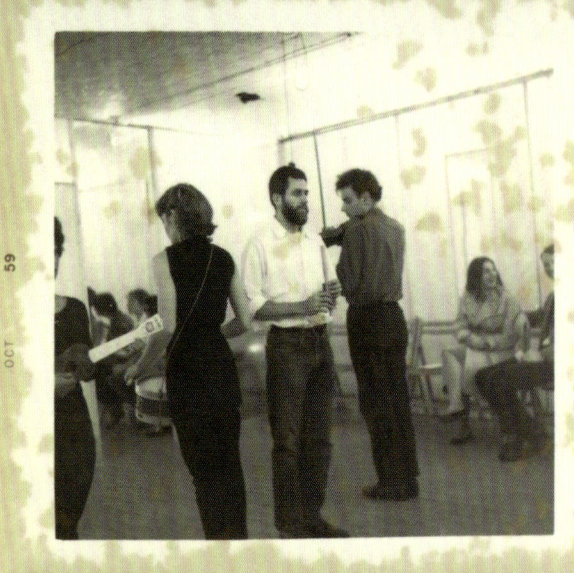

33 Movement score, p. 1

34 Concert in room 1, set 4

35 Rosalyn Montague squeezing oranges in room 1, set 5
36 Movement score, p. 2

Room 1 Set 1

Person 1

(8) (side view) turn right swing left foot slowly back and forth not too far either way 17"

(9) takes 22 steps in any cardinal direction changing as often as you wish. Each turn should be made after a near stop and should be a clean angle. Stop. (approx. 22")

(10) hands clasped behind back, not touching back tho 2"

(11) (side view) bend over arms hanging straight 10"

(12) hands on chest, elbows up 12"

(13) two steps forward 2"

(14) (side view) squat, knees together, arms on thighs. 4"

(15) (side view) arms extended 1"

(16) knees apart, hands on chest 2"

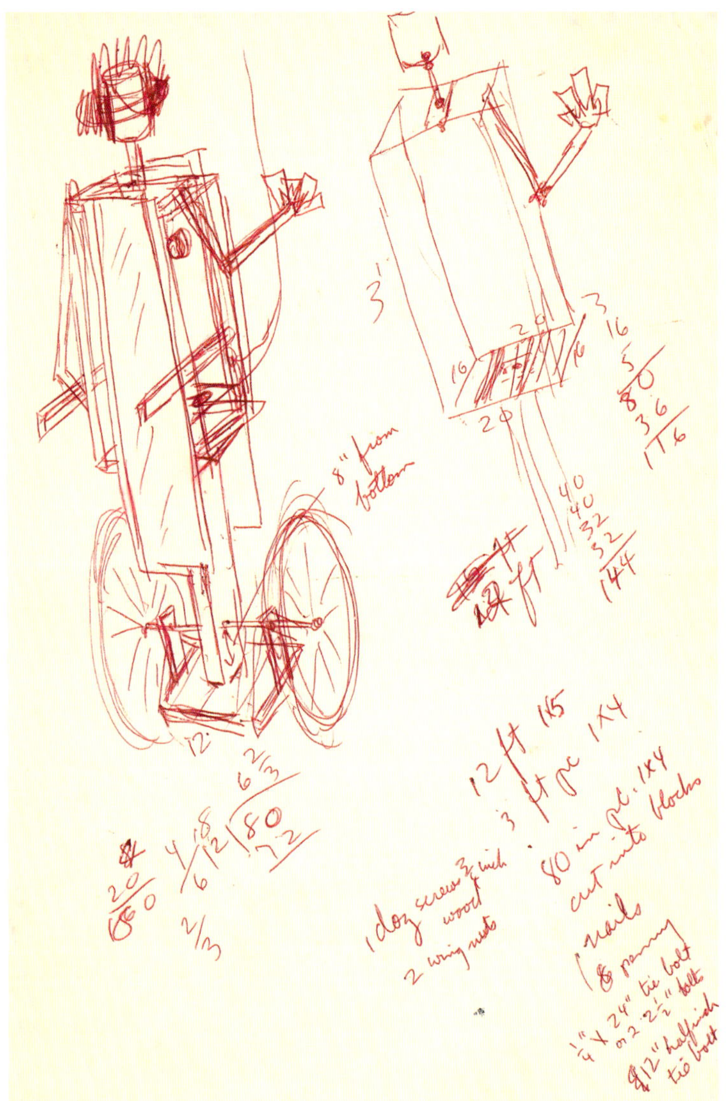

37 Sketch for Sandwich Man

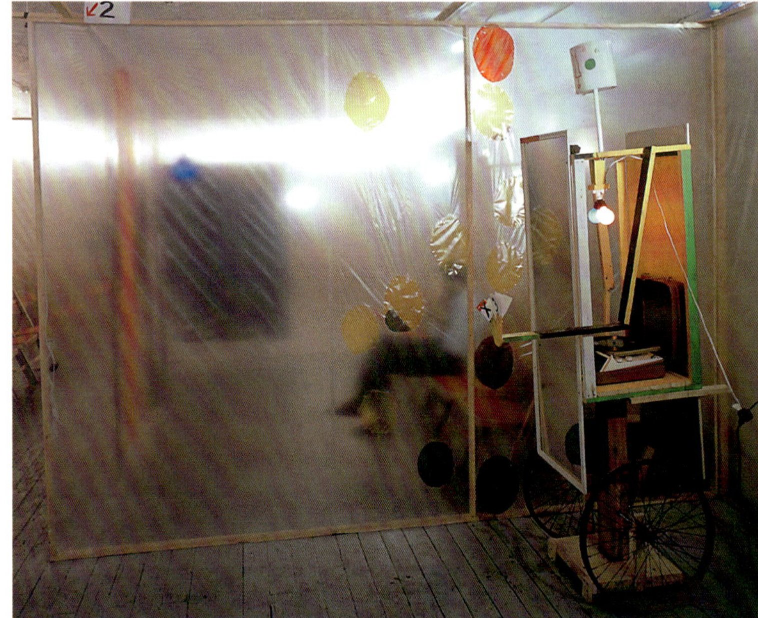

38 Sandwich Man
Photo: Scott Hyde

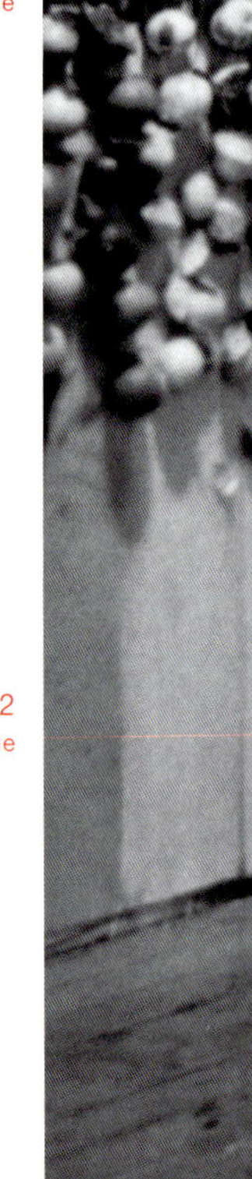

39 View of room 2
Photo: Scott Hyde

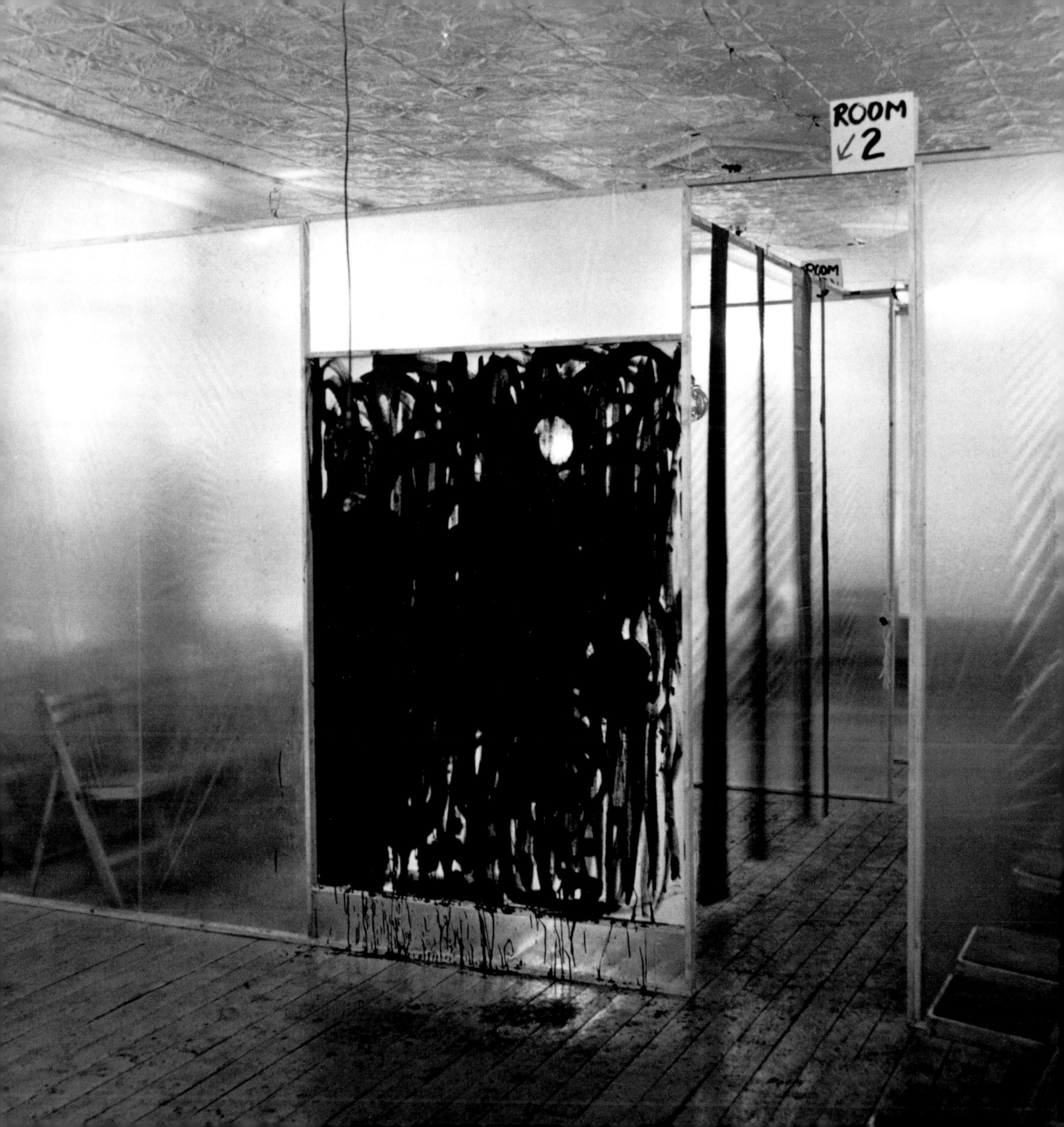
ROOM
↙2

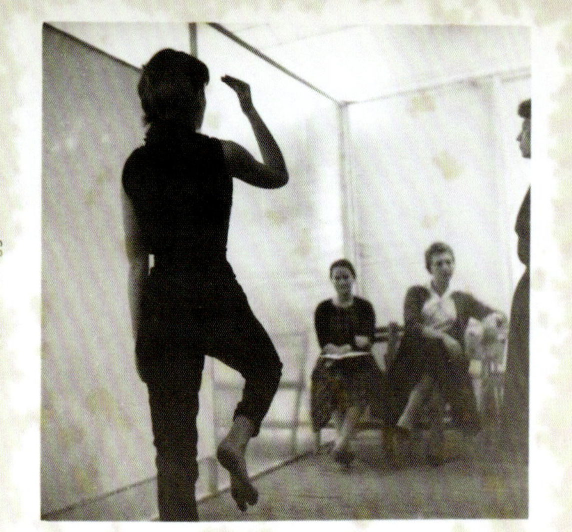

(side view)

(15)

keep arm up; with ~~other arm grasp ankle of raised foot~~. Hold for 11" (or till buzzer sounds. If at the end of the 11 count, the buzzer has not yet sounded maintain as long as possible. When tired return to straight up and down and at buzzer, walk slowly out.)

18"

40 Rosalyn Montague performing movement

41 Movement score (detail)

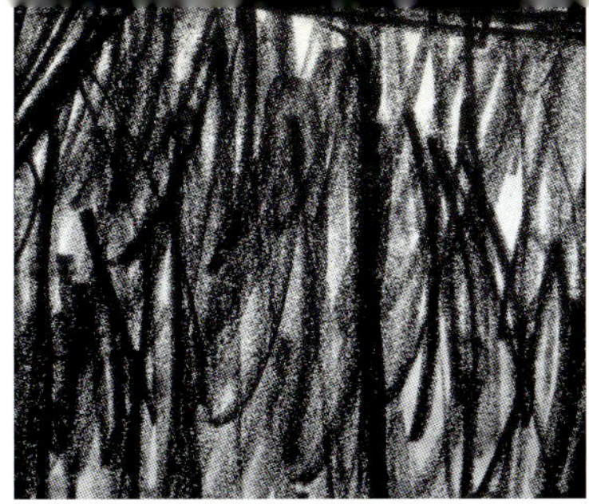

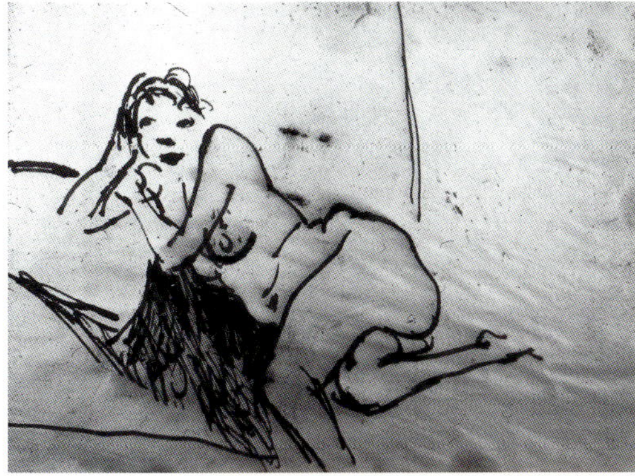

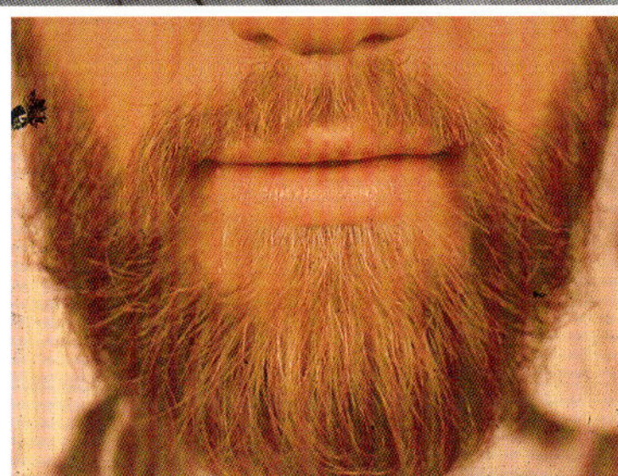

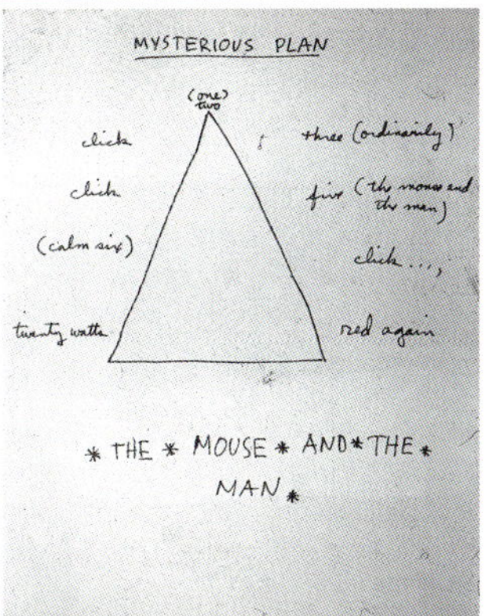

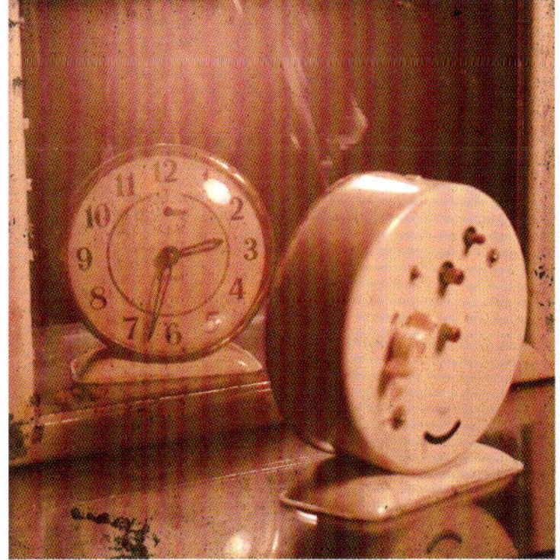

42–46 Slides shown in room 3

Lucas — Set 2 Room 3

I was about to speak yesterday on a subject most dear to you all — art. I wanted to speak then about art but I was unable to begin — for many reasons. You know with what seriousness and trembling I approach this subject. I would not treat lightly the most sacred of the soul's sanctuaries, as perhaps, perhaps unwittingly, yes unintentionally, have some of my colleagues. Thus I have thought and reflected, knowing full well how cannily the mistress of our hearts' flower can elude our very genuine, yes, certainly sincere, ~~intentions~~ to disclose her secrets. Shall we be permitted to approach, to touch, nay remove the veil? How can one not be awed and humbled before the ultimate in mysteries? Oh Hymenae! Hymenae! Yes, there are those, who, with facile word and mocking eye, would tear the veil away, make of art a toy of politics, a simple tool of causes and effects. They would have us learn the game, whose rules grasped and applied, would enable all to achieve ~~this day in the sun~~ success. These are sorry men, victims of their own design; what do they win but the dregs of a tragedy whose nature escapes them? Their prize is bitterness. The mocker mocked and was mocked in turn.

47 Text of speech read by Lucas Samaras

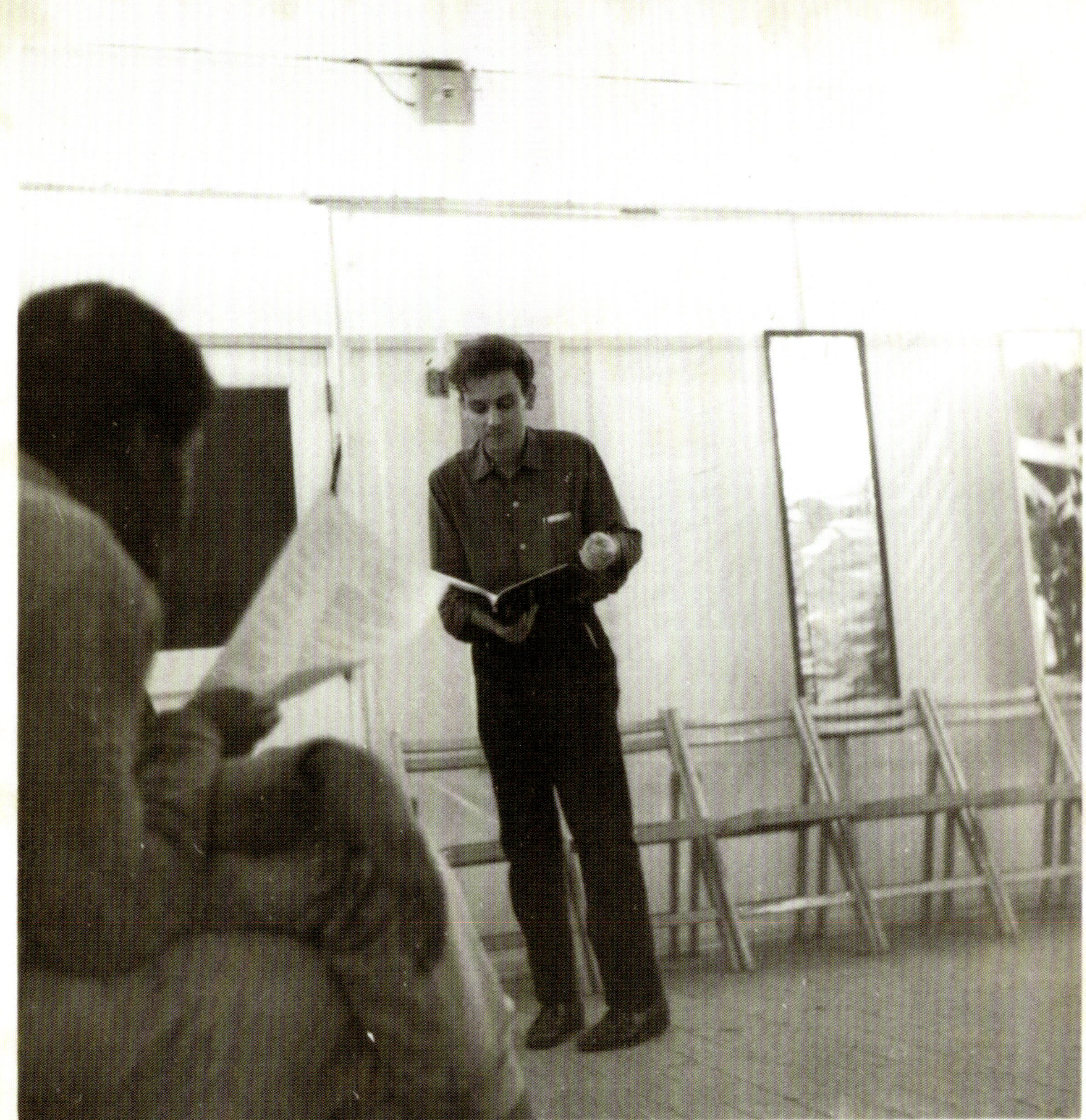

48 Lucas Samaras reading a speech

ART

Fairfield Porter

THE REUBEN GALLERY is a new gallery at 61 Fourth Avenue, New York. It plans to show *avant-garde* art that you can see nowhere else. The first exhibition is not of paintings but is an "event" consisting of eighteen "happenings," by Allan Kaprow. Kaprow has had thirteen one-man exhibitions, and he teaches art history at Rutgers University. He wishes to stretch the limits of art: he wants to make something outside the old classifications, to which one responds with several senses. Like a composer of opera, he wants to combine all the arts in one form. He is ambitious; and as a teacher conscious of history he is impatient with the brush: he resembles the critics who say, "you can't do such and such any more, it has already been done."

To see the "Eighteen Happenings" it was necessary to reserve seats in advance. During the performance different things go on in each of three different rooms, which are separated by semi-transparent plastic partitions. After two sets of events, you move, during an intermission, to another room, according to instructions given you at the door. After two more events you move to the remaining room, and so each member of the audience sees one-third of all that goes on; but you can hear and partly see what is happening in the other rooms. Actors come in, read or speak or play a musical instrument, or paint, or just move; and accompanying this are tape-recorded sounds and the activity and noise of wound-up mechanical toys. Sometimes the words spoken are drowned out by other sounds. In one room is a collage of artificial fruits, partly painted over. There are vari-colored lights.

The movements are military, disciplined and solemn: the words spoken have a similar solemnity, the fragments of ideas are romanticized, there is something about time from T. S. Eliot, phrases like "art: dear to you all" and "the mocker mocked." A game is stiffly played according to plan by two players with cubical blocks.

THE details, like the details of collage, are ready-made: reminiscences of sets by Rauschenberg for dances by Cunningham, of Cage's music (this in the quality of timing), of modern poetry, of Dada and German Expressionism. The action is monolithic, the materials of the setting flimsy, and the voices have an unrelieved seriousness. Kaprow's method is almost the opposite of most artists, literary or visual, who make something out of clichés or ordinary things or rubbish: he uses art, and he makes clichés. Kaprow debases what he quotes and what he refers to. If he wants to prove that certain things can't be done again because they have already been done, he couldn't be more convincing. The "Eighteen Happenings" devalue all art by a meaningless and deliberate surgery. And the final totality is without character, it never takes off from the sidewalk.

Avant-garde art has the merit of surprise. Kaprow's *avant-garde* "event" constantly disappoints one's expectation of surprise. Like so many science fiction movies about the future, his subject matter is the undigested immediate past.

10-24-59
The NATION

49 Review of *18 Happenings in 6 Parts*

Dear Fairfield—

It is with some hesitation that I write to you in reference to your recent review in <u>the Nation</u> of my happenings. Some of the reasons for this lie in the nature of common rules-of-the-game which I trust you can understand. Others derive from the evident differences in our respective values, values which are not apt to be mutually acceptable nor change very much in the future. That this latter is conducive to misunderstandings appears truistic —— yet so much the more reason is there for reflecting upon it, since you have judged my work, and now I am about to comment on this judgement.

For some reason that is mysterious to me there is no reviewer who has followed my professional activities so consistently as you have. Why? Is it mere coincidence? The accident of editorial assignments? I cannot believe it, for others, responding unfavorably or uninterestedly have specifically requested thereafter to be released from such assignments. . . . I therefore imagine that you are curious in some way that may be clear to you, and this causes you to return. At least you <u>come</u> to my work and in contrast to the others, it is to me a statistic of some significance.

I begin with this, thinking that

50 Draft of Kaprow's response

51–53 **The Big Laugh**
Happening, January 1960
Presented for *A Program of Happenings*
Reuben Gallery, New York

Coca-Cola, Shirley Cannonball?
Happening, February–March 1960
Presented for *The Ray Gun Spex*
Judson Gallery, New York

Sound Piece 1958
Performed at *Concert of New Music,* March 1960
Living Theater, New York

Electronic sound for Eugene Ionesco's *The Killer*
Performed March 1960
Seven Arts Playhouse, New York

Intermission Piece
Happening, June 1960
Reuben Gallery, New York

Garage Environment
Environment, September 1960
Old Bridge, New Jersey

55–60 **Apple Shrine**
Environment, November 1960
Judson Gallery, New York
Reinvented in 1991 and 1992 (twice)

51 Score for *The Big Laugh*

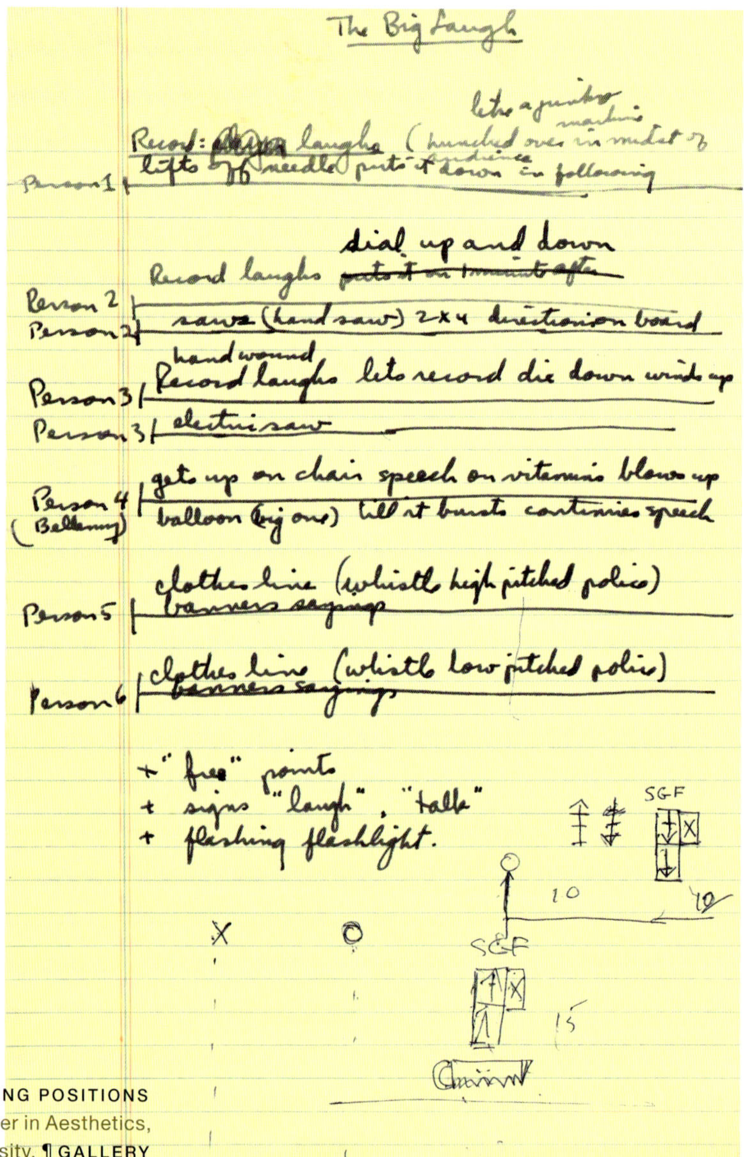

1960

LIFE EVENTS Amy Sue Kaprow, daughter, born December. ¶ TEACHING POSITIONS Assistant Professor, Department of Fine Arts, Rutgers University. Lecturer in Aesthetics, Pratt Institute, Brooklyn. ¶ AWARDS Research grant from Rutgers University. ¶ GALLERY ADMINISTRATION Director, Judson Gallery, New York. ¶ GROUP EXHIBITIONS *A Program of Happenings,* Reuben Gallery, New York, January. *The Ray Gun Spex,* Judson Gallery, New York, February–March. *The Horace Richter Collection, Contemporary American Painting and Sculpture,* Mint Museum of Art, Charlotte, North Carolina (traveled nationally), May–August. *New Forms—New Media 1,* Martha Jackson Gallery, New York, June. *New Forms—New Media 2,* Martha Jackson Gallery, New York, September–October. ¶ WRITINGS "Some Observations on Contemporary Art," in *New Forms—New Media 1,* exh. cat. (New York: Martha Jackson Gallery), n.p.

52 + 53 *The Big Laugh*

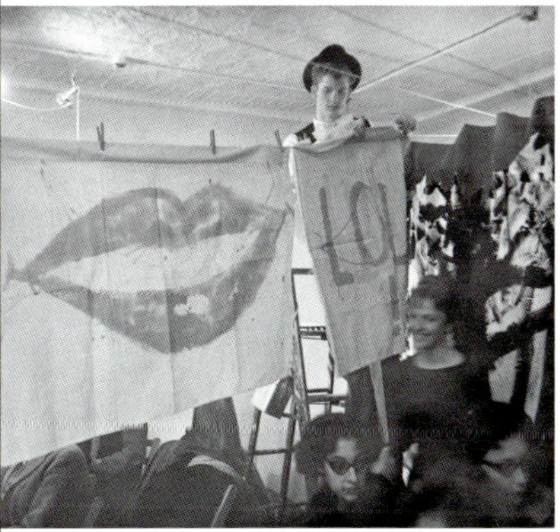

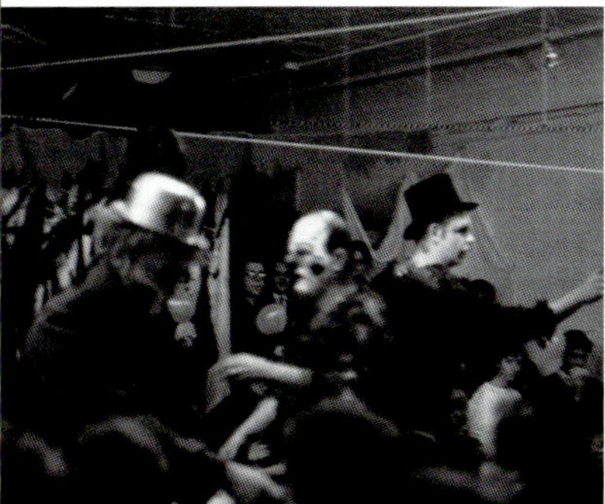

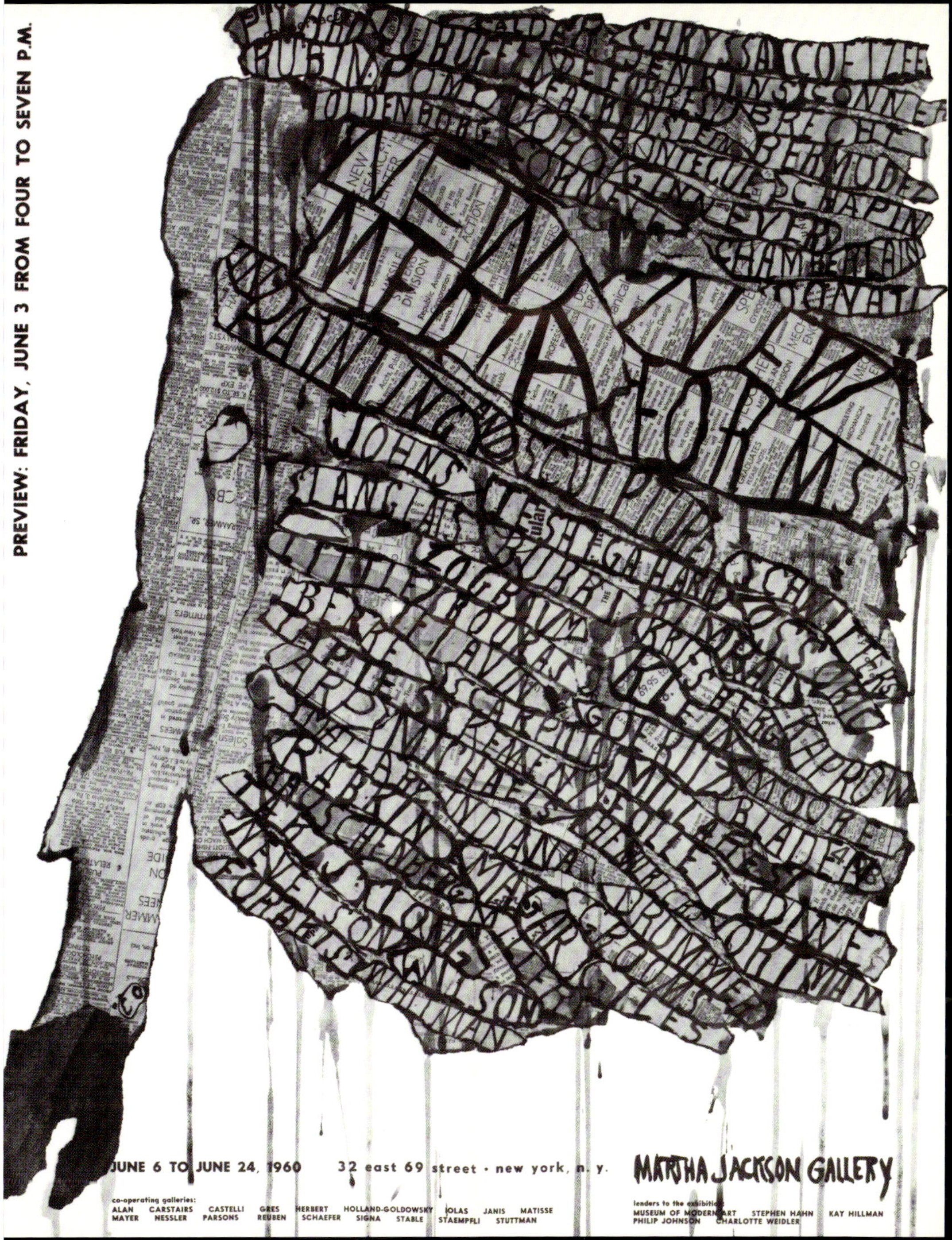

PREVIEW: FRIDAY, JUNE 3 FROM FOUR TO SEVEN P.M.

JUNE 6 TO JUNE 24, 1960 32 east 69 street · new york, n. y. MARTHA JACKSON GALLERY

co-operating galleries:
ALAN CARSTAIRS CASTELLI GRES HERBERT HOLLAND-GOLDOWSKY IOLAS JANIS MATISSE
MAYER NESSLER PARSONS REUBEN SCHAEFER SIGNA STABLE STAEMPFLI STUTTMAN

lenders to the exhibition:
MUSEUM OF MODERN ART STEPHEN HAHN KAY HILLMAN
PHILIP JOHNSON CHARLOTTE WEIDLER

54 Poster for *New Forms—New Media 1*

55 Poster for *Apple Shrine*

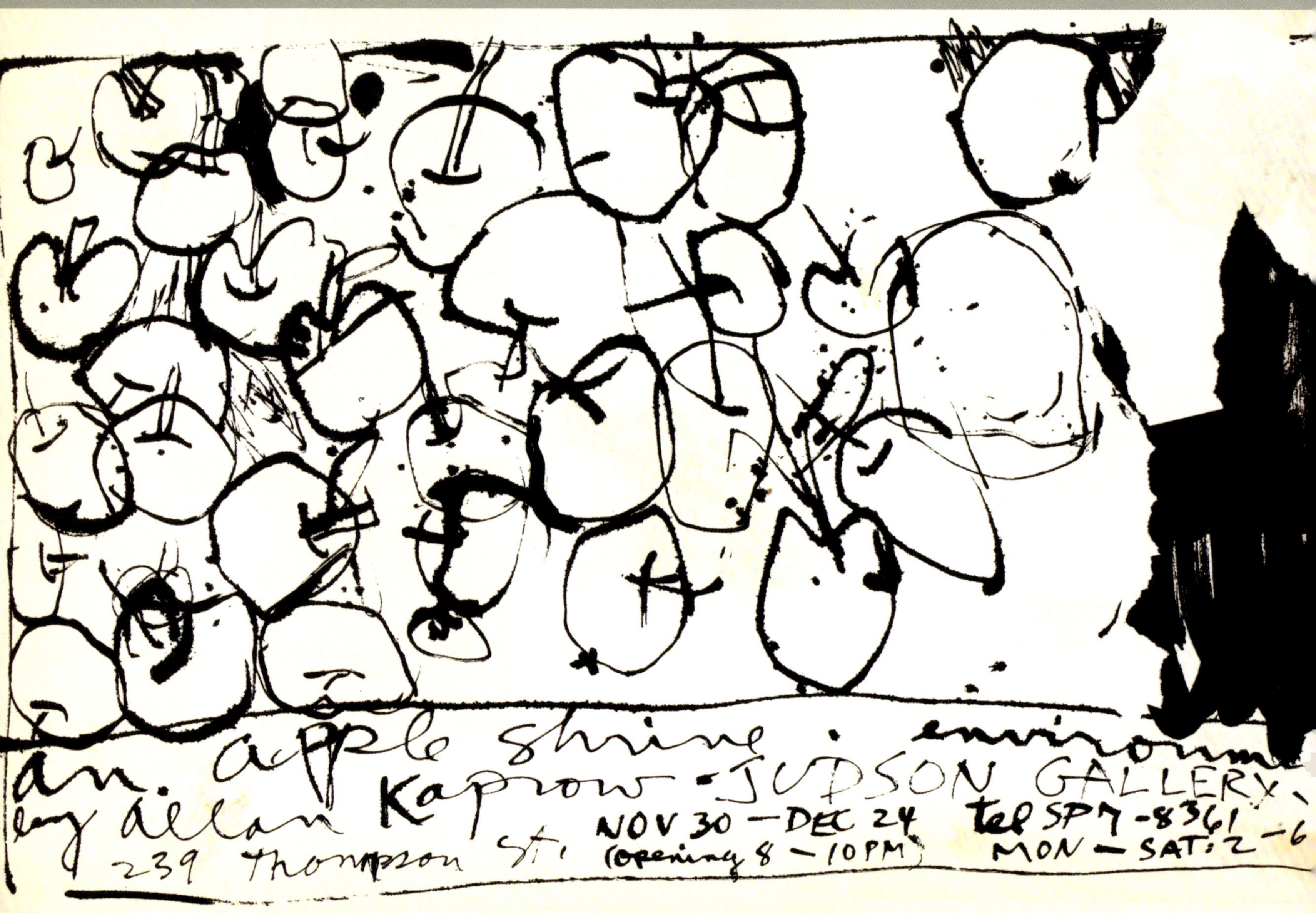

56 Altar with artificial apples
Photo: Robert R. McElroy

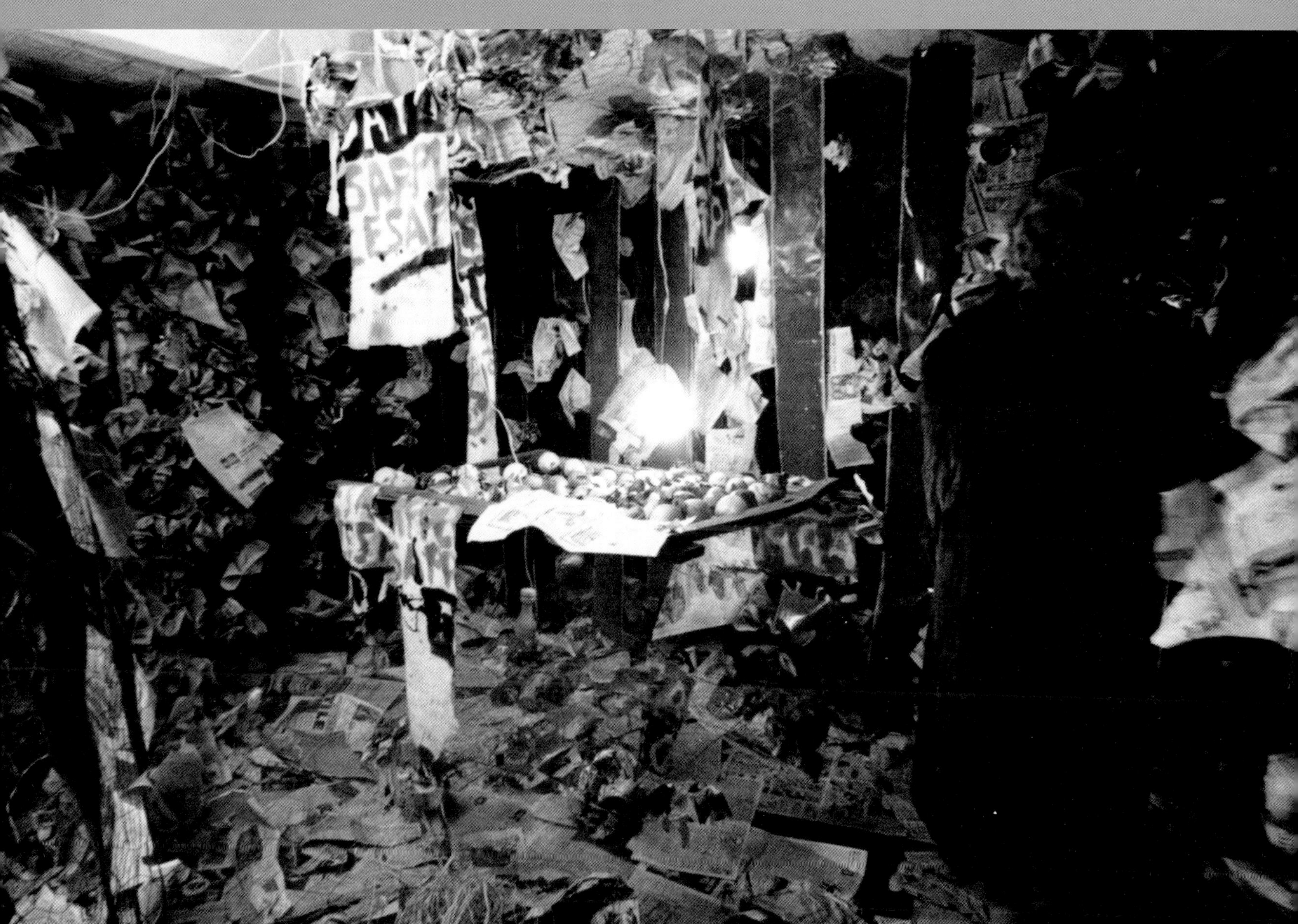

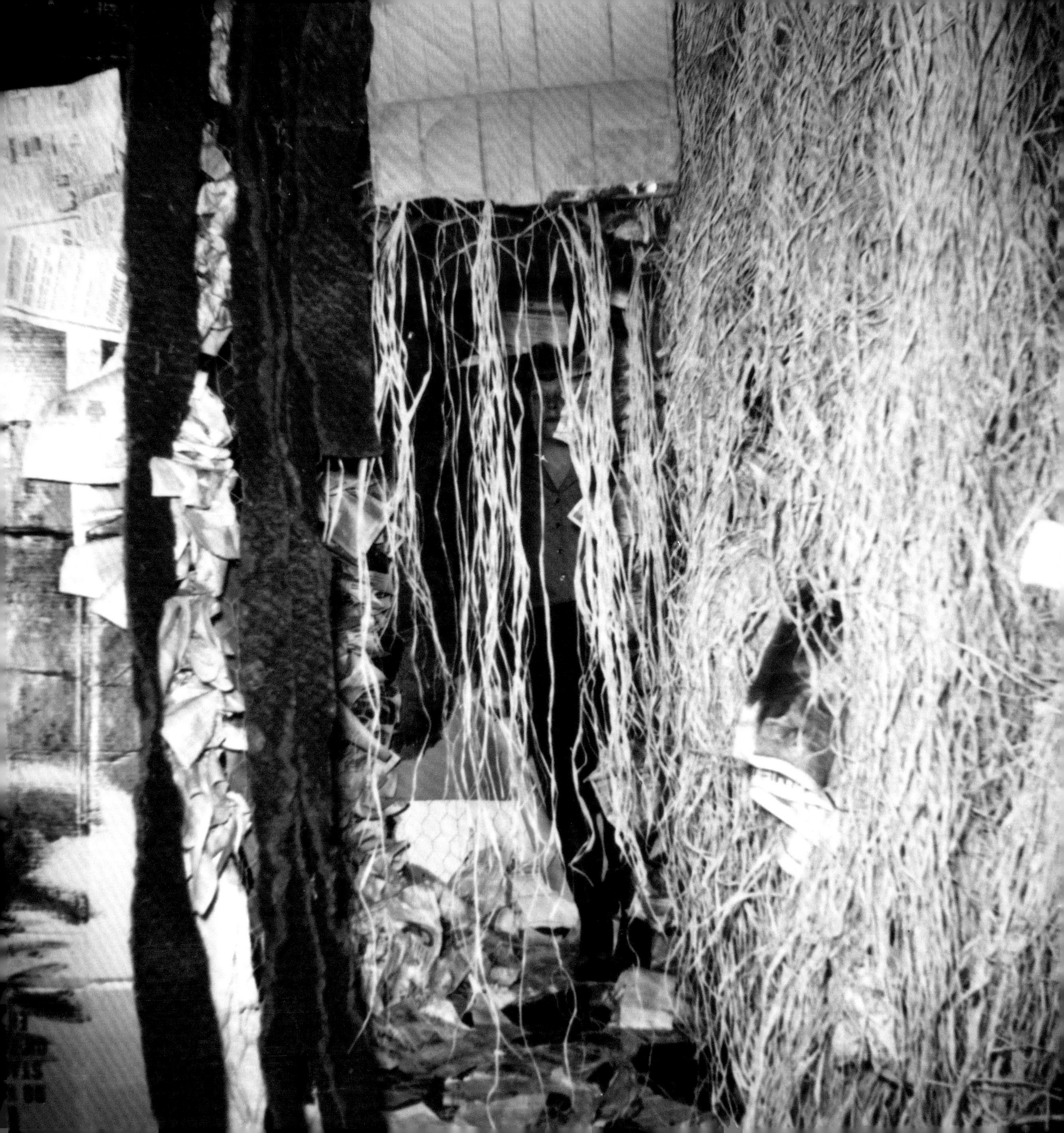

57 "Paths stuffed with paper and rags"
Photo: Robert R. McElroy

58 Score for *Apple Shrine*

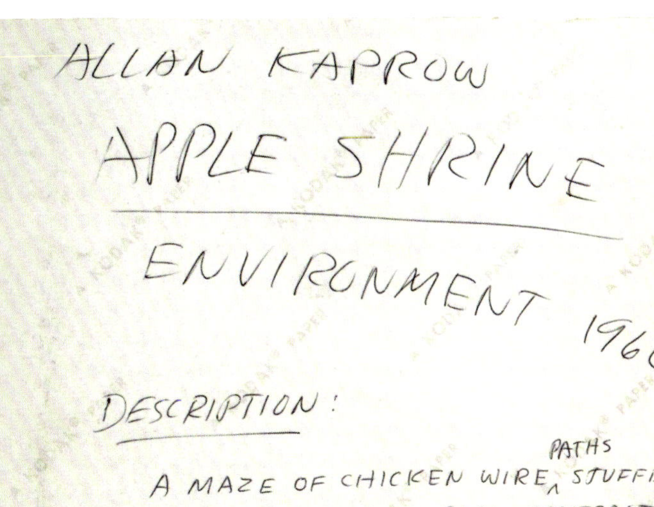

ALLAN KAPROW

APPLE SHRINE

ENVIRONMENT 1960

DESCRIPTION:

A MAZE OF CHICKEN WIRE PATHS STUFFED WITH PAPER AND RAGS. CONTRASTS OF BRIGHT AND DIM LIGHTS. FLOORS STREWN WITH RUBBLE. AN INNER ROOM WITH RED AND GREEN BANDS, MIRRORS, MORE PAPER. IN ITS CENTER, A THREE-TIERED HANGING "ALTAR" MADE OF WOOD AND CHICKEN WIRE, DECORATED WITH RAGS PRINTED WITH FRAGMENTS OF THE WORD "APPLES". ON EACH TIER, LOOSELY PLACED ARTIFICIAL APPLES. GENTLE COLORED LIGHT BULBS HUNG WITHIN THE FRUITS.

the village VOICE, *January 12, 1961*

KAPROW'S 'APPLE SHRINE'

On December 30 there closed an exhibition at the Judson Gallery by Allan Kaprow, called "An Apple Shrine." So far as I know, it received no critical reviews and was hardly noticed by the public or much of the professional art world. This was regrettable because it was an event of considerable importance.

It seemed at first surprising that it was so little noticed, for Kaprow has been well known for some years now for his "environments" and "happenings," both as an exceptionally original artist and a leader who has seen a movement develop around him. Perhaps it was the bad weather that dogged his showing, perhaps it was the holiday season, but one has strong suspicions that it may also have been part of the apparatus of the "deep freeze" that so frequently attends the early years of a radical and sometimes difficult art.

This most recent of Mr. Kaprow's environments generated one of the most densely sustained moods that has been come upon in some time. An opiate tranquility pervaded the whole with touches of unexpected excitement, causing one to feel steeped in it, even saturated.

Modern Labyrinth

This was not, however, fortuitous. It was, I should judge, induced by the plan and materials of the idea. The "Apple Shrine" was a modern labyrinth of narrow passageways constructed of chicken wire, ripped cardboard, rags, tarpaper, enormous quantities of torn and crumpled newspapers stuffed into the wire from ceiling to floor, and extending to the floor in heaps through which one slushed and waded. Intestinally wound from dark to light, almost Manichean if it were not for the softness of the atmosphere, the alleys led by a cascade of straw, some pieces of which brushed one's face. Then, a hot, bright light, revealing walls of wrapping paper dripping with black enamel; next the light slightly dimmed, and finally one emerged into the quiet of the shrine proper.

The gentleness of the light here was unforgettable. It had been somewhat cold in feeling until now with only glimpses through openings, of color and warmth, fragments of other persons moving about as though from far away. This inner area was really beautiful in that discarded sense of the word, bestowing upon the visitor a pleasant, unsought "grace." It was startling too, because it was hard to believe that such rubbish as chicken wire and newspapers (whose items could be read with an almost enchanted appropriateness, a nameless catechism of daily events), were capable of evoking such a state of attentiveness and contemplation; immediate, topical, yet suspending time to the point of something endless . . .

Four Tiers

In the center of this sanctum, hanging in four tiers of the same crude matter, was an "altar," an apple-stand, on one level of which were strewn paint spattered artificial fruit, fruit which naturally asked to be picked, faintly stimulating the memory of an old tale. Torn banners with fragments of the repeated word "apples," and a blue-and-green lighted bulb, were hung in the tiers. On the floor the newspapers were spread at random, but here smoothly. And around this enclosure were long, vertical bands of red and green in some order that appeared architectural and impossible to follow. A small mirror imbedded in the cluster of paper and wire, mistaken at first for an opening in the rough wall, suddenly revealed one's own face as if meeting a stranger.

One stayed there for a while, quietly enjoying this peaceful state, and then returned as one had come, seeing everything in reverse. A cycle of sorts was complete.

Admittedly, Mr. Kaprow's art poses problems. The exhibition is now dismantled, its materials have been carted away by the junkman, and it will not be seen again. If its vocabulary is unfamiliar, it will not remain to be judged at a later, more knowledgeable year. Its life is a present one, and only memory can carry it into the future.

Instantaneous and Dramatic

Yet I believe Allan Kaprow's art is not of itself hard to grasp, right now. On the contrary, its impact is instantaneous and dramatic. It is an art both of high seriousness and of emotional breadth. What does present a problem is its apparent lack of relation to an established cultural tradition. Beneath the surface of each confrontation with this work is the doubt that it is art at all. There is a distrust and fear of an expression which is short-lived by intention, as though this were subtly calling upon death itself. One cannot comprehend an attitude which bluntly embraces the fleeting. Perishable materials, perishable forms, perishable genius; chance, change— all conspire to damn this work and dissolve our values. Far beyond the "Apple Shrine's" actual content and humanity stands Kaprow's inadvertent quarrel with all the vapid glories, qualities and eternities which we think are History.

—Theodore Tucker
South Lincoln, Massachusetts

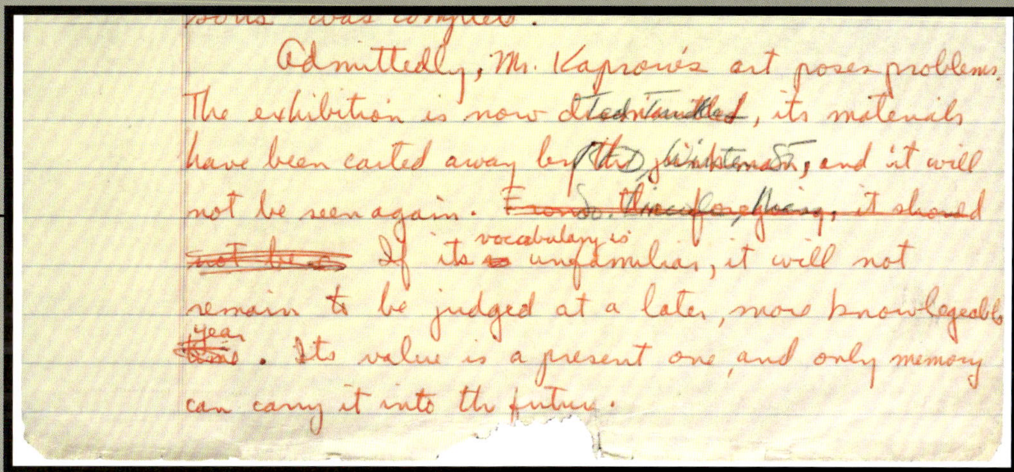

was complete.

Admittedly, Mr. Kaprow's art poses problems. The exhibition is now dismantled, its materials have been carted away by the junkman, and it will not be seen again. ~~From the foregoing, it should not be~~ If its vocabulary is unfamiliar, it will not remain to be judged at a later, more knowledgeable year. Its value is a present one, and only memory can carry it into the future.

60 Kaprow's handwritten draft (detail)

59 Review published by Kaprow under the pseudonym Theodore Tucker

TEACHING POSITIONS Assistant Professor, Department of Fine Arts, Rutgers University. Lecturer in Aesthetics, Pratt Institute, Brooklyn. Associate Professor, Department of Fine Arts, State University of New York, Stony Brook. ¶ **AWARDS** Research grant from Rutgers University. Research grant from State University of New York, Stony Brook. ¶ **GALLERY ADMINISTRATION** Codirector, Judson Gallery, New York. ¶ **GROUP EXHIBITIONS** *Art in Motion,* Stedelijk Museum, Amsterdam (traveled internationally), March–April. *Environments, Situations, Spaces,* Martha Jackson Gallery, New York, May–June. ¶ **FESTIVALS** Open House '61, University of Michigan, Ann Arbor, May. ¶ **WRITINGS** "'Happenings' in the New York Scene," *ARTnews* 60, no. 3: 36–39, 58–62. "Irving Kriesberg," in *Irving Kriesberg,* exh. cat. (New York: Jewish Museum), n.p. Statement in *Environments, Situations, Spaces,* exh. cat. (New York: Martha Jackson Gallery), n.p.

1961

STOCKROOM

This environment will require the following minimum space and materials. The minimum space, number of materials and proportions between them may be extended indefinitely whenever it seems appropriate to a given exhibition area, as long as the proportions are basically maintained.

SPACE

20 feet long by 11 feet wide by 7 feet high

MATERIALS

34 cardboard cartons, of which 7 are large (from 3 feet to over life-size), 17 are medium sized and 10 are small.

52 pieces of newspaper.

Enough newspaper and flattened cartons to cover the floor area of the environment.

1 bottle of schoolchild's black watercolor paint.

1 " " " white " "

2 inexpensive brushes (one for each bottle).

2 sticks (one for each bottle).

1 small can of commercial black spray enamel.

1 " " " " white " "

1 box of charcoal.

1 " " large, soft schoolchild's white pastel or chalk.

1 roll of commercial adhesive tape ("Scotch" or "masking" tape).

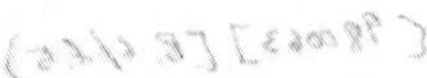

61 + 62 Score for *Stockroom,* pp. 1–2

2.

MATERIALS (continued)

1 roll of nylon (plastic) cord such as used by fishermen and decorators.

1 roll of picture wire (if necessary).

36 or more eye screws (if necessary).

38 small "S" hooks.

1 common household bulb (150 w.), socket and enough electric wire to hang it from above.

1 stepladder and 1 small table, preferably dirty.

GENERAL INSTRUCTIONS

Perhaps in view of the unfamiliar nature of such a work as this, a few suggestions regarding its composition are permitted. Basically, the work is to be conceived organically rather than geometrically, though one should not interpret these words in any absolute way. The "feel" of it should be one of artlessness or stylelessness, therefore. This of course requires of the composer the utmost in responsibility and devotion to his job. While flexibility is intended within certain limits, license is to be discouraged. The composer's sense of responsibility to what he does, furthermore, may be conceived in a spirit of either fun or gravity, as long as his feelings are natural and spontaneous.

To achieve this, it may help to consider the form of the work and the use of one's materials. Materials and their arrangement are to "grow" from each other. They are therefore to reveal as few repetitions as possible. The composer should try to avoid similar sizes of elements, similar groupings, similar heights and

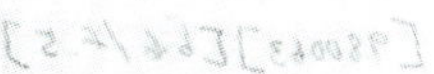

Chapel
Proposal for an Environment, January 1961
Version of *Stockroom* (1961)
For William Seitz, Museum of Modern Art, New York

A Spring Happening
Happening, March 1961
Reuben Gallery, New York

Night
Happening, May 1961
Presented for Open House '61
University of Michigan, Ann Arbor

61–65 **Stockroom**
Environment, May–September 1961
Presented for *Art in Motion*
Moderna Museet, Stockholm
Reinvented in 1991, 1992, 2006, and 2007

66–70 **Yard**
Environment, May–June 1961
Presented for *Environments, Situations, Spaces*
Sculpture garden at Martha Jackson Gallery, New York
Reinvented in 1967, 1970, 1981, 1982, 1984, 1986, 1990, 1991, 1998, 2003, 2006, and 2007

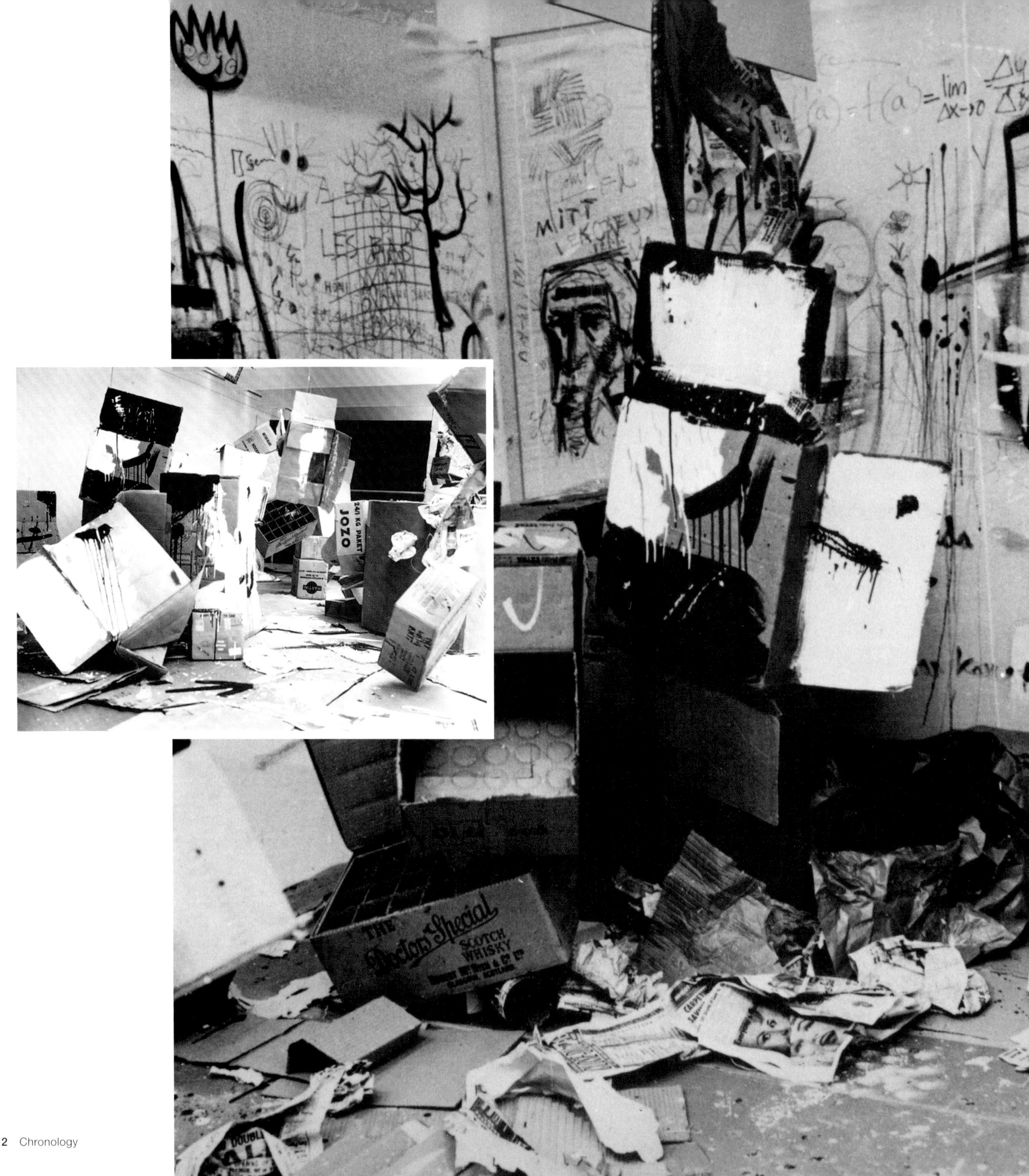
JOZO
THE
Doctor's Special
SCOTCH
WHISKY
MITT

65 Score for *Stockroom*, p. 3

3.

placements of papers and boxes, similar spaces in between them, repeated cuts, tears, crumples, scrawls, strokes, etc. This should be attended to from all views, inside the work and from without. The quality of moves should be as human as possible, ranging from hard to soft, rapid to slow, dense to open, heavy to light, restrained to excited, etc.

Any person (or small group) may secure the materials and compose the environment, except that once decided, that person (or group) should follow through until the work appears complete. The composition may then continue to change (like the seasons, like furniture in a room, or chessmen ...) from day to day.

Any visitor to the exhibition is permitted one of the following changes: He may paint, spray, scratch, draw, write or print with one color, on a box or paper, either chosen from those on the floor or those hanging. He may move a box on the floor within the environment's general floor area. He may unhook a hanging box and hang it on a free hook elsewhere, or he may interchange any two hanging boxes. A stepladder and table with materials are provided for these moves.

SPECIFIC INSTRUCTIONS

The boxes are to be hung in such a way as to permit people to move amongst them. They are to be attached by hooks to single nylon cords hanging from the ceiling. (If it is impractical to fix these cords to the ceiling, picture wires may be screwed into wall mouldings and strung tightly overhead in some irregular fashion, which will permit the nylon cords to be arranged unmechanically).

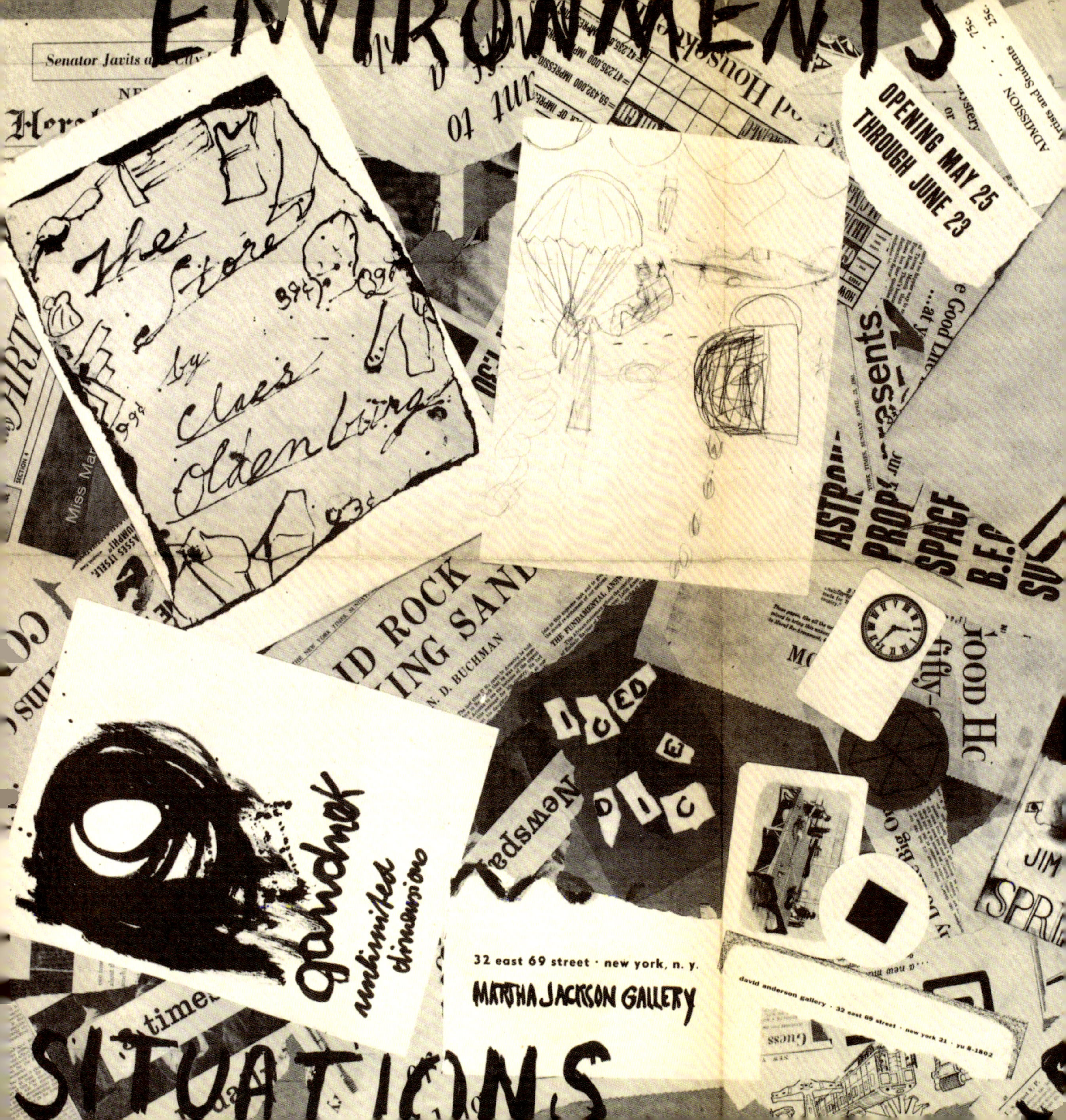
ENVIRONMENTS
OPENING MAY 25
THROUGH JUNE 23
The Store
by
claes Oldenburg
32 east 69 street · new york, n. y.
MARTHA JACKSON GALLERY
david anderson gallery · 32 east 69 street · new york 21 · yu 8-1802
SITUATIONS

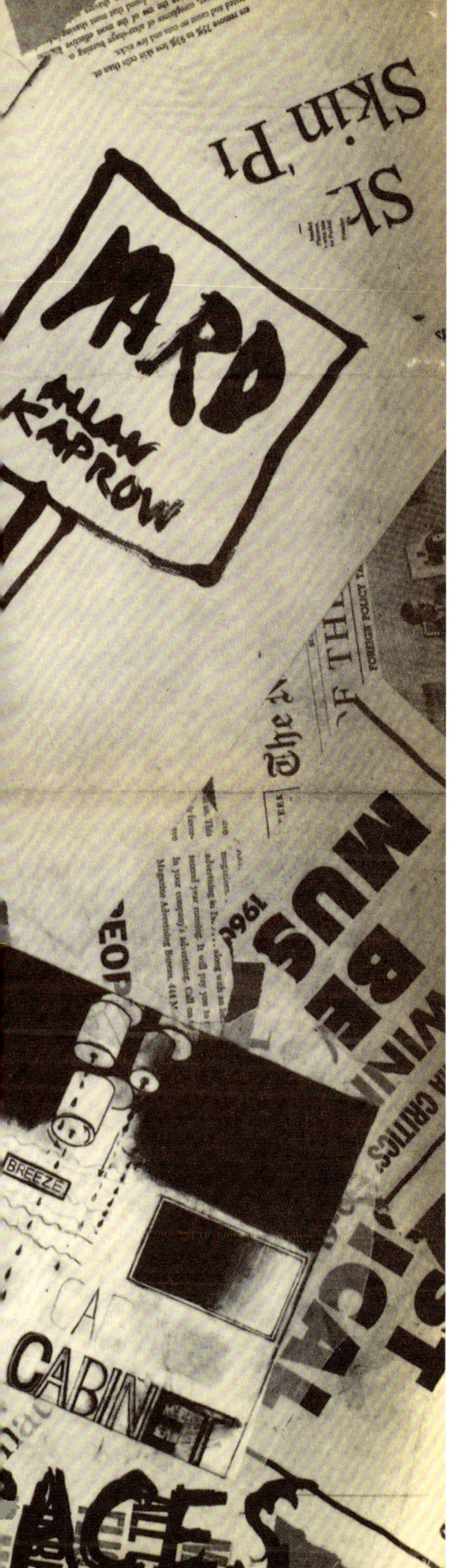

66 Poster for *Environments, Situations, Spaces*

67 Overhead view

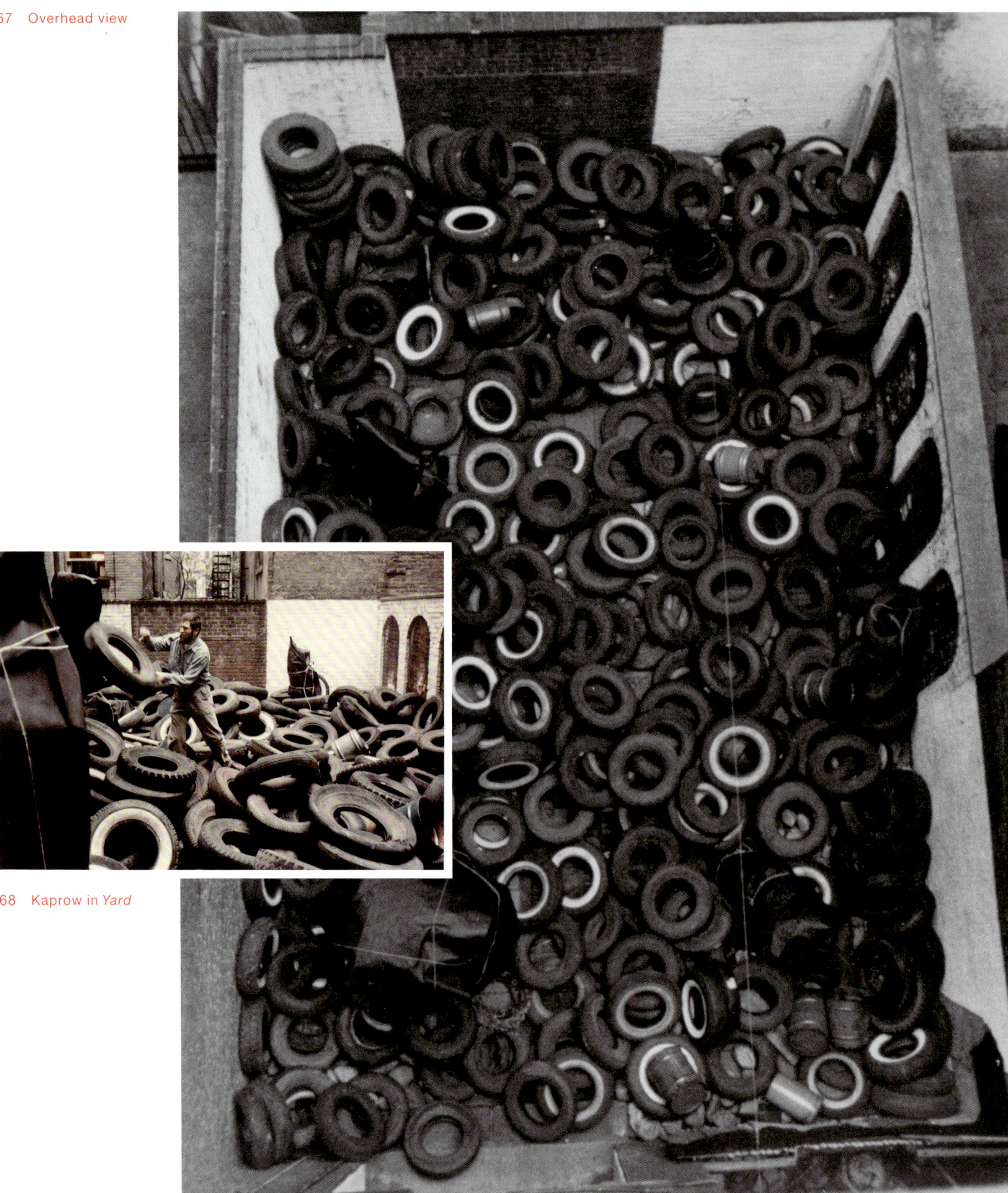

68 Kaprow in *Yard*

Allan Kaprow

Among the things I have felt to be important in the conception of my work is the idea that it could be called art, or ordinary nature. I devote great effort to balancing what I do as precariously as possible on this tightrope of identities. I find here a certain drama. And then, more crucially, life and art begin flowing together in an easy give and take.

YARD thus looks neither exactly like a junk pile nor any of the usual arts, nor even a fun-house (for in this the themes and forms are also quite conventionalized). Yet YARD could relate to any or all fo them.

Beyond this general objective, each Environment or Happening has its source in things I care deeply about. For instance, in this case, dumps, and the shanty-huts built by those strange madmen who divide their world with rats....

the village VOICE, *July* 6, 1961

'ENVIRONMENTS' at MARTHA JACKSON's

The "terrible children" invaded Martha Jackson's Gallery last May and June with more of those baffling non-commercial commodities, things youn can't use or sell or label even, which nobody could be too clear about why they should be encouraged or endured much less considered the prestige items they obviously a.e, or else why would Miss Jackson (whose commercial acumen is well known) clutter up her fashionable yard with a bunch of junky car tires that she permitted Alan Kaprow to put there?

No Dark Meanings

I don't know what Miss Jackson thought about those tires. I didn't think much myself, I mean I perceived a bunch of tires there in the yard and then asked my son if he wanted to stay and play around in them while I went upstairs to see the rest. I know Mr. Kaprow is against people finding dark serious meanings, commentaries on the state of the union, etc., in these situations, and I agree, there seems no pressing reason to find anything other than what you see; in fact the cultural references are usually a dodge and a distraction right off, a way of trying to account for what seems incomprehensible—how, say, Art and a mess of old tires could possibly be related. (And I don't mean to imply that they are, although they might be.)

Well, this was an unusual show. The gallery put out a fine brochure, tall and thin, called "Environments, Situations, Spaces," containing "statements" by each artist preceded by their handsome autographs. George Brecht is always clean as a clipped wing, airy, cheerful, and self-disappearing. He has a little white room just off the yard with a nice white chair in it, comfortable for a Cape Cod porch and adjoining Jim Dine's "Spring Cabinet." Brecht's autograph in the brochure is an inch wide. His first two statements are: A. nothing-special; b. no theory.

Inexhaustible List

Whereas Claes Oldenburg sears his page with a mud-luscious Whitmanesque catalogue of the materials of art, and for Oldenburg the list is inexhaustible because he is for an art that is everything, everything that is "that does something other than sit on its ass in a museum," and preferably everything that is *not* self-consciously refined, in other words that is raw, quick, smelly, holy, many small "sweet and stupid" acts of ungracious side-splitting, nose-blowing living that are supposed to be left for keeps in dirty abandoned corners. Oldenburg's "Store" has that unkempt look; the items hang in blobbish disregard for civilized order; the store articles are sculptured in relief with muslin strips dipped in plaster and placed over chicken wire, then painted with enamel to give the business a high dripping festive gloss.

These environments, situations, spaces are not going any place; they're not on the market for immortality; they're just not negotiable at all, except for tempting traffic with the eye and heart that is looking for more or less anything, or ready to stumble on something; and even that is saying too much, or too little, and no doubt Robert Whitman is right when he says that "this whole business has been complicated by people who say all smart things . . . "

—Jill Johnston

A Service For The Dead, II

A Happening
(performed August, 1962 as part of the Ergo Suits Festival,
Bridge-hampton, New York)

Setting: A high, grassy dune running parallel to the water's edge separates the beach from large tracts of potato fields stretching away from it in all directions. A farmhouse in the distance, and a few shacks near the dume make up the site's human community. The beach itself runs about a hundred yards down to the water. Large breakers hit the shoreline, rising and lowering with the wind.

Event: In a hollow at the foot of the inland side of the dune, near one of the shacks, a group of people stand looking. They watch the top of the dune between two high poles capped with loose clusters of tarpaper. Figures come slowly into view from the other side carrying cartons, fluttering bedspreads, wheeling a bicycle, rolling a few oil drums, and a car tire, dragging some junkmetal. They pass along the crest and then down out of sight.

Emerging from the shack, a man dragging a large bundle of something, pushes through the group of people, walks up the dune and over, disappearing. Another man, towing a gas-powered electric generator, does the same. He drags it to a spot on the beach where he begins connecting it to appropriate wires.

Someone from the seaward side of the dune comes up to the top holding a stick with a cloth tied to it and motions the group in the hollow to come. He takes a few steps down the far side and returns, still beckoning. A second man joins him.

The people then make their way through the high grass, climb the dune and descend to the beach, where they see ten more poles with tarpaper spaced randomly down to the water. There are various pieces of wood stuck into the sand here and there, each topped with a cloth marker.

Work is begun on a partially-built six foot high platform. The cloth-topped wood is fetched for this purpose, and [illegible] person who is asked to help, brings them over to the carpenters, now building loudly and matter-of-factly, banging nails and shouting orders. One of them, meanwhile, has started the generator motor, and to this noise he adds the grinding sound of an electric ratchet-wrench which he uses to tighten bolts in the construction. The carpenters carry on animatedly about getting the job done quickly, the loadbearing strength of the boards, etc., and ask the people every once in a while how it looks, and so forth.

When the job is finished, they pick up a small bed spring lying nearby and put it on top of the platform.

A shrill whistle from the dune. The carpenters turn around and, pointing, yell hey!, hey!..... Three fellows with plastic bags tied around their heads rush over the crest and roll down the dune,

TEACHING POSITIONS Associate Professor, Department of Fine Arts, State University of New York, Stony Brook. ¶ **AWARDS** Research grant from State University of New York, Stony Brook. ¶ **SOLO EXHIBITIONS** *Words,* Smolin Gallery, New York, September. ¶ **GROUP EXHIBITIONS** *Art 1963—A New Vocabulary,* Arts Council of the Young Men's-Young Women's Hebrew Association (YM-YWHA), Philadelphia, October–November. ¶ **FESTIVALS** Ergo Suits Festival, various locations, New York, August. ¶ **WRITINGS** "About 'Words,'" in *Words,* exh. booklet (New York: Smolin Gallery), n.p.

1962

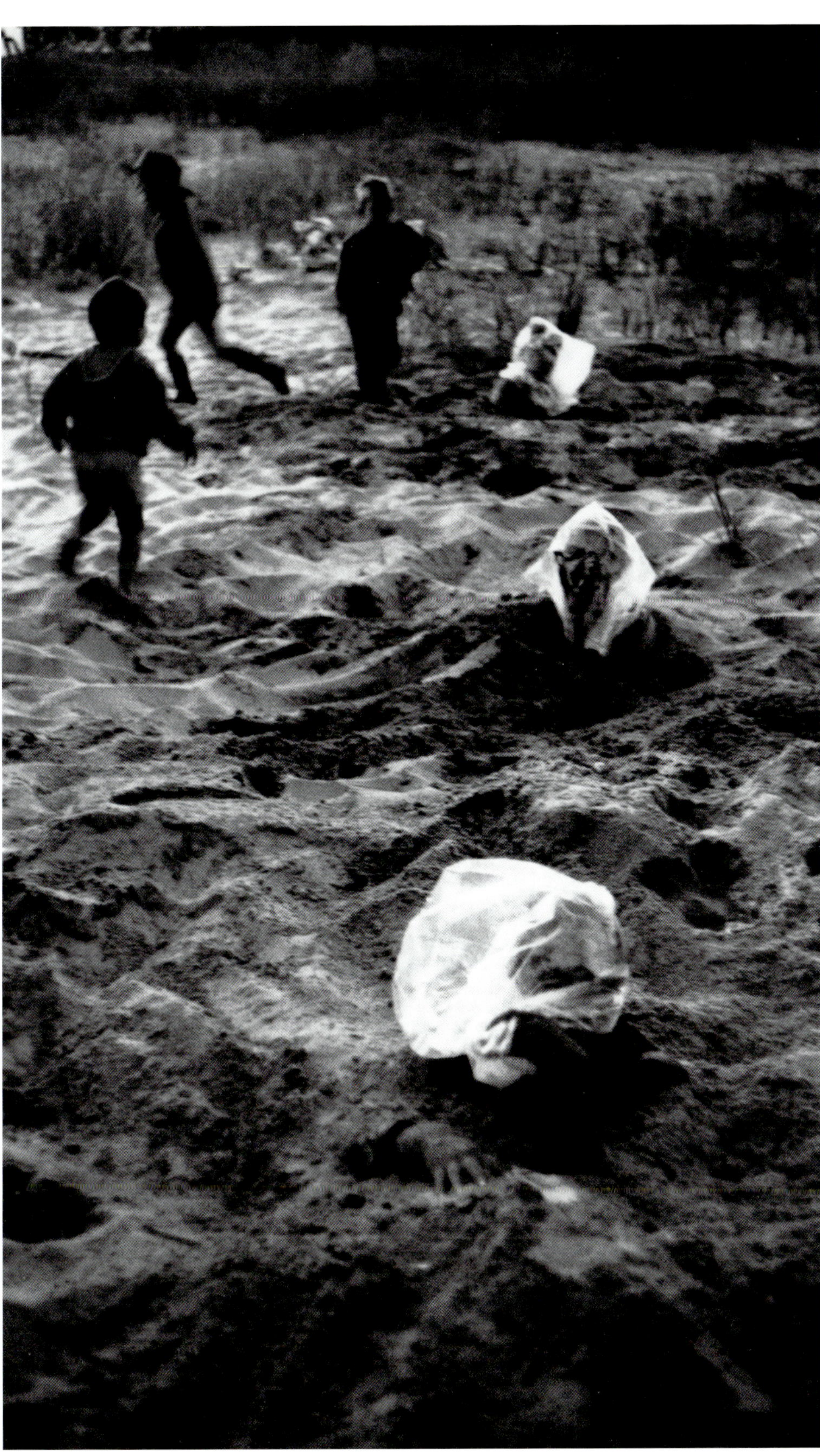

A Service for the Dead I
Happening, March 1962
Sponsored by New York Poets Theater
Maidman Playhouse, New York

Mirrors: A Happening
Happening, May 1962
Not realized

Sweeping
Happening, August 1962
Presented for Ergo Suits Festival
Woodstock, New York
Reinvented in 1988

71–73 **A Service for the Dead II**
Happening, August 1962
Presented for Ergo Suits Festival
Bridgehampton, New York

74–77 **Words**
Environment, September 1962
Smolin Gallery, New York
Reinvented in 1962, 1967 (twice), 1975, 1984, 1991, 1992, 2005, 2006, and 2007

Words
Environment, October–November 1962
Fine Arts Department, State University of New York, Stony Brook

72 Three men covered in sand
Photo: Robert R. McElroy

(Service II , cont'd)

twisting and turning, throwing up sand as they gyrate towards three large pits at the edge of the crowd. They fall into the pits, crouching so that only their heads and shoulders stick up. ~~xxxxxxxx xxxxxx~~ During this time, the carpenters walk slowly over to them and, taking up shovels, begin to fill in the [illegible] with sand. After a few shovelsfull they motion to the nearest people and ask them to take over, and suggest casually that the three men can be covered just up to their noses. They return to the platform and grab some quart bottles of beer from underneath, climb up on it and begin to drink.

As the three men are buried to the nose, wails are heard from behind the dune. A girl, all shrouded in loosely wound plastic film, appears. She stands for a moment and then she, too, falls down the embankment, but slowly this time. Just as slowly, she slithers through the sand toward the platform. Meanwhile, the carpenters are drinking heavily, but are spitting and puking mouthfuls of the beer over the side. The girl reaches the platform and lies there motionless, but the men continue drinking and spitting beer, often right on her.

They throw down their bottles, jump down, pick up the girl, lifting her onto the bed spring, and then walk to the three fellows buried in the sand and start digging them out. As they work, a large, bright light in a circular reflector made of sheets of loosely applied tinfoil, mounted at the water's edge, begins to blink. Low at first,but getting louder, are booming sounds from the dune. As each man is freed, he trudges back towards the booming and disappears over the top.

Once more the carpenters return to the platform, and this time lift the bedspring with the girl down to the ground some ten feet away. They then ~~xxxxxx~~ crumple up some paper and rags around the platform's base, add kerosene,and set it on fire.

The drumming sounds are still rather low but pulsating in the distance. A man in the crowd suddenly screams, brandishing a tree limb over his head, and rushes, yelling, to the water. He slashes at the waves, wading deeper and deeper until he sinks and is washed ashore. The booming gets louder and more insistent.

From the sounds' source, horns, pots and pans and other metallic noises, are heard joining the booming. ~~xx~~ They increase in loudness, and a ship-distress horn fills the air. The booming diminishes as these new sounds increase. Five processioners come down the dune now, and march with their soundmakers banging and blaring, past the burning platform, and stop near the girl. Withe carpenters they lift her upon their shoulders and walk slowly toward the big blinking light. One by one, with the exception of the ship-distress horn that continues to signal, their noisemakers are dropped as they carry the girl to the water. They go out as far as they can and when the first wave hits, go under and in turn are washed ashore where they lay still.

-- Allan Kaprow

Allan Kaprow
791 Glen Cove Ave.
Glen Head, N. Y.

WORDS

An Environment

Two rooms, one 9' x 9', leading railroad style into another, 6' x 6', each 8' high, constructed within a room. Doorways covered by white cloths.

Outside first room is a large electric sign saying "WORDS". Red and white lights blinking all around top of the walls. Inside, 4 lights hanging at eye level: a blue, a yellow, a green, and a white one, which alone blinks. Two vertical rows of lights, also not blinking, from floor to ceiling, on opposite walls. On the other two walls are five continuous rolls of cloth, also floor to ceiling, on which are stenciled words. Operated manually, these rolls, containing fixed elements, can be aligned variously with each other to make sense-groups or non-sense, as one wishes. Covering the other two walls are word strips on paper (lettered by a group of friends and myself and derived at random from a number of poetry books, newspapers, comic magazines, the telephone book, popular love stories, etc.; these having been shuffled, I composed them into wall-sized poems.) Overhead, are crudely-lettered signs urging the visitors to roll the rolls, to tear off more word strips from stacks nailed to a center-post, and to staple them over the ones alrady there; in addition, they are exhorted to play the victrolas and listen to the records I had made, of talk, lectures, shouts, advertizements, ramblings of nonsense etc.-- either singly or all together.

In the smaller room, painted blue, illuminated by a single, weak light bulb and covered overhead by a plastic film, the atmosphere is very close and intimate (in contrast to the brash open feeling of the first room). Many strips of cloth hang from the sheet of plastic filling the entire space; and above, through its filminess one can see crumpled newspapers scattered here and there on top. A visitor has to push through these hangings which brush his face like cobwebs. Clipped onto these hangings were many small pieces of paper with handwritten notes from, and to, different people. Near the doorway are a pencil, clips, and more paper for additional notes. Then, hanging all around the walls from strings are large colored chalks. (I and friends had written and drawn already on these walls to start things off and thereafter the visitors added whatever they wished.) Finally a record-player on the floor plays whispers when it is turned on.

This environment therefore is transformed everyday.

76 + 77 “Wall-sized poems”
Photos: Robert R. McElroy

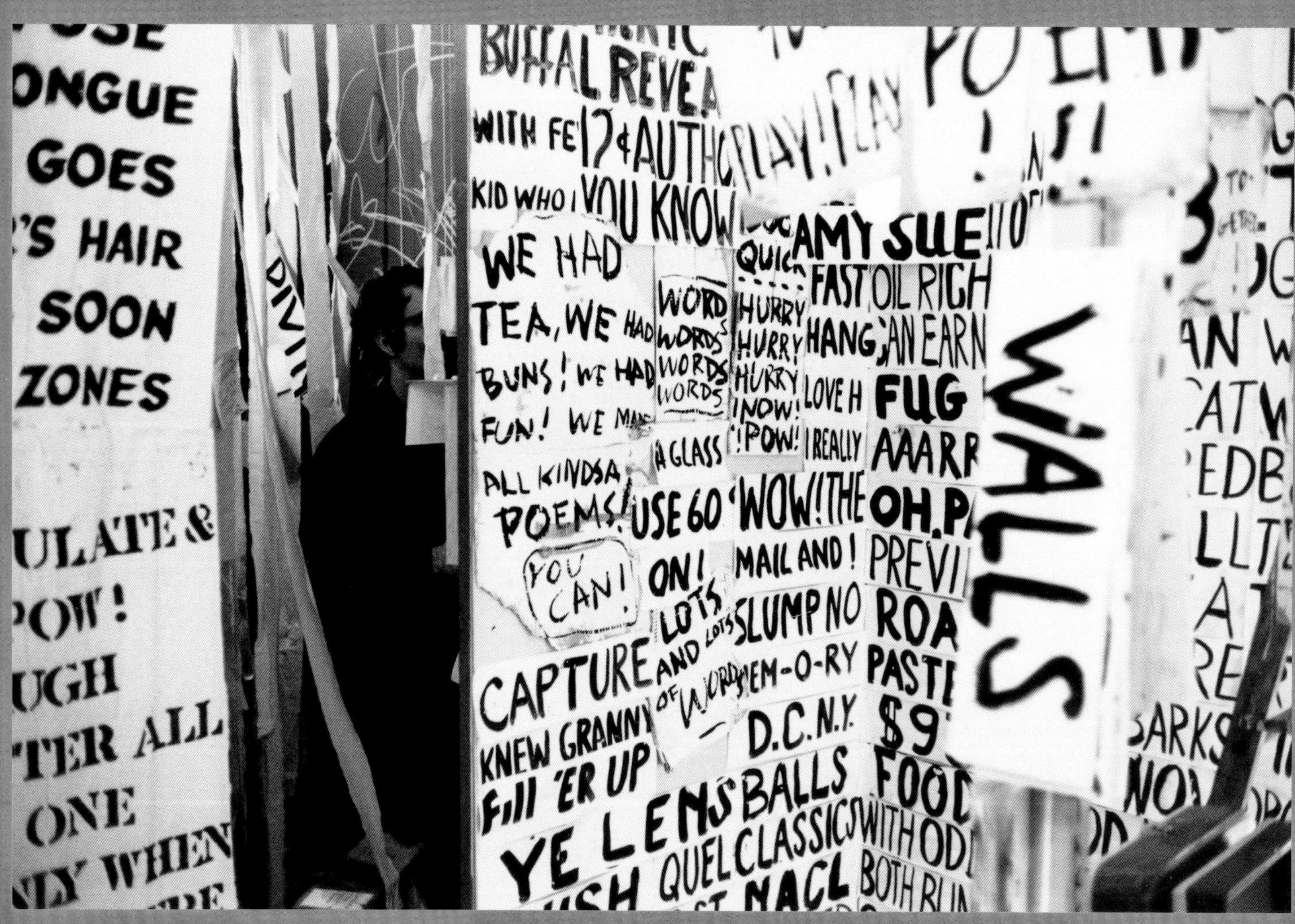

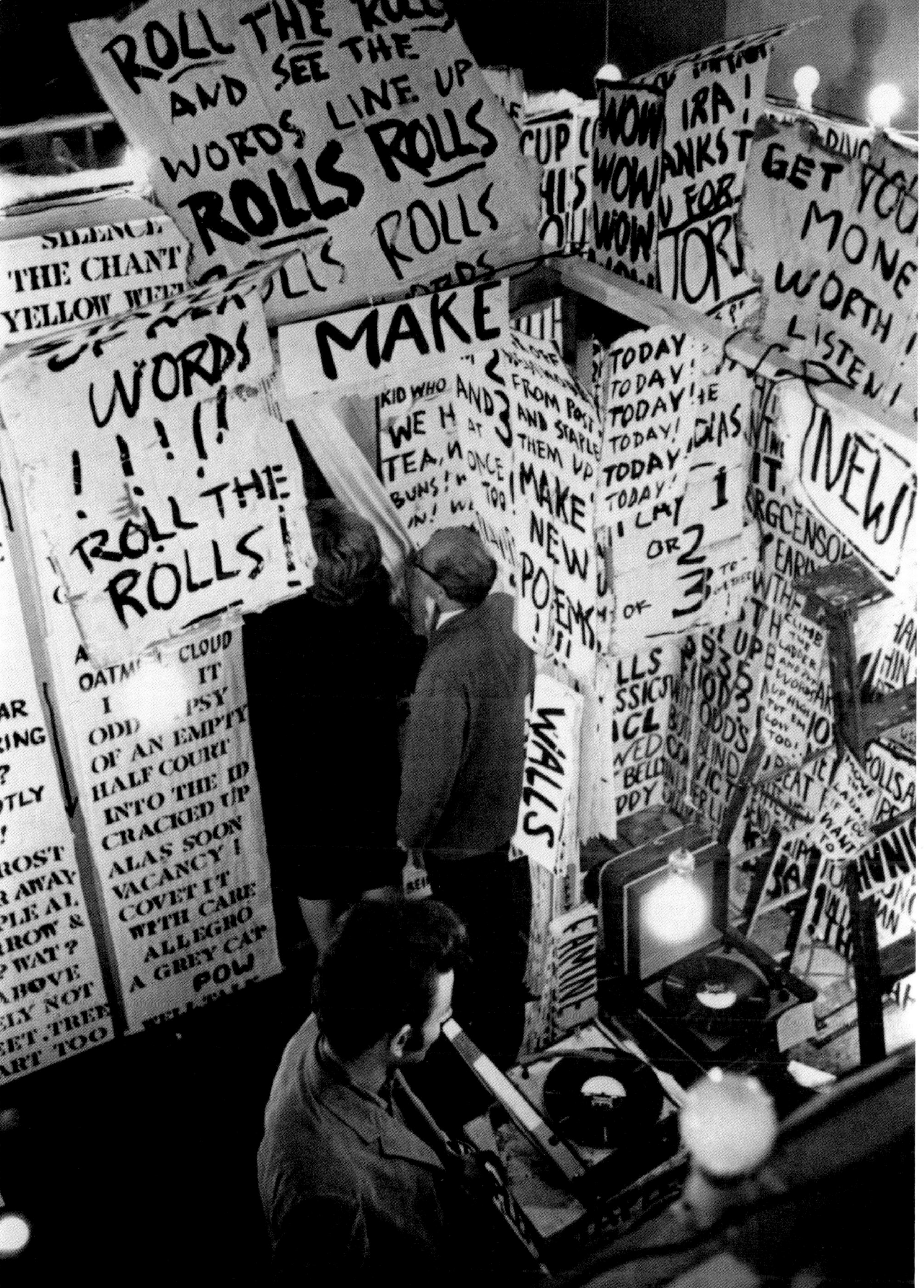

ROLL THE
AND SEE THE
WORDS LINE UP
ROLLS ROLLS
ROLLS
SILENCE
THE CHANT
MAKE
WORDS
!!!!!
ROLL THE
ROLLS!
TODAY
TODAY!
TODAY!
TODAY!
TODAY!
TODAY!
OR 2
OF 3
FROM POST
AND STAPLE
THEM UP
MAKE
NEW
KID WHO
WE H
TEA,
BUNS!
AND 3
AT
ONCE
TOO!
GET
MONE
WORTH
LISTEN!
IRA!
WOW
WOW
WOW
NEW
CLIMB
THE
LADDER
WALLS
OATM
I
ODD
OF AN EMPTY
HALF COURT
INTO THE
CRACKED UP
ALAS SOON
VACANCY!
COVET IT
WITH CARE
ALLEGRO
A GREY CAT
POW

Michael ELIAS
611 E. 6th
GR 3 5179

C H I C K E N

A Happening

A large auditorium, chairs removed, with balcony running around the sides and back, the stage curtained off. Hanging irregularly within an area of about 60 feet square are ten roughly made hollow spheres of chicken wire mesh open at the bottom and of about two feet in diameter. Suspended within each is a plucked chicken, and above them a 60 W bulb.

Off to another side of the area is a 9 ft. high construction of wood, wire mesh and tarpaper, in the form of a monstrous chicken. At another side is a 7 ft. cubic cage of wood frame and bars, covered with chicken wire. Inside it are suspended 3 closed cartons with live chickens inside and a man sitting on the floor reading a newspaper.

Besides these, there are six large tables distributed around the space. Built on top of the first, there is a telephone-booth-like wooden framework covered with semi-transparent plastic film. Inside it a young lady sits with a phonograph player and a light bulb over her head. A crudely lettered sign running around the top of this booth says "Happy Closet".

On the other five tables, fixed up with displays, salesmen sit on a chair or stool, megaphone at hand, ready to deliver a pitch and demonstration about chickens. A carnival atmosphere prevails. As the visitors enter, they hear chicken noises over a loudspeaker and intermittent band music. The salesmen rise and begin their performance.

cartons
tint
cardboard

The first has two dead chickens hanging from cords tied to the end of a sort of gallows alongside his table. He pokes at the bird with his gestures, rips out a few feathers, spreads the wings, bends the feet, etc. Then taking it down, he starts to pluck the chicken, throwing the feathers all around him, haranguing the watchers all the while he does this.

Segal

The second table has a fellow selling a live chicken tied by a rope to the chair or table leg. He holds up the chicken high, exhibits its various parts to all, swings it by its feet over his head while talking. Periodically, he turns on a vacuum sweeper (perhaps put in reverse) and vacuums the bird to show everyone how clean it is.

The third table has a rotobroiler (on a box or smaller table) and a dejected individual with glazed eyes sitting on a box with a dead chicken tied around his neck. The saleman here has a pointer and using it with much flourish and tapping, tells about cooking the chicken and how the man with the dead bird thinks he's a chicken. Everytime he taps the fellow on the head, the fellow rocks back and forth, flaps his arms, clucks loudly, then rises to his feet and crows like a rooster.

more

2.

78 Score for *Chicken*, p.1

A Happening /2

On the fourth table, three posts stick up with a cross-piece over two of them from which sespend five or more aluminum-foil wrapped broilers. On the other post is a decorated pin-wheel with a backboard of numbers running around it. The salesman spins the wheel and asks the visitors to guess the number coming up and thus win a broiler. One way or another he gets rid of most of the chickens (for example he can cheat in these ways: stopping the wheel with his finger, saying the number guessed was correct in Arabic, or was secretly right, or backwards, etc., etc., even though it doesn't correspond to the number called out).

The fifth table has on it an egg salesman, who has before him a small table or stand piled with common egg containers some with eggs, some not, some exposed to view. In addition, there is a tin can with a lit candle sticking out of the top. Nearby is an easel with a large pad of paper and some charcoal. The saleman divides his time between talking about his grade A eggs, giving out free samples (either whole dozens or an egg or two at a time), candling the eggs, most of which he throws over his shoulder letting them break wherever they land, and periodically drawing on the pad to show how an egg comes out of the chicken and how a chick grows inside it.

Above each of the preceeding, the chicken construction, the cage and the five tables, is a 60 W light bulb. And around each table are freely lettered signs appropriate to the products like, "Champeen Plucker Here!", "Yummy Eggs and Egg Artist!", "The Only Chicken Man!", A Clean Chicken for a Change!", The Great Chicken Contest!".

Then, in the center of the auditorium is a wooden platform about 6 ft. high by 7 ft. square. Its four legs extend upward above the platform surface forming corner poles. The other end of the rope is tied to the base of the platform. Chicken parts are hung around this base.

Finally, in another part of the space is a fairly high, freestanding wall of wooden crates piled on one another, about 15 feet in length. Around the front of this in a rough semi-circle are a number of chairs opened up and pointing in different directions as though they were casually left there.

Besides the small bulbs described, overhead lights are on.

The demonstrations of the salesman go on for about 20 minutes to a half hour. Then a man in the crowd suddenly dashes over to the tarpaper chicken and picking up a shovel and a sledgehammer, nearby, proceeds to demolish it violently. As he does so a spot light trains on the action. The loudspeaker becomes silent and

more

A Happening /3

they stop what they are doing, jump from their tables and walk over to watch. When the man completes his destruction, they clap and yell "Hooray!", "Whoopee!", "Marvelous!", "Yay!" all in unison, and then raise him like a hero up on their shoulders and march out through an exit. Others in the crowd start clapping and also shouting hooray.

The fellow returns directly with the salesmen and the clapping stops. He wheels in a small table with a pot or platter of hot broiled chicken parts, which he proceeds to offer, first to the accompanying salesmen, then to the public, shouting "Hee y'are! Get ya fresh roasted chicken dinnah!" etc. Threading his way among the people; the spot light (which sought him out as he entered) follows him.

During this time the girl in the Happy Closet gets up and turns on her light and plays her recording. The sounds are cluckings of chickens similar to those already heard over the loudspeaker. After a few moments she turns off both and then following a pause turns them on again, repeating this action henceforth.

When most of the cooked chicken disposed of, the vender pushes his table over to the wall of crates. All the lights except the Happy Closet go out. The spot focuses on the wall's surface. He looks at the wall for a moment, and then with nervous, jerky gestures, throws the remaining chicken pieces at it. He next heaves the pot and if it's a platter it shatters into pieces all over the floor. Then he stands on one of the opened chairs and reaches up to a nearby broiler hanging inside its mesh sphere and, unhooking it, flings it with all his might at the wall. He walks around to the other side of the crate wall and, teetering it backward and forth for a while, pushes the whole pile down onto the pot and bits of chicken remaining.

After this, with spot keeping up with him, he moves a chair under each of the remaining chickens and unhooks them. In the crowd, salesman and others form a bucket-brigade line leading to the center scaffold under the steel drum. As each chicken is unhooked it is passed along the line and the last man places it on the platform directly beneath the drum. The girl in the Happy Closet turns off her light and the record. The barrel comes down, BOOMMM! and crushes the broiler, and is raised for the next one. It is repated 8 more times. The spot light follows the action moving along the line of hands as the chicken is passed from person to person, and then up to the platform awaiting the fall of the barrel. The crusher keeps on slamming away at the pile of broilers even after the last one is tossed under it.

Another spot now illuminates the wire cage with the man inside who's been reading the newspaper all the time. The crusher now stops and the spot on it goes out. The salesmen and cooked chicken vendor walk over to it, peer in, point, ask the man what he's got in the boxes. He doesn's answer. They ask again and begin to taunt him

more

A Happening /4

and laugh, as though he was ridiculous sitting there. He throws down the newspaper, gets up and unties each of the cartons and pulls out a squawking chicken which flies madly around the cage. The salesmen laugh louder now and start to cluck like the chickens. Then the record from the Happy Closet goes on and cluckings start coming from all over the crowd, and from the technicians. The cackling swells in volume. Then the salesmen grasp the bottom of the cage and heave it over. Inside the man goes crazy and starts screaming in chicken-like noises, swinging wildly at the hysterical chickens. The cage is turned over again. And once more, it goes over, crashing, with the taunting and laughing continuing.

As the cage is turned over the second time, two cops come in from an opposite door with flashlights and fire-extinguishers. They force their way through the crowd, come up to the salesmen, grab them away from the cage and tell them and everybody else to get back. The clucking subdues slightly during this but now continues loud again in a more menacing way with a beat emerging in it.

One cop goes over to the demolished tarpaper chicken and gets a roll of tarpaper standing near it. He brings it back and with a knife rapidly cuts lengths of seven feet which the other cop takes and staples around the cage, using a stapler he pulls out of his pocket. As he does the first piece all the clucking and cackling stop. The cops roughly cover the whole cage. They then pick up the extinguishers and methodically submerge the whole cage with a fine white powder.

Except possibly for a few noises from the chickens, the only sound is the snorting and hissing from these extinguishers. When each is emptied the cops put them down, then switch on their flashlights and leave as they came. After a few moments of silence, a voice from the balcony says "Ladies and Gentlemen, the performance is concluded", and the overhead lights go on.

ms
10-29-1962

79–81 Score for *Chicken*, pp. 2–4

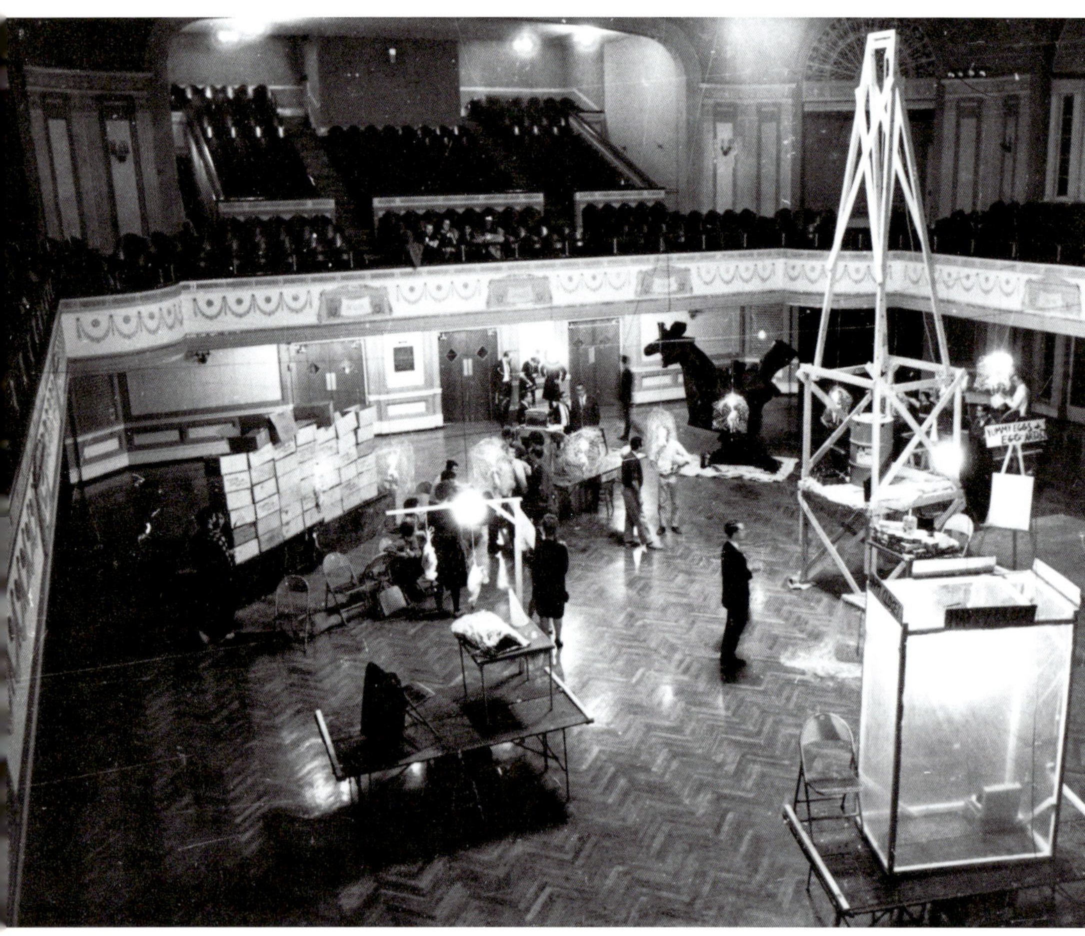

82 View of the auditorium

78–85 **Chicken**

Happening, November 1962
Presented for *Art 1963—A New Vocabulary*
Auditorium, Young Men's-Young Women's Hebrew Association, Philadelphia

Mushroom

Happening, November 1962
Sponsored by Walker Art Center
Lehmann mushroom caves, Saint Paul

86–92 **Courtyard**

Happening, November 1962
Sponsored by Smolin Gallery
Greenwich Hotel, New York

Flight, Part I, version 1

Happening, 1962
Not realized

Flight, Part I, version 2

Happening, 1962
Not realized

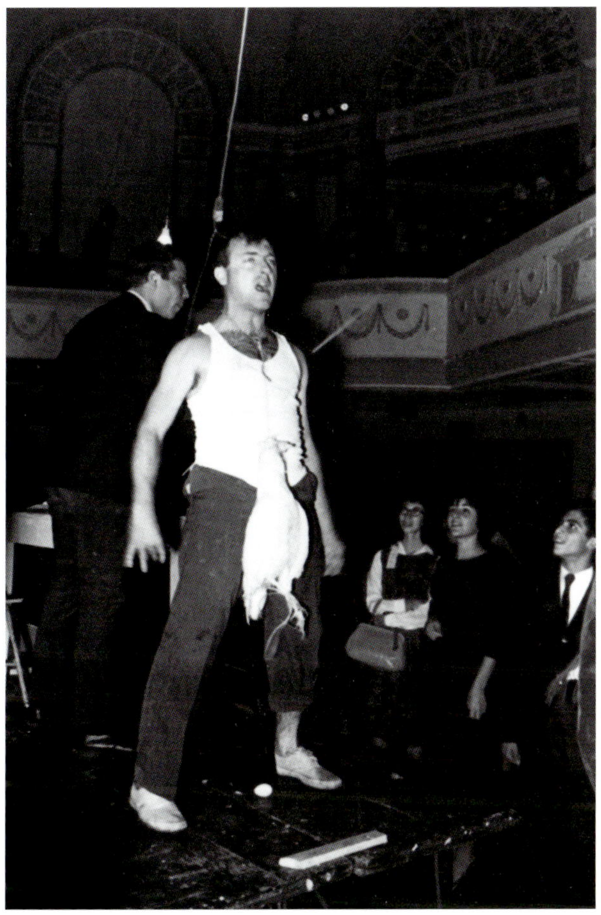

83 Participant with a dead chicken around his neck

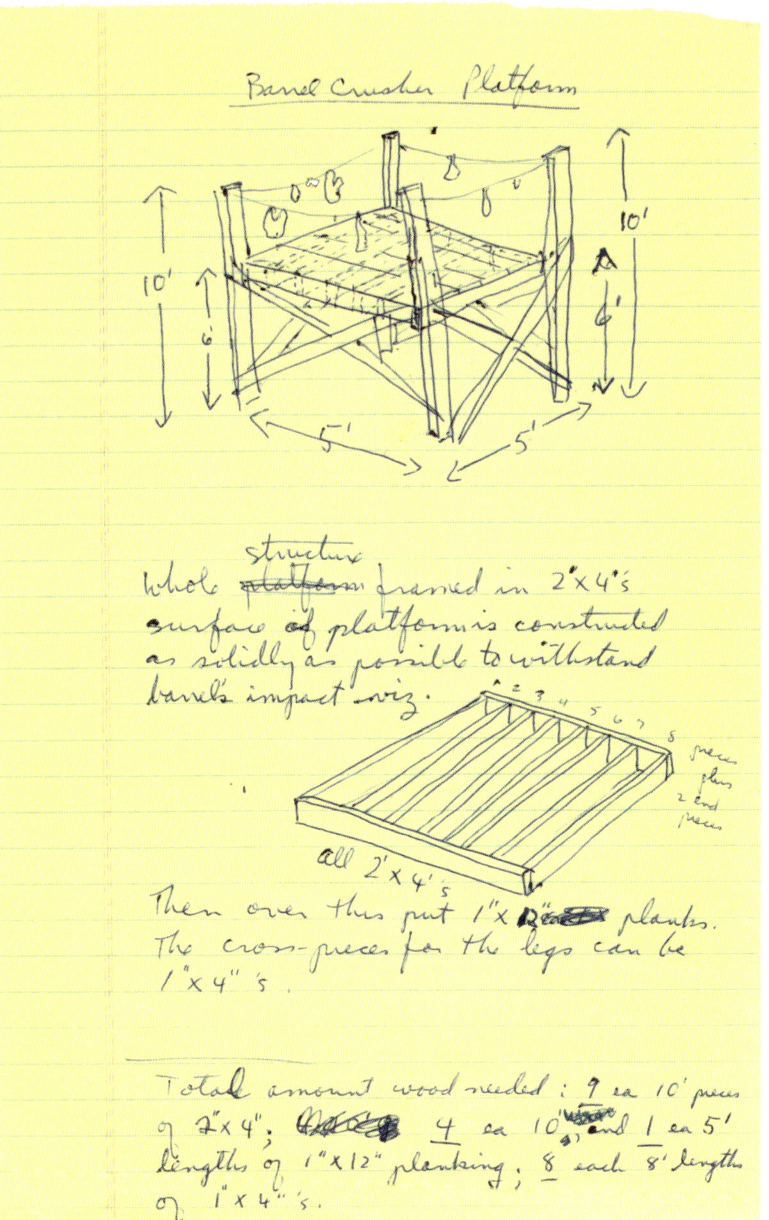

85 Drawing for the panel crusher platform

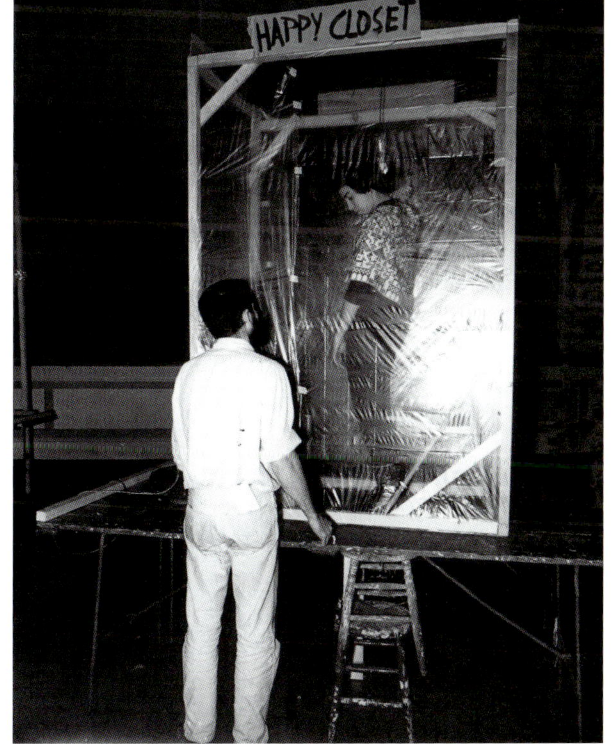

84 Happy Closet

86 Tar paper mountain

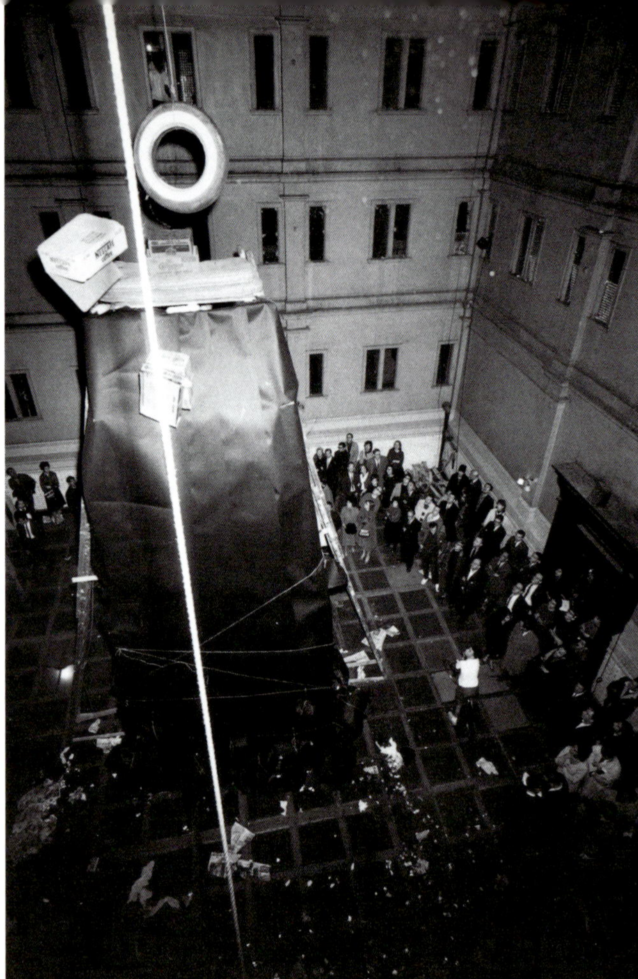

87 Poster for *Courtyard*

88 Girl in nightgown with photographers

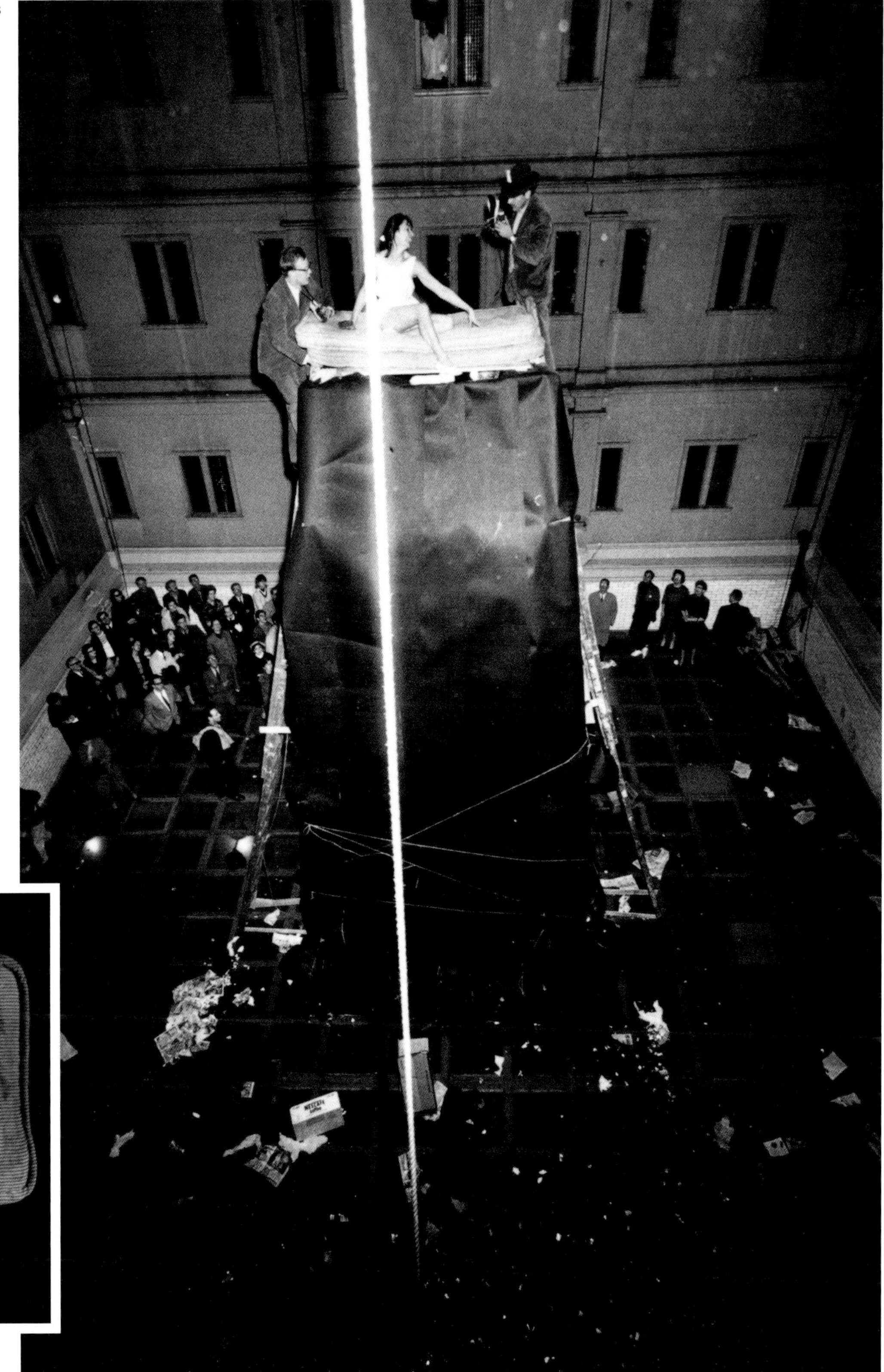

89 Girl in nightgown
Photo: Peter Moore

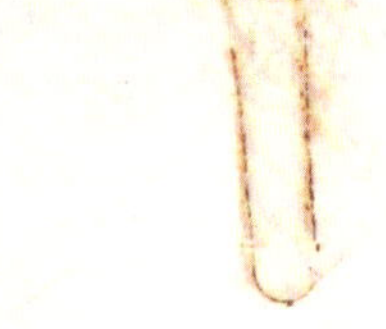

THE COURTYARD

Happening by Allan Kaprow at the Mills Hotel, N.Y.C., Nov, 1962

ACTION	LIGHTS
AS PEOPLE ENTER courtyard, a barely audible but insistent humming sound comes from various windows. Sound increases in intensity as small bits of timfoil flutter down (either from eighth floor or attic). Sound and foil increase for ½ minute, then peter out.	4 floods pointing upward
MAN WITH TRUNDLE CART comes in through glass doors and pushes through crowd, then goes out.	
TWO WORKMEN enter with brooms and large cartons... begin to sweep...hand out brooms to audience to clean up. Cartons are filled and dumped into crater by at least two trips up ladder by workemn. During this action, MAN WITH BICYCLE enters and rides through crowd, ringing handlebar bell in a quiet way.	floods go out
As clean up ends, WILD NOISES are heard inside mountain (workemn collect brooms and leave)	spots on mountain
After a few moments, MOUNTAIN ERUPTS...tar paper balls thrown out.	
VOICES AND ACTIONS from windows...apartment noise heard...people lean out of windows...flash lights, rattle dishes and silverware, dust mops, etc. During this, DISHES are thrown out of mountain, breaking on courtyard floor. (Bicycle man is still going around, ringing bell).	spots on mountain off 4 floods go on
All apartment activity stops . From windows THREE MATTRESSES are lowered to floor, followed by 5 or 6 cartons.	4 floods go off mountain spot goes on
TWO WORKMEN enter...go to mattresses and direct the action...carry mattresses and then boxes to top of mountain, forming altar-bed...then they descend and leave.	spot on top of mountain

90 Score for *Courtyard*, p. 1

92 Score for *Courtyard*, p. 2

- 2 -

TIRE swings back and forth, is pulled back just as...	spot still on mountain
...GIRL IN NIGHTGOWN enters, carrying transistor radio...walks through crowd listening to radio.	
She climbs up mountain...reclines (changing positions) on mattress...radio is heard. (At this point, the BICYCLIST stops his action and becomes a part of the crowd until end of performance)	
TWO PHOTOGRAPHERS enter...look for girl...shout "Where is she?", etc...find her...rush up ladder...ask her to pose...flash bulbs go off...they thank her....they descend and leave.	
GIRL lights candle and holds it up...	
ELECTRIC SAW sound starts high up...	
TIRE is released and puts candle out...GIRL releases white streamers down side of mountain...SAW stops.	
Sitting, GIRL catches and unties tire, clasps it to herself.	
SMOKE starts high up...SHIP DISTRESS SIGNAL begins...	floods on, pointing upward spots on mountain off
From above smoke, TORN TAR PAPER floats down...	
INVERSE MOUNTAIN descends...	halfway down, spots on mountain go on again
Girl guides it over her body with the ropes.	floods and spots out

THE END

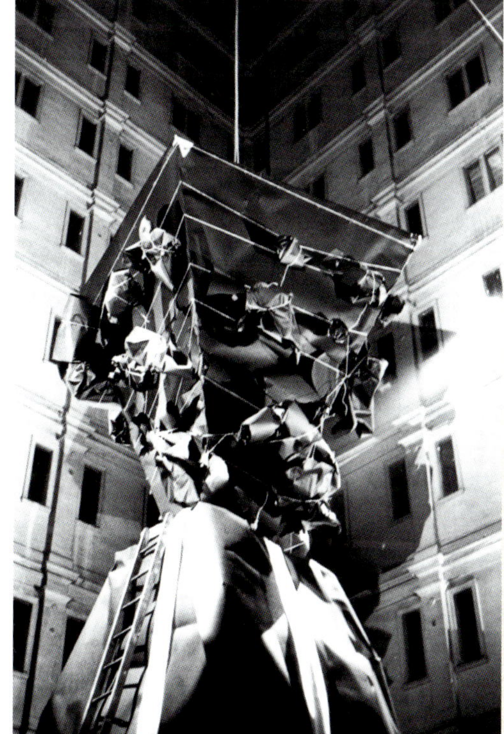

91 "Inverse mountain descends"

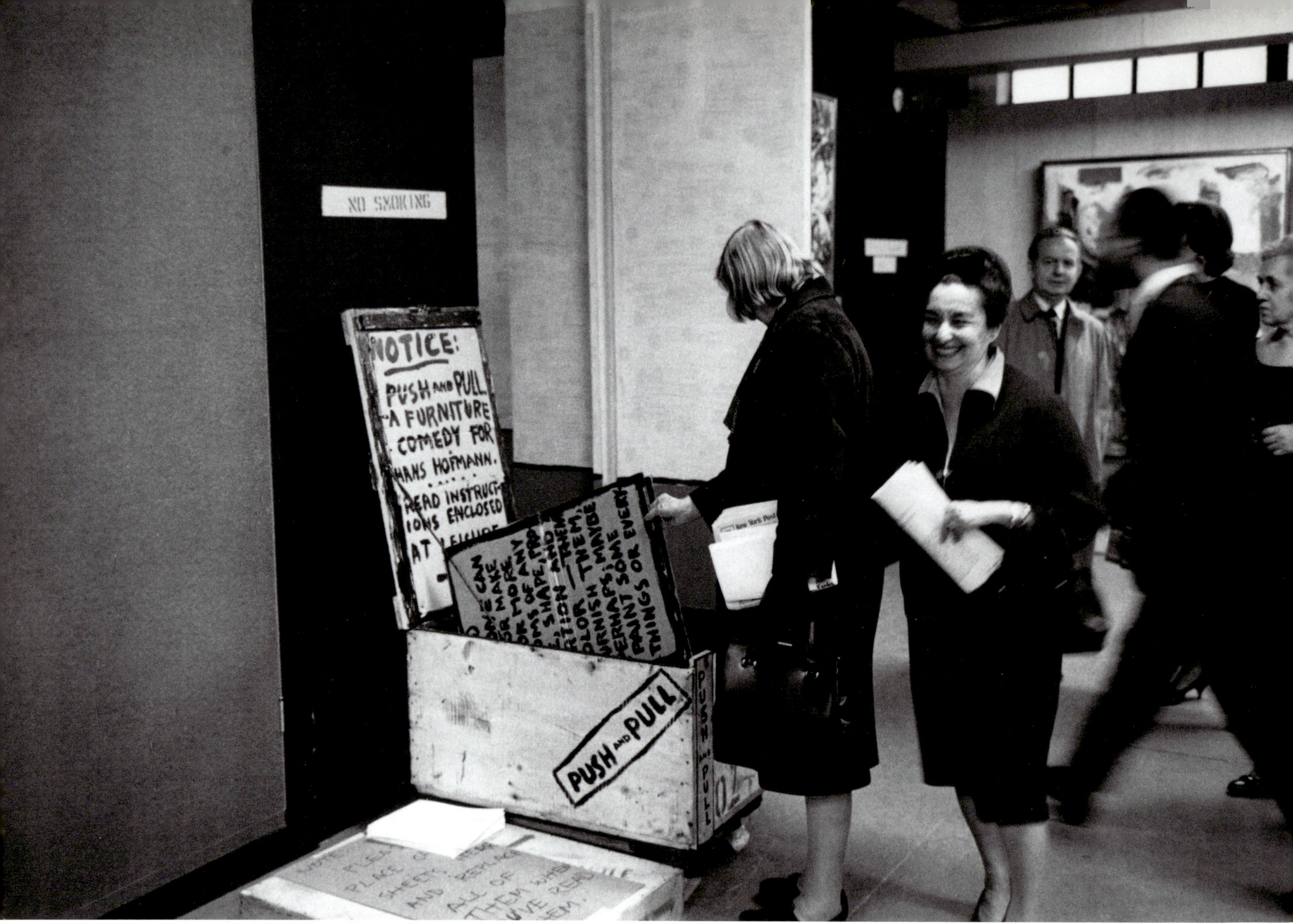

93 Entrance to *Push and Pull*

1963

TEACHING POSITIONS Associate Professor, Department of Fine Arts, State University of New York, Stony Brook. ¶ **AWARDS** Research grant from State University of New York, Stony Brook. William and Noma Copley Foundation Award. ¶ **GROUP EXHIBITIONS** *Hans Hofmann and His Students,* organized by the Museum of Modern Art, New York (traveled nationally), May 1963–April 1965. ¶ **FESTIVALS** Yam Festival, George Segal's farm, South Brunswick, New Jersey, May. ¶ **WRITINGS** "An Artist's Story of a 'Happening,'" *New York Times,* 6 October: 17. "Effect of Recent Art upon the Teaching of Art," *Art Journal* 23: 136–38. "Impurity," *ARTnews* 61, no. 9: 30–33, 52–55. "A Service for the Dead," *Art International* 7, no. 1: 46–47. Untitled essay on George Segal, in *Segal,* exh. cat. (Paris: Ileana Sonnabend Gallery), 16–19. "The World View of Alfred Jensen," *ARTnews* 62, no. 8: 28–31, 64–66.

'Push and Pull—a Furniture Comedy'

By PAUL BERG of the PICTURES Staff

Art, it appears, does not necessarily have to hang on walls. It can be the walls themselves and all the furniture and boxes and stuff and trash frequently enclosed by walls. Added up, it can turn out to be a room, a part of most people's everyday life. Two such rooms were exhibited by the Museum of Modern Art in New York as an example of new art forms called "environments" and "happenings."

The occasion was a special showing of the museum's new circulating exhibition titled "Hans Hofmann and His Students." Paintings and sculpture by 50 artists who had been students of the famous 83-year-old abstract expressionist teacher are in the exhibition. All of their work is conventional, at least in the sense that one looks at it. But one student of Hofmann's, Allan Kaprow, gave up painting in 1956 and has been exploring "environments" and "happenings," which involve elements of theater, games and audience participation. Kaprow, therefore, designed a special "environment" for the exhibition called "Push and Pull — A Furniture Comedy for Hans Hofmann."

He constructed two rooms, each about 10 by 20 feet in size and connected by a door. One room, painted black, was dimly lighted by a single blue bulb. It was filled with items that might have been stored in an attic or basement — boxes, barrels, a ladder, old clothes, old newspapers, a broken television set. The other room was painted yellow and red and brightly lit by yellow bulbs. It contained an orderly arrangement of furniture all painted yellow — a chest of drawers, three chairs, a table with a typewriter and bowl of fruit, a cot and a trunk.

At the entrance to the bright room was a wooden crate in which were piled large pieces of cardboard on which Kaprow had hand printed instructions for viewing the rooms. Visitors were invited to push and pull the furnishings around until they "made a significant composition." Objects could be moved from one room to the other, furniture rearranged, boxes opened, pictures rehung.

Soon the exhibition viewers were hard at work following Kaprow's suggestions. Their contributions, however, were closer to the unrestrained and undirected activities of children in a permissive nursery school than that of creative adults. For some of the results, turn to pages 22 and 23.

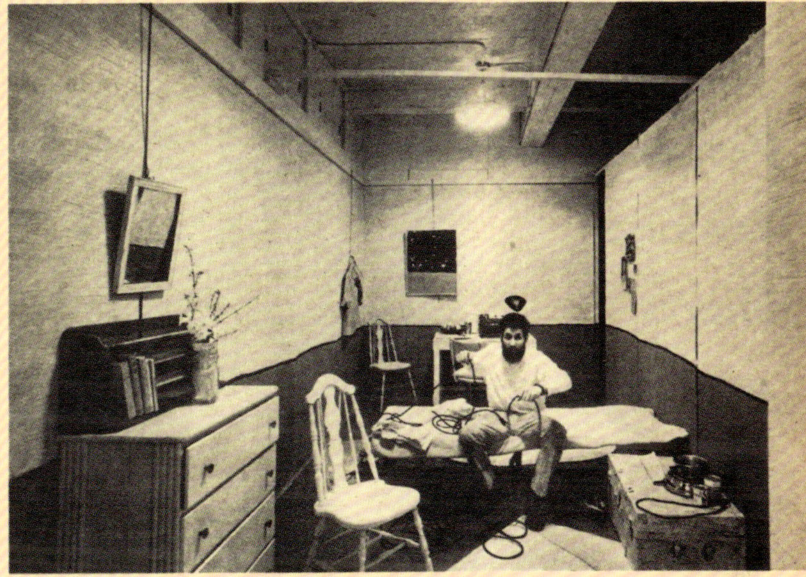

Allan Kaprow (above) unwinds a knotted electric cord as he hastily finishes work on the bright yellow room of his "Furniture Comedy." Some art critics noted that it bore a resemblance to Van Gogh's bedroom at Arles. At far end of wall at right is door leading to the dark room (below), dimly lit by a bare blue bulb and filled with an attic-like disarray of unused objects. Kaprow conceived the two rooms as expressions of opposites — light and dark, colored and non-colored, public and private, order and disorder, the conscious and subconscious.

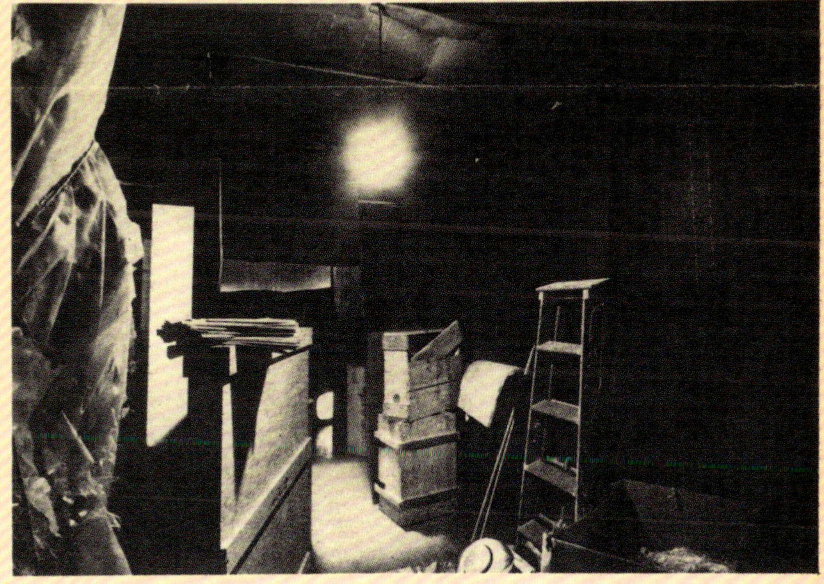

PICTURES—St. Louis Post-Dispatch, Sunday, May 19, 1963 19

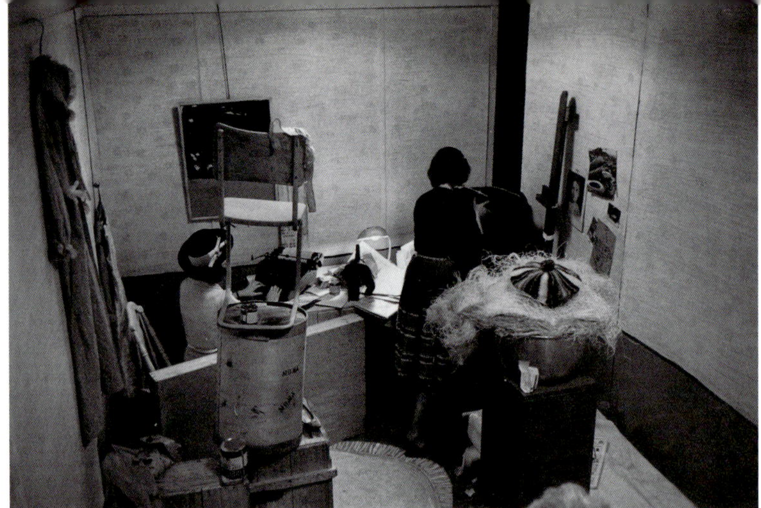

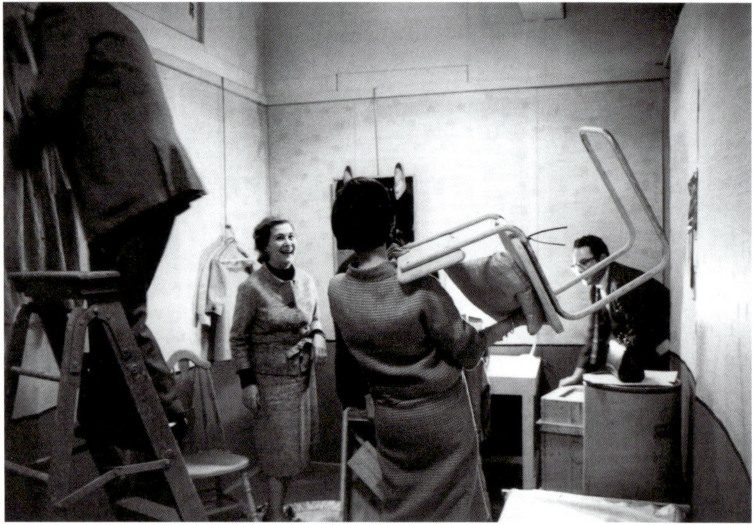

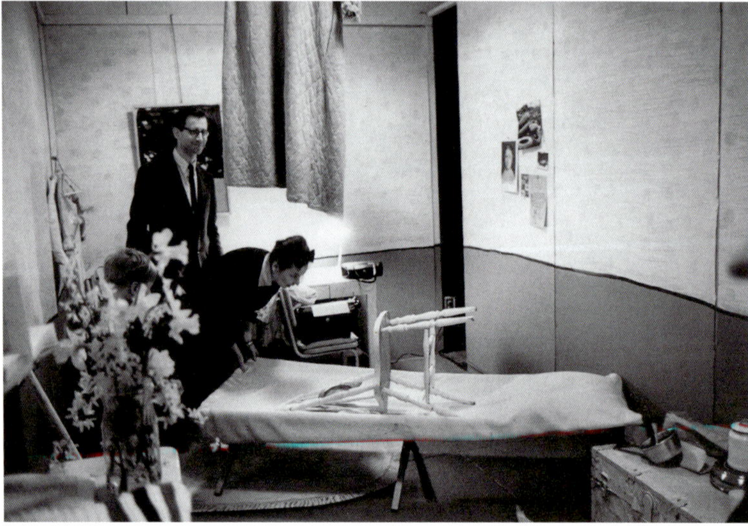

95–97 Visitors "push and pull" the furnishings

93–97 **Push and Pull: A Furniture Comedy for Hans Hofmann**
Environment, April 1963
Presented for *Hans Hofmann and His Students*
Santini Brothers warehouse, New York
Reinvented in 1965, 1967, 1977, 1986, 1991, 1998, 2002, 2006, and 2007

Tree
Happening, May 1963
Presented for Yam Festival
Sponsored by Smolin Gallery
George Segal's farm, South Brunswick, New Jersey

Bon Marché
Happening, July 1963
Sponsored by Théâtre des Nations
Bon Marché department store, Paris

Out
Happening, September 1963
Sponsored by International Drama Conference
Courtyard of McEwan Hall, Edinburgh
Reinvented in 2006

Sea
Happening, September 1963
For Edinburgh International Writer's Conference
Not realized

BIRDS

A Happening, for participants only, commissioned by the University of Southern Illinois, Carbondale, performed Febraury 16, 1964.

Setting: A patch of woods near a lake on the campus. A road leading to a small wooden bridge over a dry brook filled with rocks. On the bridge, a patio table loaded with packages of cheap white bread and strawberry jam, a bright beach umbrella opened over this. Women in trees are widely separated and some can only hear each other. Below each woman is a mass of old furniture hung on ropes.

Events

1 (Tree women swing hanging furniture, and bang trees with sticks.
(Wall men build wall of rocks on edge of bridge.
(Bread man hawks bread and jam, "Bread!, Bread!, Bread!," etc., blows toy pipe whistle.

2 (Bread man silent.
(Wall workers go to tree women, taunt them, bang with sticks and rocks on trees.
(Tree women drop furniture.

3 (Wall workers carry furniture to pile under edge of bridge
(Tree women blow police whistles.
(Wall workers bomb furniture with rocks from wall.
(Bread man resumes hawking.

Birds (cont'd

4 (Wall workers leave quietly one by one when finished.
(Bread man continues hawking.
(Tree women silent after first wall worker leaves

5 (Bread man slowly bombs rubble with bits of bread, leaves when finished.
(Tree women rhythmically yell in unison "Yah! Yah! Yah!," like crows, as Bread man does this and when he leaves they are silent.

Allan Kaprow
January, 1964

98 + 99 Score for *Birds*

LIFE EVENTS Nina Madge Kaprow, daughter, born November. ¶ TEACHING POSITIONS Associate Professor, Department of Fine Arts, State University of New York, Stony Brook. ¶ AWARDS Research grant from State University of New York, Stony Brook. ¶ FESTIVALS All Student Art Festival, University of California, Berkeley, March. Festival of Contemporary Arts, Cornell University, Ithaca, New York, May. Second Annual New York Avant-Garde Festival, Judson Hall, New York, September. ¶ WRITINGS "An Artist's Story of a 'Happening'" (originally published in 1963) and scores for *Words, Bon Marché, Sweeping, Mirrors, Push and Pull,* and *Tree,* in *Décollage/4 "Happenings,"* no. 4: n.p. "The Happening" (notes on *Household*), *Ithaca Journal,* 9 May: 8. "Nature in the Art of Irving Kriesberg," *Art International* 7, no. 10: 29–31. "Segal's Vital Mummies," *ARTnews* 62, no. 10: 30–33, 65. "Should the Artist Become a Man of the World?" *ARTnews* 63, no. 6: 34–37, 58–59. "Two Happenings" (introductory note and scenarios for *Birds* and *Orange*), *City Lights Journal,* no. 2: 255–59. "What Is an 'Environment'?" a statement in Betty Rollin, "Eat," *Vogue* 143, no. 7: 125.

1964

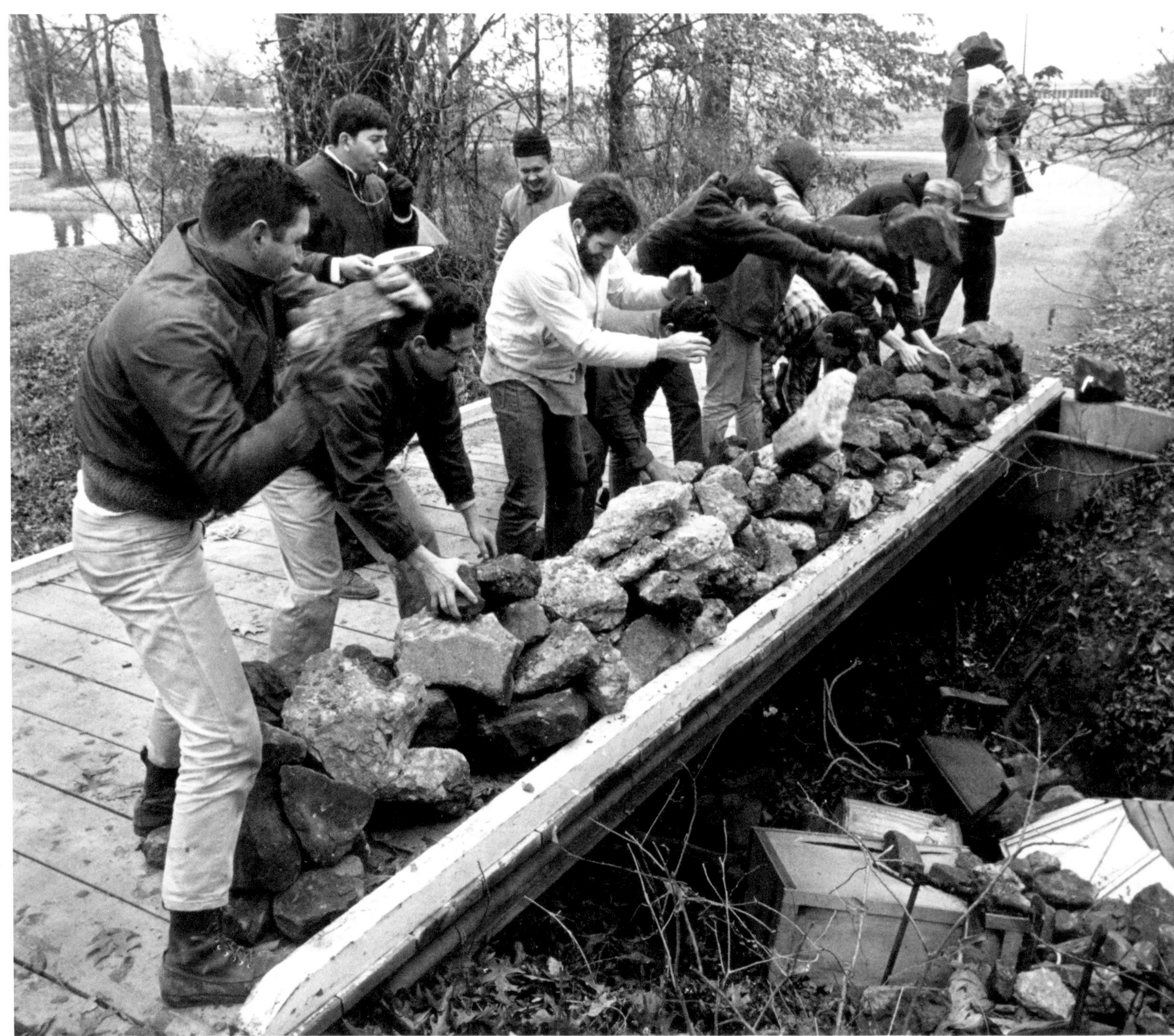

Eat

Environment, January 1964
Sponsored by Smolin Gallery
Caves of the former Ebling Brewery, South Bronx
Reinvented in 1991 and 1992 (twice)

98–100 **Birds**

Happening, February 1964
Woods near a lake, Southern Illinois University, Carbondale
Reinvented in 2006 and 2007

O R A N G E

Ladies and Gentlemen:

This is the scenario of a HAPPENING which Allan Kaprow has prepared especially for the Arts Council of Miami, Inc., to be performed on March 7, 1964, between 8:30 P.M. and 10:30 P.M. The event begins when the first guest arrives and concludes with the last one. Otherwise, there is no real "beginning" or "end". You may come at any time during these hours.

The scenario is sent to you, who are the participants, so that you may know exactly what part you will have in the HAPPENING. And also, so that you will understand that, without your serious participation, it cannot exist. "Orange" is not something to watch; nor is it intended to be mere light entertainment. It is an occurrence with an idea behind it, that has been formed in a certain time sequence and within particular spaces.

This idea has to do with a journey one might take and with the changing experiences one may have on the way. Now following is the HAPPENING'S description:

A large factory-like building of concrete, with girdered roof. A truck-loading platform inside one end of the building is the place of entry. Six automobiles with drivers, pointed the entryway, are arranged in a semi-circle.

Each traveler arrives with a ball of string and a few fresh flowers, perhaps contained in a plastic bag. He or she walks past the cars into the loading area and sees a myriad of oranges hanging by strings from the ceiling. There are a number of small tables or stands with juice-squeezers, paring knifes and paper cups on them. The traveler pulls an orange from its cord (a nail stuck through its core is all that holds it) cuts it, squeezes its juice into a cup and drinks it.

During this time, up on the platform, are three persons sitting on large metal drums, holding blank-cartridge pistols in their laps and facing the incoming visitors. A policeman is also standing to one side. Periodically (though not too often) he raises a whistle to his mouth and blows it piercingly. The pistols are aimed at the orange juice drinkers, detonated simultaneously, and are returned to the shooter's laps. Directly, these shots are answered by the car drivers who turn on their high beams and scream their horns together, for several drawn-out seconds. Then silence immediately returns and the lights go off.

The travelers next go up some steps to the left of the loading pit and come upon a shiny aluminum-foil room and enter it. Inside, bright lights reflect upon a girl in a bikini into a bath-tub orange juice. She is listening to rock-n-roll on a radio which she periodically turns on and off, one time low, another time quite loud. Each visitor gently tosses his flowers to her and passes on.

In the next part is a blank section of hallway, lit indifferently. A man is violently throwing and breaking against a wall. He only pauses to let the travelers by.

Then, a small, dark tarpaper room is entered, lit by a single weak bulb. Inside a woman is cooking long spaghetti in a big pot. She continuously winds forks-ful of it around an upright mass of the stuff, of about three feet in height. There is something vaguely human about the image being formed. Nearby, there is a similar structure of strings. The traveler unravels his own string and adds to the image in whatever way he wishes. Like the other one, it will grow more and more grotesque.

Leaving the dark room, one comes at last to a lonely, again indifferently lit (but with a few orange bulbs). It is sparsely hung with bottles of orange soda. An attendant in white uniform sits at the far end with of bottles at her side, and upon payment of a dime, gives those who wish one a soda to drink. Each time a sale is made, she rings a counter-bell; occasionally drinking herself and laughing in short bursts of raucousness or self-amusement. The effect here is of utter desolation. "Orange" is concluded.

Thereafter the travelers go to another section of the building for the remainder of the evening.

101 + 102 Score for *Orange*

101–105 **Orange**

Happening, March 1964
Sponsored by Miami Arts Council
An unused citrus warehouse, Coral Gables, Florida

106–108 **Paper**

Happening, March 1964
Presented for All Student Art Festival
A parking structure in Berkeley

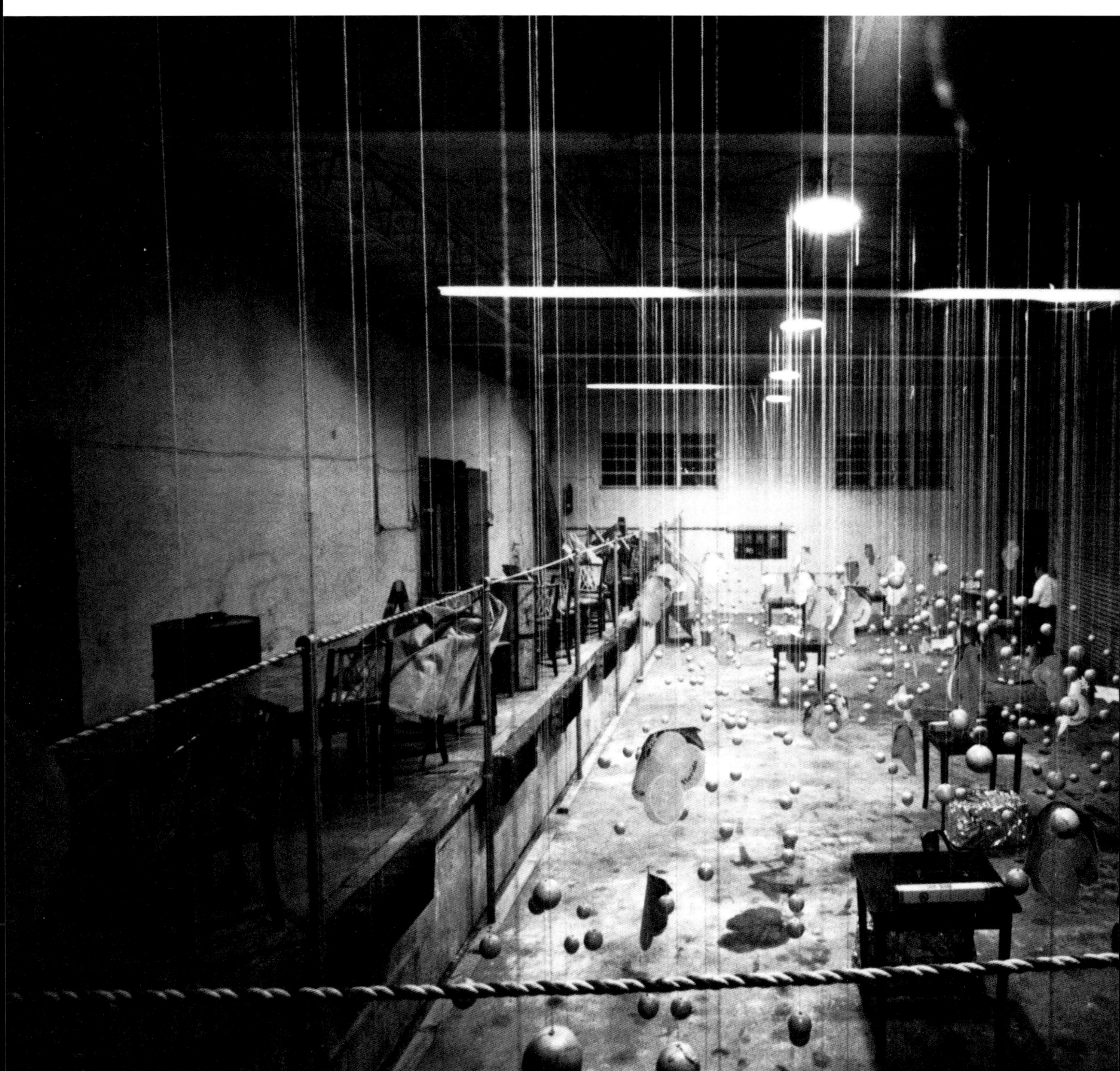

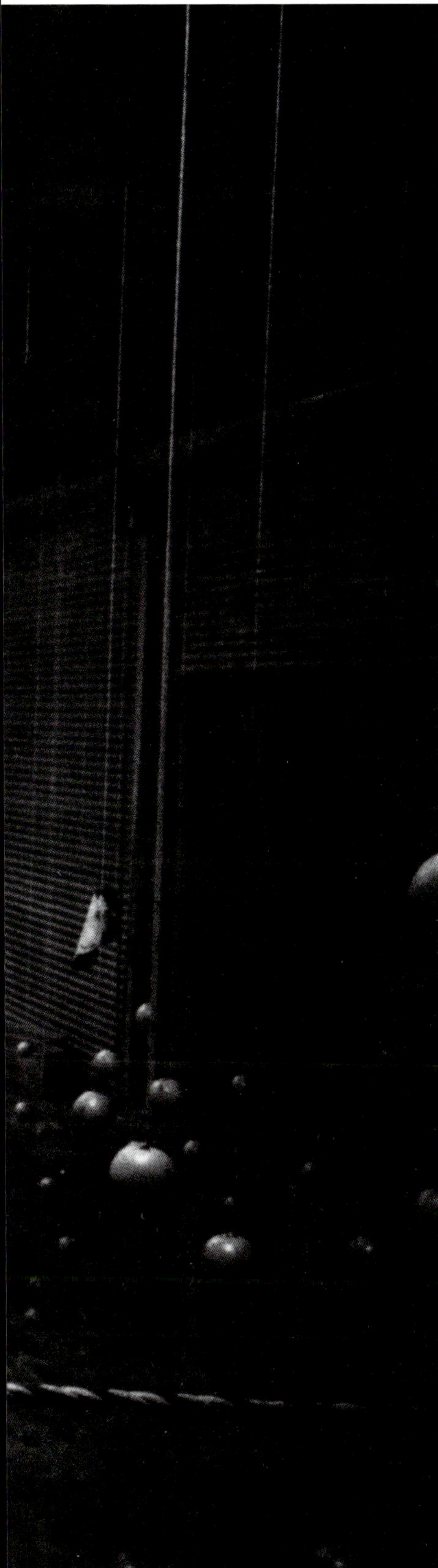

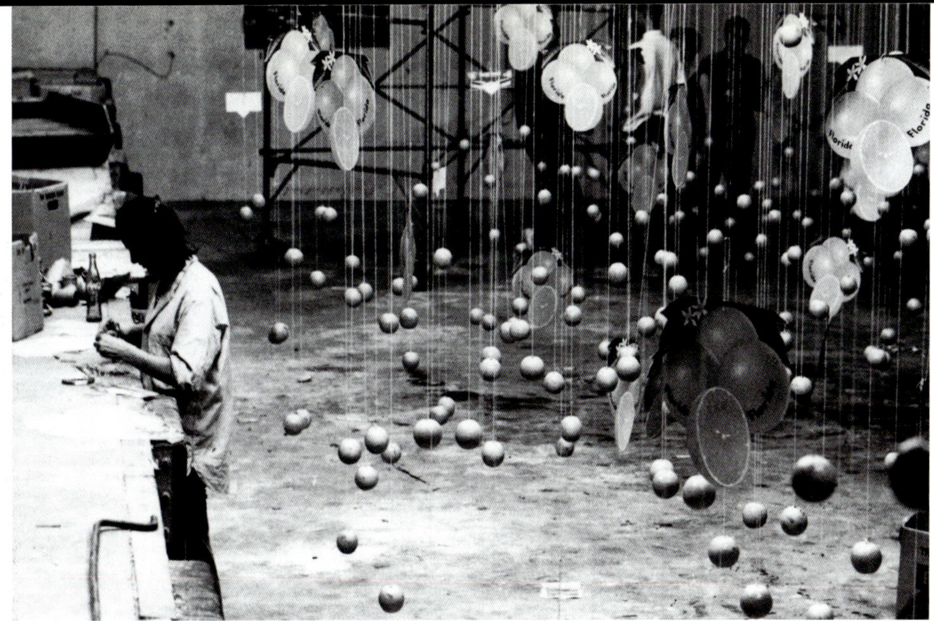

104 Participant squeezing oranges

105 The shiny aluminum-foil room

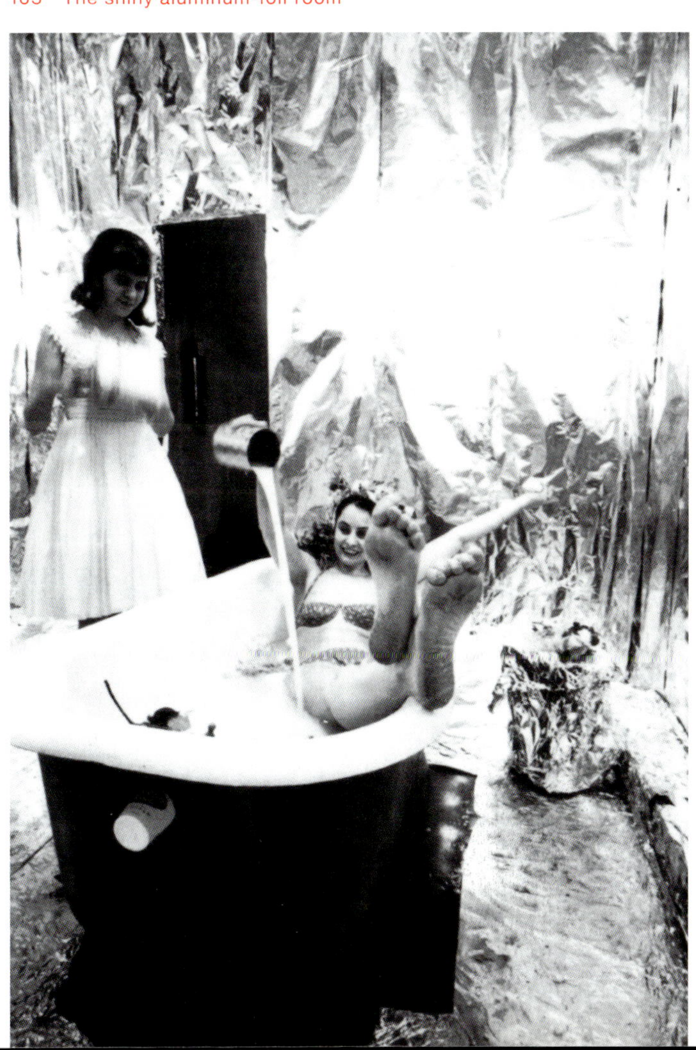

103 Oranges hanging by strings

106 + 107 Score for *Paper*

PAPER

(A Happening)

prepared for the University of California at Berkeley

SETTING

Street level of a three-tiered parking lot opposite residence halls. (During Monday afternoon and Tuesday, each participant should crumple the sheets of a full newspaper and strew it over the eastern half of the lot.) A record player is near the center and ten metal barrels are placed in line along the western end.

EVENTS

1 (Twist gal arrives, puts on rock-and-roll records, dances.

(Sweepers (25, male) with brooms arrive, sweep paper mechanically in a
(line toward western end.
(
2 (Barrel men (10) arrive and slowly tip barrels end-over-end toward sweepers
(and when wall is reached, reverse direction.
(
(Gal twists.

(Cars (25) drive in at half-minute intervals, brights on, moving slowly
(like hearses; each dumps a body (woman) which rolls to sweepers and be-
(comes part of trash line.
(
3 (Cars drive off.
(
(Barrels boom.
(
(Gal twists.

(Cars return, moving faster, find a parking spot on west side, screech
(to a stop.
(
(Drivers jump out, crouching, run wildly to another car, yelling, "Hey!,
4 (Hey!", get into next car. Repeat this twice (third time they are drivers'
(own cars). Running steps echoing, car doors slamming.
(Barrels boom.
(Gal twists.

(Drivers wait one minute, lean on horns for one steady minute.
(
(Barrels stop.
5 (
(Bodies in the paper jump up, fight violently with sweepers, who succumb.
(
(Gal twists.

2

(Barrel people get up on barrels and begin to twist.
(
(Women begin to twist also, move toward barrel people, viciously pull
(them down to the ground.
6 (
(The women load trash into barrels.
(
(Truck comes in.
(
(Gal twists.

(Women and truck driver load barrels and brooms onto truck, then get on
7 (themselves. They drive off gaily waving, calling, "Bye!, Bye!, G'Bye!"
(
(Gal twists.

8 (One minute of silence except for twist gal.

9 (Twist gal turns up volume, glides to each fallen body, kneels, kisses
(it tenderly on the lips, then walks away.

10 (Cars start motors, one after the other, drive over to the bodies, put
(them into the cars and drive off.

Allan Kaprow
March, 1964

NOTE: There may be no spectators. Those wishing to participate should dress in jeans or old clothes. A preliminary meeting to discuss the Happening, and to assign parts, will take place at room 155 Dwinelle Hall, 1:30 p.m., Tuesday the 24th.

108 Fallen body

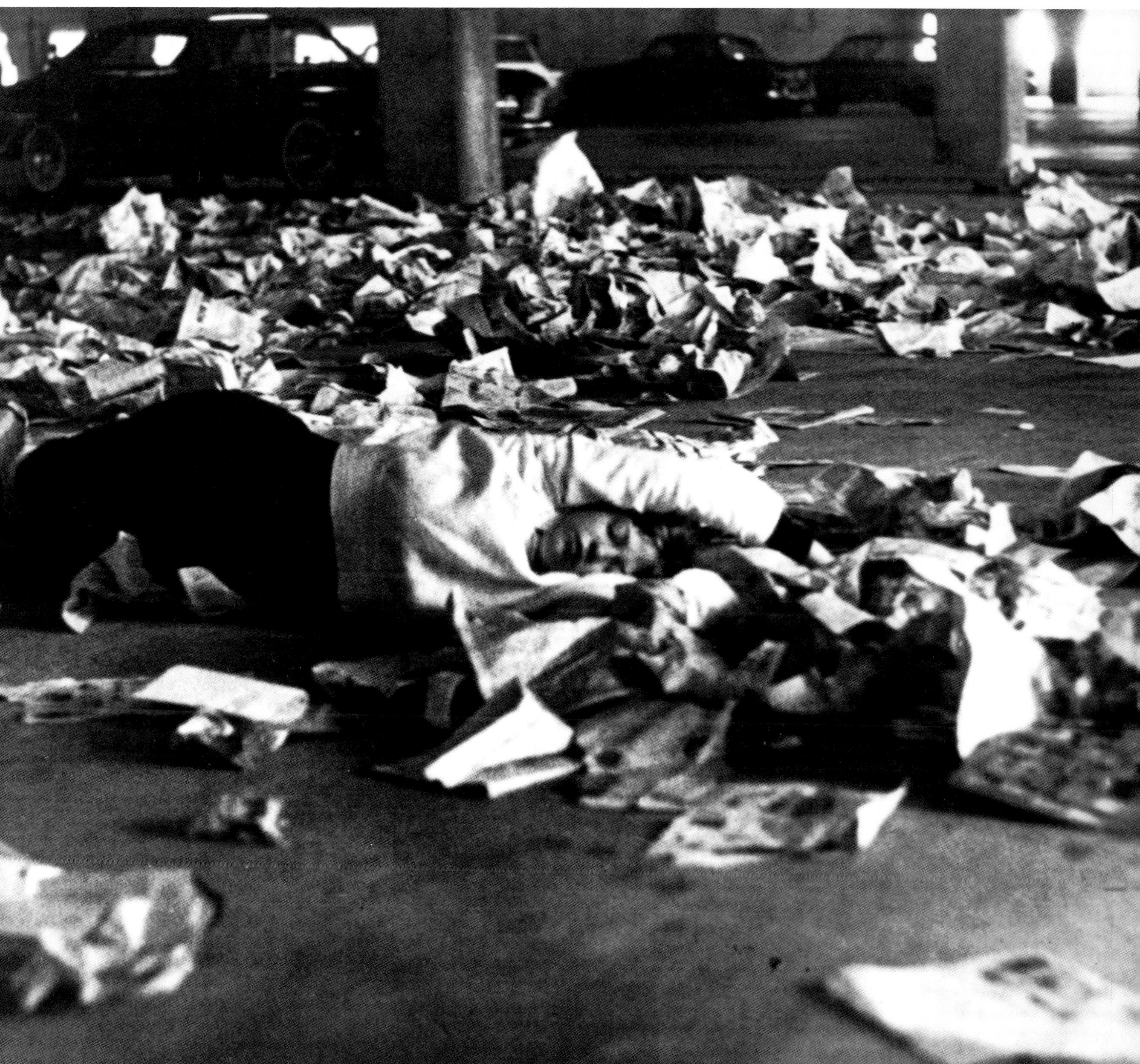

109 Movement score for *Household*

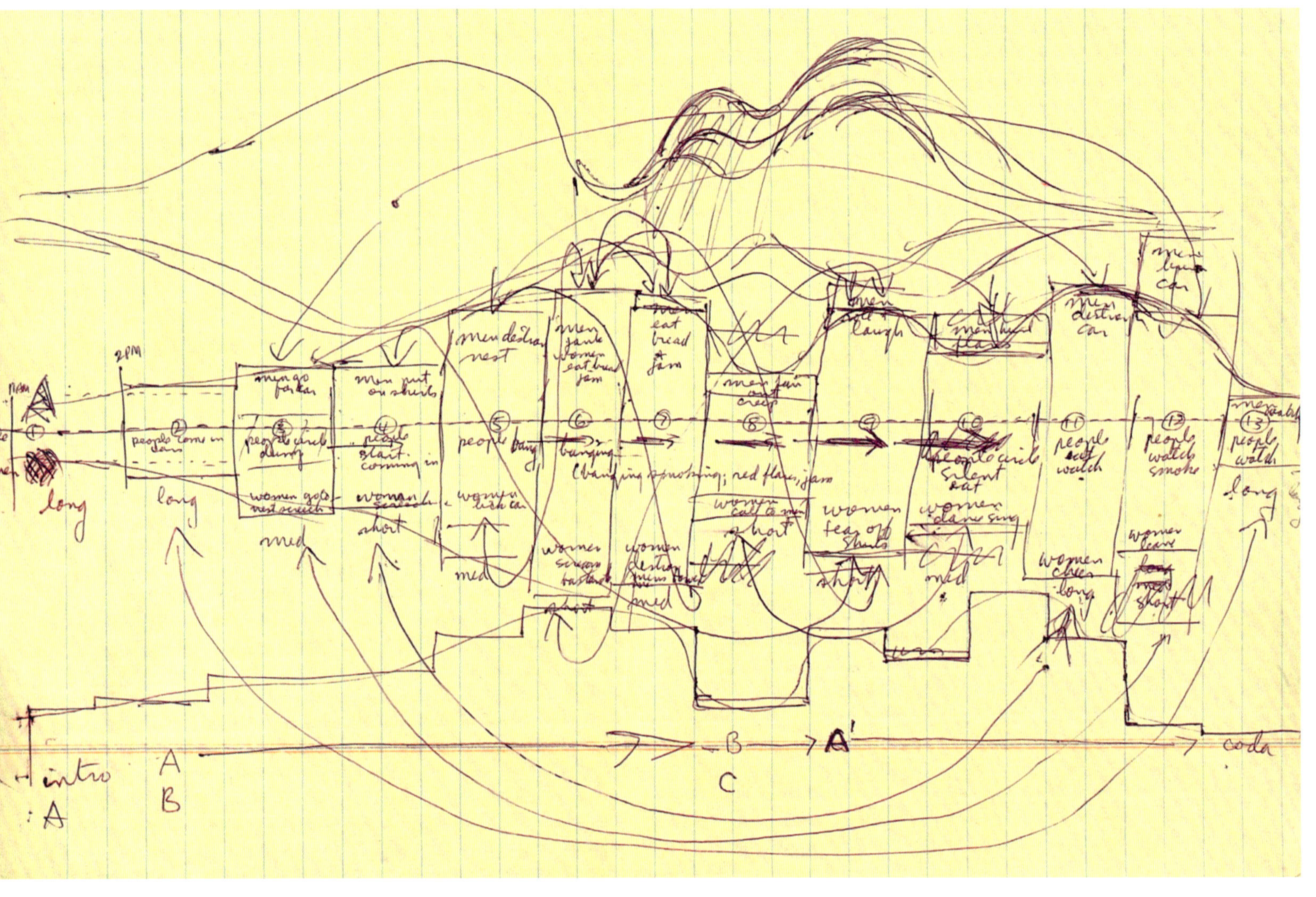

109–117 **Household**

Happening, May 1964
Presented for Festival of Contemporary Arts
City dump, Ithaca, New York
Reinvented in 2006

110 Kaprow explaining *Household*

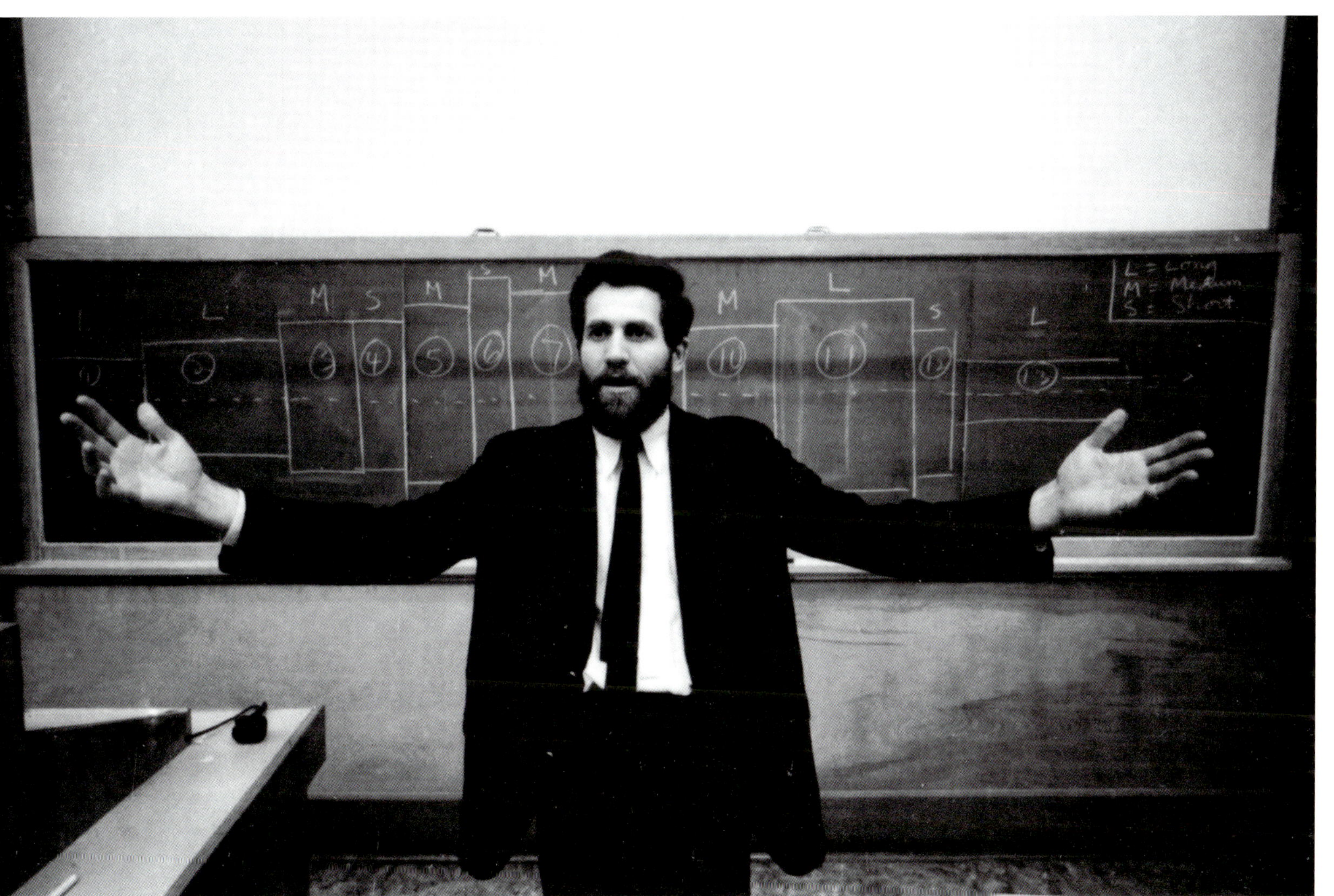

Originale

Opera Happening, September 1964
Presented for the Second Annual New York Avant-Garde Festival
Directed by Allan Kaprow
Written by Karlheinz Stockhausen
Judson Hall, New York

HOUSEHOLD

A Happening prepared for Cornell University by Allan Kaprow, May, 1964

Note: There will be no spectators of this event, which will be performed regardless of weather. Those wishing to take part in it should attend a preliminary meeting to be held (Saturday, May 2, 2 p.m., Franklin 115) where the Happening will be discussed and parts distributed.

Setting

A lonesome dump out in the country. Trash heaps all around, some smoking. Parts of dump enclosed by old, red tin fence. Trees around rest of it.

Sequence of Events

1.

11 a.m. Men build wooden tower on a trash mound. Poles topped with tarpaper clusters are stuck around it.

Women build nest of saplings and strings on another mound. Around the nest on a clothesline they hang old shirts.

2.

2 p.m. Cars arrive, towing smoking wreck, park outside dump, people get out.

Men and women work on tower and nest.

3.

People circle dump, out of sight in trees and behind tin wall, wait.

Women go inside nest and screech.

Men go for smoking wreck, roll it into dump, cover it with strawberry jam.

HOUSEHOLD
Page 2

4.

People's voices call "Hey! Hey! Hey!" all around dump.

Men go to women, put on shirts, squat down and watch them.

People very slowly start coming in toward car, still calling "Hey! Hey!"

Women screech.

5.

Women go to car and lick jam.

Men destroy nest with shouts and cursing.

People, coming in, start to pound pots and blow police whistles in slow unison.

6.

Men return to women at wreck, yank them away, eat jam with fingers, slap white bread all over sticky stuff, eat with their mouths.

Women scream at men "Bastards!, Bastards!"

People advance, banging and whistling.

7.

Women destroy men's poles and tower, laughing, yelling, "Watch this!, Watch this!"

Men eat Bread.

People advance, banging and whistling.

8.

Women go to heaps of smoking trash, call to men sweet-songy come-ons.

Men fan out, creep low to ambush women.

People advance, banging and whistling.

9.

Women jump men, rip off shirts and fling shirts into smoking trash, run to men's tower mound.

Men roll on ground laughing loud, "Hee!, Hee!, Hee!, Haw!, Haw!"

People advance, banging and whistling.

HOUSEHOLD
Page 3

10.

Women take off blouses, wave them overhead like hankies, each singing own rock-n-roll tune and twisting dreamy-like.

Men hurl red smoke-flares into smoking trash heap.

People circle smoking jam-car, become silent, squat down, eat jam sandwiches.

11.

Men go to wreck, take sledge hammers from people, pick up battering log, begin to demolish car.

Women watch from distance and cheer men for every smash.

People eat silently and watch.

12.

Men jack up car, remove wheels, set fire to it, sit down to watch, light up cigarettes.

People light up cigarettes, watch car burning.

Women run out of junk yard, waving blouses, gaily calling, "'Bye, 'Bye! G'Bye!, 'Bye!", get into cars, drive away with horns blaring steadily till out of earshot.

13.

Everyone smokes silently and watches car until it's burned up.

Then they leave quietly.

111–113 Score for *Household*

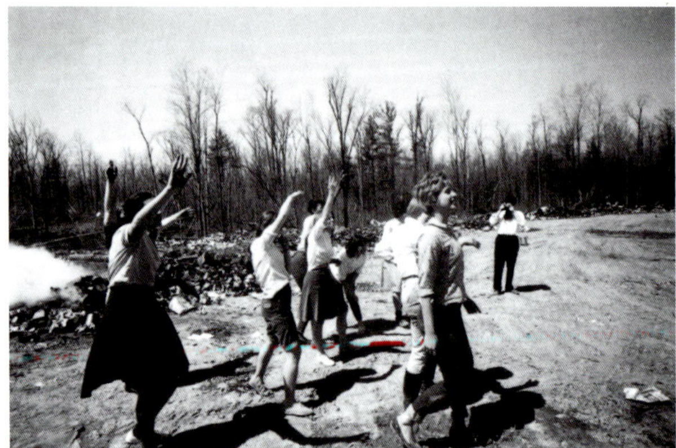

114 Women calling to the men

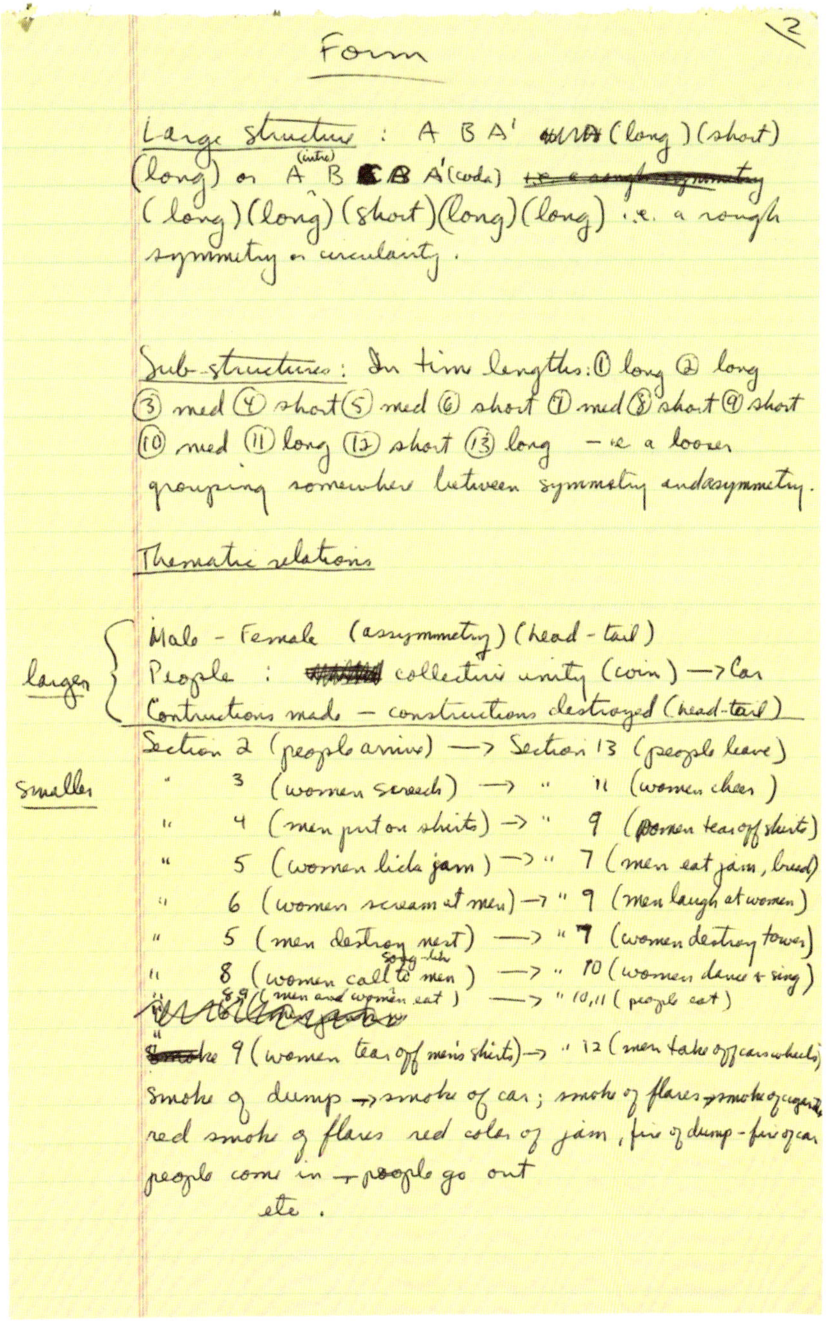

2

Form

Large structure: A B A' (long)(short)(long) or A (intro) B C B A' (coda) (long)(long)(short)(long)(long) i.e. a rough symmetry or circularity.

Sub-structures: In time lengths: ① long ② long ③ med ④ short ⑤ med ⑥ short ⑦ med ⑧ short ⑨ short ⑩ med ⑪ long ⑫ short ⑬ long — i.e. a looser grouping somewhere between symmetry and asymmetry.

Thematic relations

larger { Male - Female (assymmetry) (head - tail)
People : collective unity (coin) → Car
Contructions made — constructions destroyed (head-tail)

smaller
Section 2 (people arrive) → Section 13 (people leave)
" 3 (women screech) → " 11 (women cheer)
" 4 (men put on shirts) → " 9 (women tear off shirts)
" 5 (women lick jam) → " 7 (men eat jam, bread)
" 6 (women scream at men) → " 9 (men laugh at women)
" 5 (men destroy nest) → " 7 (women destroy tower)
" 8 (women call song-like to men) → " 10 (women dance + sing)
" 8,9 (men and women eat) → " 10,11 (people eat)
" 9 (women tear off men's shirts) → " 12 (men take off car wheels)

smoke of dump → smoke of car; smoke of flares → smoke of cigarettes
red smoke of flares red color of jam, fire of dump - fire of car
people come in → people go out
etc.

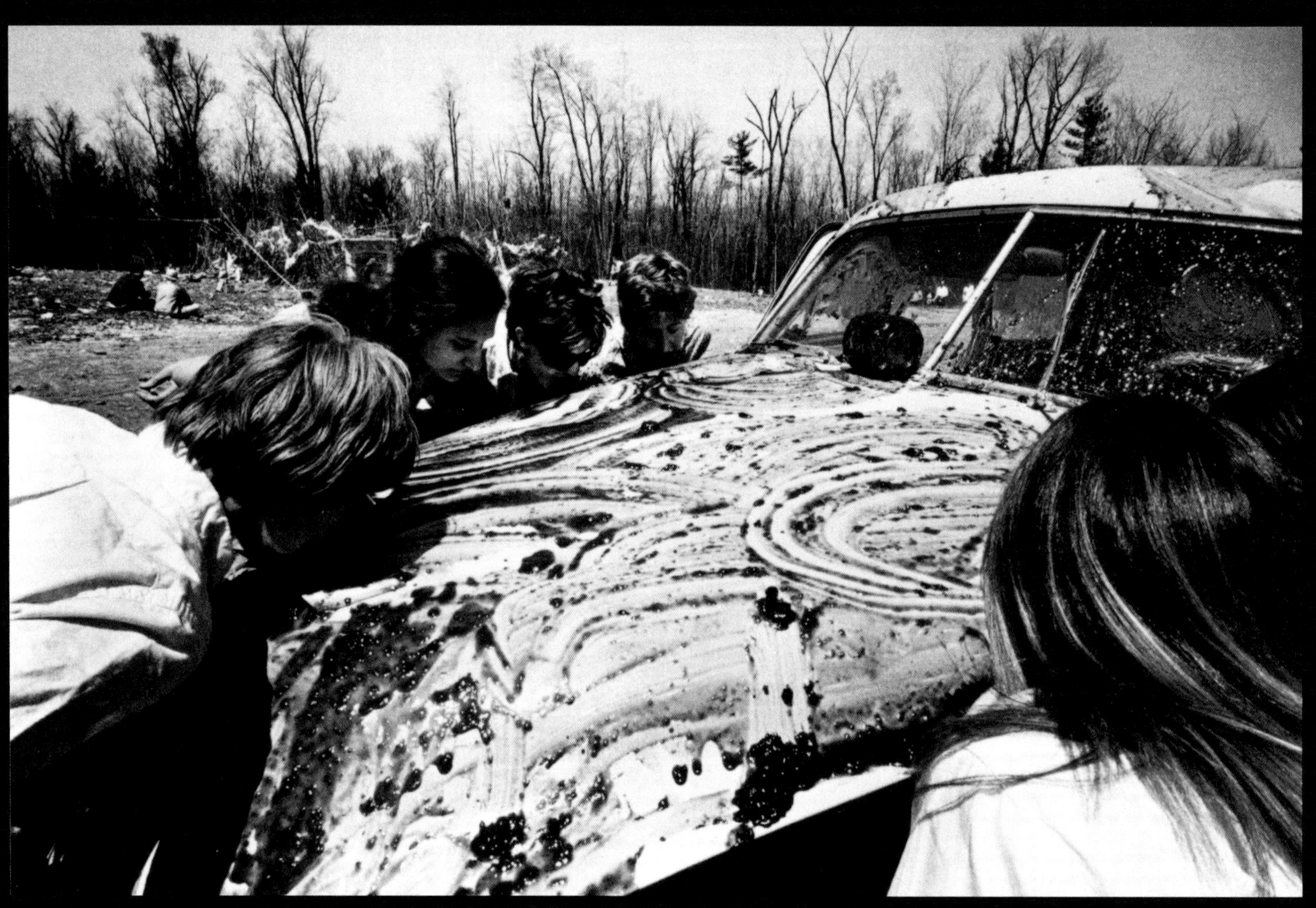

116 Women licking jam off of a car

117 Men working on the tower

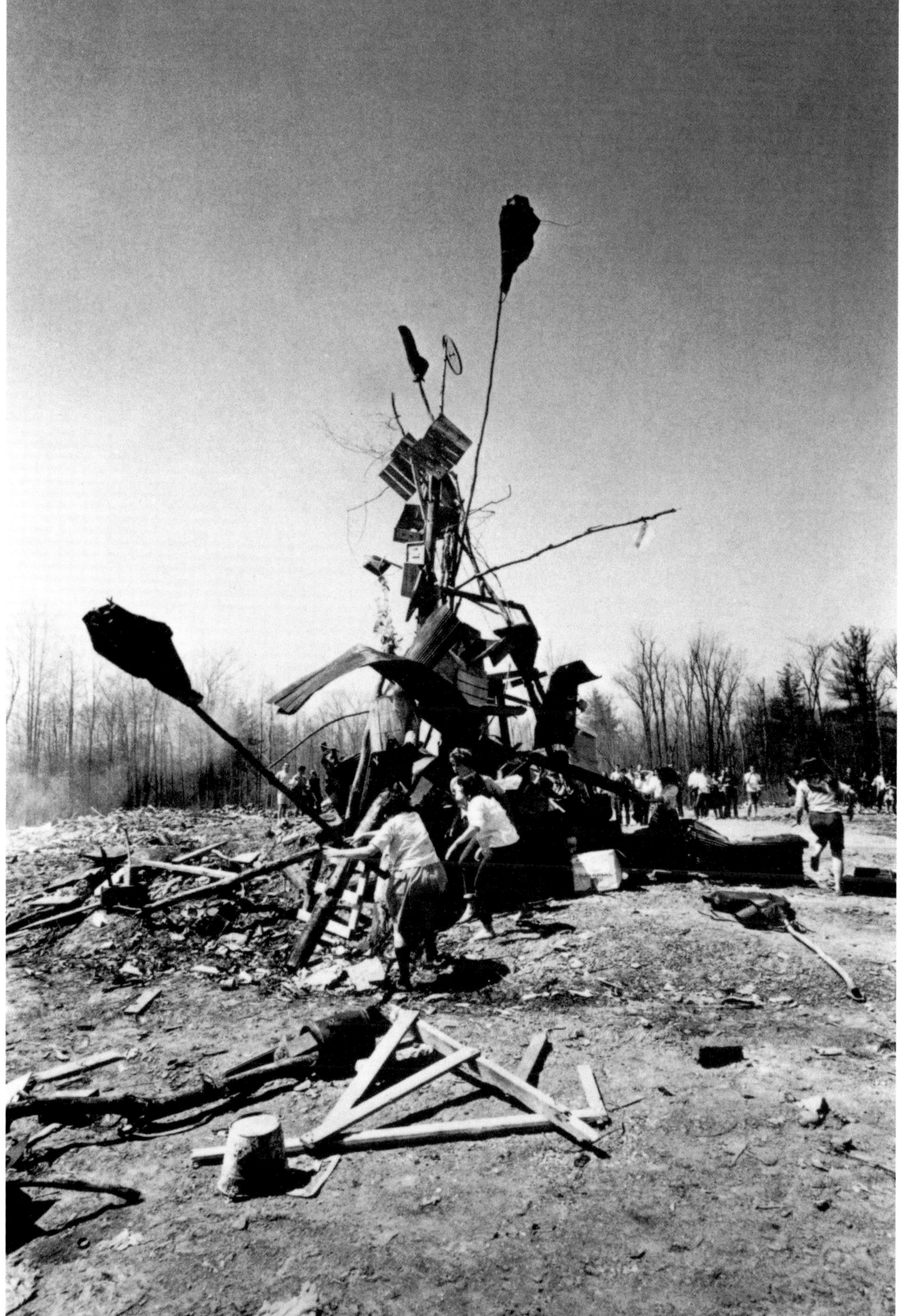

Raining

Booklet, 1965
Published by the Solomon R. Guggenheim Museum, New York

Soap

Happening, February 1965
Commissioned by Florida State University, Sarasota
Canceled due to misinterpretation of intent
Realized independently by a participant on the beach and in the city of Sarasota
Reinvented in 1989

118–123 Calling

Happening, August 1965
New York and the woods at George Segal's farm, South Brunswick, New Jersey

Push and Pull

Environment, September 1965
Reinvention for the Third Annual New York Avant-Garde Festival
Judson Hall, New York

118 Notes to *Calling*

Notes to <u>CALLING</u>:

1) Places (other than train station) and times are to be decided just prior to performance.

2) Performance should preferably take place over two days, the first in the city, and the second in the country.

3) At least twenty-one persons are necessary to perform this Happening properly. For this number six cars are required. Thus there would be three persons waiting at street corners, a car containing three people, including the driver, to pick each one up; and a matching number of second-stage cars, also manned by three people, to carry the wrapped persons to the railroad station. But this basic number of participants can be multiplied proportionately for as large a group as is desired.

4) Names used throughout are to be the names of those involved.

5) Wrappings of foil and cloth should be as thoroughly applied as possible, the face covered except for breathing gap.

6) Second-stage cars should be parked near pre-chosen wastebaskets, widely separated from each other. Drivers then proceed to part of city where first-stage cars are parked at meters. There the two drivers exchange car keys, the first-stage trio hurrying to wastebasket positions, where they enter the autos and await the arrival of the human packages. The latter, of course, are brought by the second-stage trio. Timing for this, and all other stages of the event, must be worked out exactly.

7) The cars depositing packages in wastebaskets next proceed to the homes of their drivers, where phone calls will be received.

8) After the human packages unwrap themselves at the information booth, calls should be made from a public booth to the drivers of the last-mentioned cars. Phone is allowed to ring fifty times before it is picked up. Answerer says only "yes?" Caller asks if it is <u>x</u>, (stating the right name), and <u>x</u> quietly hangs up.

9) The people hanging from ropes in the woods are those who drove and accompanied the cars the day before. An exchange of positions takes place here (underscored by the inverted positions on the ropes), with the former package people taking the active role. There should be no less than five bodies suspended, although all car people may choose to hang this way. If less than the total (of, say, eighteen), the others should sit motionless beneath each rope and join in the anwering and the calling of names. When called from afar by the package people, the answer is simply "here!", "here!", "here!" until each body is found and violated.

10) The package people, arriving at the woods, call out the names of the car people hidden over a wide area among the trees. Moving as a group, they follow the sounds of the voices and reach each dangling figure. Its clothes are rapidly cut off, and after all have been so treated, the group leaves. Each suspended person (and those sitting beneath him) should cease answering to their names when found. Gradually the answering will diminish to silence, and at that point they start to call out each other's names, like children lost.

Allan Kaprow
July, 1965

1965

TEACHING POSITIONS Associate Professor, Department of Fine Arts, State University of New York, Stony Brook. Director, Experimental Education, Institute of Contemporary Art, Boston. ¶ AWARDS Research grant from State University of New York, Stony Brook. ¶ GROUP EXHIBITIONS *Eleven from the Reuben Gallery,* Solomon R. Guggenheim Museum, New York, January. *Ten from Rutgers University,* Bianchini Gallery, New York, December–January. ¶ FESTIVALS Third Annual New York Avant-Garde Festival, Judson Hall, New York, September. ¶ THEATER Performed in "Theater Piece" by John Cage, Third Annual New York Avant-Garde Festival, Judson Hall, New York, September. ¶ WRITINGS "Barnett Newman—ein Klassiker?" in Jürgen Claus, ed., *Kunst heute: Personen, Analysen, Dokumente* (Hamburg: Rowohlt), 74–78. "Daniel Spoerri," in *Daniel Spoerri's Room No. 631 at the Chelsea Hotel,* exh. cat. (New York: Green Gallery), n.p. "Eat" (notes and drawing) and "Calling" (notes and scenario), *Tulane Drama Review* 10, no. 2: 44–49, 203–11. "The New Brunswick School," in *Ten from Rutgers University,* exh. cat. (New York: Bianchini Gallery), 3–4. Notes and scenario for *Eating,* in Susan Sontag and Allan Kaprow, "An Art of Radical Juxtaposition," *The Second Coming Magazine* 1, no. 6: 25–26. "Pop Art," *Newsletter of the Department of Fine Arts,* State University of New York, Stony Brook, November: 3–4. Statement in Katharine Kuh, "Recent Kinetic Art," in Gyorgy Kepes, ed., *The Nature and Art of Motion* (New York: George Braziller), 121–24. Statement and scripts for *18 Happenings in 6 Parts, Coca-Cola, Shirley Cannonball?, A Spring Happening,* and *Courtyard,* in Michael Kirby, *Happenings: An Illustrated Anthology* (New York: E.P. Dutton), 44–52, 55–66, 84–86, 92–93, 105–7.

119 + 120 Announcement and score for *Calling*

CALLING

A Happening for performers only.
Tentatively scheduled for Saturday,
August 21, and Sunday, August 22.

Those interested in participating
may call Allan Kaprow (telephone:
516, OR 1-6735) on Tuesday, August
17, from 9 AM to 10 PM.

CALLING

In the city, people stand at street corners and wait.

For each of them:

A car pulls up, someone calls out a name, the person gets in, they drive off.

During the trip, the person is wrapped in aluminum foil. The car is parked at a meter somewhere, is left there, locked; the silver person sitting motionless in the front seat.

Someone unlocks the car, drives off. The foil is removed from the person; he or she is wrapped in cloth or tied into a laundry bag. The car stops, the person is dumped in a public wastebasket, and the car goes away.

A waiting auto pulls over to the curb, the person is removed from the wastebasket, is hauled into the car, is taken to the information booth at Grand Central Station. The person is propped up against it and left.

The person calls out names, and hears the others brought there also call. They call out for some time. Then they work loose from their wrappings and leave the train station.

They telephone certain numbers. The phone rings and rings. Finally, it is amswered, a name is asked for, and immediately the other end clicks off.

* * * * * * * *

In the woods, the persons call out names and hear hidden answers. Here and there, they come upon people dangling upside down from ropes. They rip the people's clothes off and go away.

The naked figures call to each other in the woods for a long time, until they are tired. Silence.

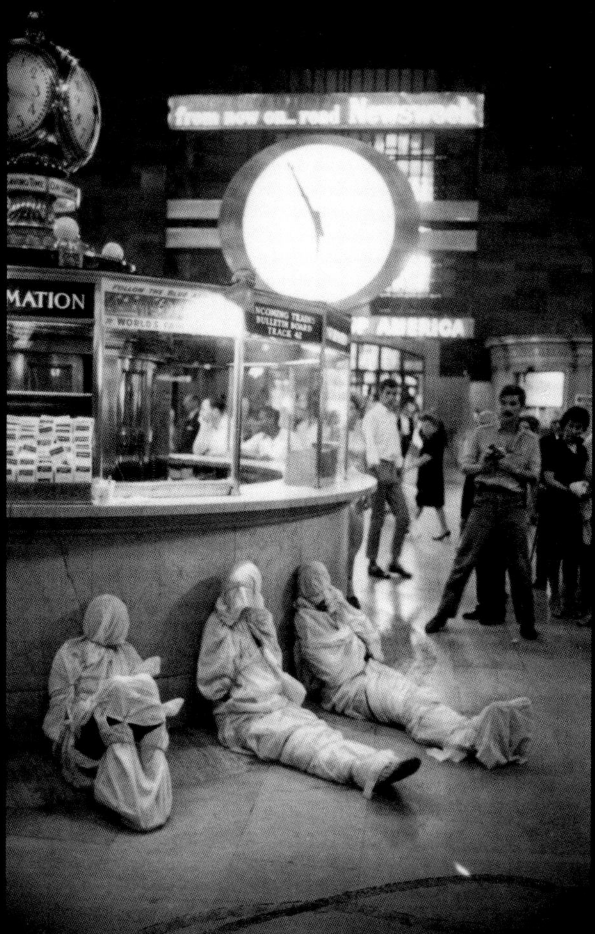

121 Participants at Grand Central Station
Photo: Peter Moore

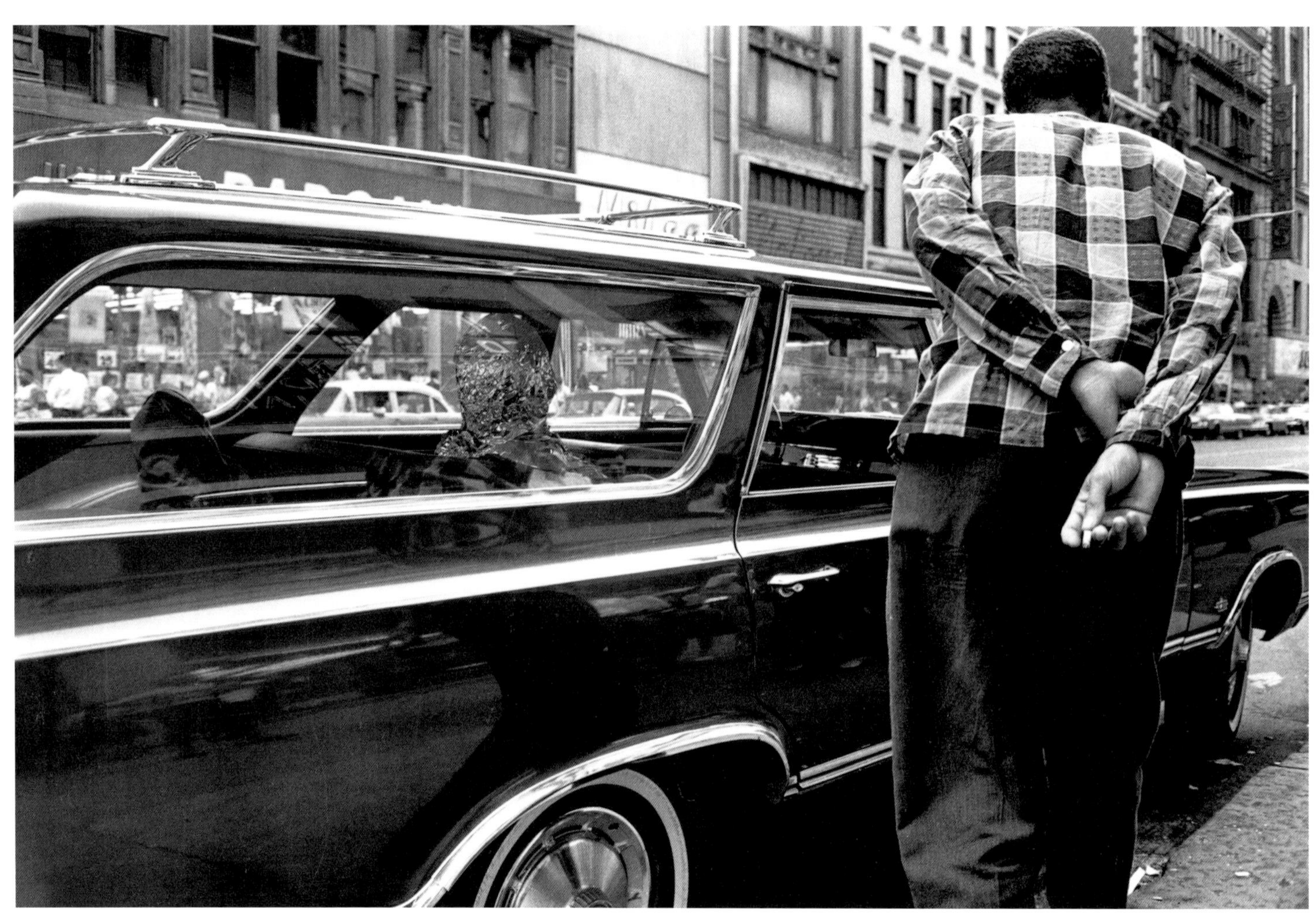

122 Jeanne-Claude Christo wrapped in aluminum foil
Photo: Peter Moore

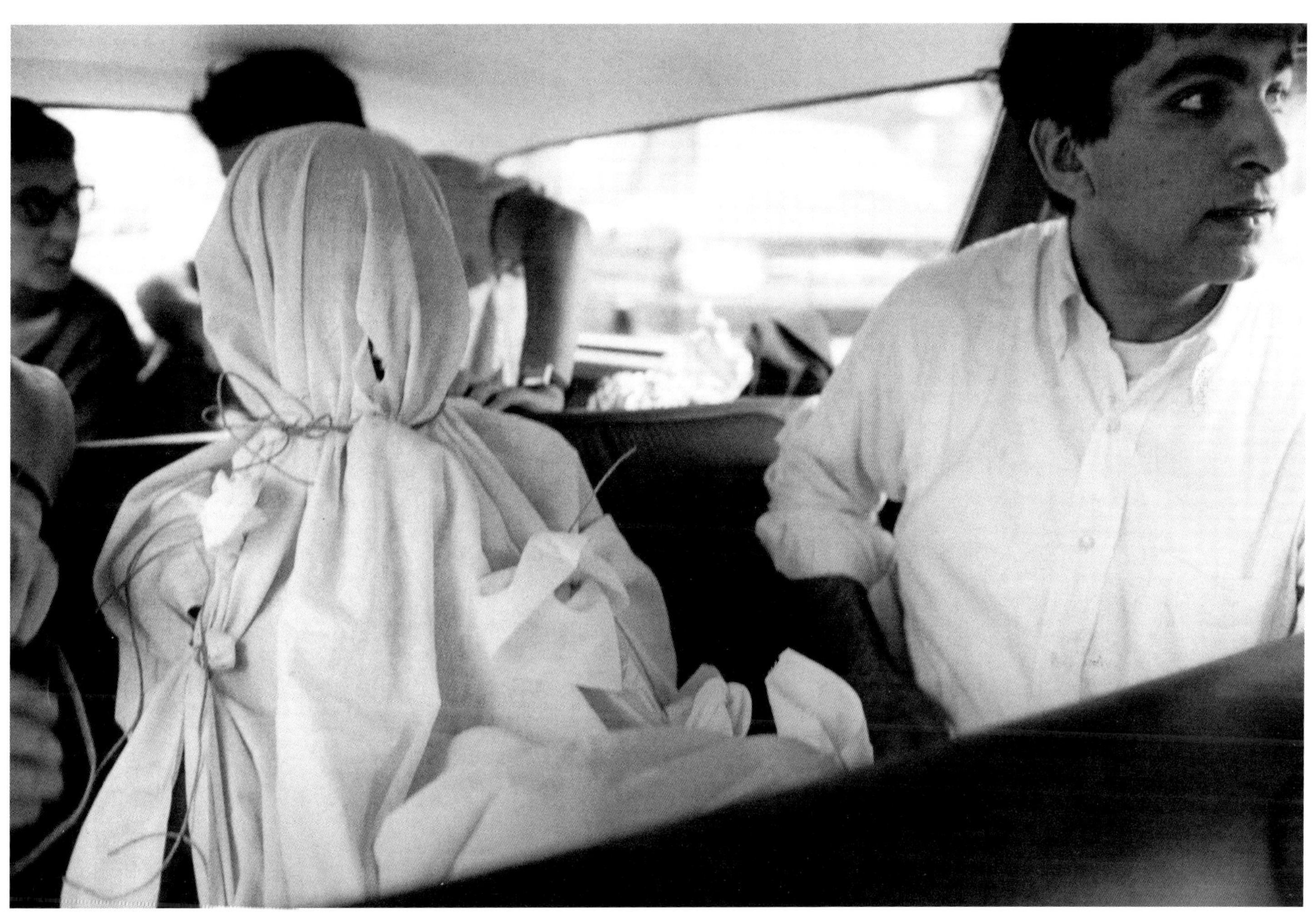

123 Participant wrapped in cloth
Photo: Peter Moore

NEW YORK

(Available Activities)

Rockets, spread over several miles, go up in red smoke, explode, scatter thousands of scraps of paper with messages.

Couples make love in hotel rooms. Before they check out, they cover everything with large sheets of black plastic film.

Warehouse or dump of used refrigerators. People bring packages of ice, transistor radios, and put them into the boxes. Radios are turned on, refrig doors are shut, people leave. On another day they turn, sit inside with radios for awhile, and quietly listen.

Couples kiss each other in the midst of the world, go on.

People stand on bridges, on street corners, watch cars pass. After two hundred red ones, they leave.

People shout in subway just before getting off, leave immediately.

On the streets, kids give paper flowers to people with pleasant faces.

On the shoulder of a stretch of highway, a fancy banquet table laid out, food in the plates, money in the saucers. Everything left there.

Everyone watches for either:
- a signal from someone.
- a light to go on in a window.
- a plane to pass directly overhead.
- an insect to land nearby.
- three motorcycles to barrel past.

Immediately afterwards, they write a careful description of the occurrence, and mail copies to each other.

An empty house. Nails are hammered halfway into all surfaces of rooms, house is locked, hammers go away.

LOS ANGELES

(Available Activities)

Cars drive into a fillings station, erupt with white foam pouring from windows.

A car is built on an isolated mountain top, from junk parts. Is left.

People shout in subway just before getting off, leave immediately.

Everyone watches for either:
- a signal from someone.
- a light to go on in a window.
- a plane to pass directly overhead.
- an insect to land nearby.
- three motorcycles to barrel past.

Immediately afterwards, they write a careful description of the occurrence, and mail copies to each other.

Warehouse or dump of used refrigerators. People bring packages of ice, transistor radios, and put them into the boxes. Radios are turned on, refrig doors are shut, people leave. On another day they return, sit inside with radios for awhile, and quietly listen.

On the streets, kids give paper flowers to people with pleasant faces.

A daytime procession of cars on a highway, brights on. Periodically, and momentarily, fifteen feet of thin plastic film streams from car's windows, is drawn back inside. Half-hour later, cars disperse.

Many shoppers begin to whistle in aisles of supermarket. After a few minutes, they go back to shopping.

Photos of supermarket and washerette projected onto clouds, into air.

People tie tarpaper around many cars in supermarket lot.

Night in the country. Many cars, moving on different roads, about a mile from a certain point, lights blinking, horns beeping sporadically, converge and disperse.

Photos of supermarket and washerette sent to everyone.

People listen to records in glass booths. They look at each other and dance.

Two people telephone each other. Phone rings once, is answered "hello". Caller hangs up. After a few minutes, other person does same. Same answer. Phone clicks off. Repeated with two rings, three rings, four rings, five rings, six rings, seven, eight, nine, etc......until a line is busy.

124 + 125 Score for *Self-Service*, pp.1–2

126 Score for *Self-Service,* p. 3

BOSTON

(Available Activities)

Many shoppers begin to whistle in aisles of supermarket. After a few minutes they go back to their shopping.

For a few moments at night, shouts, words, calls, all through bull-horns. Voices moving on the streets, from windows, around corners, in hallways, alleys.

At a supermarket (on another day) transistor radios playing rock are put into shelves of cereals, soaps, freezers, bananas, napkins, etc. Left there. On still another day, bouquets are tucked in with products.

In a neighborhood, people inflate, by mouth, a twenty foot weather balloon. It's pushed through the streets and buried in a hole at the beach. The people leave it.

Two people telephone each other. Phone rings once, is answered "hello". Caller hangs up. After a few minutes, other person does same. Same answer. Phone clicks off. Repeated with two rings, three rings, four rings, five rings, six rings, seven, eight, nine, etc......until a line is busy.

People tie tarpaper around many cars in supermarket lot.

On another day, twenty or more flash-gun cameras shoot off at same time all over supermarket; shopping resumed.

3 A.M. emptiness at a 24-hour washer-ette. Piles of clothes washed. Turning cylinders, blue-whie flour-escents. Regularly on the half-hour, loud bunch of photogs bust in, flash, leave. Home at five.

Cars drive into filling station, erupt with white foam pouring from windows.

Three Country Happening

Proposal for a Happening, Spring 1966
For Allan Kaprow (United States of America), Marta Minujín (Argentina), and Wolf Vostell (Germany)

124–128 **Self-Service**

Happening, June–September 1966
Sponsored by Harry N. Abrams, the Pasadena Art Museum, and the Institute of Contemporary Art, Boston
New York, Los Angeles, and Boston
Reinvented in 1986 and 1988

Towers

Happening, September 1966
Presented for the Fourth Annual New York Avant-Garde Festival
Central Park, New York

129–132 **Gas**

Happening, August 1966
Sponsored by Dwan Gallery and WCBS-TV
The Hamptons, Long Island, and New York

Untitled Environment

Environment, November 1966
Reinvention for *Mass-Art*
Westchester Art Society, White Plains, New York

How To Make a Happening

LP record, 1966
Recorded in conjunction with *Mass-Art*
Produced by Mass Art Inc.

1966 TEACHING POSITIONS Professor, Department of Fine Arts, State University of New York, Stony Brook. Director, Experimental Education, Institute of Contemporary Art, Boston. ¶ AWARDS Research grant from State University of New York, Stony Brook. ¶ GROUP EXHIBITIONS *Mass-Art,* Westchester Art Society, White Plains, New York, November. ¶ FESTIVALS Fourth Annual New York Avant-Garde Festival, Central Park, New York, September. ¶ WRITINGS *Assemblage, Environments & Happenings* (New York: Harry N. Abrams). "The Creation of Art and the Creation of Art Education" and "Excerpts," in *A Seminar in Art Education for Research and Curriculum Development* (University Park: Pennsylvania State University), 74–89. "Experimental Art," *ARTnews* 65, no. 1: 60–63, 77–82. "Female Art: No Games," *Village Voice,* 28 April: 12. "Hans Hofmann," *Village Voice,* 24 February: 1–2. "The Happenings Are Dead—Long Live the Happenings!" *Artforum* 4, no. 7: 36–39. "'Katei' no tame no oboegaki" (notes for *Household*), in Nakahara Yūsuke, ed., "Tokubetsu kikō: Gendai bijutsu no kanōsei" (Special contribution: The possibility of contemporary art), *Mizue,* no. 731: 10–11. Letter to the editor, *Tulane Drama Review* 10, no. 4: 281–83. Response to a questionnaire in "People Are Replying to Our Inquiry," *World Theatre* 15, no. 1: 33–35. "Self-Service: A Happening," *Soundings* 3, no. 1: 14–27. *Some Recent Happenings,* Great Bear Pamphlet no. 7 (New York: Something Else). Untitled manifesto, in Dick Higgins, ed., *Manifestos,* Great Bear Pamphlet no. 8 (New York: Something Else), 21–23.

FINAL SCHEME FOR SELF-SERVICE

The chart below indicates the distribution of all Los Angeles activities from June through September. Figures in boxes represent the number of persons who have chosen to enact a particular activity in each month. Blank spaces occur either because practical matters eliminated an activity or due to the chance-operations used in arriving at the distribution

Activities	June	July	Aug.	Sept.	Remarks
Car built on mountain top		8	5	3	Contact Eric Orr. A suggestion: women may be especially interested in helping with the upholstering of the interior of auto.
Watching for signals	18				This may be done either privately or with a few other participants. Mimeographing of descriptions at Pasadena Museum.
Warehouse of used refrigerators					
Paper flowers		9		7	Contact Margaret Koch. This activity should be done with as many kids as seems appropriate, with kids making paper flowers beforehand.
Daytime procession of cars	12		7		Contact Jim Stehn.
Whistle in supermarket.	14	20			Contact Michael Agnello.
Tarpaper around cars.	7			7	Contact Joseph Byrd. Cars should belong to participants.
Cars blinking, beeping at night.	6	9	10	7	Contact Mary Yeomans.
Photos of supermarket sent to everyone	1	2	1	2	Photographers should connect with market and laundrorette events. Contact Pasadena Museum regarding expenses.
Listen to records and dance	7	9	6	4	Contact Jesse Jacobs.
Two people telephone	9			5	Telephone calls to be arranged among participants.
Torn paper dropped	13	12	10		This is primarily a private activity.
Weather balloon		15			Contact Joseph Byrd.
Eat sandwiches in phone booths	9	15	9	10	This is a completely private activity.
Count red cars		8			This is a completely private activity.
Rockets		6			Contact Joe Mullin.

Activities continued	June	July	Aug.	Sept.	Remarks
Nails in empty house	13	[illegible]	15		Contact Gwenda Davies.
Whistle in elevator	7			7	Contact Michael Genth.
3 A.M. in washerette					Contact Walter Hopps.
Long parade of white banners, etc.	7	14	10		Contact Gwenda Davies. Bring into activity as many kids as possible.
Riding on bus searching for face	2		4	5	This is a private activity.
Bread and jam path			11	9	Contact Hal or Gretchen Glicksman
Couples kiss in world	13	15	12	15	This activity should be enacted in a way that seems appropriate to the couple.
Photos projected	1		1		Contact Walter Hopps
Shout is subway					
Cars in filling stations					

127 + 128 Final scheme for *Self-Service*

A HAPPENING

by

Charles Frazier
Mordi Gerstein
Gordon Hyatt
Allan Kaprow

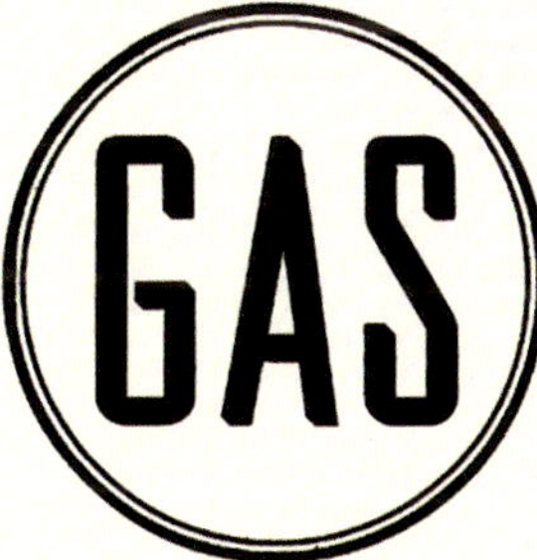

In Cooperation With The Dwan Gallery And WCBS-TV

SATURDAY, AUGUST 6 - AM

slow parade of big weather balloons, crowds pushing - hover crafts manned by the Neutron Kid and Liquid Hips - seeing eyes - flares - barrel pounders booming

SATURDAY, AUGUST 6 - PM

weather balloons rise, burst, wash ashore, messages to area - plastic skyscraper on beach, destroyed, shrill whistles - laundry uncovered, day at washerette - bulging letters go up, ride waves - sky divers descend, yells, noise - blimp hoves in - skywriter's secret word - seeing eyes

SUNDAY, AUGUST 7 - AM

"fire" written inside truck, cops spray with snow bombs - ferry trip, white sheets hung out, loud rock on car radios - seeing eyes - nurses onshore yahooing welcomes - black plastic moving across exit - nurses running off - passed by on highway, nurses stacked five-deep on hospital beds, waving, laughing

SUNDAY, AUGUST 7 - PM

bluffs above sea - fire trucks, squad cars, red flashers on, lights, intercoms - bullhorn instructions - seeing eyes - black mounds on beach - rockets released - foam pouring down cliff, past mounds into waves - crowd passing through - interviews

MONDAY, AUGUST 8 - AM

junked autos - kids' clubhouses dolled up for picnic - goodie car serving - flying machine buzzing hulks - big ballon oozing out of car body - seeing eyes - playtime

MONDAY, AUGUST 8 - PM

burial pit - black mounds moving slowly down, sea of foam rolling down - cars blaring horns every thirty seconds - blast on whistles, towers of barrels toppled into pit - pushed up incline against flow - seeing eyes still, all over bottom - regular garbage deliveries

Those interested in participating should attend a preliminary meeting at either the VFW Hall, 4 Main Street, Easthampton on Sunday, July 31 - 11 AM; or the CBS Broadcasting Center, 524 West 57 Street, New York City on Tuesday, August 2 - 8 PM (ask at desk in lobby).

129 Poster for *Gas*
(with score)

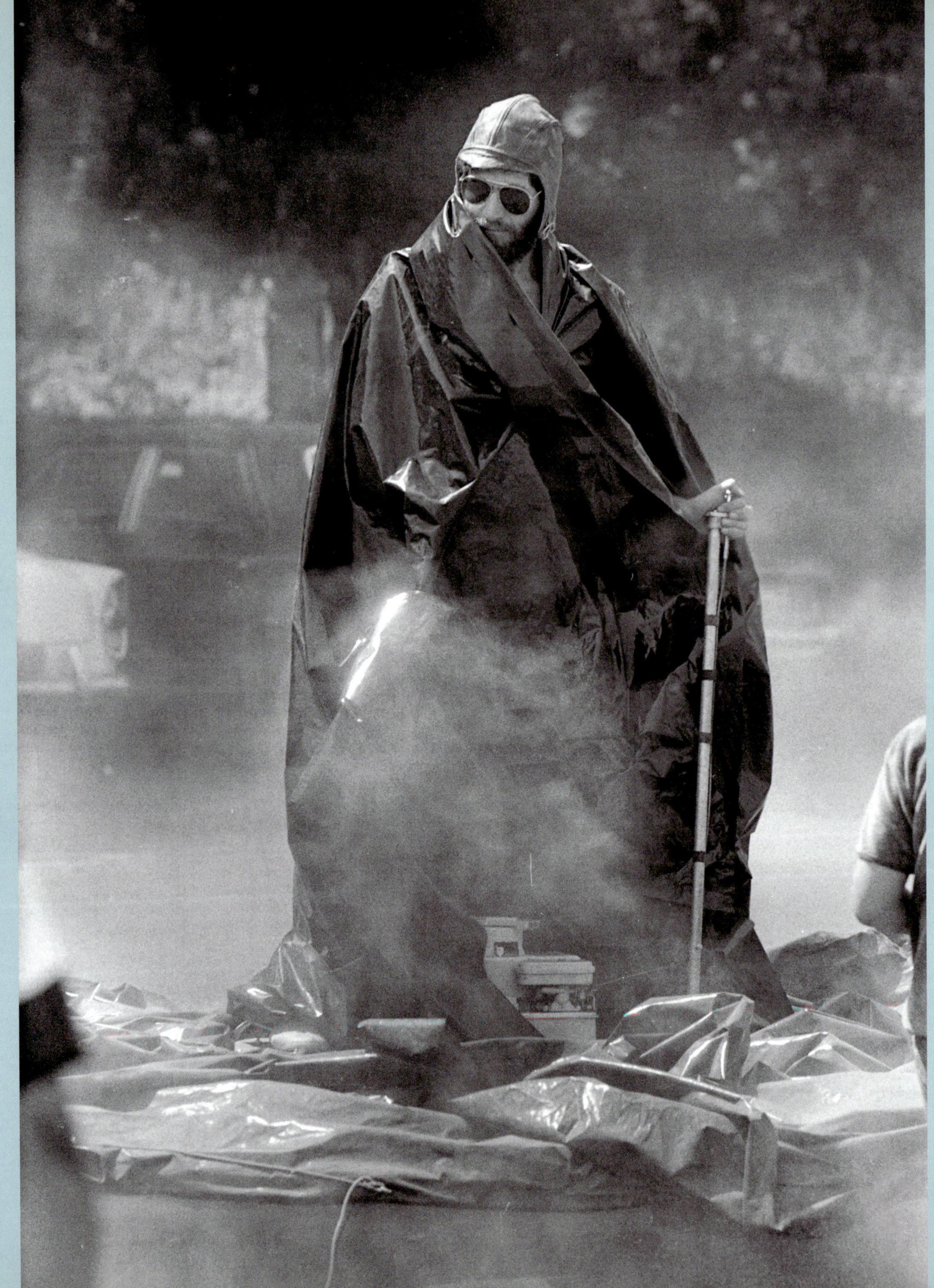

130 Kaprow as the Neutron Kid
Photo: Peter Moore

131 Slow parade of big weather balloons

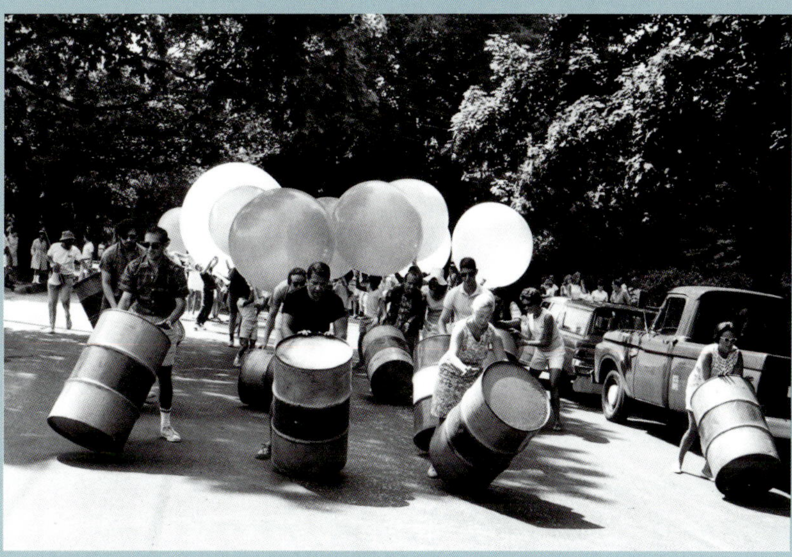

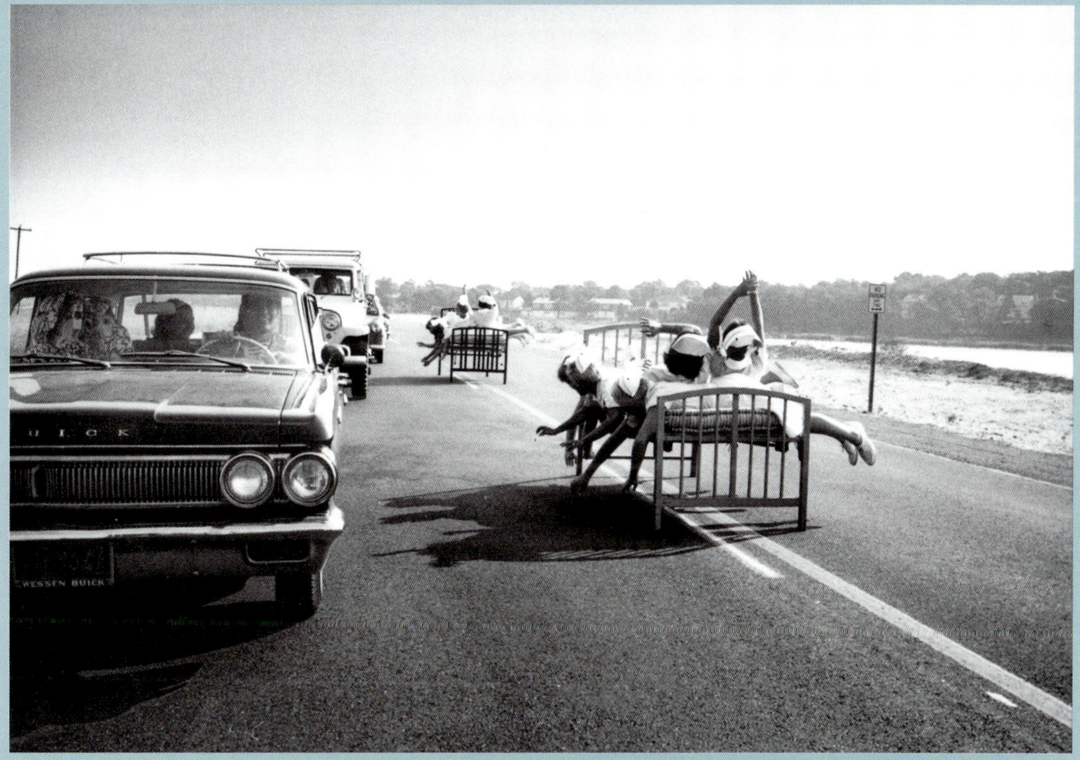

132 Nurses on hospital beds

LIFE EVENTS Marisa Tamar Kaprow, daughter, born January. Nina Madge Kaprow, daughter, died March. ¶ **TEACHING POSITIONS** Professor, Department of Fine Arts, State University of New York, Stony Brook. ¶ **AWARDS** Guggenheim Fellowship. Research grant from State University of New York, Stony Brook. ¶ **SOLO EXHIBITIONS** *Allan Kaprow,* Pasadena Art Museum, Pasadena (traveled nationally), September–October. ¶ **GROUP EXHIBITIONS** *Pictures To Be Read, Poetry To Be Seen,* Museum of Contemporary Art, Chicago, October–December. *Two Happening Concepts: Allan Kaprow and Wolf Vostell,* Museum of Contemporary Art, Chicago (traveled nationally), November–December. ¶ **FESTIVALS** Fifth Annual New York Avant-Garde Festival, Staten Island Ferryboat, New York, September. ¶ **WRITINGS** *Calling—A Big Little Book* (with Dick Higgins and Alison Knowles), limited ed. (New York: Something Else). "Communications Programming" and "Pinpointing Happenings" (with Barbara Berman), in *Allan Kaprow,* exh. cat. (Pasadena: Pasadena Art Museum), 12–19. "The End of the Concert Hall" (introduction to a dialogue between Max Neuhaus and students), *The Statesman,* 3 May: 4–5. "Gas" (program, notes, and critical analysis), in Michael Benedikt, *Theater Experiment* (New York: Doubleday), 379–87. "'Happenings' in the New York Scene" (originally published in 1961), in Alvin Kernan, ed., *The Modern American Theater: A Collection of Critical Essays* (Prentice Hall, N.J.: Spectrum), 121–30. "Pop Art: Past, Present and Future," *Malahat Review,* no. 3: 54–76. Response to a questionnaire, in Barbara Rose and Irving Sandler, "Sensibility of the Sixties," *Art in America* 55, no. 1: 45. Statement printed without title in "Jackson Pollock: An Artists' Symposium, Part 1," *ARTnews* 66, no. 2: 32–33, 59–61. *Untitled Essay and Other Works* (essay and scores for *Mushroom, Paper,* and *Interruption*), Great Bear Pamphlet no. 16 (New York: Something Else). "Where Art Thou, Sweet Muse? (I'm Hung up at the Whitney)," in Allan Kaprow and Robert Smithson, "Death in the Museum," *Arts Magazine* 41, no. 4: 40–41; reprinted as "What Is a Museum?: A Dialogue between Allan Kaprow and Robert Smithson," *Arts Yearbook,* no. 9: 94–101.

1967

Flick
Happening, February 1967
Sponsored by Angry Arts against War in Vietnam
Streets of New York

Sweep-In
Happening, April 1967
Lower East Side, New York

Interruption
Happening, May 1967
State University of New York, Stony Brook

L Gold
Proposal for a publicity campaign of Happenings, Summer 1967
For Liggett & Myers Tobacco Company

Noise
Happening, September 1967
Presented for the Fifth Annual New York Avant-Garde Festival
Automobile deck of the Staten Island Ferryboat, New York

Push and Pull
Environment, September–October 1967
Reinvention for *Allan Kaprow*
Pasadena Art Museum, Pasadena

Words
Environment, September–October 1967
Reinvention for *Allan Kaprow*
Pasadena Art Museum, Pasadena

Yard
Environment, September–October 1967
Reinvention for *Allan Kaprow*
Pasadena Art Museum, Pasadena

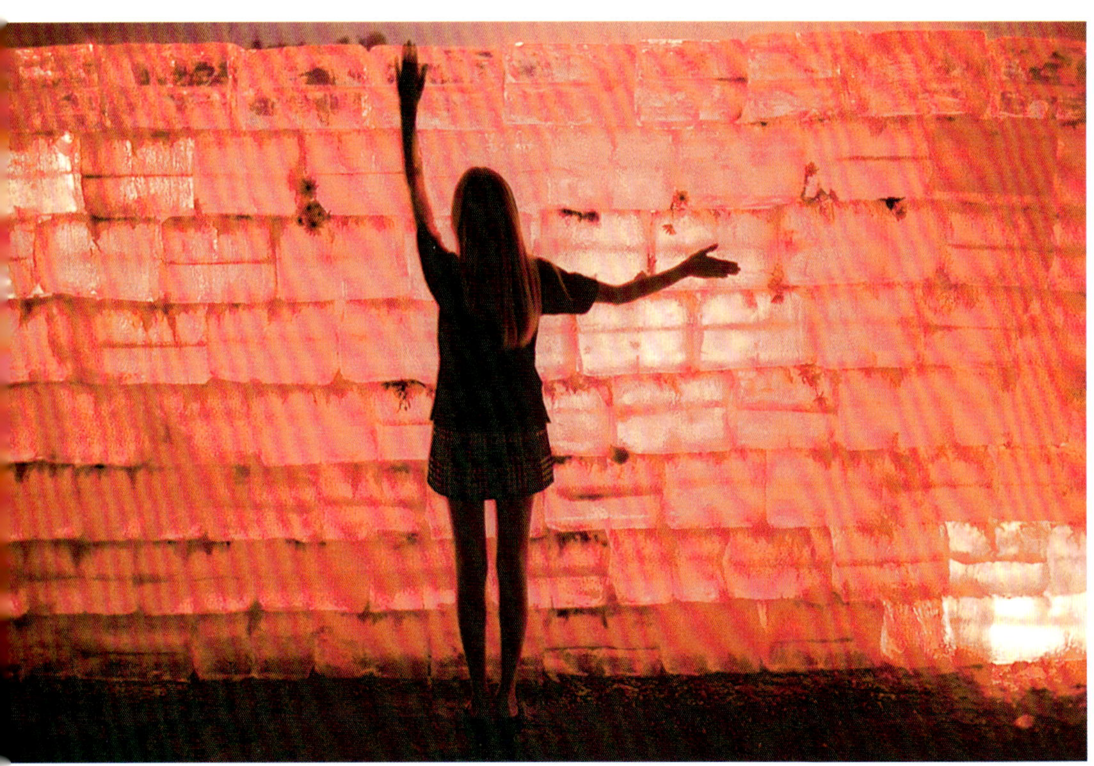

133 Woman in front of red ice

133–142 Fluids

Happening, October 1967
Presented for *Allan Kaprow*
Various locations in Pasadena and Los Angeles
Reinvented in 2005

Words

Environment, October–December 1967
Reinvention for *Pictures To Be Read, Poetry To Be Seen*
Museum of Contemporary Art, Chicago

Watching

Happening, November 1967
Presented for *Gateway to the Arts*
WCBS-TV, New York

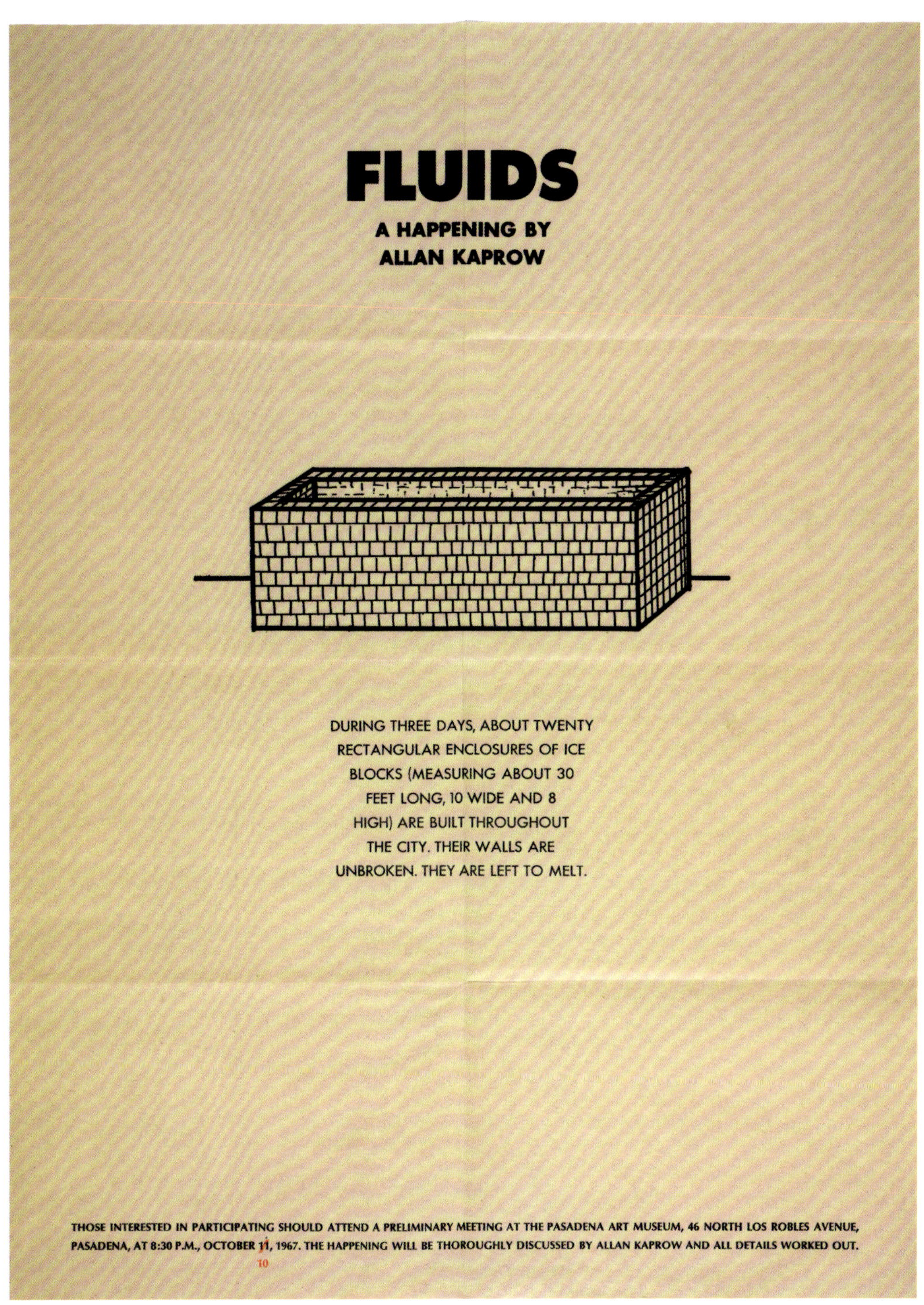

134 Poster for *Fluids*
(with score)

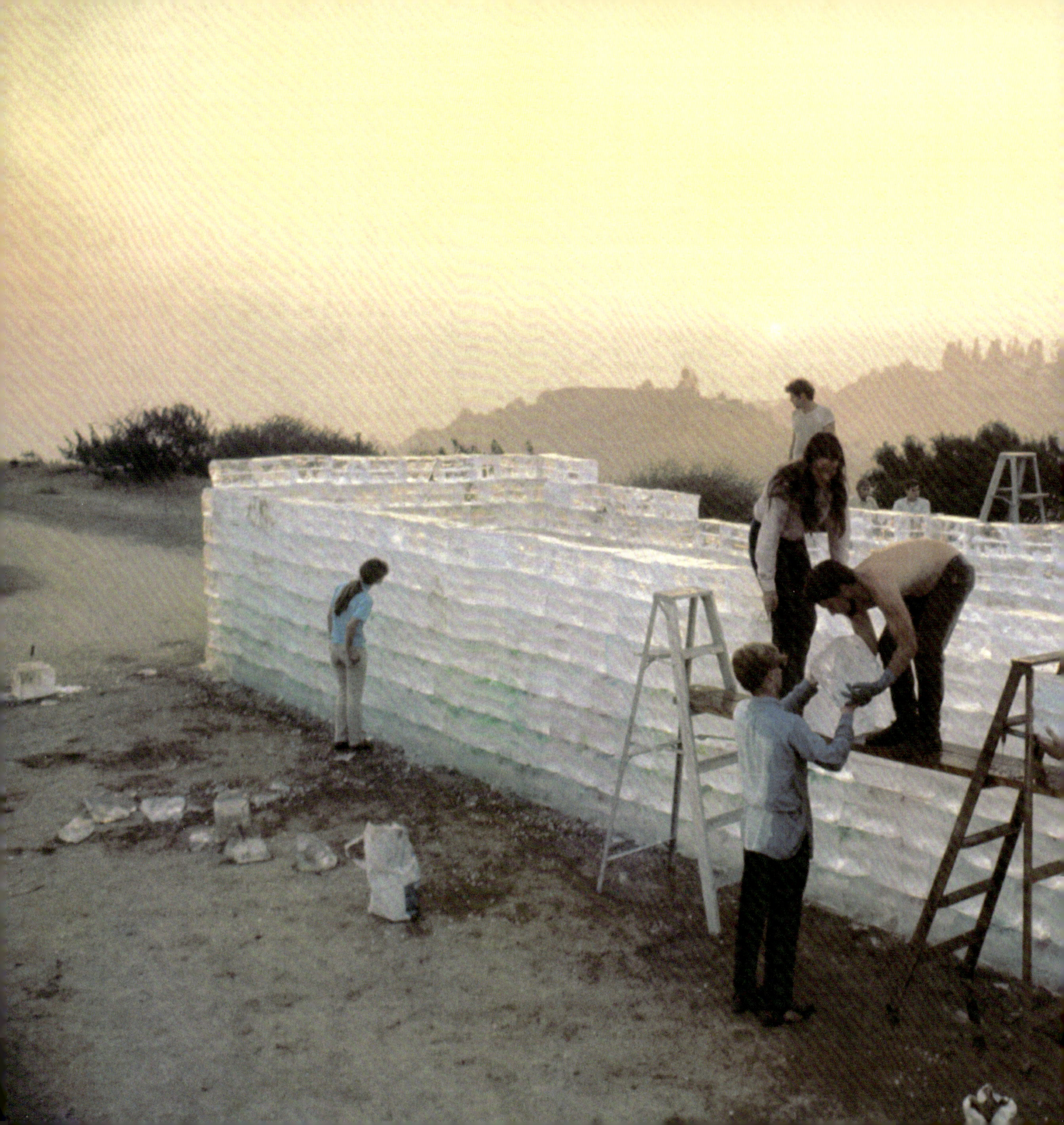

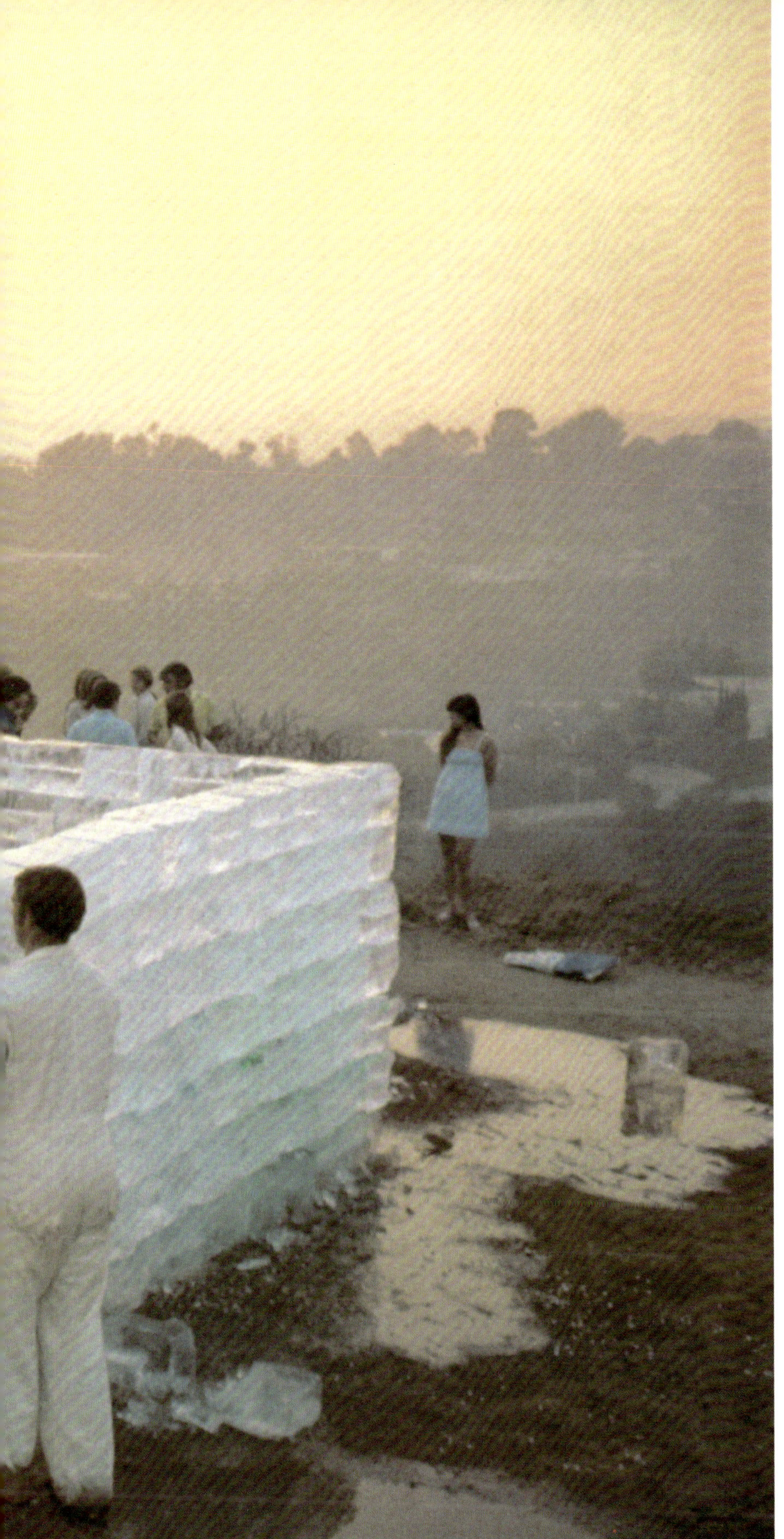

135 Trousdale Estates in Beverly Hills

273-2029 Julian

Thursday, October 12th

Allan Kaprow

1\. McDonalds Hamburger 12:00 noon
(in lot next door - South)
799 North Lake Street, Pasadena

phone: 798-0625

AK

Class of around 17 girls from Westridge School will be there to build under the direction of Barbara Smith

2\. The Play Yard (Mr. Matthiessen) 10:00 AM
5607 Rosemead Boulevard
Temple City

phone: 285-6796

3\. Pierce College (Walt Smith) 10:00 AM
6201 Winnetka
Woodland Hills

JW

phone: 347-0551

Ample supply of willing students to build structure
Someone will meet truck at gate and direct it to site of building on campus.

4\. Under two Colorado Street Bridges ~~12:00 noon~~ 2 PM
enter vacant area off El Circulo Drive
Pasadena

AK? JW?

no phone

AK

5\. Tail o'the Cock (Mr. Buchtel) 3:00 PM
447 South La Cienega Boulevard
Los Angeles 48

phone: CR 3-1200

Friday, October 13th

6\. Watts Towers (Mrs. Babbitz) 11:00 AM
East 107th Street
1 block East of Graham
Watts, Los Angeles

JW

phone: 462-8191 (Watts Committee offices on Melrose)

platform to be covered with plastic

7\. Brookside Park (Mr. Walt Moore) 2:00 PM
NE corner next to Fanny Morrison Bldg.
Pasadena

JW

AK

phone: 793-1947

enter park through parking lot - there is paved driveway

8\. Robert Colombatto Residence 3:00 PM
2000 Ashbourne
South Pasadena

phone: 799-5681

South on Chelton Way off Monterey Road - house is on North East corner Ashbourne and Chelton Way. Truck to park nest to fence - unload through gate. NO MORE VOLUNTEERS NEEDED.

9\. La Canada Rustic Stone Company (Paul Davis) 10:00 AM
301 North Lake
Pasadena

phone: SY 2-6262

JW

AK

build in Southern most driveway (there are two), as near the street as possible

138 Kaprow in front of a wall of ice

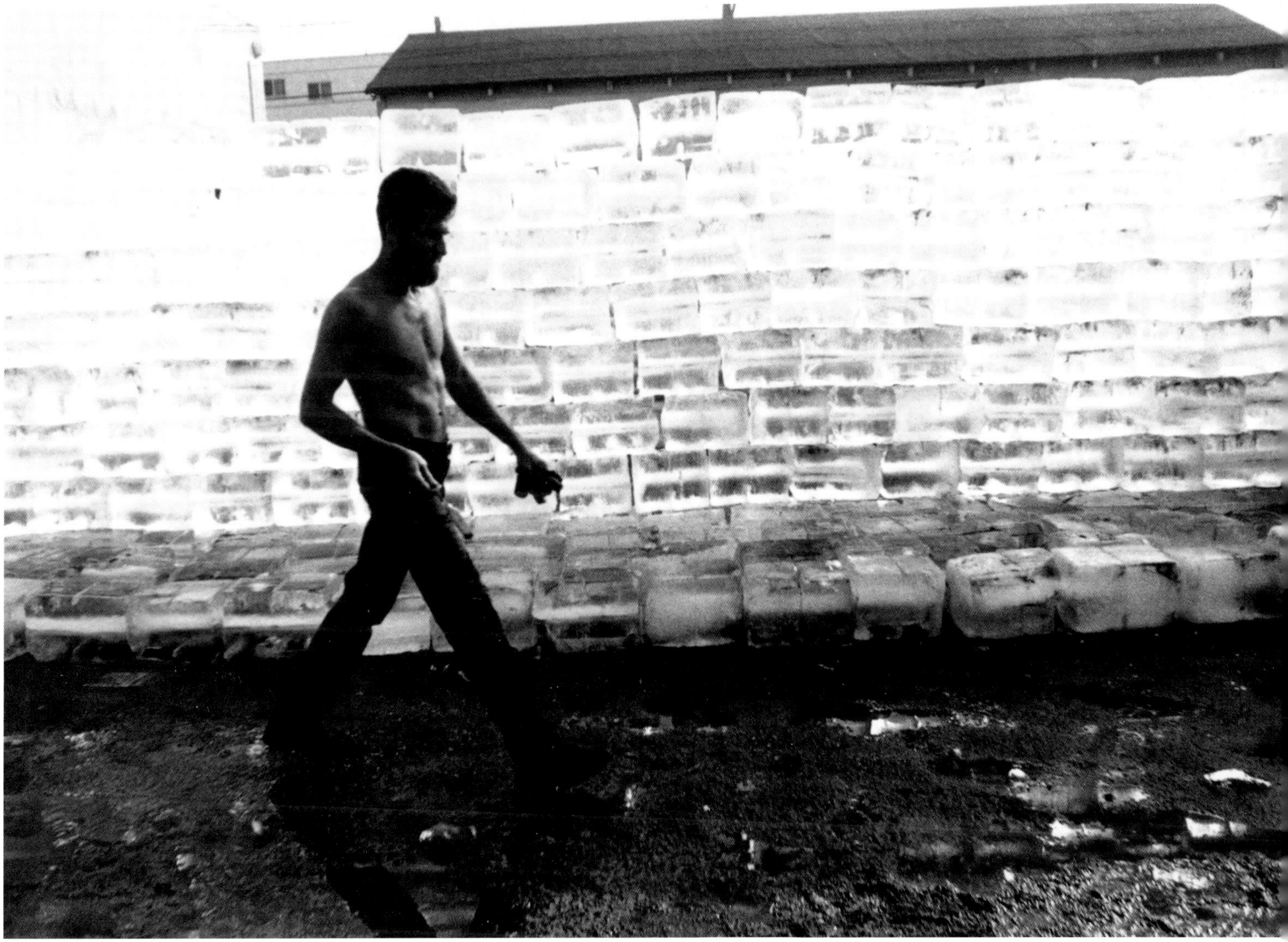

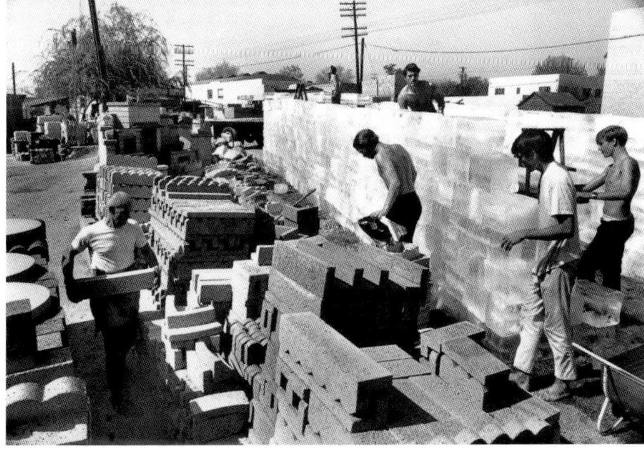

139 La Canada Rustic Stone Company in Pasadena

For immediate release (Sept 17) -18, 19, 20
UPI wire service

Iceman's Holiday?

On ____ street, ____ street ____ and ____ yesterday, identical constructions of hundred blocks of ice, resembling boxcars in shape, were built by small groups of people driving up to a street corner in a van. They did their work quietly and with dispatch, leaving immediately. No one seems to know what its all about. Rumors are that hippies or some religious sect are responsible. Meanwhile the structures are melting and are drawing crowds of perplexed onlookers.

L.A.'s
New Architecture?

It was reported in this and other newspapers yesterday that strange, unexplained activities were going on around our city. Large ice houses without doors or windows appeared in at least ten different public places around town. For no apparent reason the makers leave them upon completion without explanation and they are melting slowly. However, one professor from UCLA, Kurt von Meyer, believes they are demonstration

Theories abound: they are an ad means of promotion for an ice company, they are the spiritual offerings of a sect of local Eskimos, they are the work of a madman.

Today more such enclosures were constructed

[980063.B12.F9]

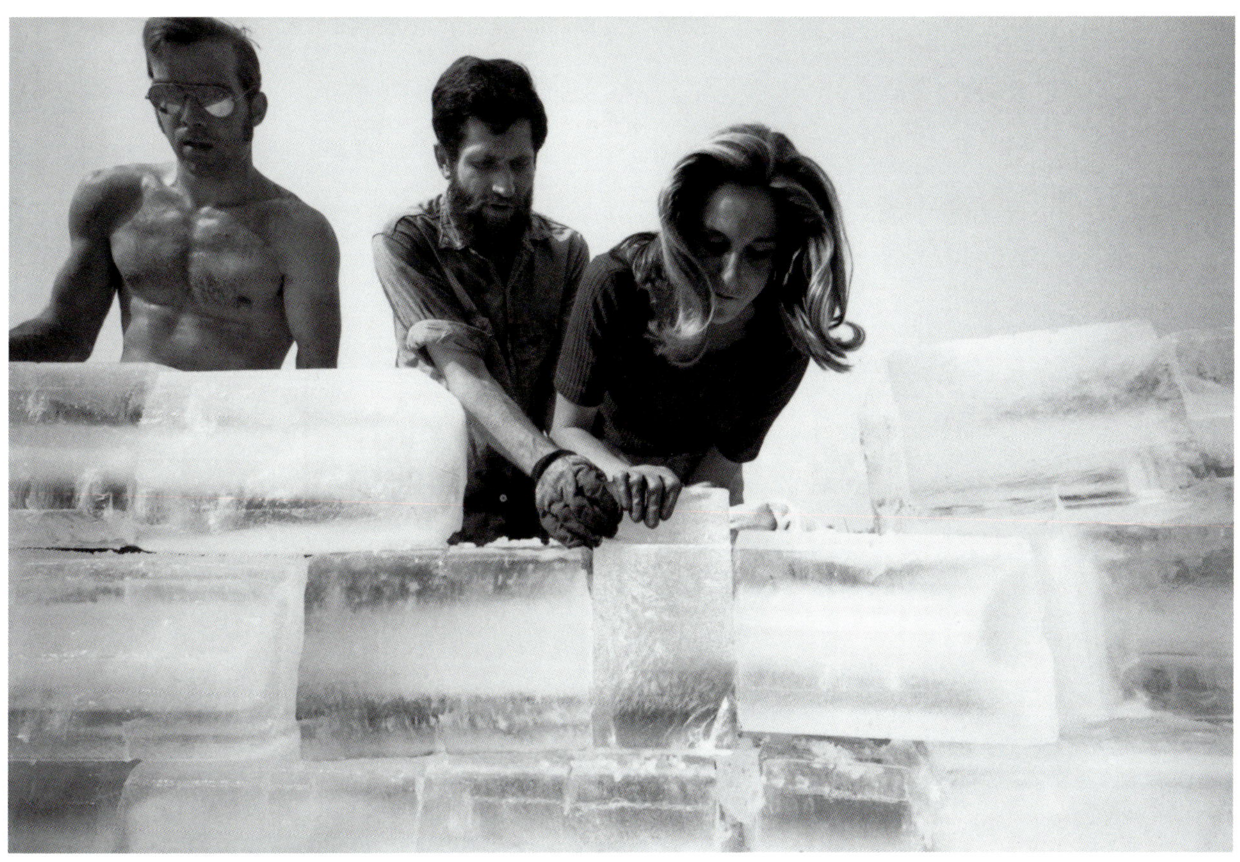

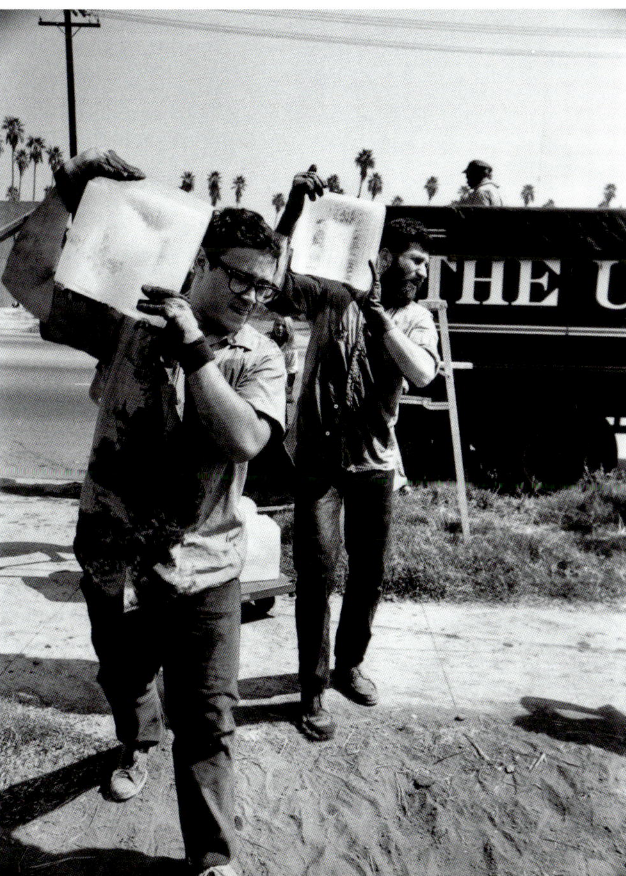

141 + 142 Colorado Street bridges in Pasadena

Moving

Happening, November 1967
Presented for *Pictures To Be Read, Poetry To Be Seen*
Unused houses in different parts of Chicago

143–144 **Moving**

Photoalbum, 1967
Published by the Museum of Contemporary Art, Chicago

PHOTOALBUM

MOVING

A HAPPENING BY ALLAN KAPROW

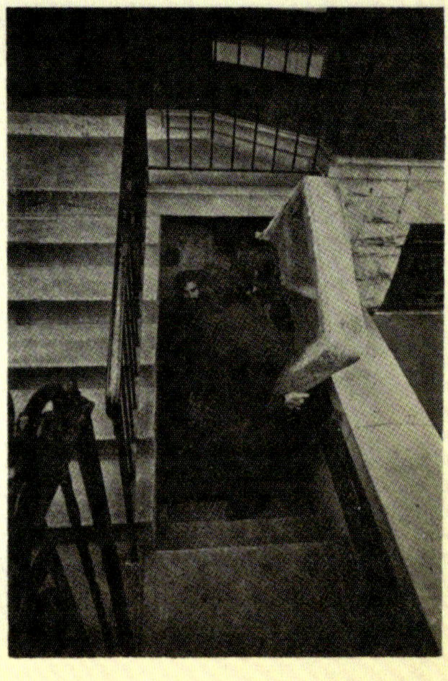

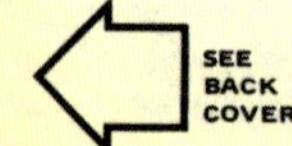

143 Front cover
Photo:
Peter Moore

SOME UNUSED HOUSES IN DIFFERENT PARTS OF THE CITY. ON EACH OF FOUR DAYS, OLD FURNITURE IS OBTAINED, AND IS PUSHED THROUGH THE STREETS TO THE HOUSES. THE FURNITURE IS INSTALLED.

On the first day, bedrooms are furnished, and slept in that night.

On the second day, dining rooms are furnished, and a meal is eaten.

On the third day, living rooms are furnished, and guests are invited to cocktails.

On the fourth day, attics are filled and their doors are locked.

Commissioned by the Museum of Contemporary Art, Chicago, November 29 to December 2, 1967. Dedicated to Milan Knizak. Photographed by Peter Moore.

144 Back cover

145 Poster for *Runner*
(with score)

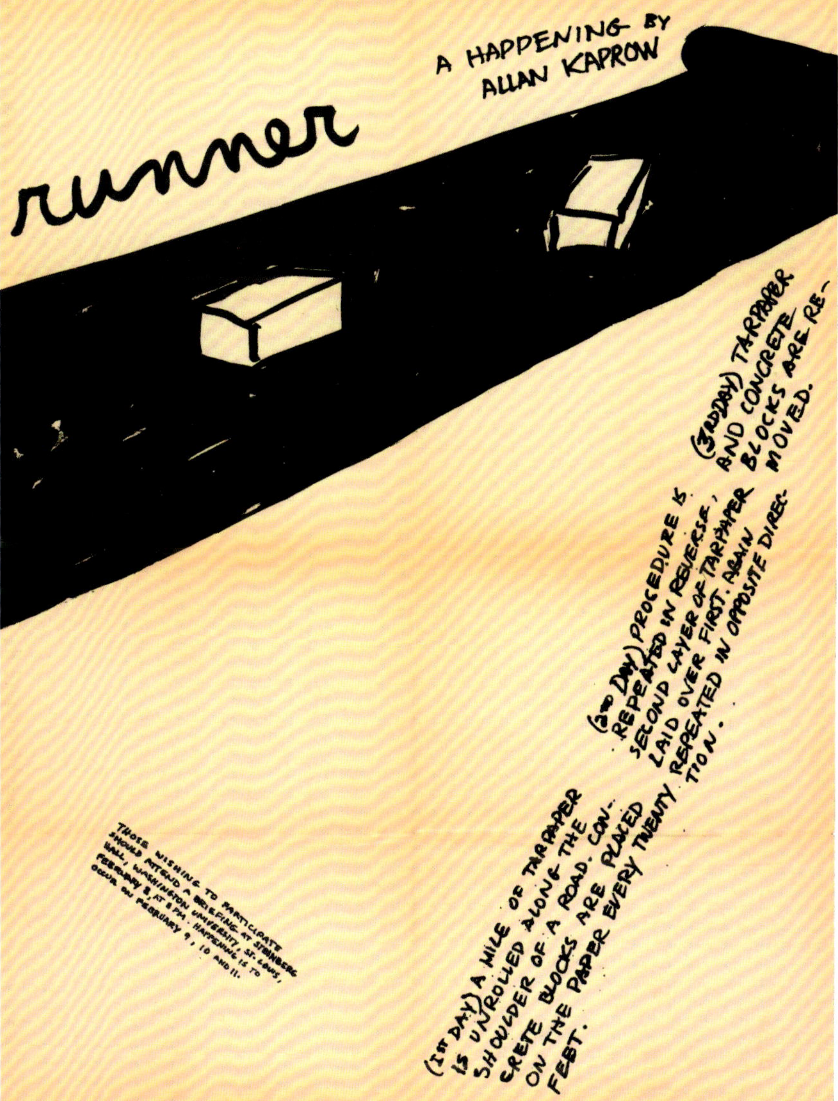

145–148 **Runner**
Happening, February 1968
Presented for *Allan Kaprow*
Washington University, Saint Louis

149–151 **Transfer**
Happening, February 1968
Sponsored by Wesleyan University
Various locations in Middletown, Connecticut, including Anderson Oil and Chemical Company, Andrus Field at Wesleyan University, Middletown Shopping Plaza, Portland Quarry, Powder Hill ski area, and South Green

Record I
Happening, Spring 1968
Commissioned by University of Texas, Austin
Not realized

152–153 **Round Trip**
Happening, March 1968
State University of New York, Albany
Reinvented in 2006

1968

TEACHING POSITIONS Professor, Department of Fine Arts, State University of New York, Stony Brook. Codirector, Project Other Ways, Berkeley Unified School District, Berkeley. ¶ AWARDS Research grant from State University of New York, Stony Brook. ¶ SOLO EXHIBITIONS *Allan Kaprow,* Washington University, Saint Louis, February–March. *Allan Kaprow,* University of Texas, Austin, March–April ¶ FESTIVALS Sixth Annual New York Avant-Garde Festival, Central Park West, New York, September. ¶ WRITINGS "Art and Education" (with Jim Hinton and Herbert Koh), *Cultural Affairs* 2: 6–17. "Fight" (score for an unrealized Happening), *Some/thing,* nos. 4 and 5: 88–90. "The Happenings Are Dead. Long Live the Happenings!" (includes scores for *Runner, Round Trip, Arrivals, Transfer, Moving, Record, Fluids,* and *Population*), *Metro,* n.s., no. 14: 144–53. "Nam June Paik," in *Nam June Paik: Electronic Art II,* exh. cat. (New York: Galeria Bonino), n.p. "On Happenings," *Arts in Society* 5: 28–37. "The Shape of the Art Environment: How Anti Form Is 'Anti Form'?" *Artforum* 6, no. 10: 32–33. ¶ INTERVIEWS "La sfida del sistema," *Metro,* n.s., no. 14: 34–71.

146 Unrolling tar paper along the road

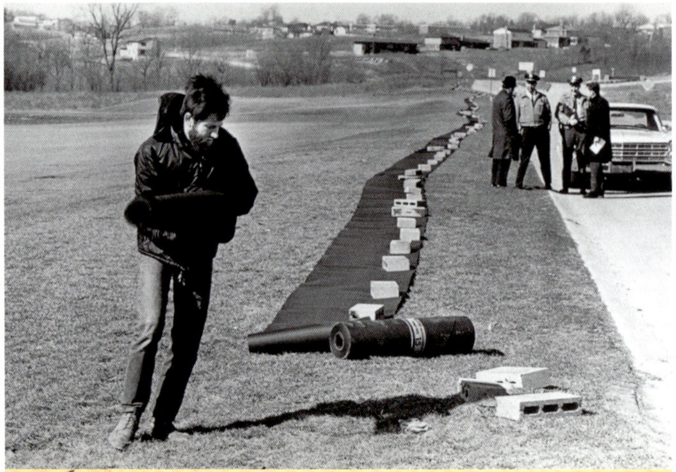

147 + 148 Explanatory notes for *Runner*

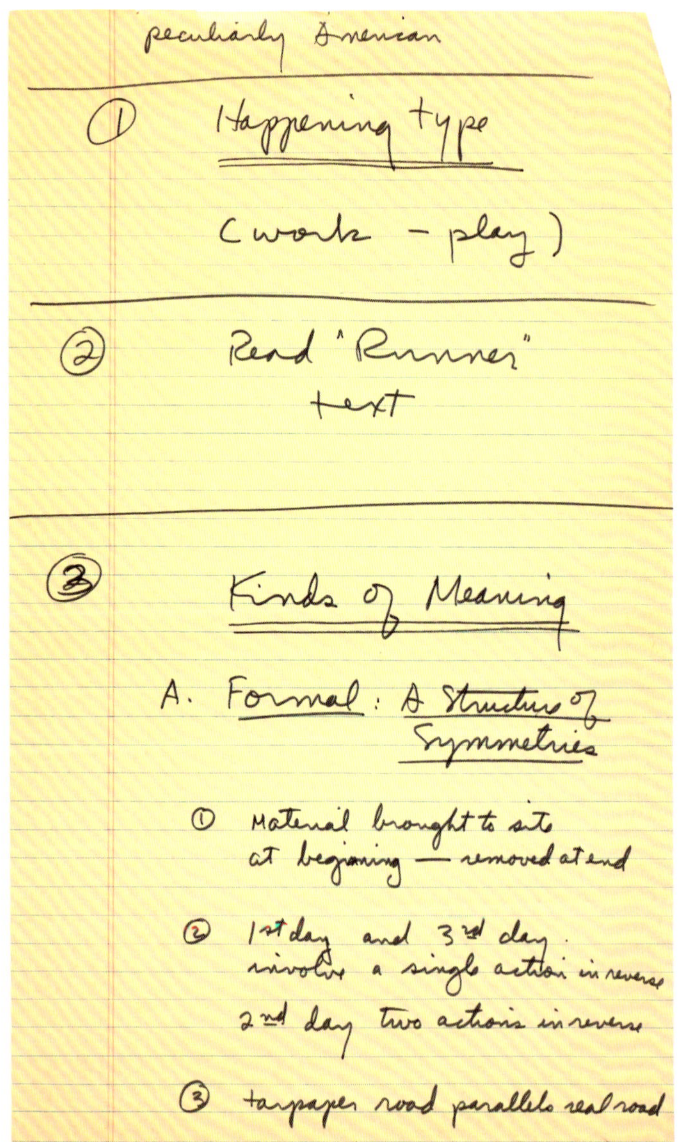

peculiarly American

① Happening type

(work – play)

② Read "Runner" text

③ Kinds of Meaning

A. Formal: A Structure of Symmetries

① Material brought to site at beginning — removed at end

② 1st day and 3rd day involve a single action in reverse

2nd day two actions in reverse

③ tarpaper road parallels real road

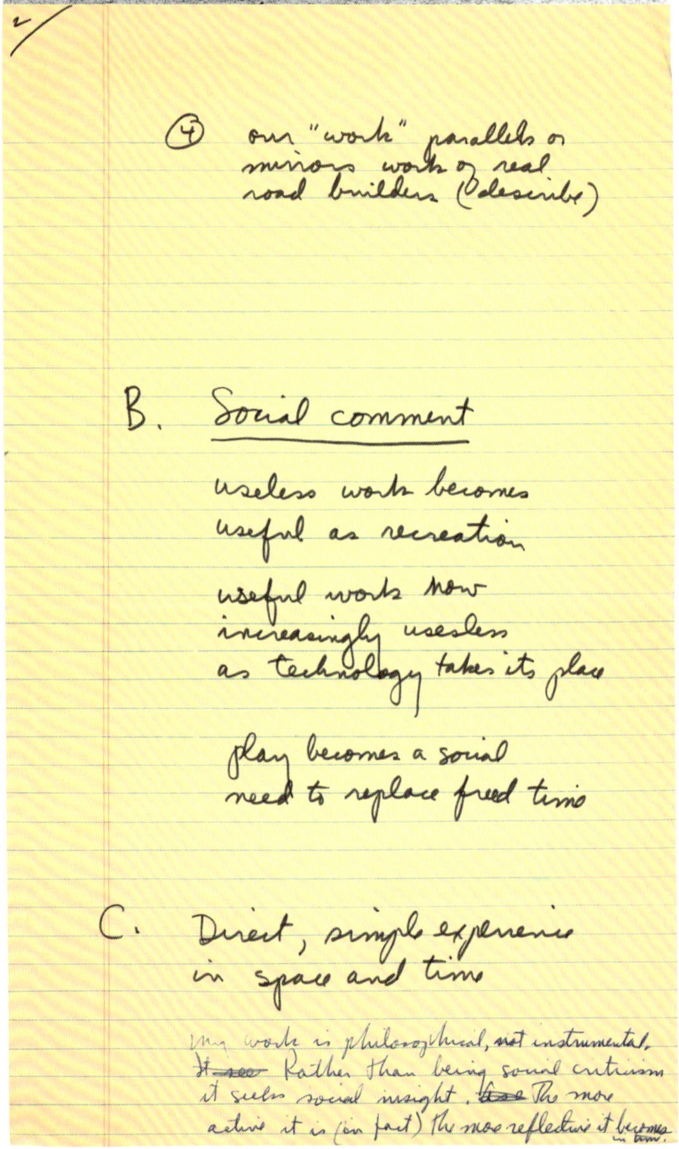

2/

④ our "work" parallels or mirrors work of real road builders (describe)

B. Social comment

useless work becomes useful as recreation

useful work now increasingly useless as technology takes its place

play becomes a social need to replace freed time

C. Direct, simple experience in space and time

My work is philosophical, not instrumental. ~~It sees~~ Rather than being social criticism it seeks social insight. ~~[illegible]~~ The more active it is (in fact) the more reflective it becomes in time.

149 Triumphal photo from *Transfer*

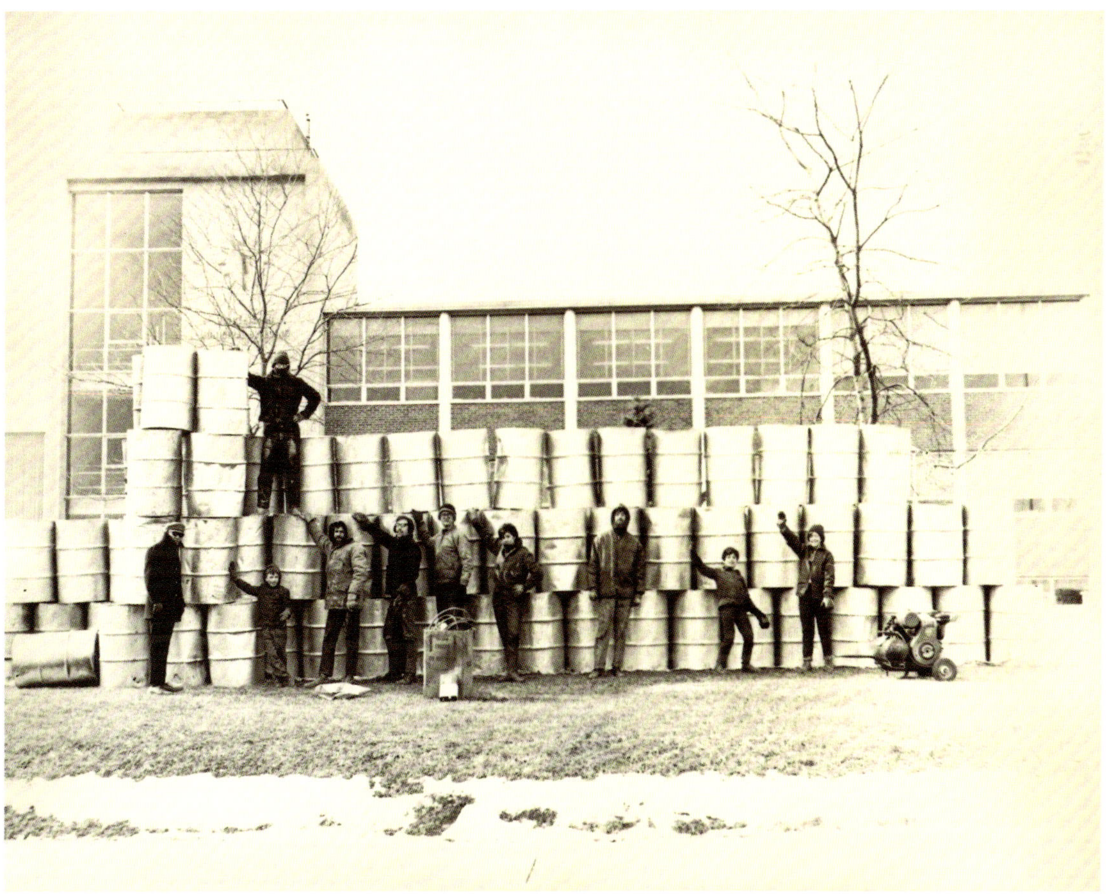

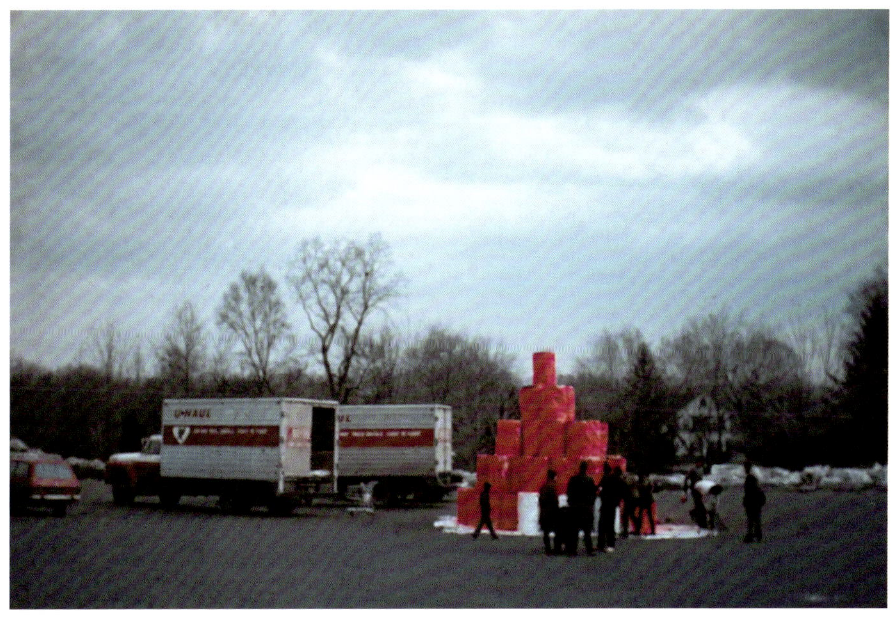

150 Day-Glo red barrels

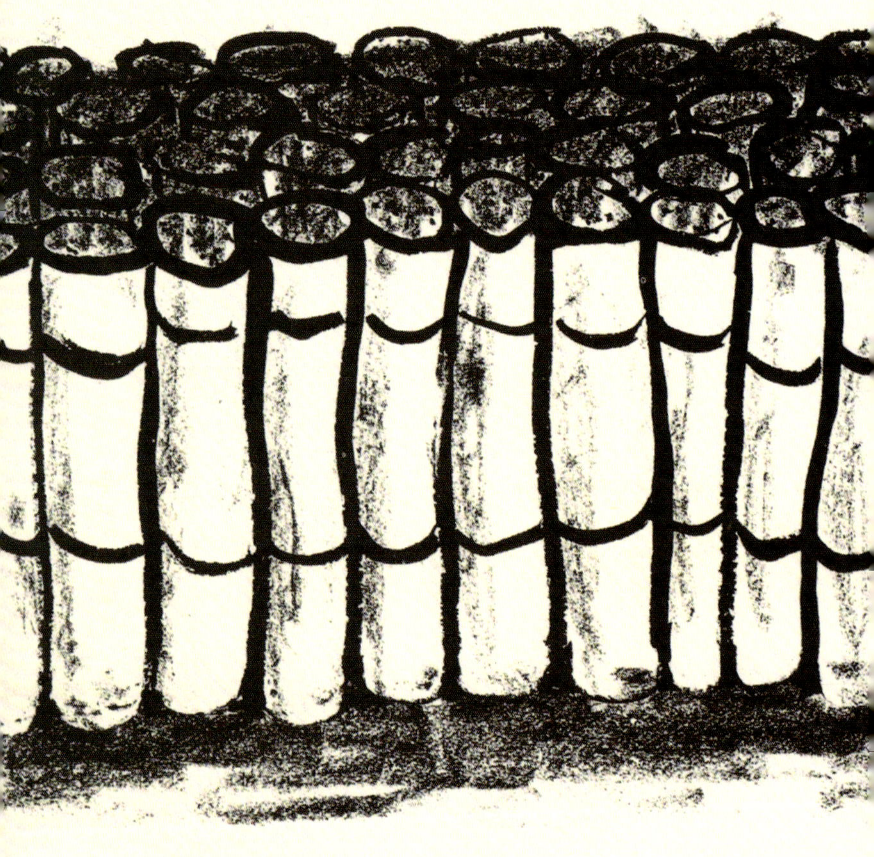

LARGE HEAP OF METAL BARRELS BEHIND CHEMICAL PLANT. PEOPLE POSE AMONG THEM FOR TRIUMPHAL PHOTO.

BARRELS LOADED ONTO TRUCKS, DRIVEN TO ANOTHER SITE. UNLOADED. STACKED NEATLY. SPRAYED SILVER. PEOPLE POSE FOR TRIUMPHAL PHOTO.

BARRELS LOADED OI
TRUCKS, DRIVEN TO
SITE. STACKED NEAT
SPRAYED WHITE. TR
UMPHAL PHOTO TAK

A HAPPENING (FOR CHRISTO)

THOSE INTERESTED IN PART

TRANSFER

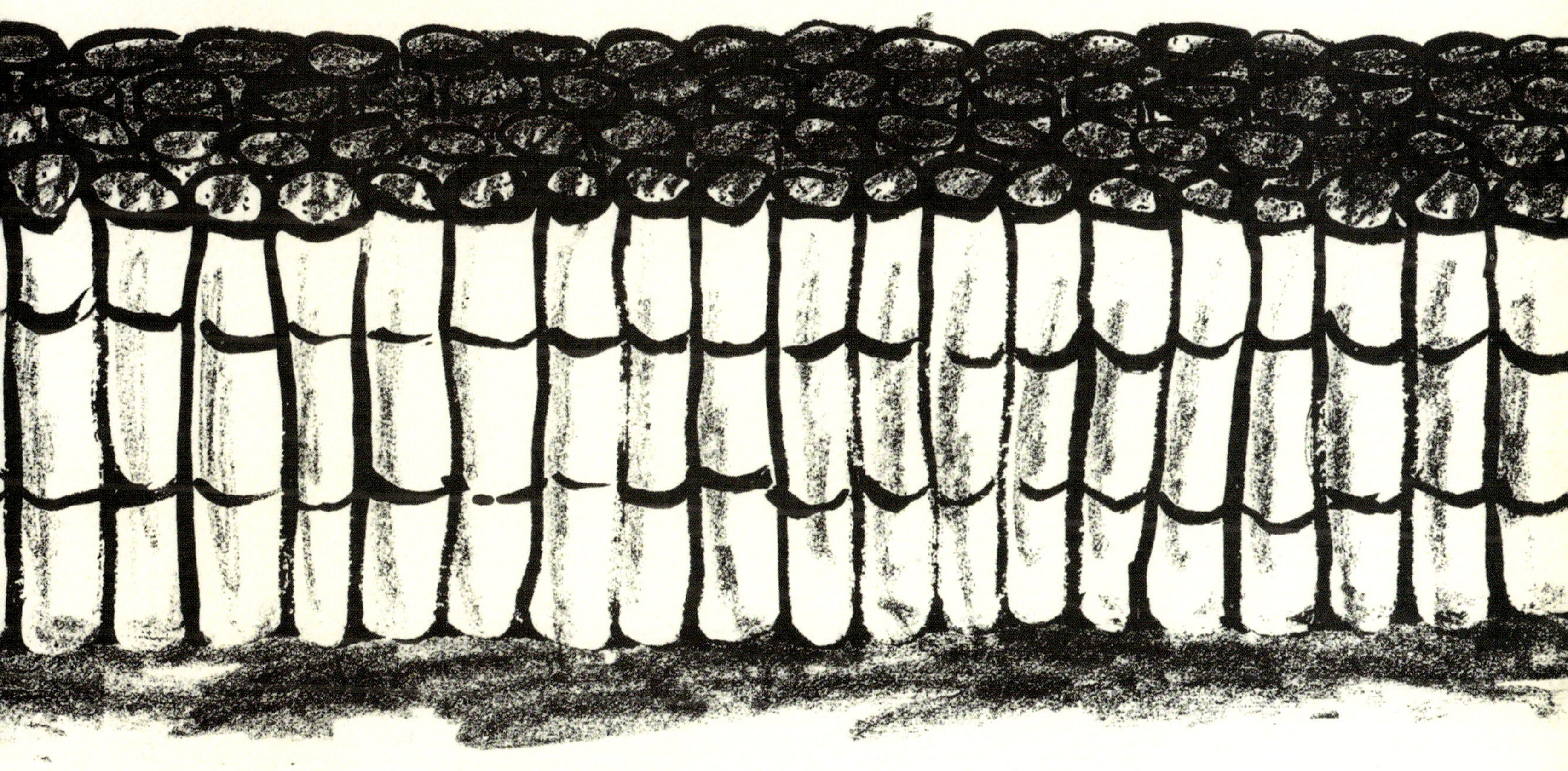

RRELS TRUCKED TO
W SITE. STACKED.
RAYED BLACK.
IUMPHAL PHOTO.

NEW SITE. BARRELS
STACKED. DA-GLO RED.
TRIUMPHAL PHOTO.

NEW SITE. BARRELS
STACKED. DA-GLO
GREEN. TRIUMPHAL
PHOTO.

NEW SITE. BARRELS
STACKED. SILVER.
TRIUMPHAL PHOTO.

NEW SITE. BARRELS
STACKED. WHITE.
TRIUMPHAL PHOTO.

BACK TO CHEMICAL
PLANT. BARRELS
DUMPED. BLACK.
TRIUMPHAL PHOTO.

ULD ATTEND A PRELIMINARY MEETING AT THE CO LOUNGE, WESLEYAN UNIVERSITY, SUNDAY, FEBRUARY 18, 1968, AT 8 PM

BY ALLAN KAPROW

152 Score for *Round Trip*

ROUND TRIP

A HAPPENING BY ALLAN KAPROW

Tiny ball of paper, cardboard,
string, rolled several blocks.
Ball enlarged with more materials.
Rolled several blocks again. Enlarged.
Rolled several blocks again.
Enlarged. Rolled several blocks. Enlarged....
Process repeated until ball is too
large to roll.

Some paper, cardboard and string,
removed. Ball rolled several
blocks. More material removed.
Rolled several blocks. More removed.
Rolled several blocks. More removed.
Rolled.... Process repeated until
there's no ball.

(Activities executed identically
by two groups, each from
opposite ends of a certain route.
Paths
crossing, each concludes
at the other's beginning.)

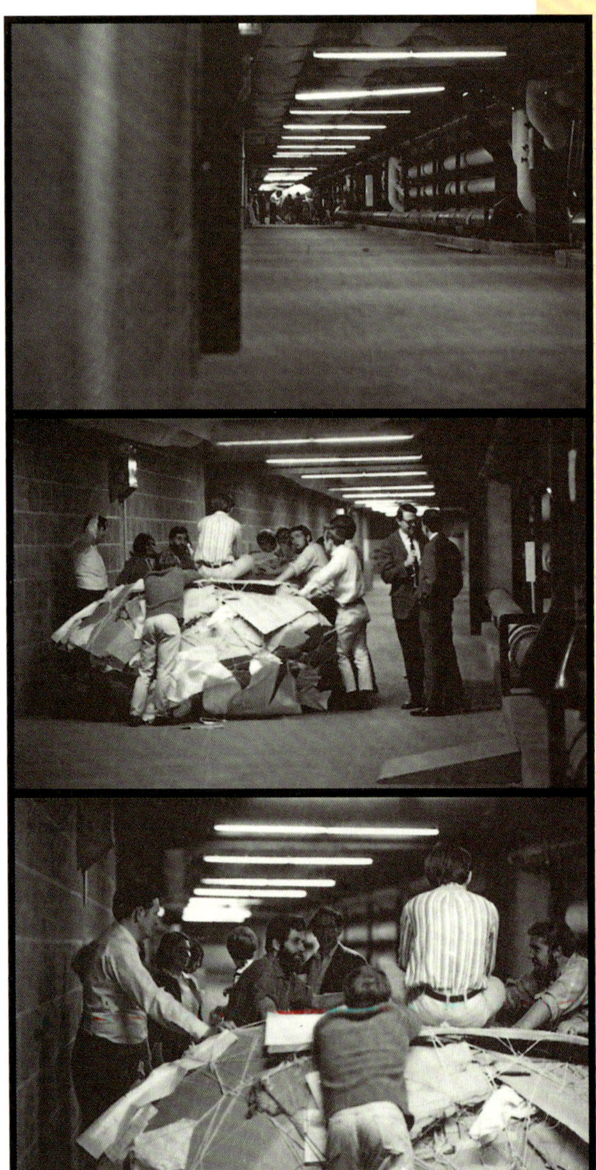

153 Contact sheet

154 Pamphlet for *Record II*
(with score)

RECORD II

FOR ROGER SHATTUCK

BREAKING BIG ROCKS
PHOTOGRAPHING THEM

SILVERING BIG ROCKS
PHOTOGRAPHING THEM

SCATTERING THE PHOTOS
WITH NO EXPLANATION

Commissioned by The University of Texas, April 3, 4, 1968. In the environs of Austin.

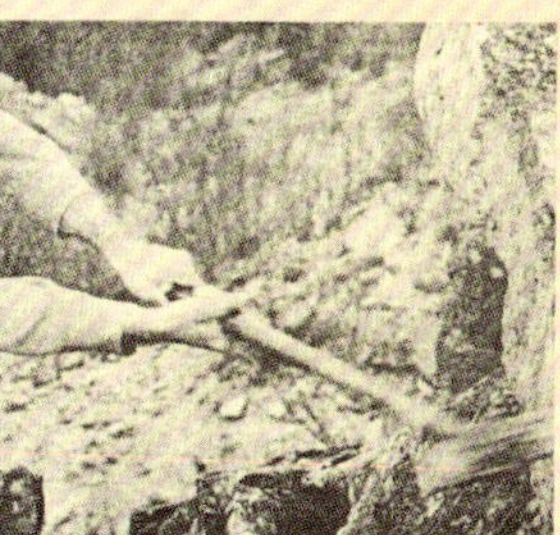

A HAPPENING BY
ALLAN KAPROW

155 Draft score for *Record II*

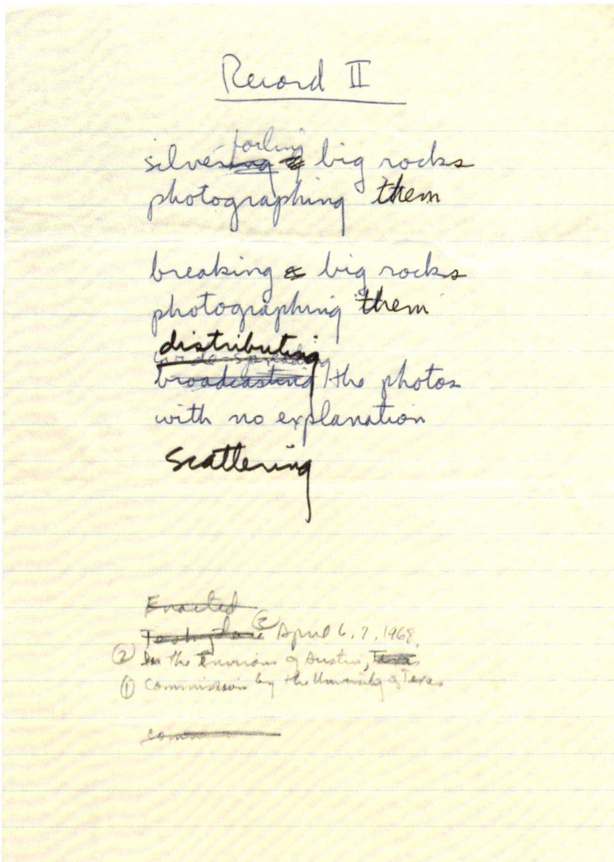

Record II

silvering big rocks
photographing them

breaking big rocks
photographing them
distributing
the photos
with no explanation
scattering

154–156 **Record II**

Happening, April 1968
Presented for *Allan Kaprow*
Quarry outside of Austin and
downtown Austin
Reinvented in 1988

Record II

Pamphlet, 1968
Published by the University
of Texas, Austin

Overtime

Happening, April 1968
Commissioned by State University
of New York, New Paltz
Not realized

157 **Arrivals**

Happening, April 1968
Abandoned airstrip near Nassau
Community College, Hempstead,
New York

Population

Happening, May 1968
Colby Junior College, New London,
New Hampshire

Overtime

Happening, May 1968
Sponsored by University of
California, San Diego
On the beach, San Diego

156 "Silvering big rocks"

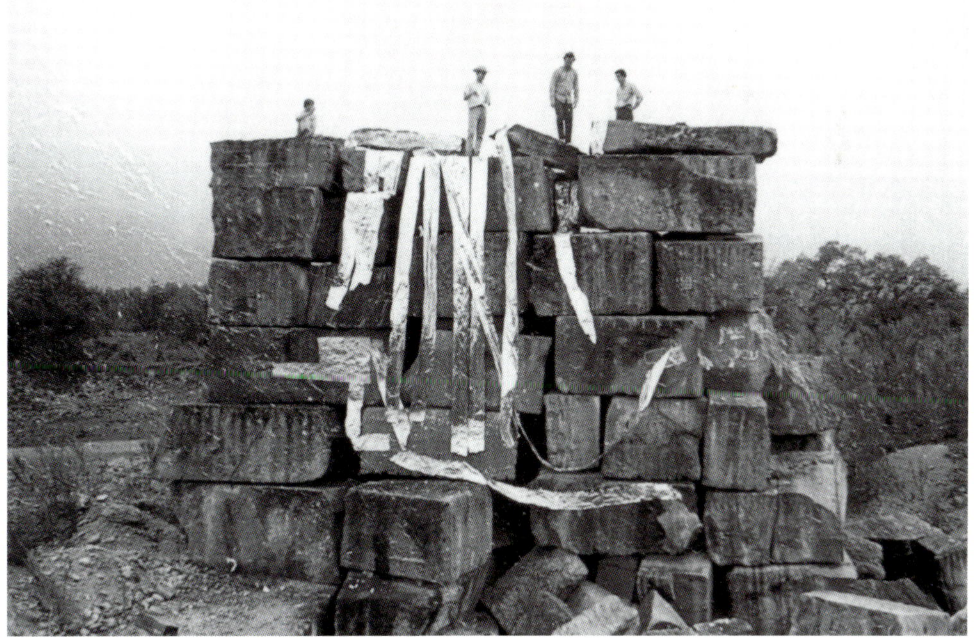

ARRIVALS

unused airstrip

tarring cracks in airstrip

painting guidelines on airstrip

cutting grass at airstrip's edge

placing mirrors on airstrip

watching for reflections of planes

157 Poster for *Arrivals* (with score)

A HAPPENING BY ALLAN KAPROW
Those interested in participating, should attend a talk given by Mr. Kaprow on April 22nd, 1968, at 3 PM, at the Firehouse Gallery, Nassau Community College, New York.

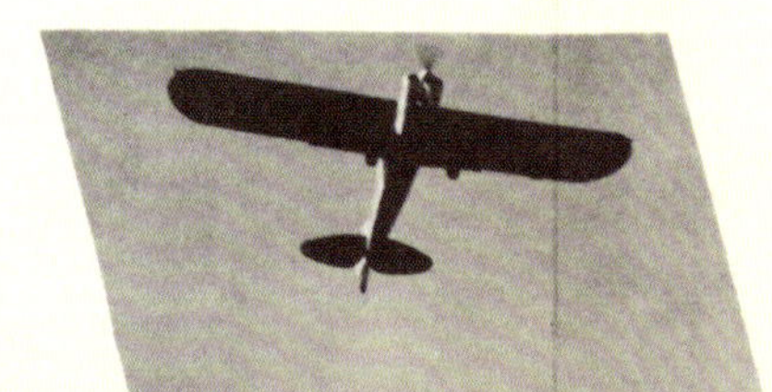

Francis S. Mason, Jr. May 27, 1968
President,
E.A.T., Inc.
9 East 16th Street
N.Y., N.Y. 10003

Dear Mr. Mason:

Thank you for sending me the announcement that E.A.T. will be submitting projects to the National Science Foundation for possible funding. Although you have in your files a number of projects which I have outlined in the past, to which you may refer, Iwwould like to ~~xxxxxx~~ sketch one more at this time. (It is one which I mentioned to Billy Klüver around 1961, written about here and there since, but as yet unrealized.) In brief, it is this:

MESSAGE UNITS

A mile or more of woods in every direction. At random, and widely separated throughout these woods, are about two hundred cheap closet door mirrors suspended from trees so that they rotate freely in the wind. Their reflections, thus changing, will continuously alter the fixity of space for any observer, human or animal. On some of them, there will be a small dial to be turned at will; it will affect the volume of a radio loudspeaker system mounted in trees or hidden amongst rocks nearby.

The radio signals will be picked up by sensitive microphones from the avilable sounds of nature; tree branches rubbing together in the wind, the weather, a bird, insects, human voices and movements in the underbrush, etc.

Explorers of these woods will come upon their reflections swinging wildly in the mirrors; where there are radio controls ~~someomay be~~ tuned audibly already so that their footsteps, their voices, nearby nature sounds etc. will be heard. These may be altered more or less in intensity and may randomly combine with those amplified elsewhere in the woods. Thus a chirping cricket may be earsplitting, and a voice may be muffled. In addition, some areas of the terrain may be radio-responsive only to the footsteps of animals and people, to sound like crackles, or thunder...

(over)

-2-

This situation may be restricted to a twenty four hour period--day and night--which would permit those who would like to experience night compared with day. Using flashlights, their reflections would suddenly be caught by a mirror, and perhaps photo cells attached to the mirrors would activate a sound response typical of the kind mentioned, or of an entirely synthetic, "feedback" type. Or, if the equipment were weatherproof, everything could be left for nature to enjoy itself!

It would be interesting, too, to shift the the whole arrangement to a cityscape, with a corresponding change in flavor of experience and participation.

. . . . .

One of the ways in which this may be of legitimate value to the National Science Foundation, is in the area of environmental research: such as sensory deprivation, overload, and mix-up of normal signal patterns. It may also provide useful information about what happens to animal and insect life when their (in this case, mostly auditory) environment is altered. Although this is not my primary concern, I do find it engaging and would be willing to cooperate with scientific researchers.

Sincerely,

Allan Kaprow

158 + 159 Score for *Message Units*

158–159 Message Units

Proposal for a Happening,
May 1968
For Experiments in Art
and Technology

Travelog

Happening, July 1968
Presented for Eighth International
Artists' Seminar
Fairleigh Dickinson University,
Madison, New Jersey

Refills

Happening, August 1968
Sponsored by Dwan Gallery
Hofstra University, Brookville,
New York

Barreling

Happening, September 1968
Presented for the Sixth Annual
New York Avant-Garde Festival
Central Park West from 95th to
67th Streets, New York

TEACHING POSITIONS Professor, Department of Fine Arts, State University of New York, Stony Brook. Associate Dean of the School of Art, California Institute of the Arts, Burbank. ¶ **CONSULTING POSITIONS** Codirector, Project Other Ways, Berkeley Unified School District, Berkeley. Founding member, Advanced Placement Committee on Art and History for the Education Testing Service, Princeton, and the College Entrance Examination Board, New York. ¶ **AWARDS** Research grant from State University of New York, Stony Brook. ¶ **SOLO EXHIBITIONS** John Gibson Gallery, New York, October. ¶ **GROUP EXHIBITIONS** *Concrete Poetry,* Fine Arts Gallery, University of British Columbia, Vancouver, March–April.

1969

160 Title sequence from *Hello*

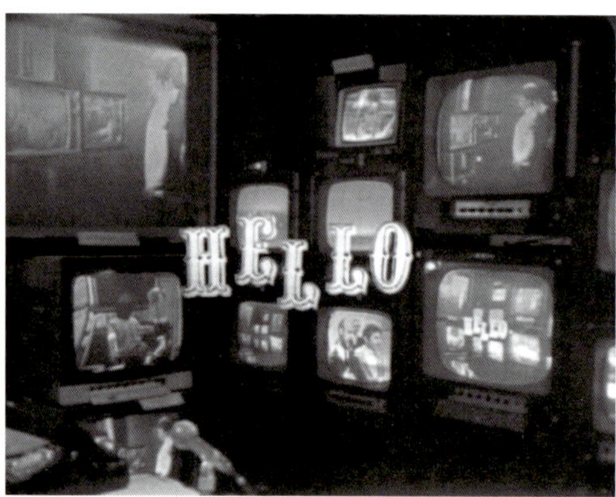

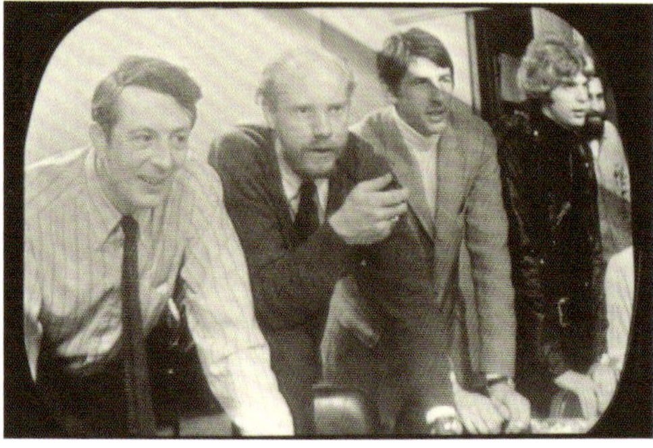

161 Participants in *Hello*

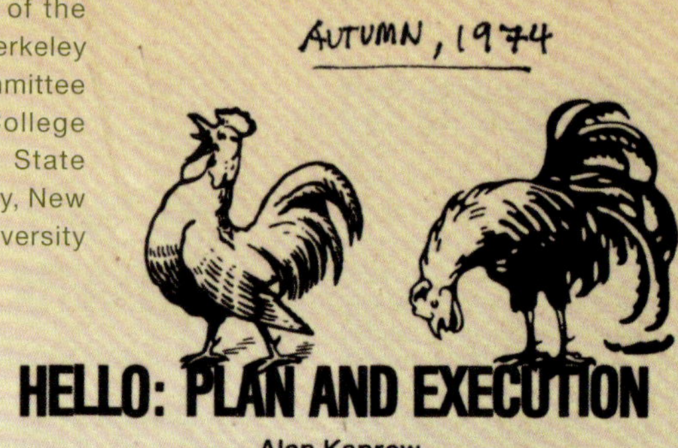

HELLO: PLAN AND EXECUTION

Alan Kaprow

A global network of simultaneously transmitting and receiving "TV Arcades." Open to the public twenty-four hours a day, like any washerette. An arçade in every big city of the world. Each equipped with a hundred or more monitors of different sizes from a few inches to wall-scale, in planar and irregular surfaces. A dozen automatically moving cameras (like those secreted in banks and airports, but now prominently displayed) will pan and fix anyone or anything that happens to come along or be in view. Including cameras and monitors if no one is present. A person will be free to do whatever he wants, and will see himself on the monitors in different ways. A crowd of people may multiply their images into a throng.

But the cameras will send the same images to all *other* arcades, at the same time or after a programmed delay. Thus what happens in one arcade may be happening in a thousand, generated a thousand times. But the built-in program for distributing the signals, visible and audible, random and fixed, could also be manually altered at any arcade. A woman might want to make electronic love to a particular man she saw on a monitor. Controls would permit her to localize (freeze) the communication within a few TV tubes. Other visitors to the same arcade may feel free to enjoy and even enhance the mad and surprising scramble by turning their dials accordingly. The world could make up its own social relations as it went along! Everybody in and out of touch all at once!

Hello in original form has never been done for obvious technical, financial and social reasons. If it ever is approximated in our lifetime, it probably will be locked into the exhibition atmosphere of a world fair and thus will be denied the casual accessibility it really needs. I rarely indulge in futuristic dreams, preferring the practicable, but this exception arose out of a fanciful conversation with Nam June Paik who likes predicting the future and did very well at it.

At the same time (the fall of 1968) I knew from Paik that I would have a chance to do a small model experiment of *Hello* at WGBH-TV in Boston, for a video program of works by artists, under a grant from the Public Broadcast Laboratory. This station, directed by Fred Barzyk was, and is, the most open and adventurous in the country. Thus I wasn't entirely dreaming.

Barzyk made it possible to set up four separate sites of video, including two at WBBH, one (I believe) at MIT, and one at a children's school in Cambridge. Five cameras and twenty-seven monitors were involved. This modified program for *Hello* went as follows:

Each of the four sites were linked together sending and receiving simultaneously, like an open conference call on the telephone. There was about an hour of time available. A group of participants at each place watched their monitors and when anyone saw someone they knew they called out Hello! (speaking the name of the person) I see you!

The engineers in the control room at WGBH, which was also one of the sites, had the additional job of randomly switching the sound and picture signals to all four sites. Thus one of the monitors at site A might get audio but no video image, two monitors at site B might have video but no audio, while C and D got normal transmission for a few minutes on all monitors. Audio and video might be divided between sites so that friends might hear but not see each other and vice-versa.

Because of this switching system which was arranged in advance, people in all four places were only in partial and brief contact with one another. It was a strange, straining yet often hilarious scramble of efforts to reach out. Surprise nearly balanced personal need.

162 Article about *Hello*

163 Poster for *Six Ordinary Happenings*
(with scores)

CHARITY

BUYING PILES OF OLD CLOTHES

WASHING THEM
IN ALL-NIGHT LAUNDROMATS

GIVING THEM BACK
TO USED-CLOTHES STORES

(MARCH 7)

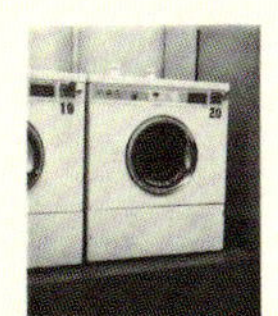

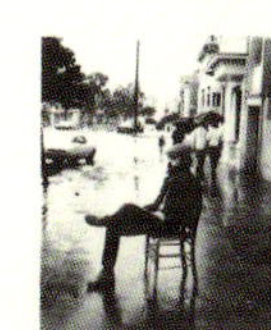

POSE

CARRYING CHAIRS THROUGH THE CITY

SITTING DOWN HERE AND THERE

PHOTOGRAPHED

PIX LEFT ON SPOT

GOING ON

(MARCH 21)

FINE!

PARKING CARS IN RESTRICTED ZONES

WAITING NEARBY FOR COP

SNAPSHOT OF GETTING TICKET

DETAILED REPORT

SENDING PIX, REPORTS, FINES TO COPS

(APRIL 4)

SIX ORDINARY HAPPENINGS

BY ALLAN KAPROW

ORDINARY PHOTOS BY CAROL BOWEN

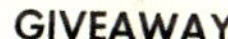

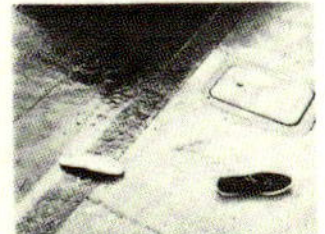

SHAPE

SHOES, BODIES
ON STREETS, SIDEWALKS, FIELDS

SPRAY PAINTING THEIR SILHOUETTES

REPORTS AND PHOTOS IN NEWSPAPER

(APRIL 18)

GIVEAWAY

STACKS OF DISHES
LEFT ON STREET CORNERS

PHOTOGRAPHED

NEXT DAY, PHOTOGRAPHED

(MAY 2)

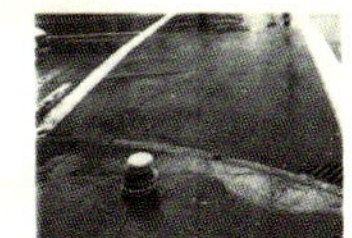

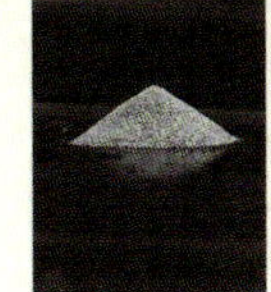

PURPOSE

(Variation on a theme of Tomas Schmit)

MAKING A MOUNTAIN OF SAND

MOVING IT REPEATEDLY
UNTIL THERE IS NO MOUNTAIN

RECORDING THE WORK SOUNDS

RERECORDING THEM
UNTIL THERE IS NO SOUND OF WORK

LISTENING TO THE TAPES

(MAY 23)

A series of events presented by OTHER WAYS. Those interested in participating in any or all, should attend preliminary meetings on the dates indicated, 8:30 p.m., at East Campus, Dwight Way (Haste Bldg., Rm. 101). The Happenings will occur on the next day(s).

160–162 **Hello**
Happening, March 1969
Presented for *The Medium Is the Medium*
WGBH-TV, Boston

163–164 **Six Ordinary Happenings**
Sponsored by Project Other Ways, Berkeley Unified School District
Berkeley, March–May 1969

Charity
Happening, March 1969
Presented for *Six Ordinary Happenings*
Various thrift stores, Berkeley and Oakland
Reinvented in 2007

Pose
Happening, March 1969
Presented for *Six Ordinary Happenings*
Various locations, Berkeley and Oakland
Reinvented in 2006 (twice) and 2007 (twice)

Fine!
Happening, April 1969
Presented for *Six Ordinary Happenings*
Restricted parking zones, Berkeley

Shape
Happening, April 1969
Presented for *Six Ordinary Happenings*
Various sidewalks, Berkeley

Giveaway
Happening, May 1969
Presented for *Six Ordinary Happenings*
Various street corners, Berkeley

Purpose
Happening, May 1969
Presented for *Six Ordinary Happenings*
Various locations, Berkeley

Click
Album, 1969
Published by Project Other Ways

164 Review of *Six Ordinary Happenings*

Hard Lessons The Easy Way

By NOEL LIEBERMAN
Tribune Staff Writer

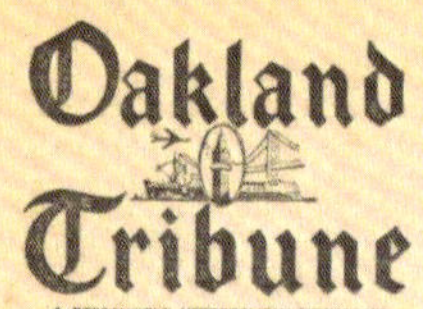

Wed., June 4, 1969 17

BERKELEY — Scores of Berkeley schools pupils are learning hard lessons the easy way.

The distress felt in growing older and insights into the difficulty of trying to leave a permanent mark on an increasingly complex world usually take years of experiences to develop and put in perspective.

Countless Berkeley pupils, however, are feeling the same things in "other ways" and attempting to cope with them.

A high school student, for instance, recently etched his silhouette on the sands of a local beach, spraying lime chalk out of a can. Winds, however, soon began to reshape the sand patterns and the youth's outline slowly faded.

An elderly man lying nearby finally became overwhelmed by his own curiosity and asked what the young man was doing. When told, he responded, "Gee, it's not going to last very long."

The young man thus, rather poignantly and symbolically, learned something of the impermanence of life and began to consider what to do about it.

The teenager was one of some 50 youngsters who recently participated in one of six "happenings" sponsored by Project Other Ways, an experimental program designed to educate through unstructured and open-ended experiences. Other Ways is being conducted through the Berkeley Unified School District.

Other students have assimilated countless maxims through such other "happenings" as leaving stacks of dishes on street corners and photographing bewildered passersby, parking cars in restricted zones and taking snapshots of policemen writing out tickets, and buying piles of old clothes, washing them in a laundromat and returning them to the store.

Such open-ended experiences are more educational than classroom discussion of traditional subjects and must become a central part of school systems in the United States, says Allan Kaprow, Project Other Ways' codirector.

Kaprow organized the project's six "happenings," while Herbert Kohl, author of the well-known "36 Children," devised a myriad of activities designed to stimulate creativity among students and teachers.

"The experience that student absorbed on the beach suggested a symbol without spelling it out verbally," Kaprow pointed out.

"Our whole culture is verbal," he added. "But experience is far more communicative without being verbal. The only way to learn what is real in our environment is by experiencing it. And, of course, there's nothing wrong with talking about our experiences later; that's when our words take on a real meaning."

Kaprow believes the classroom is "a box which serves to fragment learning" by separating students from the rest of the world. Students who acquire all their learning in the classroom "can't see any relationship to what they learned inside and what they see outside," he asserts.

"The students who took part in our happenings have had a whole range of human emotions as well as environmental experiences," Kaprow related. "They really got to know and see the town as most people don't.

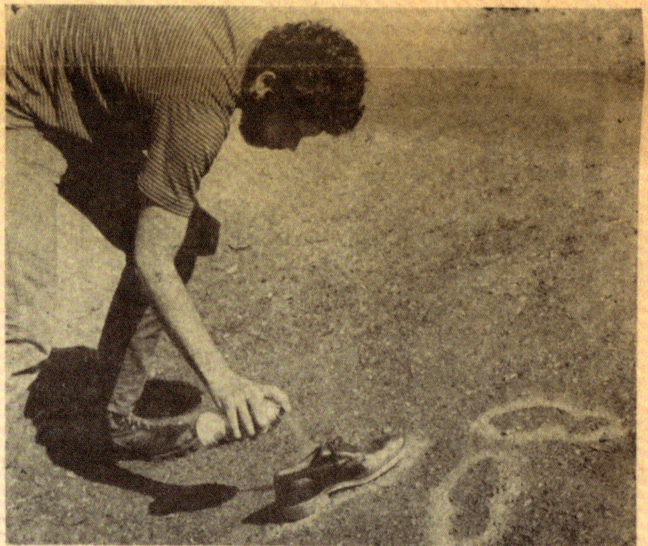

Tribune photos by Chris Kjobech

ERIC WESTHEIMER LEAVES 'FOOTPRINTS' WITH SHOE AND SPRAY CAN
It is all part of Berkeley School District's Other Ways creative arts project

"They never really had looked at it, felt it, or smelled it before, even though they might have walked or driven through it a million times."

Kaprow says "other ways" of education must become "a central part" of the American school system "so the other parts can take on a completely new meaning."

The project hopes to influence instruction by involving teachers in "hpapenings" and other activities. Teachers also attend weekly seminar sessions at the project headquarters, a storefront at 2556 Grove St.

The weekly sessions are a kind of "catharsis" geared to changing fixed attitudes about curriculum and education, Kohl explained.

"We're trying to work with teachers so they can open up and give kids more choices," Kohl said. "Right now, kids are totally disenfranchised in their relationships with teachers. They don't leave school with any real ability to determine what they want to learn at rates consistent with their best way of learning."

Teachers, Kohl added, are equally shackled by accepted, but obsolete instructional methods and bureaucratic regimen. "Other Ways" is proving a liberating factor for them, he claimed.

"Other Ways" students, many of them suspended or dropouts who felt unchallenged by regular schools, have produced a varied collection of published poems and essays, photographs and films.

The project is being funded by a $68,000 Carnegie Foundation grant. Kaprow and Kohl currently are seeking $50,000 in school district money to match another Carnegie allocation.

Take-Off
Happening, April 1969
Sponsored by University of California, San Diego
Various outdoor locations, San Diego
Reinvented in May 1969

Transplant
Happening, April 1969
University of Nevada, Los Vegas

Forecast
Happening, April 1969
Not realized

Dial
Happening, May 1969
Sponsored by San Francisco Art Institute
Telephone booths near telephone poles, San Francisco
Reinvented in 1973 and 1974, and as *Dial II* in 1971

Take-Off
Happening, May 1969
Reinvention for California State University, Sacramento
Various outdoor locations, Sacramento

165–166 **Course**
Happening, May 1969
Cedar River near Iowa City

166 Score for *Course*

COURSE

A Happening By Allan Kaprow

Digging tributaries to river

Bucketing out the water

Carrying it upstream to first tributary

Pouring it back in

Bucketing out that water

Carrying it upstream to next tributary

Pouring it back in

And so on, till no more tributaries

** ** **

Telling the world about it

(photos) (newspapers) (packages)
(recordings) (TV) (phone calls)
(letters) (bulletin boards)
(graffiti) (telegrams) (gossip)

Those interested in participating should attend a meeting at Union Yale Room, 9AM, May 9th, The University of Iowa.

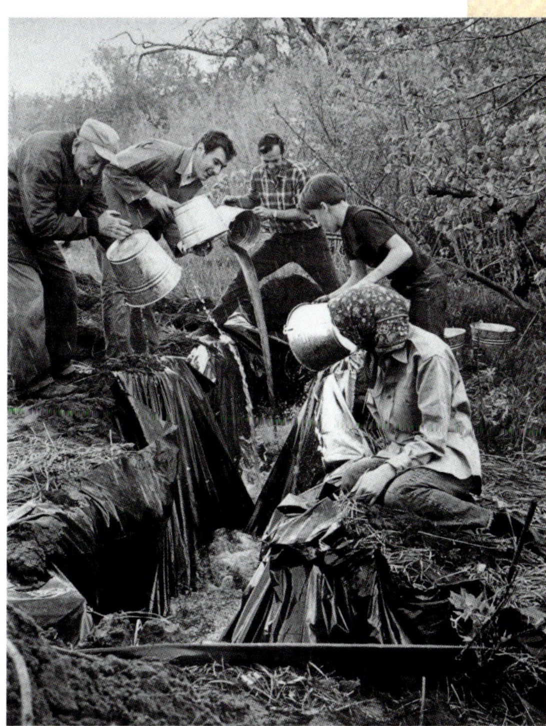

165 Participants pouring water back in

167 Invitation to *Homemovies*

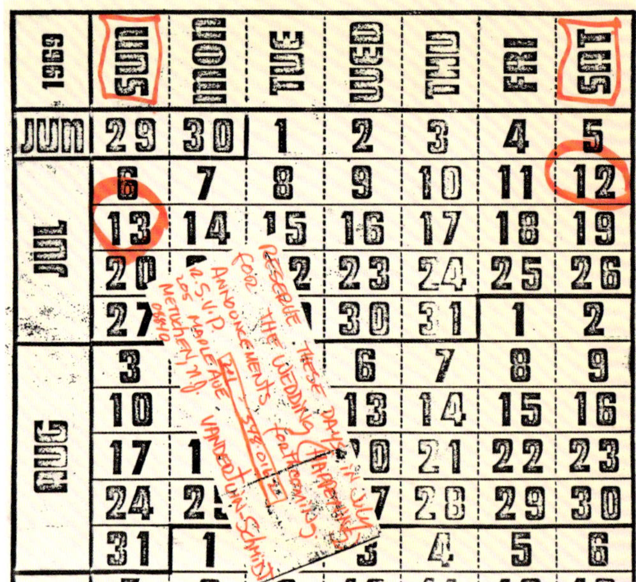

168 Poster for *Homemovies* (with score)

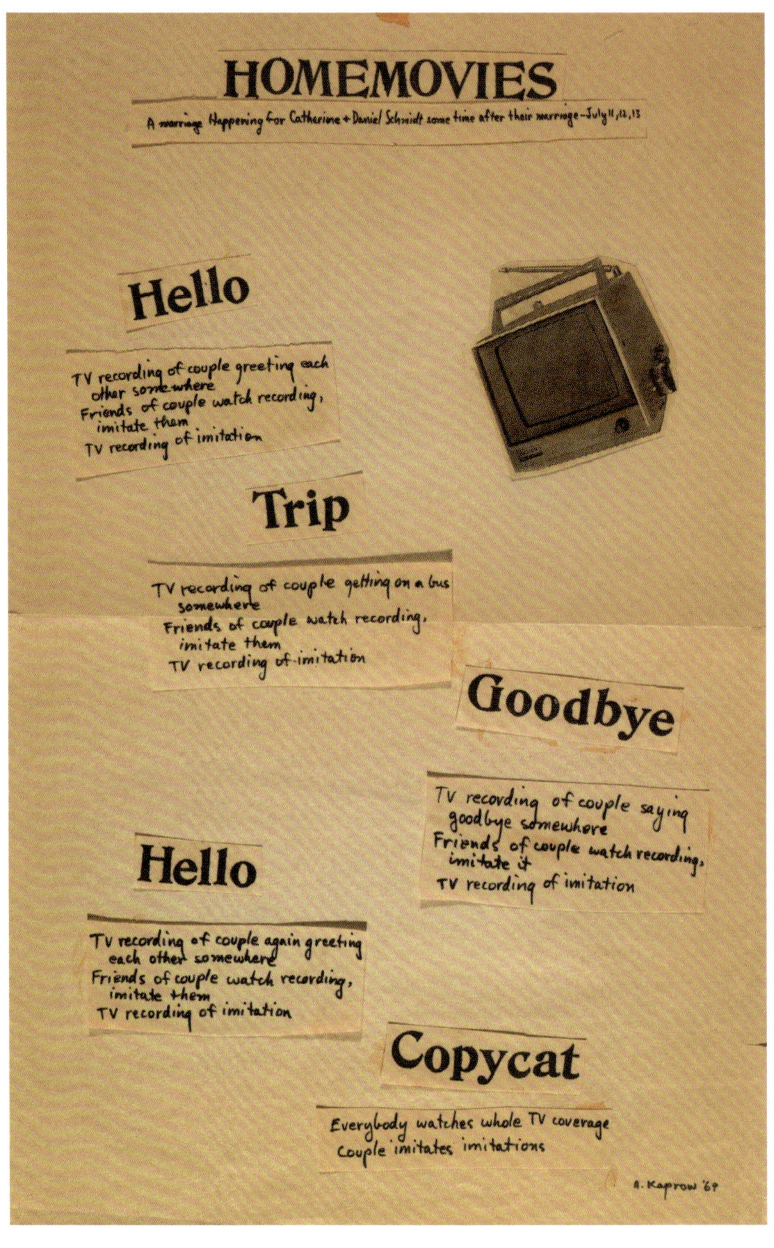

167–168 **Homemovies**
Marriage Happening, July 1969
Metuchen, New Jersey, and New York

Homemovies
Video, 1969
Length unknown

Heavenly Pass-Time
Proposal for an Activity, August 1969
For Experiments in Art and Technology's Pepsi-Cola Pavilion at Japan World Exposition '70, Osaka, Japan

Work
Activity, September 1969
Commissioned by the Jewish Museum, New York
Not realized

Home Brew
Activity, November 1969
Commissioned by KPFK-FM, Los Angeles
Not realized

Moon Sounds
Activity, December 1969
Presented for the wedding of Helga and Richard Blau
El Mirage Dry Lake, California

Solo
Activity, 1969
Not realized
Reinvented in 2006

169–174 **Days Off: A Calendar of Happenings**
Calendar, 1970
Commissioned by the Junior Council of the Museum of Modern Art, New York

Graft
Activity, January 1970
Presented for Creative Arts Festival
Various locations, Kent State University, Kent, Ohio
Reinvented in 2007

Good Morning!
Activity, May 1970
Sponsored by San Francisco State University
San Francisco
Reinvented in 2006

Supermarket Event
Activity, July–August 1970
Sponsored by Arts Council of the Aspen Institute for Humanistic Studies
A supermarket in Aspen, Colorado

169 Cover of *Days Off*
Photo: Peter Moore

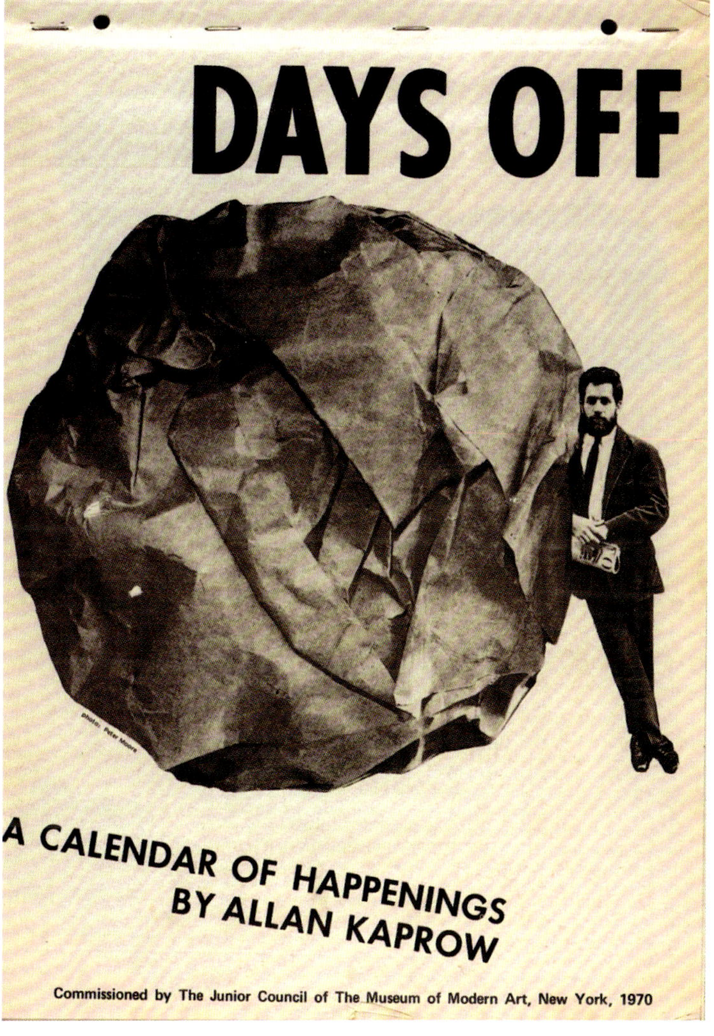

1970

TEACHING POSITIONS Associate Dean and Professor of the School of Art, California Institute of the Arts, Burbank. ¶ CONSULTING POSITIONS Codirector, Project Other Ways, Berkeley Unified School District, Berkeley. Advanced Placement Committee on Art and History for the Education Testing Service, Princeton, and the College Entrance Examination Board, New York. ¶ GROUP EXHIBITIONS *Software,* Jewish Museum, New York (traveled nationally), September–November. *Happening and Fluxus,* Kölnischer Kunstverein, Cologne, November–January. *Three Toward Infinity: New Multiple Art,* Whitechapel Art Gallery, London, November–January. ¶ FESTIVALS Creative Arts Festival, Kent State University, Kent, Ohio, January. Summer Change '70, Department of Parks and Recreation, Los Angeles County, September. ¶ WRITINGS "Inter-Office Memorandum To: All Deans," "Pasadena Freeway Project," and "(desert dry lake bed moon sounds)," in "California Institute of the Arts: Prologue to a Community," special issue, *Arts in Society* 7, no. 3: 22–23, 125–28, 166–67. "Mid Twentieth Century Environments and Happenings," in Chandler McC. Brooks, ed., *The Changing World and Man: The Cultural and Social Environment of Man, Its Significance for His Biological Performance* (Albany: Pridemark), 83–96. Scores for *Six Ordinary Happenings, Homemovies, Graft, Course,* and *Record II,* in Wolf Vostell, *Aktionen: Happenings und Demonstrationen seit 1965* (Reinbek: Rowohlt), n.p.

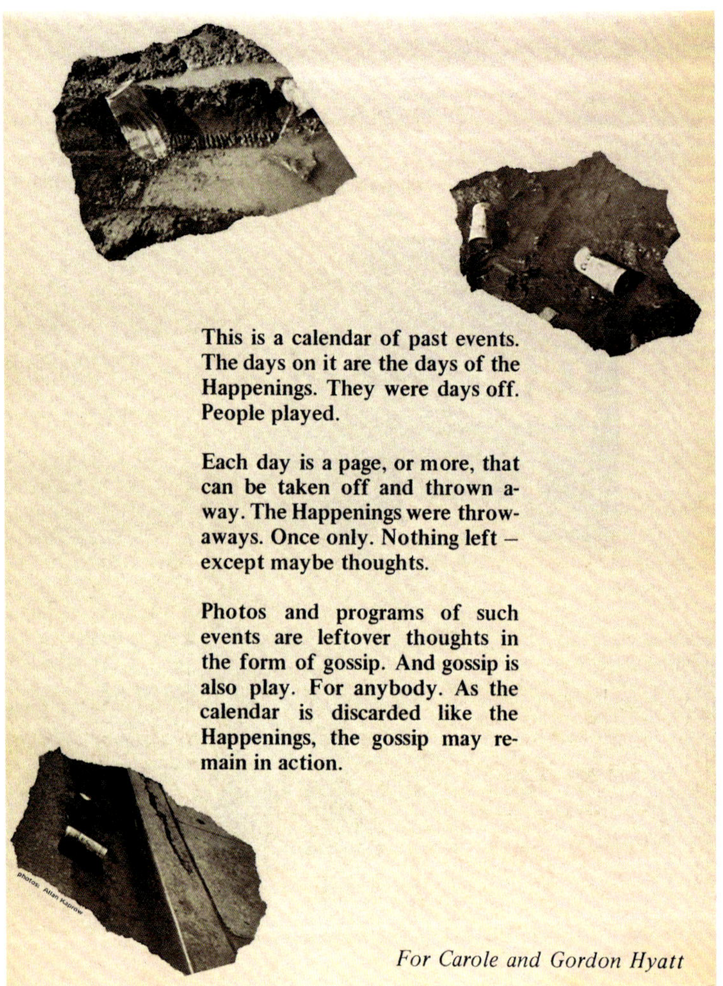

This is a calendar of past events. The days on it are the days of the Happenings. They were days off. People played.

Each day is a page, or more, that can be taken off and thrown away. The Happenings were throw-aways. Once only. Nothing left – except maybe thoughts.

Photos and programs of such events are leftover thoughts in the form of gossip. And gossip is also play. For anybody. As the calendar is discarded like the Happenings, the gossip may remain in action.

Photos: Allan Kaprow

For Carole and Gordon Hyatt

170 Preface to *Days Off*

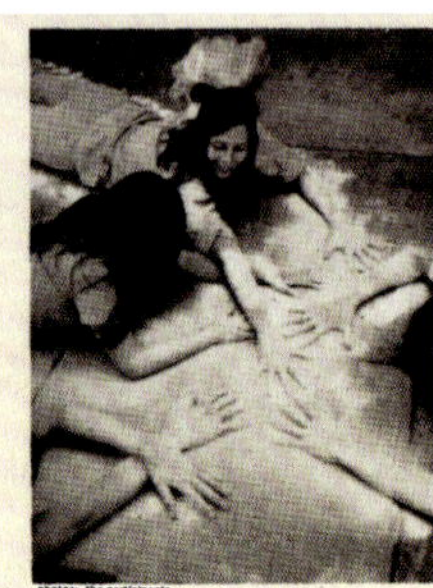

SHAPE

SHOES, BODIES
ON STREETS, SIDEWALKS, FIELDS

SPRAY PAINTING THEIR SILHOUETTES

REPORTS AND PHOTOS IN NEWSPAPER

APRIL

19

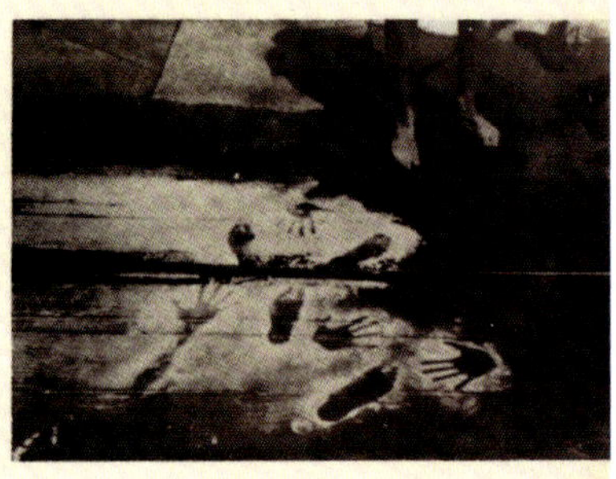

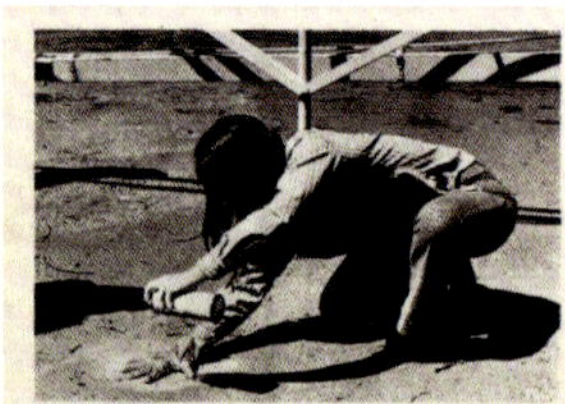

APRIL

19

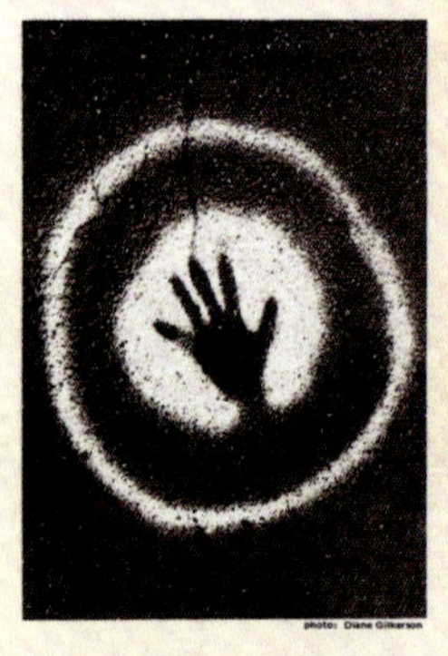

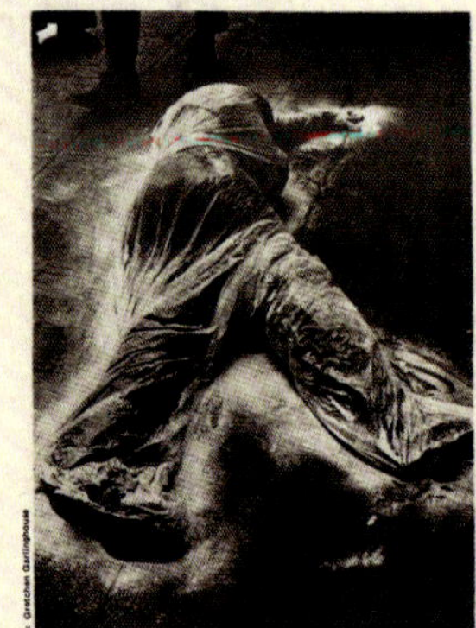

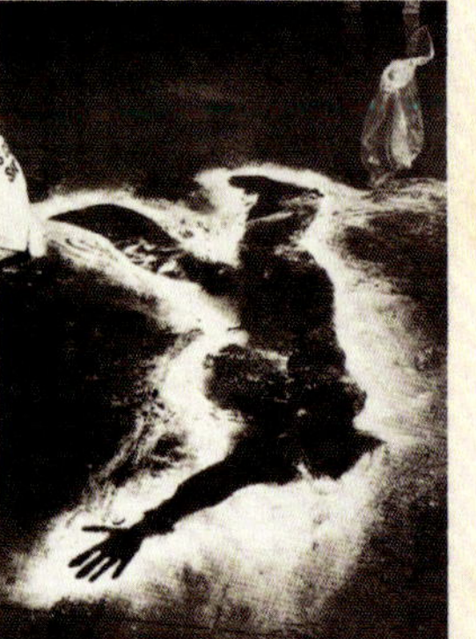

171 + 172 Calendar for 19 April (documenting *Shape*, 1969)

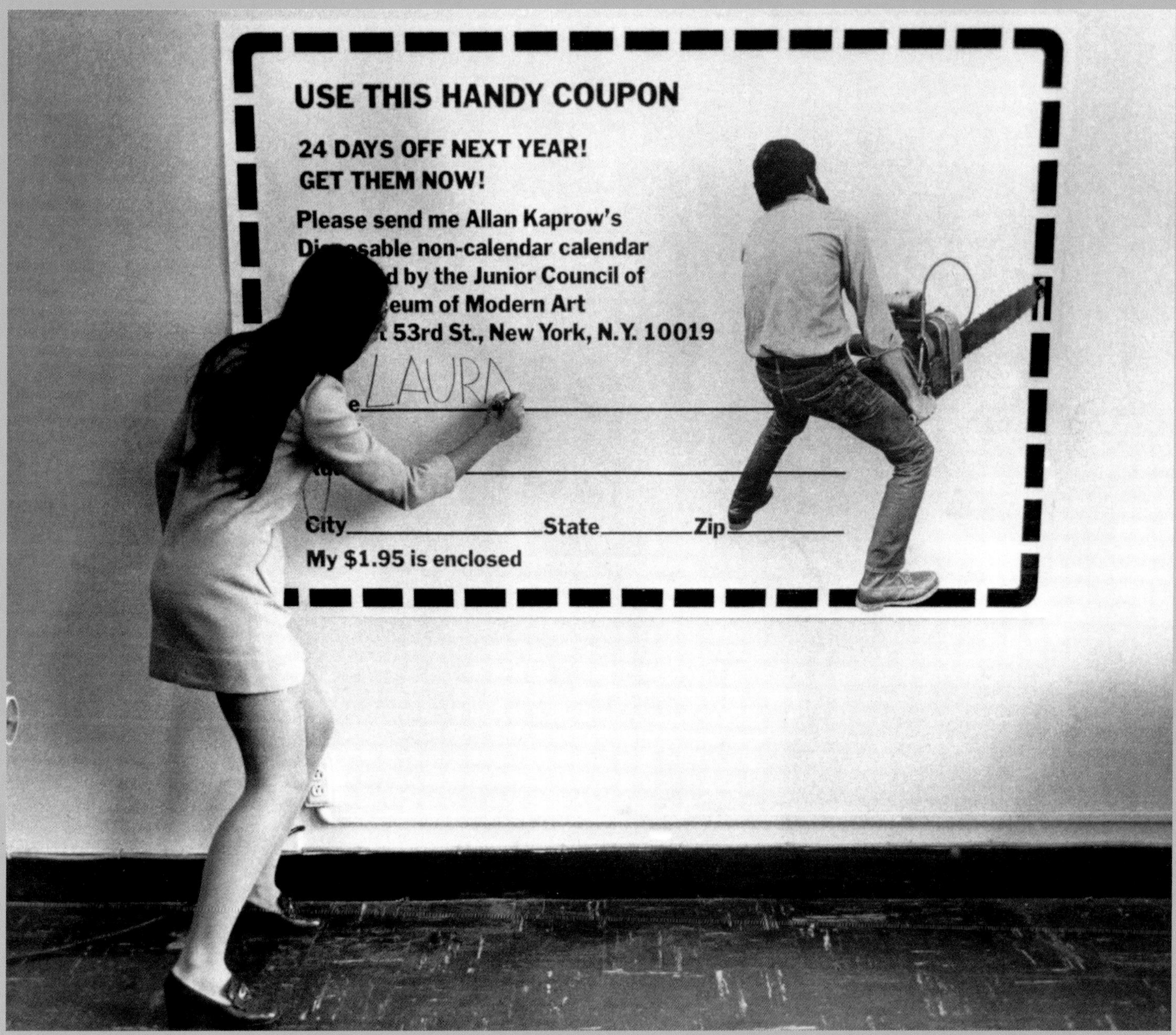
USE THIS HANDY COUPON
24 DAYS OFF NEXT YEAR!
GET THEM NOW!
Please send me Allan Kaprow's
Disposable non-calendar calendar
by the Junior Council of
eum of Modern Art
53rd St., New York, N.Y. 10019
LAURA
City
State
Zip
My $1.95 is enclosed

ALLAN KAPROW's *Days Off* is a calendar of Happenings. Oddly, where LeWitt's gallery work is crucial and published work at best superfluous, Kaprow's case is just the opposite. The published work makes his John Gibson show redundant.

Days Off is like a movie of stills. Kaprow's fine eye and sense of pace allow him to be the director of ten consecutive "still-shorts," some hilarious, some disquieting. In this hybrid medium, clearly two gifts count—skill at the individual isolated image, and skill at that image in time, as one of a series, as a moment. Kaprow has both.

His flair—or weakness, depending on one's point of view—for the collective prank should not prevent us from enjoying Kaprow's eye. Throughout the calendar, the image remains important. True, the images must be set in a verbal grid, but that grid can be kept to a minimum, something Kaprow does well. Right at the start of *Runner*, the first Happening, the second and third pages, totalling six photos, are wordless. In *Pose* six consecutive pages are virtually wordless, in *Travelog* nearly four. Though there is a verbal explanation at the beginning, when it mentions first photos and then words, we believe that order of importance. The photos are not illustrations in the old sense of mere "renderings" of text. Aptly, the calendar's cover, with its huge paper ball, is as striking visually as it is verbally.

Kaprow's eye is responsible for extraordinary images. In *Record II* he silvers parts of a stack of colossal rocks with tinfoil. Absurdity aside, purely formally the contrast between the glistening ribbons and the brute rocks is remarkable. As is the end of *Record II:* after more than twenty pages of strictly rectangular photos, each a squared-off, isolated newsview, suddenly photos are scattered pell-mell down the page, overlapping left and right and running right to the page's edge. The effect is visual anarchy. Where the eye had been used to a single, normal horizon per image, now suddenly in this grand image it sees seven, many tilted; the result is a touch of spatial vertigo. In addition to this, all the scattered photos, since seen earlier in the course of the Happening, represent moments of time once in sequence but now chucked into simultaneity like a throw of jacks; the result is a touch of temporal vertigo too. Kaprow's eye is fine indeed.

Shape, a Happening that involves placing objects, including bodies, on the ground and spray-painting their silhouettes, begins as fun and games. A girl is shown enjoying spraying her own hand. Once the idea is grasped visually and a certain empathy established by the fun, Kaprow switches his image toward the disquieting. A man lies on the ground with arm outstretched. The negative image is dark, the silhouetting paint white, giving the effect of a shadow groping its way across the floor. Later two floor effigies fight, still later two dance. Finally a dark figure bathed in a brilliant halo stands with feet apart and arms wide like some cheap but thrilling Lucifer.

Soon film and still-photography may move so close that films may freeze for longer than the split-second they often do now. They may freeze for say a half-minute or more, producing images to be experienced not just as interruption but as stillness, the director moving toward the artist. *Days Off* describes a similar movement from the other side. It shows an artist, much to his credit, moving toward being a director.

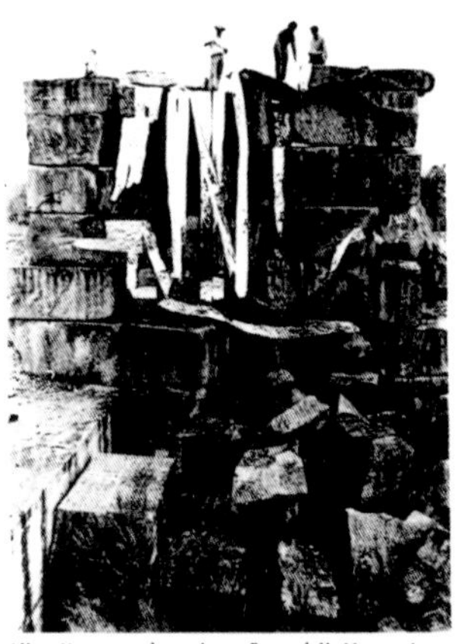

Allan Kaprow, photo from *Record II*, Happening, 1968. John Gibson Gallery.

175 Score for *Level*

LEVEL

A block of ice and a bale of straw are placed near one another somewhere.

The ice melts slowly.

The bale is reduced straw by straw until nothing remains.

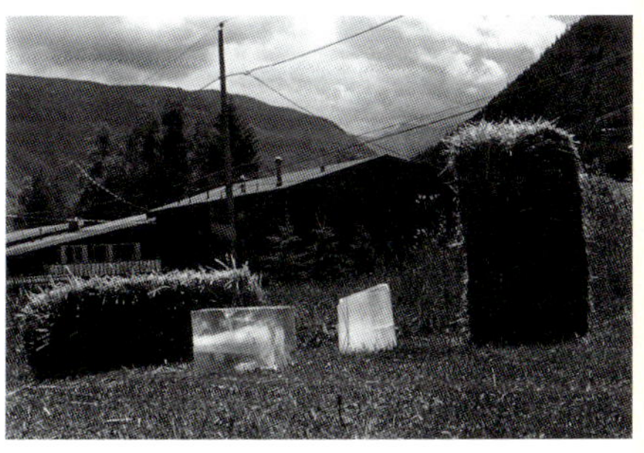

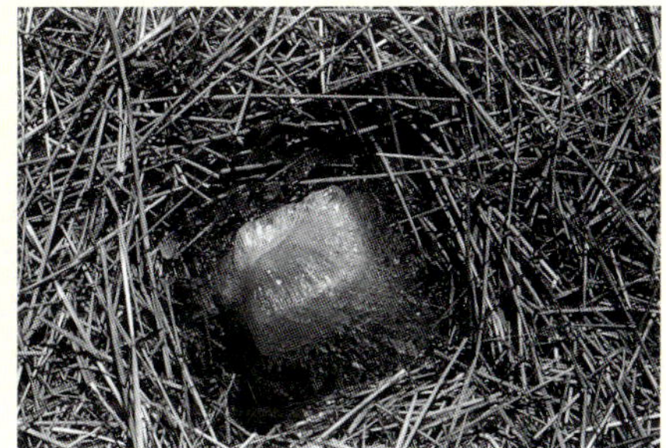

176 Blocks of ice and bales of straw
177 Ice melts slowly

An activity prepared by Allan Kaprow, and sponsored by the Arts Council of the Aspen Institute, for anyone, on Friday, August 7, 1970, Aspen, Colorado.

175–177 **Level**

Activity, August 1970
Sponsored by the Arts Council of the Aspen Institute for Humanistic Studies
A field in Aspen, Colorado
Reinvented in 2007 (twice)

Don't

Activity, September 1970
Presented for Summer Change '70
Century City Shopping Plaza, Los Angeles, and El Porto Beach, Manhattan Beach
Reinvented in 2006 and 2007 (twice)

178 Making structures of 2 x 4s

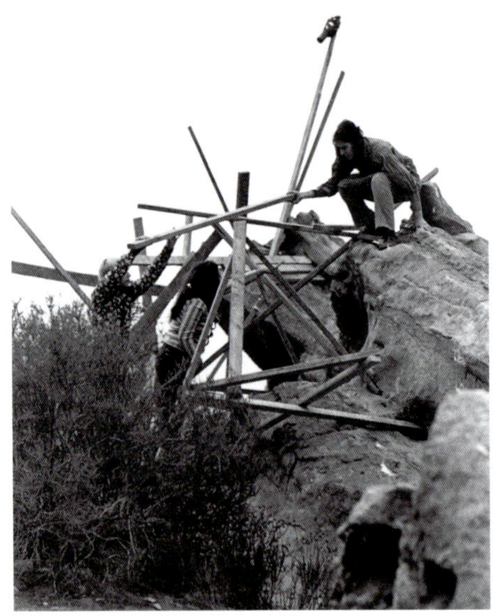

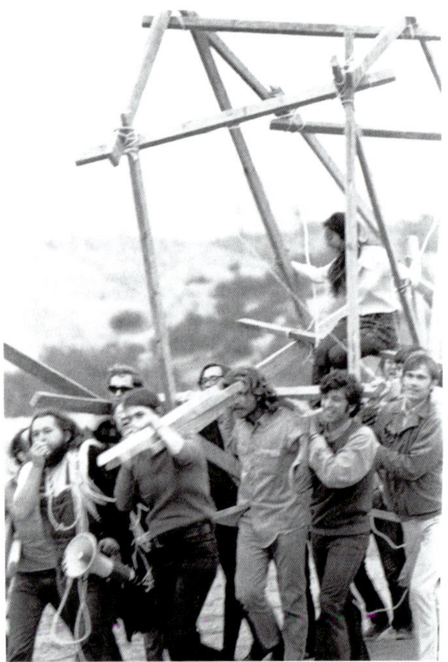

179 Post-Activity celebration

PUBLICITY

CREWS MAKING STRUCTURES OF 2X4'S AMONG THE ROCKS

ROVING BAND OF 4 VIDEO CAMERMEN

WORK CREWS WAVING FROM THE PEAKS CALLING THRU BULLHORNS FOR THE VIDEO PEOPLE--WANTING THEM TO SEE AND RECORD

VIDEO PEOPLE TRYING TO COVER EVERYTHING--ACTION, OOHS, WOWS, AHS, SMALL TALK--ALL ON TAPE

PLAYBACKS OF EVERYONE'S WORK AT EACH SITE--CAUSING MAYBE NEW IDEAS, CHANGES, RECONSTRUCTIONS--MORE RECORDINGS

CALLS AGAIN AND AGAIN ON BULLHORNS, VIDEO PEOPLE MOVING FAST, MAYBE WORK CREWS START EXCHANGING, MAYBE STRUCTURES START COMBINING

GOING ON TILL SUNDOWN OR TILL EVERYONE'S TIRED

(AT VASQUEZ ROCKS, CALIF. 10/6/70)

180 Score for *Publicity*

178–180 **Publicity**
Activity, October 1970
Sponsored by California Institute of the Arts
Vasquez Rocks, Agua Dulce, California

Sales Pitch
Proposal for an Activity, October 1970
Version of *Hello* (1969)
For Experiments in Art and Technology

Ribbon Cutting
Activity, November 1970
Presented for the dedication of the Hans Hofmann wing
University Art Museum, University of California, Berkeley

181–185 **Sawdust**
Activity, November 1970
Presented for *Happening and Fluxus*
Local carpentry shop, Cologne
Reinvented in 1986 and 2005

Sawdust
Lithograph, 1970
61 × 42.8 cm (24 × 16 ⅞ in.)
Museum am Ostwall, Dortmund, Germany

Yard
Environment, November–January 1970
Reinvention for *Happening and Fluxus*
Kölnischer Kunstverein, Cologne

186–189 **Sweet Wall**
Activity, November 1970
Sponsored by Galerie René Block
Empty lot near the Berlin wall, West Berlin
Reinvented in 1986

Car Spaces
Activity, November 1970
Sponsored by California Institute of the Arts
On the Pasadena freeway

181 Letter from Wolf Vostell

KÖLNISCHER KUNSTVEREIN
5 KÖLN 1 · JOSEF HAUBRICH-HOF 1
NÄHE NEUMARKT
FERNSPRECHER: KÖLN 217021 UND 221-3740

AUSSTELLUNGEN:
TÄGLICH VON 10–17 · FR 10–21 UHR

SEKRETARIAT:
DI–FR VON 9–17 · SA VON 9–13 · SO VON 10–13 UHR
MO GESCHLOSSEN

Dear Allan,
How are you ,so long that I didnt hear from you,you must be very active-activity.
I hope we all see you soon here-Szeeman told me today that you prefer a garage instead of the yard of the museum.
The garage is in in function underneath the museum and once I did an environment there and nobody would find the cellar.
I am coordinating the environments part,on the other side of the building there is a space more terrain vague near th several buildings,some trees around there it could be very strong.
On the other side where is the oficial entrance with yard there I suggested to put a toilet-trailer -Maciunas wanted a toilet in the building-but I think a mobil car-toilet-truck outside the museum is better.Inside (see plan) is a huge hall-there we are installing emmett williams fish-poem in several aqariums-dick higgins -1ooo symphonies for audience participation(shooting scores)-alisons house of doust-documentation and I am trying to get 6 or 7 cows to show during the time of opening the birth of an animal,a repetition from the ULM-happening 1964,where no birth took place.
Than my friend Rywelski,Galerie Art Intermedia showed me that john Gibson is offering him a show during the museums-show of your old pannels.What do you think should we install a part in the Kunstverein where we show this old fall outs.Please write me soon about that to get the transport ready from Gibson.
very cordially,yours,

(VOSTELL)

18.9.70

Konten:
Sparkasse der Stadt Köln 52752079
Bankhaus J. H. Stein, Köln 21085
Bankhaus I. D. Herstatt Köln 314290
Dresdner Bank, Köln 4-131660
Postscheckkonto Köln 10050

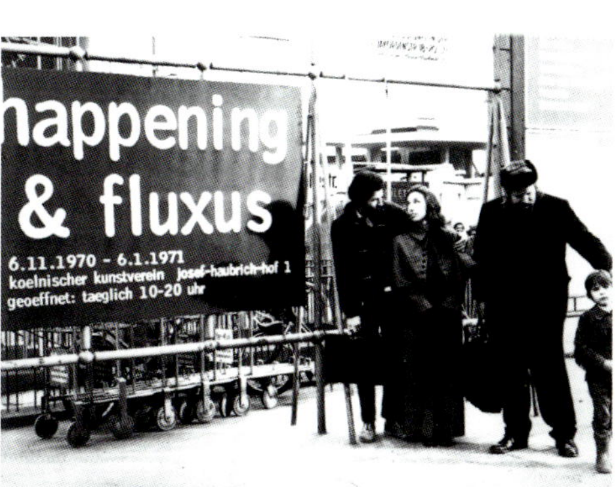

182 Poster for *Happening and Fluxus*

SAWDUST

(a dècollage for Vostell)

large wooden beams
placed separately somewhere

reducing beams to sawdust

exchanging sawdust of beams

at each place
mixing sawdust with glue
putting sawdust into molds
to form new beams

getting more from less

a.k. 7/10/70
Cologne

183 Score for *Sawdust*

184 Putting sawdust into molds

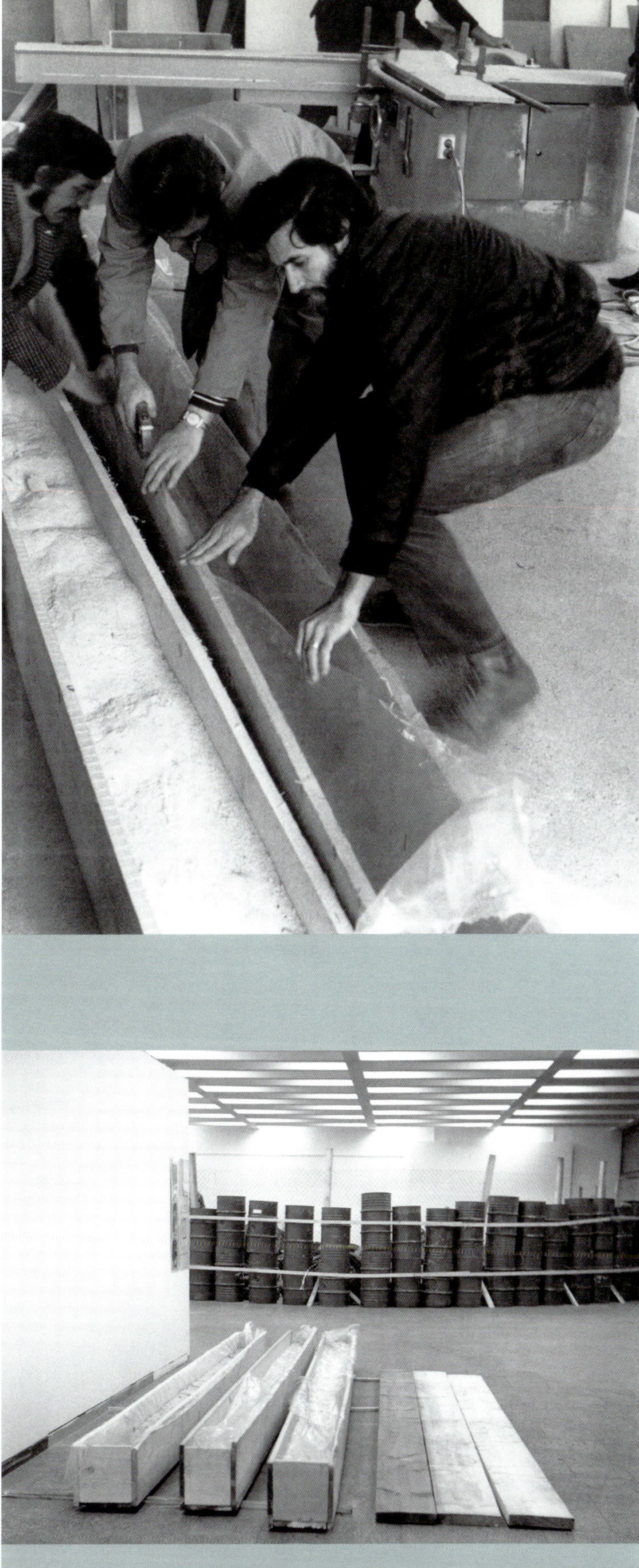

185 Molds and beams

186 Statement for *Sweet Wall*

From the Activity booklet (pub. 1976)

Some art containing political references attempts to affect social change as directly and quickly as possible. Its themes are blunt and the moral choices are clear.

In other cases, the art's political content is a metaphor intended to play upon an already awakened consciousness. The politics are implicit, and are imbedded in complexes of other human and cultural meaning. Yet this art also presumes to have some positive effect upon society; it simply doesn't specify how and when.

Both kinds of art may be valuable to the world but they are addressed to two very different kinds of consumer: the activist and the intellectual. At their extremes both are clichés, of course; but there are in fact intelligent activists and passionately committed intellectuals. One tries to serve short range goals; the other, long range.

"Sweet Wall", looking back six years, contains ironical politics. It is parody. It is for a small group of colleagues who can appreciate the humor and sadness of political life. It is for those who cannot rest politically indifferent, but who know that for every political solution there at least ten new problems.

"Sweet Wall" was free-standing. It enclosed nothing, separated no one. It was built in a desolated area close to the real Berlin Wall. The real Wall divided a city against itself. "Sweet Wall" was put up within hours and then was easily knocked down by its builders. The Berlin Wall was constructed for impregnability and will stand until either a war or a political act by a later generation removes it. The blocks of the "Sweet Wall" were bound together by fresh bread and jam (an oblique reference to the Biblical Isrealites), while those of the Berlin Wall were joined by cement.

As parody, "Sweet Wall" was about an idea of a wall. The Berlin Wall was an idea, too: it summed up in one medieval image the idealogical division of Europe. But it also directly affected the lives of more than three million residents, at least six governments, as well as countless non-Berliners who at one time or other would be involved in that city.

As an idea for a handful of people, "Sweet Wall" could be played in the mind without serious consequence at the time. Like the wall with its bread and jam, symbols could be produced and erased at will. The participants could speculate on the practical value of such freedom, to themselves and to others. That was its sweetness and its irony. The event was sponsored in November of 1970 by Galerie René Block.

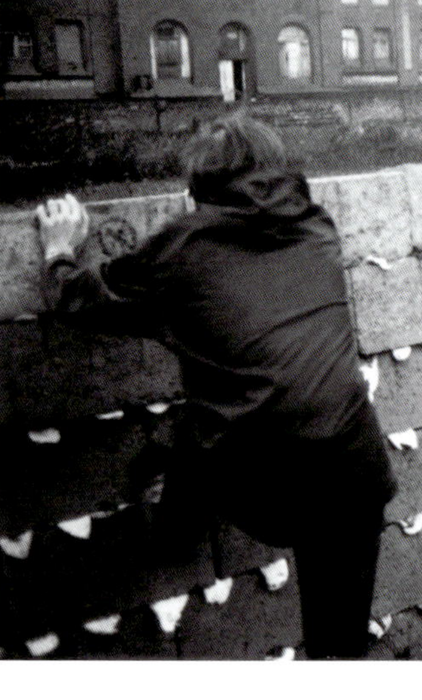

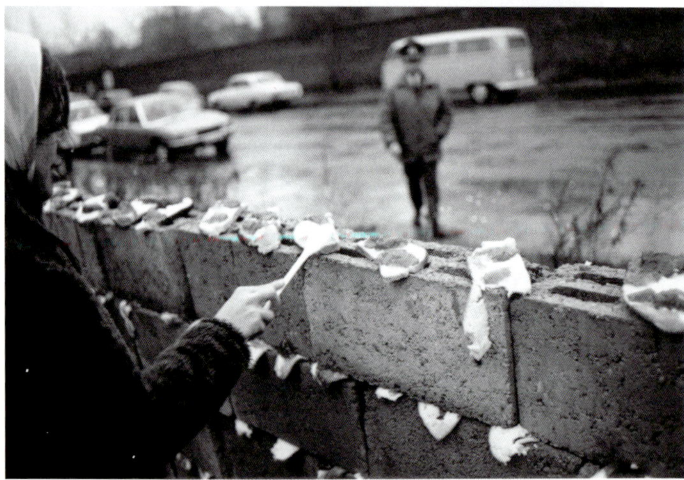

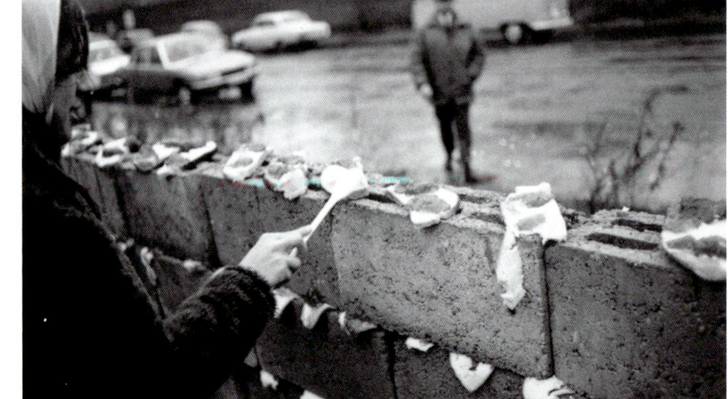

187 Spreading jam on bread

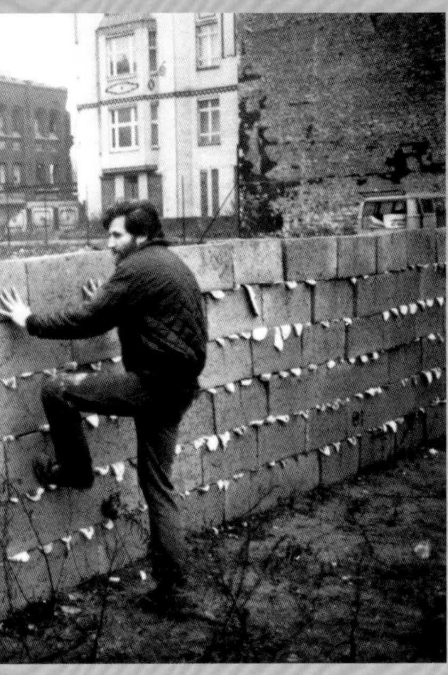

188 Knocking over the wall

SWEET WALL

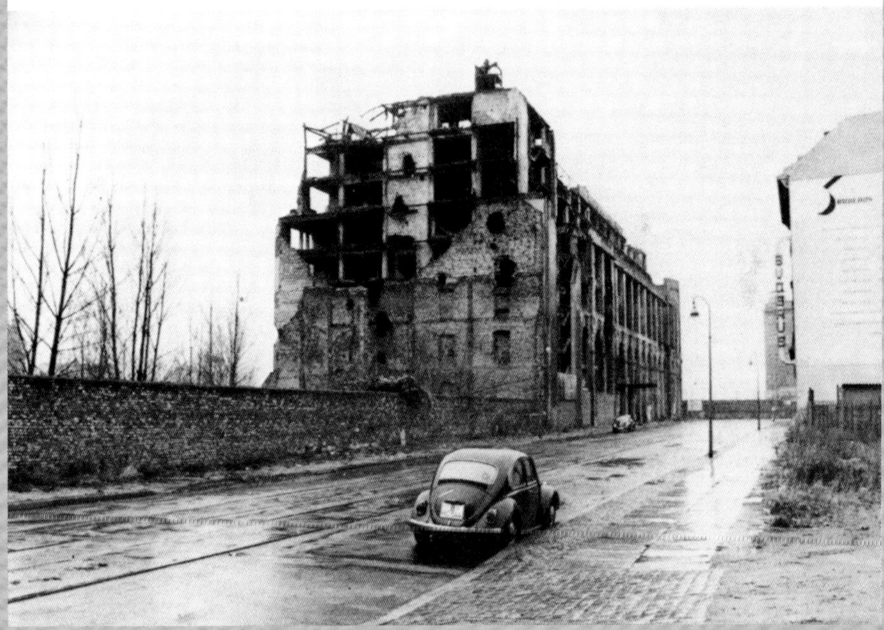

189 Title page for *Sweet Wall*
From the Activity booklet (pub. 1976)

TEACHING POSITIONS Associate Dean and Professor of the School of Art, California Institute of the Arts, Burbank and Valencia. ¶ CONSULTING POSITIONS Advanced Placement Committee on Art and History for the Education Testing Service, Princeton, and the College Entrance Examination Board, New York. ¶ AWARDS Gold Medal, Cultural Office of the City of Milan. ¶ SOLO EXHIBITIONS Galerie Inge Baecker, Bochum, October. ¶ GROUP EXHIBITIONS *Arte de sistemas,* Centro de arte y comunicación en el Museo de arte moderno, Buenos Aires, July. ¶ WRITINGS "The Education of the Un-Artist, Part I," *ARTnews* 69, no. 10: 28–31, 66–68. "Publicity" (Activity score), *Box* 1, no. 1: n.p.

1971

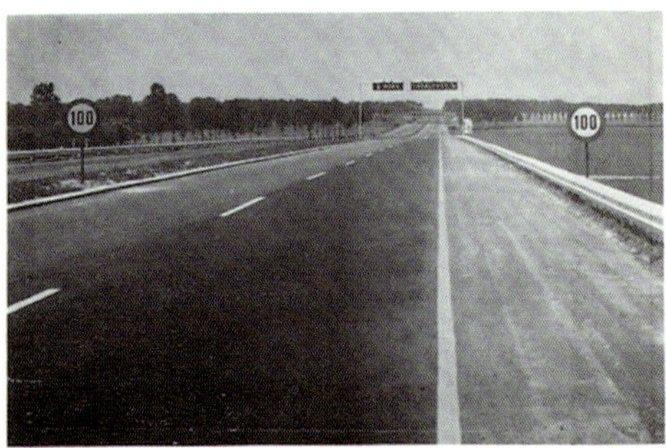

PRINT-OUT

(FOR GEORGE BRECHT)

un' azione di Allan Kaprow

Guidando delle macchine in un prato aperto fino a che queste traccino una strada

Dipingendo la strada di bianco fino a che venga cancellata

America cultura visiva
Happening di Allan Kaprow in Videotape
14 settembre - 3 ottobre 1971
Rotonda della Besana
Comune di Milano
Ripartizione iniziative culturali

Segnando una strada asfaltata con una linea bianca

Guidando delle macchine sulla linea fino a che venga cancellata

Nota: La linea si ottiene con una normale macchina da segnaletica orizzontale, utilizzando pittura ad acqua totalmente solubile. La linea deve essere lunga un miglio. La stessa pittura ad acqua viene spruzzata sulla strada nel prato, utilizzando un normale compressore. Le due attività vengono filmate e proiettate su monitors TV.

Riprese televisive: Luciano Giaccari, Studio 970-2 Varese

190 Poster for *Print-Out* (with score)

Dial II
Happening, January 1971
Reinvention of *Dial* (1969) for the California Institute of the Arts
Telephone booths near telephone poles, Valencia, California

Tracts
Activity, May 1971
A hillside above the temporary campus of California Institute of the Arts, Burbank

Tag
Activity, June 1971
Sponsored by the Aspen Design Conference
Aspen, Colorado

Labor Day
Activity, September 1971
Sponsored by Centro Apollinaire
Six points along a circular route and a racetrack, Milan

190–192 **Print-Out**
Activity, September 1971
Sponsored by Comune di Milano
Ripartizione inizitive culturali
Open fields, roads, and the Rotonda della Besana, Milan

City Works
Activity, October–November 1971
Sponsored by Galerie Inge Baecker
On the B1 freeway, Bochum

Calendar
Activity, October 1971
Sponsored by California Institute of the Arts
Valencia

193 **Scales**
Activity, October 1971
Sponsored by California Institute of the Arts
In a stairwell, Birnkrant Residence Hall, Valencia
Reinvented in 2006 and 2007 (twice)

191 Participants reading the score

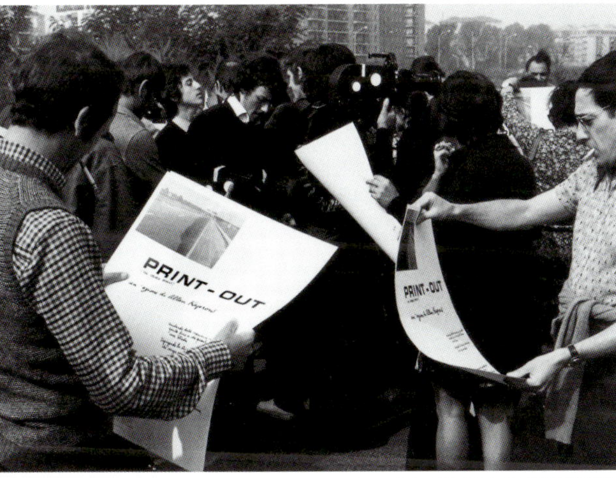

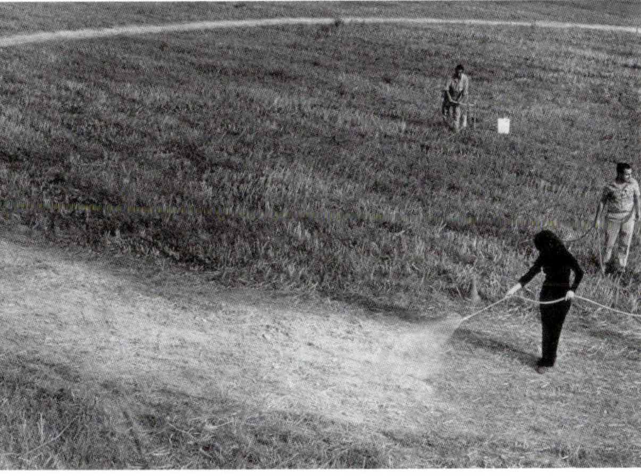

192 Spraying a line on the meadow

193 Score for *Scales*

SCALES

placing cement blocks on steps of 1st floor stairway
to form new steps going up

climbing them

carrying blocks to 2nd floor stairway

repeating placements

climbing them

carrying blocks to 3rd floor stairway

repeating placements

climbing them

*   *   *   *   *

carrying cement blocks to different 3rd floor stairway

placing them on steps going down

descending them

carrying blocks to different 2nd floor stairway

repeating placements

descending them

carying blocks to different 1st floor stairway

repeating placements

descending them

* process may continue indefinitely, either up and down or if building has more floors. — A.K. Oct.,'71

TEACHING POSITIONS Associate Dean and Professor of the School of Art, California Institute of the Arts, Valencia. ¶ **CONSULTING POSITIONS** Advanced Placement Committee on Art and History for the Education Testing Service, Princeton, and the College Entrance Examination Board, New York. ¶ **GROUP EXHIBITIONS** *Cal Arts Faculty Show,* California Institute of the Arts, Valencia, January. *Art 3 '72,* John Gibson Gallery, Basel Art Fair, Basel, Switzerland, May. *Everybody Knows: Hubert Peeters Collection,* Westfälisches Landesmuseum für Kunst und Kulturgeschichte, Münster, West Germany, September. *Operazione Vesuvio,* Henry Art Gallery, University of Washington, Seattle (traveled internationally), November–December. ¶ **WRITINGS** "Baggage" (Activity score and notes), *Source* 6, no. 1, issue 11: 94–100. "The Education of the Un-Artist, Part II," *ARTnews* 71, no. 3: 34–39. "Heavenly Passtime—Year 2000" (proposal for Experiments in Art and Technology's Pepsi-Cola Pavilion, Expo '70, Osaka, Japan), in Billy Klüver, Julie Martin, and Barbara Rose, eds., *Pavilion* (New York: E.P. Dutton), 295–97.

1972

ALLAN KAPROW VISIT

Below is a description the "telephone piece" that Allan Kaprow intends to stage while he is here. He expects it to be initiated at Waterson Towers. The piece will be completed on the following Saturday morning.

<u>MESSAGE UNITS</u>

(night) turning on a blinking light bulb
calling someone
phone ringing 10 times
when answered, saying "I've turned on the 1st blinking light bulb"
answerer saying "OK, I'll turn mine on"

turning on 2nd blinking light bulb
calling again
phone ringing 20 times
when answered, saying "I've turned on the 2nd blinking light bulb"
answerer saying "OK, I'll turn mine on"

turning on 3rd blinking light bulb
calling again
phone ringing 30 times
when answered, saying "I've turned on the 3rd blinking light bulb"
answerer saying "OK, I'll turn mine on"

turning on 4th blinking light bulb
calling again
phone ringing 40 times
when answered, saying "I've turned on the 4th blinking light bulb"
answerer saying "OK, I'll turn mine on"

(day) answerer turning off 1st blinking light bulb
calling caller
phone ringing 50 times
when answered, saying "I've turned off the 1st blinking light bulb"
answerer saying "OK, I'll turn mine off"

turning off 2nd blinking light bulb
calling again
phone ringing 60 times
when answered, saying "I've turned off the 2nd blinking light bulb"
answerer saying "OK, I'll turn mine off"

turning off 3rd blinking light bulb
calling again
phone ringing 70 times
when answered, saying "I've turned off the 3rd blinking light bulb"
answerer saying "OK, I'll turn mine off"

turning off 4th blinking light bulb
calling again
phone ringing 80 times
when answered, saying "I've turned off the 4th blinking light bulb"
answerer saying "OK, I'll turn mine off"

a.k., 2/72

Note: The program here describes a pattern for two persons; it may be doubled indefinitely to include as wish to participate.

194 + 195 Score for *Message Units*

196 Lightbulb on

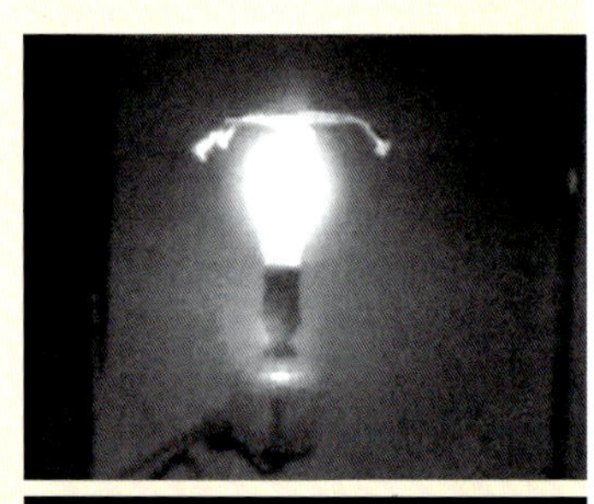

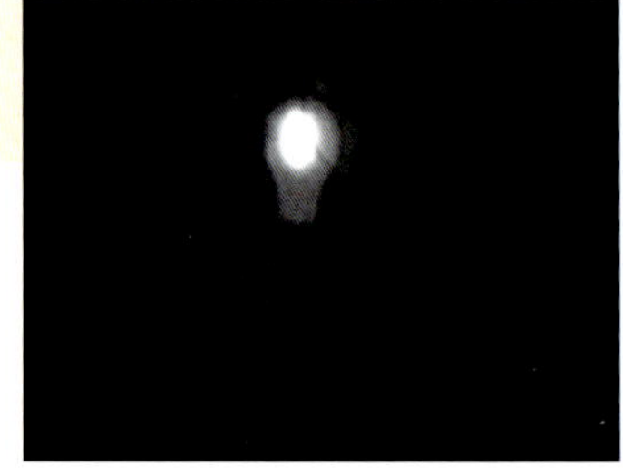

197 Lightbulb off

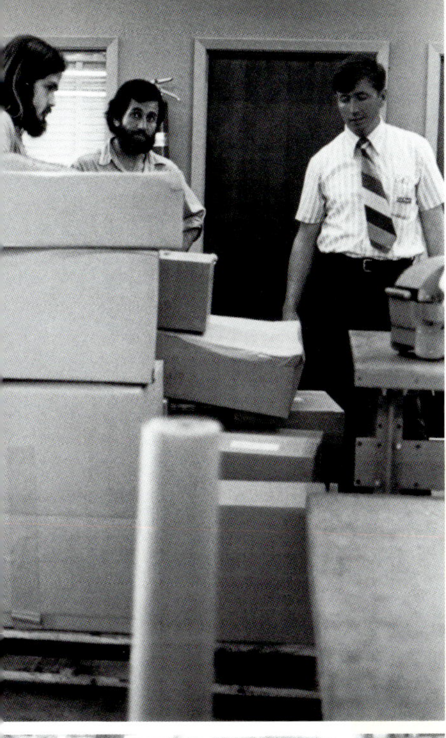

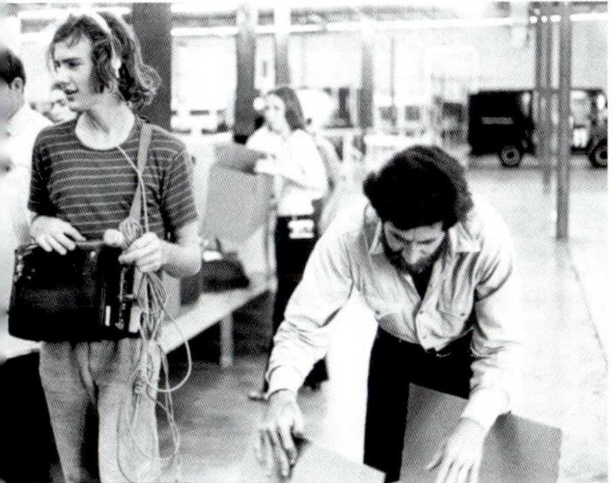

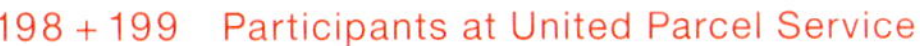

198 + 199 Participants at United Parcel Service

200 Score for *Baggage*

BAGGAGE

driving to airport
with suitcases of packaged sand
(tagged with owner's name)

leading them
on airport underground train
waiting
until train returns
removing suitcases
stacking them together

taking them at random
driving to the shore
there emptying sand

refilling suitcases with beach sand
driving them to city United Parcel Service
for delivery to owners

A.K. 4/72

194–197 **Message Units**
Activity, February 1972
Various locations, California Institute of the Arts, Valencia

198–203 **Baggage**
Activity, April 1972
Sponsored by Rice University
Various locations, Houston

Easy
Activity, May 1972
Sponsored by Colorado College
A streambed in Colorado Springs
Reinvented in 2006

204 **Meters**
Activity, May 1972
Not realized

Message Units
Activity, May 1972
Watterson Towers, Illinois State University, Normal

Meaning

① transportation piece
foot
car
train
plane
boat
truck

② recreational piece
mimics (or re-creates) the activity of the traveller - tourist - vacationer

③ recycle piece
sand packed, sent out into the world, returns
like the seasons
like the life cycle

④ about the self
"baggage" as burden

"baggage" as memory, training, beliefs etc.

attempt to get rid of it:
random redistribution of one's own bags
yet the "chickens come home to roost"
but it's different sand than went out originally
one changes after all

"sand": dreams built on shifting sands

sands of time

the beach and its constant changes in and out flow

"the return": United Parcel Service
a little bit of the self coming back
pronounced
UPS (oops!)

203 Suitcase of packaged sand

A.K., 72

METERS

(in the hills)

carrying a cube of ice in the mouth
carrying a cube of ice in the hand
walking on

swallowing the melting ice till it's gone
calling out: now!
walking on

waiting for the hand to hold no ice
calling out: now!
walking on

waiting for the hand to dry
calling out: now!
walking on

wetting a finger with saliva
holding it up till dry
calling out: now!
walking on

repeating till mouth is dry
calling out: now!
walking on

205–206 **Burbank**
Activity, September 1972
For Luther Burbank
California Institute of the Arts,
Valencia

Meteorology
Activity, September 1972
Sponsored by Galerie Inge Baecker
Banks of the Rhine river, Dusseldorf

Meteorology
Assemblage, 1972
Dimensions variable
Collection Maria and Walter Schnepel,
Bremen

Idea
Activity, September 1972
Sponsored by Portland Center for the
Visual Arts
Portland, Oregon

Flow
Collage, 1972
55.9 × 76.2 cm (22 × 30 in.)
Allan Kaprow Estate

207 **Entr'acte**
Activity, December 1972
In a public washroom at California
Institute of the Arts, Valencia
Reinvented in 2007

George Brecht Dedication Ceremony
Activity, 1972
Cologne

Copy
Activity, 1972
Not realized

Private Lines
Videoscript, 1972
Not realized

205 Score for *Burbank*

Burbank

leafless branch fixed to leafy branch
leafy branch fixed to one without
pix of leafless branch fixed to leafy branch
pix of leafy branch fixed to one without
plastic leaves fixed to leafy branch
plastic leaves fixed to one without
leafy branch fixed to leafy branch
leafless branch fixed to one without

note: each graft is to a different tree;
pix are polaroids

A.K. 9/72

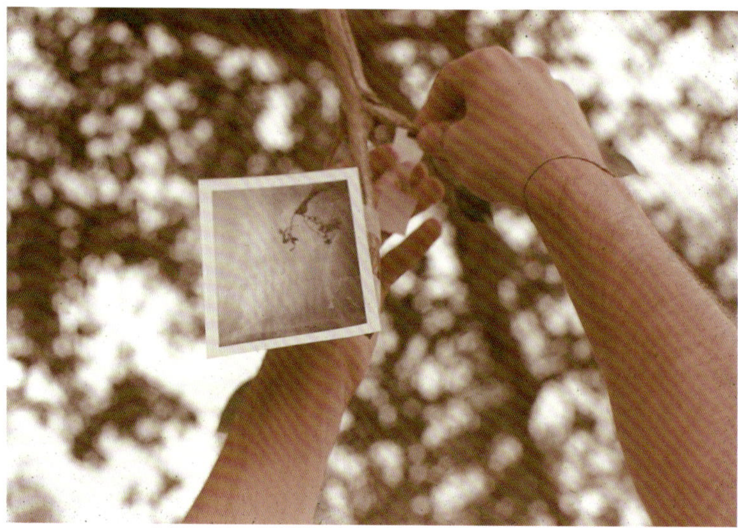

206 "Pix of leafy branch fixed to leafless branch"

ENTR'ACTE

(in a public washroom)

wet hand   shaking another hand   "shake!"

that hand shaking another   "shake!"

and so on till a hand is dry   "that's it!"

*

wet hands   drying with a towel   "finished!"

other wet hands   drying   "finished!"

and so on till towel is wet   "it's wet!"

*

towel   shaking it   passing it to other hands
"shake it!"

shaking it   passing it   "shake it!"

and so on till towel is dry   "that's it!"

ak 12/72

TEACHING POSITIONS Associate Dean and Professor of the School of Art, California Institute of the Arts, Valencia. ¶ **CONSULTING POSITIONS** Trustee and Education Committee chair, Pasadena Museum of Modern Art, Pasadena. ¶ **GROUP EXHIBITIONS** *Grafische Techniken,* Neuer Berliner Kunstverein and Kunstbibliothek, West Berlin, February–March. *ADA: Aktionen der Avantgarde,* Neuer Berliner Kunstverein, Akademie der Künste, West Berlin, September–October. *Contemporanea: Incontri internazionali d'arte,* Parcheggio di Villa Borghese, Rome, November–February. ¶ **WRITINGS** "Allan Kaprow: Jensen Mikro Makro," in *Alfred Jensen,* exh. cat. (Hannover: Kestner Gesellschaft), 33–42. "Doctor MD," in *Marcel Duchamp,* exh. cat. (New York: Museum of Modern Art), 204–5. "Stephan von Huene," in *Sound Sculpture,* exh. cat. (Vancouver: Vancouver Art Gallery), 25–26.

1973

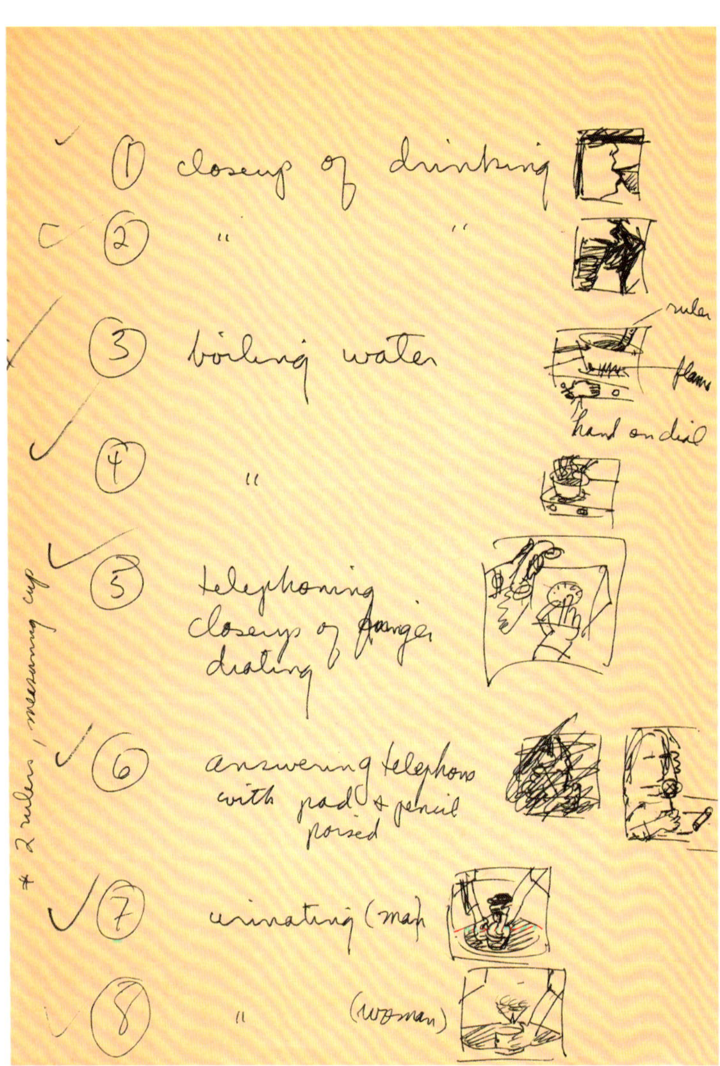

208 Sketch of photo layout

LOSS

drinking an amount of water
boiling an amount of water

waiting for an amount to be:
urinated
or
evaporated

telephoning someone doing the same;
being telephoned by someone doing the same:
to drink that amount of water
or
to add that amount of water
to the water boiling

continuing:
drinking
boiling
urinating
telephoning

until the bladder is empty
until the pot is empty

- a.k. 1/73

209 Score for *Loss*

208–210 **Loss**

Activity, January 1973
New York

Highs

Activity, February 1973
University of Kansas Museum of Art, Lawrence
Reinvented in 2006

Dial

Happening, February 1973
Reinvention for Western Washington University
Telephone booths near telephone poles, Bellingham, Washington

211–219 **Basic Thermal Units**

Activity, March 1973
Sponsored by Galerie Inge Baecker, Museum Folkwang, and Stiftung Wilhelm Lehmbruck Museum
Apartments in Essen, Duisburg, Bochum, and Remscheid, West Germany

Anniversary

Activity, May 1973
Sacramento

Clockwork

Activity, May 1973
Sponsored by California Institute of the Arts
In participants' private apartments
Reinvented in 2007

Wink

Activity, May 1973
Sponsored by California Institute of the Arts
In an elevator
Reinvented in 2007 (three times)

Creatures

Activity, September 1973
Presented for Ruhrpark Kunstwoche
Sponsored by Galerie Inge Baecker
Ruhrpark, Bochum

220–243 **Time Pieces**

Activity, September 1973
Presented for *ADA: Aktionen der Avantgarde*
Carried out independently by participants, West Berlin

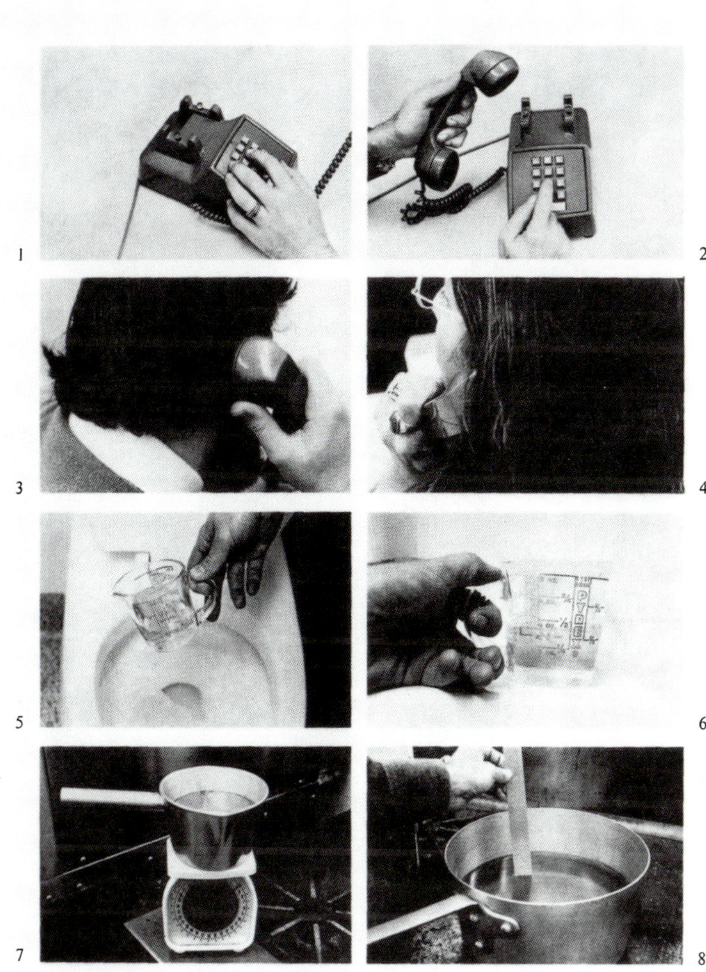

1 2 3 4 5 6 7 8

1–8. *Loss.* The eight shots included here were posed and taken some weeks after the Activity. They are intended to be *illustrations* rather than documents. Like the text of this article, they both explain something and mythify it, thus becoming a part of the evolving form of *Loss.* That is, what is lost by faulty memory is replaced by words and pictures.

210 Photo layout published in "Easy Activity" (1975)

BASIC THERMAL UNITS

(Essen)

HEATING A BODY
HEATING A ROOM

(for perhaps three hours
adding layers of clothes
one after the other
feeling the body get warm

phoning someone to raise
their apartment's heat by
the increase felt
in the warming body, e.g. 5°, 8°, 10°..

phoning repeatedly
until the body's too hot or
until the room's too hot
saying, or hearing, that
the limit is reached)

BTU's, p. 2

(Duisburg)

HEATING A ROOM
COOLING A BODY

(for perhaps three hours
increasing the temperature
of a room watching the
thermometer's rise, e. g. 5°, 8°, 10°....

phoning someone to lower
their body's heat
by shedding clothes
by applying ice packs
until the body feels 5°, 8°, 10°....cooler

phoning repeatedly
until the room's too hot or
until the body's too cold
saying, or hearing, that
the limit is reached)

BTU's, p. 3

(Bochum)

COOLING A BODY
COOLING A ROOM

(for perhaps three hours
lying in a bath
decreasing the temperature
of the water
gradually adding ice
feeling the body cool

phoning someone to lower
their room's temperature
by the decrease felt
in the cooling body, e. g. 5°, 8°, 10°....
by opening a door, a window,
by using an air-conditioner...
watching the thermometer's fall

phoning repeatedly
until the body's too or
until the room's too cold
saying, or hearing, that
the limit is reached)

BTU's, p. 4

(Remscheid)

COOLING A ROOM
HEATING A BODY

(for perhaps three hours
decreasing the temperature
of a room
by opening a door, a window,
by using an air-conditioner....
watching the thermometer's fall,
e. g., 5°, 8°, 10°....

phoning someone to raise
their body's temperature
by lying in a byth
increasing the heat
of the water
until it feels 5°, 8°, 10°....warmer

phoning repeatedly
until the room's too cold or
until the body's too hot
saying, or hearing, that
the limit is reached)

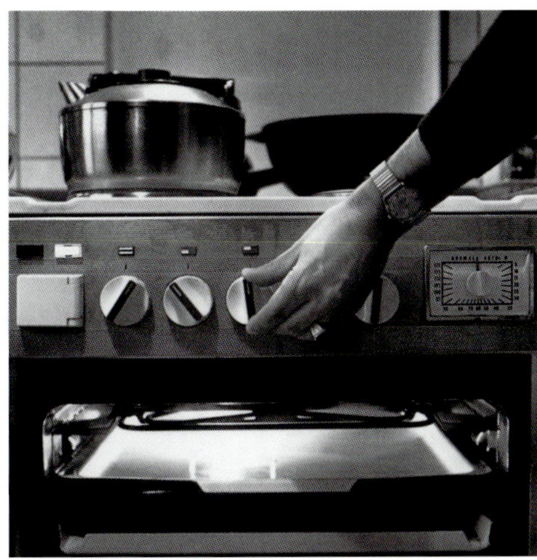

215 Increasing the temperature of a room

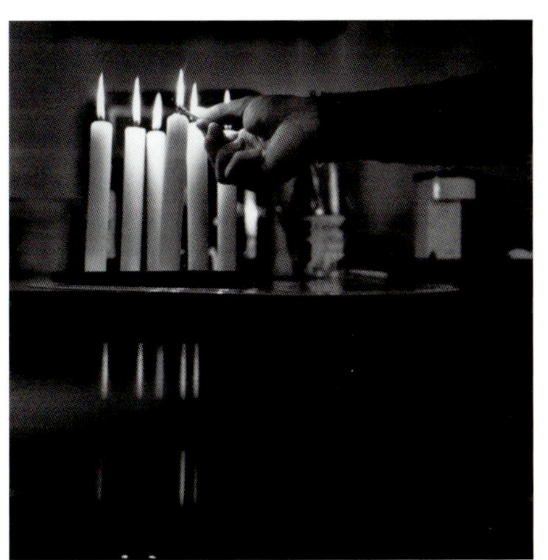

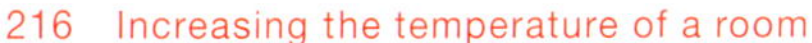

216 Increasing the temperature of a room

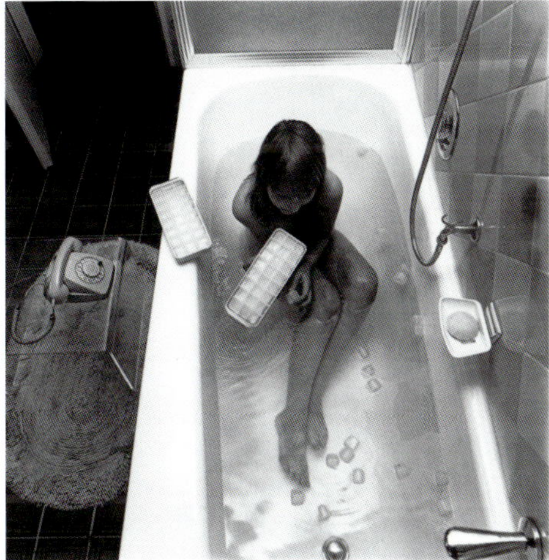

217 Gradually adding ice

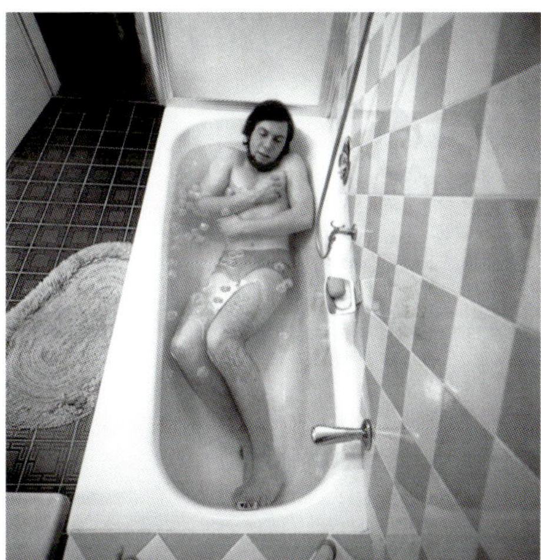

218 Feeling the body cool

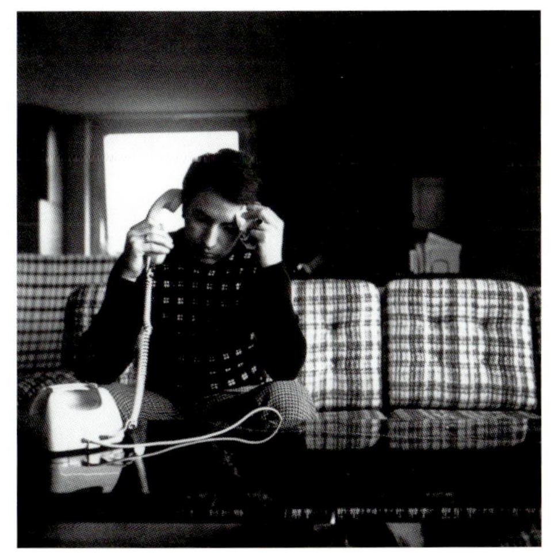

219 Phoning repeatedly

220 + 221 Score for *Time Pieces*, cover and prefatory note (details)

TIME PIECES

Note: TIME PIECES is arranged for any even number of participants. An initial meeting to discuss practicalities, and a review afterwards to exchange experiences and their implications, are considered part of the overall structure of the Activity.

222–225 Score for *Time Pieces*, pp. 1–4 (details)

PULSE EXCHANGE

turning on a tape recorder

counting aloud one's pulse for a minute
(noting count)

once again...

and again....

listening to tape

Time Pieces
Activity booklet, 1973
Produced by Neuer Berliner Kunstverein

Time Pieces
Video, 1973
B/w, approx. 30 minutes
Produced by Neuer Berliner Kunstverein
Remade in 1975

Air Condition
Activity, October 1973
Hills around California Institute of the Arts, Valencia

244–246 **Routine**
Activity, December 1973
Sponsored by Portland Center for the Visual Arts
Various locations, Portland, Oregon
Reinvented in 1988 (twice)

Routine
Film, 16 mm, 1973
B/w, sound, 18 minutes, 39 seconds
Produced by the Portland Center for the Visual Arts

telephoning a partner

counting aloud one's pulse for a minute
(noting count)
playing previous tape over phone

partner doing same

meeting somewhere

one counting aloud his/her pulse for a minute
(noting count)
once again...

other counting aloud his/her pulse for a minute
(noting count)
once again...

climbing some stairs together

turning on both tape recorders

counting aloud, and together, each other's pulse for a minute
(noting count)

listening to each tape

recorders off

counting aloud, and separately, each other's pulse for a minute
(noting count)

BREATH EXCHANGE

226–233 Score for *Time Pieces*, pp. 5–12
(details)

climbing some stairs together

turning on both tape recorders

each partner breathing into his/her mike for a minute

counting breaths
(noting count)

listening to each tape

recorders off

again, each partner breathing for a minute

counting breaths
(noting count)

breathing into each other, mouth-to-mouth, for a minute

drawing the breath in and out
(noting count)

once again...

and again....

turning on a tape recorder

breathing rapidly into mike for a minute

counting breaths
(noting count)

once again...

and again....

listening to tape

telephoning a partner

breathing rapidly into mouthpiece for a minute

counting breaths
(noting count)

playing previous tape over phone

partner doing same

PULSE-BREATH EXCHANGE

turning on a tape recorder

holding one's exhaled breath for a minute

counting pulse by tapping mike
(noting count)

once again...

and again....

listening to tape

telephoning a partner

holding inhaled breath for a minute

counting pulse by tapping mouthpiece
(noting count)

playing previous tape over phone

partner doing same

meeting somewhere

each partner holding exhaled breath for a minute

counting each other's pulse by blinking eyes
(noting count)

234–237 Score for *Time Pieces*, pp. 13–16
(details)

climbing some stairs together

turning on both tape recorders

each partner holding inhaled breath for a minute

each counting his/her pulse by tapping mike
(noting count)

listening to both tapes at once

again, climbing stairs together

holding inhaled breath for a minute

each counting his/her pulse
(noting count)

exhaling breath into plastic bag, sealing it

once again, climbing stairs together

inhaling each other's bagged breath

238 Counting pulse by tapping mike

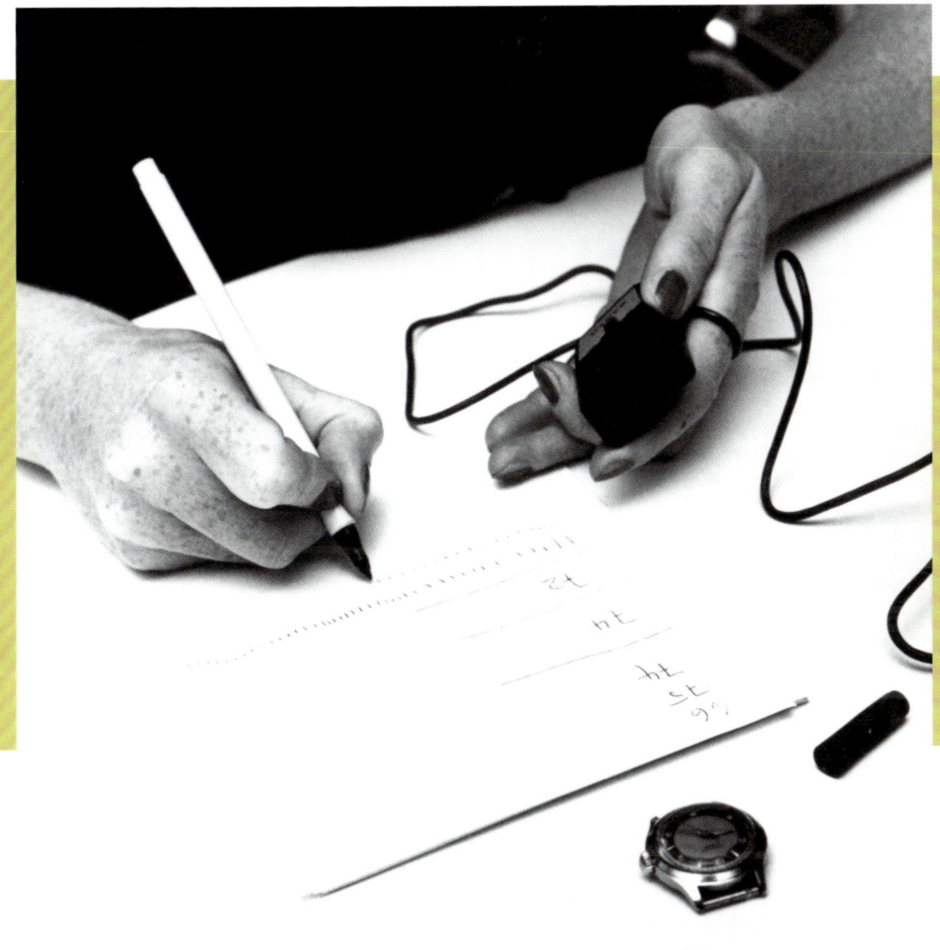

239 Breathing for a minute

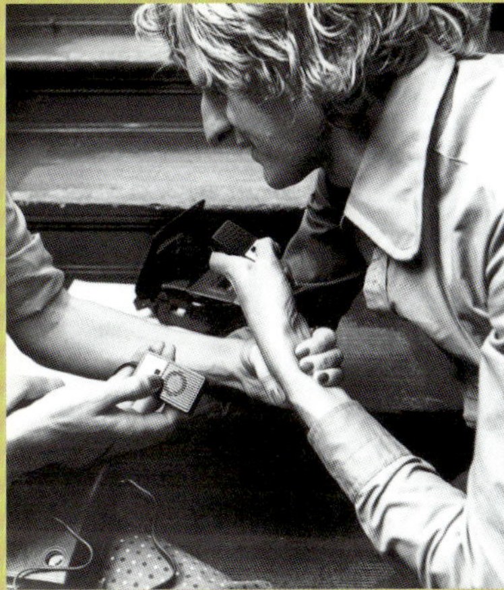

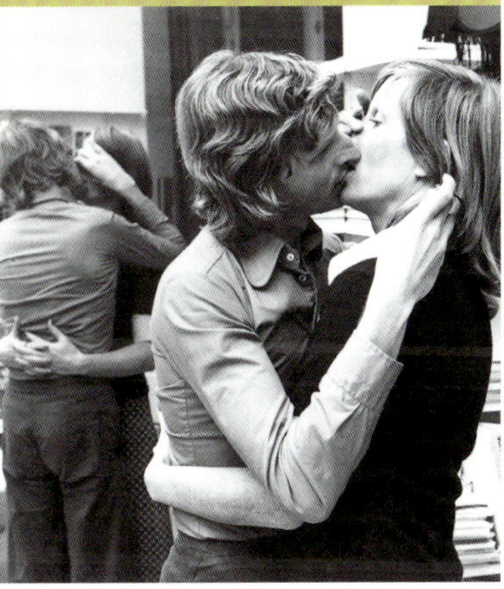

240 Breathing into each other, mouth-to-mouth

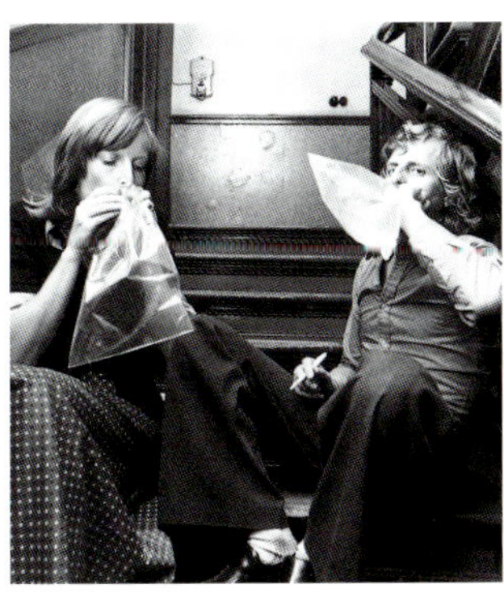

241 Exhaling into plastic bags

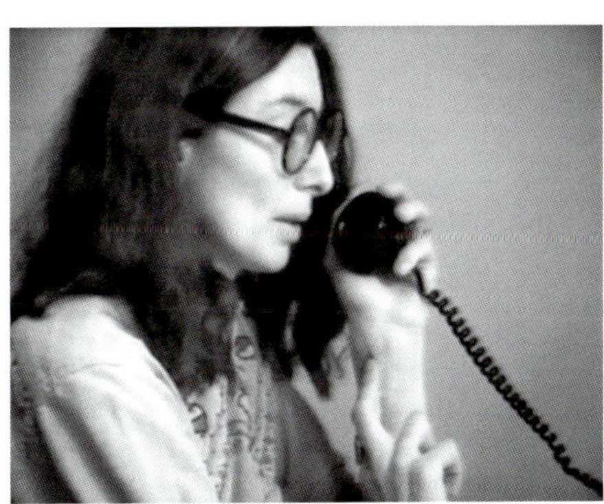

242 Breathing into a phone

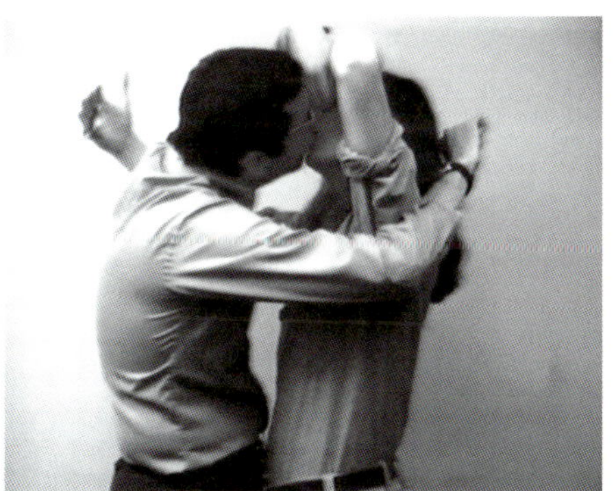

243 Breathing into each other, mouth-to-mouth

ROUTINE

1) standing somewhere —
facing a friend holding a large mirror

trying to catch one's reflection

signalling to tilt the mirror variously
until the reflection is caught

both moving apart a few steps
repeating process

moving apart again and again
repeating process
until it's no longer possible
to see oneself

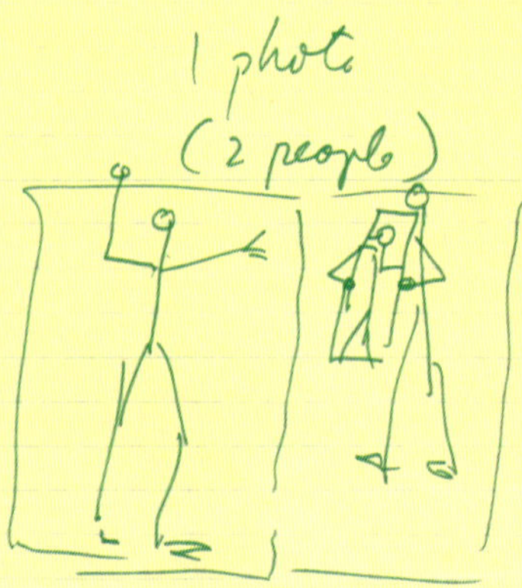

244 Score for *Routine*

245 Letter to Mary Beebe

California Institute of the Arts Valencia California 91355 805 255 1050

Nov. 5,'73

Dear Ms. Beebe:

Enclosed is the program for our upcoming Activity. If possible I'd like it retyped with a good machine, as is and on five separate sheets and staple together. Then xerox/as many copies as need to be given out at the briefing. (200?; 300?) As you remember, we estimated that if 200 come to the initial talk, then one fourth, or 50, will participate. This breakdown has tended to hold true for the last decade. So, in ordering our mirrors we should go over that figure for safety and get 74 pocket mirrors (3"x4"@ 12¢ ea.) and 37 large ones (15"x 40" @ $3.00/ea. at discount stores).

Now, as for advertising, we thought that a poster would be sufficient. It can say simply ~~[illegible]~~: ROUTINE, an Activity by Allan Kaprow, presented by the PCVA. Briefing, Sat. Dec. 1st, 8:30 PM; Activity, Sun. Dec. 2nd; Review, Sun, Dec. 2nd, 8:30 PM.

My thought is that I could come up Thursday evening, meet with photographers or video people on Friday, regarding the record we want to make, and have both Saturday and the following Monday free to make the actual film, photos or tapes (as we decide).

Please give me a call when you get this material and we'll talk further,

Sincerely,

Allan Kaprow

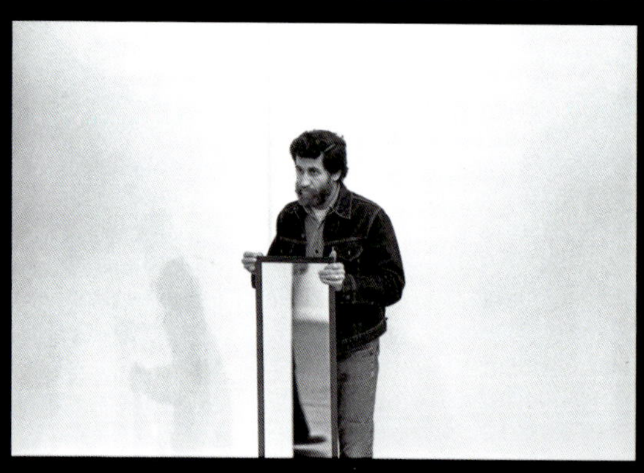

246 Kaprow explaining the Activity to participants

247–250 **Then**

Video, 1974
B/w, approx. 20 minutes
Produced by Art/Tapes/22

2nd Routine

Activity, March 1974
Sponsored by Stefanotty Gallery
On eight floors of a commercial building, New York

2nd Routine

Activity booklet, 1974
Published by Stefanotty Gallery & Anna Canepa

2nd Routine

Video, 1974
B/w, 30 minutes
Produced by Stefanotty Gallery

2nd Routine

Video, 1974
B/w, 16 minutes
Produced by Art/Tapes/22

Dial

Happening, May 1974
Reinvention for the California Institute of the Arts
Telephone booths near telephone poles, Valencia

1974

TEACHING POSITIONS Professor, California Institute of the Arts, Valencia. Professor, Visual Arts Department, University of California, San Diego. ¶ CONSULTING POSITIONS Consultant/panelist, Visual Arts Program, National Endowment for the Arts, Washington, D.C. ¶ AWARDS Annual Award and Gold Medal for "Non-Categorical Art," Skowhegan School of Painting and Sculpture, Skowhegan, Maine. Artist grant from Berliner Künstlerprogramm, Deutscher Akademischer Austauschdienst (DAAD), West Berlin. Artist grant from the National Endowment for the Arts. ¶ SOLO EXHIBITIONS Galleria La Bertesca, Milan, January. Galerie Gerald Piltzer, Paris, September. *Rarities,* Galerie Inge Baecker, Bochum, September–October. Galleria Martano, Turin, October. Galleria Martini and Ronchetti, Genoa, October. ¶ GROUP EXHIBITIONS *Word Works,* Mount San Antonio Art Gallery, Mount San Antonio College, Walnut, California, April. *Multiples: Ein Versuch die Entwicklung des Auflagenobjektes darzustellen = Multiples: An Attempt to Present the Development of the Object Edition,* Neuer Berliner Kunstverein and Kunstbibliothek, West Berlin, May–June. Stefanotty Gallery, Basel Art Fair, Basel, Switzerland, June. *Projekt '74,* Kölnischer Kunstverein, Cologne, July–September. *What's the Time?* Galerie René Block, New York, September–November. *Art/Video Confrontation '74,* ARC 2, Musée d'art moderne de la ville de Paris, November–December. *Poets of the Cities, New York and San Francisco, 1950–65,* Dallas Museum of Fine Arts (traveled nationally), November–December. ¶ WRITINGS "Easy" (Activity score), in "Happenings-Aktionismus," special issue, *Der Löwe,* no. 1: 35–43. "Easy" (introductory essay and Activity score), *Art in America* 62, no. 4: 73–75. "The Education of the Un-Artist III," *Art in America* 62, no. 1: 85–91. "Formalism: Flogging a Dead Horse," *Quadrille* 9, no. 1: 24–28. "Hello: Plan and Execution," *Art-Rite,* no. 7: 17–18. Response to a letter to the editor, *Artforum* 13, no. 3: 8. "A Stone Dropped into a Still Pond," in *Barbara Smith,* exh. cat. (La Jolla: University of California, San Diego, Art Gallery), 2–4. "L'utilité d'un passé déterminé," *Opus International,* no. 49: 68–72. "Video Art: Old Wine, New Bottle," *Artforum* 12, no. 10: 46–49. ¶ INTERVIEWS "Allan Kaprow: Pasadena 16 April 1973, Gespräch auf Tonband," in "Happenings-Aktionismus," special issue, *Der Löwe,* no. 1: 43–45.

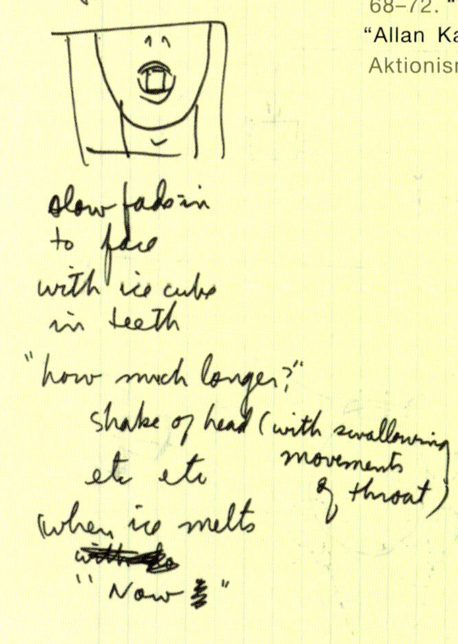

247 Sketch for *Then*

248 Mouth open

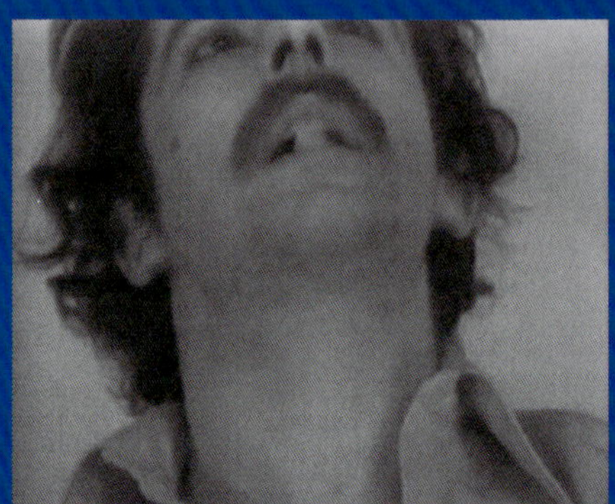

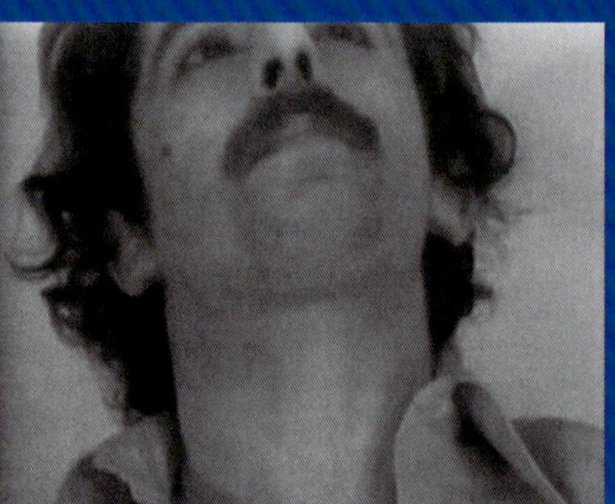

249 Mouth closed

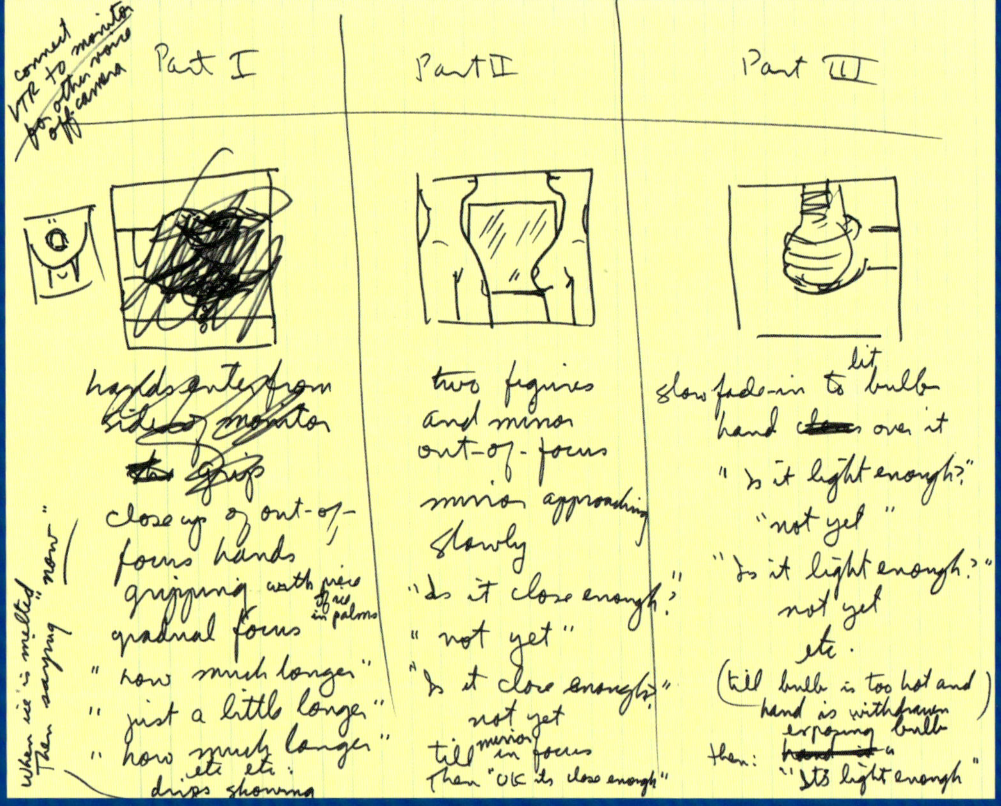

250 Sketch for *Then*

251–252 **3rd Routine**

Activity, July 1974
Presented for *Projekt '74*
Dom Hotel, Cologne

3rd Routine

Video, 1974
B/w, 60 minutes
Produced by Art/Tapes/22

Dom Hotel Köln
Rms 206–203,
107–108
with Inge
Baecker
July 17, 74

ALLAN KAPROW

3rd ROUTINE

1) A, privately making video tape of him/herself entering own apartment, greeting imagined B waiting there.

Making second tape of imagined goodbye; of leaving B in apartment.

Re-recording tapes again and again until effect is exactly right.

2) A, ~~mounting~~ leaving video camera facing front door, monitor in nearby room showing motionless image. (closed-circuit, no tape)

At appointed time, A watching monitor, waiting for B's arrival, watching and waiting longer than expected; at last seeing B's greeting on monitor.

3) A and B together, viewing tape of greeting; viewing tape of leaving.

A leaving.

B, carrying out similar process in own apartment: making ~~two~~ both tapes, waiting for A, watching A arrive, showing the tapes, taking leave of A, as A did of B.

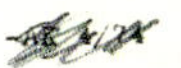

~~The Activity~~ ~~Note:~~ ~~3rd Routine~~ is carried out by two persons in their everyday world. It is built around the conventions of greetings, appointments and goodbyes; and upon the roles we adopt when we say hello, goodbye or make excuses for being late.

Video performs here as an objectification of fantasy, as a surveillance device to hide oneself behind, as an aide-mémoire and as an influence on subsequent behavior.

3rd Routine's nod to vaudeville is intentional. 4/74

-~~Allan Kaprow~~

~~Photos by Alvin Comiter~~

This tape ~~is not~~ does not a document ~~of~~ a real event. It is a condensed illustration of that event, a diagram of moves. Excluded are the psychological transactions which 3rd Routine is ~~primarily concerned with~~ about; these are in fact the personal discoveries of the participants. The viewer can ~~easily~~ too imagine them. for the most part

251 + 252 Score for *3rd Routine*

253 Score for *Affect*

From the Activity booklet *2 Measures* (pub. 1974)

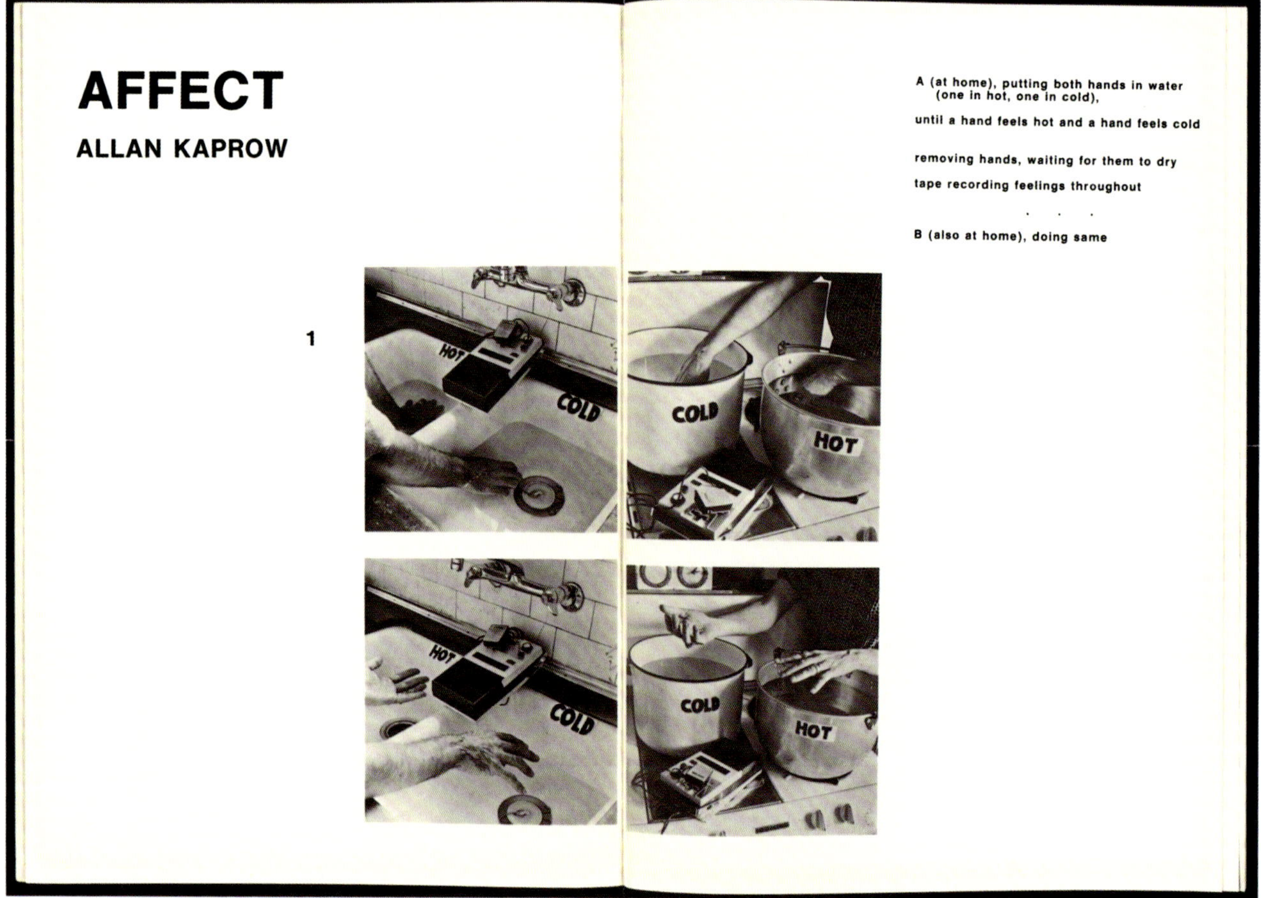

254 + 255 Score for *Affect*
From the Activity booklet *2 Measures* (pub. 1974)

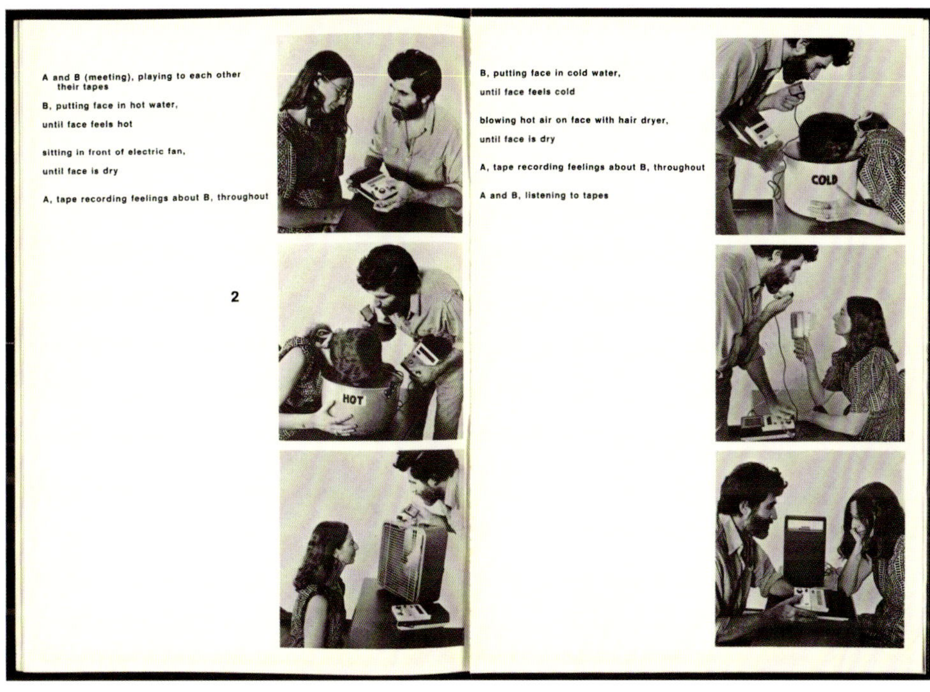
A and B (meeting), playing to each other their tapes

B, putting face in hot water,

until face feels hot

sitting in front of electric fan,

until face is dry

A, tape recording feelings about B, throughout

2

B, putting face in cold water,

until face feels cold

blowing hot air on face with hair dryer,

until face is dry

A, tape recording feelings about B, throughout

A and B, listening to tapes

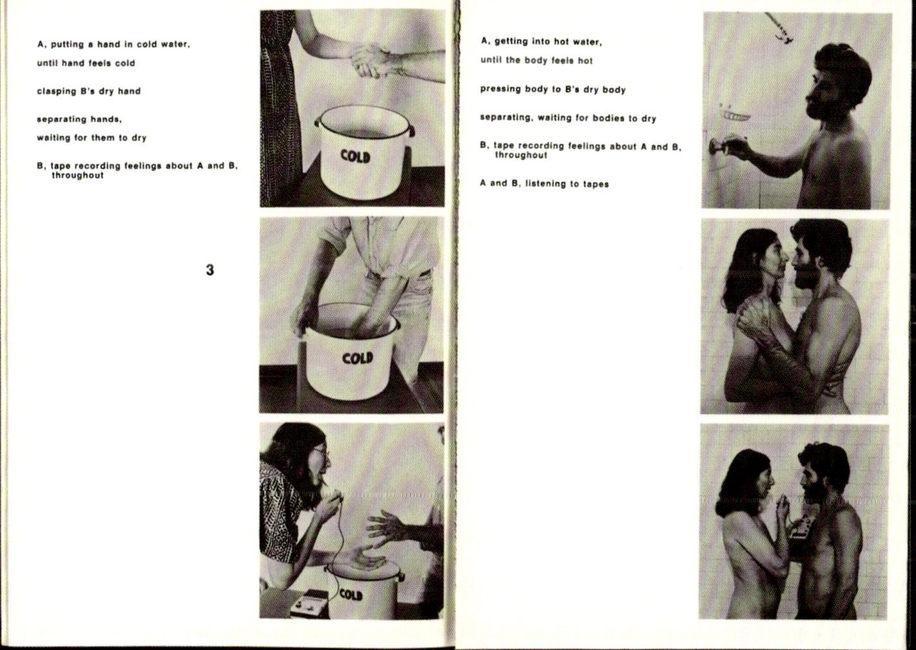
A, putting a hand in cold water,

until hand feels cold

clasping B's dry hand

separating hands,

waiting for them to dry

B, tape recording feelings about A and B, throughout

3

A, getting into hot water,

until the body feels hot

pressing body to B's dry body

separating, waiting for bodies to dry

B, tape recording feelings about A and B, throughout

A and B, listening to tapes

On Time
Activity, September 1974
Sponsored by Galerie Gerald Piltzer
An apartment at rue de Turenne
and in a car, Paris

On Time
Activity booklet, 1974
Published by Galerie Gerald Piltzer

253–255 **Affect**
Activity, October 1974
Sponsored by Galleria Martano
Eight apartments, Turin

256–259 **Take-Off**
Activity, October 1974
Sponsored by Galleria Martini
and Ronchetti
Six apartments, Genoa

2 Measures
Activity booklet, 1974
Contains scores for *Affect* and
Take-Off
Published by Martano Editore

TAKE-OFF

Put-On 1

A (at home with B), tape recording one of four statements

"I'm dressing"

"I'm undressing"

"I'm removing the bedclothes"

"I'm replacing the bedclothes"

then describing details of act, concluding with

"Now you do the same"

(A, doing as stated on tape, or ~~really~~ doing one of other three choices)

B, taking polaroid proof of A's act

(if A's statement lies, B asking A to pose for second "true" photo to deceive C; if true, asking A to pose for "false" one; selecting second shot from other three choices)

B, leaving A, taking tape and two photos to inform C

B (at C's home, choosing to deceive
or not to deceive C), playing tape,
declaring

"A told the truth...." or

"A lied, here's the proof"

then showing C true or false photo

C, recording detailed description
of act A requested on tape,
declaring

"OK, I'm (dressing, undressing, etc.)"

(C, choosing to do what A says or
doing one of other three
choices)

B, taking polaroid proof of C's act

(if C's statement lies, B asking C
to pose for second "true" photo
to deceive A; if true, asking C to
pose for "false" one; selecting
second shot from other three choices)

B, leaving C, taking tape and two photos
to inform A

B (at A's home, choosing to deceive
or not to deceive A), playing tape,
declaring

"C told the truth...." or

"C lied, here's the proof"

then showing A true or false photo

(A, believing what she/he wishes)

Put-On 2

B, occupying A's home

A, occupying C's home

C, becoming go-between

repeating above process

Put-On 3

C, occupying A's home

B, occupying C's home

A, becoming go-between

reapeating above process

TAKE-OFF is at once a parody and a series of collusions masked as deceptions (or put-ons). The central issue is trust in the truthfulness and loyalty of a confederate. The confederate is trusted to carry a desired impression to another person. But she or he is also the confederate of that other person and may not be loyal. The possibility of secrecy and intimacy exist on all sides. And betrayal.

But since all three parties become at some point go-betweens (or confidence- women/men), each one is able to take certain advantage of the others by manipulating the truth. The take-off lies in the fact that the whole Activity is a grand collusion in which each of the participants knows the scheme from the start, and knows that the others know.

TAKE-OFF was realized by nine persons using six apartments, in Genova on October 19, 1974.

Allan Kaprow

Photos: Bee Ottinger

TAKE-OFF

ALLAN KAPROW

PUT-ON 1

A (at home with B), tape recording one or four statements

"I'm dressing"

"I'm undressing"

"I'm removing the bedclothes"

"I'm replacing the bedclothes"

then describing details of act, concluding with

"Now you do the same"

(A, doing as stated on tape, or doing one of other three choices)

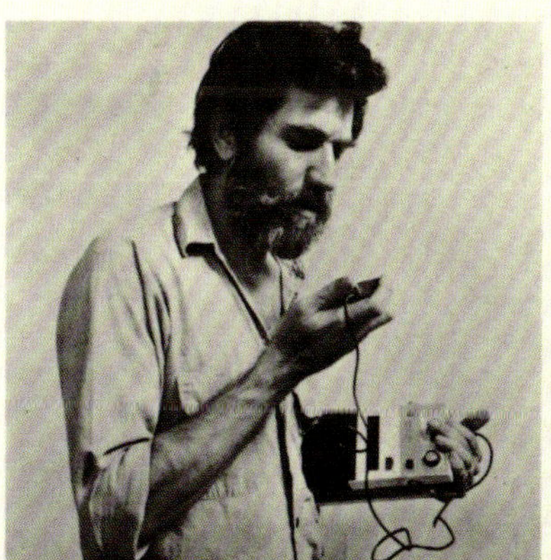

B, taking polaroid proof of A's act

(if A's statement lies, B asking A to pose for second "true" photo to deceive C; if true, asking A to pose for "false" one; selecting second shot from other three choices)

B, leaving A, taking tape and two photos to inform C

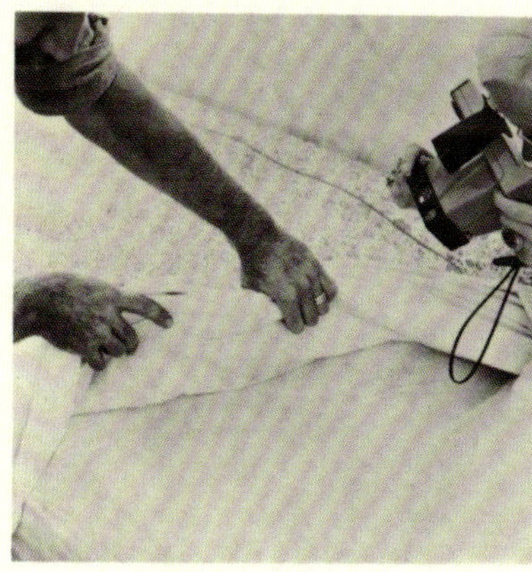

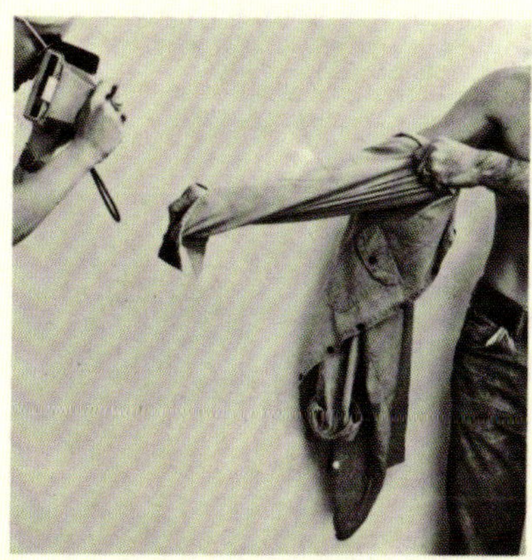

1975

TEACHING POSITIONS Professor, Visual Arts Department, University of California, San Diego. ¶ **SOLO EXHIBITIONS** *Arte Fiera '75,* Galleria Martini and Ronchetti, Bologna, May–June. ¶ **GROUP EXHIBITIONS** *Americans in Florence: Europeans in Florence,* Long Beach Museum of Art, Long Beach, January–February. *Video Art,* Institute of Contemporary Art, University of Pennsylvania, Philadelphia, January–February. *Arte-video & Multivision,* Rotonda della Besana, Milan, March. *Von Pop zum Konzept,* Neue Galerie—Sammlung Ludwig, Aachen, West Germany, April–September. *Art/'75,* Anna Canepa Video Distribution, Basel Art Fair, Basel, Switzerland, June. *Southland Video Anthology,* Long Beach Museum of Art, Long Beach, June–September. *Video Art U.S.A.,* São Paolo Biennale, São Paolo, October–December. *Internationaler Kunstmarkt,* Galerie Inge Baecker, Cologne, November. ¶ **FESTIVALS** Twelfth Annual New York Avant-Garde Festival, New York, September. ¶ **WRITINGS** Advertisement for *Echo-logy, Artforum* 13, no. 10: 9. "Air Condition" (Activity score), *Los Angeles Institute of Contemporary Art Journal,* no. 6: 34–39. "Animation: Stephan von Huene's Sound Sculptures," in John Grayson, ed., *Sound Sculpture: A Collection of Essays by Artists Surveying the Techniques; Applications; and Future Directions of Sound Sculpture* (Vancouver: A.R.C.), 24–30. "Easy Activity" (essay on *Loss*), in Frederick Hartt and Patricia Egan, eds., *Art Studies for an Editor: 25 Essays in Memory of Milton S. Fox* (New York: Harry N. Abrams), 177–82. "Routine," *Los Angeles Institute of Contemporary Art Journal,* no. 4:16–21. "Take Off: An Activity in Genova" (includes score and participant accounts), *TDR/The Drama Review* 19, no. 1: 87–94. "Warm-Ups," in *Arttransition,* exh.cat. (Cambridge: Massachusetts Institute of Technology), 14–15.

Rates of Exchange
Activity, March 1975
Sponsored by Stefanotty Gallery
Participants' own homes, New York
Reinvented in 2006

Rates of Exchange
Activity booklet, 1975
Published by D'Arc Press with Anna Canepa

Rates of Exchange
Video, 1975
B/w, sound, 46 minutes
Produced by Anna Canepa Video Distribution

260–261 **Echo-logy**
Activity, May 1975
Sponsored by Merriewold West Gallery
A stream in Far Hills, New Jersey

Echo-logy
Activity booklet, 1975
Published by D'Arc Press

Comfort Zones
Activity, June 1975
Sponsored by Galeria Vandrès, S.A.
Performed privately, Madrid

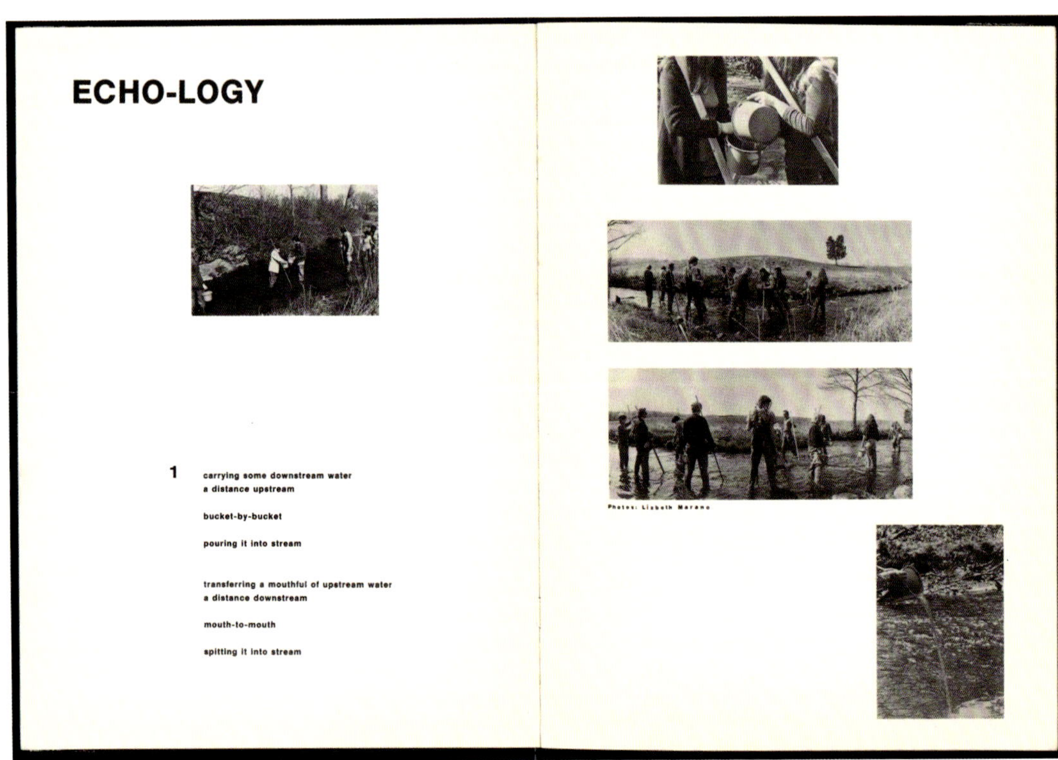

260 Score for *Echo-logy*
From the Activity booklet (pub. 1975)

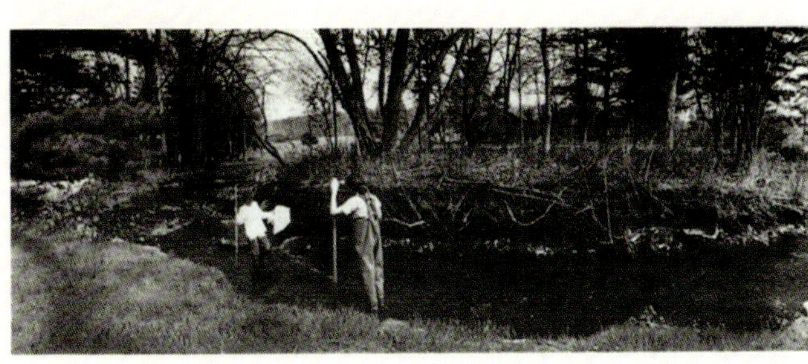

ECHO-LOGY *is concerned with natural processes. Water flowing downstream is carried mechanically upstream, is dumped and flows back. Some is lost along the way. More water is transferred downstream mouth-by-mouth, loses oxygen, is mixed with saliva and is given back to the stream to be altered again. A word is silently formed, is recognized from a distance and is passed in that manner upstream, changing its identity, and is spoken to the trees. A word shouted from person to person, so loudly as to be misunderstood, rushes downstream similarly and is silently conveyed to the air. A gas-soaked rag is evaporated in stages on its trip upstream, becoming relatively clean as it gives its fumes to the atmosphere and further chemical change. Human breaths are collected and conducted downstream by hand. Small bits escape. The growing bagful becomes stale and the container is then released to the winds. The movement is simply back and forth.*

ECHO-LOGY *was carried out by a small group of persons moving in the water of a stream in Far Hills, N.J. on the weekend of May 3rd and 4th, 1975. It was commissioned by the Merriewold West Gallery.*

9/74-4/75

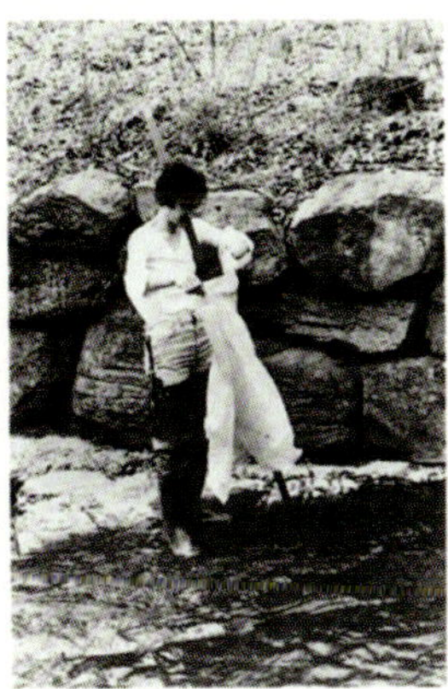

ALLAN KAPROW

261 Statement for *Echo-logy*
From the Activity booklet (pub. 1975)

Comfort Zones
Activity booklet, 1975
Published by Galeria Vandrès, S.A.

Comfort Zones
Film, 16 mm, 1975
B/w, sound, 17 minutes, 10 seconds
Produced by Galeria Vandrès, S.A.

Words
Environment, July 1975
Reinvention for a private collector
Remscheid, West Germany

262–263 **Match**
Activity, August 1975
Sponsored by Kunst- und Museumsverein Wuppertal and Von der Heydt-Museum
Over three days, Wuppertal, West Germany

Match
Activity booklet, 1975
Published by Kunst- und Museumsverein Wuppertal

262 Score for *Match*
From the Activity booklet (pub. 1975)

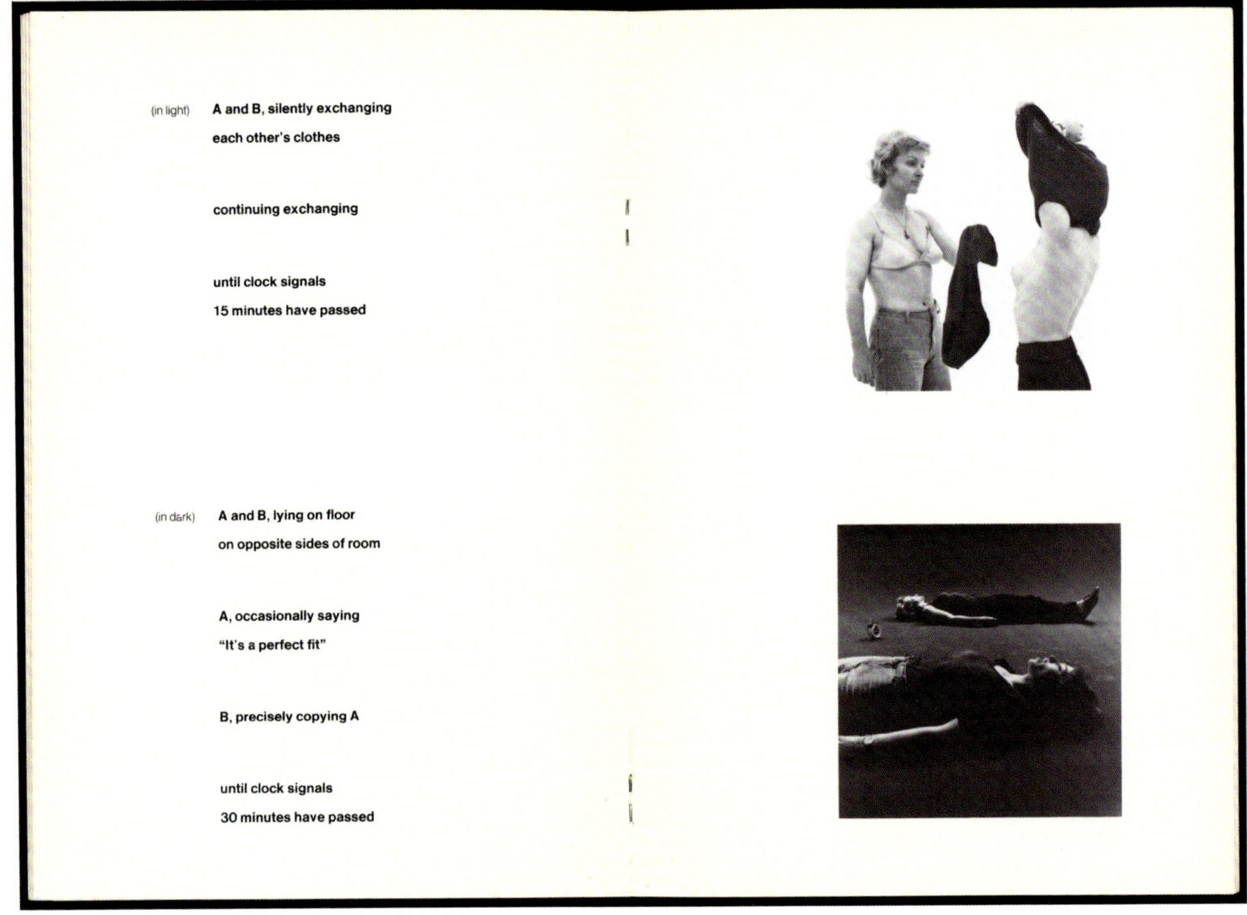

MATCH is obviously a play on the word. In the midst of the Activity xxx matches are lit and extinguished several times ~~to~~ briefly illuminate the face of a person looking into a mirror in a darkened room. It is a bit of a poke at the idea of light as enlightenment. In other parts of the piece, partners attempt to match each other's movements, sounds and, if possible, feelings. Still further, they are engaged in a "match", or contest, of temperaments, in which questions of momentary leadership and subordination may pass half-consciously between them as the piece progresses. But it is, of course, impossible to figure this out in advance.

Throughout MATCH, set periods of time delimit the partners' transactions, extending for emphasis what ordinarily would be too brief to notice — such as sipping water — and curtailing what might be pleasant to continue longer — such as changing into each other's clothes. An alarm clock blatantly announces the end of each of the twelve parts, alluding [redacted] to parrallels in everyday life. ~~Blocks of time given in advance, whether or not they are organic to any situation, influence the meaning, tone and outcome of that situation.~~

Considering MATCH structurally, light and dark are the two poles between which the parts move. A partnership [redacted] formed mainly by seeing is contrasted to one formed by using other senses. That is, gross body movements may be adequately copied with the eyes but other expressive gestures, as "true" or "truer", may be transmitted without sight. In any case, neither is favored, and traditional associations of objective and subjective states with light and dark, are ignored.

The photos here are not documents but are posed to illustrate the text. Together, text and pictures can be read as a "score" or plan of action. The actual event was carried out by a handful of couples on August 29, 30, 31, 1975, and was sponsored by the Kunst- und Museumsverein, the von der Heydt-Museum, Wuppertal, Germany.

WARM-UPS

1 A, sitting

B, standing close
asking is it warm yet

A, feeling seat, answering not yet

B, repeating question
till A says yes

A and B, holding hands, ice within
waiting for ice to melt

asking is it warm yet

answering not yet

continuing till both say yes

B, pressing hand to A's face
asking is it warm yet

A, answering not yet

B, repeating question
till A says yes

2 C, lying in bed

A (in another room),
calling is it warm yet

C, answering not yet

A, repeating question
till C says yes

C, getting out of bed

. . .

A, entering room
getting into bed
fitting self to warmth
made by C

C, asking is it warm yet

repeating question if necessary
till A says yes

C, rubbing bare feet on floor
shuffling slowly across room

A, following
asking is it warm yet
feeling the floor behind C's feet

C, answering not yet

A, repeating question
(following C, feeling floor)
till C says yes

266 Score for *Warm-Ups*, p. 3

3 B and C, standing apart
rubbing hands rapidly

asking is it warm yet

answering not yet

repeating question
till both say yes

. . .

approaching each other

repeating process
till both say yes

B and C, pressing ice
between their foreheads

waiting for ice to melt

asking is it warm yet

answering not yet

repeating question
till both say yes

B, lying on C
asking is it warm yet

C, answering not yet

B, repeating question
till C says yes

. . .

B, arising, feeling C's body

C, arising, feeling bed's warmth

– Allan Kaprow
September, 1975

267 "Rubbing bare feet on floor"

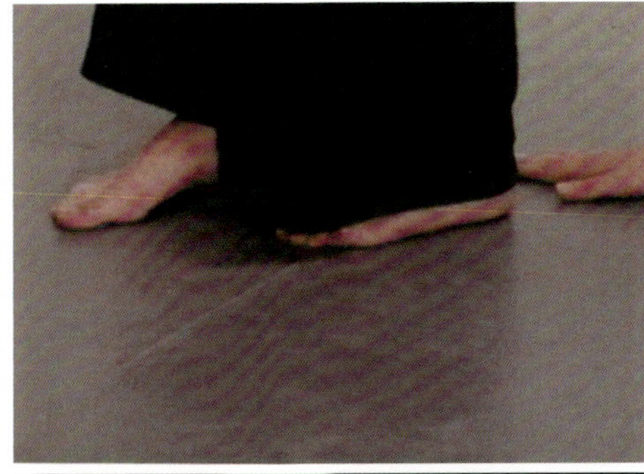

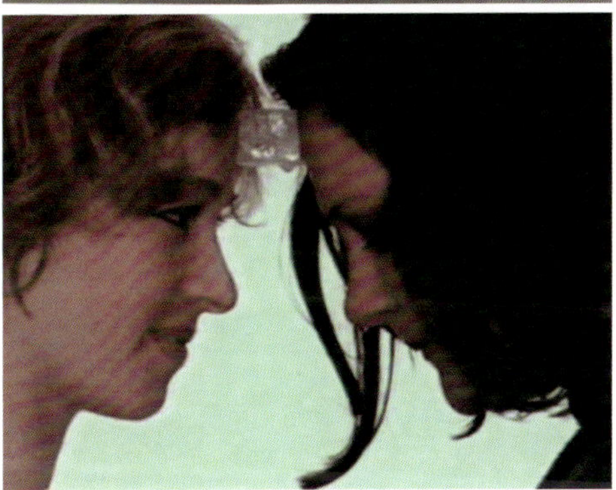

268 "Pressing ice between their foreheads"

264–268 **Warm-Ups**
Activity, October 1975
Sponsored by Center for Advanced Visual Studies
Participants' apartments, Boston
Reinvented in 2006 (twice)

Warm-Ups
Activity booklet, 1975
Published by Massachusetts Institute of Technology

Warm-Ups
Film, 16 mm, 1975
Color, sound, 14 minutes, 20 seconds
Produced by Deutscher Akademischer Austauschdienst (DAAD)

269–272 **Likely Stories**
Activity, November 1975
Sponsored by Galleria Luciano Anselmino
An apartment in Milan

Likely Stories
Activity booklet, 1975
Published by Galleria Luciano Anselmino

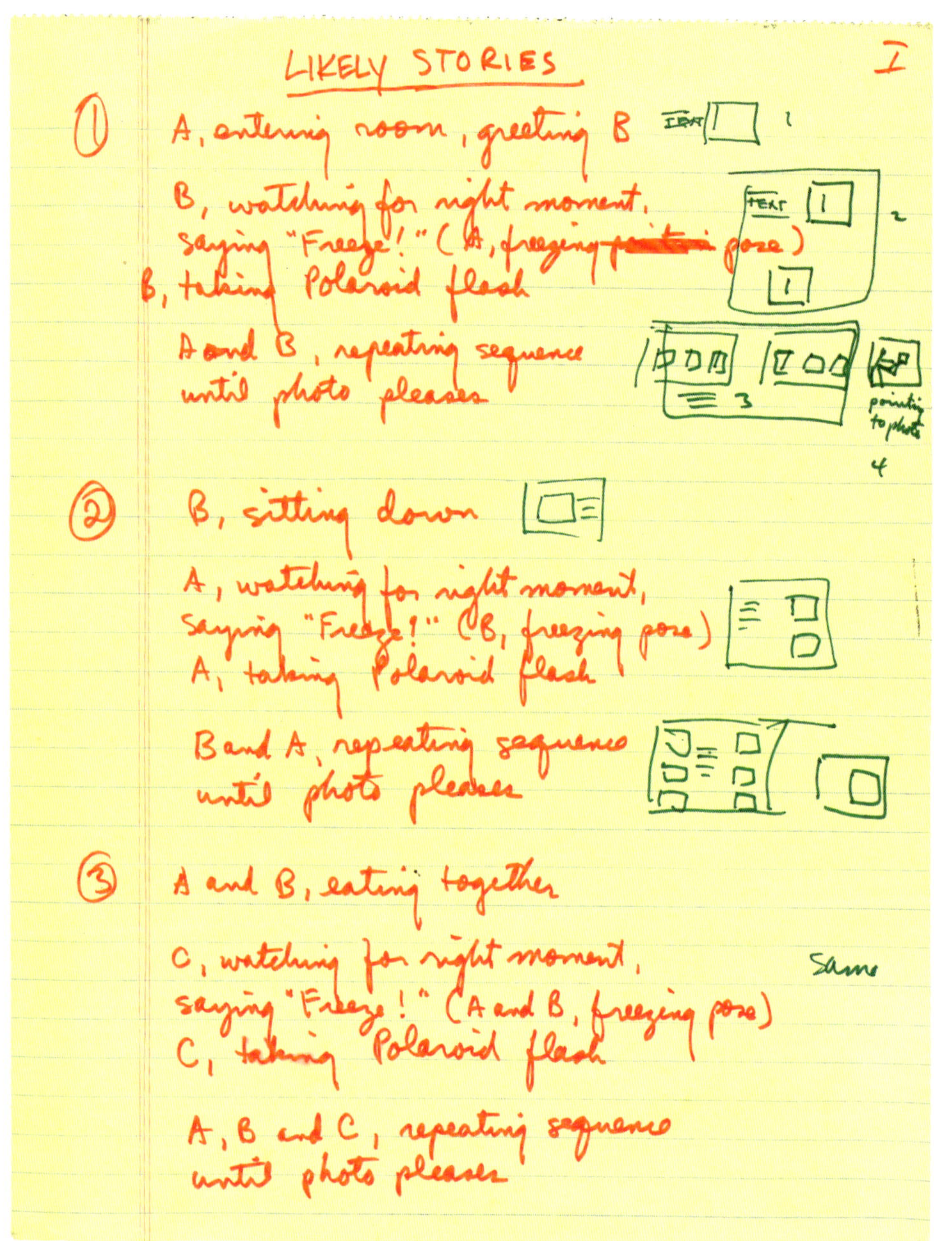

LIKELY STORIES I

(1) A, entering room, greeting B

B, watching for right moment, saying "Freeze!" (A, freezing pose)
B, taking Polaroid flash

A and B, repeating sequence until photo pleases

(2) B, sitting down

A, watching for right moment, saying "Freeze!" (B, freezing pose)
A, taking Polaroid flash

B and A, repeating sequence until photo pleases

(3) A and B, eating together

C, watching for right moment, saying "Freeze!" (A and B, freezing pose)
C, taking Polaroid flash

A, B and C, repeating sequence until photo pleases

A and C, arranging photos into story

B, watching for right moment,
saying "Freeze!" (A and C, freezing pose),
B, taking Polaroid flash

A, C and B, repeating sequence
until photo pleases

270–272 Score for *Likely Stories*
From the Activity booklet (pub. 1975)

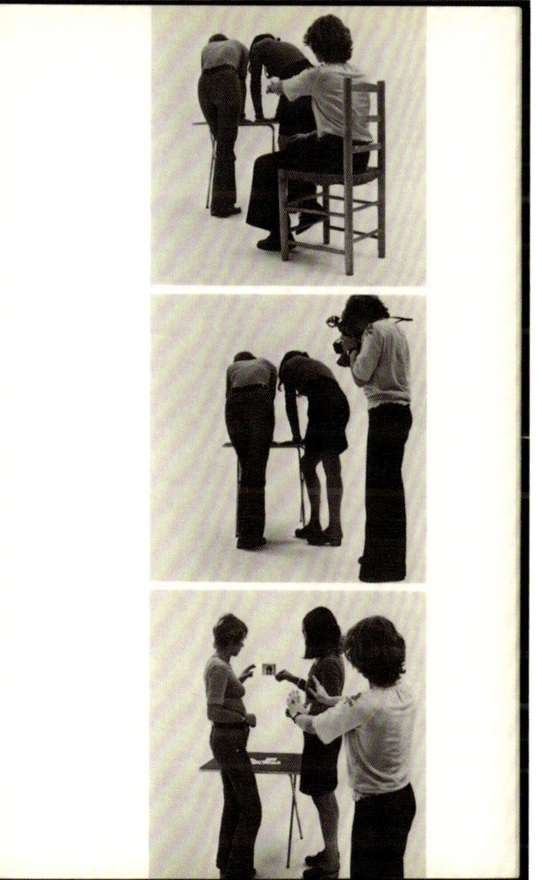

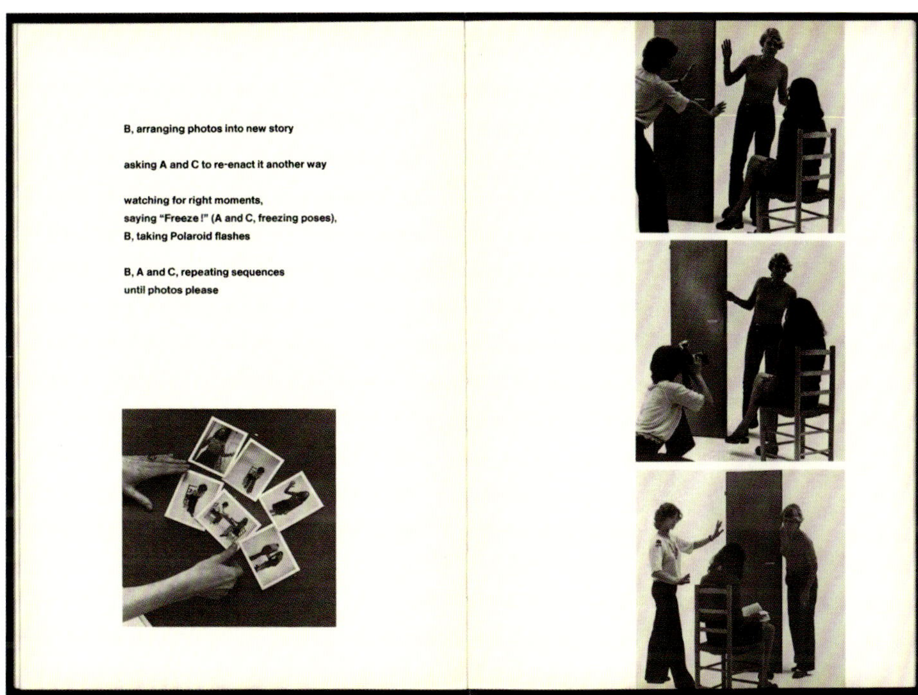

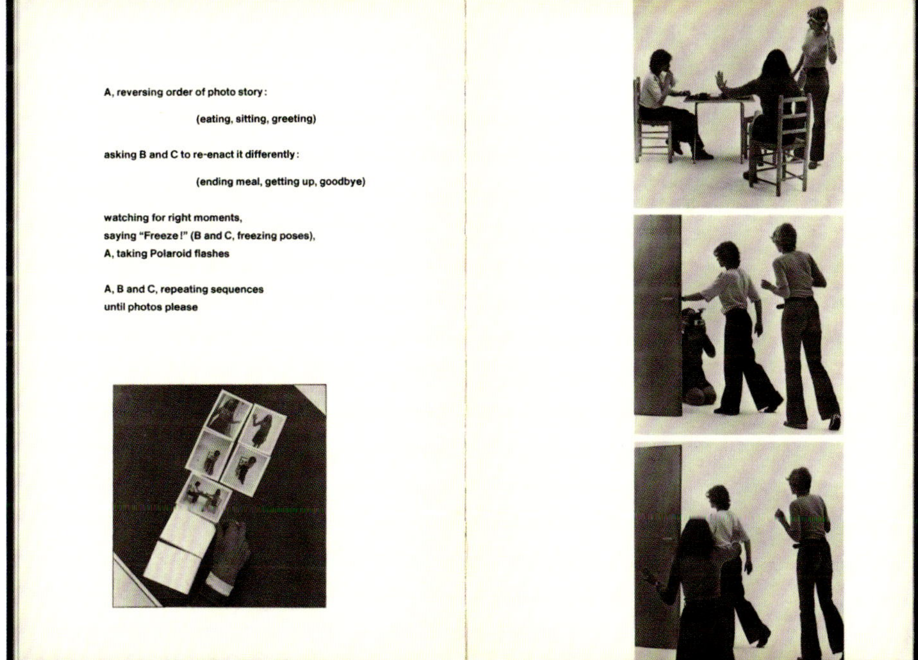

273 Introduction to *Useful Fictions*
From the Activity booklet (pub. 1975)

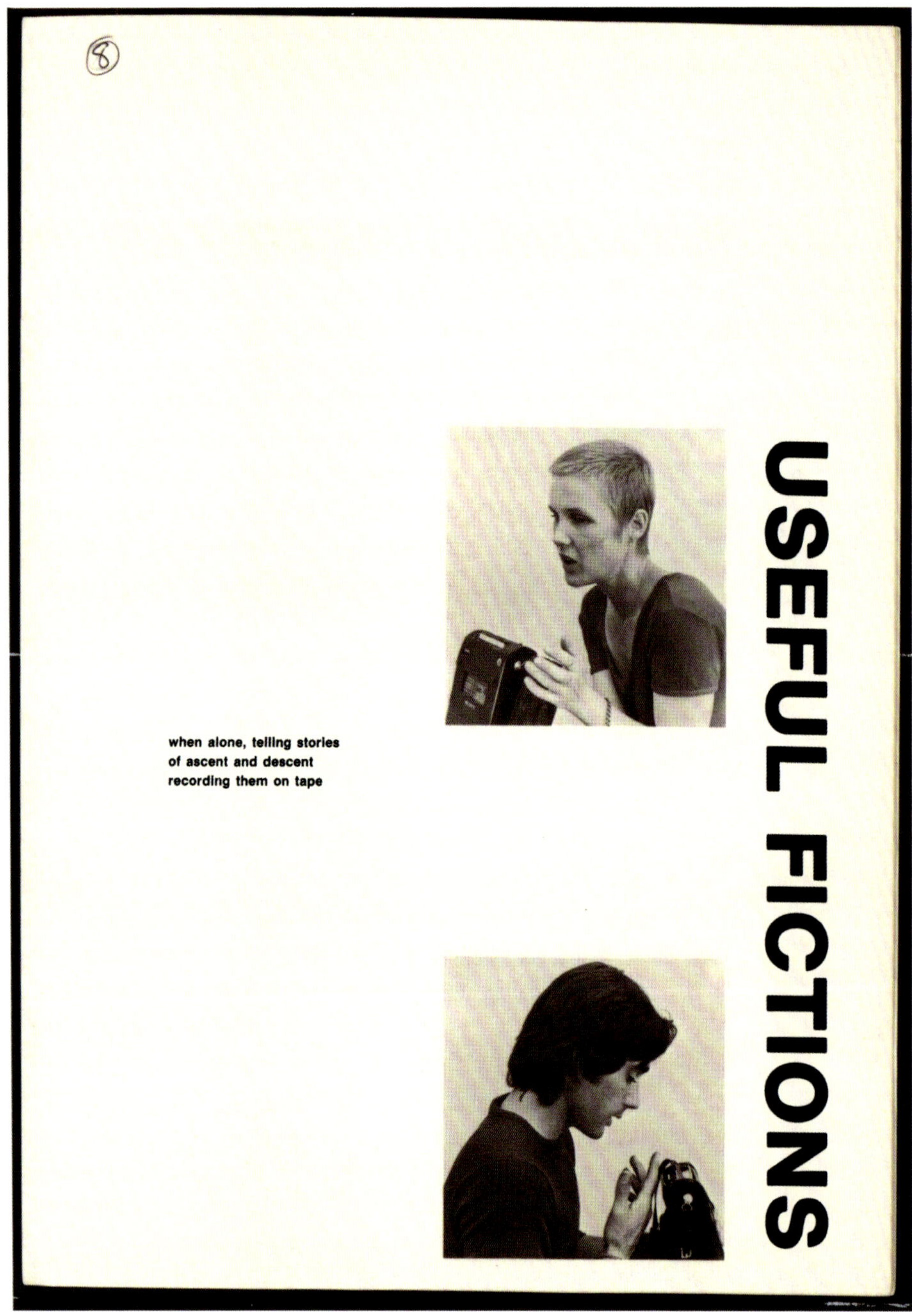

273–276 **Useful Fictions**
Activity, December 1975
Sponsored by Galleria Schema
Various locations, Florence

Useful Fictions
Activity booklet, 1975
Published by Schema Informazione

Time Pieces
Video, 1975
B/w, sound, 29 minutes
Remake of *Time Pieces* (1973)
Produced by Peter Kirby

Air Condition
Activity booklet, 1975
Published by Allan Kaprow

Routine
Activity booklet, 1975
Published by Allan Kaprow

274 Score for *Useful Fictions*
From the Activity booklet (pub. 1975)

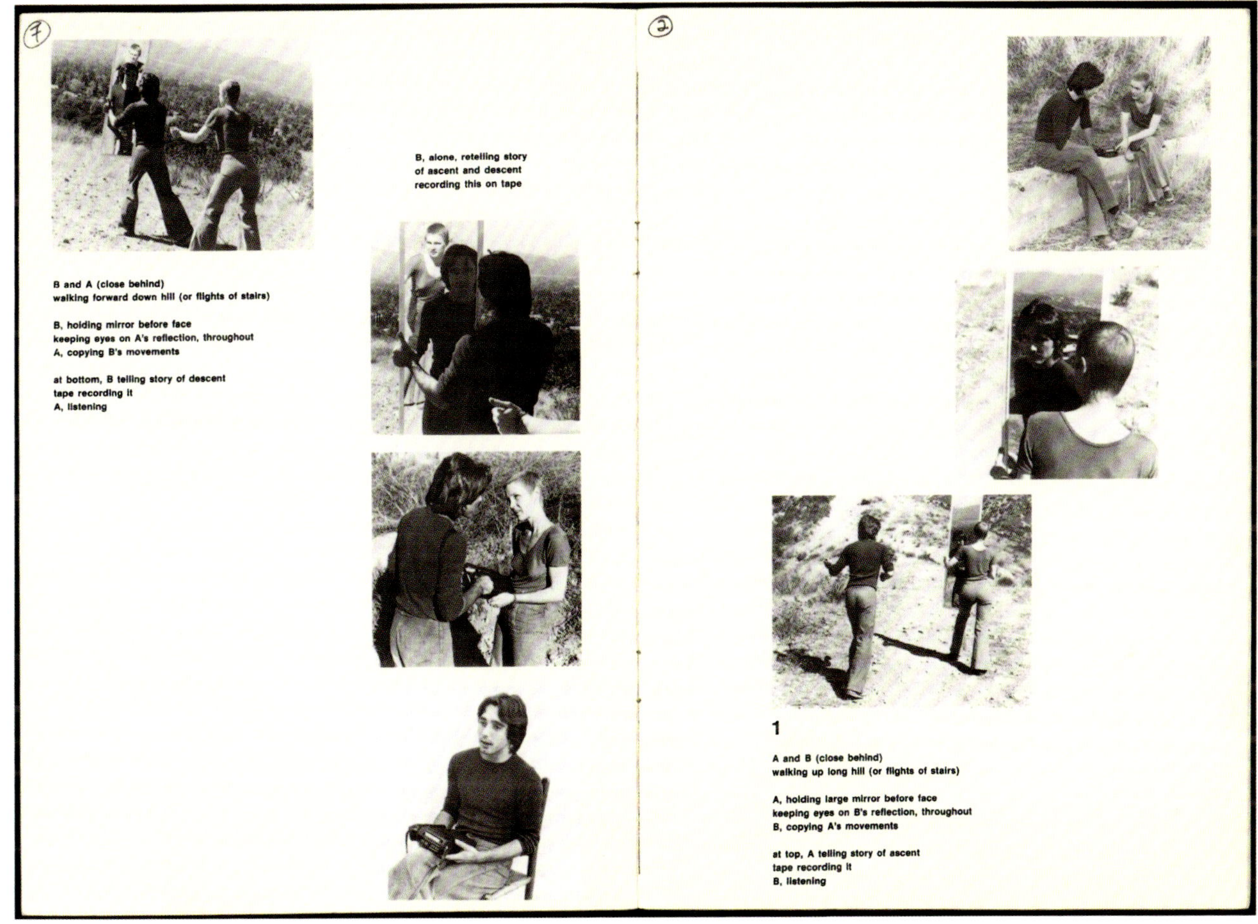

B and A (close behind)
walking forward down hill (or flights of stairs)

B, holding mirror before face
keeping eyes on A's reflection, throughout
A, copying B's movements

at bottom, B telling story of descent
tape recording it
A, listening

B, alone, retelling story
of ascent and descent
recording this on tape

1

A and B (close behind)
walking up long hill (or flights of stairs)

A, holding large mirror before face
keeping eyes on B's reflection, throughout
B, copying A's movements

at top, A telling story of ascent
tape recording it
B, listening

275 + 276 Score for *Useful Fictions*

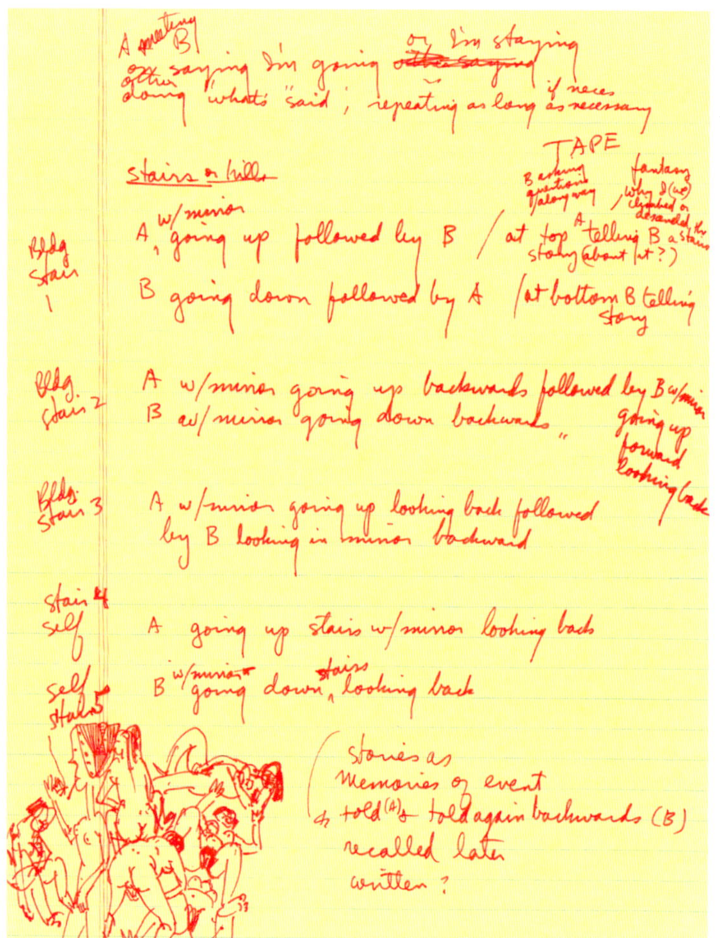

A meeting B
or saying I'm going or I'm staying
doing what's said; repeating as long as necessary

TAPE

stairs or hills

B asking questions along way / fantasy, Why I (we) climbed or descended the stairs

Bldg stair 1 — A, w/mirror, going up followed by B / at top A telling B a story (about it?)
B going down followed by A / at bottom B telling story

Bldg stair 2 — A w/mirror going up backwards followed by B w/mirror going up forward looking back
B w/mirror going down backwards "

Bldg stair 3 — A w/mirror going up looking back followed by B looking in mirror backward

stair 4 self — A going up stairs w/mirror looking back

self stair 5 — B w/mirror going down stairs, looking back

(stories as memories of event
as told (A) & told again backwards (B)
recalled later
written?

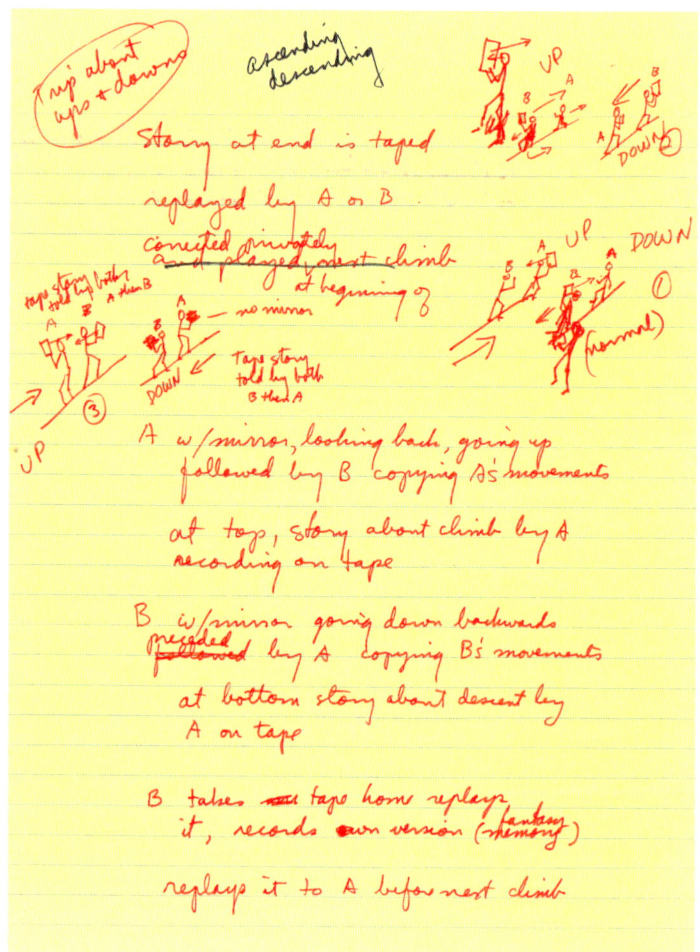

Trip about ups + downs

ascending
descending

UP
DOWN

Story at end is taped
replayed by A or B
corrected privately
~~and played, next climb~~
at beginning of

tape story told by both A then B

no mirror

DOWN

Tape story told by both B then A

UP

(normal)

A w/mirror, looking back, going up
followed by B copying A's movements

at top, story about climb by A
recording on tape

B w/mirror going down backwards
preceded ~~followed~~ by A copying B's movements

at bottom story about descent by
A on tape

B takes tape home replays
it, records own version (fantasy ~~memory~~)

replays it to A before next climb

1976

TEACHING POSITIONS Professor, Visual Arts Department, University of California, San Diego. ¶ SOLO EXHIBITIONS *Early Works,* Galerie Näechst St. Stephan, Vienna, March. Los Angeles Institute of Contemporary Art, Los Angeles, March. *Allan Kaprow: Activity-Dokumente 1968–1976,* Kunsthalle Bremen, Bremen, May. Galerie René Block, West Berlin, June. ¶ GROUP EXHIBITIONS Anthology Film Archives, New York, February. *Monumente durch Medien ersetzen,* Kunst- und Museumsverein Wuppertal, Wuppertal, West Germany, February–March. *Medium Film: Filme von Künstlern,* Künstlerprogramm des DAAD, Akademie der Künste, West Berlin, March–April. *Satisfaction,* M.L.D'Arc Gallery, New York, April. Faculty exhibition, Mandeville Gallery, University of California, San Diego, May. Fine Arts Gallery, Balboa Park, San Diego, May. *Allan Kaprow and Wolf Vostell,* Hochschule der Künste, West Berlin, September–October. *Frames of Mind,* Neuer Berliner Kunstverein, West Berlin, September. *New York—Downtown Manhattan: Soho: Ausstellungen, Theater, Musik, Performance, Video, Film,* Akademie der Künste, West Berlin, September–October. *Tenth Street Days: The Co-ops of the '50s,* 14 Sculptors Gallery, NOHO Gallery, Pleiades Gallery, Ward-Nasse Gallery, New York (simultaneous exhibition), December–January. ¶ FESTIVALS Pro Musica Nova, Radio Bremen, Bremen, May. ¶ WRITINGS "Bemerkungen zu 'Zeitverläufe,'" in *Allan Kaprow: Activity-Dokumente 1968–1976,* exh. cat. (Bremen: Kunsthalle Bremen), n.p. "Non-Theatrical Performance," *Artforum* 14, no. 9: 45–51. "Satisfaction," *Vision,* no. 3: n.p. "Testimonials" (Activity score), *Criss Cross, Double Cross* 1: 18–20.

NATURAL DISTANCES

early morning — A, walking toward sun
B, following
footsteps on tip of A's shadow
continuing until shadow shortens

high noon — B, walking toward sun
A, following,
footsteps on tip of B's shadow
continuing until shadow lengthens

late afternoon — A, walking toward sun
B, following,
footsteps on tip of A's shadow
continuing until sun sets

night — B, walking along lighted street
A, following B's shadow's rotation,
extension and diminution,
footsteps on its tip
continuing at length

Maneuvers
Activity, March 1976
Galleria Framart, Naples

Maneuvers
Activity booklet, 1976
Published by Framart Studio

7 Kinds of Sympathy
Activity, March 1976
Sponsored by Museum des 20er Jahrhunderts
Participants' own apartments, Vienna

7 Kinds of Sympathy
Activity booklet, 1976
Published by Museum des 20er Jahrhunderts

7 Kinds of Sympathy
Video, 1976
Color, sound, approx. 8 minutes
Produced by Anna Canepa Video Distribution

277 **Natural Distances**
Activity, March 1976
Los Angeles Institute of Contemporary Art, Los Angeles

278–284 **Satisfaction**
Activity, April 1976
M.L.D'Arc Gallery, New York

Satisfaction
Activity booklet, 1976
Published by M.L.D'Arc Gallery with Anna Canepa

Testimonials
Activity, April 1976
Sponsored by Galeria Foksal
Various locations, including participants' own apartments, Warsaw

Testimonials
Activity booklet, 1976
Published by Galerie Inge Baecker

277 Score for *Natural Distances*

SATISFACTION

*All transactions, excepting dialog in program, are to be verbally silent, or extremely minimal. For parts 1 and 2, persons C and D carry out elsewhere same plan as A and B.

1 *A, telephoning B, saying:
this is ——
B, replying: unh-hunh
hanging up

B, telephoning A, asking:
are you thinking of me
A, replying: unh-hunh
(or)
unh-unh
hanging up

A, telephoning B, saying:
I was thinking of you
B, replying: unh-hunh
hanging up

B, telephoning A, asking:
do you know how much
I think of you
A, replying: unh-hunh
(or)
unh-unh
hanging up

A, telephoning B, saying:
you must be thinking of me
B, replying: unh-hunh
hanging up

[???]

2 A (with B) saying to B:
praise me
(or)
look at me
(or)
comfort me
(or)
feed me
(or)
kiss me
(or)
bathe me
showing how

B, answering: unh-hunh
(or)
unh-unh
complying if agreeable

A, repeating request
or choosing another
B, answering
complying or not
till options are exhausted

3 C and D (with A and B) saying to A:

praise B
(or)
look at B
(or)
comfort B

showing how

A, answering: unh-hunh
(or)
unh-unh

complying if agreeable

C and D, nodding or shaking heads

C and D, repeating request
or choosing another
A, answering
complying or not
C and D, nodding or shaking heads
till options are exhausted

. . . .

C and D, saying to B:

feed A
(or)
kiss A
(or)
bathe A

showing how

<u>3 cont'd</u>

B, answering: unh-hunh
(or)
unh-unh

complying if agreeable

C and D, nodding or shaking heads

C and D, repeating request
or choosing another
B, answering
complying or not
C and D, nodding or shaking heads
till options are exhausted

4 C, telephoning A, saying:
this is ———

A, replying: unh-hunh

hanging up

C, again telephoning A, asking:
did you like me

A, replying: unh-hunh
(or)
unh-unh

hanging up

C, again telephoning A, saying:
I like you

A, replying: unh-hunh

hanging up

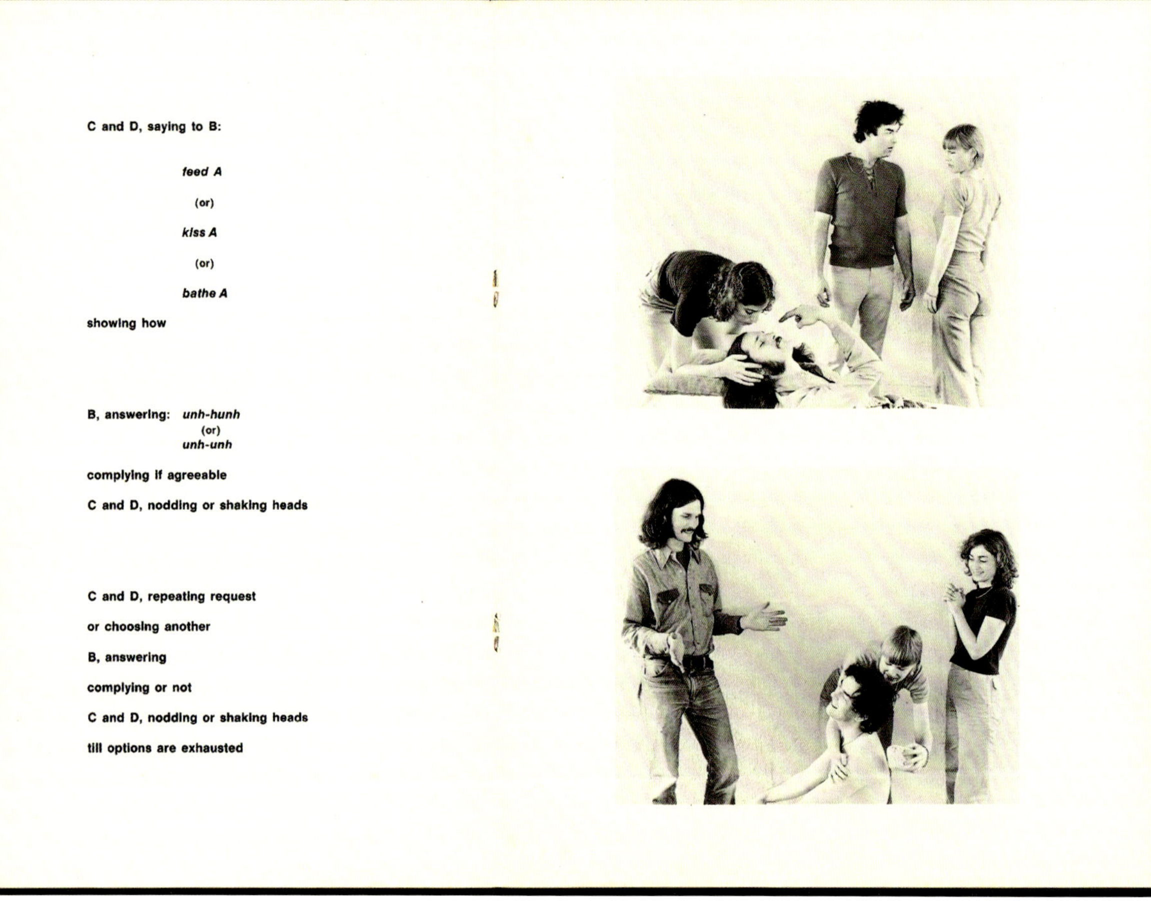

4 cont'd

. . . .

D, telephoning B, saying:
this is ——

B, replying: unh-hunh

hanging up

D, again telephoning B, asking:
did you understand me

B, replying: unh-hunh
(or)
unh-unh

hanging up

D, again telephoning B, saying:
I am really for you

B, replying: unh-hunh

hanging up

284 Notes for *Satisfaction*

Sweet Wall/Testimonials
Activity booklet, 1976
Includes Kaprow's sketches for *Testimonials*
Published by Galerie René Block

285–289 **Durations**
Activity, May 1976
Presented for Pro Musica Nova
A field near Bremen

Durations
Film, 16 mm, 1976
Color, sound, approx. 25 minutes
Produced by Anna Canepa Video Distribution and M. L. D'Arc Gallery

Galileo Galilei
Activity, June 1976
Galerie Inge Baecker, Bochum

Frame Work
Activity, August 1976
Annual meeting of the American Theater Association, Los Angeles

Pre-Socratic
Activity, August 1976
Artpark, New York State Parks Department, Lewiston, New York

Frames of Mind
Activity, September 1976
Presented for *Frames of Mind*
Neuer Berliner Kunstverein, West Berlin

Private Parts
Activity, November 1976
Center for Twentieth-Century Studies, University of Wisconsin–Milwaukee
Reinvented in 2006

DURATIONS

① marking a grassy field with a cross

(116 m. in length, lying N, S, E, W)

digging out 45 squares along cross

(each leg having 12 squares from center; size of squares increasing from 20 x 40 cm. for first 3, 40 x 40 cm. for second 3, 40 x 60 cm. for third 3, and 60 x 80 cm. for fourth 3; distances between squares increasing from 1 meter between first 3, 2 between second 3, 3 between third 3, and 4 between fourth 3)

placing grass carefully aside

② constructing columns of ice blocks on squares where grass was removed

(columns increasing in thickness from 1 block for first 3, 2 for second 3, 3 for third 3, and 6 for fourth 3; increasing regularly in height from 1 block at center to 12 at ends)

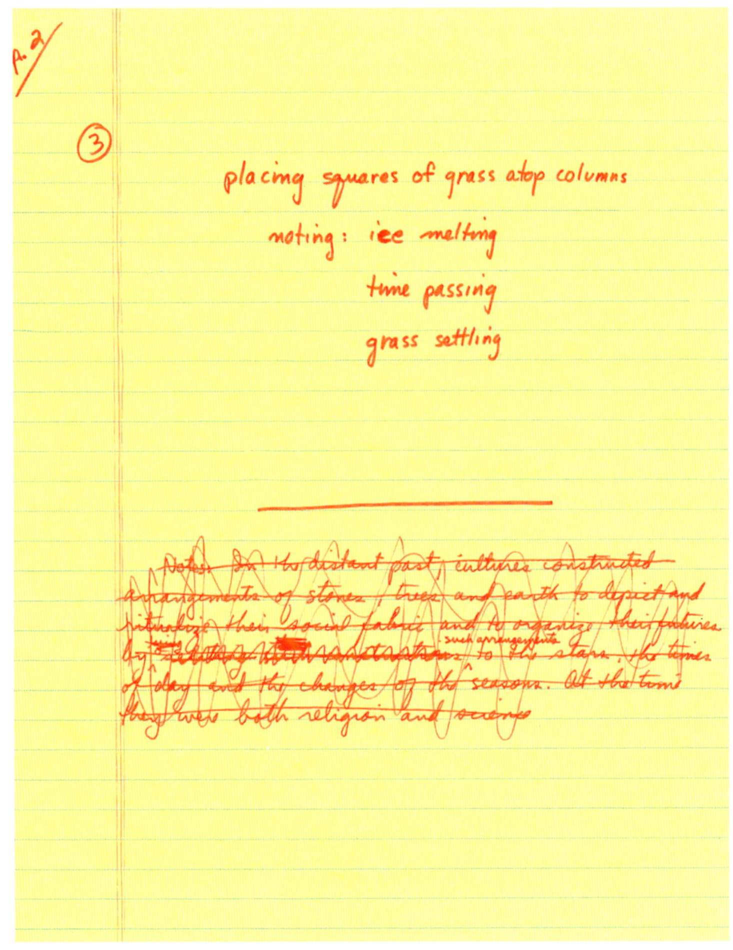

p. 2

③ placing squares of grass atop columns

noting: ice melting

time passing

grass settling

285 + 286 Score for *Durations*

287 Column of ice blocks

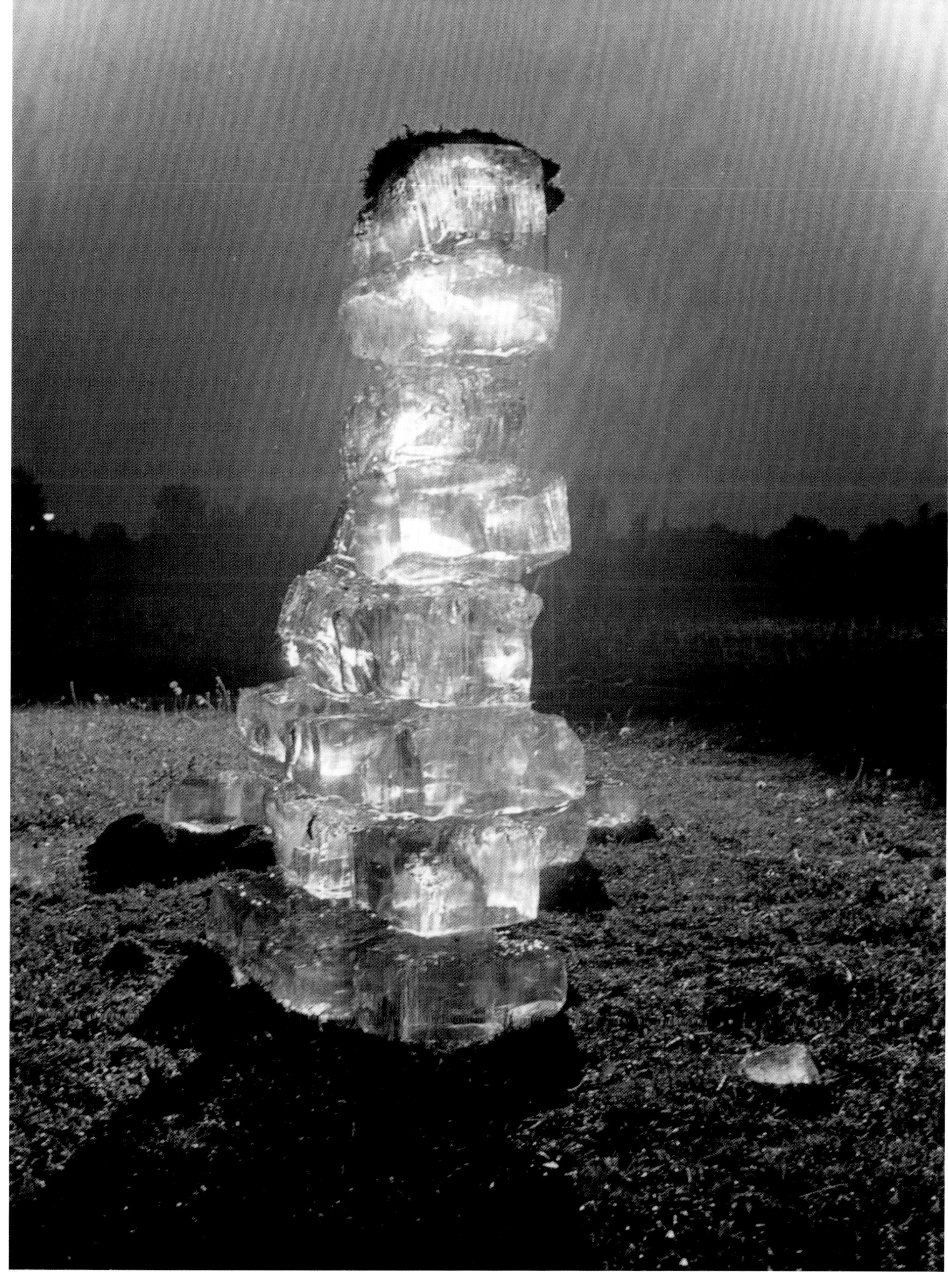

288 Sketch of ice columns

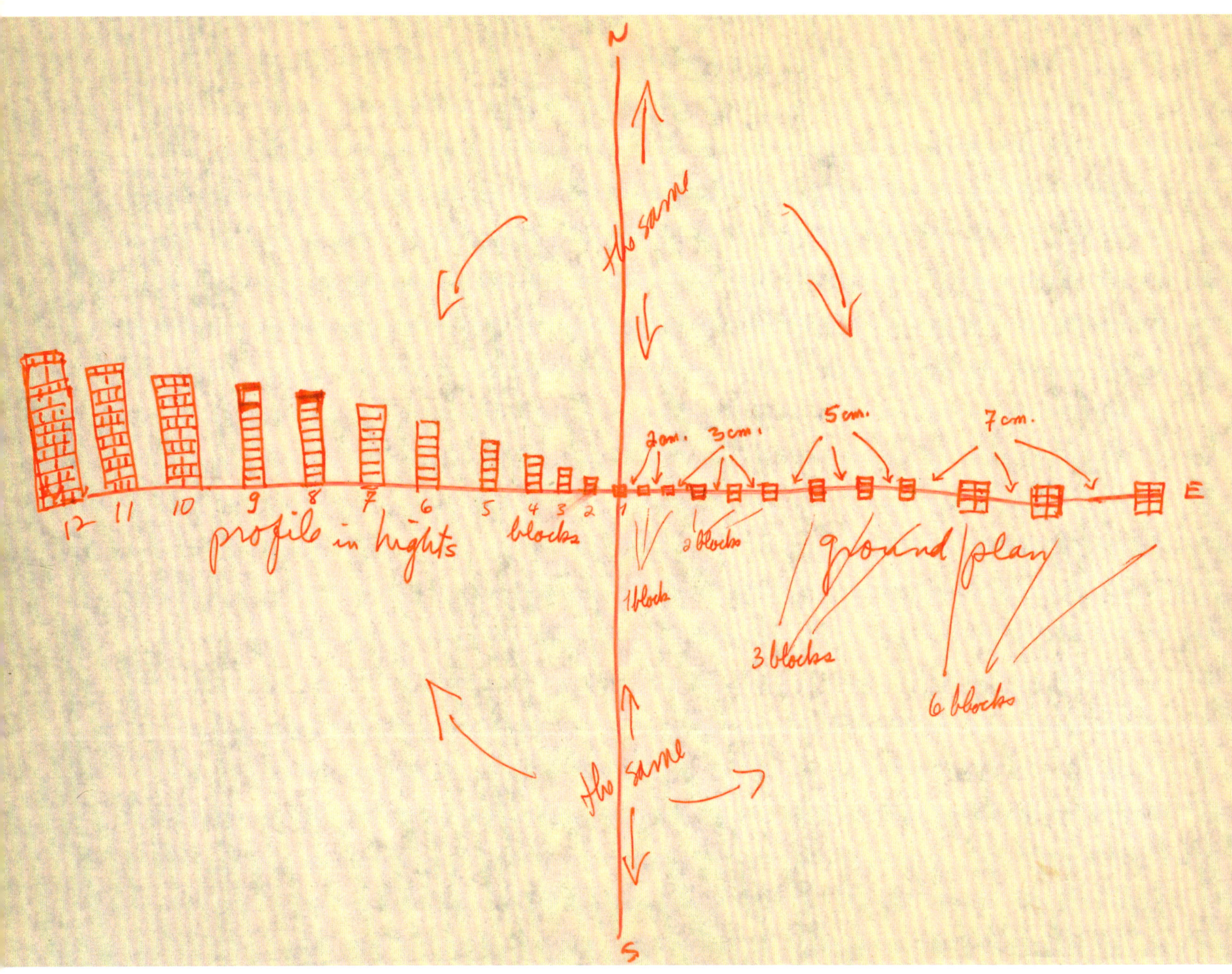

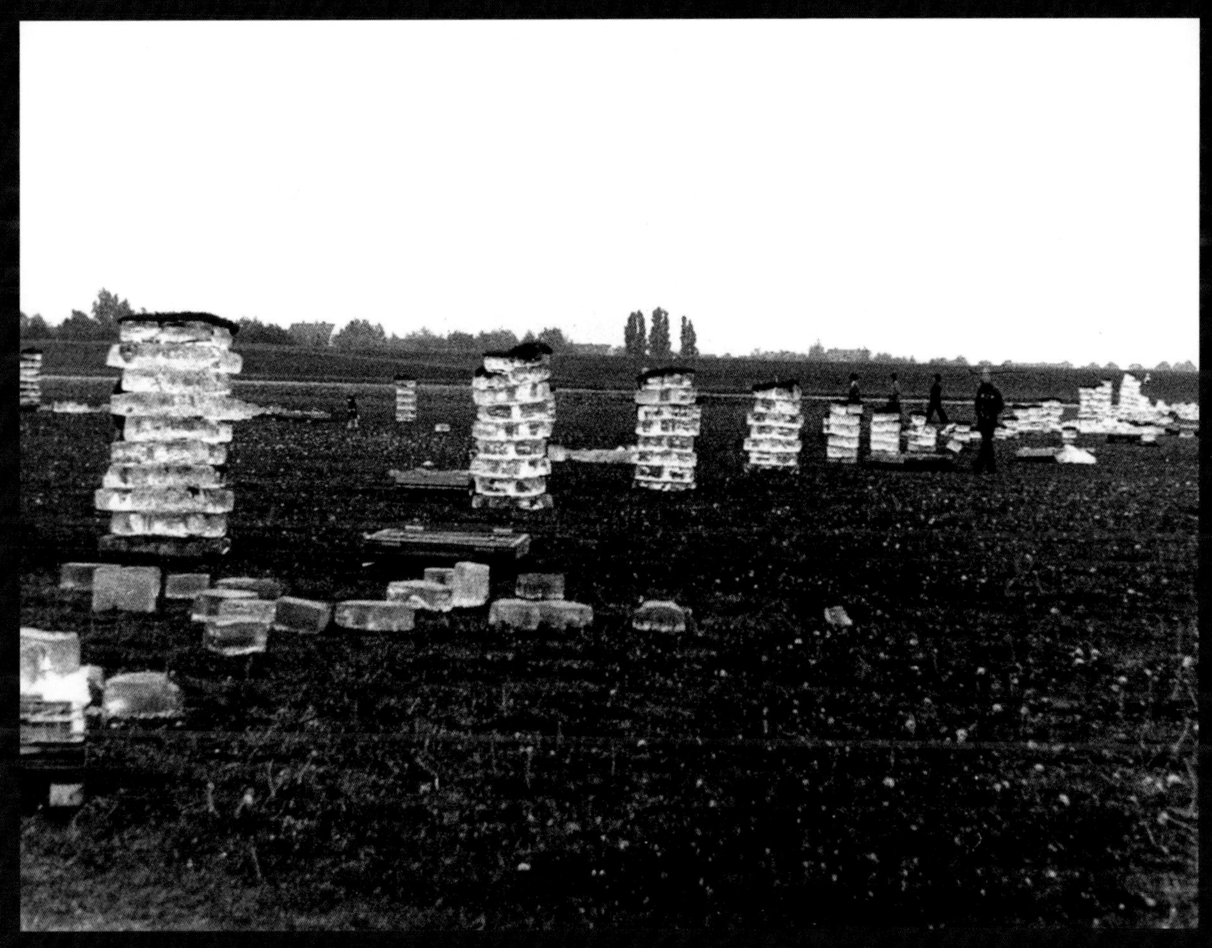

289 “Squares of grass atop columns of ice”

TEACHING POSITIONS Professor, Visual Arts Department, University of California, San Diego. ¶ **SOLO EXHIBITIONS** Galerie Zellermeyer, West Berlin, March. *Posters and Flyers of Happenings and Activities,* Other Books and So Gallery, Amsterdam, September. ¶ **GROUP EXHIBITIONS** *Allan Kaprow and Wolf Vostell,* Galerie Inge Baecker, Bochum, January–March. *The Museum of Drawers,* Museum im Prediger, Schwäbisch Gmünd, West Germany, January. *Whitney Biennial,* Whitney Museum of American Art, New York, February–April. *The Artist's Book,* Mandeville Gallery, University of California, San Diego, April–May. *Malerei und Photographie im Dialog von 1840 bis Heute,* Kunsthaus Zürich, Zurich, May–July. *Southland Video Anthology,* Los Angeles Institute of Contemporary Art, Los Angeles, May–July. *Paris—New York,* Musée national d'art moderne, Centre Georges Pompidou, Paris, June–September. ¶ **FESTIVALS** What's Cooking? I, Center for Music Experiment, University of California, San Diego, April. Thirteenth Annual New York Avant-Garde Festival, World Trade Center, New York, June. ¶ **WRITINGS** "Introduction" and "Roy Lichtenstein," in *Roy Lichtenstein at CalArts: Drawings and Collages from the Artist's Collection,* exh. cat. (Valencia: California Institute of the Arts), 7–9, 23–36. "Participation Performance," *Artforum* 15, no. 7: 24–29.

1977

290–292 **Museum Portraits**
Activity, March 1977
For Hamburger Kunsthalle, Hamburg
Not realized

Timing
Activity, April 1977
Presented for What's Cooking? I
University of California, San Diego
Reinvented in 2006

Common Senses
Video, 1977
Color, 6 minutes
Produced by Allan Kaprow
and Peter Kirby

Courtesy
Activity, June 1977
Presented for *Close Radio*
KPFK-FM, Los Angeles

Private Parts
Video, 1977
Color, sound, 17 minutes
Produced by Allan Kaprow
and Peter Kirby

Push and Pull
Environment, December 1977–
January 1978
Reinvention
Galerie Inge Baecker, Bochum

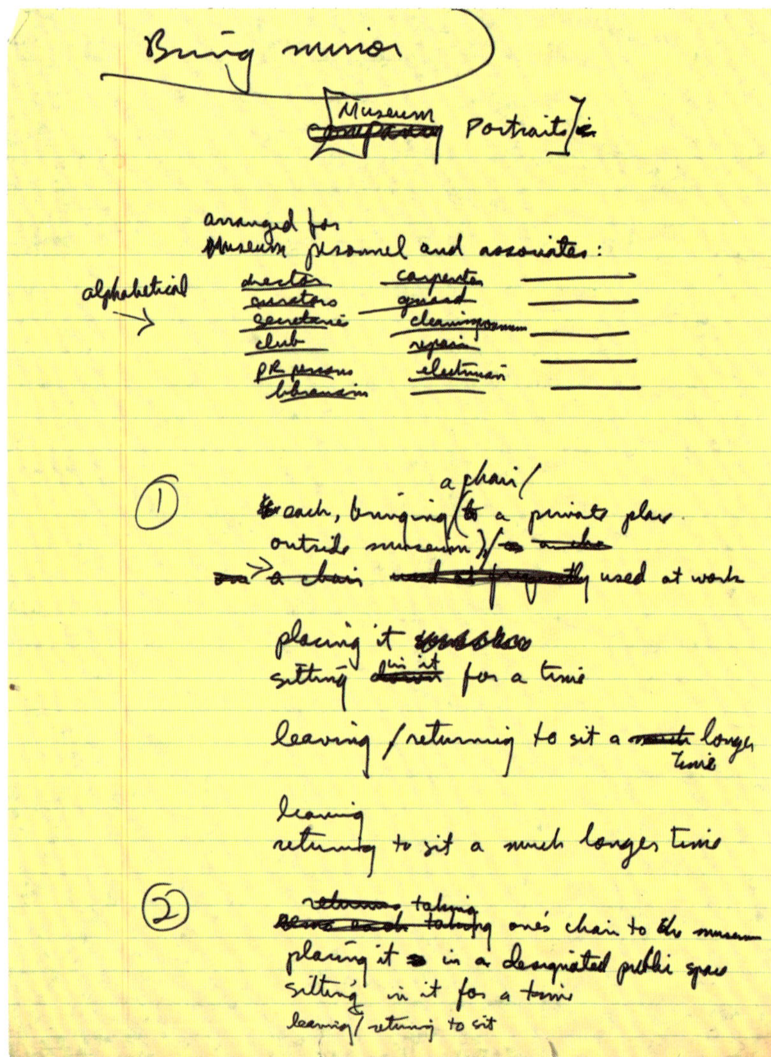

290 Score for *Museum Portraits*

Professor Allan Kaprow
270 Wigmore Drive
Pasadena, Calif. 91105

4th March, 1977
Prof.H./Lu

Dear Professor Kaprow,

we have given long and serious consideration to your project (enclosed to the letter of February 15th).

The idea has two aspects, a theoretical and a practical one. Since what you propose is playing a (serious) game, we have to ask the participants whether they agree to join the game. You understand that you are questioning people in their given or attributed roles and that your approach to their problems implies their readiness to accept this manipulation.

Now in addition to their professional manipulation they will be the victims of another one - - - !? This is what our people do not accept, and I can understand their reasons and I am sure that you will understand, why there is no chance to continue on the line drawn in your "Project for the Hamburger Kunsthalle".

Sincerely yours

(Professor Dr. Werner Hofmann)

cc: Mrs.Baecker
Galerie Baecker
Bochum

Hamburger Kunsthalle
2 Hamburg 1
Glockengießerwall
☎ 24 82 51/2607

March 11, 1977

Professor Dr. Werner Hofmann
Director, Hamburger Kunsthalle
2 Hamburg 1
Glockengiesserwall, W. Deutschland

Dear Dr. Hofmann:

I have received your letter of March 4th in which you summarily interpret and dismiss my project proposal for the Hamburger Kunsthalle.

I must tell you that you've misunderstood nearly everything. And in view of the finality of your decision, there can be no purpose in trying to explain why you have misunderstood nearly everything.

I should also point out that your letter is the first and only direct communication from you to me in the more than two years of our negotiations. (My letter of January 4th asking important questions about these negotiations went unanswered.) If you had been in contact with me during this whole period, we could easily have avoided the negative reaction you have now.

Even recently, you could have telephoned me and Inge Baecker when you received my general outline of intention. You could have asked questions before rushing to conclusions. You could have waited to see the detailed program in finished form. But you let your imagination take charge, instead.

In an ironic and unfortunate sense, this creation of fantasies is what the project was about, and you began to perform it. But you performed it helplessly, without the information and guidance that could have made it a value to you, to me, and to your colleagues. What a pity, Dr. Hofmann!

Sincerely,
Allan Kaprow, Professor

c.c. Inge Baecker, Galerie Baecker

TEACHING POSITIONS Professor, Visual Arts Department, University of California, San Diego. ¶ AWARDS Listing in *Who's Who in America.* ¶ SOLO EXHIBITIONS Museum of the University of Northern Iowa, Cedar Falls, December–January. ¶ FESTIVALS What's Cooking? II, Center for Music Experiment, University of California, San Diego, April. ¶ WRITINGS "Natural Distances" (Activity score), *New Wilderness Letter* 1, no. 3–4: 35–37. "Playing with Memory," unpublished essay written for *Art-Rite.*

1978

Two Appointments
Activity, January 1978
Sponsored by Holly Solomon Gallery
Statler Hilton and Pennsylvania Station, New York

Peeping Tom
Activity, March 1978
Performed privately with friends
La Jolla, California

Toothbrushing Piece
Activity, Spring 1978
Performed privately with friends
La Jolla, California

Ups/Downs
Activity, April 1978
Presented for What's Cooking? II
University of California, San Diego

Mantra
Activity, April 1978
Performed privately with friends
La Jolla, California

Small Exercise I
Activity, May 1978
Performed privately with friends
La Jolla, California

Small Exercise II
Activity, June 1978
Performed privately with friends
La Jolla, California

Hello/Goodbye
Activity, July 1978
Performed privately with friends
Los Angeles
Reinvented in 2006

293–296 **Standards**
Activity, January–February 1979
University of Northern Iowa, Cedar Falls-Waterloo

Blindsight
Activity, April 1979
Sponsored by Wichita State University
Various locations, including a vacant painting studio, Wichita, Kansas
Reinvented in 1998

Blindsight
Activity booklet, 1979
Published by the Department of Art Education, Wichita State University

Easy Too
Activity, July 1979
Sponsored by University of Arizona, Tucson
Tucson

Shadows
Activity, September 1979
Presented for Kunstwoche im Ihme Zentrum
Hannover

297–298 **Tire Tower**
Activity, September 1979
Presented for Bochumer Kunstwoche
Sponsored by Galerie Inge Baecker and Museum Bochum
Ruhrpark Shopping Center, Bochum

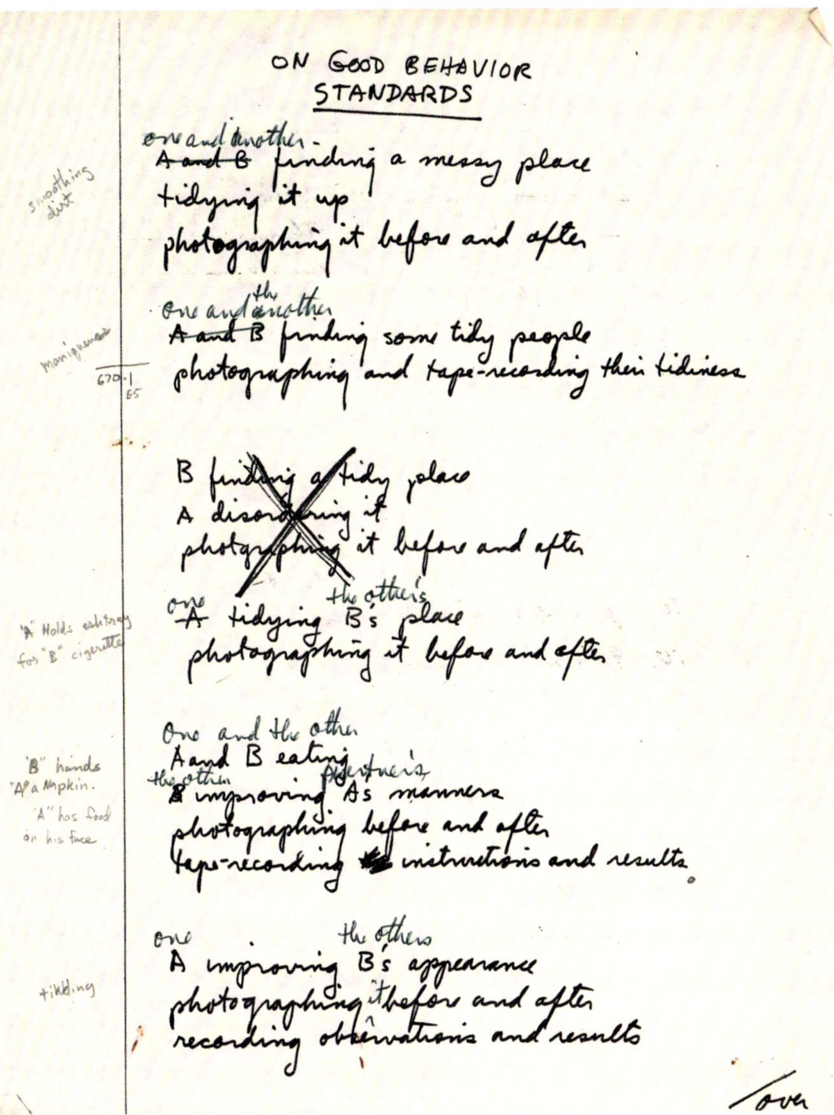
ON GOOD BEHAVIOR
STANDARDS

~~A and B~~ one and another finding a messy place
tidying it up
photographing it before and after

~~A and B~~ One and the another finding some tidy people
photographing and tape-recording their tidiness

~~B finding a tidy place~~
~~A disordering it~~
~~photographing it before and after~~

~~A~~ one tidying ~~B's~~ the other's place
photographing it before and after

One and the other
A and B eating
~~B~~ the other improving ~~A's~~ partner's manners
photographing before and after
tape-recording instructions and results.

~~A~~ one improving ~~B's~~ the others appearance
photographing it before and after
recording observations and results

/over

293 Score for *Standards*, p. 1

TEACHING POSITIONS Professor, Visual Arts Department, University of California, San Diego. Acting department chair, Fall Quarter. ¶ AWARDS Artist grant, National Endowment for the Arts. Guggenheim Fellowship. ¶ SOLO EXHIBITIONS *Ulrich Museum,* Wichita State University, Wichita, Kansas, April. *Frühe Arbeiten,* Galerie Inge Baecker, Bochum, September–October. ¶ GROUP EXHIBITIONS *Words,* Museum Bochum, Bochum (traveled internationally), January–March. *Fluxus International and Co.,* Espace Lyonnaise d'art contemporain, Lyon, April–May. *The Animal Show,* Los Angeles Contemporary Exhibitions Gallery, Los Angeles, July. *Weich und Plastisch: Soft Art,* Kunsthaus Zürich, Zurich, November–February. ¶ FESTIVALS Bochumer Kunstwoche, Bochum, September. Kunstwoche im Ihme Zentrum, Hannover, September. ¶ WRITINGS "Milan Knížák (Who Never Fell in Love with Art)," in *Unvollständige Dokumentation, 1961–1979 = Some Documentary, 1961–1979,* exh. cat. (Berlin: Ars Viva), 9–14. "Project for the Hamburger Kunsthalle," *The Dumb Ox,* no. 8: 38–41.

1979

294 Score for *Standards*, p. 2

one and the another
* A and B finding ~~another~~ tidy place
photographing it
~~improving~~ tidying their behavior
each photographing the other's improvement
~~both~~ both recording why they're improved

20 people (10 pairs)

10 polaroid cameras w flash (or 35mm cameras
30 packages of film (bl. & wh?) if instant development and printing is possible

10 portable tape recorders
10 90 min cassettes

to meet ~~Sat~~ Fri PM
do piece on Sat 9, Sun 10
meet ~~Sat~~ Sun PM

* The "tidy" image (composed)

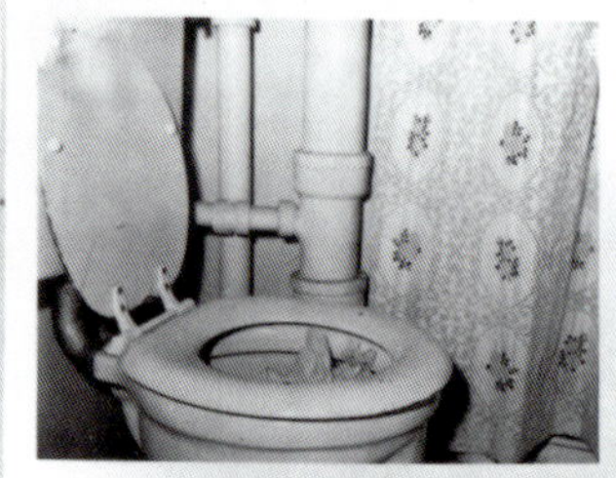
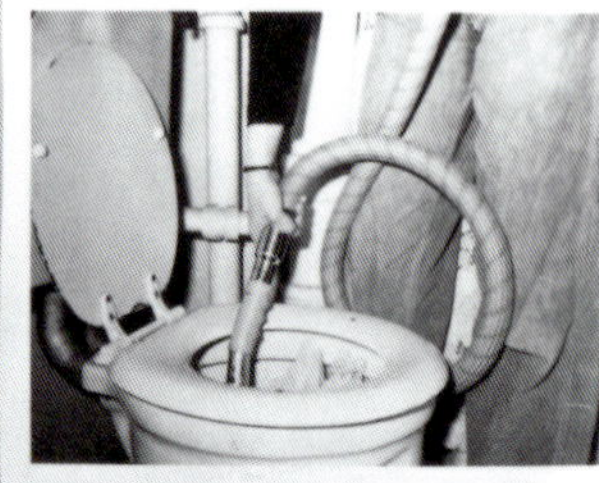
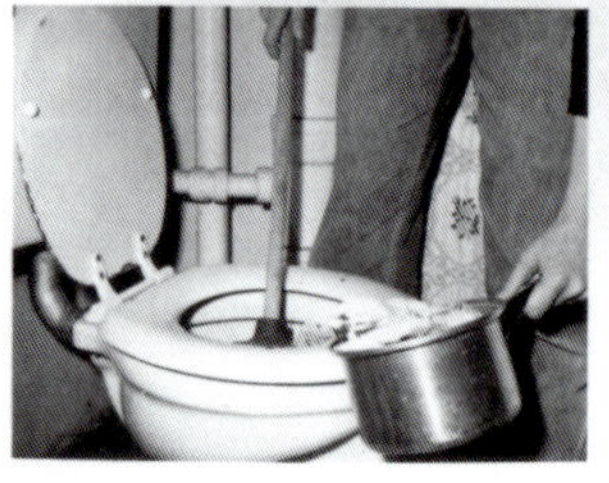
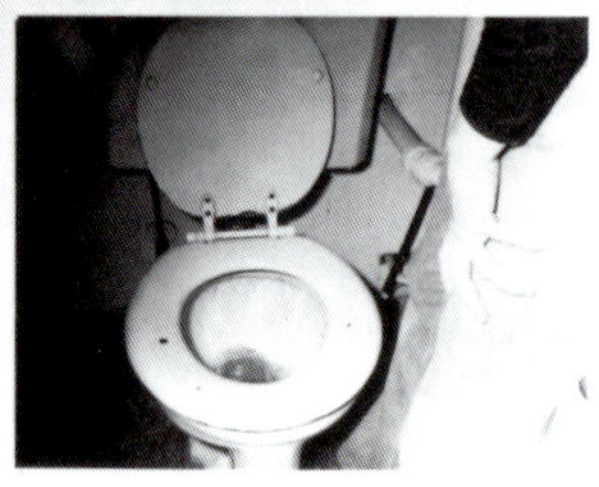

295 Finding a messy place, tidying it up

296 Improving one's appearance

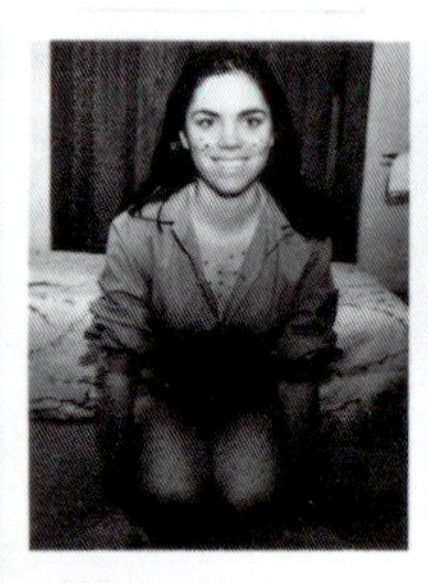
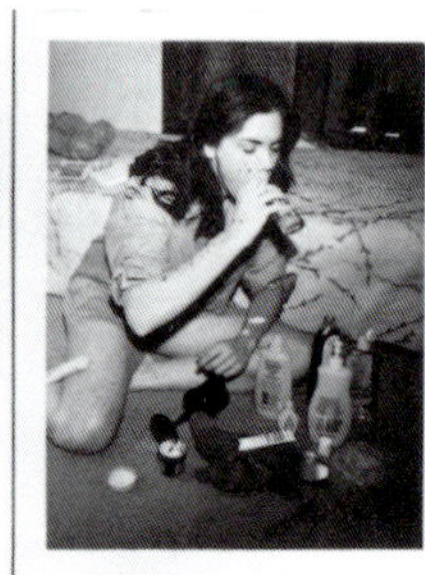
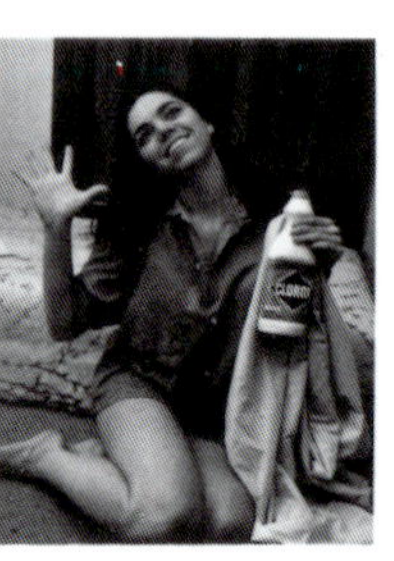

297 *Tire Tower*

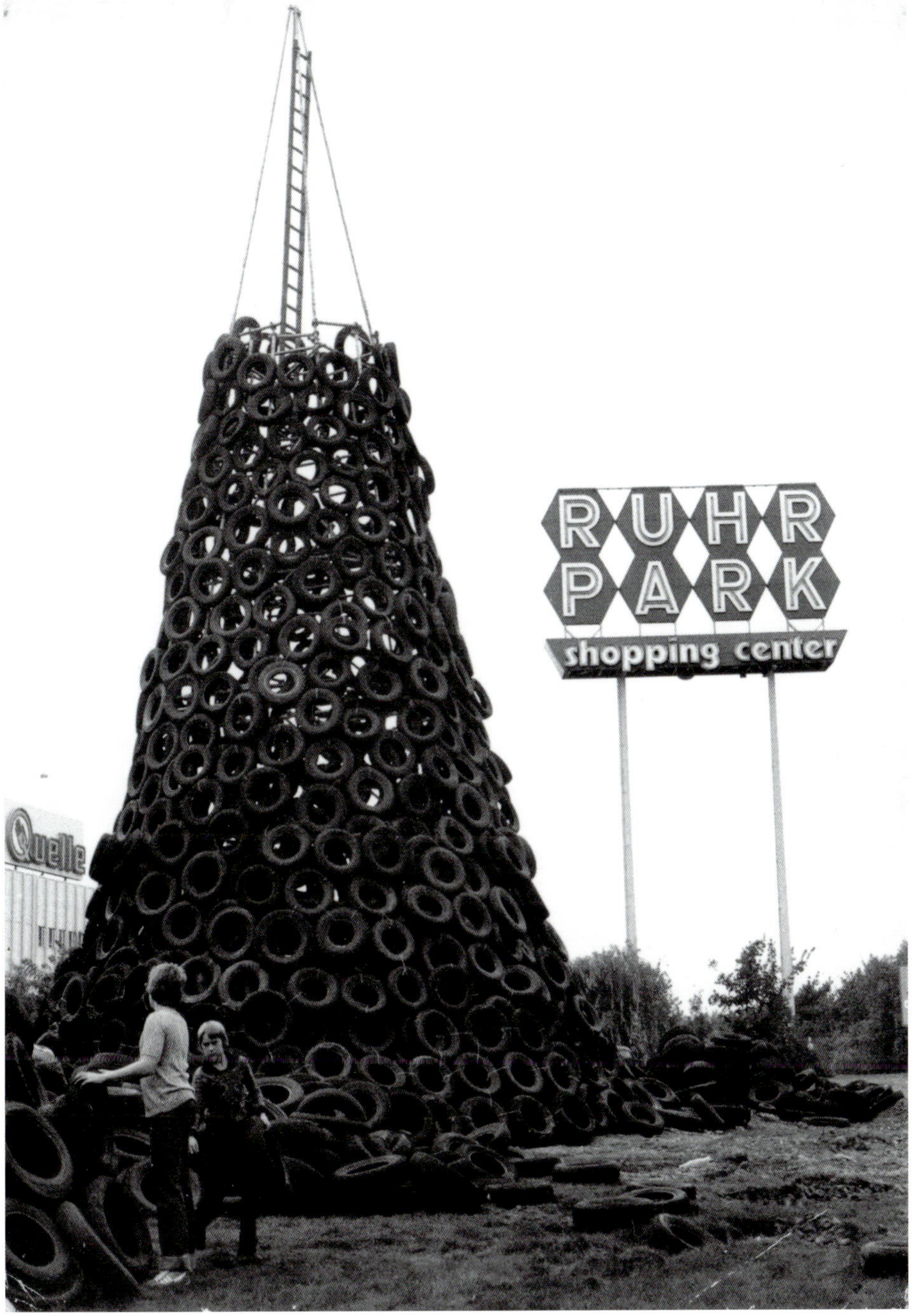

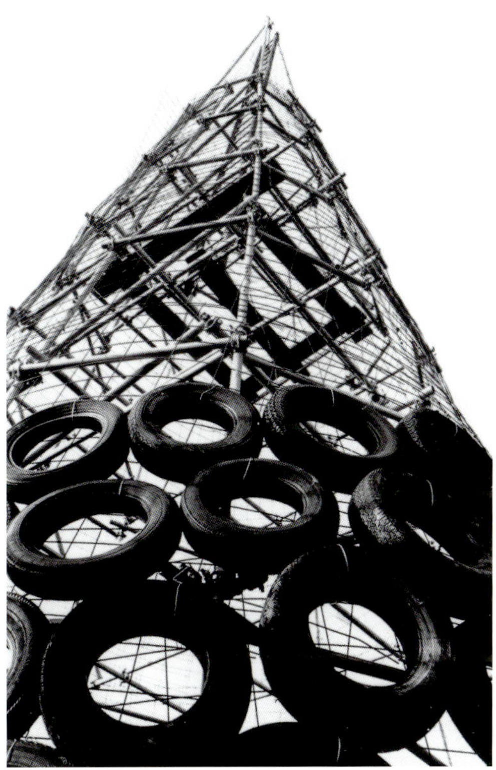

298 *Tire Tower*
(detail)

1980

TEACHING POSITIONS Professor, Visual Arts Department, University of California, San Diego. ¶ **GROUP EXHIBITIONS** *Für Augen und Ohren,* Akademie der Künste, West Berlin, January–March. *Mein Kölner Dom: Zeitgenössische Künstler sehen den Kölner Dom,* Kölnischer Kunstverein, Cologne, October–November. ¶ **FESTIVALS** Public Spirit, Los Angeles Contemporary Exhibitions, Los Angeles, May. Tel Hai '80 Arts Festival, Tel Hai College, Upper Galilee, Israel, September. Public Spirit 2, Los Angeles Contemporary Exhibitions, October. ¶ **WRITINGS** "Ein Statement," in *Mein Kölner Dom: Zeitgenössische Künstler sehen den Kölner Dom,* vol. 3 of *Der Kölner Dom im Jahrhundert seiner Vollendung,* exh. cat. (Cologne: Kölnischer Kunstverein), 78–81. "Exercise" and "Team" (Activity scores), *High Performance* 3, nos. 3–4: 52–55. "Performing Life" and facsimiles of the Activity booklets for *Routine, Maneuvers, Testimonials,* and *Standards,* in Carl E. Loeffler and Darlene Tong, eds., *Performance Anthology: Source Book for a Decade of California Performance Art* (San Francisco: Contemporary Arts), x–xii, 159–64, 208–18, 352–58. "Thoughts on Picasso in Our Time," unpublished essay commissioned by *Art in America.*

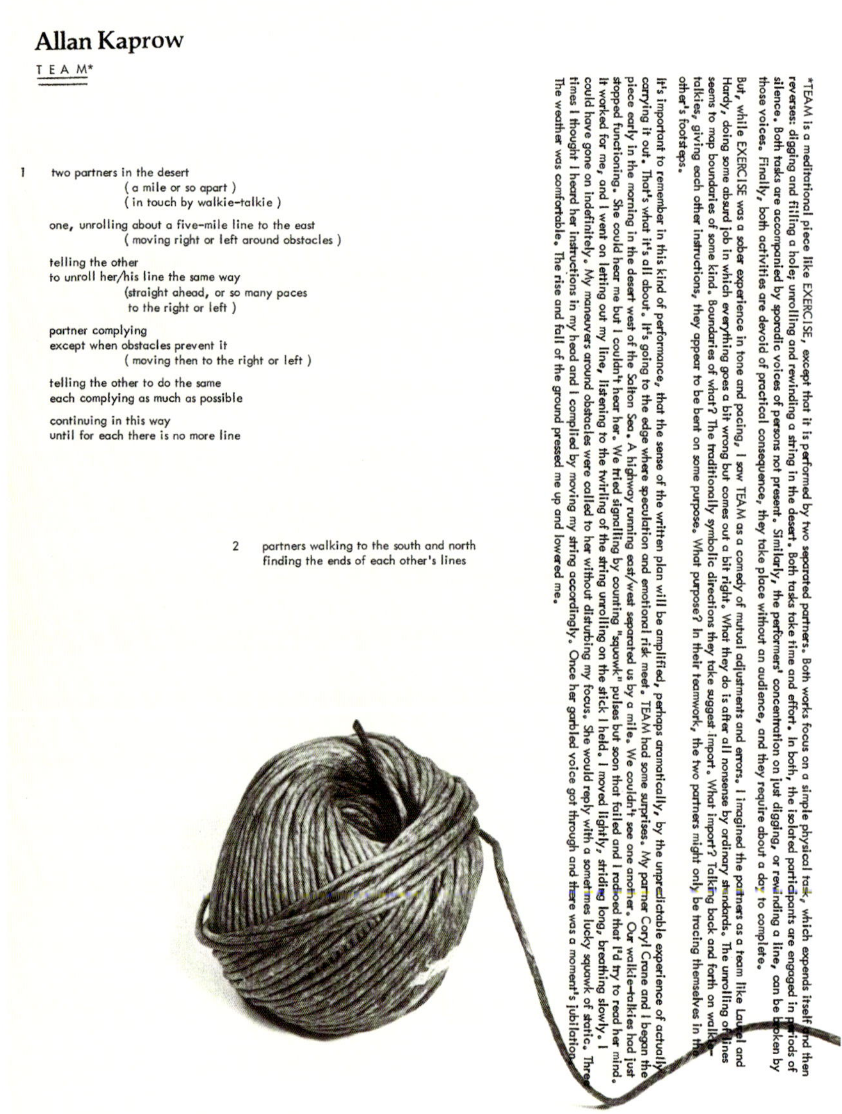

Allan Kaprow

TEAM*

1 two partners in the desert
(a mile or so apart)
(in touch by walkie-talkie)

one, unrolling about a five-mile line to the east
(moving right or left around obstacles)

telling the other
to unroll her/his line the same way
(straight ahead, or so many paces
to the right or left)

partner complying
except when obstacles prevent it
(moving then to the right or left)

telling the other to do the same
each complying as much as possible

continuing in this way
until for each there is no more line

2 partners walking to the south and north
finding the ends of each other's lines

*TEAM is a meditational piece like EXERCISE, except that it is performed by two separated partners. Both works focus on a simple physical task, which expends itself and then reverses: digging and filling a hole; unrolling and rewinding a string in the desert. Both tasks take time and effort. In both, the isolated participants are engaged in periods of silence. Both tasks are accompanied by sporadic voices of persons not present. Similarly, the performers' concentration on just digging, or rewinding a line, can be broken by those voices. Finally, both activities are devoid of practical consequence, they take place without an audience, and they require about a day to complete.

But, while EXERCISE was a sober experience in tone and pacing, I saw TEAM as a comedy of mutual adjustments and errors. I imagined the partners as a team like Laurel and Hardy, doing some absurd job in which everything goes a bit wrong but comes out a bit right. What they do is after all nonsense by ordinary standards. The unrolling of lines seems to map boundaries of some kind. Boundaries of what? The traditionally symbolic directions they take suggest import. What import? Talking back and forth on walkie-talkies, giving each other instructions, they appear to be bent on some purpose. What purpose? In their teamwork, the two partners might only be tracing themselves in the other's footsteps.

It's important to remember in this kind of performance, that the sense of the written plan will be amplified, perhaps aramatically, by the unpredictable experience of actually carrying it out. That's what it's all about. It's going to the edge where speculation and emotional risk meet. TEAM had some surprises. My partner Coryl Crane and I began the piece early in the morning in the desert west of the Salton Sea. A highway running east/west separated us by a mile. We couldn't see one another. Our walkie-talkies had just stopped functioning. She could hear me but I couldn't hear her. We tried signalling by counting "squawk" pulses but soon that failed and I radioed that I'd try to read her mind. It worked for me, and I went on letting out my line, listening to the twirling of the string unrolling on the stick I held. I moved lightly, striding long, breathing slowly. I could have gone on indefinitely. My maneuvers around obstacles were called to her without disturbing my focus. She would reply with a sometimes lucky squawk of static. Three times I thought I heard her instructions in my head and I complied by moving my string accordingly. Once her garbled voice got through and there was a moment's jubilation. The weather was comfortable. The rise and fall of the ground pressed me up and lowered me.

HIGH PERFORMANCE Fall/Winter 1980

299 Score for *Team* with Kaprow's account

Untitled Environment
Environment, January–March 1980
Reinvention for *Für Augen und Ohren*
Akademie der Künste, West Berlin

Exercise
Activity, May 1980
Presented for Public Spirit
Los Angeles

Imitations
Activity, May 1980
School of Art, Ohio University, Athens

Convoy
Activity, September 1980
Presented for Tel Hai '80 Arts Festival
Tel Hai College, Upper Galilee, Israel

299–300 **Team**
Activity, October 1980
Presented for Public Spirit 2
Anza-Borrego Badlands near the Salton Sea, California

An Archaeology of the Everyday
Activity, October 1980
Presented for *Mein Kölner Dom*
Kölnischer Kunstverein, Cologne

Making Faces
Activity, December 1980
Not realized

Coryl, on her side, veered quite off course, perhaps not aware she was followin the sun as it swung from east to south. (We had no compasses.) She couldn't connect with me. It frustrated her hearing me so clearly and not being heard. Gradually, this feeling became more noticeable to both of us. It was then getting late. I had unrolled about three miles of string and Coryl under two. It was time to cross over to find each other and our lines. Without two-way communication, this wasn't easy. I called repeatedly, now wondering if she heard me at all. I designated meeting points and she wasn't there. I had thoughts of snake bite, falls, loss of water. My meditational state was replaced with anxiety. I had to remind myself to drop my center from my shoulders to my abdomen, to breathe evenly, to concentrate on each step for itself. Coryl began to worry about me worrying about her. I stopped at a house to inquire and the owners tried reaching Coryl by CB radio. She was attempting the same thing elsewhere. No luck. When we did meet by chance at a roadside cafe, it was a relief. She was about to enlist help for a search. I saw how much fear had taken over.

We ate lunch and exchanged directions to locate each other's lines. An hour later I was lost. I came to landmarks that resembled her descriptions, but there was no string there or anywhere else I looked. The scenery was magnificent: canyons, stony hills, ravines. But everything looked the same and different. Periodically I tried to radio Coryl but by then I was out of range. Meditation alternated with concern and fatigue. I began counting strides. I knew I would not find Coryl's line. From a high hill I saw a house. Much later I reached it and got a lift to my truck. I had wandered over fifteen miles in the badlands.

I expected to see Coryl waiting there for hours. But she walked up exactly at that moment with a huge load of string. She had located my line without trouble; but following it and rewinding it took as much time as I had taken getting lost. She had been quite absorbed in the whole process, and in noticing shells and the tracks of animals. Once, though, when it seemed it would never end, involvement turned into disbelief and annoyance ("what the hell am I doing this for?"). Then back into the process. Laurel and Hardy could have laughed... This piece is dedicated to LaMonte Young whose early piece "Draw a Straight Line and Follow It" prompted the idea. —Allan Kaprow 10/80

3 re-winding the line
telling each other
to move in the directions they find it
(to the right, straight ahead
or left)

both winding
continuing to make adjustments
to the positions of each other's lines

until for each there is no more line

HIGH PERFORMANCE Fall/Winter 1980

VA 111
Winter 81

Kaprow

zazen

introduction

zazen

(inside)		(outside)	
sweeper:	sweeping the dust together	raker:	raking the leaves together
	standing still from time to time		standing still from time to time
watcher:	nearby, watching	watcher:	nearby, watching

zazen

quiet lunch

replacer: (former watcher)	replacing the dust standing still from time to time	replacer: (former watcher)	replacing the leaves standing still from time to time
watcher: (former sweeper)	nearby, watching in a mirror	watcher: (former raker)	nearby, watching in a mirror

zazen

sweeper: (who began)	sweeping the same dust together standing still from time to time	raker: (who began)	sweeping the same leaves together standing still from time to time
listener: (who began as watcher)	nearby, listening, not watching	listener: (who began as watcher)	nearby, listening, not watching

zazen

sweeper and listener:	blending the gathered dust somewhere else each standing still from time to time	raker and listener:	blending the gathered leaves somewhere else each standing still from time to time

zazen

group discussion

301 Score for *Meditation 1*

1981

TEACHING POSITIONS Professor, Visual Arts Department, University of California, San Diego. Acting department chair, Fall Quarter. ¶ CONSULTING POSITIONS Consultant/panelist, Interarts Program, National Endowment for the Arts, Washington, D.C. ¶ GROUP EXHIBITIONS *California Performance: Then and Now,* Museum of Contemporary Art, Chicago, January–February. *Westkunst: Zeitgenössische Kunst seit 1939,* Museum Ludwig, Cologne, August. *Schwarz,* Kunsthalle Düsseldorf, Dusseldorf, October–November. ¶ WRITINGS "Allan/Kaprow (An Irritating Interview with Kaprow by Allan)," unpublished self-interview, Allan Kaprow Papers, Getty Research Institute, Los Angeles; published as "Ein Interview von Allan mit Kaprow: Expeditionen ins fast alltägliche Leben," *Die Zeit,* 27 March: 47–48 (Feuilleton section).

Last March (?), at the San Diego Zen Center, the Institute for Transcultural Studies sponsored a workshop called "Performance as a Meditational (Practice?)(Discipline?)." The ~~intent~~ intent was to explore a possible bridge between the meditative aspects of my art work and the traditional practice of zazen.

I had been sitting regularly for about two years and began to be aware of ~~[illegible]~~ the ~~[illegible]~~ unintended ~~but now clear~~ Zen parallels that had been recurring all ~~[illegible]~~ in my performance work ~~of the last twenty years~~ from its beginnings in the 1950's. I was always interested in Zen but in a philosophical sense. Now ~~Now~~ I ~~wanted~~ wanted to link experimental ~~[illegible]~~ art and Zen practice in a more concrete way. ¶ Of course, older art forms in Asia such as ~~[illegible]~~ calligraphy and shakuhachi playing grew together with the evolution of Zen. But ~~[illegible]~~ the connection is less clear in ~~[illegible]~~ ~~present day~~ experimental art in the West. The ~~most~~ notable exception in the 50s the composer ~~was~~ John Cage, with whom I studied in the 50's. He introduced me to the possibility of contemporary Buddhism and it had a profound effect on my outlook ~~then~~, not simply regarding ~~[illegible]~~ the arts, but regarding living itself. ~~It took a long time~~

301–302 **Meditation 1**

Activity, March 1981

Institute for Transcultural Studies, Zen Center–San Diego, Del Mar, California

303–309 **Die Zeit Project**

Newspaper Happening, March 1981

Organized by Petra Kipphoff

In the pages of *Die Zeit*

Small Exercise 3

Activity, March 1981

Center for Music Experiment

University of California, San Diego

FAXGRAM via Graphnet

99 WEST SHEFFIELD AVENUE ■ ENGLEWOOD, NEW JERSEY 07631 201-569-7707

C071 366-1 L804 314 03/19/81 12:51 SS

6A 03/19 11:27 R144 3901-1 C071 366 03/19/81 12:43
SGD3901 GGA0978 DP2131I658
URGW CO DPHB 063
HAMBURG/TLX 63/61 19 1656

MR. ALLAN KAPROW
1225 LINDA ROSA AVE.
LOS ANGELES, CALIFORNIA

DEAR ALLAN,
THE WORLD IS OUT OF JOINT AND DIE ZEIT ALSO.
ALL OF US ARE BUSY ANSWERING THE PHONE AND LISTENING TO
QUESTIONS,
LAUGHTER, SCREAMING, CURSES OF READERS
AND COLLEAGUES. I WISH
YOU WERE HERE AND I THINK YOU WOULD ENJOY EVERY BIT OF IT.
WE ARE ALL VERY EXHAUSTED AND PLEASED
YOURS PETRA
KIPPHOFF ← Art Editor, Die Zeit

COL 1225 9004

NNNN
SUMS

376

DIE ZEIT
Nr. 14 — 27. März 1981

FEUILLETON
Seite 47

Allan Kaprow: Das Happening der falschen Photos

Ein Verwirrspiel zur Aufklärung und die Reaktionen darauf

Die ersten, die etwas merkten, waren die Drucker, die zweiten die Kollegen von den Nachrichtenagenturen, Zeitungen, Sendern, die dritten (aber sie waren nur so viel langsamer, wie die Anlieferung der Zeitung an die ersten Großstadtkioske dauerte) waren die Leser. Das ging alles ungeheuer schnell. Und die, die die Folgen dieser Entdeckung am schnellsten und intensivsten zu spüren bekamen, waren die Damen in der Telephonzentrale. Fragen, Flüche, Glückwünsche (die Reihenfolge ist ein Hinweis auf die Häufigkeit) kamen zwei Tage lang gewitterartig bei ihnen an.

Die Drucker in Ahrensburg und Neu-Isenburg riefen am Mittwoch gegen zwei Uhr morgens den Verlagsleiter an. Der versuchte vergeblich, ein paar Leute aus dem Schlaf zu telephonieren, und erreichte schließlich einen müden politischen Redakteur, der ihm, ohne Freude, bestätigte: Ja, ja, das soll so sein.

Die Dame von *dpa* rief gleich am Morgen an und war neugierig. Die Zeitungskollegen riefen etwas später an und waren mitleidig bis schadenfroh: Ogottogott, was habt ihr denn da für einen Mist gebaut. Schön, daß auch euch solche Pannen passieren!

Die Leute von *AP* sagten: Herzlichen Glückwunsch, eine fabelhafte Idee. Herr Blackstein vom Reuter-Büro Hamburg telexte: „Und ich dachte schon, mit dem Whisky wäre was nicht in Ordnung, den ich immer zum ersten Durchblättern der neuen ZEIT-Ausgabe trinke." Cheers!

Der erste geschwollen-entrüstete Anruf kam von der Pressestelle der Universität Hamburg: Man ließ wissen, daß man erbost und für solche Bilder nicht sein Geld zu entrichten bereit sei. Wir dürfen erwidern: Es lebe die Universität und ihre Bemühung um eine aufgeschlossene, phantasievolle akademische Jugend.

Und da wir schon bei den ganz einfach Empörten sind, die freilich in der Minderzahl waren, seien hier ihre Hauptvorwürfe zitiert: 1. Was sind das für abstoßende, makabre Photos (damit war wohl in erster Linie der mit der Autopsie beschäftigte Mann gemeint — auffallenderweise gelangten gerade die Entrüsteten gar nicht über dieses Photo hinaus); und 2. Es ist nicht seriös, Leser in die Irre zu führen, und das kann man auch durch keine Erklärung oder Entschuldigung wiedergutmachen; 2 a und eine Etage tiefer: Sie wollen uns wohl „verarschen".

Was eigentlich heißt und meint „seriös"? Für manche Leute offensichtlich so etwas wie „bierernst". Daß „seriös" ein Synonym für „ernsthaft" ist und daß auch ein Scherz einen ernsthaften Hintergrund haben kann, ist keine weitverbreitete Erkenntnis.

Vielleicht kann sich der eine oder andere Leser, der sich in höheren oder tieferen Körperregionen beleidigt fühlt, doch noch mit dem Gedanken vertraut machen, daß diese Aktion nicht der Irreführung, sondern der Aufklärung über die alltägliche Irreführung galt und daß eine Zeitung, die so etwas publiziert, nicht nur den Lesern etwas zumutet, sondern sich auch selber exponiert, indem sie den Leser auffordert, in Zukunft schärfer hinzuschauen — auch bei der ZEIT.

Eine etwas größere und pfiffige Gruppe von Lesern dachte, hier sei der 1. April vorverlegt, ein Test veranstaltet worden, ein Rätsel oder ein Preisausschreiben. Sollte man vielleicht die richtigen Artikel zu den Bildern finden oder die richtigen Bilder zu den Unterschriften? Ja, so etwas Ähnliches wie ein Test war das schon. Aber das Verwirrende war ja, daß nichts zu irgend etwas passen wollte.

Ein Architekt in Berlin schaffte sich, nachdem er telephonisch aufgeklärt war, gleich fünf weitere Exemplare der ZEIT an und legte sie ins Tiefkühlfach, Kunstwerke für schlechte Zeiten. Ein Ingenieur aus Berlin schrieb am 19., also wenige Stunden nachdem er die Zeitung gesehen und die Bilder exakt aufgelistet hatte, einen langen, nachdenklichen Brief: „Zuerst glaubte ich an ein Versehen, doch dann las ich mir die Texte zu den einzelnen Bildern genauer durch und merkte, daß hier kein Versehen vorlag ... Nun drängten sich bei mir einige Fragen auf ..." Wie dieser sorgfältige und geduldige Leser reagierten viele.

Herr Kurt-Jürgen Maaß schickte, per Eilboten, sein Photo, um unserem „offensichtlich erschöpften" Photoarchiv auszuhelfen, und schlug vor, sein Konterfei wahlweise zu einem Artikel über Hausbesetzungen, steigende Ölpreise, Sonderangebote für den Sommerurlaub oder Erfolge mit neuen Medikamenten zu verwenden. Ein beweglicher Mann, der die Sache begriffen hat.

Auch mit Henri Nannen vom STERN ging das große Herz durch, als er schrieb: „Man merkt der neuen ZEIT einigen Streß an ... Wenn das kein Happening ist, dann zeigt es, daß Euer Bildervorrat offenbar beschränkt ist. Auch dann bin ich gern bei Ihnen und stelle das STERN-Bildarchiv zu ermäßigten Sätzen zur Verfügung."

Es ist die Aktion eines Happening-Künstlers, und die ZEIT-Graphiker hoffen, daß das Angebot dennoch gilt.

Wenn man versucht, diese ersten Reaktionen ein bißchen zu bündeln (was schade ist, denn so bunt und individuell geht's bei Lesern nicht oft zu), dann zeigen sich sechs überwiegende Reaktionen und Interpretationen:

- ein riesiges Malheur
- ein Sabotage-, Rache- oder Protestakt
- ein Aprilscherz, Test oder Preisausschreiben
- eine Sparmaßnahme
- eine Unverschämtheit
- eine Sache, bei der etwas dahintersteckt — vielleicht ein Hinweis auf die „Beliebigkeit der Photodokumente" (so ein Leser).

„Ich weiß nicht, was soll es bedeuten", schreiben Ulrike und Reinhard Löw. Wir hoffen, daß sie und andere jetzt etwas mehr wissen.

Wir jedenfalls haben durch Allan Kaprows Aktion viel erlebt und viel erfahren.

Zum Beispiel über uns selber. Manche Redakteure, die zunächst und als alles noch Plan und Theorie war, amüsiert schienen und bereit mitzuspielen, zuckten dann doch zusammen, als es Ernst wurde, redaktionellen Platz kostete (gerade in *dieser* Nummer!), das „falsche" Photo vielleicht gar in dem eigenen Artikel zu stehen kam. Das setzte sich fort beim Umbruch — jeder hatte das irgendwie anders verstanden, und alles wurde noch einmal durchdiskutiert. Und wie man schließlich sehen kann, zeigt sich die Aktion Kaprows in jedem Ressort auf andere Weise, hat das „Moderne Leben" enthusiastisch und total, die „Wirtschaft" eher verschämt mitgemacht — die Welt ist auch bei der ZEIT in Ordnung.

Wir haben auch etwas erfahren über unsere Leser. Wer, außer mit der Familie und dem Krämer, vorwiegend mit Kollegen, Spezialisten und Fachleuten hier oder anderswo spricht und sich dann an den Schreibtisch setzt, der denkt, wenn er beim Schreiben an irgend jemanden denkt, manchmal an Menschen, öfter noch an andere Spezialisten. Die Art und Weise, in der ZEIT-Leser auf die Kaprow-Aktion als wütende, fragende, neugierige, amüsierte Menschen reagiert haben, war für uns überraschend, verblüffend, überwältigend. Wir müssen zugeben: ganz so stürmisch und vielfältig hatten wir uns das nicht vorgestellt. Keiner im Hause, der nicht Kommentare oder Spekulationen von außerhalb zu hören bekommen hat. Die Mitglieder der ZEIT-Redaktion sahen auf einmal Menschen vor sich und nicht nur Standesvertreter oder statistische Mittelwerte mit diesen und jenen Lesegewohnheiten.

Im Jahr 1977 verpackte, verwickelte und verhüllte Christo die Mitglieder des Feuilletons der ZEIT, zum Jahresbeginn 1978 durchsetzte Horst Janßen den Feuilletonteil mit seinen Zeichnungen. Jetzt hat Allan Kaprow die ganze Zeitung ein wenig aus den Fugen gebracht, und ihre Leser auch. „Wer sich darüber entrüstet, zeigt nur, daß ihm das Spiel in die Glieder gefahren ist, er bestätigt nur die Absicht des Autors", kommentierte die „Süddeutsche Zeitung". Und der „Spiegel" schrieb: „Wenn er (Kaprow) tatsächlich das Bewußtsein der ZEIT-Leser erweitert, dann müssen sich wohl auf die nächste Aktion einige ZEIT-Schreiber gefaßt machen: auf die Aktion gegen den gedankenlosen Gebrauch der Sprache."

Eine gute Idee, die dem Erfinder fürs eigene „Spiegel"-Blatt vorbehalten bleiben soll.

Petra Kipphoff

Drei Photos wurden in der vorigen Ausgabe der ZEIT in vier Ressorts je einmal gedruckt – ohne in den Textzusammenhang zu passen, dafür mit wechselnden Unterschriften. Im Interview mit sich selbst erklärt Kaprow seine Idee.

Ein Interview von Allan mit Kaprow

Expeditionen ins fast alltägliche Leben

Allan: Zunächst ein bißchen Hintergrund. Sie waren ein moderner Maler in der New Yorker Nachkriegsszene. Sodann schreibt man Ihnen die Erfindung des Happenings und seiner Theorie in den späten fünfziger Jahren zugute. Im nächsten Jahrzehnt wurde es zu einem internationalen Phänomen. Bei Ihrer Art des Happenings führten die Teilnehmer bestimmte, geplante Aktionen miteinander und innerhalb ihrer alltäglichen Umgebung durch.

Da wurden zum Beispiel quer durch Los Angeles große, hausartige Strukturen aus Eisblöcken gebaut, und dann beobachtete man sie, wie sie schmolzen. Eine Steinmauer wurde neben der Berliner Mauer errichtet. Die Steine wurden mit Brot und Marmelade beschossen, und dann wurde die Mauer umgestoßen. Krankenhausbetten mit richtigen Schwestern darin wurden in die Mitte einer Autobahn gerollt. Feuerlöschschaum wallte von hohen Kliffs herunter und hüllte die Spaziergänger unten am Strand ein. Leerstehende Wohnungen wurden vorübergehend zum Zuhause, als Happening-Teilnehmer altes Mobiliar durch die Straßen schoben und diese Wohnungen für eine Nacht belegten. Sie verließen die Wohnungen dann einer nach dem andern.

Bei solchen Veranstaltungen gab es keine Proben, keine Wiederholungen und kein Publikum. Kunstgalerien, Museen und Bühnen wurden gemieden. Statt dessen benutzte man die Häuser der Teilnehmer, die Landschaft, Fabriken, Straßen, Autos, Autobushaltestellen und Keller. Sie benutzten auch Telephone, den Postdienst, den Körper und den Kopf als „Plätze" zur Aufführung Ihrer Happenings.

Und jetzt eine Frage. In ganz einfachen Worten: Was hat Sie dazu bewegt, die Malerei zu verlassen, und was hält Ihr Interesse lebendig an diesen Happenings, dieser Kunst, die solange dauert, wie sie dauert?

Kaprow: In der Mitte der fünfziger Jahre war ich angewidert von dem wachsenden politischen und künstlerischen Konservativismus der Welt. Mein jugendlicher Traum war es gewesen, der wichtigste Künstler meiner Zeit zu werden. Das erscheint im Rückblick ziemlich jugendlich-romantisch, aber es sagt etwas über meine angeborene Neugierde für das Experiment. Ich hatte Kunstgeschichte und Philosophie studiert, und so hatte ich gewisse Informationen über das, was es in den Künsten schon gegeben hat. Um der modernste aller Künstler zu sein, beschloß ich nichts zu

● Fortsetzung nächste Seite

 DIE ZEIT — Nr. 13 — 20. März 1981

Jugendstrafanstalt Hahnöversand

Sie kommen fast alle wieder zurück

Erfahrungen aus einem Sozialpraktikum: Eine radikale Reform des Strafvollzugs tut not / Von Jost Peyer

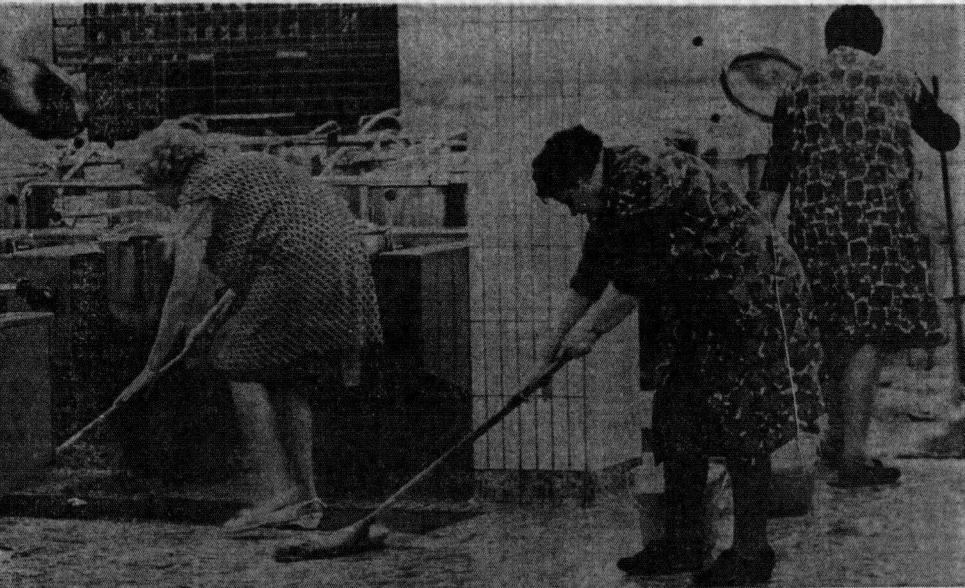

Ein Experiment zur Verbesserung des Sozialklimas. Diese Frauen, Ehefrauen von reichen Industriellen, übernehmen eine Woche lang Arbeiten im Dienstleistungsgewerbe. Während die Welt schläft, fegen und schrubben sie die Böden und Labore ihrer Männer, um „die öffentliche Aufmerksamkei auf die Forderungen der vernachlässigten Industriearbeiter zu lenken“.
Aufnahme: Stefan Mose

Die Jugendstrafanstalt Hahnöversand bei Hamburg ist eine offene Anstalt. Wer hier „sitzt“, gehört schon zu den Privilegierten unter den jugendlichen Kriminellen. Er bekommt eine Berufsausbildung und wird psychologisch betreut. Dennoch werden die meisten von ihnen wieder rückfällig. Woran liegt das?

☆

Offene Jugendstrafanstalt Hahnöversand bei Hamburg; mein erster Tag auf der „Insel“, die für die nächsten vier Wochen mein Praktikumsplatz ist. Ich stehe vor der Tür von Haus 2, einer von vier Gefangenenunterkünften. Die Eingangstür hat keinen Drücker, nur ein überdimensionales Schloß. Der Beamte vom Aufsichtsdienst, der „Hausvater“, kommt und schließt auf. Drinnen auf dem Flur stehen zwei Gefangene gelangweilt herum, der eine zerreißt ein auf der Heizung liegendes Schulheft, der andere schlägt mit dem zugehörigen Lineal so lange auf das Steinsims, bis es zerbricht.

Die Gefangenen, die ich aus der Lehrwerkstatt mitgebracht habe, werden in ihren Zellen eingeschlossen. Einer von den „Jungs“ zeigt mir seine Zelle: 2,50 mal 3,50 Meter, vergittertes Fenster, Tisch, Bett, Waschbecken, Klo, Schrank, ein Sessel, ein Stuhl, alles sauber und akkurat. „Klein, aber fein“, meint er, „die Wände hat gerade der Maler gemacht, meine Zelle ist noch eine von den besseren!“ Er hat recht, andere Zellen machen einen völlig verwahrlosten Eindruck. Der „Hausvater“ erscheint in der Tür, er will abschließen. Wohl zum hundertstenmal an diesem Tag holt er sein Schlüsselbund aus der Tasche und entläßt mich mit dem wohlmeinenden Ratschlag: „Es gibt drei Dinge, auf die Sie im Knast aufpassen müssen — Schlüssel, Sägen und Feilen!“

Zucht und Ordnung

Hahnöversand ist eine offene Strafanstalt, es gibt keine Gefängnismauer, die äußere Sicherheit ist eher lax. Hierher kommen Gefangene, mit denen es der Staat besonders gut meint. „Im Vergleich zu Neumünster ist das hier 'ne Trinkerheilanstalt“, erzählt Dirk, der, obwohl er erst 19 Jahre alt ist, schon fast vier Jahre Knasterfahrung hat. Seine Tätowierungen zeugen von der Langeweile des Knastalltags und sind „Kunstwerk“ und Statussymbol zugleich. Dirk ist einer von etwa hundert Gefangenen auf „H.-Sand“, ihnen steht etwa ebensoviel Personal gegenüber (darunter auch ein Psychologe), das sich im Schichtdienst ablöst. Die Jugendlichen sind zwischen 15 und 23 Jahre alt, sie verbüßen Strafen von einigen Monaten bis zu vier Jahren. Die Belegschaft ist bunt gemischt, Automatenknacker, Rauschgiftsüchtige und wegen Körperverletzung Verurteilte sitzen hier ein.

Die ersten drei bis vier Wochen verbringen die Jugendlichen im Zugangshaus zur Beobachtung, sie werden damit beschäftigt, überstehenden Grat von Gummihalterungen für Autokühler abzuschneiden. „Nach zwei Wochen träumst du von Gummi!“ sagt einer.

Eine regelrechte Lehre können die Jugendlichen in mehreren Berufen wie Maurer, Maler, Maschinenschlosser, Tischler und Landwirt absolvieren. Nur wenige machen jedoch den Abschluß, weil die Strafzeit kürzer als die Lehrzeit ist.

Der Betrieb in der Metall-Lehrwerkstatt gleicht dem in einer Lehrwerkstatt außerhalb der Anstalt. Um 16.30 Uhr ist Feierabend, die Sägen und Feilen werden nachgezählt, danach bringen die Ausbilder die Gefangenen „auf Haus“, wo sie von den Hausvätern übernommen werden. Nach dem Abendbrot stehen Fernsehen und manchmal Sport zur Auswahl. Je nach Fernsehplan, der für jede Woche neu zusammengestellt wird, ist zwischen 21 und 23 Uhr Einschluß bis zum nächsten Morgen, das Licht wird gelöscht.

Das Wochenende ist arbeitsfrei. Aber auch dann dürfen die Gefangenen sich nur unter Aufsicht auf dem Gelände bewegen, ein Beamter muß beim Sport oder Spazierengehen dabei sein. An jedem zweiten Sonntag ist Besuchstag — für die „Knackis“, wie sie sich selbst nennen, ein besonderes Ereignis. Die „Gastgeber“ sind sichtlich nervös, sie haben sich frisch eingekleidet und gekämmt und für eine Stunde Kontakt zur Außenwelt und zu den alten Freunden.

Gegen Ende der Haftzeit gibt es Urlaub über das Wochenende oder auch länger, um die Wiedereingliederung zu fördern.

„Zucht und Ordnung werden hier groß geschrieben, du hast nur das Recht, das zu machen, was die dir sagen“, sagt ein Jugendlicher. Anpassung an die Hausordnung ist das Wichtigste, ein Stufensystem von I bis IV, das bei Wohlverhalten eine frühere Höherstufung und damit Entlassung in Aussicht stellt, lehrt die Häftlinge, sich unterzuordnen, im Knastjargon: zu „klingeln“. „Man steht immer unter freiwilligem Zwang“, sagt Jörn, 21 Jahre alt, wegen Körperverletzung hinter Gittern.

Eine Einsicht in das von ihnen begangene Unrecht entwickeln die meisten jugendlichen Strafgefangenen in der Anstalt nicht, für ihre Straftaten interessieren sich meist nur die Mitgefangenen: Da wird kräftig mit den alten Brüchen geprahlt und werden neue im Geist vorbereitet. Resignierende Erkenntnis eines Gefangenen: „Der Knast macht die Leute ja nur noch schlimmer!“ Das abschließende Urteil eines anderen über den Jugendvollzug: „Ist alles nur Rache und Vergeltung hier.“

Einer von fünf Gefangenen, die ich beaufsichtigen sollte, war „auf Flucht“ gegangen. In den Obstgärten von Jork verlor sich seine Spur, ein Beamter, den ich bei der Suche begleitete, meinte: „Über kurz oder lang landen sie doch fast alle wieder im Knast, wegen solcher Eierdiebe macht die Polizei keine Großfahndung!“ Statistiken geben ihm recht.

Fast alle Jugendlichen haben nach ihrer Entlassung einen Job oder eine Lehrstelle, für eine Wohnung sorgt die Sozialarbeiterin der Anstalt. Trotzdem werden zwei Drittel der jugendlichen Ersttäter wieder rückfällig. Die Gründe für ihr Scheitern sind so unterschiedlich wie die Tätertypen, die der Jugendstrafvollzug unter einen Hut bringen muß. Mancher schafft es nicht, morgens regelmäßig um sechs Uhr aufzustehen, er verliert seinen Arbeitsplatz; andere können kein Geld „herumliegen“ sehen oder geraten im Alkoholrausch erneut in Schlägereien, wieder andere sehen sich bei ihrer Entlassung einem Schuldenberg gegenüber, angesichts dessen sie sich nach „schnellen“ Verdienstmöglichkeiten umsehen. Die alten Freunde sind wieder da, man trinkt zusammen, die abschreckende Erinnerung an den Knast verblaßt schnell. Pläne werden geschmiedet nach dem Motto: Diesmal stellen wir es so an, daß man uns nicht erwischt!

Lieber Wohngruppen

Verbesserungen wie die Möglichkeit, daß Straftäter in der Anstalt eine Berufsausbildung bekommen, haben sich also nur unwesentlich auf die Rückfallquote ausgewirkt. Sollte man da nicht zum alten Verwahrungsvollzug zurückkehren?

Die Gründe für die relative Erfolglosigkeit des Jugendstrafvollzugs sind wohl darin zu suchen, daß eine persönliche Fehlentwicklung der Straftäter sich nicht wie eine Krankheit durch eine (wenn auch mehrjährige) „Kur“ beseitigen läßt. Der Jugendanstalt verbleibt die undankbare Aufgabe zu retten, was so nicht mehr zu retten ist. In der Haft sind Jugendliche aus den unterschiedlichsten Bevölkerungsschichten mit den unterschiedlichsten Straftaten — „Hauer Hascher, Klauer“ — auf engem Raum zusammengeschlossen. Gemeinsam ist ihnen nur, daß sie mit den Wertvorstellungen dieser Gesellschaft in Konflikt gekommen sind. Die meisten sehen sich als Opfer, nicht als Täter. Zusammengehalten wird diese brisante Mischung von einer rigiden Hausordnung, die im wesentlichen die Sicherheit der Anstalt im Auge hat. Die Vollzugsbeamten geraten dabei in einen Zwiespalt. Einerseits müssen sie kontrollieren und einschließen, mit einem Wort: mißtrauisch sein. Das trägt ihnen das Mißtrauen der Gefangenen ein. Andererseits sollen sie gemäß dem gesetzlich vorgeschriebenen Resozialisierungsvollzug Vertrauen gewinnen, offen sein. Im Zweifelsfall siegt das Sicherheitsdenken, der Gefangene wird durch die starre Ordnung entmündigt, er fällt einer „dressierten Gewöhnung“ (Zitat aus einem Urteil) anheim — nicht förderlich für das Leben in Freiheit für Menschen, die ohnehin wenig Selbstvertrauen haben.

Es gibt Alternativen: In den USA leben jugendliche Straftäter und Sozialarbeiter auch in Wohngruppen zusammen, die Bewährungshilfe wurde verbessert. Diese Versuche waren effektiver und billiger. 1972 gar schloß der US-Bundesstaat Massachusetts sämtliche Jugendstrafanstalten.

er (es) verdient.

Der Freiheitsbegriff dagegen erlebt eine erstaunliche Konjunktur; man kann damit kaum falsch liegen, wenn man ihn gegen den Interventionsstaat, gegen den Sozialismus oder für das freie Unternehmertum verwendet. Man darf ihn nur nicht gegen den konservativen Staat ins Feld führen. Die Gefahr der Bindungslosigkeit, der Auflösung von Ordnungen droht dann. Für solches Unterfangen ist das ehrbare Wort Freiheit verboten; es wird ersetzt durch andere, polemisch aufgeladene Begriffe wie etwa Emanzipation.

ohne seine Freiheit in Frage zu stellen." Der Kanzler räumt ein, der Bestand an „Grundwerten" sei schutzbedürftig. Wie aber der Staat den Schutz organisiere, das entscheide sich im Prozeß der politischen Willensbildung; und der Kanzler vertraut dabei offenbar den „ethosbezogenen gesellschaftlichen Kräften" sehr stark, er baut vor allem auf die Kirchen.

So werde, meint dagegen Kohl, der Staat zum bloßen Notar von Mehrheitsmeinungen. Die gesellschaftlichen Grundwerte müßten wieder aktualisiert werden, und das sei Aufgabe des Staates. Die Grundwerte erhalten hier freilich

feiert. Die Freiheit gegen die staatliche Ordnung gewendet, wie sie eine extensive Interpretation des Grundgesetzes ergibt, wird als Schwund der Ethik unter Verdacht gestellt. Dieser Widerspruch ist nirgendwo genau ausdiskutiert. Die Spannungen, Friktionen rücken kaum ins Blickfeld. Daß die moderne Wirtschaft den Gesetzen des Marktes unterliegt, wo das Recht des Stärkeren gilt, und den Gesetzen der Effizienz gehorcht, die notwendigerweise Instrumentalisierung bedeuten, läßt sich kaum bestreiten. Daß dies aber mit einem konservativen wert- und würdebezogenen Menschenbild sich nicht nahtlos

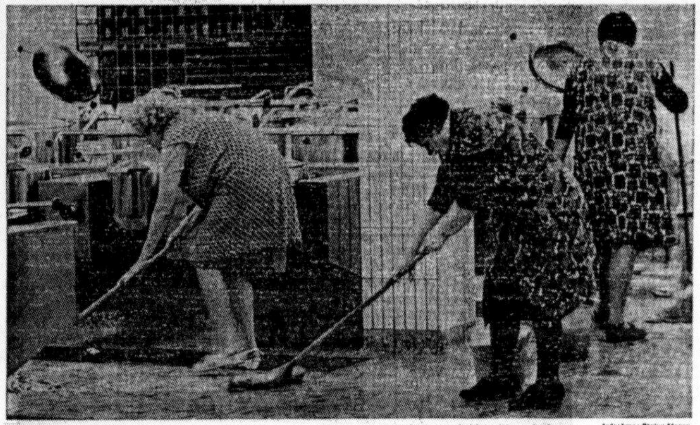

Aufnahme: Stefan Moses

(Business)

Are mops and pails obsolete? Several firms are introducing prototypes of automated cleaning services for industry and home. Expensive at the moment, such computer-programmed devices are expected, within the next decade, to cut the cost of menial labor by 50%.

er (es) verdient.

Der Freiheitsbegriff dagegen erlebt eine erstaunliche Konjunktur; man kann damit kaum falsch liegen, wenn man ihn gegen den Interventionsstaat, gegen den Sozialismus oder für das freie Unternehmertum verwendet. Man darf ihn nur nicht gegen den konservativen Staat ins Feld führen. Die Gefahr der Bindungslosigkeit, der Auflösung von Ordnungen droht dann. Für solches Unterfangen ist das ehrbare Wort Freiheit verboten; es wird ersetzt durch andere, polemisch aufgeladene Begriffe wie etwa Emanzipation.

ohne seine Freiheit in Frage zu stellen." Der Kanzler räumt ein, der Bestand an „Grundwerten" sei schutzbedürftig. Wie aber der Staat den Schutz organisiere, das entscheide sich im Prozeß der politischen Willensbildung; und der Kanzler vertraut dabei offenbar den „ethosbezogenen gesellschaftlichen Kräften" sehr stark, er baut vor allem auf die Kirchen.

So werde, meint dagegen Kohl, der Staat zum bloßen Notar von Mehrheitsmeinungen. Die gesellschaftlichen Grundwerte müßten wieder aktualisiert werden, und das sei Aufgabe des Staates. Die Grundwerte erhalten hier freilich

feiert. Die Freiheit gegen die staatliche Ordnung gewendet, wie sie eine extensive Interpretation des Grundgesetzes ergibt, wird als Schwund der Ethik unter Verdacht gestellt. Dieser Widerspruch ist nirgendwo genau ausdiskutiert. Die Spannungen, Friktionen rücken kaum ins Blickfeld. Daß die moderne Wirtschaft den Gesetzen des Marktes unterliegt, wo das Recht des Stärkeren gilt, und den Gesetzen der Effizienz gehorcht, die notwendigerweise Instrumentalisierung bedeuten, läßt sich kaum bestreiten. Daß dies aber mit einem konservativen wert- und würdebezogenen Menschenbild sich nicht nahtlos

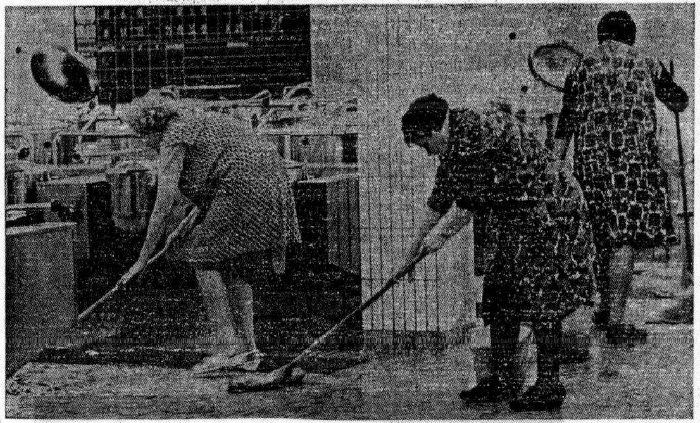

Aufnahme: Stefan Moses

(Culture)

True-to-life Happening. A group of well-known artists quietly washed the floors of an office building, after dark. Purpose? To experience work as a meditational practice. Is this the ultimate magic for the working masses, or is it food for thought?

307 Culture section
(caption translated)

308 Politics section
(caption translated)

(Politics)

Arbeit macht frei? Dirty jobs like these are not spoken about, but over ten million of them provide Western Europe with cheap services. However, they cost the taxpayer billions in medical insurance and other forms of social welfare. Who really benefits? Who really pays?

Aufnahme: Stefan Moses

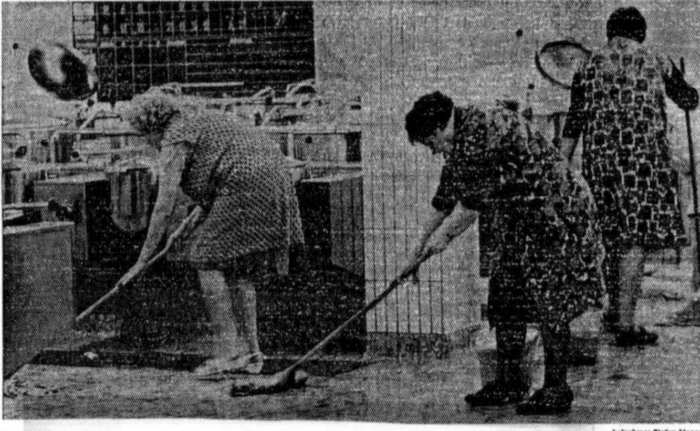

(Economics)

These women work at night to clean a computer center. Soon, technology will provide cleaning, and other simple services, automatically. Menial labor may become a thing of the past. Where will these women find work? Will the future eliminate the working class, or transform it?

Aufnahme: Stefan Moses

309 Economics section
(caption translated)

January 30th, 198I

Dear

Please forgive this photocopied letter; it's the most efficient way to contact a number of my friends with the same message.

I'm coming to England and the Continent in the Spring for a personal project that interests me. I'd like you to be involved if you can.

The idea is to visit certain of my friends living in England, Germany, Holland, France and Italy, and make for each of them a unique Activity. The visits would be short - 3 or 4 days - and the pieces would be very simple, emerging from the situation itself. After each event we'd tell our stories of what occurred, which I'd like to collect for a small book at the end of my travels.

Basically I want to try an alternative to the art market and, instead, make art for those I enjoy being with.

So I'd like to make a piece for you. All I'd ask from you is your hospitality for the period of my visit. I'll be travelling with my friend Coryl Crane (some of you know her), who is a stained-glass artist, and who will be studying the cathedrals and making contacts in her field during our tour.

Our itinerary is England (Essex and London), April 8-2I; Berlin April 21-28; Hamburg April 28-May 2; Amsterdam May 2-7; Cologne May 7-12; Paris May 12-17; Pouillac (Dordogne) May 17-22; Florence May 22-27; Munich May 27-June 2; Berlin June 2-6. (The outside dates in each place would be arrival and departure days of course).

If you're interested and will be at home during the appropriate dates, please telegraph me with one word "OKAY" and I'll be in touch with you soon afterward. If it's not possible telegraph the word "REGRETS". Naturally, I hope you find the idea attractive and will be at home. But do let me know soon!

Fond regards,

Allan

Allan Kaprow

Allan Kaprow
1225 Linda Rosa Avenue
Eagle Rock
Los Angeles, CA 90041

310 **European Tour**

Seven Activities, April–June 1981
England, Germany, Holland, France, and Italy

Just Walking on the Edge

Activity, April 1981
For Rita Donnagh and Richard Hamilton
Oxfordshire, United Kingdom

311 **Leaving No Footprints**

Activity, May 1981
For Barbara Glas and Ludwig Thürmer
West Berlin

Drawing on Stories

Activity, May 1981
For Shula Koren, Yaël Koren, Nimrod Koren, and Shlomo Koren
Amsterdam

312–313 **Quiet Please**

Activity, May 1981
For José-Anne De Kock and Pierre Restany
Paris

314 **Going/Staying**

Activity, May 1981
For Marianne Filliou, Marcelline Filliou, and Robert Filliou
Pouillac-Le Moustier, France

311 Score for *Leaving No Footprints*

II

going for a walk
leaving your footprints in some grass

lifting each blade of grass
leaving no footprints

G K 5/81

A piece for Barbara Glas and Ludwig Thürmer, performed by them, Coryl Crane, Ralf Wudtke, ~~Stephan von Huene~~ and myself, May 1, 1981,
Allan Kaprow — Berlin

Weighty Matters
Activity, May 1981
For Giancarlo Bicocchi and Maria Gloria Bicocchi
Florence

Our Life Together (Scenes for a Movie)
Activity, May 1981
For Danny Keller
Munich

Performance as a Meditational Practice (with Pauline Oliveros)
Activity, June 1981
Institute for Transcultural Studies, Zen Center, Los Angeles

Meditation 2
Activity, August 1981
A street piece for 80 Langton Street, San Francisco

Small Exercise 4
Activity, October 1981
A street piece for ESPACE DbD, Los Angeles

315–316 **Exercise 6**
Activity, October 1981
Not realized

Yard
Environment, October–November 1981
Reinvention for *Schwarz*
Kunsthalle Düsseldorf, Dusseldorf

Maybe the Shortest Parade
Activity, November 1981
Sponsored by Washington Project for the Arts
7th Street between E Street and Pennsylvania Avenue, Washington, D.C.

I 4

QUIET PLEASE
(A SOAP OPERA IN 8 PARTS)
(for video tape)

(~~silently~~)

silently going into a room / alone or with one or more others
one person after the other } camera following

staying there as long as desired

camera fixed on door of room [~~cut~~]

person (or group) emerging

~~close up~~ saying something about what happened (~~without sound~~)
(silently mouthing the words

camera close up of mouth [~~cut~~]

each person doing same until all are ~~completed~~ finished

Part 1 of a piece for José-Anne DeKock and Pierre Restany, carried out by ~~myself~~ Coryl Crane and myself, in Paris May 14, 1981

Part II

some friends walking around a block
beginning at different times
going in alternate directions

one friend seeing another from a distance

both stopping, each silently mouthing a message
forming the words again if signalled
both writing them down

continuing around the block
one friend seeing another from a distance
coming closer this time
both stopping, each silently mouthing a longer message
repeating it if signalled
each writing it down

continuing around the block
one friend seeing another from a distance
coming even closer this time
both stopping, each silently mouthing yet a longer message
repeating it if signalled
each writing it down

later sharing the written messages

Part 2 of a piece for José-Anne DeKock and Pierre Restany ~~perfo~~ carried out by them, Coryl Crane and myself, in Paris May 14, 1981 — AK

going: when it's time
staying: at the point of a turn
going: when the wind passes your face
staying: at the descent
going: when the cloud passes the tree
staying: when you have an itch
going: when you hear a word
staying: at the ascent
going: past the edge
staying: when your feet hurt
staying: anyway
going: any way

---

a piece for Marianne, Marcelline and Robert Filliou, carried out by them, Coryl Crane and myself, May 21, 1981, at Pouillac-Le Moustier, France.

— Allan Kaprow

EXERCISE 6

1) (in the street)

some listeners

others, here and there,
each observing a traffic light
(from far or near)

each adjusting their breathing
to its changes

doing this for some time

then moving on to another light
(breathing with its changes)
hammering a nail into a piece of wood
when the light is green

stopping when it's red

repeating process five or six times
each time seeking another light

listeners listening
perhaps following the sources
of the hammering

2) (in a quiet place)

all together

waiting until the quiet is heard

someone, then, hammering a nail into a piece of wood
waiting again to hear the quiet

someone, hammering another nail
waiting..., hammering a nail

repeating process five or six times
until the quiet is very loud

someone, then, taking up an electric saw
cutting into a piece of wood

until someone shouts stop

a.k. 10/81

TEACHING POSITIONS Professor, Visual Arts Department, University of California, San Diego. ¶ **CONSULTING POSITIONS** Consultant/panelist, Interarts Program, National Endowment for the Arts, Washington, D.C. ¶ **GROUP EXHIBITIONS** *Photo recycling Photo; oder, Die Fotografie im Zeitalter ihrer technischen Reproduziebarkeit,* Universität Kassel, Kassel, June. *Performance as Photograph/Photograph as Performance: The Value of Preserving Human Activity,* Grunwald Center for the Graphic Arts at the Frederick S. Wight Gallery, University of California, Los Angeles, September–November. *Wiesbaden Fluxus 1962–1982,* Museum Wiesbaden Nassauischer Kunstverein, Wiesbaden, West Germany (traveled internationally), September–November. *Extended Uses of Photography,* University of California, Los Angeles, October. *Kunst wird Material,* Nationalgalerie, West Berlin, October–December. *Hans Hofmann as Teacher: Drawings by Hofmann and His Students,* organized by the American Federation of Arts, New York (traveled in North America), December 1982–July 1984. ¶ **THEATER** Set design for *Stacked Deck* (a play by Dick Higgins), Los Angeles County Museum of Art, Los Angeles, January. ¶ **WRITINGS** "Anmerkungen zu *Yard,*" in *Kunst wird Material,* exh. cat. (West Berlin: Nationalgalerie), 42–45. "Bilder für die 'ZEIT,' 20.3.1981" (on the *Die Zeit Project* and selected reader responses), in Floris M. Neusüss, ed., *Photo recycling Photo,* exh. cat. (Kassel: Bermuda-Dreieck für Fotografie, Universität Kassel), 36–39. "Company" (Activity score), in Brian Buczak et al., eds., *Black and White* (New York: Money for Food), 21.

1982

317 **Company**
Activity, April 1982
Ballantine Hall, Rutgers University
Reinvented in 1988

Give Me Your Jacket
Activity, July 1982
Sponsored by the 80 Langton Street Workshop Group
Golden Gate Bridge, San Francisco

After Dinner Speeches
Activity, August 1982
De Benneville Pine Camp, De Benneville, California

Yard
Environment, October–December 1982
Reinvention for *Kunst wird Material*
Nationalgalerie, West Berlin

Photoplay
Activity, October–November 1982
Los Angeles and San Diego
Reinvented in 2007 (twice)

Tail Wagging Dog
Activity, December 1982
Sponsored by University of California, San Diego
The hills behind Del Mar, California

Carpet Bagging
Activity, December 1982
Not realized

COMPANY

A person locates a bare room and sits in it for a long time. Then she or he brings into the room a cement block and sits with it for a long time. A second block is brought in, a third, a fourth, a fifth and so on, up to the number corresponding to the person's age. At each addition, the person sits with the blocks for a long time. Then, one by one the blocks are removed. The person sits, as before, at each stage, for a long time, until the room is empty. Then, she or he sits in the empty room.

Allan Kaprow
1981-82

A unique performance prepared especially for the celebration of the 20th Anniversary of Rutgers Visual Arts M.F.A., Mason Gross School of the Arts.

The room and cement blocks will be located through the ground floor door of Ballantine Hall on George Street near Hamilton Street from Monday, April 5th to Thursday, April 15th. There will be a meeting between all the participants and Allan Kaprow on April 15th at 4:30 in Room 204, Downtown Art Building, 358 George Street to share experiences and discuss the work.

To sign up for participation check the door of Ballantine Hall.

317 Score for *Company*

Clean Graffiti
Activity, January 1983
Sponsored by University of California, San Diego
A semi-industrial area east of San Diego

Putting On Your Face
Activity, February 1983
Various locations, University of California, San Diego

Building Muscles
Activity, March 1983
Rancho Santa Fe, California

Give Me Your Money!
Activity, April 1983
University of California, San Diego

Lots of Work
Activity, May 1983
Rancho Santa Fe, California

Six Spots for Television
Television spots, May–June 1983
Presented for *Video as Attitude*
Broadcast on local Santa Fe and Albuquerque television stations

Trading Dirt
Activity, October 1983–September 1985
San Diego and Los Angeles
Reinvented in 1989

1983

LIFE EVENTS Divorced from Vaughan Rachel, April. ¶ TEACHING POSITIONS Professor, Visual Arts Department, University of California, San Diego. ¶ CONSULTING POSITIONS Consultant/panelist, Interarts Program, National Endowment for the Arts, Washington, D.C. ¶ GROUP EXHIBITIONS *Video as Attitude,* Santa Fe Museum of Art, Santa Fe, and the Museum of the University of New Mexico, Albuquerque, May–June. *Video Art: A History, Part Two,* Museum of Modern Art, New York, November. ¶ WRITINGS "Animation" (originally published in 1975) and "Als ich Stephan von Huene und seine Arbeit kennenlernte," in *Stephan von Huene: Klangskulpturen,* exh. cat. (Baden-Baden: Staatliche Kunsthalle Baden-Baden), 8–9, 39. "The Real Experiment," *Artforum* 22, no. 4: 37–43.

ALLAN KAPROW: Text [for LAVA exhibition brochure] "DRAG"

dragging behind you a concrete block

tied to a rope

going on

when meeting someone you know,

picking up the block and

carrying it

going on

when meeting someone you know,

putting down the block and

pushing it ahead of you

going on

when meeting someone you know,

once again dragging the block

behind you

going on

repeating sequence indefinitely or

until there's no more time

[the above in larger-- e.g. 14-point-- type]
[the narrative text to follow beneath, in smaller-- e.g. 8-point-- type]

ALLAN KAPROW: Text-- 2

[The following, beneath the performance instructions, to be set in smaller-- e.g. 8-point-- type]

This piece was an end-of-the-term gift to students in a performance class at U.C. San Diego, in June 1984. The full-size concrete blocks were dragged, carried, and pushed around the university campus for about three hours. I was, as usual, one of the participants. It was slow work, especially the pushing part, when you were either scrunched down on the ground shoving the block with your hands, or nudging it inch-by-inch with your shoe.

Afterwards, some of the group said the blocks became very heavy and exhausting work (few realized they could rest any time they wished...). Some cheated actively by dragging their blocks over pathway steps so that they broke into smaller (and thus lighter) pieces. Others were embarrassed by the absurdity of taking around a mass of cement as if it were a dog on a leash; they sought woods and backways where they wouldn't be seen. Still others went directly to the most public thoroughfares and buildings, where they could be noticed by friends and cause a stir. Everyone understood that such different behaviors might be self-portraits.

I said that it was hard work for me, also, but I enjoyed the revealing conversations I had along the way, conversations that never would have happened if I hadn't been attached to my block by a rope. I was amused as well to see that I'd spread my "burdens" so equitably among my friends; and that they were very good about sharing them.

We didn't get around to talking about the building-block subject matter and its relation to the suburban landscape, but that was part of the piece, too.

--Allan Kaprow

1984

TEACHING POSITIONS Professor, Visual Arts Department, University of California, San Diego. ¶ CONSULTING POSITIONS Consultant/panelist, Interarts Program, National Endowment for the Arts, Washington, D.C. ¶ GROUP EXHIBITIONS Faculty exhibition, Mandeville Gallery, University of California, San Diego, May–June. *Skowhegan Celebration Exhibition,* Hirschl and Adler Modern, New York, May–June. *A Private Act in a Public Place,* Zwerglgartenpavillion, Salzburg, August. *Blam! The Explosion of Pop, Minimalism, and Performance, 1958–1964,* Whitney Museum of American Art, New York, September–December. *Video: A Retrospective,* Long Beach Museum of Art, Long Beach, September–January.

320 Score for *A Private Act in a Public Place*
(with statement)

A PRIVATE ACT IN A PUBLIC PLACE

A Short Note

This environment was arranged collectively by myself and the students of the Experimental Performance class of the International Summer Academy, Salzburg.

We began with a simple plan:
" Find one or more chairs and mirrors, sit down and look at yourself. "
Since we would do this together, and in a gallery, it also meant looking at each other looking at ourselves.
That is a private act in a public place.

When you sit down and think about this or that, you may be reflective (thoughtful).
When you look into a mirror your are reflecting in a different sense:
the mirror takes into itself a part of you;
and when you leave, it gives you up.
Without people, this environment reflects itself.

I want to thank everyone who has taken part in this collaborative experiment:
my assistent Coryl Crane, the members of the class, Stacey Allen, Edda Figl, Oliver Grassmann, Anna Hauer, Anne Hutter, Christine Kaindl, Elisabeth Kamenicek, Gernot Lechner, Bettina Schmeidl-Grubbauer Joachim Wally, Marlene Wiesbauer, Freya Wisböck, Gudrun Zander

and those friends who have contributed furniture, mirrors, valuable assistence and good ideas,
Elfie and Volker Heiß, Ines und Maria Höllwarth, Eva Kiefer, Hans Müller Beppo Pliem, Ina Stegen, Treffpunkt, W.A.B.E., und Barbara Wally.

Allan Kaprow

August 1984

Please Help Yourself
Activity, May 1984
Hirschl and Adler Modern,
New York

318–319 **Drag**
Activity, June 1984
University of California, San Diego
Reinvented in 2007

A Much Better Idea
Activity, July 1984
Rancho Santa Fe, California

320 **A Private Act in a Public Place**
Activity, August 1984
Sponsored by the International Summer Academy
Streets of Salzburg

321–324 **Yard**
Environment, September–December 1984
Reinvention for *Blam!*
Sculpture Court, Whitney Museum of American Art, New York

325–326 **Words**
Environment, September–December 1984
Reinvention for *Blam!*
Whitney Museum of American Art, New York

Aug 12, 84

1200 noon
Corner B'way / Canal (City Bank) (!)
#6 Ave Lex line
RR also (only local)

Dear Barbara —

Your proposal is insane! but as I telegrammed, it's possible if we all can work intensively well before the actual floor work begins. "Words" is the most difficult piece to reassemble because there's so much hands-on work to be done. Here's the general plan.

First: "Yard" can be done in the pit. The proportions are different but can be an advantage for maximum impact. Entry should be from the side wall for appropriate feeling of the scale and mass of tires. A rough wooden fence should be made as sketched on plan, with 3'2" opening accessed by steps.

Inside, we'll need quite a lot of tires: easily 1,000 of them. The walls and floor should be completely covered with tarpaper (though when I see the space again this might be modified somewhat). Wooden inner forms to cover with tarpaper and rope will be constructed in the floor areas, as approximately indicated on plan, i.e.

tarpaper

forms, say, 10' high

note: each mound is different in height and volume

to be anchored to floor

Vincent Hum

So, what must be arranged in advance are: used tires to be delivered and removed (dumps don't like to have them back!); enough rolls of tarpaper to cover space and mounds (3 rolls are sufficient, I think, for the mounds alone); 1,000 feet roll of heavy hemp twine 3/16" thick approximately; enough scrap wood (2"x4"'s, 2"x3"'s, 2"x2"'s for the inner forms, plus anchoring tape to adhere to the floor (or equivalent method); rough construction lumber (used if possible) for the fence and steps; wire mesh for the fence, say, 8'x16' of it. (The fence will keep

2/ the tires inside, since people will play with them and otherwise throw them outside into the galleries....)

Second: "Words" was, and should be, ~~small in scale~~; it needs psychological compression to make sense. It had two spaces: a "public" one full of "noise", auditory and visual; and a "private" one, smaller yet, darker, and quiet — both roughly equivalent to everyone's outer and inner experiences. So, I've reduced the space you've allowed by cutting off the triangle in it (as you'll see by the plan modification I'm sending back). That gives us a room 9'x10', and one 10'x7'; about the same as the original. Outside the entry was a cardboard sign in the form of a 5 or 6' box of cartonboard lit from within with the cut-out words in freehand saying "Words" — see the photo in my book.

Inside the public room were word-strips randomly combined in rows covering the walls. On the far wall separating the larger from the smaller room, were two flanking cloth rolls with words stencilled on them. (These were to be rolled and aligned, or not, ad lib.) Tacked to a center pole were stacks of additional word strips, to be taken by visitors and added (by staple guns provided along the walls) to those already there on the walls. Throughout the space were roughly torn cartonboard signs advising you to "make words!" "roll the rolls!" etc. A stepladder was provided for this process; at any moment three or four people could be tacking away.... ¶At the same time, around the center post (a 2"x2") were small tables with three children's record players; and signs advising one to play one or more of them at any time, singly or at once. These players had records of me saying words in various ways set upon their turntables.

Around the top edge of this public room were alternating red + white 25 watt bulbs flashing on and off (like a second-hand car lot, I thought). These added to the visual noise. (PLEASE SEE P. 6 FOR DRAWING)

The second, private, room was entered by a central doorway

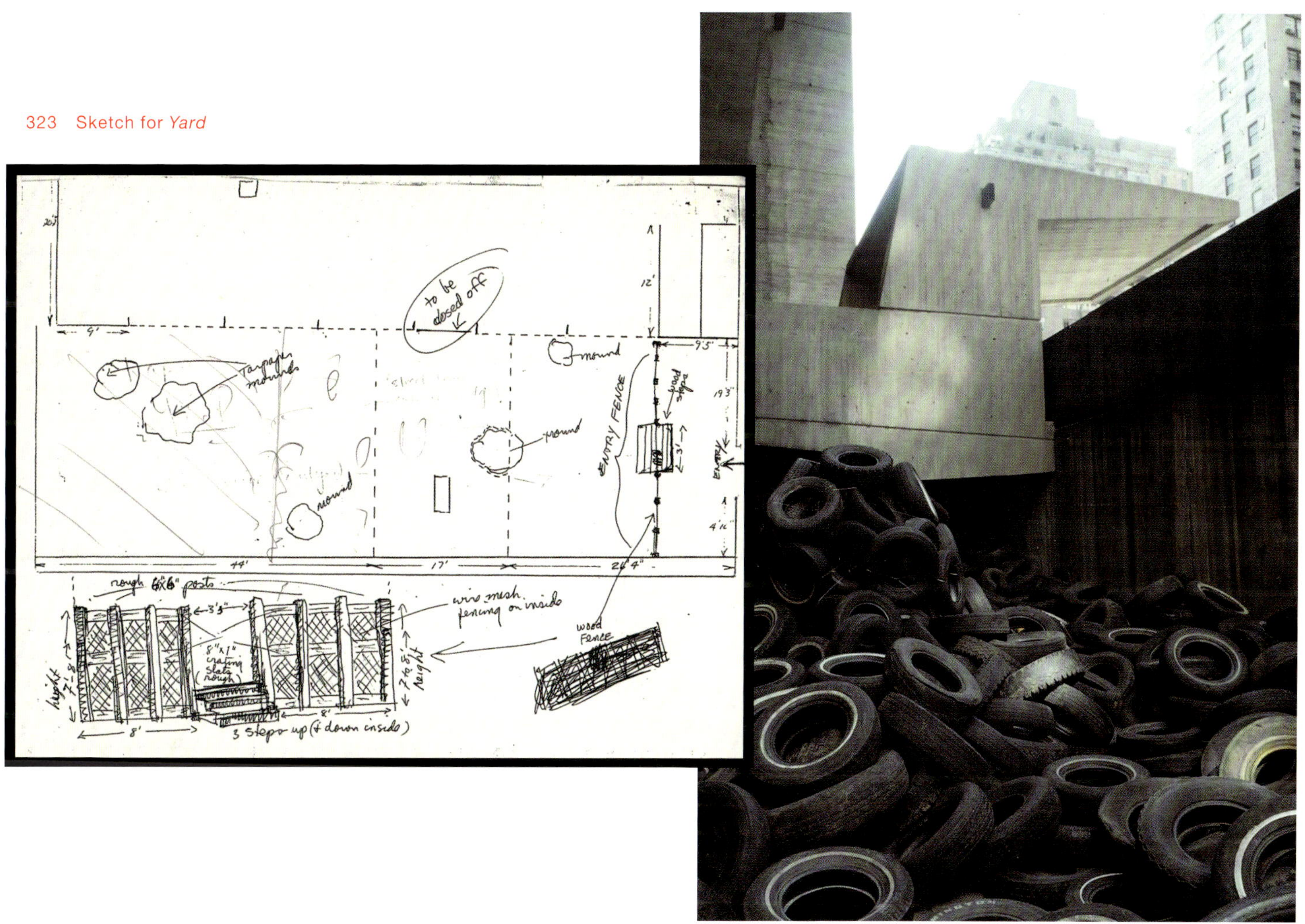

323 Sketch for *Yard*

324 *Yard*

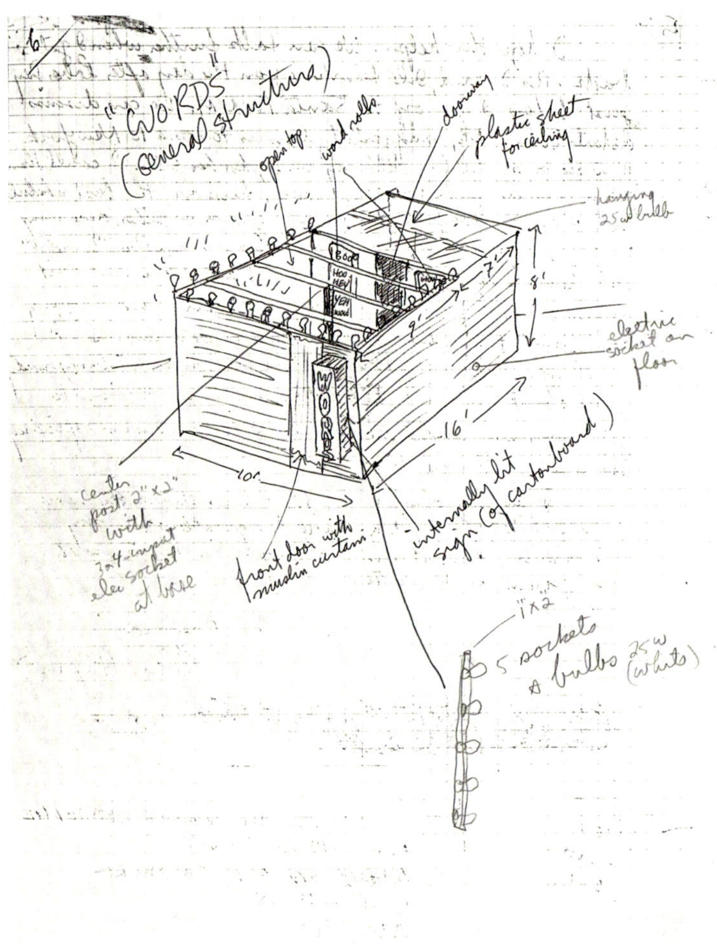

325 Sketch for *Words*

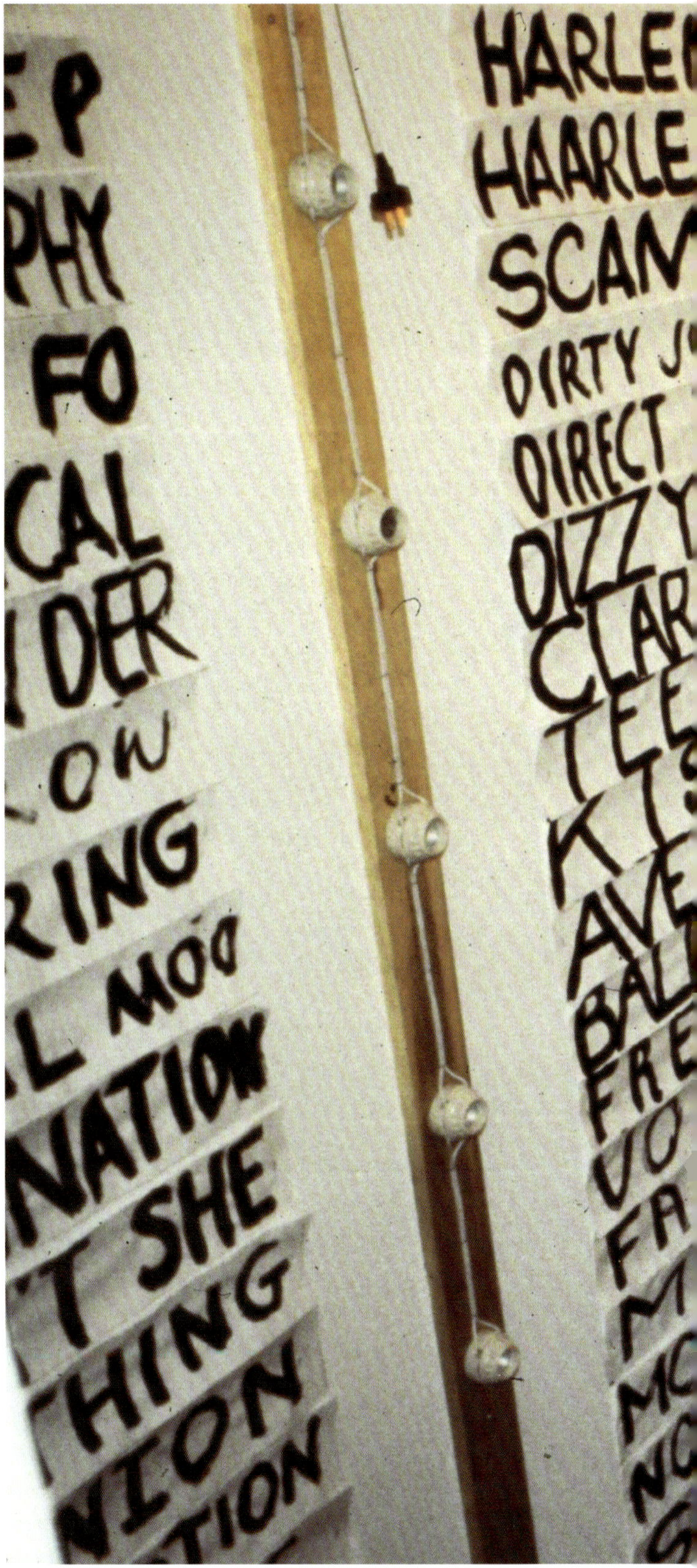

326 *Words*

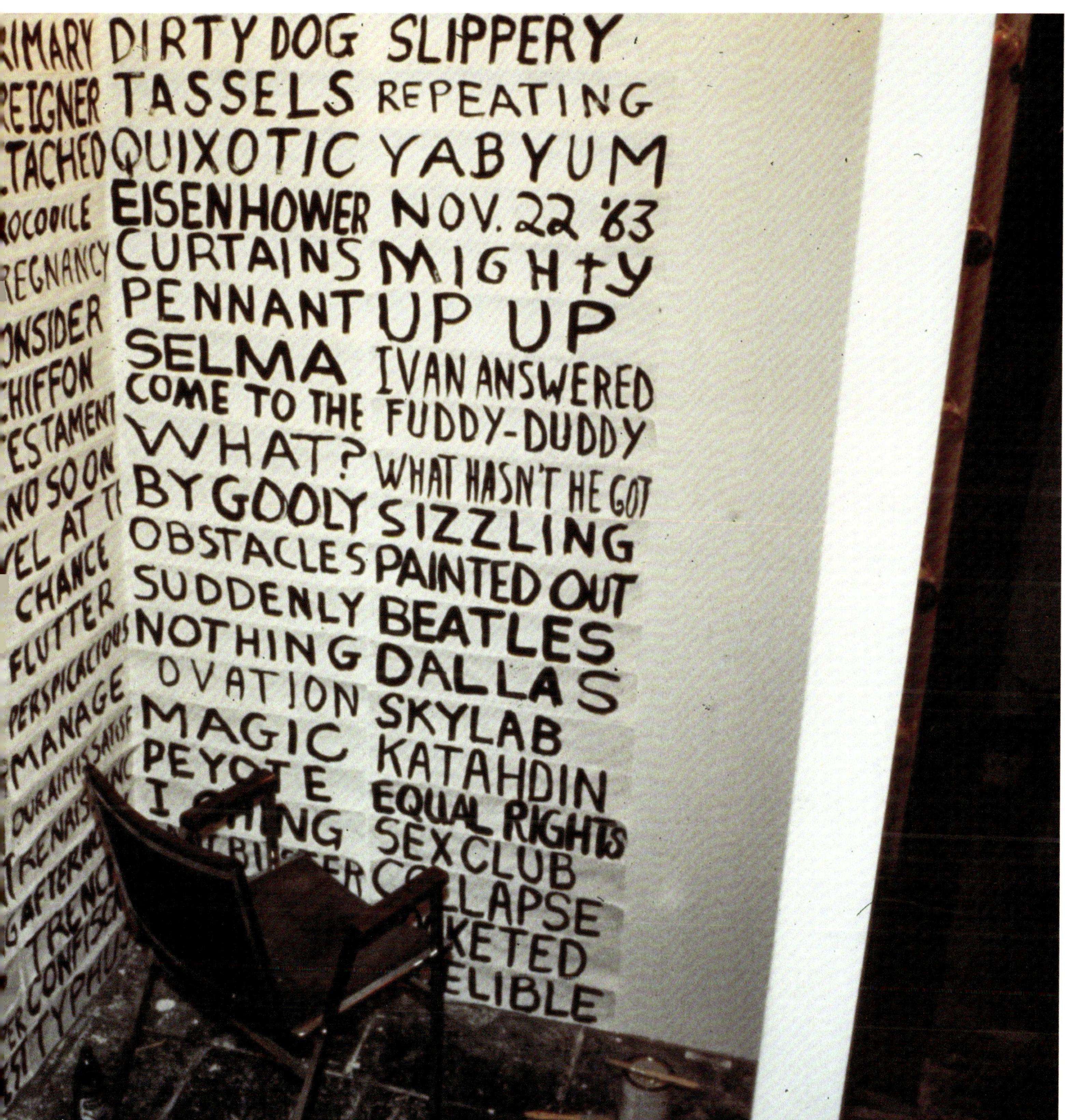

DIRTY DOG
TASSELS
QUIXOTIC
EISENHOWER
CURTAINS
PENNANT
SELMA
COME TO THE
WHAT?
BY GOOLY
OBSTACLES
SUDDENLY
NOTHING
OVATION
MAGIC
SLIPPERY
REPEATING
YABYUM
NOV. 22 '63
MIGHTY
UP UP
IVAN ANSWERED
FUDDY-DUDDY
WHAT HASN'T HE GOT
SIZZLING
PAINTED OUT
BEATLES
DALLAS
SKYLAB
KATAHDIN
EQUAL RIGHTS
SEX CLUB
CHANCE
FLUTTER
PERSPICACIOUS
MANAGE

TEACHING POSITIONS Department Chair and Professor, Visual Arts Department, University of California, San Diego. ¶ CONSULTING POSITIONS Consultant/panelist, Interarts Program, National Endowment for the Arts, Washington, D.C. ¶ GROUP EXHIBITIONS *To the Astonishing Horizon: New Approaches to Landscape by Southern Californians,* Design Center of Los Angeles, Los Angeles, January–February. *Fotografie, Geduld und Langeweile,* Goethe Institute, Paris, March–April. *Wirken und Wirkung: Ein Salut von 80 Künstlern,* DAADgalerie, West Berlin, November–January. *Zugehend auf eine Biennale des Friedens,* Kunsthaus und Kunstverein Hamburg, Hamburg, December–January. ¶ WRITINGS Notes and photographs from the *Die Zeit Project,* in Renate Heyne, ed., *Fotografie, Geduld und Langeweile = Photographie, patience et ennui,* exh. cat. (Paris: Goethe-Institut), 12–14. ¶ INTERVIEWS "Environments and Happenings" (previously unpublished transcript of a radio interview with Allan Kaprow and George Segal), in Jeanne Siegel, *Artworks: Discourse on the 60s and 70s* (Ann Arbor: UMI Research), 166–78.

1985

A Sea Event
Activity, February 1985
Scripps Institute of Oceanography, La Jolla, California

René Block Said Don't Call This the Milky Way and I Agreed
Activity, December 1985–January 1986
Presented for *Zugehend auf eine Biennale des Friedens*
Kunsthaus und Kunstverein Hamburg, Hamburg

Spit
Activity, December 1985
Hochschule für Kunst, Hamburg
Reinvented as *Another Spit Piece* in 2007

Piece for Coryl's Birthday
Activity, December 1985
Encinitas, California

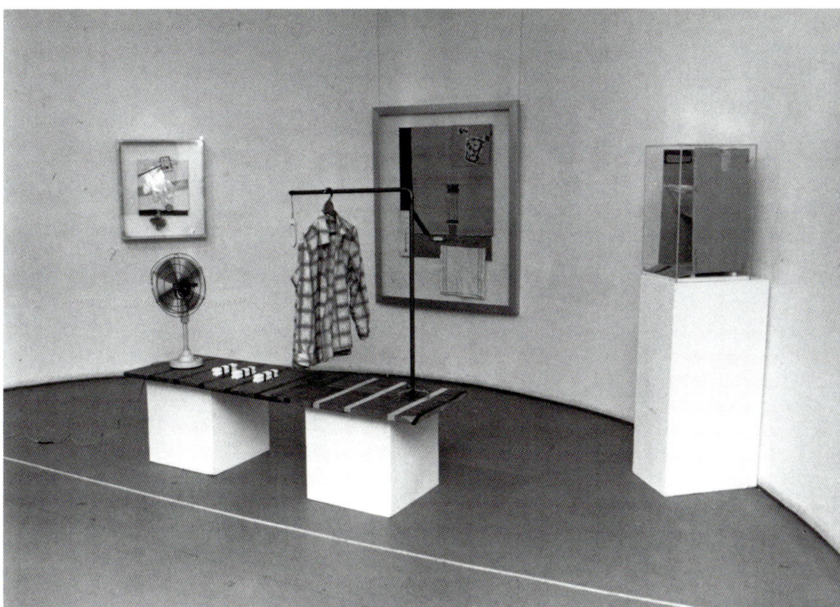

327 Installation view of *Allan Kaprow*

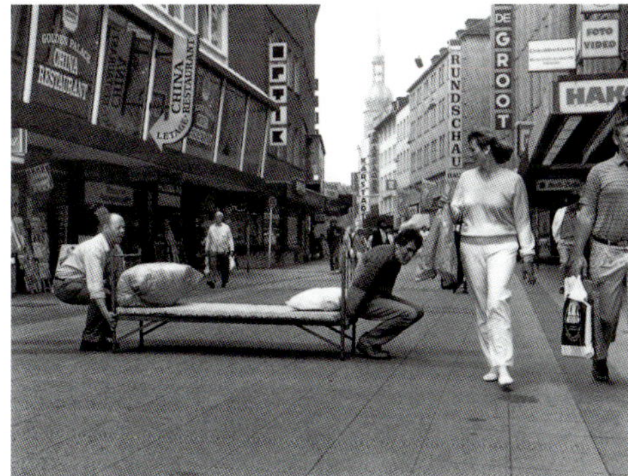

328 *The Perfect Bed*

1986

TEACHING POSITIONS Department chair and Professor, Visual Arts Department, University of California, San Diego. ¶ CONSULTING POSITIONS Consultant/panelist, Interarts Program, National Endowment for the Arts, Washington, D.C. ¶ AWARDS Arties Award from Franklin Furnace "for dissolving the boundaries between art and life, artist and audience, and arts disciplines." ¶ SOLO EXHIBITIONS *Allan Kaprow: Collagen, Environments, Videos, Broschüren, Geschichten, Happening- und Activity-Dokumente, 1956–1986,* Museum am Ostwall, Dortmund, West Germany, August–October. ¶ GROUP EXHIBITIONS *Sammlung Feelisch Privat,* Museum am Ostwall, Dortmund, West Germany, February–March. *Das Automobil in der Kunst, 1886–1986: Malerei, Graphik, Skulptur, Happening, Plakat, Karikatur, Photographie, Trivialkunst, Design, Architektur,* Haus der Kunst, Munich, August–October. *Die 60er Jahre: Kölns Weg zur Kunstmetropole: Vom Happening zum Kunstmarkt,* Kölnischer Kunstverein, Cologne, August–November. *Fröhliche Wissenschaft: Das Archiv Sohm,* Staatsgalerie, Stuttgart, November–January. ¶ FESTIVALS La Comida del Arte, Venice, California, October. ¶ WRITINGS "Art Which Can't Be Art" and "Stories: 1981–1985," in *Allan Kaprow: Collagen, Environments, Videos, Broschüren, Geschichten, Happening- und Activity-Dokumente, 1956–1986,* exh. cat. (Dortmund: Museum am Ostwall), 17–19, 117–19. "Postscript to *Useful Fictions*" (includes score), *The Act* 1, no. 1: 7–13.

327–332 **The Perfect Bed**
Activity, August–October 1986
Presented for *Allan Kaprow*
Various streets, Dortmund, West Germany

333 **Sweet Wall**
Activity, August–October 1986
Reinvention for *Allan Kaprow*
Museum am Ostwall, Dortmund, West Germany

Self-Service
Happening, August–October 1986
Reinvention for *Allan Kaprow*
Museum am Ostwall, Dortmund, West Germany

Sawdust
Activity, August–October 1986
Reinvention for *Allan Kaprow*
Museum am Ostwall, Dortmund, West Germany

Fresh Air
Environment, August–October 1986
Reinvention of *Untitled Environment* (1958) for *Allan Kaprow*
Museum am Ostwall, Dortmund, West Germany

Yard
Environment, August–October 1986
Reinvention for *Allan Kaprow*
Museum am Ostwall, Dortmund, West Germany

UNIVERSITY OF CALIFORNIA, SAN DIEGO

BERKELEY · DAVIS · IRVINE · LOS ANGELES · RIVERSIDE · SAN DIEGO · SAN FRANCISCO SANTA BARBARA · SANTA CRUZ

VISUAL ARTS DEPARTMENT (B-027) LA JOLLA, CALIFORNIA 92093

Jan 6, 86

Dear Wolfgang —

It was wonderful seeing you in Hamburg! I'm glad we had a chance to talk about the coming exhibition in a quiet atmosphere. The general plan is much clearer now. As you requested, here is a basic structure for the show — and later we can shift around the details.

The exhibition can contain five parts: selected pictorial works from 1956–58 (I would eliminate the work of the previous decade 1945–55 as it is a bit traditional); three reconstructed "environments"; a selection of Activity programs (booklets and photomontages); a selection of films and videotapes of Activities; and a new event to occur outside of the Museum.

1) Pictorial Works (1956–1958) (Essentially those in European collections)

A) Modernes Museum, Palais Liechtenstein, Vien: "Baby" (large collage).
B) Centre Pompidou, Paris: "Stained Glass Window" (large collage).
C) Städt. Museum, Mönchengladbach: "Untitled" (large collage).
D) Sammlung H. Peeters, Brugge: "Tobacco King", "Hysteria", "Kiosk" (small collage; large collage; assemblage) Please contact Herr Peeters soon; I heard that he has sold the "Kiosk"!
E) Sammlung Feelisch, Remscheid: (diverse collages/assemblages)
F) Collection A. Kaprow (in Galerie Baecker, Köln), "Veronica" (medium size collage)

P. 2 / Feelisch

UNIVERSITY OF CALIFORNIA, SAN DIEGO

BERKELEY · DAVIS · IRVINE · LOS ANGELES · RIVERSIDE · SAN DIEGO · SAN FRANCISCO SANTA BARBARA · SANTA CRUZ

VISUAL ARTS DEPARTMENT (B-027) LA JOLLA, CALIFORNIA 92093

Jan 6, '86 cont'd.

2) Selected Documents, paste-ups, Booklets (scores) of Activities (1957(?)–1986)
(Items to be decided later) (approximately ten for walls and vitrines)

3) Selected Films and Video tapes (1974–1984)
(Items to be decided later) (approx. five for daily showing on videotape only — including film by Karl Gerbe — so please contact him in Bochum ....

4) Reconstructed Environments
A) "Words", 1962
B) "Eat", 1963
C) "Push and Pull", 1963

5) New Piece
(For friends; documents to be seen in Museum, perhaps via telephone, video, reports, communiqués ....)

. . . .

The exhibition, as I understand, will open in autumn 1986. Mid-September would be best for my university duties (as you know I'm the chairman of the Department and it's extremely difficult for me to be absent for too long). I should come to Dortmund in the latter part of May for a preliminary, short 1-week meeting with you and Dr. Thiemann, to look at the museum space and to fix all details.*

Regarding the catalogue, which we discussed, its structure can parallel that of the exhibition, in 5 parts, with photos and texts from each part. (You should contact the collectors and museums which

* Then, in the latter part of August I would come to actually work on the exhibition.

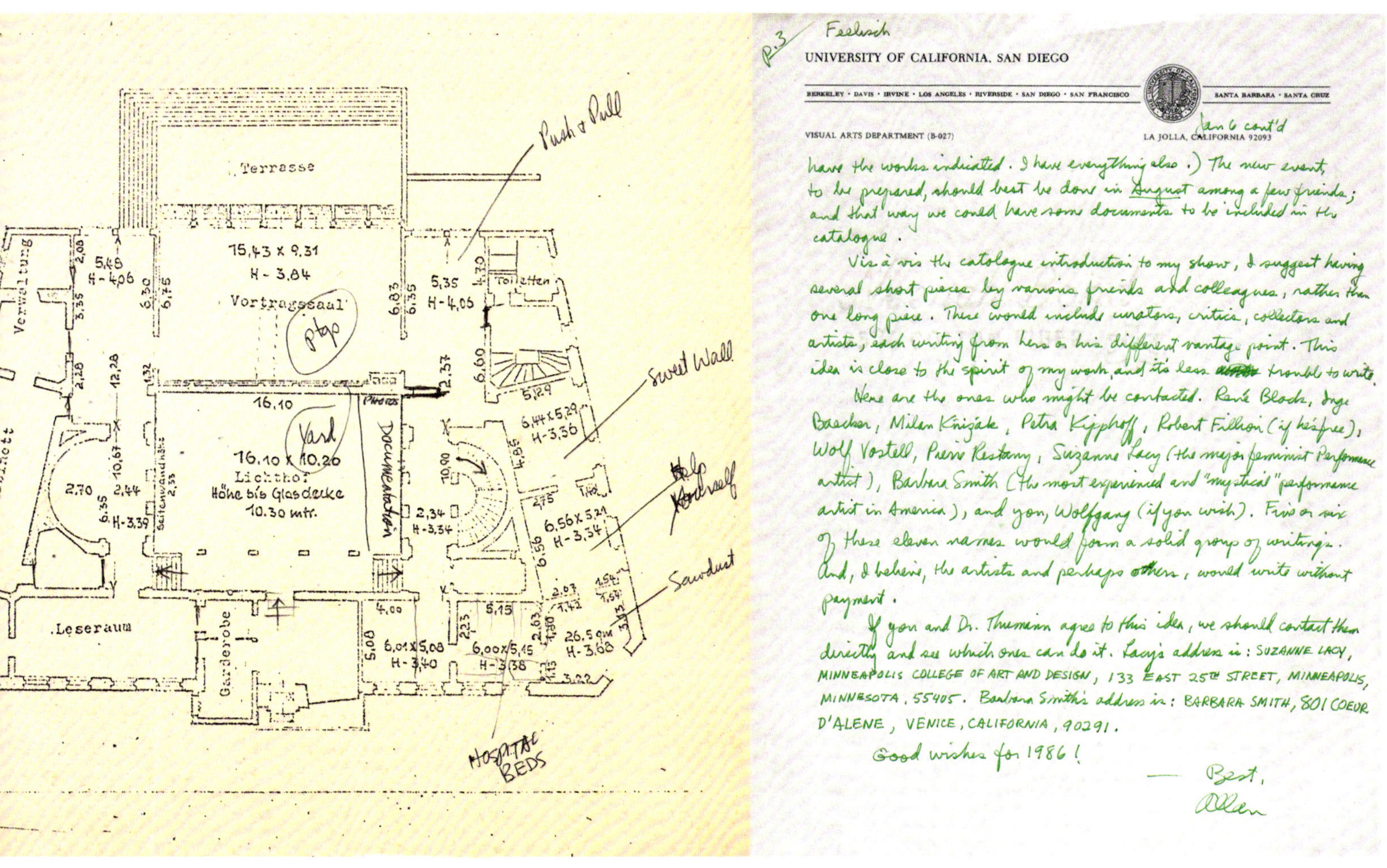

p. 3 Feelisch

UNIVERSITY OF CALIFORNIA, SAN DIEGO

BERKELEY · DAVIS · IRVINE · LOS ANGELES · RIVERSIDE · SAN DIEGO · SAN FRANCISCO · SANTA BARBARA · SANTA CRUZ

VISUAL ARTS DEPARTMENT (B-027) LA JOLLA, CALIFORNIA 92093

Jan 6 cont'd

have the works indicated. I have everything else.) The new event, to be prepared, should best be done in August among a few friends; and that way we could have some documents to be included in the catalogue.

Vis à vis the catalogue introduction to my show, I suggest having several short pieces by various friends and colleagues, rather than one long piece. These would include curators, critics, collectors and artists, each writing from hers or his different vantage point. This idea is close to the spirit of my work, and it's less trouble to write.

Here are the ones who might be contacted. René Block, Inge Baecker, Milan Knížák, Petra Kipphoff, Robert Filliou (if he's free), Wolf Vostell, Pierre Restany, Suzanne Lacy (the major feminist Performance artist), Barbara Smith (the most experienced and "mystical" performance artist in America), and you, Wolfgang (if you wish). Five or six of these eleven names would form a solid group of writings. And, I believe, the artists and perhaps others, would write without payment.

If you and Dr. Thiemann agree to this idea, we should contact them directly and see which ones can do it. Lacy's address is: SUZANNE LACY, MINNEAPOLIS COLLEGE OF ART AND DESIGN, 133 EAST 25TH STREET, MINNEAPOLIS, MINNESOTA, 55405. Barbara Smith's address is: BARBARA SMITH, 801 COEUR D'ALENE, VENICE, CALIFORNIA, 90291.

Good wishes for 1986!

— Best,
Allan

Push and Pull

Environment, August–October 1986
Reinvention for *Allan Kaprow*
Museum am Ostwall, Dortmund, West Germany

The Conference as Performance

Activity, October 1986
In a conference room, Richmond Museum of Art, Richmond, Virginia

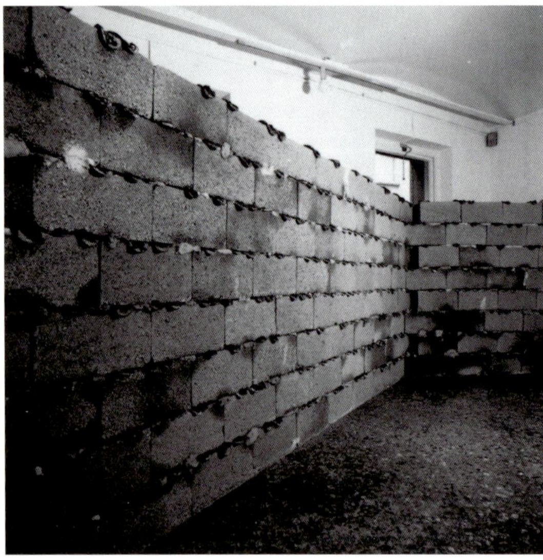

333 *Sweet Wall*

334–335 **Apples and Oranges**

Activity, October 1986
Presented for La Comida del Arte
Venice, California
Reinvented in 2006

334 Score for *Apples and Oranges*

APPLES and ORANGES
(For Barbara Smith)

1) Two persons are matched, and will appear at an address at a certain time.

They'll be directed to a room. On a table, lying on a plate, is some bread. On another plate are some dollar bills.

One person takes the bread. The other, the money.

2) Whoever takes the bread leaves the house and, by breaking the bread into tiny bits, drops a trail of crumbs to somewhere, and waits.

Whoever takes the money waits ten minutes, then goes outside to follow the trail of bread crumbs.

While following the trail, the dollar bills are torn into tiny bits like the bread crumbs, and are dropped along the way.

The two persons meet if possible; but both will return to the house within exactly 45 minutes of their arrival.

3) The two will be directed to a room. On a table are two plates as before, with bread and money on them, respectively. One person will give the bread to the other. The other will give the money.

. . . . . .

Note: There is usually no need for prior guidance in such pieces as this. But since I will not see the participants beforehand, one condition may be urged: notice everything! At 10:30 PM there will be a review and discussion. This is part of the piece.

- ak

CONJUNCTIONS OF FOOD AND ART

ARTWEEK
NOV. 16, 1986

Venice, CA / **Ruth Askey**

Three presentations in the *La Comida Del Arte* series proved that performance events can be either rarefied experiences or annoying interludes. Produced by Barbara Smith and performed by six artists during a six-month period, this "food/art series" has three more events ahead: Shiro Ikegawa on November 22, Sheila Pinkel on December 20 and Leslie Labowitz on January 24, 1987.

Money and food were the focus of the three initial participatory events. Richard Newton's *Drive-in Saturday Night* kicked off the season with hourly shows on two nights. In this piece, the accoutrements were the best part, the food and the "movie," disappointing. Old Cadillac convertibles were arranged to face a film screen in the corner of a Venice school playground. The night was beautiful. A big moon hung over the Marina del Rey highrises, and the night had an end-of-summer chill. Traffic assistants dressed in Russian uniforms directed car parking and unloading, guiding groups of viewers to waiting Eldorados with their tops down. (It was thirty dollars a carload, so if you got a big car and five friends together, it came to five dollars each. More about money later.) As soon as the film began, cute French-style waitresses hurriedly served dry, unidentifiable sandwiches in baskets. The film was an outpouring of meaningless clips that included 1930s cartoons like *Heckle and Jeckle*, meandering art talk and repeated shots of Charles Christopher Hill, up to his neck in water, saying "When I'm warm, I'm happy." We weren't. Newton's concept was attractive but the content was disappointing.

In contrast, Barbara Smith's performance was a thoughtful, meditative event followed by a sumptuous dinner. Fall winds swept through her garden as we took seats around a burning pit. Titled *Ting: The Cauldron*, the performance

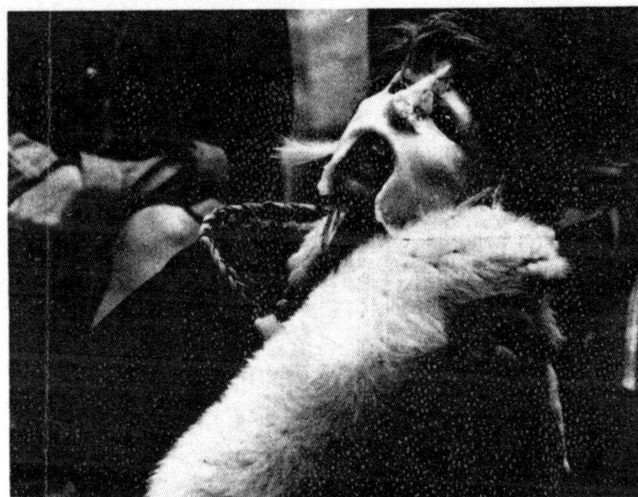

Barbara Smith, *Ting: The Cauldron*, 1986, performance, Venice, CA. Photo: David Friedman.

evoked mystical ritual as Smith paced and undulated to sounds drawn from musical history. Taped African, Greek, Andalusian, Renaissance and modern music was the background for the chanting sounds and songlike cries of Smith and four women who represented the cardinal points—East, West, South and North. Faces covered with half-masks suggested animal heads, and talismans hung from the women's clothes like good-luck pieces. Their self-designed costumes were decorated with crystals, feathers, iridescent shells, horns, fur and beads. In the final moments, Smith took a baked squash from the smoking pit, broke its enclosing clay shell and cut it open. She served it with dried fruit, saying that the mixture represented a melding of sun-ripened fruits with earth-grown vegetables—male and female symbols uniting. We ate from individual seashells, and wine was served. The meditation ended and the banquet began. We moved to tables where garlic-drenched steamed shrimp were passed out, along with a salad of carrot, papaya, melon and red onion, corn in husks, steamed halibut, more squash and, for dessert, pumpkin cake and whipped cream mixed with candied ginger and apricot liqueur. In four hours, we'd enjoyed a spiritual ritual, eaten delicious food and talked to friends.

Allan Kaprow's "artlike life" piece melded natural experiences, social interaction and self-analysis. *Apples and Oranges* was a joyful event. The night was warm and balmy; matched partners met and determined which would take a loaf of bread and which would tear up five one-dollar bills. Both would leave a trail—bread first, followed by the torn dollar bills—through the streets of Venice Beach. Partners could meet again along the way or back at the starting place, at Smith's house. Everyone was concerned about tearing up money and littering, yet walking around a neighborhood filled with well-tended, pre-1930 bungalows, friendly people and good air was a happy experience. When we returned empty-handed, there was another loaf of bread and five more dollar bills to be divided. Each of us had different neighborhood experiences. A business substructure formed, made up of little boys with paper bags who collected the pieces of dollar bills in hopes of gluing them together. In the evening, the group met to discuss the event. Each participant was expected to pay at least ten dollars for this performance and, at the door, was asked to donate an additional amount—up to thirty dollars—that s/he felt the performance would be worth. Everyone had different rationales. "Well, all I had was $11.39 so that's what you got." "It's a Kaprow event, so it's worth $27.50 and not a penny more!" "I couldn't really afford the ten dollars, so I didn't tear up all the dollar bills and kept a couple." Kaprow feels that "the purpose of lifelike art is therapeutic, to reintegrate the piecemeal reality we take for granted. Not just intellectually, but directly, as experience—in this moment, in this house."

Early publicity for *La Comida Del Arte* said that the charge for each event would be thirty dollars. Complaints about the price came from everyone, and the cost was modified somewhat with Newton's "carload bargain" and Kaprow's "pay what it's worth" approach. At thirty dollars, however, Smith's ceremony/banquet was a hot value. It was an afternoon to be remembered.☐

For further information about times and locations of events in this series, call 213-687-7302.

335 Review of *Apples and Oranges*

1987

LIFE EVENTS Married Coryl Crane, February. ¶ TEACHING POSITIONS Department chair and Professor, Visual Arts Department, University of California, San Diego. ¶ CONSULTING POSITIONS Consultant/panelist, Interarts Program, National Endowment for the Arts, Washington, D.C. ¶ GROUP EXHIBITIONS *Grüsse an Beuys von 199 Künstlern,* Städtisches Museum Haus Koekkoek, Kleve, West Germany, February–March. *Sieben Künstler des DAAD, Berlin,* Zellermeyer Galerie, West Berlin, March–April. *Models and Concepts for the Arena,* Museum of Seasonal Change project, Imperial Bank Building, San Diego, April–May. *Auf ein Wort!: Aspekte Visueller Poesie und Visueller Musik,* Gutenberg Museum Mainz, Mainz, West Germany (traveled in Germany), May–August. *A Tribute to John Cage,* Carl Solway Gallery, Chicago International Art Exposition, Chicago, May. *Berlinart, 1961–1987,* Museum of Modern Art, New York (traveled nationally), June–September. *Documenta 8,* Museum Fridericianum and the Orangerie, Kassel, June–September. ¶ WRITINGS "Apples and Oranges" (Activity score), in *La Comida del Arte: A Food/Art Series* (Venice, Calif.: Barbara Smith), n.p. "The Conference as Performance," *Dialogue* 10, no. 6: 23–25, 27. Excerpt from "Homework," in "The Future of Hedonism and Sport," special issue, *New Observations,* no. 46: 8–9. "February 1, 1987: Letter" and "Right Living," in Arthur Solway, Carl Solway, and Allan Kaprow, eds., *A Tribute to John Cage: Prepared Box for John Cage,* exh. cat. (Cincinnati: Carl Solway Gallery), 41a–41b.

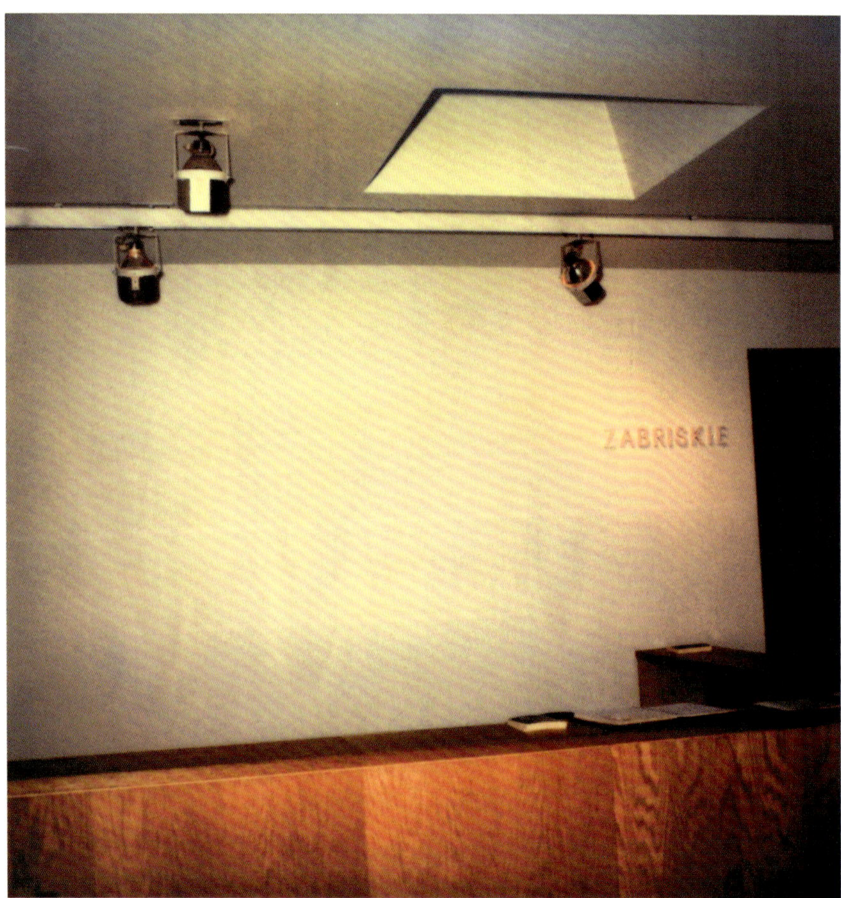

336 Front desk at the Zabriskie Gallery

ZABRISKIE GALLERY
724 FIFTH AVENUE, NEW YORK 10019
(212) 307-7430

October 14, 1987

"Office Boy"
Nov., 1987

Alan Kaprow
4975 Saratoga Avenue
Dan Diego, CA 92107

Dear Alan:

This is to confirm our agreement to employ you as a gallery assistant for two weeks, November 16-28. Your pay will be $750 for this period, or $75 per day. Your hours will be 10:00 AM - 6:00 PM, working Monday through Friday of the first week, and Monday-Wednesday, and Friday-Saturday of the second (that Thursday is Thanksgiving, when even Zabriskie is closed). You will work at the front desk, and will be trained by Editha Carpenter, who recently has moved to New York from our Paris gallery. I expect you to become friendly with our computer terminal at this station. I enclose a polaroid of your future post. Your job requirements include a neat appearance and courteous demeanor, the ability to say "No" to a range of frequently asked questions (e.g., May I use your bathroom?, Are you looking at slides?, Can you get to other galleries by the stairs?, Can you add me to the mailing list?), and highly developed lunch delivery skills. Should things not work out at "the front" you will be tranfered to "the back", where you will assist in the tracking, packing, and moving of art, both light and heavy. I think, Alan, that this will be a fine learning experience as you enter the art world of the late eighties, and I look forward to assisting in you re-education.

Sincerely,

Virginia

Virginia M. Zabriskie
VMZ/bja

ZABRISKIE GALLERY
724 FIFTH AVENUE, NEW YORK 10019
(212) 307-7430

December 19, 1987

Dear Alan:

I thought that you might want to hear a couple of anecdotes about your time here. First, the woman who owns the David Smith drawings, Gloria Gil, was in with her daughter, Sally. Gloria loved the way the show was hung (and actually commented on the placement of the numbers above the pictures, remarking that it made it more like book pages), and when I told them that you had hung and lit the show, Sally excitedly said that you had been her teacher at UCSD. Nice coincidence, I think.

More to the point of developing gossip, last night I was at a party and speaking with Carolee Schneeman. She said that she had been at a party or dinner in late November and people were talking about how you now were working at Zabriskie. No one knew what the story was, but she said that there was speculation of your having left teaching and now had gotten a job in a gallery -- a real change of life sort of thing. I loved it. So word did get around in interesting ways.

I hope that this finds you and Coryl well, and enjoying the holidays. Happy New Year to you both.

Sincerely,

Bruce

Bruce Altshuler

Home
(212) 982-7836
Holly Hughes

337 Letter from Virginia Zabriskie
338 Letter from Bruce Altshuler

Burdens
Activity, March 1987
Sponsored by Pennsylvania State University Museum of Art
Various public places, including shopping centers and cafeterias, University Park, Pennsylvania

Whether Weather
Model, April–May 1987
For *Models and Concepts for the Arena*
Imperial Bank, San Diego

Red Carpet for the Public
Activity, June–September 1987
Presented for *Documenta 8*
Museum Fridericianum, Kassel

Blending into the Environment
Activity, June–September 1987
Presented for *Documenta 8*
On the stairs between the Operaplatz and the Orangerie, Kassel

336–338 **Office Boy**
Activity, November 1987
Zabriskie Gallery, New York

1988

LIFE EVENTS Bram Adam Crane-Kaprow, son, born September. ¶ **TEACHING POSITIONS** Professor, Visual Arts Department, University of California, San Diego. ¶ **SOLO EXHIBITIONS** *Allan Kaprow: Precedings,* Center for Research in Contemporary Art, University of Texas, Arlington, April. ¶ **GROUP EXHIBITIONS** *Marcel Duchamp und die Avantgarde seit 1950,* Museum Ludwig, Cologne, January–March. *Affiches, Collages, Décollages,* Galerie Zabriskie, Paris, May–June. *Art after Silence,* Walters Hall Gallery, Rutgers University, June–July. ¶ **WRITINGS** "Horse Feathers Still," in *Nouveau Realistes,* exh. cat. (New York: Zabriskie Gallery), 7–9. "Piece for Museum" (includes 1961 and 1987 versions in both German and English) and "Interview with Dieter Daniels," in *Übrigens sterben immer die Anderen: Marcel Duchamp und die Avantgarde seit 1950,* exh. cat. (Cologne: Museum Ludwig), 194, 195–211.

PRECEDINGS

The conversion of an event into an exhibit becomes a species of mythology. 1975

An artist concerned with "life-like" art is an artist who does and doesn't make art. 1986

Allan Kaprow

"Precedings," a retrospective reinvention of selected 'happenings' by Allan Kaprow, will take place April 12th through the 16th, 1988, at the UTA Center for Research in Contemporary Art (CRCA), University of Texas at Arlington. Organized by CRCA with major financial support from the Lannan Foundation, and with technical support from the UTA Media Center, **"Precedings"** will examine 30 years of Kaprow's "life-like" art events.

Over a four-night period - from Tuesday, April 12th through Friday, April 15th - Kaprow will "reinvent his career" in the form of four lecture/performances, to be held in the Studio Theatre of the UTA Fine Arts Building. During the days, several 'activities,' including "Sweeping" (1962) and "Company" (1985) will take place on or near the grounds of UTA.

Following these, on Saturday, April 16th, a two-part symposium called "Precedings: Art as Participation, 1958 - 1988" will be held at UTA, also in the Studio Theatre. Besides Mr. Kaprow, its participants will include: David Antin, Franticek Deak, Michael Kirby, Jeff Kelley, Suzanne Lacy, Lucy Lippard, Robert C. Morgan, Claes Oldenburg, Jim Pomeroy, Moira Roth, George Segal, Richard Schechner, Ingrid Sischy, and Barbara Smith. The symposium will be composed of two panels which will consider the changing nature of participation in art prior to and since 1970, and will thereby extend the questions raised by Kaprow's life-like art.

Events Schedule: Activities & Lecture/Performances

Date	Time	What	Where
Mon, Mar 28, through Wed, April 13	8 hour intervals	"Company," 1985*	Stairwell UTA Art Dept
Tues, April 12	8 pm	Lecture/Performance #1: *"The Art/Life Frame"*	Studio Theatre UTA
Wed, Apr 13	1 pm	First Participants Meeting for "Sweeping," 1962**	Studio Theatre UTA
	8 pm	Lecture/Performance #2: *"The Making of Meaning and the Experience of Meaning-Making"*	Studio Theatre UTA
Thurs, Apr 14	1 pm	Participants Meeting for "Company"	Studio Theatre UTA
	8 pm	Lecture/Performance #3: *"The Social, Personal Ethical, and Artistic Implications of 'Life-Like' Art"*	Studio Theatre UTA
Fri, Apr 15	1 pm	Second Participants Meeting for "Sweeping"	Studio Theatre UTA
	8 pm	Lecture/Performance #4: *"The Reinvention of One's Past, and the Transformation of a Present Self."*	Studio Theatre UTA

* Contact UTA Art Department at (817) 273-2891 about sign-up times; reservations will be taken for 8 hour blocks.

** Mr. Kaprow requests that you bring something to sweep with.

A Symposium: "Art as Participation, 1958-88"

Date	Time	What	Where
Sat, April 16	9:00 am	Coffee	Studio Theatre
	9:30 am	Welcome: Jeff Kelley	
	9:45 am	Introduction: David Antin	
	10:05 am	Panel Discussion: "Art as Participation: the '50s & '60s" Panelists: David Antin (Moderator), Franticek Deak, Allan Kaprow, Michael Kirby, Claes Oldenburg, George Segal, Richard Schechner, & Barbara Smith.	
	11:30 am	Audience Questions	
	12:00 pm	Lunch	
	2:00 pm	Welcome Back: Jeff Kelley	
	2:15 pm	Introduction: Robert C. Morgan	
	2:35 pm	Panel Discussion: "Art as Participation: the '70s & '80s" Panelists: Moira Roth (Moderator), Allan Kaprow, Jeff Kelley, Suzanne Lacy, Lucy Lippard, Robert C. Morgan, Jim Pomeroy, & Ingrid Sischy.	
	4:00 pm	Audience Questions	
	4:30 pm	Summary: Moira Roth	

All events are free and open to the public

CPS-3-88

Precedings is a retrospective consideration of 30 years of Allan Kaprow's "life-like" art and critical writing

Tues. Apr 12, through Sat. Apr 16, 1988 Studio Theatre, Fine Arts Building, and the grounds of UTA

UTA Center for Research in Contemporary Art (CRCA)

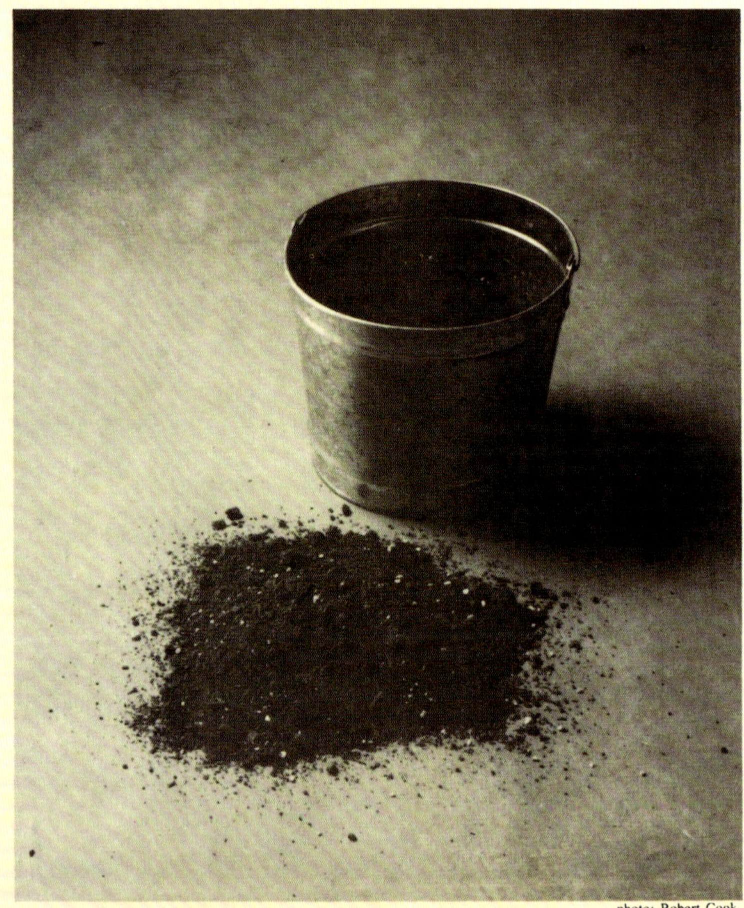

photo: Robert Cook

339 Conference folder from *Allan Kaprow: Precedings*

339–341 Self-Service

Happening, February–April 1988
Reinvention for *Allan Kaprow: Precedings*
At random over a three-month period

Record II

Happening, February 1988
Reinvention for *Allan Kaprow: Precedings*
A quarry outside of Austin

18 Happenings in 6 Parts

Happening, March 1988
Reinvention for *Allan Kaprow: Precedings*
Sponsored by Zabriskie Gallery
Throughout New York

Routine

Activity, March 1988
Reinvention for *Allan Kaprow: Precedings*
Mills College and California College of Arts and Crafts, Oakland

Blindsight

Activity, March–April 1988
Reinvention for *Allan Kaprow: Precedings*
An elementary school in Arlington, Texas

Company

Activity, March–April 1988
Reinvention for *Allan Kaprow: Precedings*
A stairwell at the Art Department, University of Texas, Arlington

340 + 341 Scores for reinventions

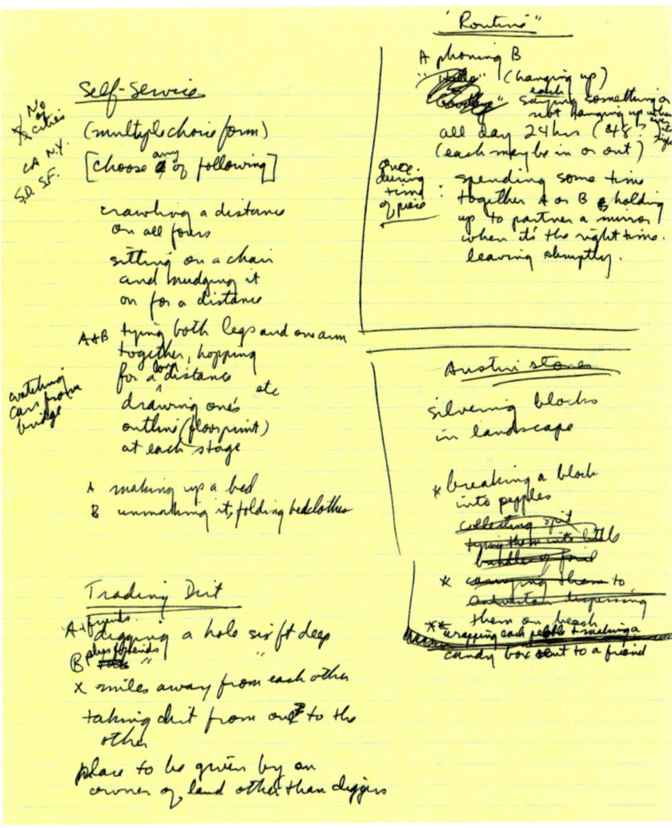
Self-Service
(multiple choice form)
[choose any of following]
crawling a distance on all fours
sitting on a chair and nudging it on for a distance
A+B tying both legs and one arm together, hopping for a long distance etc
drawing one's outline (floorprint) at each stage
A making up a bed
B unmaking it, folding bedclothes
Trading Dirt
digging a hole six ft deep
x miles away from each other
taking dirt from one to the other
place to be given by an owner of land other than diggers
"Routine"
A phoning B
all day 24 hrs (48?)
(each may be in or out)
spending some time together A or B holding up to partner a mirror when it's the right time.
leaving abruptly.
Austin stones
silvering blocks in landscape
x breaking a block into pebbles
candy box sent to a friend

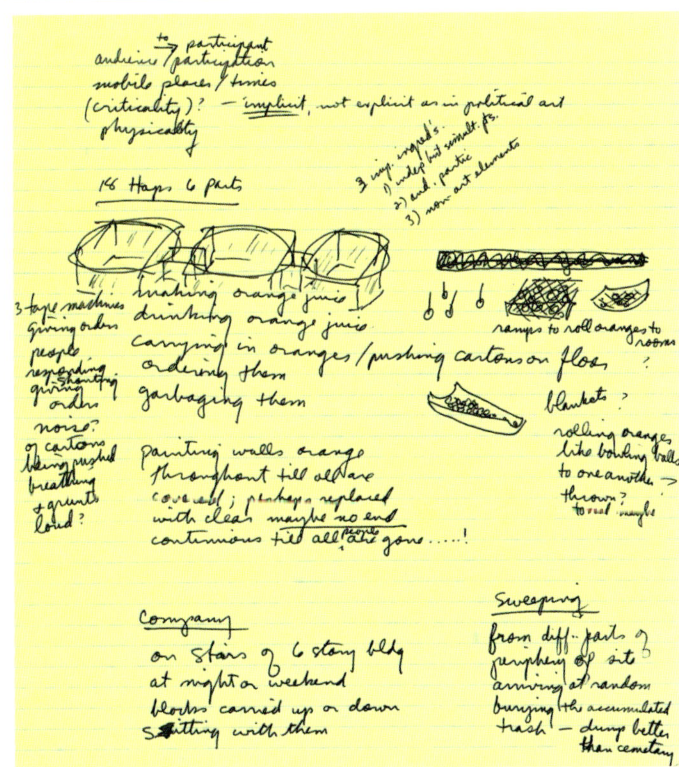
audience/participation → participant
mobile places/times
(criticality)? — implicit, not explicit as in political art
physicality
18 Haps 6 parts
3 imp. ingred's: 1) indep but simult. pts. 2) aud. partic. 3) non art elements
making orange juice
drinking orange juice
carrying in oranges/pushing cartons on floor
ordering them
garbaging them
ramps to roll oranges to rooms
blankets?
rolling oranges like bowling balls to one another → thrown? maybe
painting walls orange throughout till all are covered; perhaps replaced with clear maybe no end
continuous till all are gone.....!
3 tape machines giving orders
people responding shouting giving orders
noise? of cartons being pushed
breathing + grunts loud?
Company
on stairs of 6 story bldg
at night or weekend
blocks carried up or down
sitting with them
Sweeping
from diff. parts of periphery of site
arriving at random
burying the accumulated trash — dump better than cemetery

Sweeping

Happening, April 1988
Reinvention for *Allan Kaprow: Precedings*
Studio Theater, University of Texas, Arlington

Routine

Activity, May 1988
Reinvention for *Allan Kaprow: Precedings*
University of Texas, Arlington

342 **What's Watts' Watts?**

Activity, October 1988
Presented for *Fluxlux*, Robert Watts's funeral
Bangor, Pennsylvania

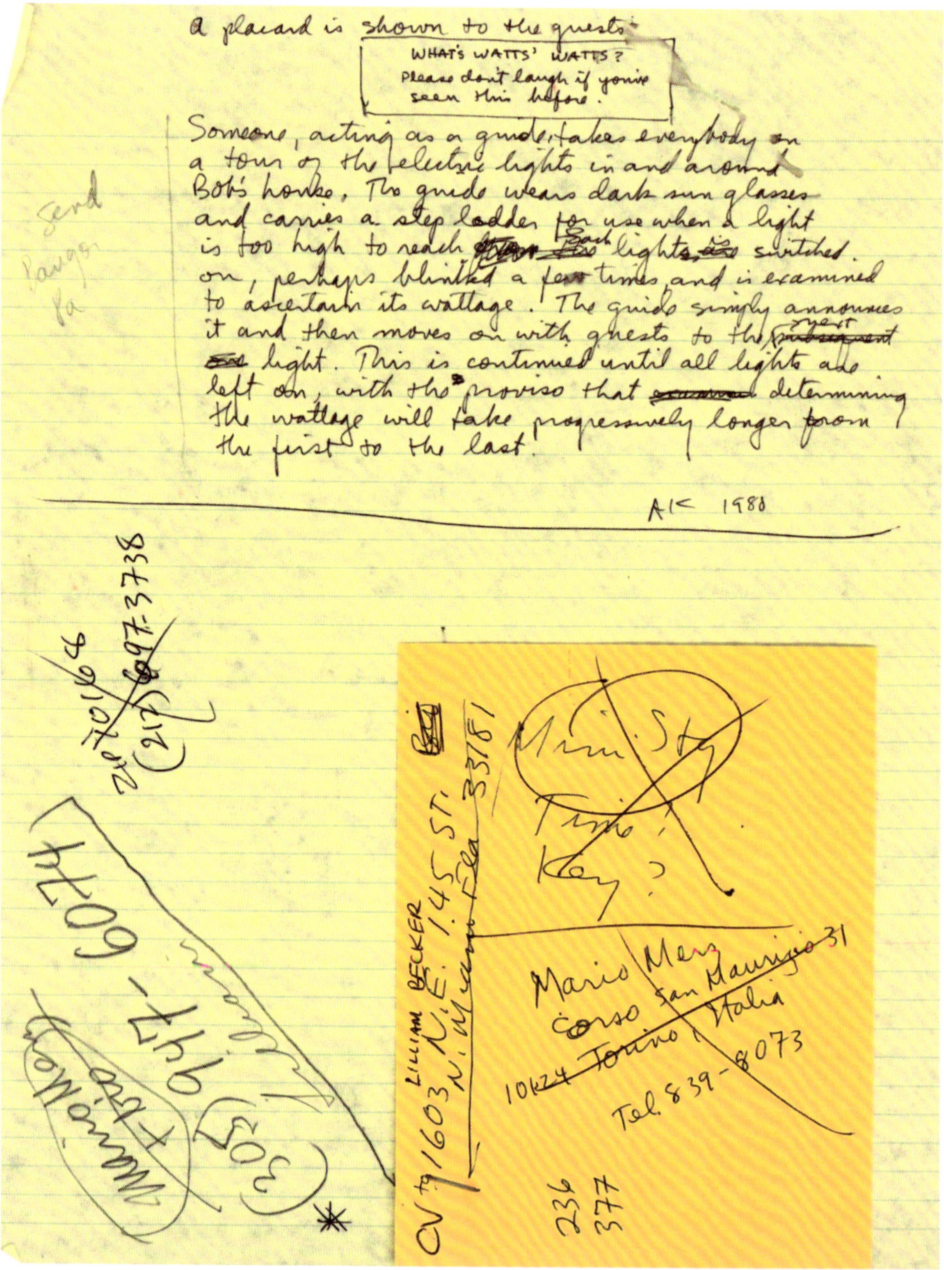
A placard is shown to the guests:
WHAT'S WATTS' WATTS?
Please don't laugh if you've seen this before.
Someone, acting as a guide, takes everybody on a tour of the electric lights in and around Bob's house. The guide wears dark sun glasses and carries a step ladder for use when a light is too high to reach. Each light is switched on, perhaps blinked a few times, and is examined to ascertain its wattage. The guide simply announces it and then moves on with guests to the next light. This is continued until all lights are left on, with the proviso that determining the wattage will take progressively longer from the first to the last.
AK 1988

342 Score for *What's Watts' Watts?*

1989

TEACHING POSITIONS Professor, Visual Arts Department, University of California, San Diego. ¶ **GROUP EXHIBITIONS** *Theater of the Object: Reconstructions, Re-creations, Reconsiderations, 1958–1972,* Alternative Museum, New York, May–June. *Happenings & Fluxus,* Galerie 1900–2000, Paris (traveled in France), June–July. *The Junk Aesthetic,* Whitney Museum of American Art at the Equitable Center, New York, June–August. *Fluxus 1962–1989,* Bonner Kunstverein, Bonn, August. *Art Cologne,* Galerie Inge Baecker, Cologne, November. ¶ **WRITINGS** "The Disturbing Lesson of Andy Warhol," unpublished essay commissioned by the Museum of Modern Art, New York, for *Andy Warhol: A Retrospective.* "Saubere Graffiti" (translation of *Clean Graffiti*), in Johannes Stahl, ed., *An der Wand: Graffiti zwischen Anarchie und Galerie* (Cologne: Dumont), 198. "Soap" (includes 1965 and 1989 versions), in Peter Frank, ed., *Theater of the Object: Reconstructions, Re-creations, Reconsiderations, 1958–1972,* exh. cat. (New York: Alternative Museum), 16–17.

Trading Dirt
Activity, April 1989
Reinvention for *Allan Kaprow: Precedings*
Sponsored by Koninklijke Academie van Beeldende Kunsten
Coast of the Netherlands

Border Work
Activity, April 1989
Sponsored by City Sites Projects and California College of Arts and Crafts
Lafayette Elementary School, Oakland

Soap
Happening, May–June 1989
Reinvention for *Theater of the Object*
Alternative Museum, New York

343–344 **Taking a Shoe for a Walk**
Activity, August 1989
Presented for *Fluxus, 1962–1989*
Throughout Bonn
Reinvented in 2006

A L L A N   K A P R O W

~~"Putting the Baby to sleep"~~

Bonn, den 13. August 1989

Taking A Shoe For A Walk (in honor of Fluxus)

pulling a shoe on a string through the city

examining the shoe from time to time, to see if it's worn out

wrapping your own shoe, after each examination,
with layers of bandage or tape, in the amount you
think the shoe on the string is worn out

repeating, adding to your shoe more layers of bandage
or tape, until, at the end of the walk, the shoe you are
pulling appears completely worn out

Einen Schuh ausführen

Einen Schuh an einer Schnur durch die Stadt ziehen.

Den Schuh von Zeit zu Zeit untersuchen, um zu sehen,
ob er verbraucht ist.

Nach jeder Untersuchung den eigenen Schuh mit Mullbinden
in der Stärke bandagieren, in der der gezogene Schuh Ihrer
Ansicht nach verbraucht ist.

Wiederholen; den eigenen Schuh weiter mit Mullbinden und
Pflaster bandagieren, bis am Ende der Promenade der
Schuh, den Sie ziehen, völlig verbraucht aussieht.

343 Score for *Taking a Shoe for a Walk*

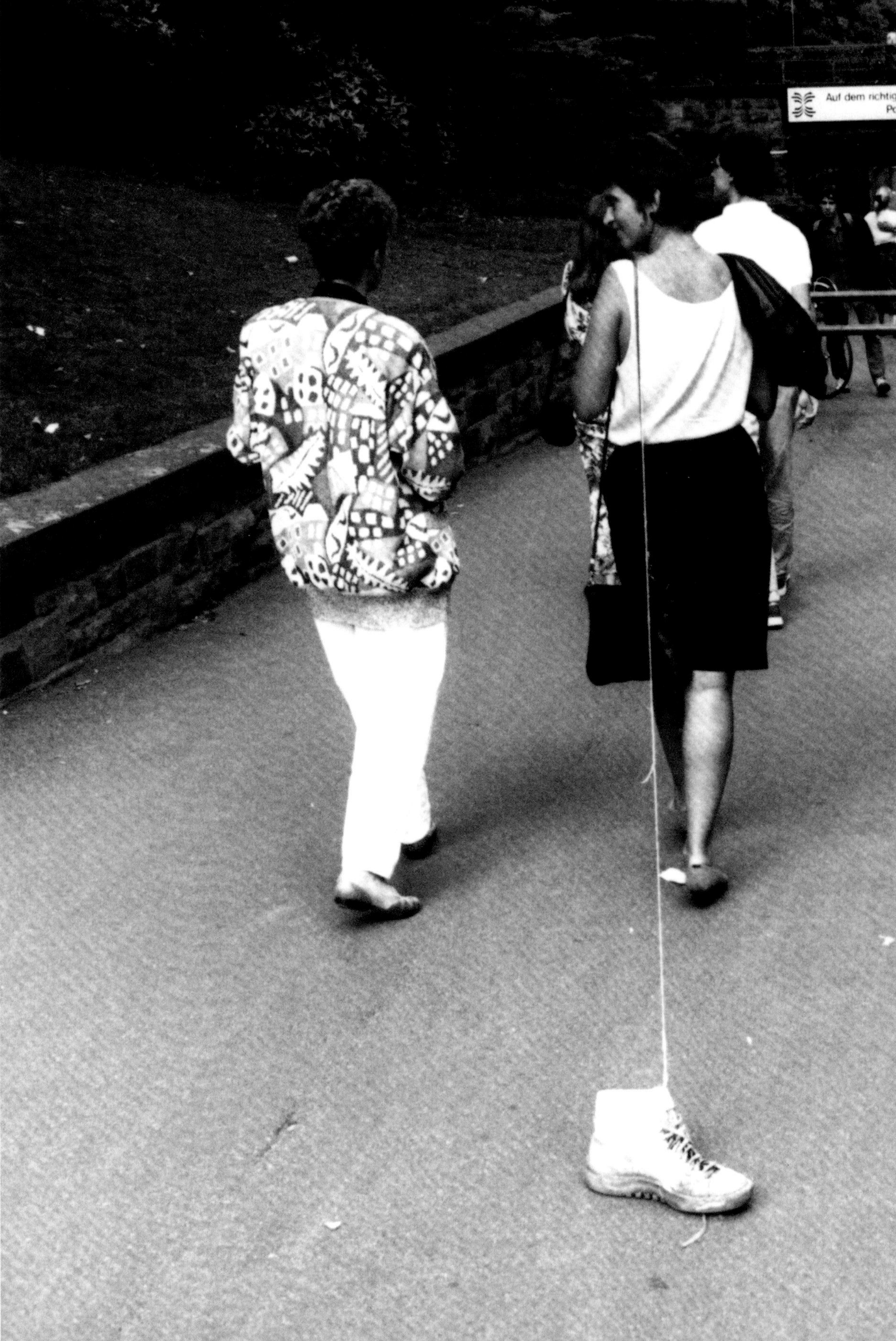

344 Pulling a shoe on a string through the city

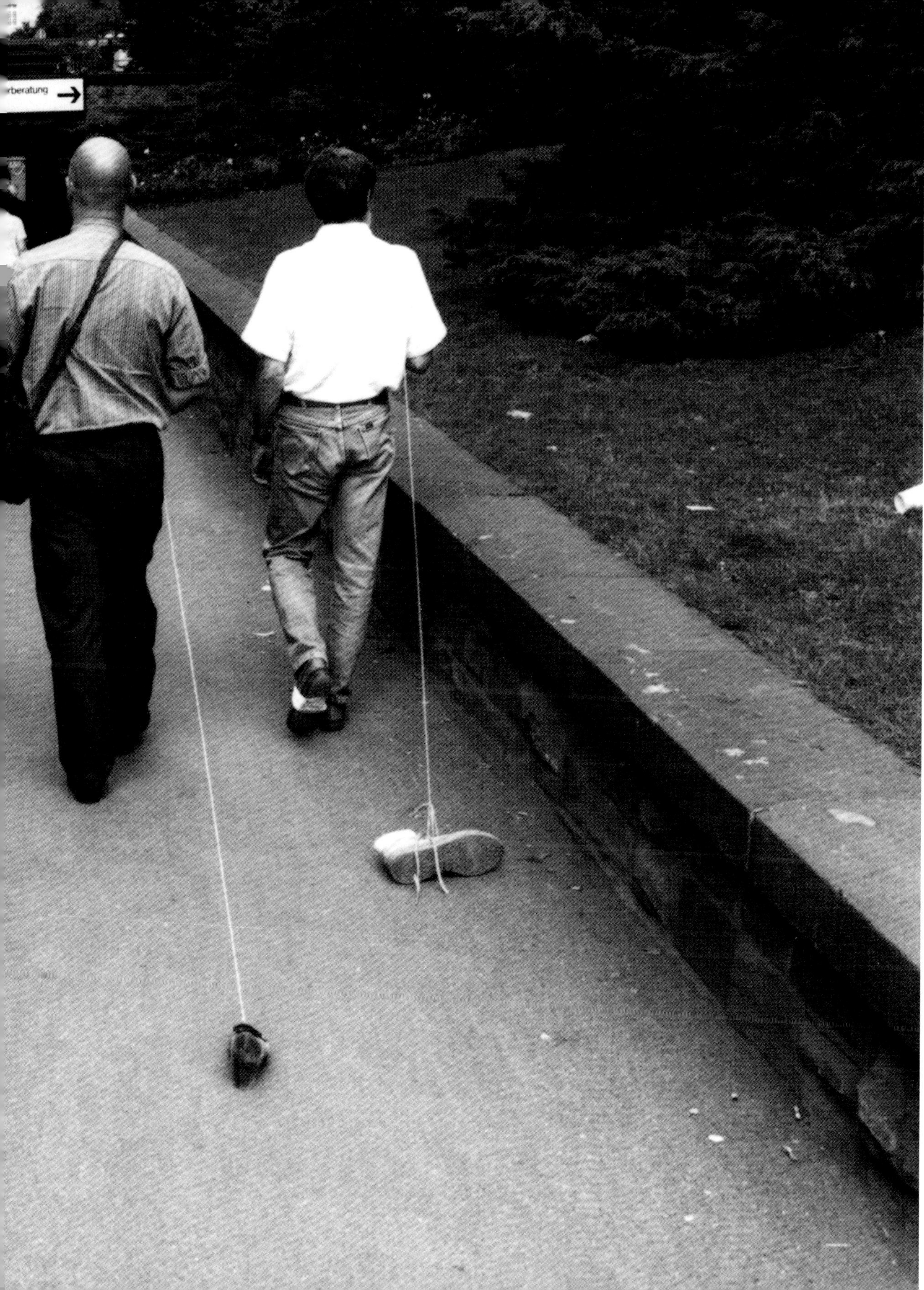
rberatung

TEACHING POSITIONS Professor, Visual Arts Department, University of California, San Diego. ¶ GROUP EXHIBITIONS *The Readymade Boomerang,* Eighth Biennale of Sydney, April–June. *Collages,* Musée d'Unterlinden, Colmar, France, June–September. *Ubi Fluxus Ibi Motus,* Biennale di Venezia, Venice, June–September. *The Readymade Boomerang Print Portfolio,* Queensland Art Gallery, Queensland, November–February. ¶ FESTIVALS The Meeting of the Worlds, Joensuu, Finland, June. ¶ WRITINGS "The Meaning of Life," *Artforum* 28, no.10: 144–49. "Meeting at the Market: Allan Kaprow's Account," in *Kohtaamisia rajojen tiellä = Encounters on the Road of Borders: Documenting a Collaborative Performance Directed by Suzanne Lacy* (Helsinki: n.p.), 36. "A Scenario" (unrealized Activity for The Exploratorium, San Francisco), in *Expanding the Exploratorium: A Resource Handbook for Thinking about Institutional Growth, A Record of Symposium Proceedings, Workshops, and Discussions, 1988–1989* (n.p.), 19. "Tail Wagging Dog," *The Act* 2, no. 1: 10–12.

1990

Yard

Environment, April–June 1990
Reinvention for *The Readymade Boomerang*
Art Gallery of New South Wales, Sydney

Meeting at the Market

Activity, June 1990
Presented for The Meeting of the Worlds
Joensuu, Finland

345 *Apple Shrine*

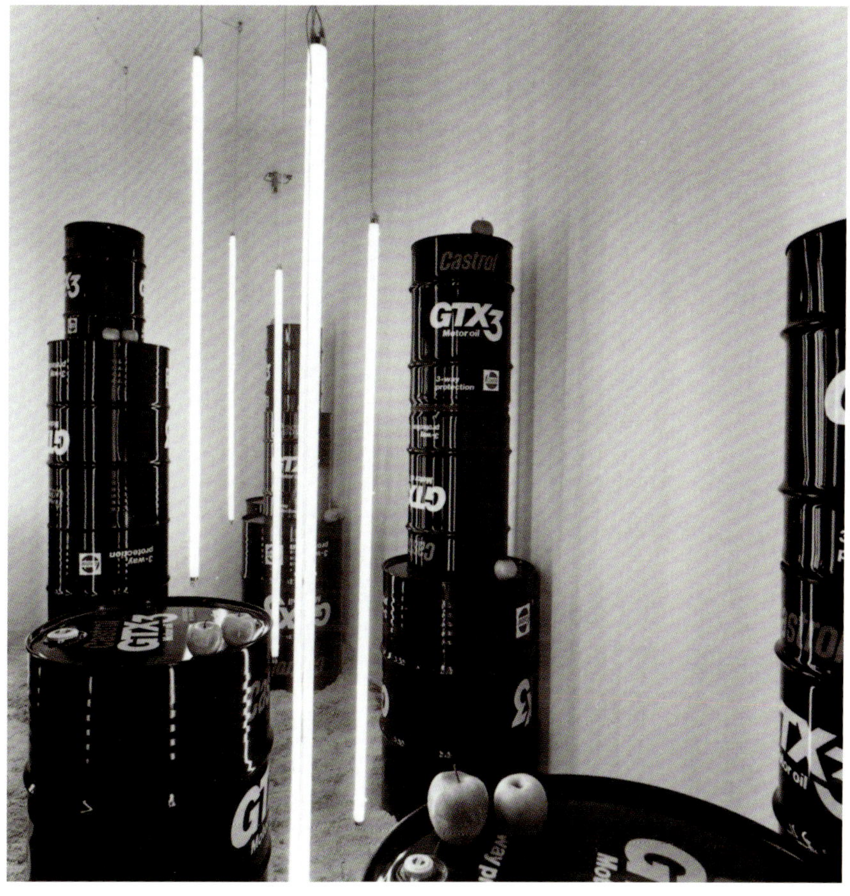

Kaprow-Négyesy Project
Activity, September 1991
Mandeville Center, Recital Hall, and Media Center, University of California, San Diego

345 **Apple Shrine**
Environment, October–November 1991
Reinvention for *7 Environments*
Fondazione Mudima, Milan

346–348 **Beauty Parlor**
Environment, October–November 1991
Reinvention of *Untitled Environment* (1958) for *7 Environments*
Fondazione Mudima, Milan

349 **Yard**
Environment, October–November 1991
Reinvention for *7 Environments*
Fondazione Mudima, Milan

350 **Eat**
Environment, October–November 1991
Reinvention for *7 Environments*
Fondazione Mudima, Milan

TEACHING POSITIONS Professor, Visual Arts Department, University of California, San Diego. ¶ SOLO EXHIBITIONS *7 Environments,* Fondazione Mudima, Milan, October–November. ¶ GROUP EXHIBITIONS *A dall'Est all'Ovest e ritorno,* Studio Oggetto, Milan, May. *Pop Art: A Continuing History,* Royal Academy of Arts, London (traveled internationally), September–December. *Thirtieth Anniversary Series,* John Gibson Gallery, New York, October–November. ¶ WRITINGS "Bon Marché," in John Howell, ed., *Breakthroughs: Avant-Garde Artists in Europe and America, 1950–1990,* exh. cat. (New York: Rizzoli), 150–55. *Bull Shit,* no. 1 (news bulletin for *7 Environments,* Fondazione Mudima, Milan). "Introduction to a Theory" and descriptions of Environments, in *7 Environments,* exh. cat. (Milan: Fondazione Mudima). "Nam June Paik" (originally published in 1968), in Toni Stooss and Thomas Kellein, eds., *Nam June Paik: Video Time–Video Space,* exh. cat. (Ostfildern, Germany: Cantz), 114. "Pierre Restany" (facsimile of handwritten article), in *Pierre Restany: Le coeur et la raison,* exh. cat. (Morlaix, France: Musée des Jacobins), 141. "Shaking Barrels," in Pierre Joris, ed., *Joy! Praise!: A Festschrift for Jerome Rothenberg on the Occasion of His Sixtieth Birthday* (Encinitas, Calif.: Ta'wil), 42.

1991

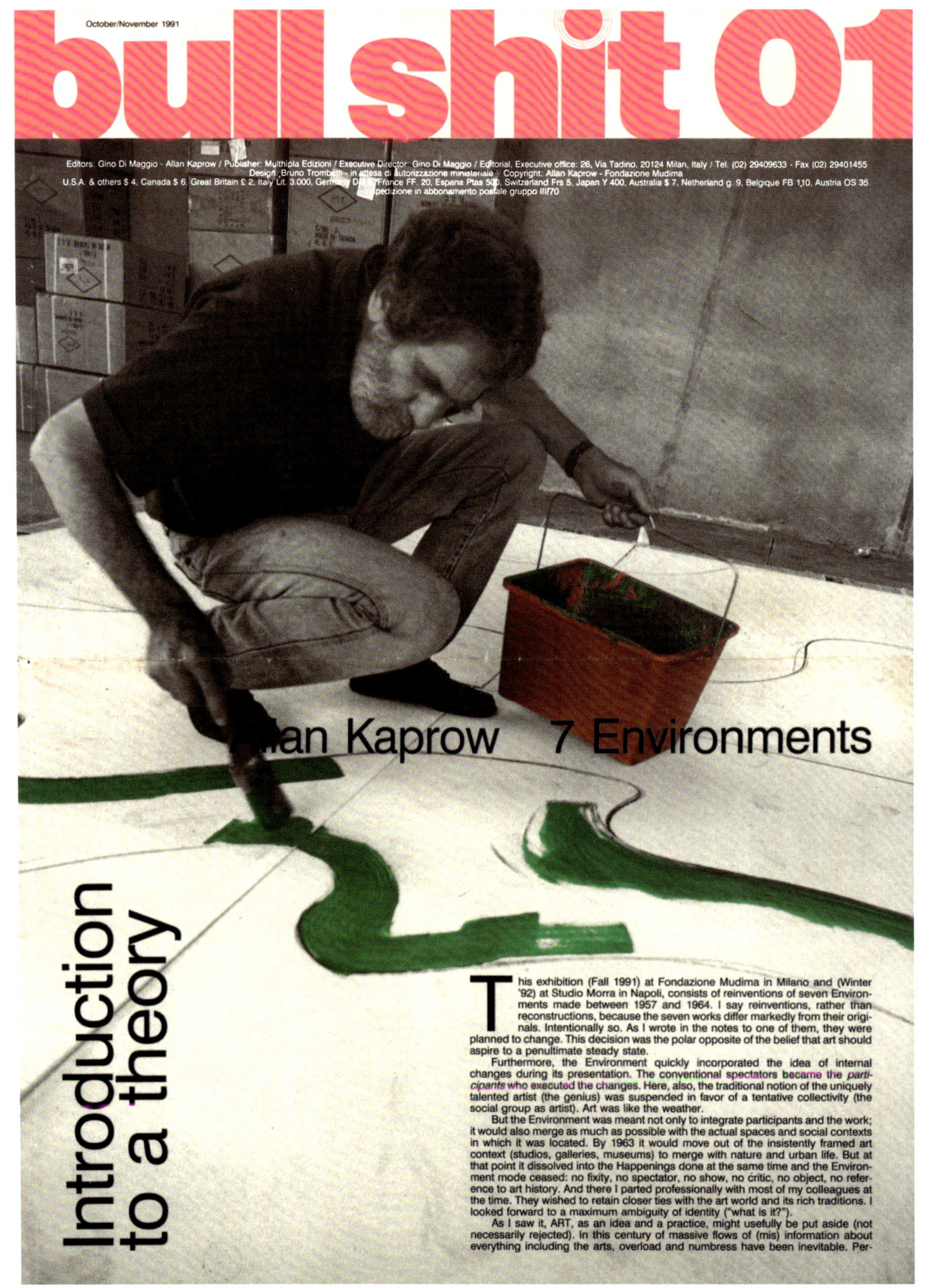

October/November 1991

bull shit 01

Editors: Gino Di Maggio - Allan Kaprow / Publisher: Multhipla Edizioni / Executive Director: Gino Di Maggio / Editorial, Executive office: 26, Via Tadino, 20124 Milan, Italy / Tel. (02) 29409633 - Fax (02) 29401455
Design: Bruno Trombetti - in attesa di autorizzazione ministeriale · Copyright: Allan Kaprow - Fondazione Mudima
U.S.A. & others $ 4, Canada $ 6, Great Britain £ 2, Italy Lit. 3.000, Germany DM 6, France FF. 20, Espana Ptas 500, Switzerland Frs 5, Japan Y 400, Australia $ 7, Netherland g. 9, Belgique FB 1,10, Austria OS 35
Spedizione in abbonamento postale gruppo III/70

Allan Kaprow 7 Environments

Introduction to a theory

This exhibition (Fall 1991) at Fondazione Mudima in Milano and (Winter '92) at Studio Morra in Napoli, consists of reinventions of seven Environments made between 1957 and 1964. I say reinventions, rather than reconstructions, because the seven works differ markedly from their originals. Intentionally so. As I wrote in the notes to one of them, they were planned to change. This decision was the polar opposite of the belief that art should aspire to a penultimate steady state.

Furthermore, the Environment quickly incorporated the idea of internal changes during its presentation. The conventional spectators became the *participants* who executed the changes. Here, also, the traditional notion of the uniquely talented artist (the genius) was suspended in favor of a tentative collectivity (the social group as artist). Art was like the weather.

But the Environment was meant not only to integrate participants and the work; it would also merge as much as possible with the actual spaces and social contexts in which it was located. By 1963 it would move out of the insistently framed art context (studios, galleries, museums) to merge with nature and urban life. But at that point it dissolved into the Happenings done at the same time and the Environment mode ceased: no fixity, no spectator, no show, no critic, no object, no reference to art history. And there I parted professionally with most of my colleagues at the time. They wished to retain closer ties with the art world and its rich traditions. I looked forward to a maximum ambiguity of identity ("what is it?").

As I saw it, ART, as an idea and a practice, might usefully be put aside (not necessarily rejected). In this century of massive flows of (mis) information about everything including the arts, overload and numbress have been inevitable. Per-

346 Cover of *Bull Shit*, no. 1 (1991)

348 Drawings for *Beauty Parlor* and *Apple Shrine*

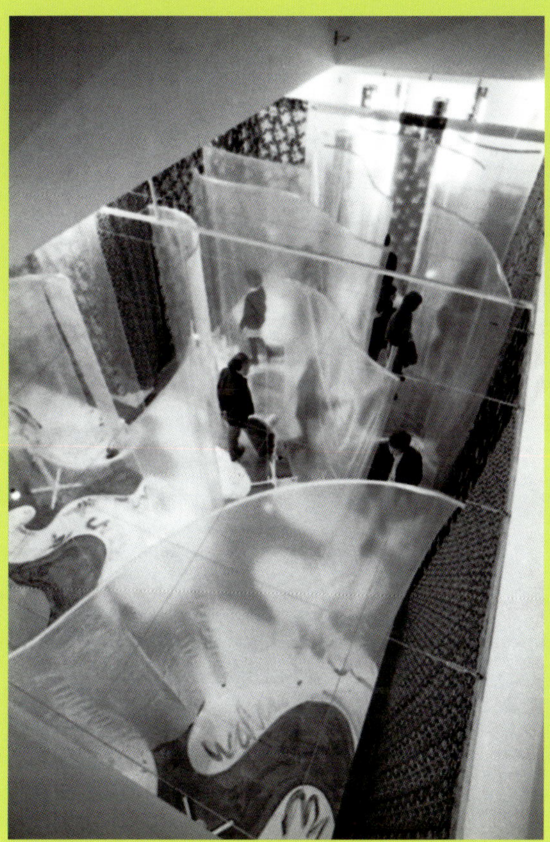

347 *Beauty Parlor*

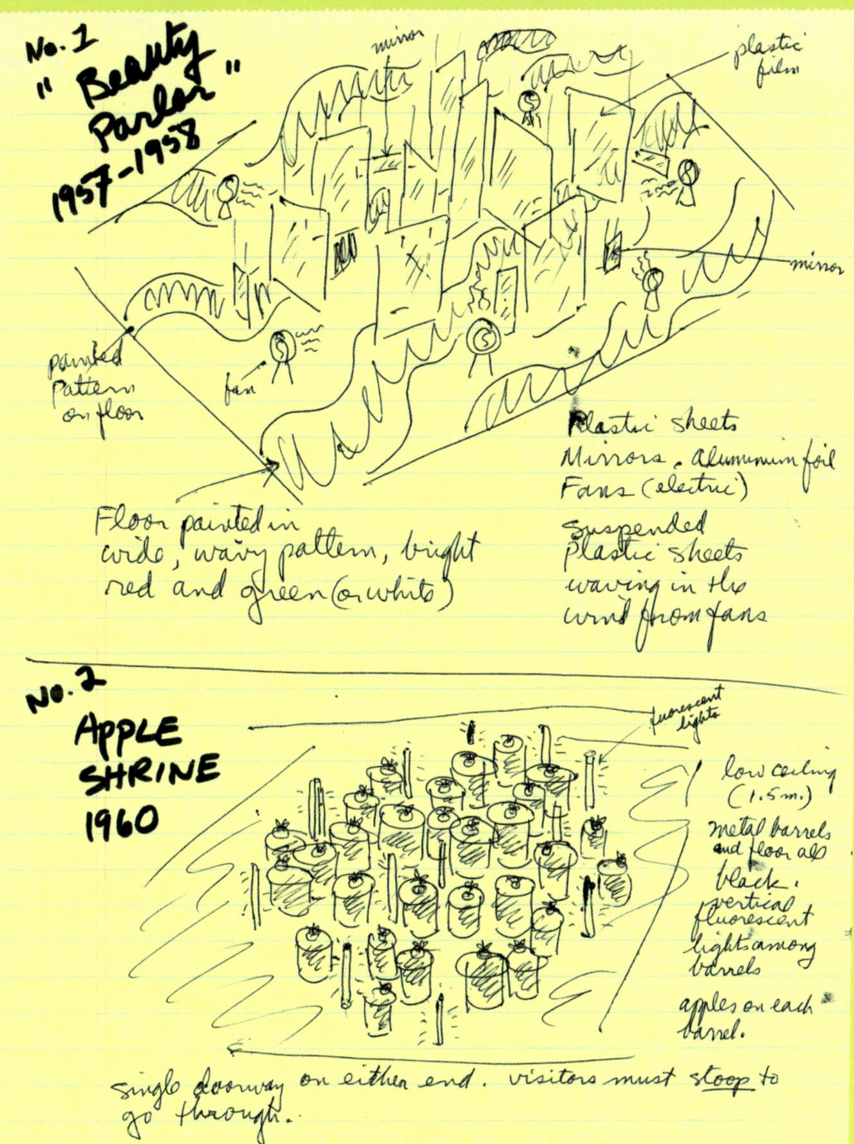

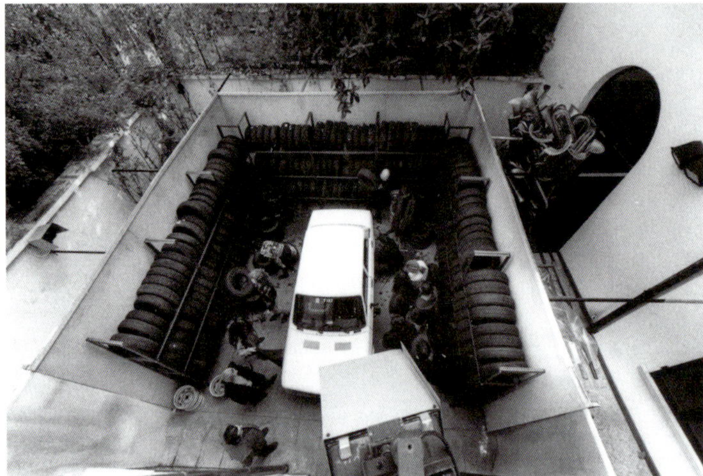

349 *Yard*

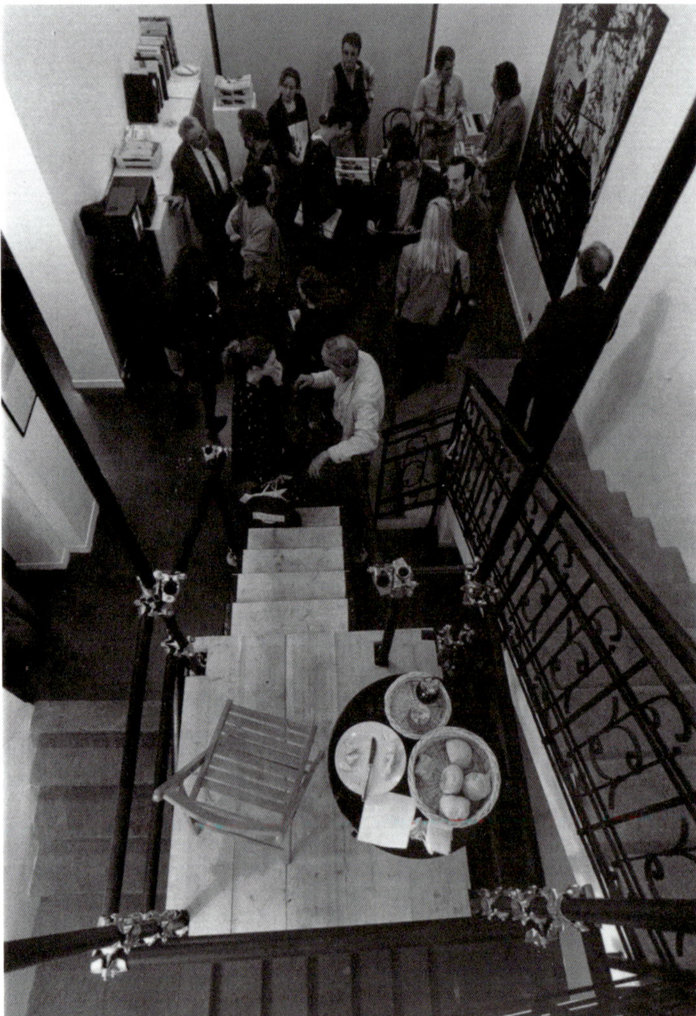

350 *Eat*

Words
Environment, October–November 1991
Reinvention for *7 Environments*
Fondazione Mudima, Milan

Push and Pull
Environment, October–November 1991
Reinvention for *7 Environments*
Fondazione Mudima, Milan

Stockroom
Environment, October–November 1991
Reinvention for *7 Environments*
Fondazione Mudima, Milan

Cabin
Environment, October–November 1991
Presented for *7 Environments*
At the entrance to Fondazione Mudima, Milan

Asleep on the Job
Television spot, October 1991
Color, sound, 2 minutes
Broadcast on local San Diego television stations

Apple Shrine
Environment, January–February 1992
Reinvention for *7 Environments*
Studio Morra, Naples

Dead End
Environment, January–February 1992
Reinvention of *Untitled Environment* (1958) for *7 Environments*
Studio Morra, Naples

Eat
Environment, January–February 1992
Reinvention for *7 Environments*
Studio Morra, Naples

Stockroom
Environment, January–February 1992
Reinvention for *7 Environments*
Studio Morra, Naples

Eat
Environment, September–October 1992
Reinvention for *4 Environments*
A factory building, Montreuil/Bois

Apple Shrine
Environment, September–October 1992
Reinvention for *4 Environments*
L'Espace Donguy, Paris

Words
Environment, September–October 1992
Reinvention for *4 Environments*
L'Espace Donguy, Paris

Short Circuit
Environment, September–October 1992
Reinvention of *Untitled Environment* (1958) for *4 Environments*
L'Espace Donguy, Paris

1992

TEACHING POSITIONS Professor, Visual Arts Department, University of California, San Diego. ¶ SOLO EXHIBITIONS *7 Environments,* Studio Morra, Naples, January–February. *4 Environments,* La Zonmééé, Montreuil/Bois, and l'Espace Donguy/APEGAC, Paris, September–October. ¶ GROUP EXHIBITIONS *Video Works by UCSD Faculty and Graduate Alumni,* Mandeville Gallery, University of California, San Diego, January–February. *The Power of the City,* Whitney Museum of American Art, Federal Reserve Plaza, New York, May–July. *Special Collections: The New Photographic Order from Pop to Now,* International Center of Photography, New York, July–October. *Zeitkunst: Sammlung Feelisch Remscheid,* Städtische Galerie Remscheid, Remscheid, Germany, September–November. *Parallel Visions: Modern Artists and Outsider Art,* Los Angeles County Museum of Art, Los Angeles (traveled internationally), October–January. *Pop Art,* Montreal Museum of Fine Arts, Montreal, October–January. *Hand-Painted Pop: American Art in Transition, 1955–62,* The Museum of Contemporary Art, Los Angeles (traveled nationally), December–March. ¶ WRITINGS "Oublions l'Art," *Kanaleurope,* no. 4: 24–26.

351 Poster for *Beauty Parlor 2* (with statement)

BEAUTY PARLOR(2)

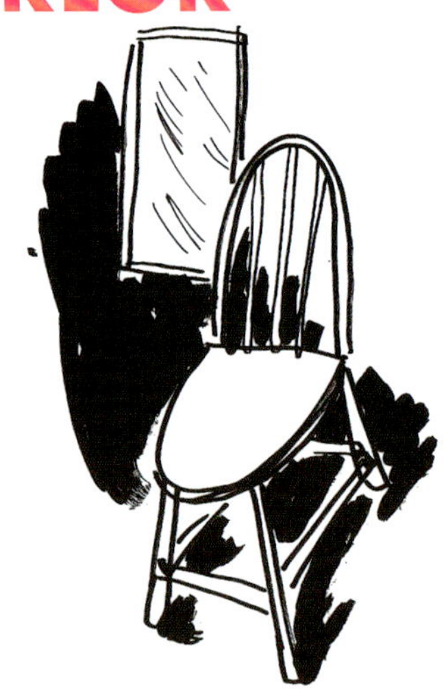

Beauty Parlor is a reinvention of 2 merged, untitled Environments presented at the Hansa Gallery in New York in 1958. It is quite different from its prototypes. For one, it is site-specific, occupying 3 floors of a large, active printing firm in an industrial section of Manhattan. The 1958 Environments were installed in the neutral space of an art gallery on Central Park South. For another, *Beauty Parlor* is inherently participatory. The 1958 works were certainly space-filling, but they only tentatively engaged the visitors in simple actions such as turning on an electric fan or moving some objects around. They were mostly intact without such moves. This Environment can't function without focused participation.

Beauty Parlor has been reinvented 3 times in the past: as *Fresh Air* at the Museum am Ostwall, Dortmund, 1986; as *Beauty Parlor* (1) at the Fondazione Mudima, Milan, 1990; and as *Dead End* at Studio Morra, Naples, 1991. Indeed, the idea from the start was to have each Environment change whenever it might be remade in the future. So, in the majority of cases, I have reinvented more or less freely. That way, the changes were always fresh.

Today, when there is a revival of interest among historians in the innovations in the arts of the late 1950s and 1960s, participation and reinvention are ways to keep history in the present.

—Allan Kaprow

Organized by the John Gibson Gallery and the Trident Group, at 315 Spring St., New York, N.Y., Tuesdays to Fridays, 1 PM to 5 PM, April 13 to April 23, 1993. For information call (212) 925-1192

352 Participant in Environment

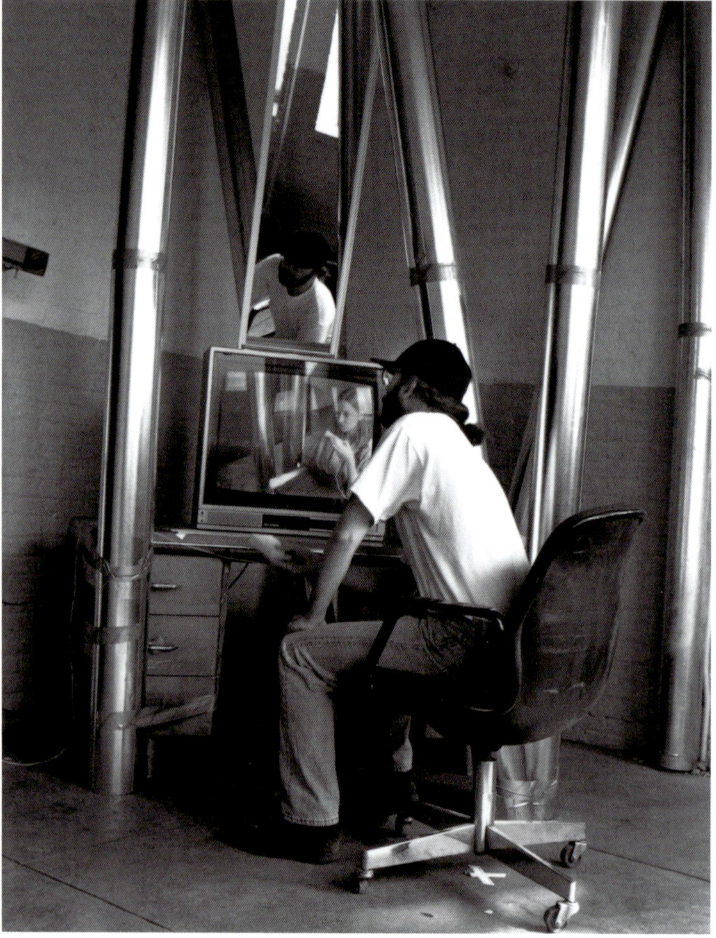

1993

TEACHING POSITIONS Professor Emeritus, Visual Arts Department, University of California, San Diego. ¶ AWARDS Honorary member of Phi Beta Kappa. ¶ SOLO EXHIBITIONS John Gibson Gallery, New York, April. ¶ GROUP EXHIBITIONS *In the Spirit of Fluxus,* Walker Art Center, Minneapolis (traveled internationally), February–June. *La biennale di Venezia: XLV esposizione internationale d'arte: Punti cardinali dell'arte,* Venice, June–October. *Action/Performance and the Photograph,* Turner/Krull Galleries, Los Angeles, July–September. *2ème biennale d'art contemporain: Et tous ils changent le monde,* Musée d'art contemporain Lyon, Lyon, September–October. *Photographic: Works of the Sixties and Seventies,* Zabriskie Gallery, New York, September. *Rolywholyover, A Circus,* The Museum of Contemporary Art, Los Angeles (traveled internationally), September–November. *Sampler: Southern California Video Collection,* David Zwirner Gallery, New York, November–December. ¶ WRITINGS *Essays on the Blurring of Art and Life,* ed. Jeff Kelley (Berkeley: Univ. of California Press). "L'expérience réelle" (translation of "The Real Experiment," originally published in 1983), in *Et tous ils changent le monde: 2ème biennale d'art contemporain,* exh. cat. (Paris: Réunion des Musées Nationaux), 122–31. "Quotes: 'On Photographing Happenings' and 'On the Photograph as Instruction for Action'" (written 22 July 1976), in Craig Krull and Robert C. Morgan, eds., *Action/Performance and the Photograph,* exh. cat. (Los Angeles: Turner/Krull Galleries), n.p. "Right Living" (originally published in 1987), *TDR/The Drama Review* 37, no. 2: 12–14.

BEAUTY PARLOR 2

(1993 reinvention of 1991 version; of Fresh Air 1986; of Untitled 1958)

6 places are located on the 3 floors of a printing firm. Each place consists of a unique chair surrounded loosely by 8 or more vertical stovepipes. Facing the chairs are a video monitor and camera. Above each monitor hangs a mirror.

The video screens show another chair in another location, either occupied by someone or not. Visitors are invited to sit in the chairs. If they see someone sitting in the chair shown on their monitor, they are urged to acknowledge that person, and vice versa. Then they describe to each other where they are located and carry their respective chairs to the other's place, where they sit down facing the camera and repeat their acknowledgements for as long as desired.

If, however, the chair in the monitor is not occupied, the visitor is encouraged to sit down and wait. When and if another visitor sits down in the empty chair, the above process can follow. If waiting becomes difficult, the visitor is free to try another chair among the 5 floors of the firm. Trying all 6 chairs could be interesting

The mirrors are available.

— AK 1993

AK 93

353 Score for *Beauty Parlor 2*

351–355 Beauty Parlor 2

Environment, April 1993
Reinvention of *Untitled Environment* (1958)
Sponsored by John Gibson Gallery and the Trident Group
Trident Group Printing Firm, New York

5 Minute Delay (Barriers)

Activity, September–October 1993
Presented for *2ème biennale d'art contemporain*
Outside Halle Tony Garnier, Lyon

Squeezeplay

Activity, September–October 1993
Presented for *La biennale di Venezia*
Venice

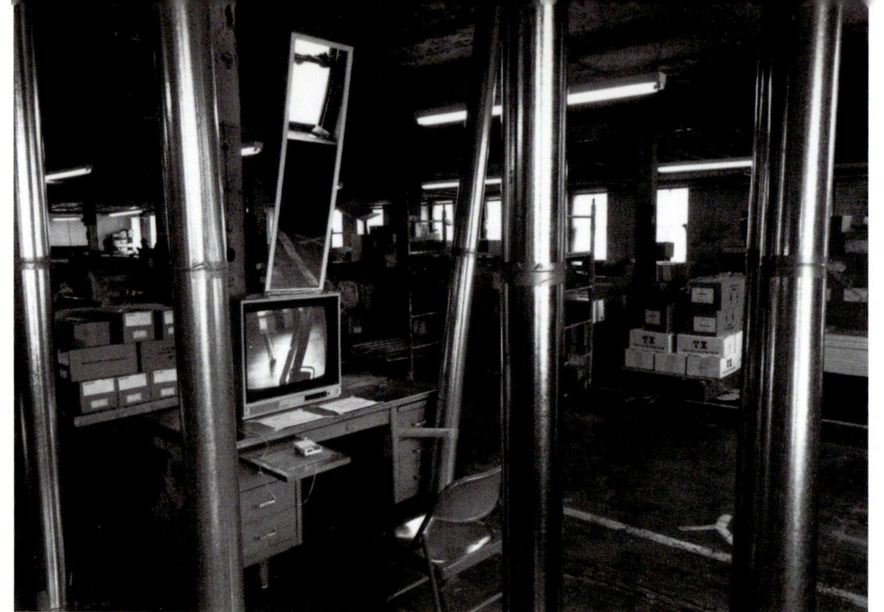

354 Video monitor, stove pipes, and mirror

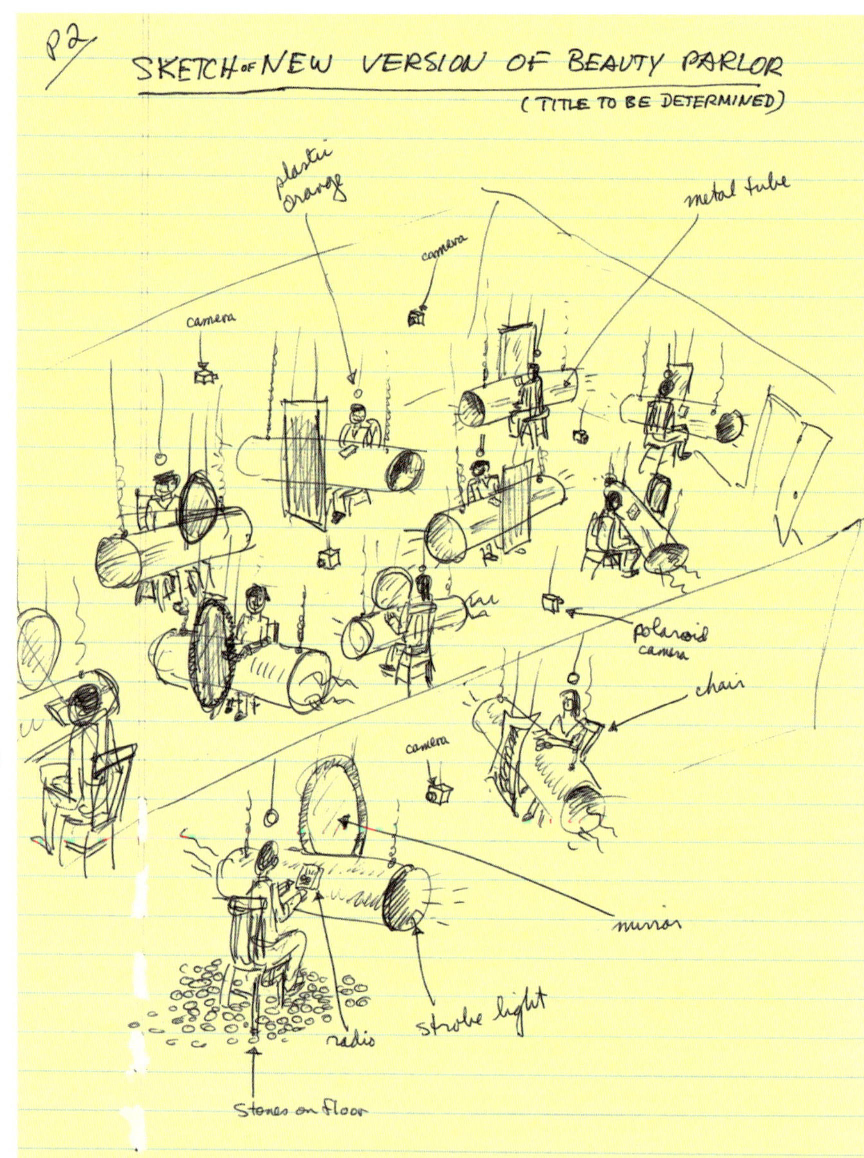

355 Sketch for *Beauty Parlor 2*

Untitled Event

Activity, June 1994
Presented for "Performance '94"
Saint Norbert Arts and Cultural Center, Manitoba

A Waste of Time

Activity, 1994
For *Minima Media*
A former textile factory in Leipzig

Assemblage (after a 1958 sketch)

Activity, September–November 1994
Prepared for *Hors limites*
Galerie Beaubourg, Centre Georges Pompidou, Paris

1994

TEACHING POSITIONS Professor Emeritus, Visual Arts Department, University of California, San Diego. ¶ SOLO EXHIBITIONS *Work in Progress by Allan Kaprow,* Galerie Beaubourg, Centre Georges Pompidou, Paris, September–November. ¶ GROUP EXHIBITIONS *Garbage,* Real Art Ways, Hartford, Connecticut, April–May. *Cloaca Maxima,* Museum der Stadtentwässerung, Zurich, June–October. *Kunst als Kommunikation: Multiples, Publikationen und Briefe aus der Sammlung Feelisch,* Institut für Lippische Landeskunde, Schieder-Schwalenberg, Germany, June–July. *inSITE94,* exhibited at arts institutions, alternative spaces, and public places throughout the San Diego/Tijuana region, September–October. *Borderline,* Galerie J & J Donguy, Paris, October. *Minima Media: Medienbiennale Leipzig '94,* Hochschule für Grafik und Buchkunst Leipzig, Leipzig, October–November. *Hors limites: L'art et la vie, 1952–1994,* Musée national d'art moderne, Centre Georges Pompidou, Paris, November–January. *Neo-Dada: Redefining Art, 1958–1962,* Scottsdale Center for the Arts, Scottsdale, Arizona (traveled nationally), November–January. ¶ SYMPOSIA "Performance '94," Saint Norbert Arts and Cultural Centre, Manitoba, June. ¶ WRITINGS *Work in Progress by Allan Kaprow,* exh. cat. (Brugge, Belgium: Walleyndruk 800). ¶ INTERVIEWS "Allan Kaprow entretien par Jacques Donguy," in *Hors limites: L'art et la vie, 1952–1994,* exh. cat. (Paris: Centre Georges Pompidou), 64–71.

1995 **TEACHING POSITIONS** Professor Emeritus, Visual Arts Department, University of California, San Diego. ¶ **SOLO EXHIBITIONS** *Allan Kaprow: Photographs, Text and Posters from Happenings,* John Gibson Gallery, New York, May–June. ¶ **GROUP EXHIBITIONS** Faculty exhibition, University of California, San Diego, April–May. *No! Art,* Neue Gesellschaft für Bildende Kunst, Berlin, October–November. *Save/Give: Life Is Art Enough,* Museum Fridericianum, Kasseler Kunstverein, Kassel, October–November. *Beat Culture and the New America: 1950–1965,* Whitney Museum of American Art, New York (traveled nationally), November–February. *Jahresgabe,* Bonner Kunstverein, Bonn, November. ¶ **WRITINGS** "Success and Failure When Art Changes," in Suzanne Lacy, ed., *Mapping the Terrain: New Genre Public Art* (Seattle: Bay), 152–58.

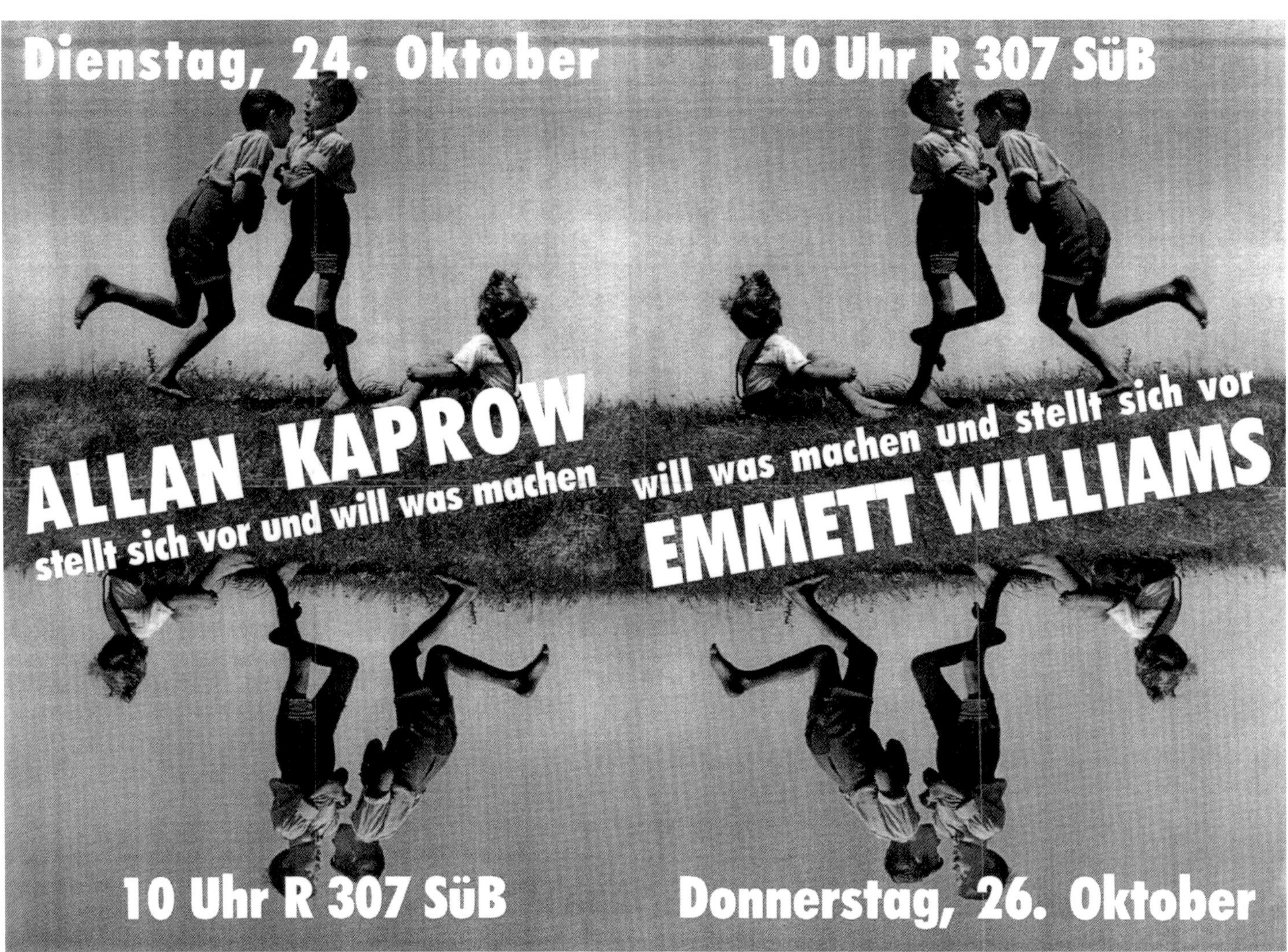

356 Poster for *Fall*

Waxworks
Activity, May 1995
Presented for *Allan Kaprow: Photographs, Text and Posters from Happenings*
John Gibson Gallery, New York

356–357 **Fall**
Activity, October 1995
Presented for *Save/Give*
Streets of Kassel
Reinvented in 2006

Assemblage of Hundreds
Activity, November 1995
Presented for the Museum Fundraiser Gala
Children's Museum of San Diego, San Diego

FALL

2 friends walking the streets
filling a bag with leaves

when bag is full, still walking,
1 friend, closing eyes,
guided by the other,
drops a leaf, then another,
until the bag is empty

eyes opened
the other friend's closed
guided as before
following the leaves, 1 by 1,
back to their beginning

(Kassel, late October '95)

Allan Kaprow

357 Score for *Fall*

TEACHING POSITIONS Professor Emeritus, Visual Arts Department, University of California, San Diego. ¶ SOLO EXHIBITIONS *Allan Kaprow,* Kunsthalle Palazzo, Basel, Switzerland, May–June. ¶ GROUP EXHIBITIONS *Die Welt ist wie ein zerbrochener Spiegel,* Galerie Inge Baecker, Cologne, January–April. *Do It,* Municipal Art Museum, Reykjavik, March–May. *Styki/Contact Prints,* Galeria Foksal, Warsaw, July–September. *Generations: The Lineage of Influence in Bay Area Art,* Richmond Art Center, San Francisco, September–November. ¶ WRITINGS *L'art et la vie confondus* (Paris: Musée National d'Art Moderne, Centre Georges Pompidou). "Deus Ex Machina," in Jacques Donguy, *Tag-Surfusion* (Fontenay-sous-Bois, France: L'Évidence), 56–57. "Experimental Art and Its Possibility" (lecture transcript), in Hedy Graber and Philip Ursprung, eds., *Allan Kaprow,* exh. cat. (Liestal, Switzerland: Kunsthalle Palazzo), 25–33. "Maestro Maciunas" (German translation of the unpublished manuscript "Maestro Maciunas" [1993]), in Emmett Williams et al., eds., *Mr. Fluxus: Ein Gemeinschaftsporträt von George Maciunas, 1931–1978* (Wiesbaden: Harlekin Art), 344–48. "Untitled Guidelines for Happenings" (excerpted from *Assemblage, Environments & Happenings*), in Kristine Stiles and Peter Selz, eds., *Theories and Documents of Contemporary Art: A Sourcebook of Artists' Writings* (Berkeley: Univ. of California Press), 709–14. "Verkefni" (translation of "Chores"), in *"Do it" heildarútgáfa,* exh. cat. (Reykjavik: Kjarvalsstaðir), n.p.

1996

Easy Chairs 1 and Easy Chairs 2
Activity, March 1996
Sponsored by the University of Iowa
Iowa City

If the Shoe Fits, Sign It

Activity, April 1997
Presented for *Allan Kaprow*
Grossmont College, El Cajon, California

Vital Fluids

Environment, September–November 1997
Reinvention of *Untitled Environment* (1958) for *The Hansa Gallery (1952–1959) Revisited*
Zabriskie Gallery, New York

1997

TEACHING POSITIONS Visiting professor, Fondazione Antonio Ratti, Como, Italy. Professor Emeritus, Visual Arts Department, University of California, San Diego. ¶ SOLO EXHIBITIONS *Allan Kaprow,* Hyde Gallery, Grossmont College, El Cajon, California, April. *Photo-Text: Plans of Happenings 1960s–1970s,* Archivio Conz, Verona, April–May. *Just Doing,* Fondazione Antonio Ratti, Como, Italy (traveled in Italy), July. *Allan Kaprow: Activity-Fotos aus den 60ern und 70ern,* Galerie Inge Baecker, Cologne, September–November. *Allan Kaprow: Installation,* Biblioteca Comunale, Como, Italy, October–November. ¶ GROUP EXHIBITIONS *Sunshine & Noir: Art in Los Angeles, 1960–97,* Louisiana Museum of Modern Art, Humlebaek, Denmark (traveled internationally), May–September. *The Hansa Gallery (1952–1959) Revisited,* Zabriskie Gallery, New York, September–November. *Konkrete Poesie Konzept Kunst,* Kunstverein Rosenheim, Rosenheim, Germany, September–October. *The Pop '60s: Transatlantic Crossing,* Centro Cultural de Belém, Lisbon, September–November. *Trash: Quando i Riffuti Diventano Arte,* Museo di Arte Moderna e Contemporanea di Trento e Rovereto, Rovereto, Italy, September–January. *Do It,* Kunsthallen Nikolaj, Copenhagen Contemporary Art Center, Copenhagen (organized by the Independent Curators Incorporated, New York; traveled internationally), October–January. *Fluxus and Arte Povera,* Andrea Contini Galleria, Genoa, November. ¶ WRITINGS "Chores," in Hans-Ulrich Obrist and Bruce Altshuler, eds., *Do It,* exh. cat. (New York: Independent Curators Incorporated), 87. "Just Doing," *TDR/The Drama Review* 41, no. 3: 101–6. "Il valore dell'irrilevante," *Il Sole 24 ORE,* 13 July: 34.

1998

TEACHING POSITIONS Professor Emeritus, Visual Arts Department, University of California, San Diego. ¶ **GROUP EXHIBITIONS** *Out of Actions: Between Performance and the Object, 1949–1979,* Geffen Contemporary at The Museum of Contemporary Art, Los Angeles (traveled internationally), February–May. *Fluxus und Happening der 60er und 70er Jahre,* Galerie Inge Baecker, Cologne, March–April. *Double Trouble: The Patchett Collection,* Museum of Contemporary Art, San Diego (traveled internationally), June–September. *1950–1970: Cinquanta opere dalla Collezione Lanfranchi e dall'Archivio Conz,* Galleria Communale d'Arte Contemporanea, Todi, Italy, October–January. *Poèmes à petite vitesse,* Musée d'art contemporain Lyon, Lyon, October–November. ¶ **FESTIVALS** Beyond the Pink, The Museum of Contemporary Art, Los Angeles, February.

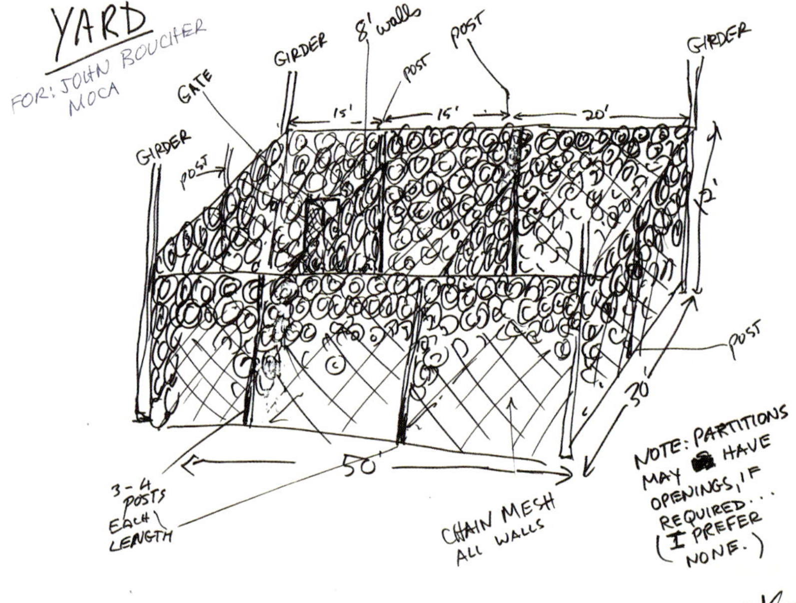

358 Drawing of *Yard*

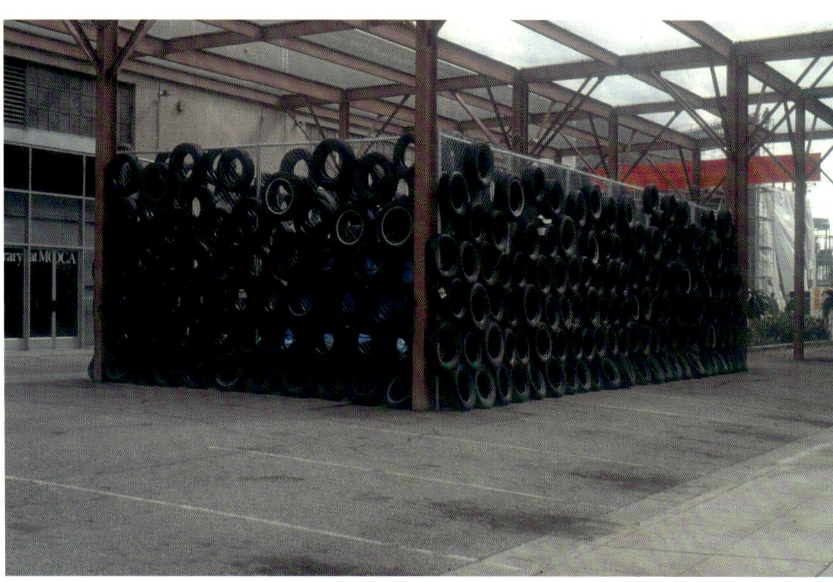

359 Photo of *Yard*

358–361 **Yard**
Environment, February–May 1998
Reinvention for *Out of Actions*
Geffen Contemporary at
The Museum of Contemporary
Art, Los Angeles

Push and Pull
Environment, February–March 1998
Reinvention for *Out of Actions*
Visitors Gallery, The Museum of
Contemporary Art, Los Angeles

Untitled Occurrences
Activity, February 1998
Presented for Beyond the Pink
The Museum of Contemporary
Art, Los Angeles

To: Kristine Stiles, FAX: (919) 688-8935 May 23, 97

Dear Kristine –

Thanks for your sympathetic letter urging me to participate in Paul Schimmel's "Out of Actions" show.

The problem of my participation emerged from two basic issues; one philosophical and the other practical. They are both intertwined:

First, the non-art contexts essential to the Environments and Happenings after 1959 were [are] incompatible with gallery/museum presentation needs. Moreover, such works were meant to change constantly — by physically active participation; and then in appearance, materials and concept each time they might be re-realized. This runs counter to the idea of the unique → artwork!

Second, from a realistic point of view, such a participatory and changeable nature cannot be supervised and maintained by gallery/museum staffs. Vandalism and breakage are common. Obvious questions of training, attention and assistance, insurance, transportation and costs, would be faced at each step of Paul's show. Neither Paul nor any other museum director could take on that responsibility.

Then, vis à vis your preference for including "18 Happenings", that piece was far more a set of events, than even an Environment. And you "can't put an event on the wall" (said Mary McCarthy)

We've got to accept that a museum is governed by culturally-ingrained habits of spectatorship (shsh! don't touch, just look), not by physically-direct involvement. No visitors (nor the all-imposing guards) could, or would, know what else to do. And without such involvement, there would be no work.

So, with all my good wishes for the show, I was ready to withdraw, as I have elsewhere.

go to p. 2

P. 2

Additionally, your concern that if I did what was essential to the work, I "would stand out like a sore thumb" is hardly my interest or desire for drama. Integrity to what the work was, and still is, historically, is all that concerned me — as much as respect for the integrity of Paul's objectives.

It is simply a plain fact that such works as my Environments and Happenings are very different from most other artists' apparently-related productions. If that makes my work "stand out like a sore thumb" when grouped among improper comparisons, then we should hasten to correct the error, not fudge it over.

In any case, I learned that there was a chance for me to use the street in front of the Temporary/Contemporary/Geffen museum, and I proposed making the "Yard" there (the one with the tires). This idea was the most practical of all, and the least costly. Paul agreed.

So we may have resolved our dilemma into a workable compromise.

— Thanks again!
Allan

CC: Paul Schimmel
MOCA

TEACHING POSITIONS Professor Emeritus, Visual Arts Department, University of California, San Diego. ¶ GROUP EXHIBITIONS *Off-Limits: Rutgers University and the Avant-Garde, 1957–63,* Newark Museum, Newark, New Jersey, February–May. *Radical Past: Contemporary Art and Music in Pasadena, 1960–1974,* Armory Center for the Arts (and other venues), Pasadena, February–April. *W(H)ALE: A Remake Portfolio,* Kunsthalle Bremen, Bremen, March–May. *The American Century: Art and Culture, Part 2, 1950–2000,* Whitney Museum of American Art, New York, September–February. *Experiments in the Everyday: Allan Kaprow and Robert Watts—Events, Objects, Documents,* Miriam and Ira D. Wallach Art Gallery, Columbia University (traveled nationally), October–December.

1999

Kids' Stories on the Sidewalks

Activity, April 1999
Children's Museum of San Diego, San Diego

Tracer
Activity, April 2000
Presented for *Time: Suspend Your Flight*
Bergen Kunstmuseum, Bergen, Norway

Safety Controls
Activity, April–June 2000
Presented for *Over the Edges*
Street corners, Ghent, Belgium

No Rules . . . Except
Activity, September 2000–September 2001
Presented for *Made in California: NOW*
Boone Children's Gallery, Los Angeles County Museum of Art–West, Los Angeles

Courtesy
LP record, 2000
One-sided, orange vinyl, 16 minutes
Recorded for *Close Radio,* KPFK-FM, June 1977
Volume 11, Slowscan Editions, s Hertogenbosch, The Netherlands

2000

TEACHING POSITIONS Professor Emeritus, Visual Arts Department, University of California, San Diego. ¶ GROUP EXHIBITIONS *Over the Edges: The Corners of Ghent,* Stedelijk Museum voor Actuele Kunst, Ghent, Belgium, April–June. *Time: Suspend Your Flight,* Bergen Kunstmuseum, Bergen, Norway (traveled internationally), April–May. *RE-PLAY: Beginnings of International Media Art in Austria,* Generali Foundation, Vienna, May–August. *La collection: Installations l'exotisme sans partage,* Musée d'art contemporain Lyon, Lyon, June–September. *Das Lied von der Erde,* Museum Fridericianum, Kassel, June–October. *Made in California: NOW,* Los Angeles County Museum of Art, Los Angeles, September 2000–September 2001. *HYPERMENTAL: Rampant Reality, 1950–2000: From Salvador Dali to Jeff Koons,* Kunsthaus Zürich, Zurich (traveled internationally), November–January.

TEACHING POSITIONS Professor Emeritus, Visual Arts Department, University of California, San Diego. ¶ SOLO EXHIBITIONS *Allan Kaprow: Activity-Fotos aus den 60ern und 70ern,* Galerie Inge Baecker, Cologne, September–November. ¶ GROUP EXHIBITIONS *Accrochage,* Galerie Inge Baecker, Cologne, February–March. *Between Sound and Vision,* Gallery 400, College of Architecture and the Arts, University of Illinois, Chicago, February–March. *After the Beginning and Before the End: Instruction Drawings,* Bergen Kunstmuseum, Bergen, Norway, March–May. *Les années pop,* Musée national d'art moderne, Centre Georges Pompidou, Paris, March–June. *Leonardo in azione e poesia,* Museo Ideale Leonardo Da Vinci, Florence, April–December. *Dennis Hopper: A System of Moments,* Österreichisches Museum für angewandte Kunst, Vienna, May–October. *A Sport and a Pastime,* Greene Naftali Gallery, New York, June–July.

2001

Postal Regulations

Activity, June–July 2001
Presented for *A Sport and a Pastime*
Greene Naftali Gallery, New York

Push and Pull
Environment, June 2002–October 2003
Reinvention for *The Collection*
Museum Moderner Kunst Stiftung Ludwig, Vienna

2002

TEACHING POSITIONS Professor Emeritus, Visual Arts Department, University of California, San Diego. ¶ SOLO EXHIBITIONS *Happening und Fluxus der 60er und 70er Jahre,* Galerie Inge Baecker, Cologne, May–June. ¶ GROUP EXHIBITIONS *Passenger: The Viewer as Participant,* Astrup Fearnley Museet for Moderne Kunst, Oslo, January–April. *Fluxus and Friends: The Walter and Maria Schnepel Collection,* Neues Museum, Weserburg, Bremen, May–June. *The Collection,* Museum Moderner Kunst Stiftung Ludwig, Vienna, June–October. *Representing Nature,* Museum of Contemporary Art, Chicago, August–January.

TEACHING POSITIONS Professor Emeritus, Visual Arts Department, University of California, San Diego. ¶ **GROUP EXHIBITIONS** *Critical Mass: Happenings, Fluxus, Performance, Intermedia and Rutgers University, 1958–1972,* Mead Art Museum, Amherst, Massachusetts (traveled nationally), February–June. *Collection: Nouvelle presentation,* Musée d'art contemporain Lyon, Lyon, April–August. *A Happening Place,* Gershman Y, Philadelphia, April–June. *European Art Expo,* Dusseldorf, July. *Living Theater/Labyrinths of the Imaginary,* Castel Sant'Elmo, Naples, July–September. *Work Ethic,* Baltimore Museum of Art, Baltimore (traveled nationally), October–January.

2003

Yard

Environment, July–September 2003
Reinvention for *Living Theater/Labyrinths of the Imaginary*
Castel Sant'Elmo, Naples

2004

TEACHING POSITIONS Professor Emeritus, Visual Arts Department, University of California, San Diego. ¶ **GROUP EXHIBITIONS** *That Bodies Speak Has Been Known for a Long Time,* Generali Foundation, Vienna, January–April. *Topographies,* San Francisco Art Institute, San Francisco (traveled in California), March–May. *Life as Art: Dedicated to Allan Kaprow,* Vlepo Gallery, Staten Island, October. *Attraversare Genova: Percorsi e linguaggi internazionali del contemporaneo, anni '60–'70,* Museo d'Arte Contemporanea di Villa Croce, Genoa, November–February. ¶ **WRITINGS** "Chores (1996)" (originally published in 1997), in Hans Ulrich Obrist, ed., *Do It* (New York: Eflux), 172–73.

TEACHING POSITIONS Professor Emeritus, Visual Arts Department, University of California, San Diego. ¶ SOLO EXHIBITIONS *Allan Kaprow,* Hauser & Wirth, Zurich, August–October. *A Short History of Performance, Part III: Allan Kaprow,* Whitechapel Art Gallery, London, October. ¶ GROUP EXHIBITIONS *Yoko Ono: Horizontal Memories,* Astrup Fearnely Museet for Moderne Kunst, Oslo, January–May. *Marking Time,* Los Angeles Contemporary Exhibitions Gallery, Los Angeles, February–May. *Recent Acquisitions from the Athenaeum's Artists' Books and Artworks Collection,* Athenaeum Music and Arts Library, La Jolla, California, February–March. *Generations of Art—10 Years at FAR,* Fondazione Antonio Ratti, Como, Italy, April–July. *Covering the Real: Art and the Press Picture from Warhol to Tillmans,* Kunstmuseum Basel, Basel, Switzerland, May–August. *Art Unlimited, Art/36/Basel,* Basel, Switzerland, June. *ARTissima 12,* Fondazione Torino Musei, Turin, November.

2005

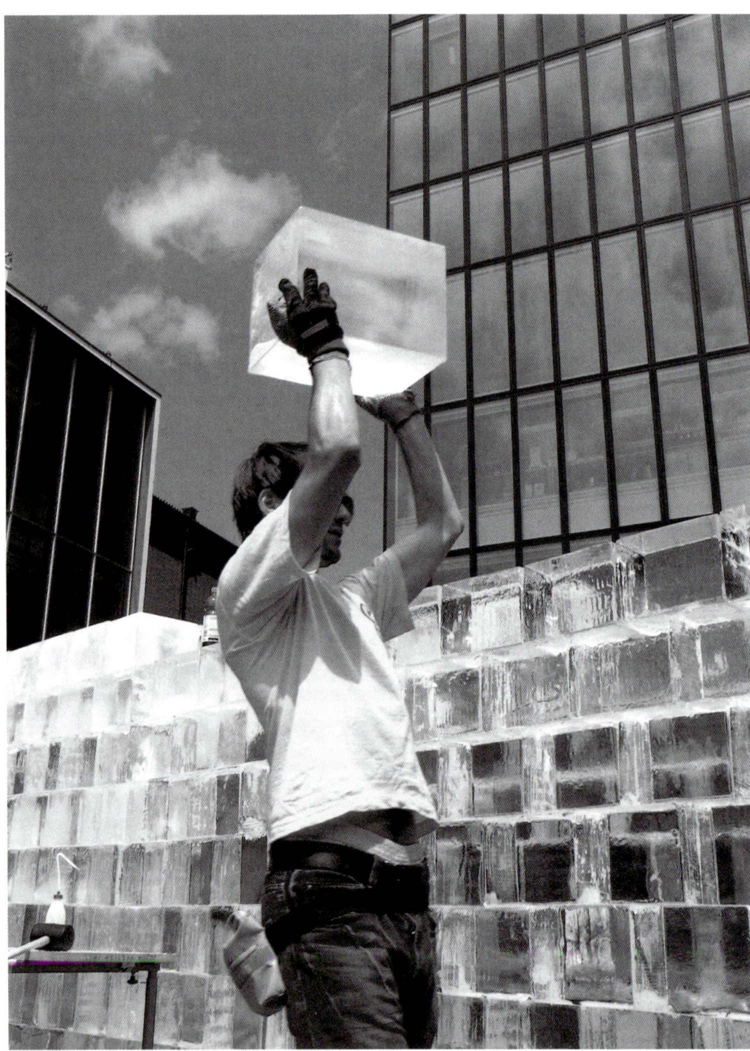

362 Participant carrying ice

362–363 **Fluids**
Happening, June 2005
Reinvention for *Art Unlimited, Art/36/Basel*
Basel, Switzerland

Sawdust
Activity, August–October 2005
Reinvention for *Allan Kaprow*
Galerie Hauser & Wirth, Zurich

Words
Environment, August–October 2005
Composed entirely of sound
Reinvention for *Allan Kaprow*
Galerie Hauser & Wirth, Zurich

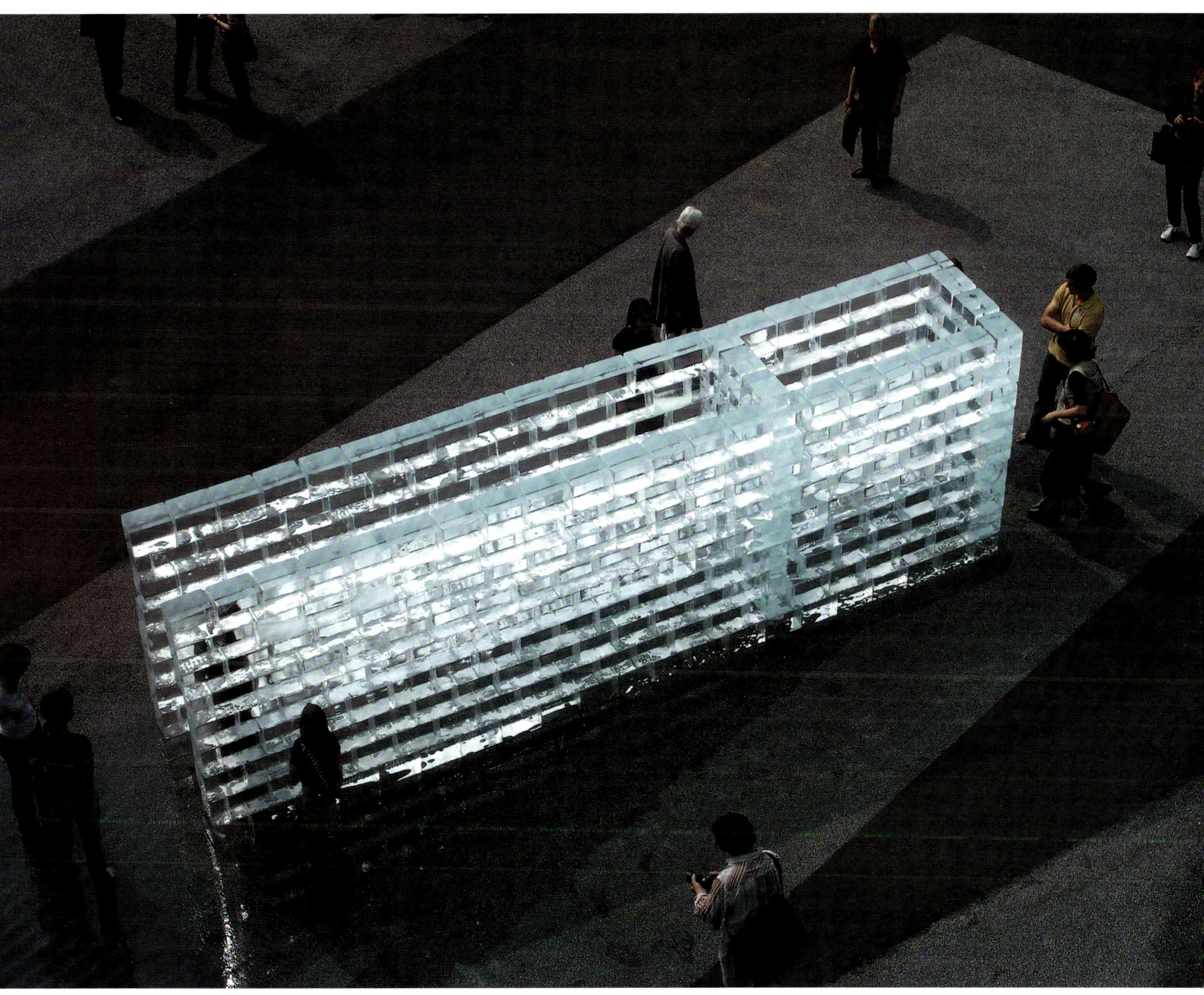

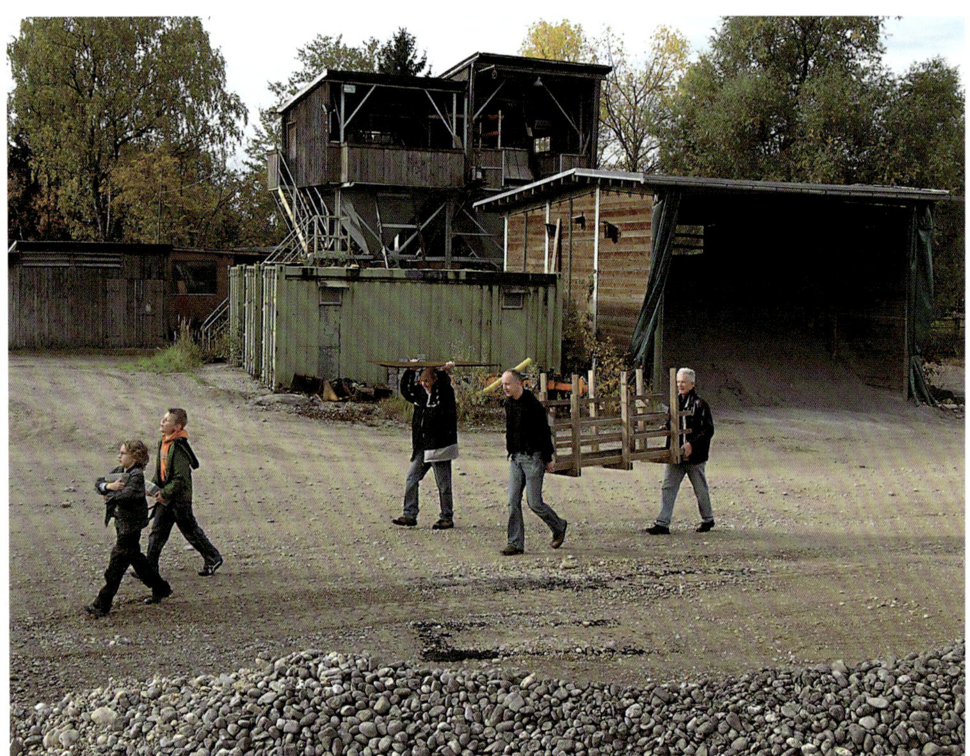

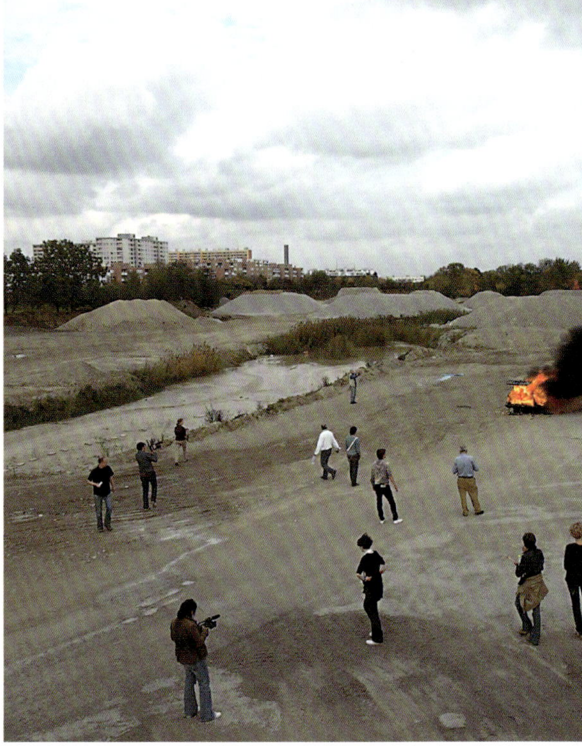

364 + 365 *Household*

LIFE EVENTS Died 5 April, Encinitas, California. ¶ TEACHING POSITIONS Professor Emeritus, Visual Arts Department, University of California, San Diego. ¶ SOLO EXHIBITIONS *Allan Kaprow—Kunst als Leben,* Haus der Kunst, Munich (traveled internationally), October–January. ¶ GROUP EXHIBITIONS *Art, Life & Confusion,* 47th October Salon, Belgrade Cultural Center, Belgrade, September–November.

2006

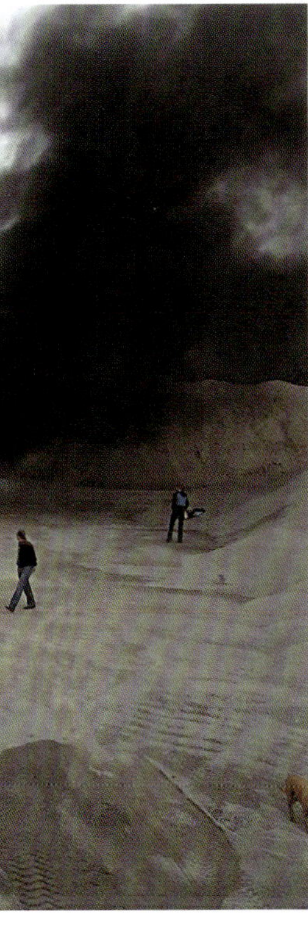

Warm-Ups
Activity, July 2006
Version by Clara Eggebrecht, Anna Klug, and Connie Mahler
Reinvention for *Allan Kaprow—Kunst als Leben*
Haus der Kunst, Munich

Warm-Ups
Activity, July 2006
Version by Aysegül Cihangir, Pernilla Henrikson, and Julia Westner
Reinvention for *Allan Kaprow—Kunst als Leben*
Munich

Round Trip
Happening, July 2006
Version by Stephanie Rosenthal
Reinvention for *Allan Kaprow—Kunst als Leben*
Munich

Yard
Environment, September–November 2006
Reinvention for *Art, Life & Confusion*
A former Turkish bath in Belgrade

Taking a Shoe for a Walk
Activity, October 2006
Version by Jörg von Brincken and the Performancegruppe der Theaterwissenschaft München OKA
Reinvention for *Allan Kaprow—Kunst als Leben*
Munich

Fall
Activity, October 2006
Version by Jörg von Brincken and the Performancegruppe der Theaterwissenschaft München OKA
Reinvention for *Allan Kaprow—Kunst als Leben*
Englischer Garten, Munich

Private Parts
Activity, October 2006
Version by Jörg von Brincken and the Performancegruppe der Theaterwissenschaft München OKA
Reinvention for *Allan Kaprow—Kunst als Leben*
A subway station, Munich

Pose
Happening, October 2006
Version by Jörg von Brincken and the Performancegruppe der Theaterwissenschaft München OKA
Reinvention for *Allan Kaprow—Kunst als Leben*
Munich

Out
Happening, October 2006
Version by Bo Christian Larsson
Reinvention for *Allan Kaprow—Kunst als Leben*
Haus der Kunst, Munich

Don't
Activity, October 2006
Version by Verena Bader, Regina Hemmerich, Judith Hummel, I-Ting Liao, Achim Sauter, Esther-Marie Schmitt, Julia Westner, and Isabelle Zahradnyik
Reinvention for *Allan Kaprow—Kunst als Leben*
Sendliger-Tor-Platz, Munich

Easy
Activity, October 2006
Version by Jörg von Brincken and the Performancegruppe der Theaterwissenschaft München OKA
Reinvention for *Allan Kaprow—Kunst als Leben*
Banks of the Isar river, Munich

364–365 Household
Happening, October 2006
Version by Bo Christian Larsson
Reinvention for *Allan Kaprow—Kunst als Leben*
Kieswerk Mächler gravel plant in a suburb of Munich

Hello/Goodbye
Activity, November 2006
Version by Jörg von Brincken and the Performancegruppe der Theaterwissenschaft München OKA
Reinvention for *Allan Kaprow—Kunst als Leben*
Various locations, Munich

Good Morning!
Activity, November 2006
Version by Petra Arres, Verena Bader, Clara Eggebrecht, Judith Hummel, Esther-Marie Schmitt, Mascha Solowjowa, and Julia Westner
Reinvention for *Allan Kaprow—Kunst als Leben*
Munich

Solo
Activity, November 2006
Version by Jörg von Brincken and the Performancegruppe der Theaterwissenschaft München OKA
Reinvention for *Allan Kaprow—Kunst als Leben*
Munich

18 Happenings in 6 Parts
Happening, November 2006
Directed by André Lepecki
Curated by Stephanie Rosenthal
Reenactment for *Allan Kaprow—Kunst als Leben*
Haus der Kunst, Munich

Scales
Activity, November 2006
Version by Stephanie Rosenthal
Reinvention for *Allan Kaprow—Kunst als Leben*
Haus der Kunst, Munich

Rates of Exchange
Activity, November 2006
Version by Jörg von Brincken and the Performancegruppe der Theaterwissenschaft München OKA
Reinvention for *Allan Kaprow—Kunst als Leben*
Theaterwissenschaft, Ludwig-Maximilians-Universität, Munich

Timing
Activity, November 2006
Version by Jörg von Brincken and the Performancegruppe der Theaterwissenschaft München OKA
Reinvention for *Allan Kaprow—Kunst als Leben*
Theaterwissenschaft, Ludwig-Maximilians-Universität, Munich

Highs
Activity, November 2006
Version by Jörg von Brincken and the Performancegruppe der Theaterwissenschaft München OKA
Reinvention for *Allan Kaprow—Kunst als Leben*
Theaterwissenschaft, Ludwig-Maximilians-Universität, Munich

Birds
Happening, December 2006
Version by Bo Christian Larsson
Reinvention for *Allan Kaprow—Kunst als Leben*
Haus der Kunst, Munich

366 Pose
Happening, December 2006
Version by Julienne Lorz
Reinvention for *Allan Kaprow—Kunst als Leben*
Haus der Kunst, Munich

366 *Pose*

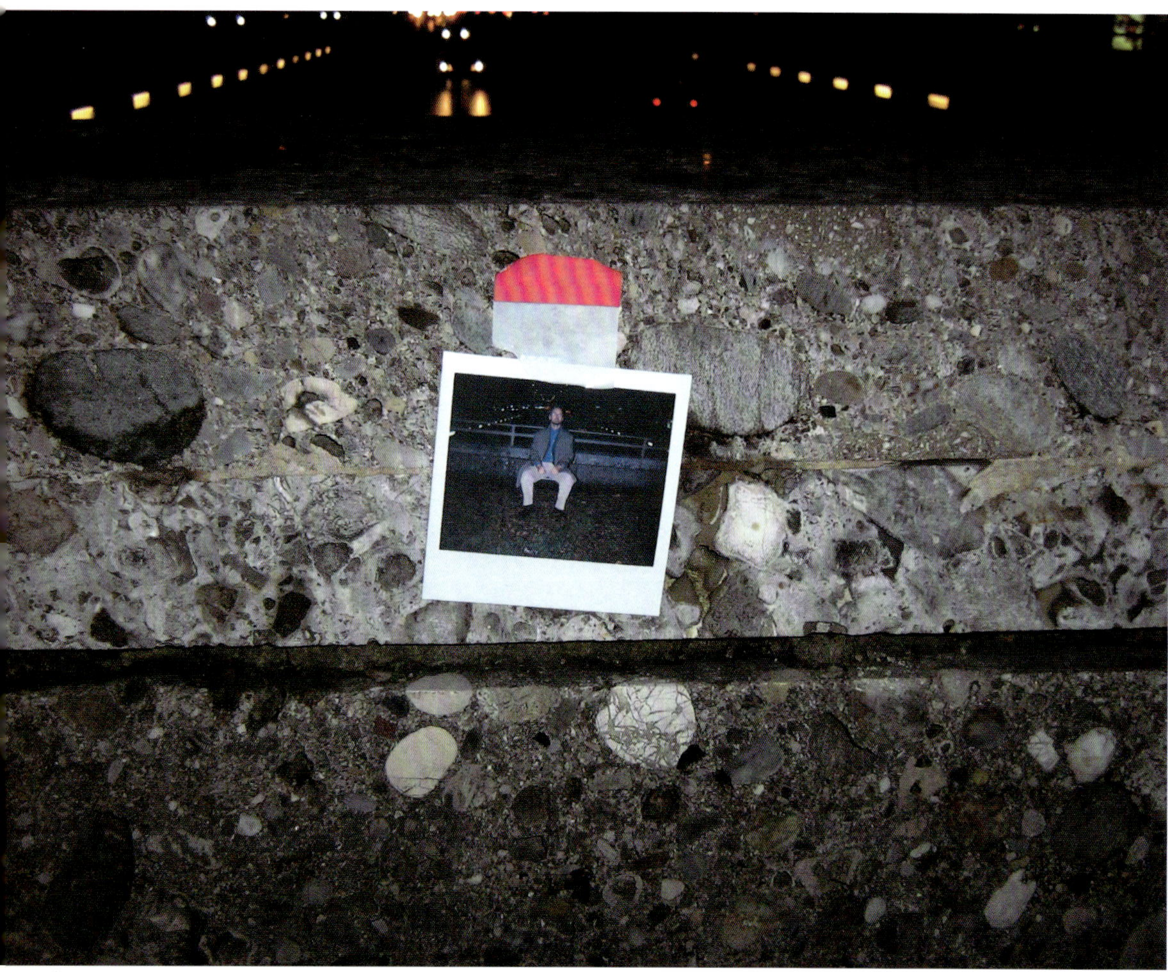

Apples and Oranges

Activity, December 2006
Version by Jörg von Brincken and the Performancegruppe der Theaterwissenschaft München OKA
Reinvention for *Allan Kaprow—Kunst als Leben*
Munich

Words

Environment, October 2006–February 2007
Version by Klasse Jetelová
Reinvention for *Allan Kaprow—Kunst als Leben*
Haus der Kunst, Munich

Stockroom

Environment, October 2006–February 2007
Version by Studio Römer
Reinvention for *Allan Kaprow—Kunst als Leben*
Haus der Kunst, Munich

Push and Pull

Environment, October 2006–February 2007
Version by 97.Tagsitzung der Klasse Pitz
Reinvention for *Allan Kaprow—Kunst als Leben*
Haus der Kunst, Munich

SOLO EXHIBITIONS *Allan Kaprow—Kunst als leven,* Van Abbemuseum, Eindhoven (traveled internationally), February–April.

2007

Scales
Activity, January 2007
Version by Jörg von Brincken and the Performancegruppe der Theaterwissenschaft München OKA
Reinvention for *Allan Kaprow—Kunst als Leben*
Ludwig-Maximilians-Universität, Munich

Level
Activity, January 2007
Version by Jörg von Brincken and the Performancegruppe der Theaterwissenschaft München OKA
Reinvention for *Allan Kaprow—Kunst als Leben*
Ludwig-Maximilians-Universität, Munich

Wink
Activity, January 2007
Version by Stephanie Rosenthal
Reinvention for *Allan Kaprow—Kunst als Leben*
Haus der Kunst, Munich

Clockwork
Activity, January 2007
Version by Jörg von Brincken and the Performancegruppe der Theaterwissenschaft München OKA
Reinvention for *Allan Kaprow—Kunst als Leben*
Munich

Wink
Activity, January 2007
Version by Jörg von Brincken and the Performancegruppe der Theaterwissenschaft München OKA
Reinvention for *Allan Kaprow—Kunst als Leben*
Munich

Another Spit Piece
Activity, February 2007
Version by Jörg von Brincken and the Performancegruppe der Theaterwissenschaft München OKA
Reinvention of *Spit* (1985) for *Allan Kaprow—Kunst als Leben*
Munich

Push and Pull
Environment, February 2007
Version by Eva Meyer-Hermann
Reinvention for *Allan Kaprow—Kunst als leven*
Van Abbemuseum, Eindhoven

367–368 Yard
Environment, February 2007
Version by Eva Meyer-Hermann
Reinvention for *Allan Kaprow—Kunst als leven*
Van Abbemuseum, Eindhoven

Stockroom
Environment, February 2007
Version by Eva Meyer-Hermann
Reinvention for *Allan Kaprow—Kunst als leven*
Van Abbemuseum, Eindhoven

Words
Environment, February 2007
Version by Eva Meyer-Hermann
Reinvention for *Allan Kaprow—Kunst als leven*
Van Abbemuseum, Eindhoven

Graft
Activity, February 2007
Version by Sandra Bradvic
Reinvention for *Allan Kaprow—Kunst als leven*
Van Abbemuseum, Eindhoven

Entr'acte
Activity, February 2007
Version by Upiek Sumanti Riptonigrum
Reinvention for *Allan Kaprow—Kunst als leven*
Heuvel Galerie, Eindhoven

Photoplay
Activity, February 2007
Version by Ger Achterbosch
Reinvention for *Allan Kaprow—Kunst als leven*
Van Abbemuseum, Eindhoven

Scales
Activity, February 2007
Version by Riet Meisen
Reinvention for *Allan Kaprow—Kunst als leven*
Van Abbemuseum, Eindhoven

Pose
Happening, March 2007
Version by Frans van Roy
Reinvention for *Allan Kaprow—Kunst als leven*
City center, Eindhoven

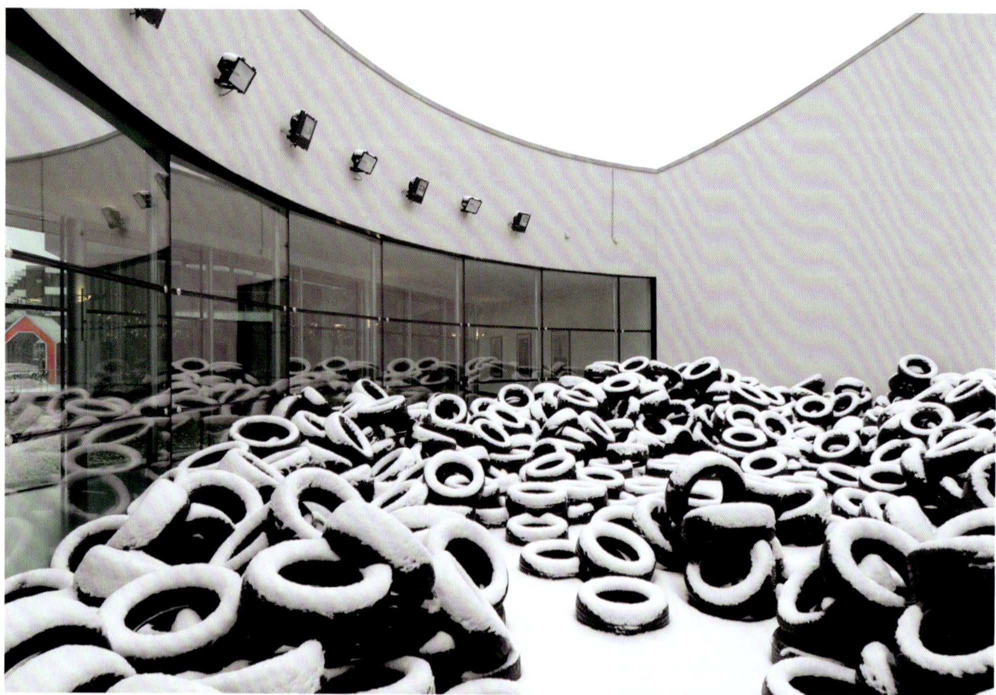

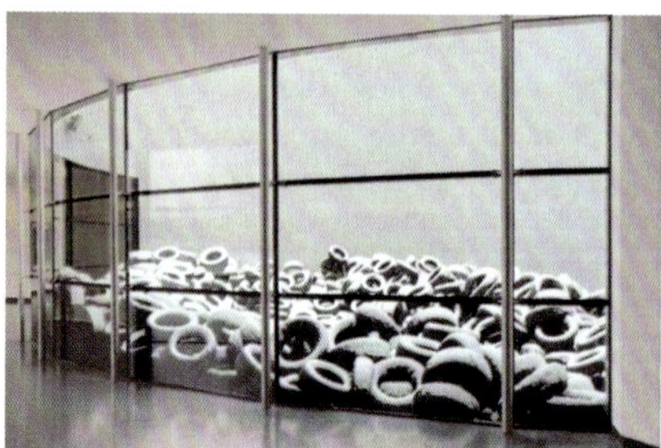

367 + 368 *Yard*

Pose
Happening, March 2007
Version by Frans van Roy
Reinvention for *Allan Kaprow—Kunst als leven*
City center, Eindhoven

Wink
Activity, March 2007
Version by Peter van Donk
Reinvention for *Allan Kaprow—Kunst als leven*
Van Abbemuseum, Eindhoven

Don't
Activity, March 2007
Version by Maggie Watkins
Reinvention for *Allan Kaprow—Kunst als leven*
Market Place, Piazza, and the Heuvel Galerie/Church, Eindhoven

Photoplay
Activity, March 2007
Version by Cor Quintus
Reinvention for *Allan Kaprow—Kunst als leven*
Van Abbemuseum, Eindhoven

Drag
Activity, March 2007
Version by Alice Pessers
Reinvention for *Allan Kaprow—Kunst als leven*
City center, Eindhoven

Birds
Happening, March 2007
Version by Noël Beterams
Reinvention for *Allan Kaprow—Kunst als leven*
Technische Universiteit, Eindhoven

Level
Activity, March 2007
Version by Willem-Jan Renders
Reinvention for *Allan Kaprow—Kunst als leven*
At the entrance to the Van Abbemuseum, Eindhoven

Charity
Happening, April 2007
Version by Herman Jentjens
Reinvention for *Allan Kaprow—Kunst als leven*
Hoogstraat, Eindhoven

Don't
Activity, April 2007
Version by Maggie Watkins
Reinvention for *Allan Kaprow—Kunst als leven*
Market Place, Piazza, and the Heuvel Galerie/Church, Eindhoven

Illustration Credits

Every effort has been made to identify and contact the copyright holders of images published in this book. Should you discover what you consider to be an unattributed photograph by a known photographer, please contact the publisher. The works of Allan Kaprow are © Allan Kaprow Estate, courtesy Hauser & Wirth Zürich London. Photographs of items in the Allan Kaprow Papers (980063), held by the Research Library at the Getty Research Institute, Los Angeles, are courtesy the Research Library and the J. Paul Getty Trust. The following sources have granted additional permission to reproduce illustrations in this book:

page 1 Kaprow at home, 1967. Allan Kaprow Papers (box 76, folder 6). Photo: Julian Wasser

page 4 Sketch of Sandwich Man for *18 Happenings in 6 Parts.* Allan Kaprow Papers (box 5, folder 6)

page 5 Kaprow discussing *Chicken* with participants. Allan Kaprow Papers (box 7, folder 9). Photo: Ed Sabol

page 359 Page from a notebook for *18 Happenings in 6 Parts.* Allan Kaprow Papers (box 5, folder 6)

page 368 Kaprow at the opening of *Allan Kaprow* at the Pasadena Art Museum, 1967. Allan Kaprow Papers (box 76, folder 6). Photo: Julian Wasser

Schimmel

fig. 1 The Rita and Taft Schreiber Collection, given in loving memory of her husband, Taft Schreiber, by Rita Schreiber. Art © 2007 The Pollock-Krasner Foundation/Artists Rights Society (ARS), New York. Photo: Brian Forrest

fig. 2 Copyright © 1960 renewed 1988 by Henmar Press Inc. C. F. Peters Corporation, Sole Selling Agent. Used by permission. All rights reserved. Photo: Geoffrey Clements. © 1998 Whitney Museum of American Art, New York. Purchased with funds from an anonymous donor

fig. 3 Photo © MUMOK, Museum Moderner Kunst Stiftung Ludwig Wien, formerly Sammlung Hahn, Köln

fig. 4 Allan Kaprow Papers (box 112, folder 1). Photo: W. F. Gainfort

fig. 5 Art © Robert Rauschenberg/Licensed by VAGA, New York, NY. Photo: Eric Pollitzer

fig. 6 Allan Kaprow Papers (box 4, folder 12). Photo: George Franklin Hurych. Courtesy Dwight Hurych

fig. 7 Art © 1954 Shiraga Kazuo. Photo: Courtesy Hyogo Prefectural Museum of Modern Art

fig. 8 Allan Kaprow Papers (box 5, folder 11). Photo: Anita Reuben Simons

figs. 9, 10 Allan Kaprow Papers (box 5, folder 11). Photos © 2007 Vaughan Rachel/Artists Rights Society (ARS), New York

fig. 11 Allan Kaprow Papers (box 5, folder 11). Photo: Anita Reuben Simons

fig. 12 Allan Kaprow Papers (box 6, folder 7). Photo © Robert R. McElroy/Licensed by VAGA, New York, NY

fig. 13 Allan Kaprow Papers (box 6, folder 7). Photo © Ken Heyman-Woodfin Camp

figs. 14, 15 Allan Kaprow Papers (box 6, folder 4). Photo © Robert R. McElroy/Licensed by VAGA, New York, NY

Potts

fig. 1 From Allan Kaprow, *Assemblage, Environments & Happenings* (New York: Harry N. Abrams, 1966), 136–37. Left: Photo © Lawrence Shustak. Right: Art © Robert Rauschenberg/Licensed by VAGA, New York, NY. Photo courtesy Portable Gallery Press, Inc.

figs. 2–4 Allan Kaprow Papers (box 7, folder 6). Photos © Lawrence Shustak

fig. 5 Allan Kaprow Papers (box 7, folder 4). Photo © Robert R. McElroy/Licensed by VAGA, New York, NY

fig. 6 Allan Kaprow Papers (box 7, folder 4). Photo by Peter Moore © Estate of Peter Moore/VAGA, New York, NY

fig. 7 Allan Kaprow Papers (box 7, folder 5). Photo © Robert R. McElroy/Licensed by VAGA, New York, NY

Phillips

fig. 1 Allan Kaprow Papers (box 24, folder 3)

figs. 2, 3 From Allan Kaprow, *Time Pieces,* Activity booklet (Berlin: Neuer Berliner Kunstverein, 1973), n.p. Allan Kaprow Papers (box 24, folder 3). Photos: Alvin Comiter

fig. 4 Allan Kaprow Papers (box 24, folder 3)

fig. 5 From Allan Kaprow, *Time Pieces,* Activity booklet (Berlin: Neuer Berliner Kunstverein, 1973), n.p. Allan Kaprow Papers (box 24, folder 3). Photo: Alvin Comiter

fig. 6 Allan Kaprow Papers (box 24, folder 4). Photo © Jürgen Müller-Schneck

fig. 7 Allan Kaprow Papers (flat file, folder 4). Photo © Jürgen Müller-Schneck

fig. 8 Allan Kaprow Papers (flat file, folder 4). Photos: Alvin Comiter

Leddy

fig. 1 Allan Kaprow Papers (box 76, folder 6). Photo: Julian Wasser

figs. 2, 3 Allan Kaprow Papers (box 17, folder 3)

fig. 4 Allan Kaprow Papers (box 18, folder 3)

figs. 5, 6 From Allan Kaprow, *Two Measures,* Activity booklet (Turin: Martano Editore, 1974), n.p. Allan Kaprow Papers (box 25, folder 7). Photos: Bee Ottinger

fig. 7 From Allan Kaprow, *Satisfaction,* Activity booklet (New York: M. L. D'Arc Gallery with Anna Canepa, 1976), n.p. Allan Kaprow Papers (box 27, folder 5). Photo: Bee Ottinger

Rosenthal

figs. 1, 2 Photos: Marion Vogel, www.marion-vogel.com.de

figs. 3, 4 Photos: Wilfried Petzi

figs. 5, 6 Photos: M. Solokhov

fig. 7 Photo: Stephanie Rosenthal

fig. 8 Photo: Regina Wohlfarth

figs. 9, 10 Photos © Andreas Lang. Haus der Kunst, *Household,* version by Bo Christian Larsson

Meyer-Hermann

fig. 1 Art © Nam June Paik Estate. Photo: Fredrik Marsh

figs. 2, 3 Art © Carl Andre/Licensed by VAGA, New York, NY. Photos: Eva Meyer-Hermann

fig. 4 From "What Is a Museum? A Dialogue between Allan Kaprow and Robert Smithson," *Arts Yearbook,* no. 9 (1967): 95. © Arts Yearbook. Left: Photo by Ezra Stoller © ESTO. Right: Photographer unknown

fig. 5 Allan Kaprow Papers (box 24, folder 4). Photo © Jürgen Müller-Schneck

figs. 6–15 Van Abbemuseum, Eindhoven, The Netherlands. Photos: Peter Cox, Eindhoven, The Netherlands

Chronology

figs. 1, 2 Photos: Barbora Gerny
fig. 3 Photo: Mary Kristen
fig. 4 Photo: Patric
figs. 5–7 Photos: Barbora Gerny
fig. 8 Martica Sawin, review of Urban Gallery solo exhibition, *Art Digest* 29, no. 16 (1955): 30. Loose clipping, Allan Kaprow Papers (box 38, folder 3)
fig. 9 Photo: Mary Kristen
fig. 10 Photo: Archivio F. Conz, Verona
fig. 11 Photo: ARTnews LLC, February 1957, courtesy of the publisher. Published as an illustration to Irving Sandler, review of Hansa Gallery exhibition, *ARTnews* 56, no. 10 (1957): 10. Loose clipping, Allan Kaprow Papers (box 38, folder 5)
fig. 12 Allan Kaprow Papers (box 3, folder 3)
fig. 13 Photo: Barbora Gerny
fig. 14 Photo: Museum Ludwig, ML1446. Courtesy Rheinisches Bildarchiv Köln
fig. 15 Photo: Mary Kristen
fig. 16 Allan Kaprow Papers (box 4, folder 12). Photo © Robert R. McElroy/Licensed by VAGA, New York, NY
fig. 17 Allan Kaprow Papers (box 112, folder 3). Photo © Robert R. McElroy/Licensed by VAGA, New York, NY
fig. 18 Van Abbemuseum, Eindhoven, The Netherlands. Photo: Peter Cox, Eindhoven, The Netherlands
fig. 19 Allan Kaprow Papers (box 112, folder 3). Photo © Robert R. McElroy/Licensed by VAGA, New York, NY
fig. 20 Allan Kaprow Papers (box 112, folder 4). Photo: Jon Henry. Courtesy Susan Henry-Young and Nancy Henry, daughters
figs. 21, 22 Allan Kaprow Papers (box 4, folder 7)
fig. 23 Allan Kaprow Papers (box 4, folder 14)
figs. 24, 25 Allan Kaprow Papers (box 4, folder 7)
fig. 26 Allan Kaprow Papers (box 112, folder 4). Photo: Jon Henry. Courtesy Susan Henry-Young and Nancy Henry, daughters
fig. 27 James R. Mellow, review of *Untitled Environment, Arts,* no. 8 (1958): 61. Loose clipping, Allan Kaprow Papers (box 38, folder 6). Reproduced courtesy *Arts Magazine*
fig. 28 Allan Kaprow Papers (box 112, folder 4). Photo: Jon Henry. Courtesy Susan Henry-Young and Nancy Henry, daughters
figs. 29–31 Allan Kaprow Papers (flat file folder 1)
fig. 32 Allan Kaprow Papers (box 5, folder 6a)
fig. 33 Allan Kaprow Papers (box 5, folder 6)
fig. 34 Allan Kaprow Papers (box 5, folder 8). Photos © 2007 Vaughan Rachel/Artists Rights Society (ARS), New York
fig. 35 Allan Kaprow Papers (box 5, folder 8). Photo: Anita Reuben Simons
figs. 36, 37 Allan Kaprow Papers (box 5, folder 6)
fig. 38 Allan Kaprow Papers (box 112, folder 7). Photo © Scott Hyde/ Licensed by VAGA, New York, NY
fig. 39 Allan Kaprow Papers (box 5, folder 11). Photo © Scott Hyde/ Licensed by VAGA, New York, NY
fig. 40 Allan Kaprow Papers (box 5, folder 9). Photo © 2007 Vaughan Rachel/Artists Rights Society (ARS), New York
fig. 41 Allan Kaprow Papers (box 5, folder 9a)
figs. 42–46 Allan Kaprow Papers (box 112, folder 6). Photographer unknown
fig. 47 Allan Kaprow Papers (box 5, folder 9)
fig. 48 Allan Kaprow Papers (box 5, folder 9). Photo © 2007 Vaughan Rachel/Artists Rights Society (ARS), New York
fig. 49 Fairfield Porter, review of *18 Happenings in 6 Parts, The Nation* 189, no. 13 (1959): 260. Loose clipping, Allan Kaprow Papers (box 38, folder 7). Reprinted with permission from the October 14, 1959 issue of *The Nation* magazine. For subscription information, call 1-800-333-8536. Portions of each week's *The Nation* magazine can be accessed at http://www.thenation.com
fig. 50 Allan Kaprow Papers (box 5, folder 12)
fig. 51 Allan Kaprow Papers (box 6, folder 1)
figs. 52, 53 Allan Kaprow Papers (box 6, folder 1). Photo: Anita Reuben Simons
figs. 54, 55 Allan Kaprow Papers (box 36)
figs. 56, 57 Allan Kaprow Papers (box 6, folder 4). Photos © Robert R. McElroy/Licensed by VAGA, New York, NY
fig. 58 Allan Kaprow Papers (box 6, folder 4)
fig. 59 Theodore Tucker [pseud., Allan Kaprow], "Kaprow's 'Apple Shrine,'" *Village Voice,* 12 January 1961. Allan Kaprow Papers (box 36)
fig. 60 Allan Kaprow Papers (box 6, folder 4)
figs. 61, 62 Allan Kaprow Papers (box 6, folder 5)
fig. 63 Allan Kaprow Papers (box 6, folder 5). Photo: Vera Spoerri-Mercer
fig. 64 Allan Kaprow Papers (box 6, folder 5). Photographer unknown
fig. 65 Allan Kaprow Papers (box 6, folder 5)
fig. 66 Allan Kaprow Papers (flat file folder 4)
fig. 67 Allan Kaprow Papers (box 6, folder 7). Photo © Ken Heyman-Woodfin Camp
fig. 68 Allan Kaprow Papers (box 112, folder 11). Photo © Ken Heyman-Woodfin Camp
fig. 69 Allan Kaprow Papers (box 6, folder 7)
fig. 70 Jill Johnston, "'Environments' at Martha Jackson's," review of *Yard, Village Voice,* 6 July 1961. Allan Kaprow Papers (box 6, folder 6)
fig. 71 Allan Kaprow Papers (box 7, folder 1)
fig. 72 Allan Kaprow Papers (box 7, folder 3). Photo © Robert R. McElroy/Licensed by VAGA, New York, NY
fig. 73 Allan Kaprow Papers (box 7, folder 1)
figs. 74, 75 Allan Kaprow Papers (box 7, folder 5)
figs. 76, 77 Allan Kaprow Papers (box 7, folder 5). Photos © Robert R. McElroy/Licensed by VAGA, New York, NY
figs. 78–81 Allan Kaprow Papers (box 7, folder 9)
figs. 82–84 Allan Kaprow Papers (box 7, folder 9). Photos: Ed Sabol
fig. 85 Allan Kaprow Papers (box 7, folder 9)
fig. 86 Allan Kaprow Papers (box 7, folder 6). Photo © Lawrence Shustak
fig. 87 Allan Kaprow Papers (box 7, folder 6)
fig. 88 Allan Kaprow Papers (box 7, folder 6). Photo © Lawrence Shustak
fig. 89 Allan Kaprow Papers (box 7, folder 7). Photo by Peter Moore © Estate of Peter Moore/VAGA, New York, NY
fig. 90 Allan Kaprow Papers (box 7, folder 6)
fig. 91 Allan Kaprow Papers (box 7, folder 6). Photo © Lawrence Shustak
fig. 92 Allan Kaprow Papers (box 7, folder 6)
fig. 93 Allan Kaprow Papers (box 8, folder 2). Photographer unknown
fig. 94 Paul Berg, "Push and Pull: A Furniture Comedy," review of *Push and Pull, Saint Louis Post-Dispatch,* Sunday magazine, 19 May 1963. Allan Kaprow Papers (box 8, folder 2). Photos: Paul Berg/*St. Louis Post-Dispatch.* Reprinted with permission of the *St. Louis Post-Dispatch,* copyright 2008
figs. 95–97 Allan Kaprow Papers (box 8, folder 2). Photos: Paul Berg/ *St. Louis Post-Dispatch*
figs. 98, 99 Allan Kaprow Papers (box 8, folder 1)
fig. 100 Allan Kaprow Papers (box 8, folder 1). Photo: Ben Gelman/ *The Southern Illinoisan*
figs. 101, 102 Allan Kaprow Papers (box 9, folder 2)
figs. 103–5 Allan Kaprow Papers (box 9, folder 2). Photos: Terry S. Lindquist

figs. 106, 107 Allan Kaprow Papers (box 9, folder 3)
fig. 108 Allan Kaprow Papers (box 9, folder 3). Photo: Florian Steiner
fig. 109 Allan Kaprow Papers (box 9, folder 1a)
fig. 110 Allan Kaprow Papers (box 9, folder 1b). Photographer unknown
figs. 111–13 Allan Kaprow Papers (box 9, folder 1a)
fig. 114 Allan Kaprow Papers (box 9, folder 1b). Photo: Sol Goldberg
fig. 115 Allan Kaprow Papers (box 9, folder 1a)
figs. 116, 117 Allan Kaprow Papers (box 9, folder 1b). Photos: Sol Goldberg
figs. 118–20 Allan Kaprow Papers (box 9, folder 7)
figs. 121–23 Photos by Peter Moore © Estate of Peter Moore/VAGA, New York, NY
figs. 124–28 Allan Kaprow Papers (box 9, folder 9)
fig. 129 Allan Kaprow Papers (flat file folder 1)
fig. 130 Photo by Peter Moore © Estate of Peter Moore/VAGA, New York, NY
figs. 131, 132 Allan Kaprow Papers (box 11, folder 2). Photos © Burton Berinsky
fig. 133 Photo: Julian Wasser
fig. 134 Allan Kaprow Papers (flat file folder 1)
fig. 135 Photo: Julian Wasser
figs. 136, 137 Allan Kaprow Papers (box 12, folder 9)
fig. 138 Allan Kaprow Papers (box 113, folder 10). Photo: Julian Wasser
fig. 139 Allan Kaprow Papers (box 12, folder 10). Photo: Julian Wasser
fig. 140 Allan Kaprow Papers (box 12, folder 9)
figs. 141, 142 Allan Kaprow Papers (box 12, folder 10). Photos: Julian Wasser
fig. 143 From Allan Kaprow, *Moving,* photoalbum (Chicago: Museum of Modern Art, 1967), n.p. Allan Kaprow Papers (box 12, folder 5). Photo by Peter Moore © Estate of Peter Moore/VAGA, New York, NY
fig. 144 From Allan Kaprow, *Moving,* photoalbum (Chicago: Museum of Modern Art, 1967), n.p. Allan Kaprow Papers (box 12, folder 5)
fig. 145 Allan Kaprow Papers (box 14, folder 2)
fig. 146 Allan Kaprow Papers (box 14, folder 2). Photo: John Millaire
figs. 147, 148 Allan Kaprow Papers (box 14, folder 2)
figs. 149, 150 Allan Kaprow Papers (box 14, folder 1). Photographs by Andrew Glantz/Zenith Design
fig. 151 Allan Kaprow Papers (flat file folder 1)
fig. 152 Allan Kaprow Papers (box 14, folder 3)
fig. 153 Allan Kaprow Papers (box 14, folder 3). Photo: Mick Brady
fig. 154 Allan Kaprow Papers (box 13, folder 7). Photo: Howard J. Smagula
fig. 155 Allan Kaprow Papers (box 13, folder 7)
fig. 156 Allan Kaprow Papers (box 13, folder 7). Photo: Howard J. Smagula
fig. 157 Allan Kaprow Papers (flat file folder 1)
figs. 158, 159 Allan Kaprow Papers (box 13, folder 9)
fig. 160 Video still from *Hello.* Allan Kaprow Papers (box 86)
fig. 161 Allan Kaprow Papers (box 13, folder 10)
fig. 162 Alan Kaprow, "Hello: Plan and Execution," *Art-Rite,* no. 7 (1974): 17. Allan Kaprow Papers (box 13, folder 10)
fig. 163 Allan Kaprow Papers (box 16, folder 3). Photos: Carol Bowen
fig. 164 Noel Lieberman, "Hard Lessons the Easy Way," *Oakland Tribune,* 4 June 1969: 18. Allan Kaprow Papers (box 16, folder 4). Photo: Chris Kiobech. Courtesy of the *Oakland Tribune*
fig. 165 Allan Kaprow Papers (box 16, folder 8). Photo: Nancy Brush
fig. 166 Allan Kaprow Papers (box 16, folder 8)
figs. 167, 168 Allan Kaprow Papers (box 17, folder 3)
fig. 169 Allan Kaprow Papers (box 23, folder 5). Photo by Peter Moore © Estate of Peter Moore/VAGA, New York, NY
fig. 170 Allan Kaprow Papers (box 23, folder 5). Photos: Allan Kaprow
fig. 171 Allan Kaprow Papers (box 23, folder 5). Photographs by participants
fig. 172 Allan Kaprow Papers (box 23, folder 5). Photos: Gretchen Garlinghouse, Diane Gilkerson, and Deborah Patten
fig. 173 Allan Kaprow Papers (box 23, folder 5). Photo © Charles Gatewood
fig. 174 © Artforum, December 1969, "Allan Kaprow," by Jean-Louis Bourgeois. Allan Kaprow Papers (box 39, folder 3)
fig. 175 Allan Kaprow Papers (box 18, folder 3)
figs. 176, 177 Allan Kaprow Papers (box 114, folder 12). Photographer unknown
figs. 178, 179 Allan Kaprow Papers (box 18, folder 6). Photographer unknown
fig. 180 Allan Kaprow Papers (box 18, folder 6)
fig. 181 © 2007, ProLitteris, Zurich. Allan Kaprow Papers (box 18, folder 9)
fig. 182 Allan Kaprow Papers (box 18, folder 10). Photo © Werner Krüger
fig. 183 Allan Kaprow Papers (box 18, folder 9)
figs. 184, 185 Allan Kaprow Papers (box 18, folder 10). Photos © Werner Krüger
fig. 186 Allan Kaprow Papers (box 19, folder 1)
figs. 187–89 Allan Kaprow Papers (box 19, folder 1). Photos: Dick Higgins. Courtesy Hannah Higgins
figs. 190–92 Allan Kaprow Papers (box 19, folder 7). Photos © Gérald Minkoff, Geneva
fig. 193 Allan Kaprow Papers (box 19, folder 9)
figs. 194, 195 Allan Kaprow Papers (box 20, folder 1)
figs. 196, 197 Video stills from *Messages Units.* Allan Kaprow Papers (box 87).
figs. 198, 199 Allan Kaprow Papers (box 20, folder 3). Photos: Jim Caldwell or Bob Covington
figs. 200–202 Allan Kaprow Papers (box 20, folder 3)
fig. 203 Allan Kaprow Papers (box 20, folder 3). Photo: Jim Caldwell or Bob Covington
fig. 204 Allan Kaprow Papers (box 20, folder 4)
fig. 205 Allan Kaprow Papers (box 20, folder 5)
fig. 206 Allan Kaprow Papers (box 20, folder 5). Photographer unknown
fig. 207 Allan Kaprow Papers (box 20, folder 8)
figs. 208, 209 Allan Kaprow Papers (box 20, folder 13)
fig. 210 From Allan Kaprow, "Easy Activity," in *Art Studies for an Editor: 25 Essays in Memory of Milton S. Fox* (New York: H. N. Abrams, 1975), 177–82. Allan Kaprow Papers (box 20, folder 13). Photographer unknown
figs. 211–14 Allan Kaprow Papers (box 20, folder 17)
figs. 215–19 Allan Kaprow Papers (box 21, folder 2). Photos: Lothar Wolleh, courtesy Estate Lothar Wolleh, Berlin
figs. 220–37 Allan Kaprow Papers (box 24, folder 3)
figs. 238–41 Allan Kaprow Papers (box 24, folder 4). Photos © Jürgen Müller-Schneck
figs. 242, 243 Video stills from *Time Pieces* (1975). Allan Kaprow Papers (box 89)
figs. 244, 245 Allan Kaprow Papers (box 24, folder 3)
fig. 246 Allan Kaprow Papers (box 24, folder 9). Photo: Alvin Comiter
fig. 247 Allan Kaprow Papers (box 25, folder 1)
figs. 248, 249 Video stills from *Then.* Allan Kaprow Papers (box 89)
fig. 250 Allan Kaprow Papers (box 25, folder 1)
figs. 251, 252 Allan Kaprow Papers (box 25, folder 4)
figs. 253–55 From Allan Kaprow, *Two Measures,* Activity booklet (Turin: Martano Editore, 1974), n.p. Allan Kaprow Papers (box 25, folder 7). Photos: Bee Ottinger
figs. 256–58 Allan Kaprow Papers (box 25, folder 6)
fig. 259 From Allan Kaprow, *Two Measures,* Activity booklet (Turin: Martano Editore, 1974), n.p. Allan Kaprow Papers (box 25, folder 7). Photos: Bee Ottinger
figs. 260, 261 From Allan Kaprow, *Echo-logy,* Activity booklet (New York: D'Arc Press, 1975), n.p. Allan Kaprow Papers (box 26, folder 6). Photos © 1975 Lizbeth Marano
fig. 262 From Allan Kaprow, *Match,* Activity booklet (Wuppertal: Kunst- und Museumsverein, 1975), n.p. Allan Kaprow Papers (box 26, folder 8). Photos © Jürgen Müller-Schneck

fig. 263 Allan Kaprow Papers (box 26, folder 8)

figs. 264–66 Allan Kaprow Papers (box 26, folder 9)

figs. 267, 268 Video stills of *Warm-Ups.* Allan Kaprow Papers (box 90)

fig. 269 Allan Kaprow Papers (box 26, folder 9)

figs. 270–72 From Allan Kaprow, *Likely Stories,* Activity booklet (Milan: Luciano Anselmino, 1975), n.p. Allan Kaprow Papers (box 26, folder 10). Photos © Jürgen Müller-Schneck

figs. 273, 274 From Allan Kaprow, *Useful Fictions,* Activity booklet (Florence: Schema Informazione, 1975), n.p. Allan Kaprow Papers (box 27, folder 1). Photos: Bee Ottinger

figs. 275, 276 Allan Kaprow Papers (box 27, folder 1)

fig. 277 Allan Kaprow Papers (box 27, folder 2)

figs. 278–81 Allan Kaprow Papers (box 27, folder 5)

fig. 282 From Allan Kaprow, *Satisfaction,* Activity booklet (New York: M. L. D'Arc Gallery with Anna Canepa, 1976), n.p. Allan Kaprow Papers (box 27, folder 5). Photos: Bee Ottinger

figs. 283, 284 Allan Kaprow Papers (box 27, folder 5)

figs. 285, 286 Allan Kaprow Papers (box 27, folder 6)

fig. 287 Allan Kaprow Papers (box 27, folder 6). Photo © Dr. Joseph Somogyi

fig. 288 Allan Kaprow Papers (box 27, folder 6)

fig. 289 Allan Kaprow Papers (box 27, folder 6). Photo © Dr. Joseph Somogyi

fig. 290 Allan Kaprow Papers (box 29, folder 3)

fig. 291 Allan Kaprow Papers (box 29, folder 3). Reproduced courtesy Werner Hofmann

fig. 292 Allan Kaprow Papers (box 29, folder 3)

figs. 293, 294 Allan Kaprow Papers (box 28, folder 11)

fig. 295 Allan Kaprow Papers (box 28, folder 14). Photo: Rebecca Cummins

fig. 296 Allan Kaprow Papers (box 28, folder 14). Photo: Susan Pamperin

figs. 297, 298 Allan Kaprow Papers (box 29, folder 7). Photographer unknown

figs. 299, 300 Allan Kaprow, "Team," *High Performance* 3, nos. 3–4 (1980): 54–55. Courtesy Arts in the Public Interest/*High Performance*

figs. 301, 302 Allan Kaprow Papers (box 30, folder 1)

fig. 303 Allan Kaprow Papers (box 30, folder 2). Reproduced courtesy Petra Kipphoff

figs. 304–9 Allan Kaprow Papers (box 30, folder 2). © Die Zeit, Nr. 13 & 14 1981, courtesy Zeitverlag Gerd Bucerius GmbH & Co. KG. Photos: Stefan Moses

fig. 310 Allan Kaprow Papers (box 30, folder 3)

fig. 311 Allan Kaprow Papers (box 30, folder 5)

figs. 312, 313 Allan Kaprow Papers (box 30, folder 7)

fig. 314 Allan Kaprow Papers (box 30, folder 8)

figs. 315, 316 Allan Kaprow Papers (box 31, folder 2)

fig. 317 Allan Kaprow Papers (box 31, folder 5)

figs. 318, 319 Allan Kaprow Papers (box 31, folder 10)

fig. 320 Allan Kaprow Papers (box 31, folder 11)

fig. 321, 322 Allan Kaprow Papers (box 31, folder 12)

fig. 323 Allan Kaprow Papers (box 31, folder 7)

fig. 324 Allan Kaprow Papers (box 115, folder 15). Installation view of *Yard* (1961), reconstructed in 1984 in the Whitney Museum of American Art Sculpture Court as part of the exhibition *Blam! The Explosion of Pop, Minimalism, and Performance, 1958–1964,* Whitney Museum of American Art, New York, September–December 1984. Photo: Geoffrey Clements. Courtesy of the Whitney Museum of American Art

fig. 325 Allan Kaprow Papers (box 31, folder 12)

fig. 326 Installation view of *Words* (1962), reconstructed in 1984 as part of the exhibition *Blam! The Explosion of Pop, Minimalism, and Performance, 1958–1964,* Whitney Museum of American Art, New York, September–December 1984. Photo: Geoffrey Clements. Courtesy of the Whitney Museum of American Art

fig. 327 Allan Kaprow Papers (box 31, folder 15). Photo © Alfred Koch

fig. 328 Allan Kaprow Papers (box 31, folder 15). Courtesy Wolfgang Feelisch. Photo: Müller + Schmitz

figs. 329–32 Allan Kaprow Papers (box 31, folder 15)

fig. 333 Allan Kaprow Papers (box 31, folder 15). Photo © Alfred Koch

fig. 334 Allan Kaprow Papers (box 31, folder 17)

fig. 335 Ruth Askey, "Conjunctions of Food and Art," *Artweek,* 16 November 1986: 11. Allan Kaprow Papers (box 40, folder 3). Reprinted with the permission of *Artweek*

figs. 336, 337 Allan Kaprow Papers (box 32, folder 1). Courtesy Virginia Zabriskie, Zabriskie Gallery

fig. 338 Allan Kaprow Papers (box 32, folder 1). Courtesy Bruce Altshuler

fig. 339 Allan Kaprow Papers (box 32, folder 4). Photo: Robert Cook. Courtesy of the Gallery at the University of Texas at Arlington, formerly known as the CRCA

figs. 340, 341 Allan Kaprow Papers (box 32, folder 4)

fig. 342 Allan Kaprow Papers (box 32, folder 7)

fig. 343 Allan Kaprow Papers (box 32, folder 9)

fig. 344 Allan Kaprow Papers (box 32, folder 9). Photo © Wolfgang Traeger, D-Volxheim

fig. 345 Allan Kaprow Papers (box 32, folder 15). Photo: Enrico Cattaneo

fig. 346 Cover of *Bull Shit,* no. 1 (1991). Allan Kaprow Papers (box 32, folder 14). Photo: Vincenzo Coronati (Milano). Reproduced courtesy Fondazione Mudima

fig. 347 Allan Kaprow Papers (box 33, folder 1). Photo: Enrico Cattaneo

fig. 348 Allan Kaprow Papers (box 32, folder 14)

fig. 349 Allan Kaprow Papers (box 33, folder 1). Photo: Archivio Fotografico Garghetti, Milano

fig. 350 Allan Kaprow Papers (box 33, folder 1). Photo: Enrico Cattaneo

fig. 351 Allan Kaprow Papers (flat file, folder 3)

fig. 352 Allan Kaprow Papers (box 33, folder 4). Photo: Courtesy John Gibson

fig. 353 Allan Kaprow Papers (box 33, folder 4)

fig. 354 Allan Kaprow Papers (box 33, folder 4). Photo: Courtesy John Gibson

fig. 355 Allan Kaprow Papers (box 33, folder 4)

fig. 356 Allan Kaprow Papers (box 33, folder 10). Photo: Jürgen O. Olbrich. Publishing rights controlled by Verwerungs-gesellschaft Bild-Kunst, Bonn, Germany (info@bildkunst.de). © 2007, ProLitteris, Zurich

fig. 357 Allan Kaprow Papers (box 33, folder 10)

fig. 358 Allan Kaprow Papers (box 34, folder 1)

fig. 359 Installation view of *Yard* (1961), reconstructed in 1998 in front of the Geffen Contemporary at The Museum of Contemporary Art, Los Angeles, as part of the exhibition *Out of Actions: Between Performance and the Object, 1949–1979,* Geffen Contemporary at The Museum of Contemporary Art, Los Angeles, 8 February–10 May 1998. Photo: Brian Forrest. Courtesy of The Museum of Contemporary Art, Los Angeles

figs. 360, 361 Allan Kaprow Papers (box 34, folder 1)

figs. 362, 363 Photos © Allan Kaprow Estate. Courtesy Hauser & Wirth Zürich London

figs. 364, 365 Photos © Andreas Lang. Haus der Kunst, *Household,* version by Bo Christian Larsson

fig. 366 Photo: Steffi Kiesl

figs. 367, 368 Van Abbemuseum, Eindhoven, The Netherlands. Photos: Peter Cox, Eindhoven, The Netherlands

Abstracted Still Life. Painting, 1952
Affect. Activity, 1974. See also *2 Measures*
After Dinner Speeches. Activity, 1982
Air Condition. Activity, 1973; Activity booklet, 1975
Anniversary. Activity, 1973
Another Spit Piece. Activity, 2007 (reinvention of *Spit*)
Apples and Oranges. Activity, 1986, 2006
Apple Shrine. Environment, 1960, 1991, 1992 (two versions)
An Archaeology of the Everyday. Activity, 1980
Arrivals. Happening, 1968
Artist in Studio. Painting, 1954
Asleep on the Job. Television spot, 1991
Assemblage. Activity, 1994
Assemblage of Hundreds. Activity, 1995
Baby. Collage, 1957
Baggage. Activity, 1972
Banjo Player. Assemblage, 1955–56
Barreling. Happening, 1968
Barriers. See *5 Minute Delay*
Basic Thermal Units. Activity, 1973
Beauty Parlor. Environment, 1991 (reinvention of *Untitled Environment*)
Beauty Parlor 2. Environment, 1993 (reinvention of *Untitled Environment*)
The Big Laugh. Happening, 1960
Birds. Happening, 1964, 2006, 2007
Blending into the Environment. Activity, 1987
Blindsight. Activity, Activity booklet, 1979; Activity, 1988
Blue and White Nudes in Interior. Painting, 1955
Blue Blue Blue. Collage, 1956
Bon Marché. Happening, 1963
Border Work. Activity, 1989
Bouquet. Collage, 1956
Building Muscles. Activity, 1983
Burbank. Activity, 1972
Burdens. Activity, 1987
Cabin. Environment, 1991
Caged Pheasant #1. Collage, 1956
Caged Pheasant #2. Collage, 1956
Calendar. Activity, 1971
Calling. Happening, 1965
Carpet Bagging. Activity, 1982 (not realized)
Car Spaces. Activity, 1970
Chapel. Proposal for an Environment, 1961 (version of *Stockroom*)
Charity. Happening, 1969, 2007
Chicken. Happening, 1962
City Works. Activity, 1971
Clean Graffiti. Activity, 1983
Click. Album, 1969
Clockwork. Activity, 1973, 2007
Coca-Cola, Shirley Cannonball? Happening, 1960
Collage No. 2. Collage, 1957
Comfort Zones. Activity, Activity booklet, film, 1975
Common Senses. Video, 1977
Communication. Happening, 1958
Company. Activity, 1982, 1988
The Conference as Performance. Activity, 1986
Convoy. Activity, 1980
Copy. Activity, 1972 (not realized)
Course. Happening, 1969
Courtesy. Activity, 1977; LP record, 2000
Courtyard. Happening, 1962
Creatures. Activity, 1973
Days Off. Calendar, 1970
Dead End. Environment, 1992 (reinvention of *Untitled Environment*)
Dial. Happening, 1969, 1973, 1974. See also *Dial II*
Dial II. Happening, 1971 (reinvention of *Dial*)
Don't. Activity, 1970, 2006, 2007 (two versions)
Drag. Activity, 1984, 2007
Drawing on Stories. Activity, 1981
Durations. Activity, film, 1976
Easy. Activity, 1972, 2006
Easy Chairs 1 and Easy Chairs 2. Activity, 1996
Easy Too. Activity, 1979
Eat. Environment, 1964, 1991, 1992 (two versions)
Echo-logy. Activity, Activity booklet, 1975
18 Happenings in 6 Parts. Happening, 1959, 1988, 2006
Electronic sound for Eugene Ionesco's *The Killer.* Performance, 1960
Entr'acte. Activity, 1972, 2007
European Tour. Series of Activities, 1981. See also *Drawing on Stories; Going/Staying; Just Walking on the Edge; Leaving No Footprints; Our Life Together (Scenes for a Movie); Quiet Please; Weighty Matters*
Exercise. Activity, 1980
Exercise 6. Activity, 1981 (not realized)
Fall. Activity, 1995, 2006
Figures in Landscape. Painting, 1953
Figures in Yellow Interior. Painting, 1954
Fine! Happening, 1969
5 Minute Delay. Activity, 1993
Flick. Happening, 1967
Flight, Part I, version 1. Happening, 1962 (not realized)
Flight, Part I, version 2. Happening, 1962 (not realized)
Flow. Collage, 1972
Fluids. Happening, 1967, 2005
Forecast. Happening, 1969 (not realized)
Frames of Mind. Activity, 1976
Frame Work. Activity, 1976
Fresh Air. Environment, 1986 (reinvention of *Untitled Environment*)
From James Joyce's Ulysses. Painting, 1956
Galileo Galilei. Activity, 1976
Garage Environment. Environment, 1960
Gas. Happening, 1966
George Brecht Dedication Ceremony. Activity, 1972
George Washington Bridge (Front View). Painting, 1955
George Washington Bridge (Side View). Painting, 1955
Giveaway. Happening, 1969
Give Me Your Jacket. Activity, 1982
Give Me Your Money! Activity, 1983
Going/Staying. Activity, 1981
Good Morning! Activity, 1970, 2006
Graft. Activity, 1970, 2007
Grandma's Boy. Assemblage, 1957
Heavenly Pass-Time. Proposal for an Activity, 1969
Hello. Happening, 1969. See also *Sales Pitch*
Hello/Goodbye. Activity, 1978, 2006
Hero. Assemblage, ca. 1955–56
Highs. Activity, 1973, 2006
Homage to Monet. Painting, 1955
Home Brew. Activity, 1969 (not realized)
Homemovies. Marriage Happening, video, 1969
Household. Happening, 1964, 2006
How To Make a Happening. LP record, 1966
Hysteria. Collage, 1956
Idea. Activity, 1972
If the Shoe Fits, Sign It. Activity, 1997
Imitations. Activity, 1980
Intermission Piece. Happening, 1960
Interruption. Happening, 1967
In the Art. Collage, 1956
Just Walking on the Edge. Activity, 1981
Kaprow-Négyesy Project. Activity, 1991
Kids' Stories on the Sidewalks. Activity, 1999
Labor Day. Activity, 1971
Laughs and Balloons. Happening, 1959
Leaning into the Light. Painting, 1956
Leaving No Footprints. Activity, 1981
Level. Activity, 1970, 2007 (two versions)
L Gold. Proposal for a publicity campaign of Happenings, 1967
Likely Stories. Activity, Activity booklet, 1975
Loss. Activity, 1973
Lots of Work. Activity, 1983
Magenta Nude. Painting, 1954
Making Faces. Activity, 1980 (not realized)
Maneuvers. Activity, Activity booklet, 1976
Mantra. Activity, 1978
Match. Activity, Activity booklet, 1975
Maybe the Shortest Parade. Activity, 1981
Meditation 1. Activity, 1981
Meditation 2. Activity, 1981
Meeting at the Market. Activity, 1990
Message Units. Activity, 1972 (two versions)
Message Units. Proposal for a Happening, 1968
Meteorology. Activity, Assemblage, 1972
Meters. Activity, 1972 (not realized)
Mirrors: A Happening. Happening, 1962 (not realized)
Model in Leotard Leaning on Sawhorse. Drawing, 1954 (two versions)
Moon Sounds. Activity, 1969
Moving. Happening, photoalbum, 1967
A Much Better Idea. Activity, 1984
Museum Portraits. Activity, 1977 (not realized)
Mushroom. Happening 1962
Music. Tape score, 1957
Natural Distances. Activity, 1976
Night. Happening, 1961

Noise. Happening, 1967
No Rules . . . Except. Activity, 2000–2001
Office Boy. Activity, 1987
The Oldtimer. Collage, 1957
On Time. Activity, Activity booklet, 1974
Orange. Happening, 1964
Originale. Opera Happening, 1964
Our Life Together (Scenes for a Movie). Activity, 1981
Out. Happening, 1963, 2006
Overtime. Happening, 1968
Paper. Happening, 1964
Pastorale. Happening, 1958
Peeping Tom. Activity, 1978
Penny Arcade. Assemblage, 1956
People. Collage, 1956
The Perfect Bed. Activity, 1986
Performance as a Meditational Practice. Activity, 1981
Photoplay. Activity, 1982, 2007 (two versions)
Piece for Coryl's Birthday. Activity, 1985
Please Help Yourself. Activity, 1984
Population. Happening, 1968
Pose. Happening, 1969, 2006 (two versions), 2007 (two versions)
Postal Regulations. Activity, 2001
Pre-Socratic. Activity, 1976
Print-Out. Activity, 1971
A Private Act in a Public Place. Activity, 1984
Private Lines. Videoscript, 1972 (not realized)
Private Parts. Activity, 1976, 2006; video, 1977
Publicity. Activity, 1970
Purpose. Happening, 1969
Push and Pull. Environment, 1963, 1965, 1967, 1977, 1986, 1991, 1998, 2002, 2006, 2007
Putting On Your Face. Activity, 1983
Quiet Please. Activity, 1981
Raining. Booklet, 1965
Rates of Exchange. Activity, Activity booklet, video, 1975; Activity, 2006
Rearrangeable Panels. Assemblage, 1957–59
Reclining Nude, Head on Cushion. Drawing, 1952–53
Reclining Nude Gazing Out. Drawing, 1952–53
Record I. Happening, 1968 (not realized)
Record II. Happening, pamphlet, 1968; Happening, 1988
Red Carpet for the Public. Activity, 1987
Red Dancers. Painting, 1955
Red Forest. Painting, 1953
Refills. Happening, 1968
René Block Said Don't Call This the Milky Way and I Agreed. Activity, 1985–86
Ribbon Cutting. Activity, 1970
Roulette. Tape score, 1957
Round Trip. Happening, 1968, 2006
Routine. Activity, film, 1973; Activity booklet, 1975; Activity, 1988 (two versions)
Runner. Happening, 1968
Safety Controls. Activity, 2000
Sales Pitch. Proposal for an Activity, 1970 (version of *Hello*)
Satisfaction. Activity, Activity booklet, 1976
Saw. Tape score, 1957
Sawdust. Activity, lithograph, 1970; Activity, 1986, 2005
Scales. Activity, 1971, 2006, 2007 (two versions)
Sea. Happening, 1963 (not realized)
A Sea Event. Activity, 1985
Seated Model in Leotard in Studio. Drawing, 1954
Seated White Figure. Painting, 1954
2nd Routine. Activity, Activity booklet, video (two versions), 1974
Self-Service. Happening, 1966, 1986, 1988
A Service for the Dead I. Happening, 1962
A Service for the Dead II. Happening, 1962
7 Kinds of Sympathy. Activity, Activity booklet, video, 1976
Shadows. Activity, 1979
Shape. Happening, 1969
Short Circuit. Environment, 1992 (reinvention of *Untitled Environment*)
Six Ordinary Happenings. Series of Happenings, 1969. See also *Charity; Fine!; Giveaway; Pose; Purpose; Shape*
Six Spots for Television. Television spots, 1983
Small Exercise I. Activity, 1978
Small Exercise II. Activity, 1978
Small Exercise 3. Activity, 1981
Small Exercise 4. Activity, 1981
Small Red Dancers. Painting, 1955
Soap. Happening, 1965 (canceled), 1989
Solo. Activity, 1969 (not realized), 2006
Sound Piece, 1958. Performance, 1960
Spit. Activity, 1985. See also *Another Spit Piece*
A Spring Happening. Happening, 1961
Squeezeplay. Activity, 1993
Stained Glass Window. Collage, 1956
Standards. Activity, 1979
Still Life on Table. Painting, 1953
Stockroom. Environment, 1961, 1991, 1992, 2006, 2007. See also *Chapel*
Subway with Self-Portrait. Painting, 1956
Supermarket Event. Activity, 1970
Sweep-In. Happening, 1967
Sweeping. Happening, 1962, 1988
Sweet Wall. Activity, 1970, 1986. See also *Sweet Wall/Testimonials*
Sweet Wall/Testimonials. Activity booklet, 1976
Tag. Activity, 1971
Tail Wagging Dog. Activity, 1982
Take-Off. Activity, 1974. See also *2 Measures*
Take-Off. Happening, 1969 (two versions)
Taking a Shoe for a Walk. Activity, 1989, 2006
Team. Activity, 1980
Testimonials. Activity, Activity booklet, 1976. See also *Sweet Wall/Testimonials*
Then. Video, 1974
3rd Routine. Activity, video, 1974
Three Country Happening. Proposal for a Happening, 1966
Three White Dancers. Painting, 1955
Throat and Cough Piece. Sound score, 1957–58
Time Pieces. Activity, Activity booklet, video, 1973; video, 1975
Timing. Activity, 1977, 2006
Tire Tower. Activity, 1979
Tobacco King. Collage, 1956
Toothbrushing Piece. Activity, 1978
Towers. Happening, 1966
Tracer. Activity, 2000
Tracts. Activity, 1971
Trading Dirt. Activity, 1983–85, 1989
Transfer. Happening, 1968
Transplant. Happening, 1969
Travelog. Happening, 1968
Tree. Happening, 1963
Two Appointments. Activity, 1978
Two Fighting Bulls. Painting, 1952
2 Measures. Activity booklet (with scores for *Affect* and *Take-Off*), 1974
Untitled. Collage, 1956
Untitled (Mountain). Assemblage, 1959
Untitled (Still Life). Painting, 1955
Untitled (The Cherry Orchard). Painting, 1955
Untitled Environment. Environment, 1958 (two versions), 1966, 1980. See also *Dead End; Fresh Air; Beauty Parlor; Beauty Parlor 2; Short Circuit; Vital Fluids*
Untitled Event. Activity, 1994
Untitled Occurrences. Activity, 1998
Ups/Downs. Activity, 1978
Useful Fictions. Activity, Activity booklet, 1975
Veronica. Collage, 1956
Vital Fluids. Environment, 1997 (reinvention of *Untitled Environment*)
Warm-Ups. Activity, Activity booklet, film, 1975; Activity, 2006 (two versions)
A Waste of Time. Activity, 1994
Watching. Happening, 1967
Waxworks. Activity, 1995
Weighty Matters. Activity, 1981
What's Watts' Watts? Activity, 1988
Whether Weather. Model, 1987
White and Brown Figures. Painting, 1954
Wink. Activity, 1973, 2007 (three versions)
Woman out of Fire. Assemblage, 1955–56
Words. Environment, 1962 (two versions), 1967 (two versions), 1975, 1984, 1991, 1992, 2005, 2006, 2007
Work. Activity, 1969 (not realized)
Yard. Environment, 1961, 1967, 1970, 1981, 1982, 1984, 1986, 1990, 1991, 1998, 2003, 2006, 2007
Yellow Flowers. Collage, 1955
Die Zeit Project. Newspaper Happening, 1981

Index

Page numbers for illustrations appear in *italic*. Artworks are by Kaprow unless otherwise noted.

FACIAL EXPRESSIONS
~~GESTURES~~

SMILES: THERE ARE SIX BASIC TYPES OF SMILES: TIGHT-LIPPED MEDIUM LENGTH AND BROAD; MOUTH OPEN, LOWER LIP MOVING (UPPER FIRM) MEDIUM LENGTH AND BROAD; UPPER LIP MOVING (LOWER FIRM) MEDIUM LENGTH AND BROAD.

1. 1. DIAG. 1. 2.

LOWER LIP MOVES OPEN

UPPER LIP MOVES OPEN

1. 2.

FIRM LIPS TOGETHER

THESE SIX TYPES ARE FURTHER VARIED BY THREE DEGREES OF ATTACK: FAST, MEDIUM AND SLOW, AND BY DURATIONS FROM 1" TO 15" FOR

Annette Leddy is a senior cataloger in Special Collections at the Getty Research Institute. She has published in diverse areas, including fiction, journalism, and literary criticism. The Allan Kaprow Papers are among the many modern and contemporary collections she has cataloged. She also cocurated, with JoAnne Paradise, the Getty Research Institute exhibition *A Tumultuous Assembly: Visual Poems of the Italian Futurists* (2006).

Eva Meyer-Hermann is an independent curator based in Cologne, Germany, and was formerly senior curator at the Van Abbemuseum in Eindhoven. Together with Stephanie Rosenthal, she cocurated the traveling exhibition *Allan Kaprow—Art as Life* (2006). Specializing in comprehensive surveys and retrospectives, her exhibitions include *Carl Andre: Sculptor 1996* (1996), *Jason Rhoades: The Purple Penis and the Venus* (1998), *Paul McCarthy: Dimensions of the Mind* (1999), *Martin Kippenberger* (2003), and *Andy Warhol: Other Voices, Other Rooms* (2007).

Andrew Perchuk is assistant director for Contemporary Programs and Research at the Getty Research Institute. He is a former Getty Fellow and a Henry Luce/ACLS Fellow. Formerly curator at the Alternative Museum, New York, he organized exhibitions such as *Maureen Connor: Discreet Objects* (1995) and *X-PRZ: Malcolm X* (Part I, 1993; Part II, 1995). He coedited *The Masculine Masquerade* (1996) and is a frequent contributor to journals of contemporary art. He is currently editing a volume on the filmmaker and anthologist Harry Smith.

Glenn Phillips is senior project specialist and consulting curator in the department of Contemporary Programs and Research at the Getty Research Institute, where he develops exhibitions, film series, and symposia related to art of the twentieth and twenty-first centuries. He has organized numerous exhibitions of video and performance art in Los Angeles, including *Pioneers of Brazilian Video Art, 1973–1983* (2004), *Marking Time* (2005), *Surveying the Border: Three Decades of Video Art about the United States and Mexico* (2005), *Reckless Behavior* (2006), *Radical Communication: Japanese Video Art 1968–1988* (2007), and *Evidence of Movement* (2007). He also coedited the book *Seeing Rothko* (2005). He is currently working on an exhibition and a book about the history of video in California.

Alex Potts is Max Loehr Collegiate Professor in the Department of History of Art at the University of Michigan, Ann Arbor. His scholarly interests range from modern and contemporary installation and sculpture to the artistic culture of the Enlightenment and early nineteenth century. His publications include *Flesh and the Ideal: Winckelmann and the Origins of Art History* (1994), *The Sculptural Imagination: Figurative, Modernist, Minimalist* (2000), and *Johann Joachim Winckelmann: History of the Art of Antiquity* (2006). His current research examines the changes taking place in the artistic culture of postwar Europe and America that led to a radical questioning of the nature and status of the art object in the late 1950s and early 1960s.

Stephanie Rosenthal is curator of contemporary art at Haus der Kunst, Munich, where she has organized exhibitions on a range of topics, including *Haim Steinbach: North East South West* (1999), *Hand-Arbeit* (2000), *Stories: Erzählstrukturen in der zeitgenössischen Kunst* (2002), *Wolfgang Laib: Retrospektive* (2003), *Abigail O'Brien: Die Sieben Sakramente* (2004), *Aernout Mik: Dispersions* (2004), *Nic Hess: Guten Morgen Deutschland!* (2004), and *Paul McCarthy: LaLa Land Parody Paradise* (2005). In addition, she teaches at Ludwig-Maximilians-Universität in Munich, offering seminars in which she investigates mediation strategies in contemporary art.

Paul Schimmel has been the chief curator of The Museum of Contemporary Art, Los Angeles, since 1990. He has organized such award-winning exhibitions as *The Interpretive Link: Abstract Surrealism into Abstract Expressionism, Works on Paper, 1938–1948* (1986), *Hand-Painted Pop: American Art in Transition, 1955–62* (1992), *Out of Actions: Between Performance and the Object, 1949–1979* (1998), *Willem de Kooning: Tracing the Figure* (2002), and *Robert Rauschenberg: Combines* (2006).

Exhibition Venues

Haus der Kunst, Munich, 17 October 2006–21 January 2007
Van Abbemuseum, Eindhoven, 10 February–22 April 2007
Kunsthalle Bern, 2 June–26 August 2007
Museo d'Arte Contemporanea di Villa Croce, Genoa,
29 November 2007–10 February 2008
The Museum of Contemporary Art, Los Angeles, 23 March—30 June 2008

Exhibition Acknowledgments

The exhibition *Allan Kaprow—Art as Life* was organized by the Haus der Kunst, Munich, with the cooperation of the Van Abbemuseum, Eindhoven, and was supported by the Andy Warhol Foundation for the Visual Arts. Concept: Eva Meyer-Hermann and Stephanie Rosenthal

Haus der Kunst, Munich

Director: Chris Dercon
Finance Director: Marco von Matuschka
Curator: Stephanie Rosenthal
Assistant: Julienne Lorz
Organization: Tina Köhler, with Cassandre Schmidt
Technical Supervision: Anton Köttl
Press: Elena Heitsch

Van Abbemuseum, Eindhoven

Director: Charles Esche
Deputy Director: Ulrike Erbslöh
Guest Curator: Eva Meyer-Hermann
Project Leader: Inge Borsje
Project Assistant: Marjon Flinterman
Education: Willem Jan Renders
Head Technician: Theo Wajon
Registrar: Martha Fritzsche
Communication: Nicole de Boer
External Relations: Marijke Roef

Kunsthalle Bern

Director: Philippe Pirotte
Guest Curator: Stephanie Rosenthal
Assistant and Organizer: Karin Minger
Technical Supervisor: Werner Schmied
Head of Administration: Yvonne Gyatso
Education: Ines Schweinlin

Museo d'Arte Contemporanea di Villa Croce, Genoa

Director: Sandra Solimano
Guest Curator: Stephanie Rosenthal
Assistant: Francesca Serrati
Technical Supervisor: Paolo Scacchetti
Head of Administration: Ezio Brenzini
Comune di Genova, Assessorato alla Cultura,
Direzione Cultura, Settore Musei

The Museum of Contemporary Art, Los Angeles

Director: Jeremy Strick
Curatorial Team: Philipp Kaiser, Paul McCarthy, Andrew Perchuk, and Paul Schimmel
Director of Education: Suzanne Isken
Senior Education Program Manager: Aandrea Stang

MOCA's presentation was made possible by generous support from the Getty Foundation.

Additional support was provided by the Hillcrest Foundation, Catharine and Jeffrey Soros, Elaine and Bram Goldsmith, The MOCA Contemporaries, Betye Monell Burton, the Dedalus Foundation, Contemporary Collectors—Orange County, Bronya and Andy Galef, Joan and Irwin Jacobs, Laura and James Maslon, and Debbie and Elliot Webb.

89.9 KCRW is the Official Media Sponsor of MOCA.

Other books featuring the holdings of the Research Library at the Getty Research Institute

China on Paper: European and Chinese Works from the Late Sixteenth to the Early Nineteenth Century
Edited by Marcia Reed and Paola Demattè
ISBN 978-0-89236-869-3 (hardcover)

Art, Anti-Art, Non-Art: Experimentations in the Public Sphere in Postwar Japan, 1950–1970
Edited by Charles Merewether with Rika Iezumi Hiro
ISBN 978-0-89236-866-2 (hardcover)

Lucien Hervé: Building Images
Olivier Beer
ISBN 978-0-89236-754-2 (hardcover)

Had gadya: The Only Kid: Facsimile of El Lissitzky's Edition of 1919
Edited by Arnold J. Band
ISBN 978-0-89236-744-3 (paper)

Aldo Rossi: I quaderni azzurri
Edited by Francesco Dal Co
ISBN 978-0-89236-589-0 (boxed set)

Devices of Wonder: From the World in a Box to Images on a Screen
Barbara Maria Stafford and Frances Terpak
ISBN 978-0-89236-590-6 (paper)

Making a Prince's Museum: Drawings for the Late-Eighteenth-Century Redecoration of the Villa Borghese
Carole Paul
ISBN 978-0-89236-539-5 (paper)

Maiolica in the Making: The Gentili/Barnabei Archive
Catherine Hess
ISBN 978-0-89236-500-5 (paper)

Incendiary Art: The Representation of Fireworks in Early Modern Europe
Kevin Salatino
ISBN 978-0-89236-417-6 (paper)

Irresistible Decay: Ruins Reclaimed
Michael S. Roth with Claire Lyons and Charles Merewether
ISBN 978-0-89236-468-8 (paper)

Russian Modernism
Compiled by David Woodruff and Ljiljana Grubišić
ISBN 978-0-89236-385-8 (paper)

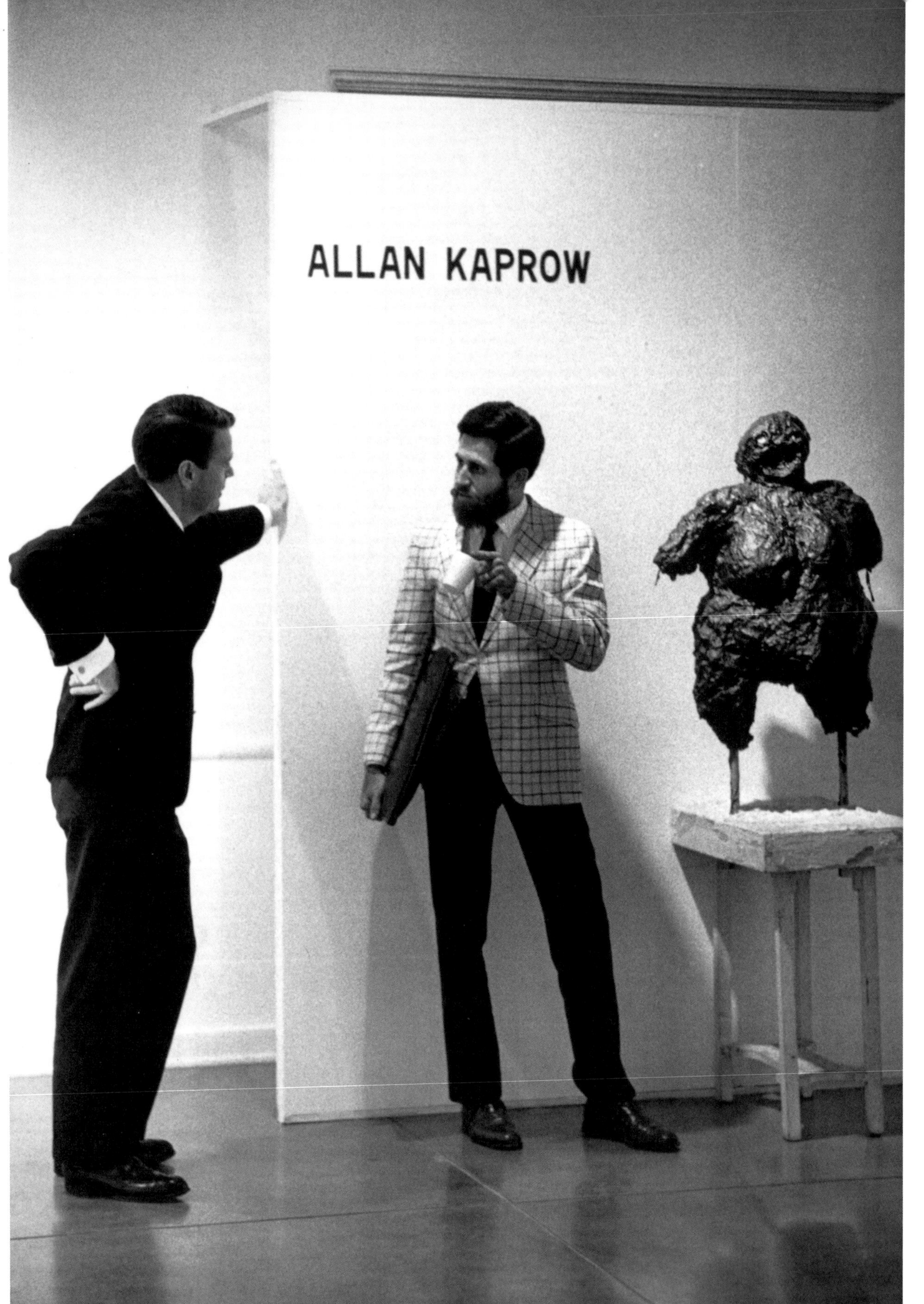
ALLAN KAPROW